W9-DDD-508

A complete index of all Prefaces and Plays appears at the end of Volume VI. Most of the Prefatory and Post-script material adjoins the play which it interprets. When Prefaces are not connected, they can be located by referring to the Table of Contents of the Volume in which the play appears.

BERNARD SHAW

COMPLETE PLAYS
WITH PREFACES

VOLUME VI

TAKEN IN THE REVOLVING STUDY IN THE GARDEN
AYOT ST. LAWRENCE, HERTFORDSHIRE

BERNARD SHAW

COMPLETE PLAYS WITH PREFACES

Volume VI

DODD, MEAD & COMPANY

NEW YORK

1963

CONTENTS

CONTENTS

"IN GOOD KING CHARLES'S GOLDEN DAYS"

A HISTORY LESSON IN THREE SCENES
(A TRUE HISTORY THAT NEVER HAPPENED)

Written in 1939

First Performed Malvern 1939

PREFACE

IN providing a historical play for the Malvern Festival of 1939 I departed from the established practice sufficiently to require a word of explanation. The "histories" of Shakespear are chronicles dramatized; and my own chief historical plays, Cæsar and Cleopatra and St Joan, are fully documented chronicle plays of this type. Familiarity with them would get a student safely through examination papers on their periods.

STAGE CHAPTERS OF HISTORY

A much commoner theatrical product is the historical romance, mostly fiction with historical names attached to the stock characters of the stage. Many of these plays have introduced their heroines as Nell Gwynn, and Nell's principal lover as Charles II. As Nell was a lively and lovable actress, it was easy to reproduce her by casting a lively and lovable actress for the part; but the stage Charles, though his costume and wig were always unmistakeable, never had any other resemblance to the real Charles, nor to anything else on earth except what he was not: a stage walking gentleman with nothing particular to say for himself.

Now the facts of Charles's reign have been chronicled so often by modern historians of all parties, from the Whig Macaulay to the Jacobite Hilaire Belloc, that there is no novelty left for the chronicler to put on the stage. As to the romance, it is intolerably stale: the spectacle of a Charles sitting with his arm round Nell Gwynn's waist, or with Moll Davis seated on his knee, with the voluptuous termagant Castlemaine raging in the background, has no interest for me, if it ever had for any grown-up person.

But when we turn from the sordid facts of Charles's reign, and from his Solomonic polygamy, to what might have happened to him but did not, the situation becomes interesting and fresh. For instance, Charles might have met that human prodigy Isaac Newton. And Newton might have met that prodigy of another sort, George Fox, the founder of the morally mighty Society of Friends, vulgarly called the Quakers. Better again, all three might have met. Now anyone who considers a hundred and fiftieth edition of

3

"IN KING CHARLES'S GOLDEN DAYS"

Sweet Nell of Old Drury more attractive than Isaac Newton had better avoid my plays: they are not meant for such. And anyone who is more interested in Lady Castlemaine's hips than in Fox's foundation of the great Cult of Friendship should keep away from theatres and frequent worse places. Still, though the interest of my play lies mainly in the clash of Charles, George, and Isaac, there is some fun in the clash between all three and Nelly, Castlemaine, and the Frenchwoman Louise de Kéroualle, whom we called Madame Carwell. So I bring the three on the stage to relieve the intellectual tension.

NEWTON'S RECTILINEAR UNIVERSE

There is another clash which is important and topical in view of the hold that professional science has gained on popular credulity since the middle of the nineteenth century. I mean the eternal clash between the artist and the physicist. I have therefore invented a collision between Newton and a personage whom I should like to have called Hogarth; for it was Hogarth who said "the line of beauty is a curve," and Newton whose first dogma it was that the universe is in principle rectilinear. He called straight lines right lines; and they were still so called in my school Euclid eighty years ago. But Hogarth could not by any magic be fitted into the year 1680, my chosen date; so I had to fall back on Godfrey Kneller. Kneller had not Hogarth's brains; but I have had to endow him with them to provide Newton with a victorious antagonist. In point of date Kneller just fitted in.

But I must make an exception to this general invitation. If by any chance you are a great mathematician or astronomer you had perhaps better stay away. I have made Newton aware of something wrong with the perihelion of Mercury. Not since Shakespear made Hector of Troy quote Aristotle has the stage perpetrated a more staggering anachronism. But I find the perihelion of Mercury so irresistible as a laugh catcher (like Weston-super-Mare) that I cannot bring myself to sacrifice it. I am actually prepared to defend it as a possibility. Newton was not only a lightning calculator with a monstrous memory: he was also a most

4

ingenious and dexterous maker of apparatus. He made his own telescope; and when he wanted to look at Mercury without being dazzled by the sun he was quite clever enough to produce an artificial eclipse by putting an obturator into the telescope, though nobody else hit on that simple device until long after. My ignorance in these matters is stupendous; but I refuse to believe that Newton's system did not enable him to locate Mercury theoretically at its nearest point to the sun, and then to find out with his telescope that it was apparently somewhere else.

For the flash of prevision in which Newton foresees Einstein's curvilinear universe I make no apology. Newton's first law of motion is pure dogma. So is Hogarth's first law of design. The modern astronomers have proved, so far, that Hogarth was right and Newton wrong. But as the march of science during my long lifetime has played skittles with all the theories in turn I dare not say how the case will stand by the time this play of mine reaches its thousandth performance (if it ever does). Meanwhile let me admit that Newton in my play is a stage astronomer: that is, an astronomer not for an age but for all time. Newton as a man was the queerest of the prodigies; and I have chapter and verse for all his contradictions.

CHARLES'S GOLDEN DAYS
As to Charles, he adolesced as a princely cosmopolitan vagabond of curiously mixed blood, and ended as the first king in England whose kingship was purely symbolic, and who was clever enough to know that the work of the regicides could not be undone, and that he had to reign by his wits and not by the little real power they had left him. Unfortunately the vulgarity of his reputation as a Solomonic polygamist has not only obscured his political ability, but eclipsed the fact that he was the best of husbands. Catherine of Braganza, his wife, has been made to appear a nobody, and Castlemaine, his concubine, almost a great historical figure. When you have seen my play you will not make that mistake, and may therefore congratulate yourself on assisting at an act of historical justice.

Let us therefore drop the popular subject of The Merry

5

"IN KING CHARLES'S GOLDEN DAYS"

Monarch and his women. On the stage, and indeed off it, he is represented as having practically no other interest, and being a disgracefully unfaithful husband. It is inferred that he was politically influenced by women, especially by Louise de Kéroualle, who, as an agent of Louis XIV, kept him under the thumb of that Sun of Monarchs as his secret pensioner. The truth is that Charles, like most English kings, was continually in money difficulties because the English people, having an insuperable dislike of being governed at all, would not pay taxes enough to finance an efficient civil and military public service. In Charles's day especially they objected furiously to a standing army, having had enough of that under Cromwell, and grudged their king even the lifeguards which were the nucleus of such an army. Charles, to carry on, had to raise the necessary money somewhere; and as he could not get it from the Protestant people of England he was clever enough to get it from the Catholic king of France; for, though head of the Church of England, he privately ranked Protestants as an upstart vulgar middle-class sect, and the Catholic Church as the authentic original Church of Christ, and the only possible faith for a gentleman. In achieving this he made use of Louise: there is no evidence that she made use of him. To the Whig historians the transaction makes Charles a Quisling in the service of Louis and a traitor to his own country. This is mere Protestant scurrility: the only shady part of it is that Charles, spending the money in the service of England, gave *le Roi Soleil* no value for it.

The other mistresses could make him do nothing that his goodnature did not dispose him to do, whether it was building Greenwich Hospital or making dukes of his bastards. As a husband he took his marriage very seriously, and his sex adventures as calls of nature on an entirely different footing. In this he was in the line of evolution, which leads to an increasing separation of the unique and intensely personal and permanent marriage relation from the carnal intercourse described in Shakespear's sonnet. This, being a response to the biological decree that the world must be peopled, may arise irresistibly between persons who could

6

not live together endurably for a week but can produce excellent children. Historians who confuse Charles's feelings for his wife with his appetite for Barbara Villiers do not know chalk from cheese biologically.

THE FUTURE OF WOMEN IN POLITICS

The establishment of representative government in England is assumed to have been completed by the enfranchisement of women in 1928. The enormous hiatus left by their previous disenfranchisement is supposed to have been filled up and finished with. As a matter of fact it has only reduced Votes For Women to absurdity; for the women immediately used their vote to keep women out of Parliament. After seventeen years of it the nation, consisting of men and women in virtually equal numbers, is misrepresented at Westminster by 24 women and 616 men. During the Suffragette revolt of 1913 I gave great offence to the agitators by forecasting this result, and urging that what was needed was not the vote, but a constitutional amendment enacting that all representative bodies shall consist of women and men in equal numbers, whether elected or nominated or co-opted or registered or picked up in the street like a coroner's jury.

THE COUPLED VOTE

In the case of elected bodies the only way of effecting this is by the Coupled Vote. The representative unit must be not a man *or* a woman but a man *and* a woman. Every vote, to be valid, must be for a human pair, with the result that the elected body must consist of men and women in equal numbers. Until this is achieved it is idle to prate about political democracy as existing, or ever having existed, at any known period of English history.

It is to be noted that the half-and-half proportion is valid no matter what the proportion of women to men is in the population. It never varies considerably; but even if it did the natural unit would still be the complete couple and not its better (or worse) half.

The wisdom or expediency of this reform is questioned on various grounds. There are the people who believe that the soul is a masculine organ lacking in women, as certain

7

physical organs are, and is the seat of male political faculty. But, so far, dissection, spectrum analysis, the electronic microscope, have failed to discover in either sex any specific organ or hormone that a biologist can label as the soul. So we christen it The Holy Ghost or The Lord of Hosts and dechristen it as a Life Force or *Élan Vital*. As this is shared by women and men, and, when it quits the individual, produces in both alike the dissolution we call death, democratic representation cannot be said to exist where women are not as fully enfranchised and qualified as men. So far no great harm has been done by their legal disabilities because men and women are so alike that for the purposes of our crude legislation it matters little whether juries and parliaments are packed with men or women; but now that the activities of government have been greatly extended, detailed criticism by women has become indispensable in Cabinets. For instance, the House of Lords is more representative than the House of Commons because its members are there as the sons of their fathers, which is the reason for all of us being in the world; but it would be a much more human body if it were half-and-half sons and daughters.

All this went on with the approval of the women, who formed half the community, and yet were excluded not only from the franchise but from the professions and public services, except the thrones. Up to a point this also did not matter much; for in oligarchies women exercise so much influence privately and irresponsibly that the cleverest of them are for giving all power to the men, knowing that they can get round them without being hampered by the female majority whose world is the kitchen, the nursery, and the drawingroom if such a luxury is within their reach.

But representation on merely plangent Parliamentary bodies is not sufficient. Anybody can complain of a grievance; but its remedy demands constructive political capacity. Now political capacity is rare; but it is not rarer in women than in men. Nature's supply of five per cent or so of born political thinkers and administrators are all urgently needed in modern civilization; and if half of that natural supply is cut off by the exclusion of women from Parliament and

PREFACE

Cabinets the social machinery will fall short and perhaps break down for lack of sufficient direction. Competent women, of whom enough are available, have their proper places filled by incompetent men: there is no Cabinet in Europe that would not be vitally improved by having its male tail cut off and female heads substituted.

But how is this to be done? Giving all women the vote makes it impossible because it only doubles the resistance to any change. When it was introduced in England not a single woman was returned at the ensuing General Election, though there were women of proved ability in the field. They were all defeated by male candidates who were comparative noodles and nobodies.

Therefore I suggest and advocate The Coupled Vote, making all votes invalid except those for a bisexed couple, and thus ensuring the return of a body in which men and women are present in equal numbers. Until this is done, adult suffrage will remain the least democratic of all political systems. I leave it to our old parliamentary hands to devise a plan by which our electorate can be side-tracked, humbugged, cheated, lied to, or frightened into tolerating such a change. If it has to wait for their enlightenment it will wait too long.

Malvern
1939

Ayot Saint Lawrence
1945

"IN GOOD KING CHARLES'S GOLDEN DAYS"

ACT I

THE library in the house of Isaac Newton in Cambridge in the year 1680. It is a cheerful room overlooking the garden from the first floor through a large window which has an iron balcony outside, with an iron staircase down to the garden level. The division of the window to the left as you look out through it is a glass door leading to these stairs, making the room accessible from the garden. Inside the room the walls are lined with cupboards below and bookshelves above. To the right of the window is a stand-up writing desk. The cupboards are further obstructed by six chairs ranged tidily along them, three to the right of the window and three to the left (as you look out). Between them a table belonging to the set of chairs stands out in the middle with writing materials on it and a prodigious open Bible, made for a church lectern. A comfortable chair for the reader faces away from the window. On the reader's left is a handsome armchair, apparently for the accommodation of distinguished visitors to the philosopher.

Newton's housekeeper, a middle aged woman of very respectable appearance, is standing at the desk working at her accounts.

A serving maid in morning deshabille comes in through the interior door, which is in the side wall to the left of the window (again as you look out through it).

THE MAID. Please, Mrs Basham, a Mr Rowley wants to know when the master will be at home to receive him.

MRS BASHAM. Rowley? I dont know him. This is no hour to call on Mr Newton.

THE MAID. No indeed, maam. And look at me! not dressed to open the door to gentlefolk.

MRS BASHAM. Is he a gentleman? Rowley is not much of a name.

THE MAID. Dressed like a nobleman, maam. Very tall and very dark. And a lot of dogs with him, and a lackey. Not a person you could shut the door in the face of, maam. But very condescending, I must say.

MRS BASHAM. Well, tell him to come back at half past eleven; but I can't promise that Mr Newton will be in. Still, if he likes to come on the chance. And without his dogs, mind. Our Diamond would fight with them.

THE MAID. Yes, maam: I'll tell him [*going*].

MRS BASHAM. Oh, Sally, can you tell me how much is three times seven. You were at school, werent you?

SALLY. Yes, maam; but they taught the boys to read, write, and cipher. Us girls were only taught to sew.

MRS BASHAM. Well, never mind. I will ask Mr Newton. He'll know, if anybody will. Or stop. Ask Jack the fish hawker. He's paunching the rabbit in the kitchen.

SALLY. Yes, maam. [*She goes*].

MRS BASHAM. Three sixpences make one and sixpence and three eightpences make two shillings: they always do. But three sevenpences! I give it up.

Sally returns.

SALLY. Please, maam, another gentleman wants Mr Newton.

MRS BASHAM. Another nobleman?

SALLY. No, maam. He wears leather clothes. Quite out of the common.

MRS BASHAM. Did he give his name?

SALLY. George Fox, he said, maam.

MRS BASHAM. Why, thats the Quaker, the Man in Leather Breeches. He's been in prison. How dare he come here wanting to see Mr Newton? Go and tell him that Mr Newton is not at home to the like of him.

SALLY. Oh, he's not a person I could talk to like that, maam. I dursnt.

MRS BASHAM. Are you frightened of a man that would call a church a steeple house and walk into it without taking off his hat? Go this instant and tell him you will raise the street against him if he doesnt go away. Do you hear. Go and do as I tell you.

SALLY. I'd be afraid he'd raise the street against us. I will do my best to get rid of him without offence. [*She goes*].

MRS BASHAM [*calling after her*] And mind you ask Jack how much three times seven is.

"IN KING CHARLES'S GOLDEN DAYS"

SALLY [outside] Yes'm.

Newton, aged 38, comes in from the garden, hatless, deep in calculation, his fists clenched, tapping his knuckles together to tick off the stages of the equation. He stumbles over the mat.

MRS BASHAM. Oh, do look where youre going, Mr Newton. Someday youll walk into the river and drown yourself. I thought you were out at the university.

NEWTON. Now dont scold, Mrs Basham, dont scold. I forgot to go out. I thought of a way of making a calculation that has been puzzling me.

MRS BASHAM. And you have been sitting out there forgetting everything else since breakfast. However, since you have one of your calculating fits on I wonder would you mind doing a little sum for me to check the washing bill. How much is three times seven?

NEWTON. Three times seven? Oh, that is quite easy.

MRS BASHAM. I suppose it is to you, sir; but it beats me. At school I got as far as addition and subtraction; but I never could do multiplication or division.

NEWTON. Why, neither could I: I was too lazy. But they are quite unnecessary: addition and subtraction are quite sufficient. You add the logarithms of the numbers; and the antilogarithm of the sum of the two is the answer. Let me see: three times seven? The logarithm of three must be decimal four seven seven or thereabouts. The logarithm of seven is, say, decimal eight four five. That makes one decimal three two two, doesnt it? What's the antilogarithm of one decimal three two two? Well, it must be less than twentytwo and more than twenty. You will be safe if you put it down as—

Sally returns.

SALLY. Please, maam, Jack says it's twentyone.

NEWTON. Extraordinary! Here was I blundering over this simple problem for a whole minute; and this uneducated fish hawker solves it in a flash! He is a better mathematician than I.

MRS BASHAM. This is our new maid from Woolsthorp, Mr Newton. You havnt seen her before.

NEWTON. Havnt I? I didnt notice it. [*To Sally*] Youre from Woolsthorp, are you? So am I. How old are you?

SALLY. Twentyfour, sir.

NEWTON. Twentyfour years. Eight thousand seven hundred and sixty days. Two hundred and ten thousand two hundred and forty hours. Twelve million six hundred and fourteen thousand, four hundred minutes. Seven hundred and fiftysix million eight hundred and sixtyfour thousand seconds. A long long life.

MRS BASHAM. Come now, Mr Newton: you will turn the child's head with your figures. What can one do in a second?

NEWTON. You can do, quite deliberately and intentionally, seven distinct actions in a second. How do you count seconds? Hackertybackertyone, hackertybackertytwo, hackertybackertythree and so on. You pronounce seven syllables in every second. Think of it! This young woman has had time to perform more than five thousand millions of considered and intentional actions in her lifetime. How many of them can you remember, Sally?

SALLY. Oh sir, the only one I can remember was on my sixth birthday. My father gave me sixpence: a penny for every year.

NEWTON. Six from twentyfour is eighteen. He owes you one and sixpence. Remind me to give you one and sevenpence on your next birthday if you are a good girl. Now be off.

SALLY. Oh, thank you, sir. [*She goes out*].

NEWTON. My father, who died before I was born, was a wild, extravagant, weak man: so they tell me. I inherit his wildness, his extravagance, his weakness, in the shape of a craze for figures of which I am most heartily ashamed. There are so many more important things to be worked at: the transmutations of matter, the elixir of life, the magic of light and color, above all, the secret meaning of the Scriptures. And when I should be concentrating my mind on these I find myself wandering off into idle games of speculation about numbers in infinite series, and dividing curves into indivisibly short triangle bases. How silly! What a waste of time, priceless time!

MRS BASHAM. There is a Mr Rowley going to call on you at half past eleven.

NEWTON. Can I never be left alone? Who is Mr Rowley? What is Mr Rowley?

MRS BASHAM. Dressed like a nobleman. Very tall. Very dark. Keeps a lackey. Has a pack of dogs with him.

NEWTON. Oho! So that is who he is! They told me he wanted to see my telescope. Well, Mrs Basham, he is a person whose visit will be counted a great honor to us. But I must warn you that just as I have my terrible weakness for figures Mr Rowley has a very similar weakness for women; so you must keep Sally out of his way.

MRS BASHAM. Indeed! If he tries any of his tricks on Sally I shall see that he marries her.

NEWTON. He is married already. [*He sits at the table*].

MRS BASHAM. Oh! That sort of man! The beast!

NEWTON. Shshsh! Not a word against him, on your life. He is privileged.

MRS BASHAM. He is a beast all the same!

NEWTON [*opening the Bible*] One of the beasts in the Book of Revelation, perhaps. But not a common beast.

MRS BASHAM. Fox the quaker, in his leather breeches, had the impudence to call.

NEWTON [*interested*] George Fox? If he calls again I will see him. Those two men ought to meet.

MRS BASHAM. Those two men indeed! The honor of meeting you ought to be enough for them, I should think.

NEWTON. The honor of meeting me! Dont talk nonsense. They are great men in their very different ranks. I am nobody.

MRS BASHAM. You are the greatest man alive, sir. Mr Halley told me so.

NEWTON. It was very wrong of Mr Halley to tell you anything of the sort. You must not mind what he says. He is always pestering me to publish my methods of calculation and to abandon my serious studies. Numbers! Numbers! Numbers! Sines, cosines, hypotenuses, fluxions, curves small enough to count as straight lines, distances between two

15

points that are in the same place! Are these philosophy?
Can they make a man great?

*He is interrupted by Sally, who throws open the door
and announces visitors.*

SALLY. Mr Rowley and Mr Fox.

*King Charles the Second, aged 50, appears at the door,
but makes way for George Fox the Quaker, a big man with
bright eyes and a powerful voice in reserve, aged 56. He is
decently dressed; but his garments are made of leather.*

CHARLES. After you, Mr Fox. The spiritual powers before the temporal.

FOX. You are very civil, sir; and you speak very justly.
I thank you [*he passes in*].

Sally, intensely impressed by Mr Rowley, goes out.

FOX. Am I addressing the philosopher Isaac Newton?

NEWTON. You are, sir. [*Rising*] Will your noble friend
do me the honor to be seated in my humble dwelling?

Charles bows and takes the armchair with easy grace.

FOX. I must not impose on you by claiming the gentleman as my friend. We met by chance at your door; and his
favorite dog was kind enough to take a fancy to me.

CHARLES. She is never mistaken, sir. Her friends are my
friends, if so damaged a character as mine can claim any
friends.

NEWTON [*taking a chair from the wall and placing it
near his table to his left*] Be seated, Mr Fox, pray.

FOX. George Fox at your service, not Mister. But I am
very sensible of your civility. [*He sits*].

NEWTON [*resuming his seat at the table*] It seems that
it is I who am at your service. In what way can I oblige you?

FOX. As you remind me, I have come here uninvited.
My business will keep while you discharge yours with this
nobleman—so called.

CHARLES. I also am uninvited, Pastor. I may address you
so both truthfully and civilly, may I not?

FOX. You have found the right word. I tended my
father's sheep when I was a child. Now I am a pastor of
men's souls.

CHARLES. Good. Well, Pastor, I must inform you I have

no business here except to waste our host's invaluable time and to improve my own, if he will be good enough to allow me such a liberty. Proceed then with your business; and take no notice of me. Unless, that is, you would prefer me to withdraw.

FOX. I have no business in this world that all men may not hear: the more the better.

CHARLES. I guessed as much; and confess to an unbounded curiosity to hear what George Fox can have to say to Isaac Newton. It is not altogether an impertinent curiosity. My trade, which is a very unusual one, requires that I should know what Tom, Dick and Harry have to say to oneanother. I find you two gentlemen much more interesting and infinitely more important.

MRS BASHAM [*posted behind Newton's chair*] What is your business, Mr Rowley? Mr Newton has much to do this morning. He has no time for idle conversation.

NEWTON. I had forgotten to make this lady known to you, gentlemen. Mrs Basham: my housekeeper, and the faithful guardian of my hours.

CHARLES. Your servant, Mistress Basham.

FOX. God be with you, woman.

NEWTON. Mr Rowley is a gentleman of great consequence, Mrs Basham. He must not be questioned as if he were Jack the fish hawker. His business is his father's business.

CHARLES. No, no. My father's business is abolished in England: he was executed for practising it. But we keep the old signboard up over the door of the old shop. And I stand at the shop door in my father's apron. Mrs Basham may ask me as many questions as she pleases; for I am far less important now in England than Jack the fish hawker.

MRS BASHAM. But how do you live, sir? That is all I meant to ask.

CHARLES. By my wits, Mistress Basham: by my wits. Come, Pastor: enough of me. You are face to face with Isaac Newton. I long to hear what you have to say to him.

FOX. Isaac Newton: I have friends who belong to the new socalled Royal Society which the King has established, to enquire, it seems, into the nature of the universe. They tell me things that my mind cannot reconcile with the word of God as revealed to us in the Holy Scriptures.

NEWTON. What is your warrant for supposing that revelation ceased when King James's printers finished with the Bible?

FOX. I do not suppose so. I am not one of those priest-ridden churchmen who believe that God went out of business six thousand years ago when he had called the world into existence and written his book about it. We three sitting here together may have a revelation if we open our hearts and minds to it. Yes: even to you, Charles Stuart.

CHARLES. The mind of Charles Stuart is only too open, Pastor.

MRS BASHAM. What did you call the gentleman, Mr Fox?

CHARLES. A slip of the tongue, Mistress Basham. Nowhere in Holy writ, Pastor, will you find any disapproval of Paul when he changed his name from Saul. Need you be more scrupulous than the apostles?

FOX. It is against my sinful nature to disoblige any man; so Mr Rowley you shall be if you so desire. But I owed it to you to let you know that I was not deceived by your new name.

CHARLES. I thank you, Pastor. Your sinful nature makes you the best mannered man in the kingdom. And now, what about the revelations?

FOX. I am troubled. I cannot conceive that God should contradict himself. How must the revelation of today be received if it be contrary to the revelation of yesterday? If what has been revealed to you, Isaac Newton, be true, there is no heaven above us and no hell beneath us. The sun which stood still upon Gibeon and the moon in the Valley of Ajalon had stood still since the creation of the world.

NEWTON. Do not let that trouble you, Pastor. Nothing has ever stood still for an instant since the creation of the world: neither the sun, the moon, the stars, nor the smallest particle of matter, except on two occasions.

CHARLES. Two! I remember only one.

NEWTON. Yes, sir: two. The first was when the sun stood still on Gibeon to give Joshua time to slaughter the Amorites. The second was when the shadow on the dial of Ahaz went ten degrees backward as a sign from God to good King Hezekiah who was dying of a boil until the prophet Isaiah made them put a lump of figs on it.

MRS BASHAM. There is nothing like a poultice of roasted figs to cure a gumboil. And to think that is because it is in the Holy Bible! I never knew it.

NEWTON. On reflection, the sun has stopped three times; for it must have stopped for an infinitesimal moment when it turned back, and again when it resumed its course.

FOX. I thank God that you are not an unbeliever and would not make me one.

NEWTON. My good friend, there is nothing so wonderful that a philosopher cannot believe it. The philosopher sees a hundred miracles a day where the ignorant and thoughtless see nothing but the daily round, the common task. Joshua was an ignorant soldier. Had he been a philosopher he would have known that to stop the nearest speck of dust would have served his turn as well as to stop the sun and moon; for it could not have stopped without stopping the whole machinery of the heavens. By the way, Mrs Basham, the fact that the sun and moon were visible at the same time may help me to fix the day on which the miracle occurred. [To the others] Excuse me, gentlemen: I have written a chronological history of the world; and the dates give me some trouble.

CHARLES. Did not the late Archbishop Ussher fix the dates of everything that ever happened?

NEWTON. Unfortunately he did not allow for the precession of the equinoxes. I had to correct some of his results accordingly.

CHARLES. And, saving the pastor's presence, what the divvle is the precession of the equinoxes?

FOX. I am sinful enough to be glad that you are as ignorant as myself. I suffer greatly from shame at my ignorance.

NEWTON. Shame will not help you, Pastor. I spend my

19

life contemplating the ocean of my ignorance. I once boasted of having picked up a pebble on the endless beach of that ocean. I should have said a grain of sand.

CHARLES. I can well believe it. No man confronted with the enormity of what he does not know can think much of what he does know. But what is the precession of the equinoxes? If I fire off those words at court the entire peerage will be prostrate before the profundity of my learning.

MRS BASHAM. Oh, tell the gentlemen, Mr Newton; or they will be here all day.

NEWTON. It is quite simple: a child can understand it. The two days in the year on which the day and night are of equal duration are the equinoxes. In each successive sidereal year they occur earlier. You will see at once that this involves a retrograde motion of the equinoctial points along the ecliptic. We call that the precession of the equinoxes.

FOX. I thank you, Isaac Newton. I am as wise as I was before.

MRS BASHAM. You ought to be ashamed of yourself, Mr Newton, injuring the poor gentlemen's brains with such outlandish words. You must remember that everybody is not as learned as you are.

NEWTON. But surely it is plain to everybody—

MRS BASHAM. No: it isnt plain to anybody, Mr Newton.

SALLY [bursting in] Mr Rowley: theres a lady in a coach at the door wants to know are you ready to take a drive with her.

CHARLES. Any name?

SALLY. No, sir. She said youd know.

CHARLES. A duchess, would you say?

SALLY. Oh no, sir. Spoke to me quite familiar.

CHARLES. Nelly! Mr Newton: would you like to be introduced to Mistress Gwynn, the famous Drury Lane actress?

MRS BASHAM [turning imperatively to Charles] Oh, I couldnt allow that, Mr Rowley. I am surprised at you mentioning such a person in my presence.

CHARLES. I apologize. I did not know that you disapproved of the playhouse, Mrs Basham.

"IN KING CHARLES'S GOLDEN DAYS"

MRS BASHAM. I do not disapprove of the playhouse, sir. My grandfather, who is still alive and hearty, was befriended in his youth by Mr William Shakespear, a well-known player and writer of comedies, tragedies, and the like. Mr Shakespear would have died of shame to see a woman on the stage. It is unnatural and wrong. Only the most abandoned females would do such a thing.

CHARLES. Still, the plays are more natural with real women in them, are they not?

MRS BASHAM. Indeed they are not, Mr Rowley. They are not like women at all. They are just like what they are; and they spoil the play for anyone who can remember the old actors in the women's parts. They could make you believe you were listening to real women.

CHARLES. Pastor Fox: have you ever spoken with a female player?

FOX [*shuddering*] I! No, sir: I do not frequent such company.

CHARLES. Why not, Pastor? Is your charity so narrow? Nell is no worse than Mary Magdalen.

MRS BASHAM. I hope Mary Magdalen made a good end and was forgiven; though we are nowhere told so. But I should not have asked her into my house. And at least she was not on the stage. [*She retires behind Newton's chair*].

CHARLES. What do you say, Pastor? Is Nelly not good enough for you?

FOX. Sir: there is nobody who is not good enough for me. Have I not warned our Christian friends who are now captives in Barbary not to forget that the life of God and the power of God are in their heathen masters the Turks and the Moors as well as in themselves? Is it any the less in this player woman than in a Turk or a Moor? I am not afraid of her.

CHARLES. And you, Mr Newton?

NEWTON. Women enter a philosopher's life only to disturb it. They expect too much attention. However, Mistress Gwynn has called to take you away, not to interrupt my work on fluxions. And if you will condescend to go down to her she need not come up to us. [*He rises in dismissal of*

"IN KING CHARLES'S GOLDEN DAYS"

the King].

CHARLES [*rising*] I see I must take my leave.

Nelly dashes in. Sally withdraws.

NELLY. Rowley darling: how long more are you going to keep me waiting in the street?

CHARLES. You are known to everyone present, Mistress Gwynn, I think. May I make our host known to you? The eminent philosopher, Mr Newton.

NELLY [*going past Charles to Newton*] I dont know what a philosopher is, Mr Newton; but you look one, every inch. Your servant, sir. [*She curtsies to him*].

NEWTON. Yours, madam. I am ashamed that you should have been kept waiting at the wrong side of my door.

NELLY. It is an honor to be seen at your door, Mr Newton. [*Looking round her*] And who keeps your house so beautifully? I thought philosophers were like Romish priests, not allowed to marry.

NEWTON. Is my house beautifully kept? I have never noticed it. This is Mrs Basham, my housekeeper. [*He sits resignedly*].

NELLY. You never noticed it! You dont deserve such a housekeeper. Your servant, Mrs Basham.

Mrs Basham bows stiffly, trying not to be flattered.

CHARLES. The other gentleman is the famous founder of the sect of Quakers.

FOX. Of Friends, Friend Rowley.

NELLY [*running to Fox*] I know. I know. The man in the leather breeches.

FOX [*stubbornly seated*] I am also known as George Fox.

NELLY [*clapping him on the shoulder*] What of that? Anybody might be George Fox; but there is only one man in the leather breeches. Your servant, George.

FOX. Yours, Nelly.

NELLY. There! Nelly! [*She goes to the wall for a chair and plants it at Fox's left, quite close*]. If I may add you to the list of my beaus I shall be the proudest woman in London.

FOX. I did not found the order of beaus. I founded that

22

of Friends.

NELLY. Ten times better. Our beaus are our foes: they care for nothing but to steal our honor. Pray for me, Friend Fox: I think you have God by the ear closer than the bishops.

FOX. He is closer to you than you have placed yourself to me. Let no priest come between you.

CHARLES. We must not waste any more of Mr Newton's time, Mistress Gwyn. He is at work on fluxions.

NELLY. On what?

CHARLES. Fluxions I think you said, Mr Newton.

NELLY. What are fluxions?

CHARLES. Mr Newton will tell you. I should be glad to know, myself.

NEWTON. Fluxions, Madam, are the rates of change of continuously varying quantities.

NELLY. I must go home and think about that, Mr Philosopher.

NEWTON [*very seriously*] I shall be much indebted to you, Madam, if you will communicate to me the result of your reflections. The truth is, I am not quite satisfied that my method—or perhaps I had better say the notation of my method—is the easiest that can be devised. On that account I have never cared to publish it.

NELLY. You really think I could teach you something, Mr Newton? What a compliment! Did you hear that, Rowley darling?

NEWTON. In these very simple matters one may learn from anyone. And you, Madam, must have very remarkable mental powers. You repeat long parts from memory in the theatre. I could not do that.

NELLY. Bless me, so I do, Mr Newton. You are the first man I ever met who did not think an actress must be an ignorant ninny—except schoolboys, who think she is a goddess. I declare you are the wisest man in England, and the kindest.

CHARLES. And the busiest, Nelly. Come. He has given us as much of his time as we have any right to ask for.

NELLY. Yes, I know. I am coming. [*She rises and goes to Charles, whose left arm she takes*]. May I come again,

23

Mr Newton?

NEWTON [*rising*] No no no no no, Madam. I cannot entertain ladies. They do not fit into my way of life. Mr Rowley: you are well known to be as interested in ladies as I am interested in the Scriptures; and I thank you for bringing this very attractive sample for my diversion—

NELLY [*as if tasting a sweet*] Oh!

NEWTON [*continuing*]—but sufficient unto the day is the evil thereof—

NELLY [*in violent protest*] Oh!!!

NEWTON. —and I beg you will bring no more ladies here until I have time to set aside a day of relaxation for their reception.

NELLY. We must go, Rowley darling. He doesnt want us.

CHARLES. You are fortunate, Mr Newton, in suffering nothing worse than Nell. But I promise you your house shall be a monastery henceforth.

As Charles and Nell turn to the door to go out, the Duchess of Cleveland, 39, formerly Lady Castlemaine, and born Barbara Villiers, bursts into the room and confronts them in a tearing rage.

BARBARA. Ah! I have caught you, have I, with your trull. This is the scientific business which made it impossible for you to see me this morning.

CHARLES. Be silent for a moment, Barbara, whilst I present you to Mr Newton, the eminent philosopher, in whose house you are an uninvited guest.

BARBARA. A pretty house. A pretty philosopher. A house kept for you to meet your women in.

MRS BASHAM [*coming indignantly to the middle of the room*] Oh! Mr Newton: either this female leaves the house this instant or I do.

BARBARA. Do you know, woman, that you are speaking of the Duchess of Cleveland?

MRS BASHAM. I do not care who I am speaking of. If you are the Duchess of Cleveland and this house were what you said it was you would be only too much at home in it. The house being what it is you are out of place in it. You go or I go.

BARBARA. You insolent slut, I will have you taken to the Bridewell and whipped.

CHARLES. You shall not, Barbara. If you do not come down with me to your carriage without another word, I will throw you downstairs.

BARBARA. Do. Kill me; and be happy with that low stage player. You have been unfaithful to me with her a thousand times.

NEWTON. Patience, patience, patience. Mrs Basham: the lady is not in a state of reason: I will prove to you that what she says has no sense and need not distress us. [*To Barbara*] Your Grace alleges that Mr Rowley has been unfaithful to you a thousand times.

BARBARA. A hundred thousand times.

NEWTON. For each unfaithfulness allow a day—or shall I say a night? Now one hundred thousand nights are almost two hundred and seventyfour years. To be precise, 273 years 287 days, allowing 68 days for Leap Year every four years. Now Mr Rowley is not 300 years old: he is only fifty, from which you must deduct at least fifteen years for his childhood.

BARBARA. Fourteen.

NEWTON. Let us say fourteen. Probably your Grace was also precocious. How many years shall we strike off your age for the days of your innocence?

NELL. Five at most.

BARBARA. Be silent, you.

NEWTON. Say twelve. That makes you in effect about twentyeight.

BARBARA. Have I denied it?

NELL. Flatterer!

NEWTON. Twentyeight to Mr Rowley's thirtysix. Your Grace has been available since, say, the year 1652, twentyeight years ago. My calculation is therefore correct.

BARBARA. May I ask what you mean by available?

NEWTON. I mean that the number of occasions on which

Mr Rowley could possibly be unfaithful to you is ten thousand two hundred and twenty plus seven for leap years. Yet you allege one hundred thousand occasions, and claim to have lived for nearly three centuries. As that is impossible, it is clear that you have been misinformed about Mistress Gwynn.

Nell claps vigorously.

BARBARA [*to Newton*] Are you mocking me, sir?

NEWTON. Figures cannot mock, because they cannot feel. That is their great quality, and their great fault. [*He goes to the door*]. And now may I have the honor of conducting your Grace to your coach—or is it one of those new fangled sedan chairs? Or would your Grace prefer to be thrown down my humble staircase by Mr Rowley? It has twentyfour steps, in two flights.

BARBARA. I will not leave this house until that player woman has gone first. [*She strides past them and plants herself in Newton's chair*].

NELL. After all, dear, it's Mr Newton's house and not ours. He was in the act of putting me out when you burst in. I stayed only because I wanted to see you in one of those tantrums of yours that Rowley so often tells me about. I might copy them on the stage.

BARBARA. He dares talk to you about me!!

NELL. He talks to me about everything, dear, because I let him get in a word occasionally, which is more than you do.

BARBARA [*to Charles*] Will you stand there and let me be insulted by this woman?

CHARLES [*with conviction*] Barbara: I am tired of your tantrums. I made you a duchess: you behave like a streetwalker. I pensioned you and packed you off to Paris; you have no business to be here. Pastor: what have you to say to all this? You are the oldest and wisest person present, are you not?

FOX. Fiftysix. And still a child in wisdom.

BARBARA [*contemptuously, noticing Fox for the first time*] What does this person know about women?

FOX. Only what the woman in myself teaches me.

26

NELL. Good for leather breeches! What do you think of her, George?

FOX. She prates overmuch about unfaithfulness. The man Rowley cannot be unfaithful to her because he has pledged no faith to her. To his wife only can he be unfaithful.

CHARLES. Wrong, Pastor. You do not know my wife. To her only I can never be unfaithful.

NELL. Yes: you are kind to us; but we are nothing to you. [*Sighing*] I would change places with her.

BARBARA. Will you order this common player to be silent in my presence?

NELL. It is not fair of her to keep mentioning my profession when I cannot decently mention hers.

With a scream of rage the duchess rises to fly at Nell, but is seized by Fox, who drags down her raised fists and throws her back into the chair.

FOX [*sternly*] Woman: behave yourself. In any decent English village you would go to the ducking stool to teach you good manners and gentle speech. You must control yourself—

He is interrupted by the clangor of a church bell, which has a terrible effect on him.

FOX [*in a thundering voice, forgetting all about the duchess*] Ha! I am called: I must go.

He makes for the door but is stopped by Charles, who, releasing Nell, shuts it quickly and posts himself with his back to it.

CHARLES. Stop. You are going to brawl in church. You will be thrown into prison; and I shall not be able to save you.

FOX. The bell, the bell. It strikes upon my life. I am called. Earthly kings cannot stay me. Let me pass.

CHARLES. Stand back, Mr Fox. My person is sacred.

NEWTON. What is the matter?

CHARLES. The church bell: it drives him mad. Someone send and stop it.

The bell stops.

FOX. God has stopped it. [*He falls on his knees and col-*

27

lapses, shivering like a man recovering from a fit.

Charles and Newton help him to his feet and lead him back to his chair.

FOX [*to Charles*] Another stroke, and I should not have answered for your life.

BARBARA. You must control yourself, preacher. In any decent English village you would be put in the stocks to teach you good manners.

FOX. Woman: I have been put in the stocks; and I shall be put there again. But I will continue to testify against the steeple house and the brazen clangor of its belfries.

MRS BASHAM. Now Mr Fox. You must not say such things here.

FOX. I tell you that from the moment you allow this manmade monster called a Church to enter your mind your inner light is like an extinguished candle; and your soul is plunged in darkness and damned. There is no atheist like the Church atheist. I have converted many a poor atheist who would have been burnt or hanged if God had not sent him into my hands; but I have never converted a churchman: his answer to everything is not his God, but the Church, the Church, the Church. They burn each other, these churchmen: they persecute: they do wickednesses of which no friend of God would be capable.

MRS BASHAM. The Popish Church, not the Protestant one, Mr Fox.

FOX. All, all, all of them. They are all snares of the devil. They stand between Man and his Maker, and take on themselves divine powers when they lack divine attributes. Am I to hold my peace in the face of this iniquity? When the bell rings to announce some pitiful rascal twaddling in his pulpit, or some fellow in a cassock pretending to bind and loose, I hear an Almighty Voice call "George Fox, George Fox: rise up: testify: unmask these impostors: drag them down from their pulpits and their altars; and let it be known that what the world needs to bring it back to God is not Churchmen but Friends, Friends of God, Friends of man, friendliness and sincerity everywhere, superstition and pulpit playacting nowhere."

28

"IN KING CHARLES'S GOLDEN DAYS"

CHARLES. Pastor: it is not given to every man as it has been to you to make a religion for himself. A readymade Church is an indispensable convenience for most of us. The inner light must express itself in music, in noble architecture, in eloquence: in a word, in beauty, before it can pass into the minds of common men. I grant you the clergy are mostly dull dogs; but with a little disguise and ritual they will pass as holy men with the ignorant. And there are great mysteries that must be symbolized, because though we feel them we do not know them, Mr Newton having not yet discovered their nature, in spite of all his mathematics. And this reminds me that we are making a most unwarrantable intrusion on our host's valuable time. Mr Newton: on my honor I had no part in bringing upon you this invasion of womanhood. I hasten to take them away, and will wait upon you at some happier moment. Come, ladies: we must leave Mr Newton to his mathematics. [*He is about to go to the door. Barbara rises to accompany him*].

NEWTON [*stopping him*] I must correct that misunderstanding, sir. I would not have you believe that I could be so inhospitable as to drive away my guests merely to indulge in the trifling pursuit of mathematical calculation, which leads finally nowhere. But I have more serious business in hand this morning. I am engaged in a study of the prophecies in the book of Daniel. [*He indicates the Bible*]. It may prove of the greatest importance to the world. I beg you to allow me to proceed with it in the necessary solitude. The ladies have not wasted my time: I have to thank her Grace of Cleveland for some lights on the Book of Revelation suggested to me by her proceedings. But solitude—solitude absolutely free from the pleasant disturbance of ladies' society—is now necessary to me; and I must beg you to withdraw.

Sally, now dressed in her best, throws the door open from without, and proudly announces—

SALLY. Her Grace the Duchess of Portsmouth.

Louise de Kéroualle, a Frenchwoman who at 30 retains her famous babyish beauty, appears on the threshold.

NEWTON [*beside himself*] Another woman! Take her

away. Take them all away. [*He flings himself into his chair at the table and buries his face in his hands*].

CHARLES. Louise: it is unlike you to pursue me. We are unwelcome here.

LOUISE [*coming over to him*] Pursue you! But I have never been so surprised in my life as to find you here. And Nelly! And her Grace of Cleveland back from Paris! What are you all doing here? I came to consult Mr Newton, the alchemist. [*Newton straightens up and stares*]. My business with him is private: it is with him, not with you, chéri. I did not know he was holding a reception.

CHARLES. Mr Newton is not an alchemist.

LOUISE. Pardon me: he is.

CHARLES. Mr Newton: are you an alchemist?

NEWTON. My meditations on the ultimate constitution of matter have convinced me that the transmutation of metals, and indeed of all substances, must be possible. It is occurring every day. I understand that you, Mr Rowley, have a private laboratory at Whitehall, in which you are attempting the fixation of mercury.

CHARLES. Without success, Mr Newton. I shall give it up and try for the philosopher's stone instead.

FOX. Would you endanger your souls by dabbling in magic? The scripture says "Thou shalt not suffer a witch to live." Do you think that God is fonder of sorcerers and wizards than of witches? If you count the wrath of God as nothing, and are above the law by your rank, are you not ashamed to believe such old wives' tales as the changing of lead into gold by the philosopher's stone?

NEWTON. Pastor Fox: I thank you for your wellmeant warning. Now let me warn you. The man who begins by doubting the possibility of the philosopher's stone soon finds himself beginning to doubt the immortality of the soul. He ends by doubting the existence of the soul. There is no witchcraft about these things. I am as certain of them as I am of the fact that the world was created four thousand and four years before the birth of our Lord.

FOX. And what warrant have you for that? The Holy

Bible says nothing of your four thousand and four. It tells us that the world was created "in the beginning": a mighty word. "In the beginning"! Think of it if you have any imagination. And because some fool in a steeplehouse, dressed up like a stage player in robes and mitre, dares to measure the days of the Almighty by his kitchen clock, you take his word before the word of God! Shame on you, Isaac Newton, for making an idol of an archbishop! There is no credulity like the credulity of philosophers.

NEWTON. But the archbishop has counted the years! My own chronology of the world has been founded on his calculation. Do you mean to tell me that all the labor I have bestowed on that book has been wasted?

FOX. Sinfully wasted.

NEWTON. George Fox: you are an infidel. Leave my house.

FOX [*rising*] Your philosophy has led you to the conclusion that George Fox is an infidel. So much the worse for your philosophy! The Lord does not love men that count numbers. Read second Samuel, chapter twentyfour: the book is before you. Good morning; and God bless you and enlighten you. [*He turns to go*].

CHARLES. Stay, Pastor. [*He makes Fox sit down again and goes to Newton, laying a hand on his shoulder*]. Mr Newton: the word infidel is not one to be used hastily between us three. Old Tom Hobbes, my tutor, who was to me what Aristotle was to Alexander the Great, was called an infidel. You yourself, in spite of your interest in the book of Daniel, have been suspected of doubting whether the apple falls from the tree by the act of God or by a purely physical attraction. Even I, the head of the Church, the Defender of the Faith, stand between the Whigs who suspect me of being a Papist and the Tories who suspect me of being an atheist. Now the one thing that is true of all three of us is that if the common people knew our real minds they would hang us and bury us in unconsecrated ground. We must stand together, gentlemen. What does it matter to us whether the world is four thousand years old, or, as I should guess, ten thousand?

NEWTON. The world ten thousand years old! Sir: you are mad.

NELL [*shocked*] Rowley darling: you mustnt say such things.

BARBARA. What business is it of yours, pray? He has always defied God and betrayed women. He does not know the meaning of the word religion. He laughed at it in France. He hated it in Scotland. In England he believes nothing. He loves nothing. He fears nothing except having to go on his travels again, as he calls it. What are ten thousand years to him, or ten million?

FOX. Are ten million years beyond the competence of Almighty God? They are but a moment in His eyes. Four thousand years seem an eternity to a mayfly, or a mouse, or a mitred fool called an archbishop. Are we mayflies? Are we mice? Are we archbishops?

MRS BASHAM. Mr Fox: I have listened to too much blasphemy this morning. But to call an archbishop a mitred fool and compare him to a mouse is beyond endurance. I cannot believe that God will ever pardon you for that. Have you no fear of hell?

FOX. How shall I root out the sin of idolatry from this land? Worship your God, woman, not a dressed-up priest.

MRS BASHAM. The archbishop is not a graven image. And when he is officiating he is not in the likeness of anything in the heavens above or on the earth beneath. I am afraid you do not know your catechism, Mr Fox.

CHARLES [*laughing*] Excellent, Mrs Basham. Pastor: she has gravelled you with the second commandment. And she has put us to shame for quarrelling over a matter of which we know nothing. By the way, where were we when we began to quarrel? I have clean forgotten.

LOUISE. It was my business with Mr Newton, I think. Nellie: will you take our sovereign lord away and leave me to speak with the alchemist in private?

CHARLES. Mr Newton: not for worlds would I deprive you of a *tête-à-tête* with her Grace of Portsmouth. Pastor: you will accompany us. Nellie: you will come with the pastor. But first I must throw the Duchess of Cleveland downstairs [*moving towards her*].

BARBARA [*screaming and making for the door*] Coward! Help! Murder! [*She rushes out*].

CHARLES. Your servant, Mrs Basham.

Mrs Basham curtsies. Charles salutes her and goes out.

NELL [*beckoning to Fox*] Come on, leather breeches.

FOX [*rising and going towards the door*] Well, what you are, God made you. I am bound to be your friend.

NELL [*taking his arm as he passes*] I am proud of your friendship, George.

They go out arm in arm.

Louise, being now the person of highest rank present, follows them as far as the armchair, in which she seats herself with distinguished elegance.

LOUISE [*to Mrs Basham*] Madam: may I have a moment alone with the alchemist?

NEWTON. You certainly may not, your Grace. I will not have Mr Locke and his friends accuse me of having relations with women. If your business cannot be discussed before Mrs Basham it cannot be discussed with me. And you will please not speak of me as "the alchemist" as you might speak of the apothecary or the chimney sweep. I am by profession—if it can be called a profession—a philosopher.

LOUISE. Pardon: I am not habituated to your English manners. It is strange to me that a philosopher should need a chaperon. In France it is I who should need one.

NEWTON. You are quite safe with me and Mrs Basham, madam. What is your business?

LOUISE. I want a love charm.

NEWTON. A what?

LOUISE. A love charm. Something that will make my lover faithful to me if I drop it into his tay. And mind! it must make him love me, and not love everybody. He is far too amorous already of every pretty woman he meets. I make no secret of who he is: all the world knows it. The love charm must not do him any harm; for if we poison the king we shall be executed in the most horrible manner. It must be something that will be good for him.

33

NEWTON. And peculiar to yourself? Not to Mistress Gwynn?

LOUISE. I do not mind Nellie: she is a dear, and so helpful when there is any trouble or illness. He picked her up out of the gutter; but the good God sometimes drops a jewel there: my nurse, a peasant woman, was worth a thousand duchesses. Yes: he may have Nellie: a change is sometimes good for men.

MRS BASHAM [*fearfully shocked*] Oh! Mr Newton: I must go. I cannot stay and listen to this French lady's talk. [*She goes out with dignity*].

LOUISE. I shall never understand the things that Englishwomen are prudish about. And they are so extraordinarily coarse in other things. May I stay, now that your chaperon has gone?

NEWTON. You will not want to stay when I tell you that I do not deal in love potions. Ask the nearest apothecary for an aphrodisiac.

LOUISE. But I cannot trust a common apothecary: it would be all over the town tomorrow. Nobody will suspect you. I will pay any price you like.

NEWTON. I tell you, madam, I know nothing about such things. If I wished to make you fall in love with me—which God forbid!—I should not know how to set about it. I should learn to play some musical instrument, or buy a new wig.

LOUISE. But you are an alchemist: you must know.

NEWTON. Then I am not an alchemist. But the changing of Bodies into Light and Light into Bodies is very conformable to the Course of Nature, which seems delighted with Transmutations.

LOUISE. I do not understand. What are transmutations?

NEWTON. Never mind, madam. I have other things to do than to peddle love charms to the King's ladies.

LOUISE [*ironically*] Yes: to entertain the Duchess of Cleveland and Mistress Gwynn, and hire a mad preacher to amuse them! What else have you to do that is more important than my business with you?

NEWTON. Many other things. For instance, to ascertain

the exact distance of the sun from the earth.

LOUISE. But what a waste of time! What can it possibly matter whether the sun is twenty miles away or twentyfive?

NEWTON. Twenty or twentyfive!!! The sun is millions and millions of miles from the earth.

LOUISE. Oh! Oh!! Oh!!! You are quite mad, Monsieur Nieuton. At such a distance you could not see it. You could not feel its heat. Well, you cannot see it so plainly here as in France, nor so often; but you can see it quite plainly sometimes. And you can feel its heat. It burns your skin, and freckles you if you are sandy-haired. And then comes a little cloud over it and you shiver with cold. Could that happen if it were a thousand miles away?

NEWTON. It is very very large, madam. It is one million three hundred thousand times heavier than the earth.

LOUISE. My good Monsieur Nieuton: do not be so fanciful. [*Indicating the window*] Look at it. Look at it. It is much smaller than the earth. If I hold up a sou—what you call a ha-pen-ny—before my eye, it covers the sun and blots it out. Let me teach you something, Monsieur Nieuton. A great French philosopher, Blaise Pascal, teached me this. You must never let your imagination run away with you. When you think of grandiose things—hundreds of millions and things like that—you must continually come down to earth to keep sane. You must see: you must feel: you must measure.

NEWTON. That is very true, madam. Above all, you must measure. And when you measure you find that many things are bigger than they look. The sun is one of them.

LOUISE [*rising and going to the table to coax him*] Ah! You are impossible. But you will make me a love potion, will you not?

NEWTON. I will write you a prescription, madam.

He takes a sheet of paper and writes the prescription. Louise watches as he writes.

LOUISE. Aqua? But aqua is only water, monsieur.

NEWTON. Water with a cabalistic sign after it, madam.

LOUISE. Ah, parfaitement. And this long magical word, what is it? Mee-kah-pah-nees. What is that?

NEWTON. Mycapaynis, madam. A very powerful life-giving substance.

LOUISE. It sounds wonderful. Is it harmless?

NEWTON. The most harmless substance in the world, madam, and the most precious.

LOUISE. Truly you are a great man, Monsieur Nieuton, in spite of your millions of miles. And this last word here?

NEWTON. Only sugar, to sweeten the micapanis, but with the cabalistic sign after it. Here is your love charm, madam. But it is not a potion: the apothecary will make it into pills for you.

LOUISE [taking the paper and tucking it into the bosom of her dress] Good. That is better, much better. It is so much easier to make men take pills than drink potions. And now, one thing more. You must swear to give this prescription to no other woman of the court. It is for me alone.

NEWTON. You have my word of honor, madam.

LOUISE. But a word of honor must be a gentleman's word of honor. You, monsieur, are a bourgeois. You must swear on your Bible.

NEWTON. My word is my word, madam. And the Bible must not be mixed up with the magic of micapanis.

LOUISE. Not black magic, is it? I could not touch that.

NEWTON. Neither black nor white, madam. Shall we say grey? But quite harmless, I assure you.

LOUISE. Good. And now I must make you a little present for your pills. How much shall it be?

NEWTON. Keep your money for the apothecary, madam: he will be amply satisfied with five shillings. I am sufficiently rewarded by the sound scientific advice you have given me from your friend Blaise Pascal. He was anticipated by an Englishman named Bacon, who was, however, no mathematician. You owe me nothing.

LOUISE. Shall I give one of the new golden guineas to the lady I shocked if I meet her on the stairs?

NEWTON. No. She would not take it.

LOUISE. How little you know the world, Monsieur! Nobody refuses a golden guinea.

NEWTON. You can try the experiment, madam. That

would be the advice of your friend Pascal. [*He goes to the door, and opens it for her*].

LOUISE. Perhaps I had better make it two guineas. She will never refuse that.

NEWTON [*at the door, calling*] Sally!

LOUISE [*with a gracious inclination of her head*] Monsieur—

NEWTON. I wish your Grace good morning.

SALLY [*at the door*] Yes, sir?

NEWTON. Shew her Grace the Duchess of Portsmouth to her chair or whatever it is.

LOUISE. Au plaisir de vous revoir, Monsieur le philosophe.

The Duchess goes out, Sally making her a rustic curtsey as she passes, and following her out, leaving Newton alone.

NEWTON [*greatly relieved*] Ouf!

He returns to his place at the table and to his Bible, which, helped by a marker, he opens at the last two chapters of the book of Daniel. He props his head on his elbows.

NEWTON. Twelve hundred and ninety days. And in the very next verse thirteen hundred and thirtyfive days. Five months difference! And the king's daughter of the south: who was she? And the king of the south? And he that cometh against him? And the vile person who obtains the kingdom by flatteries? And Michael? Who was Michael? [*He considers this a moment; then suddenly snatches a sheet of paper and writes furiously*].

SALLY [*throwing open the door, bursting with pride*] His Royal Highness the Duke of York.

The Duke, afterwards James II, comes in precipitately.

JAMES [*imperiously*] Where is his Majesty the King?

NEWTON [*rising in ungovernable wrath*] Sir: I neither know nor care where the King is. This is my house; and I demand to be left in peace in it. I am engaged in researches of the most sacred importance; and for them I require solitude. Do you hear, sir? solitude!

JAMES. Sir: I am the Duke of York, the King's brother.

NEWTON. I am Isaac Newton, the philosopher. I am also an Englishman; and my house is my castle. At least it was

37

until this morning, when the whole court came here uninvited. Are there not palaces for you and the court to resort to? Go away.

JAMES. I know you. You are a follower of the arch infidel Galileo!

NEWTON. Take care, sir. In my house the great Galileo shall not be called an infidel by any Popish blockhead, prince or no prince, Galileo had more brains in his boots than you have in your whole body.

JAMES. Had he more brains in his boots than the Catholic Church? Than the Pope and all his cardinals, the greatest scholars of his day? Is there more learning in your head than in the libraries of the Vatican?

NEWTON. Popes and cardinals are abolished in the Church of England. Only a fool would set up these superstitious idolaters against the Royal Society, founded by your royal brother for the advancement of British science?

JAMES. A club of damnable heretics. I shall know how to deal with them.

NEWTON [*rising in a fury and facing him menacingly*] Will you leave my house, or shall I throw you out through the window?

JAMES. You throw me out! Come on, you scum of a grammar school.

They rush at one another, and in the scuffle fall on the floor, Newton uppermost. Charles comes in at his moment.

CHARLES. Odsfish, Mr Newton, whats this? A wrestling match?

Newton hastily rolls off James. The two combatants remain sitting on the floor, staring up at Charles.

CHARLES. And what the divvle are you doing here, Jamie? Why arnt you in Holland?

JAMES. I am here where I have been thrown by your friend and protégé, the infidel philosopher Newton.

CHARLES. Get up, man: dont play the fool. Mr Newton: your privilege with me does not run to the length of knocking my brother down. It is a serious matter to lay hands on a royal personage.

NEWTON. Sir: I had no intention of knocking your royal

brother down. He fell and dragged me down. My intention was only to throw him out of the window.

CHARLES. He could have left by the door, Mr Newton.

NEWTON. He could; but he would not, in spite of my repeated requests. He stayed here to heap insults on the immortal Galileo, whose shoe latchet he is unworthy to unloose.

He rises and confronts the King with dignity.

CHARLES. Will you get up, Jamie, and not sit on the floor grinning like a Jackanapes. Get up, I tell you.

JAMES [*rising*] You see what comes of frequenting the houses of your inferiors. They forget themselves and take liberties. And you encourage heretics. I do not.

CHARLES. Mr Newton: we are in your house and at your orders. Will you allow my brother and myself to have this room to ourselves awhile?

NEWTON. My house is yours, sir. I am a resolute supporter of the Exclusion Bill because I hope to prove that the Romish Church is the little horn of the fourth beast mentioned by the prophet Daniel. But the great day of wrath is not yet come. Your brother is welcome here as long as you desire it.

Newton goes out. Charles takes the armchair. When he is seated James takes Newton's chair at the table.

JAMES. That fellow is crazy. He called me a Popish blockhead. You see what comes of encouraging these Protestants. If you had a pennorth of spunk in you you would burn the lot.

CHARLES. What I want to know is what you are doing here when you should be in Holland. I am doing what I can to stop this Exclusion Bill and secure the crown for you when I die. I sent you to Holland so that your talent for making yourself unpopular might be exercised there and not here. Your life is in danger in London. You had no business to come back. Why have you done it?

JAMES. Charles: I am a prince.

CHARLES. Oh, do I not know it, God help you!

JAMES. Our father lost his head by compromising with Protestants, Republicans, Levellers and Atheists. What did he gain by it? They beheaded him. I am not going to share his fate by repeating that mistake. I am a Catholic; and I am civil to none but Catholics, however unpopular it may make me. When I am king—as I shall be, in my own right, and not by the leave of any Protestant parliamentary gang—I shall restore the Church and restore the monarchy: yes, the monarchy, Charles; for there has been no real Restoration: you are no king, cleverly as you play with these Whigs and Tories. That is because you have no faith, no principles: you dont believe in anything; and a man who doesnt believe in anything is afraid of everything. Youre a damned coward, Charles. I am not. When I am king I shall reign: these fellows shall find what a king's will is when he reigns by divine right. They will get it straight in the teeth then; and Europe will see them crumble up like moths in a candle flame.

CHARLES. It is a funny thing, Jamie, that you, who are clever enough to see that the monarchy is gone and that I keep the crown by my wits, are foolish enough to believe that you have only to stretch out your clenched fist and take it back again. I sometimes ask myself whether it would not be far kinder of me to push the Exclusion Bill through and save you from the fate of our father. They will have your head off inside of five years unless you jump into the nearest fishing smack and land in France.

JAMES. And leave themselves without a king again! Not they: they had enough of that under old Noll's Major-Generals. Noll knew how to rule: I will say that for him; and I thank him for the lesson. But when he died they had to send for us. When they bully you you give in to them and say that you dont want to go on your travels again. But by God, if they try to bully me I will threaten to go on my travels and leave them without a king. That is the way to bring them down on their marrowbones.

CHARLES. You could not leave them without a king. Protestant kings—Stuart kings—are six a penny in Europe today. The Dutch lad's grandfather-in-law was our grandfather. Your daughter Mary is married to him. The Elector of Hanover has the same hook on to grandfather James.

40

Both of them are rank Protestants and hardened soldiers, caring for nothing but fighting the French. Besides Mary there is her sister Anne, Church of England to the backbone. With the Protestants you do not succeed by divine right: they take their choice and send for you, just as they sent for me.

JAMES. Yes, if you look at it in that way and let them do it. Charles: you havnt the spirit of a king: that is what is the matter with you. As long as they let you have your women, and your dogs, and your pictures, and your music, and your chemical laboratory, you let them do as they like. The merry monarch: thats what you are.

CHARLES. Something new in monarchs, eh?

JAMES. Psha! A merry monarch is no monarch at all.

CHARLES. All the same, I must pack you off to Scotland. I cannot have you here until I prorogue parliament to get rid of the Exclusion Bill. And you will have to find a Protestant husband for Anne: remember that.

JAMES. You pretend you are packing me off to save me from my Catholic unpopularity. The truth is you are jealous of my popularity.

CHARLES. No, Jamie: I can beat you at that game. I am an agreeable sort of fellow: old Newcastle knocked that into me when I was a boy. Living at the Hague on two hundred and forty pounds a year finished my education in that respect. Now you, Jamie, became that very disagreeable character a man of principle. The people, who have all sorts of principles which they havnt gathered out of your basket, will never take to you until you go about shouting No Popery. And you will die rather than do that: wont you?

JAMES. Certainly I shall; and so, I trust, would you. Promise me you will die a Catholic, Charles.

CHARLES. I shall take care not to die in an upstart sect like the Church of England, and perhaps lose my place in Westminster Abbey when you are king. Your principles might oblige you to throw my carcase to the dogs. Meanwhile, however popular you may think yourself, you must go and be popular in Scotland.

JAMES. I am popular everywhere: thats what you dont

understand because you are not a fighting man; and I am. In the British Isles, Charles, nothing is more popular than the navy; and nobody is more popular than the admiral who has won a great naval victory. Thats what I have done, and you havnt. And that puts me ahead of you with the British people every time.

CHARLES. No doubt; but the British people do not make kings in England. The crown is in the hands of the damned Whig squirearchy who got rich by robbing the Church, and chopped off father's head, crown and all. They care no more for your naval victory than for a bunch of groundsel. They would not pay for the navy if we called it ship money, and let them know what they are paying for.

JAMES. I shall make them pay. I shall not be their puppet as you are. Do you think I will be in the pay of the king of France, whose bitter bread we had to eat in our childhood, and who left our mother without firewood in the freezing winter? And all this because these rebellious dogs will not disgorge enough of their stolen wealth to cover the cost of governing them! If you will not teach them their lesson they shall learn it from me.

CHARLES. You will have to take your money where you can get it, Jamie, as I do. French money is as good as English. King Louis gets little enough for it: I take care of that.

JAMES. Then you cheat him. How can you stoop?

CHARLES. I must. And I know that I must. To play the king as you would have me I should need old Noll's army; and they took good care I should not have that. They grudge me even the guards.

JAMES. Well, what old Noll could do I can do; and so could you if you had the pluck. I will have an army too.

CHARLES. Of Protestants?

JAMES. The officers will be Catholics. The rank and file will be what they are ordered to be.

CHARLES. Where will you get the money to pay them? Old Noll had the city of London and its money at his back.

JAMES. The army will collect the taxes. How does King Louis do it? He keeps the biggest army in Europe; and he keeps you into the bargain. He hardly knows what a parliament is. He dragoons the Protestants out of France into Spitalfields. I shall dragoon them out of Spitalfields.

CHARLES. Where to?

JAMES. To hell, or to the American plantations, whichever they prefer.

CHARLES. So you are going to be the English Louis, the British Roi Soleil, the sun king. This is a deuced foggy climate for sun kings, Jamie.

JAMES. So you think, Charles. But the British climate has nothing to do with it. What is it that nerves Louis to do all these things? The climate of the Catholic Church. His foot is on the rock of Saint Peter; and that makes him a rock himself.

CHARLES. Your son-in-law Dutch Billy is not afraid of him. And Billy's house is built, not on a rock, not even on the sands, but in the mud of the North Sea. Keep your eye on the Orangeman, Jamie.

JAMES. I shall keep my eye on your Protestant bastard Monmouth. Why do you make a pet of that worthless fellow? Know you not he is longing for your death so that he may have a try for the crown while this rascally Popish plot is setting the people against me?

CHARLES. For my death! What a thought! I grant you he has not the makings of a king in him: I am not blind to his weaknesses. But surely he is not heartless.

JAMES. Psha! there is not a plot in the kingdom to murder either of us that he is not at the bottom of.

CHARLES. He is not deep enough to be at the bottom of anything, Jamie.

JAMES. Then he is at the top. I forgive him for wanting to make an end of me: I am no friend of his. But to plot against you, his father! you, who have petted him and spoilt him and forgiven him treason after treason! for that I shall not forgive him, as he shall find if ever he falls into my hand.

CHARLES. Jamie: this is a dreadful suspicion to put into my mind. I thought the lad had abused my affection until it was exhausted; but it still can hurt. Heaven keep him out of your hand! that is all I can say. Absalom! O Absalom:

my son, my son!

JAMES. I am sorry, Charles; but this is what comes of bringing up your bastards as Protestants and making dukes of them.

CHARLES. Let me tell you a secret, Jamie: a king's secret. Peter the fisherman did not know everything. Neither did Martin Luther.

JAMES. Neither do you.

CHARLES. No; but I must do the best I can with what I know, and not with what Peter and Martin knew. Anyhow, the long and the short of it is that you must start for Scotland this very day, and stay there until I send you word that it is safe for you to come back.

JAMES. Safe! What are you afraid of, man? If you darent face these Protestant blackguards, is that any reason why I should run away from them?

CHARLES. You were talking just now about your popularity. Do you know who is the most popular man in England at present?

JAMES. Shaftesbury, I suppose. He is the Protestant hero just as Nelly is the Protestant whoor. I tell you Shaftesbury will turn his coat as often as you crack your whip. Why dont you crack it?

CHARLES. I am not thinking of Shaftesbury.

JAMES. Then who?

CHARLES. Oates.

JAMES. Titus Oates! A navy chaplain kicked out of the service for the sins of Sodom and Gomorrah! Are you afraid of him?

CHARLES. Yes. At present he is the most popular man in the kingdom. He is lodged in my palace at Whitehall with a pension of four hundred pounds a year.

JAMES. What!!!

CHARLES. And I, who am called a king, cannot get rid of him. This house is Isaac Newton's; and he can order you out and throw you out of the window if you dont go. But my house must harbor the vilest scoundrel in Europe while he parades in lawn sleeves through the street with his No Popery mob at his heels, and murders our best Catholic families with his brazen perjuries and his silly Popish plot that should not impose on a rabbit. No man with eyes in his head could look at the creature for an instant without seeing that he is only half human.

JAMES. Flog him through the town. Flog him to death. They can if they lay on hard enough and long enough. The same mob that now takes him for a saint will crowd to see the spectacle and revel in his roarings.

CHARLES. That will come, Jamie. I am hunting out his record; and your man Jeffries will see to it that the poor divvle shall have no mercy. But just now it is not Oates that we have to kill: the people would say that he was murdered by the Catholics and run madder than ever. They blame the Catholics now for the Great Fire of London and the plague. We must kill the Popish Plot first. When we have done that, God help Titus Oates! Meanwhile, away with you to Scotland and try your cat-o-ninetails on the Covenanters there.

JAMES. Well, I suppose I must, since England is governed by its mob instead of by its king. But I tell you, Charles, when I am king there shall be no such nonsense. You jeer at me and say that I am the protector of your life, because nobody will kill you to make me king; but I take that as the highest compliment you could pay me. This mob that your Protestant Republicans and Presbyterians and Levellers call the people of England will have to choose between King James the Second and King Titus Oates. And James and the Church—and there is only one real Church of God—will see to it that their choice will be Hobson's choice.

CHARLES. The people of England will have nothing to do with it. The real Levellers today, Jamie, are the lords and the rich squires—Cromwell's sort—and the moneyed men of the city. They will keep the people's noses to the grindstone no matter what happens. And their choice will be not between you and Titus Oates, but between your daughter Mary's Protestant husband and you.

JAMES. He will have to cross the seas to get here. And I, as Lord High Admiral of England, will meet him on the seas and sink him there. He is no great general on land: on water he is nothing. I have never been beaten at sea.

CHARLES. Jamie, Jamie: nothing frightens me so much as your simple stupid pluck, and your faith in Rome. You think you will have the Pope at your back because you are a Catholic. You are wrong: in politics the Pope is always a Whig, because every earthly monarch's court is a rival to the Vatican.

JAMES. Do you suppose that if Orange Billy, the head of the Protestant heresy in Europe, the anti-Pope you might call him, dared to interfere with me, a Catholic king, the Pope could take his part against me in the face of all Europe! How can you talk such nonsense? Do you think Mary would share the crown if he tore it from her father's head? Rochester called you the king that never said a foolish thing and never did a wise one; but it seems to me that you talk silly-clever nonsense all day, though you are too wise: that is, too big a coward, ever to risk a fight with the squirearchy. What are they in France? Lackeys round the throne at Versailles: not one of them dare look King Louis straight in the face. But in France there is a real king.

CHARLES. He has a real army and real generals. And taxes galore. Old Noll went one better than Louis: he was a general himself. And what a general! Preston, Dunbar, Worcester: we could do nothing against him though we had everything on our side, except him. I have been looking for his like ever since we came back. I sometimes wonder whether Jack Churchill has any military stuff in him.

JAMES. What! That henpecked booby! I suppose you know that he got his start in life as your Barbara's kept man?

CHARLES. I know that the poor lad risked breaking his bones by jumping out of Barbara's window when she was seducing him and I came along unexpectedly. I have always liked him for that.

JAMES. It was worth his while. She gave him five thousand pounds for it.

CHARLES. Yes: I had to find the money. I was tremendously flattered when I heard of it. I had no idea that Barbara put so high a price on my belief in her faithfulness, in which, by the way, I did not believe. Poor Barbara was never alone with a pretty fellow for five minutes without finding out how much of a man he was. I threw Churchill in her way purposely to keep her in good humor. What struck me most in the affair was that Jack bought an annuity with the money instead of squandering it as any other man of his age would have done. That was a sign of solid ability. He may be henpecked: what married man is not? But he is no booby.

JAMES. Meanness. Pure meanness. The Churchills never had a penny to bless themselves with. Jack got no more education than my groom.

CHARLES. Latin grammar is not much use on the battle-field, as we found out. Turenne found Jack useful enough in Spain; and Turenne was supposed to be France's greatest general. Your crown may depend on Jack: by the time I die he will be as old a soldier as Oliver was at Dunbar.

JAMES. Never fear. I shall buy him if he's worth it.

CHARLES. Or if you are worth it. Jack is a good judge of a winner.

JAMES. He has his price all the same.

CHARLES. All intelligent men have, Jamie.

JAMES. Psha! Dont waste your witticisms on me: they butter no parsnips. If he can pick a winner he had better pick me.

CHARLES. There are only two horses in the race now: the Protestant and the Catholic. I have to ride both at once.

JAMES. That was what Father tried to do. See what he got by it!

CHARLES. See what I get by it! Not much, perhaps; but I keep my head on my shoulders. It takes a man of brains to do that. Our father unfortunately tried his hand at being also a man of blood, as Noll called him. We Stuarts are no good at that game: Noll beat us at it every time. I hate blood and battles: I have seen too much of them to have any dreams of glory about them. I am, as you say, no king. To be what you call a king I lack military ambition; and I lack cruelty. I have to manage Protestants who are so frightfully cruel that I dare not interfere with Protestant judges who are merciless. The penalty for high treason is so abominable that only a divvle could have invented it, and a nation of

47

divvles crowd to see it done. The only time I risked my
crown was when I stopped them after they had butchered
ten of the regicides: I could bear no more. They were not
satisfied: they dug up the body of old Noll, and butchered
it rather than have their horrible sport cut short.

JAMES. Serve the rascals right! A good lesson for them
and their like. Dont be such a mollycoddle, Charles. What
you need is a bit of my sea training to knock the nonsense out
of you.

CHARLES. So you will try your luck as a man of blood,
will you?

JAMES. I will do what is necessary. I will fight my
enemies if they put me to it. I will take care that those who
put me to it shall not die easy deaths.

CHARLES. Well, that will seem very natural to the mob.
You will find plenty of willing tools. But I would not light
the fires of Smithfield again if I were you. Your pet Jeffries
would do it for you and enjoy it; but Protestants do not like
being burnt alive.

JAMES. They will have to lump it if they fly in the face
of God.

CHARLES. Oh, go to Scotland: go to Jericho. You sicken
me. Go.

JAMES. Charles! We must not part like this. You know
you always stand by me as far as you dare. I ought not to
talk to you about government and kingcraft: you dont understand these matters and never will; and I do understand them. I have resolved again and again not to mention
them to you; for after all we are brothers; and I love you
in spite of all the times you have let me down with the
Protestants. It is not your fault that you have no head for
politics and no knowledge of human nature. You need not
be anxious about me. I will leave for Scotland tomorrow.
But I have business in London tonight that I will not post-
pone for fifty thousand Titus Oateses.

CHARLES. Business in London tonight! The one redeeming point in your character, Jamie, is that you are not a man
of principle in the matter of women.

JAMES. You are quite wrong there: I am in all things a

48

man of principle and a good Catholic, thank God. But being human I am also a man of sin. I confess it; and I do my penances!

CHARLES. The women themselves are worse penances than any priest dare inflict on you. Try Barbara: a week with her is worse than a month in hell. But I have given up all that now. Nelly is a good little soul who amuses me. Louise manages my French affairs. She has French brains and manners, and is always a lady. But they are now my friends only: affectionate friends, family friends, nothing else. And they alone are faithful to the elderly king. I am fifty, Jamie, fifty: dont forget that. And women got hold of me when I was fourteen, thirtysix years ago. Do you suppose I have learnt nothing about women and what you call love in that time? You still have love affairs: I have none. However, I am not reproaching you: I am congratulating you on being still young and green enough to come all the way from Holland for a night in London.

Mrs Basham returns, much perturbed.

MRS BASHAM. Mr Rowley: I must tell you that I cannot receive any more of your guests. I have not knives nor plates nor glasses enough. I have had to borrow chairs from next door. Your valet, Mr Chiffinch, tells who ever has any business with you this morning to come on here. Mr Godfrey Kneller, the new Dutch painter, with a load of implements connected with his trade, had got in in spite of me: he heard the noise your people were making. There are the two ladies and the player woman, and yourself and your royal brother and Mr Fox and the painter. That makes seven; and Mr Newton makes eight and I make nine. I have nothing to offer them but half a decanter of sherry that was opened last Easter, and the remains of a mouldy cake. I have sent Sally out with orders that will run away with a fortnight's housekeeping money; and that wont be half what theyll expect. I thought they were all going away when they came downstairs; but the French lady wanted to look through Mr Newton's telescope; and the jealous lady wouldnt leave until the French lady left; and the player woman is as curious as a magpie and makes herself as much at home as if she lived here. It has ended in their all staying. And now Mr Newton is explaining everything and shewing off his telescope and never thinking what I am to do with them! How am I to feed them?

CHARLES. Dont feed them, Mrs Basham. Starve them out.

MRS BASHAM. Oh no: I cant do that. What would they think of us? Mr Newton has his position to keep up.

CHARLES. It is the judgment of heaven on you for turning away my pretty spaniels from your door this morning.

MRS BASHAM. There were twelve of them, sir.

CHARLES. You would have found them much better company than nine human beings. But never mind. Sally will tell all the tradesmen that Mr Newton is entertaining me and my brother. They will call themselves Purveyors to his Majesty the King. Credit will be unlimited.

JAMES. Remember that this is Friday: a fast day. All I need is three or four different kinds of fish.

MRS BASHAM. No, sir: in this house you will have to be content with a Protestant dinner. Jack the fish hawker is gone. But he left us a nice piece of cod; and thats all youll get, sir.

CHARLES. Jamie: we must clear out and take the others with us. It seems we cannot visit anyone without ruining them.

JAMES. Pooh! What can a few pounds more or less matter to anybody?

CHARLES. I can remember when they meant a divvle of a lot to me, and to you too. Let us get back to Newmarket.

MRS BASHAM. No, sir: Mr Newton would not like that: he knows his duties as your host. And if you will excuse me saying so, sir: you all look as if a plain wholesome dinner would do you no harm for once in a way. By your leave I will go to look after it. I must turn them all out of the laboratory and send them up here while I lay the table there.

She goes out.

JAMES. "A nice piece of cod!" Among nine people!

CHARLES. "Isnt that a dainty dish to set before a king?"

50

Your fast will be a real fast, Jamie, for the first time in your life.

JAMES. You lie. My penances are all real.

CHARLES. Well, a hunk of bread, a lump of cheese, and a bottle of ale are enough for me or for any man at this hour.

All the rest come back except Mrs Basham, Barbara, and Newton. Fox comes first.

FOX. I have made eight new friends. But has the Lord sent them to me? Such friends! [*He takes his old seat, much perplexed*].

NELL [*coming in*] Oh, Rowley darling, they want me to recite my big speech from The Indian Emperor. But I cant do that without proper drapery: its classical. [*Going to the Duke*] And what is my Jamie doing here?

LOUISE [*taking a chair from the wall and planting it at Charles's right, familiarly close*] Why not give us a prologue? Your prologues are your best things. [*She sits*].

CHARLES and JAMES. Yes, yes: a prologue.

All are now seated, except Nell.

NELL. But I cant do a prologue unless I am in breeches.

FOX [*rising*] No. Eleanor Gwyn: how much more must I endure from you? I will not listen to a prologue that can be spoken only by a woman in breeches. And I warn you that when I raise my voice to heaven against mummery, whether in playhouse or steeplehouse, I can drown and dumb the loudest ribald ranter.

CHARLES. Pastor: Mistress Gwyn is neither a ribald nor a ranter. The plays and prologues in which she is famous are the works of the greatest poet of the age: the poet Laureate, John Dryden.

FOX. If he has given to the playhouse talents that were given to him for the service of God, his guilt is the deeper.

CHARLES. Have you considered, Pastor, that the playhouse is a place where two or three are gathered together?

NELL. Not when I am playing, Rowley darling. Two or three hundred, more likely.

FOX [*resuming his seat in the deepest perplexity*] Sir:

51

you are upsetting my mind. You have forced me to make friends with this player woman; and now you would persuade me that the playhouse is as divine as my meeting house. I find your company agreeable to me, but very unsettling.

CHARLES. The settled mind stagnates, Pastor. Come! Shall I give you a sample of Mr Dryden at his best?

NELL. Oh yes, Rowley darling: give us your pet speech from Aurengzebe.

LOUISE. Yes yes. He speaks it beautifully. He is almost as good an actor as King Louis; and he has really more of the grand air.

CHARLES. Thank you, Louise. Next time leave out the almost. My part is more difficult than that of Louis.

JAMES. Pray silence for his Majesty the King, who is going to make a fool of himself to please the Quaker.

CHARLES. Forgive Jamie, ladies and gentlemen. He will give you his own favorite recitation presently; but the King comes first. Now listen. [*He rises. They all rise, except Fox*]. No, pray. My audience must be seated. [*They sit down again*].

Charles recites the pessimistic speech from Aurengzebe as follows:

When I consider life, 'tis all a cheat;
Yet, fooled with hope, men favor the deceit;
Trust on, and think tomorrow will repay:
Tomorrow's falser than the former day;
Lies worse; and, while it says we shall be blest
With some new choice, cuts off what we possessed.
Strange cozenage! None would live past years again;
Yet all hope pleasure in what yet remain;
And from the dregs of life think to receive
What the first sprightly running could not give.
I'm tired of waiting for this chemic gold
Which fools us young, and beggars us when old.

Nell and Louise applaud vigorously.

CHARLES. What do you think of that, Pastor? [*He sits*].

FOX. It is the cry of a lost soul from the bottomless blackness of its despair. Never have I heard anything so terrible. This man has never lived. I must seek him out and shew him the light and the truth.

NELL. Tut tut, George! The man in the play is going to be killed. To console himself he cries Sour Grapes: that is all. And now what shall I give you?

JAMES. Something oldfashioned. Give him a bit of Shakespear.

NELL. What! That author the old actors used to talk about. Kynaston played women in his plays. I dont know any. We cannot afford them nowadays. They require several actors of the first quality; and—would you believe it, George?—those laddies will not play now for less than fifteen shillings a week.

FOX [*starting up again*] Fifteen shillings a week to a player when the servants of God can scarce maintain themselves alive by working at mechanical trades! Such wickedness will bring a black judgment on the nation. Charles Stuart: have you no regard for your soul that you suffer such things to be done?

CHARLES. You would not grudge these poor fellows their fifteen shillings if you knew what women cost.

FOX. What manner of world is this that I have come into? Is virtue unknown here, or is it despised? [*He gives it up, and relapses into his seat*].

JAMES. Mr Dryden has an answer for that. [*He recites, seated*].

How vain is virtue which directs our ways
Through certain danger to uncertain praise!
The world is made for the bold impious man
Who stops at nothing, seizes all he can.
Justice to merit does weak aid afford;
She trusts her balance, and ignores her sword.
Virtue is slow to take whats not her own,
And, while she long consults, the prize is gone.

FOX. I take no exception to this. I have too good reason to know that it is true. But beware how you let these bold impious fellows extinguish hope in you. Their day is short; but the inner light is eternal.

JAMES. I am safe in the bosom of my Church, Pastor.

53

LOUISE. Take the gentleman's mind off his inner light, Nell. Give us a speech.

NELL. They dont want a speech from me. Rowley began talking about speeches because he wanted to do one himself. And now His Highness the Duke of York must have his turn.

JAMES. Are we poor devils of princes not to have any of the good things, nor do any of the pleasant things, because we are Royal Highnesses? Were you not freer and happier when you sold oranges in Drury Lane than you are now as a court lady?

FOX. Did you sell oranges in Drury Lane?

NELL. They say I did. The people like to believe I did. They love me for it. I say nothing.

CHARLES. Come! Give us one of Cydara's speeches from The Indian Emperor. It was in that that you burst on the world as the ambitious orange girl.

NELL. A wretched part: I had to stand mum on the stage for hours while the others were spouting. Mr Dryden does not understand how hard that is. Just listen to this, the longest speech I had.

May I believe my eyes! What do I see?
Is this her hate to him? her love to me?
'Tis in my breast she sheathes her dagger now.
False man: is this thy faith? Is this thy vow?
Then somebody says something.

CHARLES.
What words, dear saint, are these I hear you use?
What faith? what voice? are those which you accuse?

NELL. "Those which you accuse": thats my cue.
More cruel than the tiger o'er his spile
And falser than the weeping crocodile
Can you add vanity to guilt, and take
A pride to hear the conquests which you make?
Go: publish your renown: let it be said
The woman that you love you have betrayed—
Rowley darling: I cannot go on if you keep laughing at me. If only Mr Dryden had given me some really great lines, like the ones he gave to Montezuma. Listen.

"IN KING CHARLES'S GOLDEN DAYS"

Still less and less my boiling spirits flow
And I grow stiff, as cooling metals do.
Farewell, Almira.

FOX. Now do you tell me that living men and women, created by God in His likeness and not in that of gibbering apes, can be bribed to utter such trash, and that others will pay to hear them do it when they will not enter a meeting house for a penny in the plate to hear the words of God Himself? What society is this I am in? I must be dreaming that I am in hell.

NELL. George: you are forgetting yourself. You should have applauded me. I will recite no more for you. [*She takes a chair from the wall and seats herself beside Louise, on her right*].

CHARLES. He does not understand, Nell. Tell him the story of the play, and why Montezuma says such extravagant things.

NELL. But how can I, Rowley darling? I dont know what it is all about: I know only my part and my cue. All I can say is that when Montezuma speaks those lines he drops dead.

FOX. Can you wonder that he does so? I should drop dead myself if I heard such fustian pass my lips.

JAMES. Is it worse than the fustian that passes the lips of the ranters in your conventicles?

FOX. I cannot deny it: the preachers are a greater danger than the players. I had not thought of this before. Again you unsettle my mind. There is one Jeremy Collier who swears he will write such a book on the profaneness and immorality of the stage as will either kill the theatre or shame it into decency; but these lines just uttered by Eleanor Gwyn are not profane and immoral: they are mad and foolish.

LOUISE. All the less harmful, monsieur. They are not meant to be taken seriously; and no one takes them so. But your Huguenot ranters pretend to be inspired; and foolish people are deluded by them. And what sort of world would they make for us if they got the upper hand? Can you name a single pleasure that they would leave us to make life

55

worth living?

FOX. It is not pleasure that makes life worth living. It is life that makes pleasure worth having. And what pleasure is better than the pleasure of holy living?

JAMES. I have been in Geneva, blasphemously called the City of God under that detestable Frenchman Calvin, who, thank God, has by now spent a century in hell. And I can testify that he left the wretched citizens only one worldly pleasure.

CHARLES. Which one was that?

JAMES. Moneymaking.

CHARLES. Odsfish! that was clever of him. It is a very satisfying pleasure, and one that lasts til death.

LOUISE. It does not satisfy me.

CHARLES. You have never experienced it, Louise. You spend money: you do not make it. You spend ten times as much as Nelly; but you are not ten times as happy. If you made ten times as much as she, you would never tire of it and never ask for anything better.

LOUISE. Charles: if I spent one week making money or even thinking about it instead of throwing it away with both hands all my charm would be gone. I should become that dull thing, a plain woman. My face would be full of brains instead of beauty. And you would send me back to France by the next ship, as you sent Barbara.

CHARLES. What if I did? You will soon be tired of me; for I am an ugly old fellow. But you would never tire of moneymaking.

NELL. Now the Lord be praised, my trade is one in which I can make money without losing my good looks!

LOUISE [to Charles] If you believe what you say, why do you not make money yourself instead of running after women?

CHARLES. Because there is a more amusing occupation for me.

LOUISE. I have not seen you practise it, Charles. What is it?

CHARLES. Kingcraft.

JAMES. Of which you have not the faintest conception.

CHARLES. Like Louise, you have not seen me practise it. But I am King of England; and my head is still on my shoulders.

NELL. Rowley darling: you must learn to keep King Charles's head out of your conversation. You talk too much of him.

CHARLES. Why is it that we always talk of my father's head and never of my great grandmother's? She was by all accounts a pretty woman; but the Protestants chopped her head off in spite of Elizabeth. They had Strafford's head off in spite of my father. And then they had his own off. I am not a bit like him; but I have more than a touch in me of my famous grandfather Henry the Fourth of France. And he died with a Protestant's dagger in his heart: the deadliest sort of Protestant: a Catholic Protestant. There are such living paradoxes. They burnt the poor wretch's hand off with the dagger in it, and then tore him to pieces with galloping horses. But Henry lay dead all the same. The Protestants will have you, Jamie, by hook or crook: I foresee that: they are the real men of blood. But they shall not have me. I shall die in my bed, and die King of England in spite of them.

FOX. This is not kingcraft: it is chicanery. Protestantism gives the lie to itself: it overthrows the Roman Church and immediately builds itself another nearer home and makes you the head of it, though it is now plain to me that your cleverness acknowledges no Church at all. You are right there: Churches are snares of the divvle. But why not follow the inner light that has saved you from the Churches? Be neither Catholic nor Protestant, Whig nor Tory: throw your crown into the gutter and be a Friend: then all the rest shall be added to you

They all laugh at him except Charles.

CHARLES. A crown is not so easy to get rid of as you think, Pastor. Besides, I have had enough of the gutter: I prefer Whitehall.

JAMES [*to Fox*] You would like to have a king for your follower, eh?

FOX. I desire Friends, not followers. I am simple in my

tastes. I am not schooled and learned as you two princes are.

CHARLES. Thank your stars for that, Pastor: you have nothing to unlearn.

FOX. That is well said. Too often have I found that a scholar is one whose mind is choked with rubbish that should never have been put there. But how do you come to know this? Things come to my knowledge by the grace of God; yet the same things have come to you who live a most profane life and have no sign of grace at all.

CHARLES. You and I are mortal men, Pastor. It is not possible for us to differ very greatly. You have to wear leather breeches lest you be mistaken for me.

Barbara storms in with a sheet of drawing paper in her hand.

BARBARA [*thrusting the paper under Charles's nose*] Do you see this?

CHARLES [*scrutinizing it admiringly*] Splendid! Has Mr Kneller done this? Nobody can catch a likeness as he can.

BARBARA. Likeness! You have bribed him to insult me. It makes me look a hundred.

CHARLES. Nonsense, dear. It is you to the life. What do you say, Jamie? [*He hands the drawing to James*].

JAMES. It's you, duchess. He has got you, wrinkle for wrinkle.

BARBARA. You say this to my face! You, who have seen my portrait by Lilly!

NELL. You were younger then, darling.

BARBARA. Who asked you for your opinion, you jealous cat?

CHARLES. Sit down; and dont be silly, Barbara. A woman's face does not begin to be interesting until she is our age.

BARBARA. Our age! You old wreck, do you dare pretend that you are as young as I am?

CHARLES. I am only fifty, Barbara. But we are both getting on.

BARBARA. Oh! [*With a scream of rage she tears the drawing to fragments and stamps on them*].

58

CHARLES. Ah, that was wicked of you: you have destroyed a fine piece of work. Go back to France. I tell you I am tired of your tantrums.

Barbara, intimidated, but with a defiant final stamp on the drawing, flings away behind James to one of the chairs against the cupboards, and sits there sulking.

Newton comes in from the garden, followed by Godfrey Kneller, a Dutchman of 34, well dressed and arrogant. They are both almost as angry as Barbara.

NEWTON. Mr Kneller: I will dispute with you no more. You do not understand what you are talking about.

KNELLER. Sir: I must tell you in the presence of His Majesty you are a most overweening, a most audacious man. You presume to teach me my profession.

CHARLES. What is the matter, Mr Newton?

NEWTON. Let it pass, Mr Rowley. This painter has one kind of understanding: I have another. There is only one course open to us both; and that is silence. [*Finding his chair occupied by the Duke of York he takes another from beside Barbara and seats himself at the side of the table on the Duke's left*].

CHARLES. Mr Newton is our host, Mr Kneller; and he is a very eminent philosopher. Will you not paint his picture for me? That can be done in silence.

KNELLER. I will paint his picture if your Majesty so desires. He has an interesting head: I should have drawn it this morning had not Her Grace of Cleveland insisted on my drawing her instead. But how can an interesting head contain no brain: that is the question.

CHARLES. Odsfish, man, he has the greatest brain in England.

KNELLER. Then he is blinded by his monstrous conceit. You shall judge between us, sir. Am I or am I not the greatest draughtsman in Europe?

CHARLES. You are certainly a very skilful draughtsman, Mr Kneller.

KNELLER. Can anyone here draw a line better than I?

CHARLES. Nobody here can draw a line at all, except the Duchess of Cleveland, who draws a line at nothing.

"IN KING CHARLES'S GOLDEN DAYS"

BARBARA. Charles—

CHARLES. Be quiet, Barbara. Do you presume to contradict your King.

KNELLER. If there is a science of lines, do I not understand it better than anyone?

CHARLES. Granted, Mr Kneller. What then?

KNELLER. This man here, this crazy and conceited philosopher, dares to assert in contradiction of me, of ME! that a right line is a straight line, and that everything that moves moves in a straight line unless some almighty force bends it from its path. This, he says, is the first law of motion. He lies.

CHARLES. And what do you say, Mr Kneller?

KNELLER. Sir: I do not say: I know. The right line, the line of beauty, is a curve. My hand will not draw a straight line: I have to stretch a chalked string on my canvas and pluck it. Will you deny that your duchess here is as famous for her beauty as the Psyche of the divine Raphael? Well, there is not a straight line in her body: she is all curves.

BARBARA [outraged, rising] Decency, fellow! How dare you?

CHARLES. It is true, Barbara. I can testify to it.

BARBARA. Charles: you are obscene. The impudence! [She sits].

KNELLER. The beauty, madam. Clear your mind of filth. There is not a line drawn by the hand of the Almighty, from the rainbow in the skies to the house the snail carries on his back, that is not a curve, and a curve of beauty. Your apple fell in a curve.

NEWTON. I explained that.

KNELLER. You mistake explanations for facts: all you science-mongers do. The path of the world curves, as you yourself have shewn; and as it whirls on its way it would leave your apple behind if the apple fell in a straight line. Motion in a curve is the law of nature; and the law of nature is the law of God. Go out into your garden and throw a stone straight if you can. Shoot an arrow from a bow, a bullet from a pistol, a cannon ball from the mightiest cannon the King can lend you, and though you had the strength of

60

Hercules, and gunpowder more powerful than the steam which hurls the stones from Etna in eruption, yet cannot you make your arrow or your bullet fly straight to its mark.

NEWTON [*terribly perturbed*] This man does not know what he is saying. Take him away; and leave me in peace.

CHARLES. What he says calls for an answer, Mr Newton.

JAMES. The painter is right. A cannon ball flies across the sea in curves like the arches of a bridge, hop, hop, hop. But what does it matter whether it flies straight or crooked provided it hits between wind and water?

NEWTON. To you, admiral, it matters nothing. To me it makes the difference between reason and madness.

JAMES. How so?

NEWTON. Sir: if what this man believes be true, then not only is the path of the cannon ball curved, but space is curved; time is curved; the universe is curved.

KNELLER. Of course it is. Why not?

NEWTON. Why not! Only my life's work turned to waste, vanity, folly. This comes of admitting strangers to break into my holy solitude with their diabolical suggestions. But I am rightly rebuked for this vice of mine that led me to believe that I could construct a universe with empty figures. In future I shall do nothing but my proper work of interpreting the scriptures. Leave me to that work and to my solitude. [*Desperately, clutching his temples*] Begone, all of you. You have done mischief enough for one morning.

CHARLES. But, Mr Newton, may we not know what we have done to move you thus? What diabolical suggestions have we made? What mischief have we done?

NEWTON. Sir: you began it, you and this infidel quaker. I have devoted months of my life to the writing of a book— a chronology of the world—which would have cost any other man than Isaac Newton twenty years hard labor.

CHARLES. I have seen that book, and been astounded at the mental power displayed in every page of it.

NEWTON. You may well have been, Mr Rowley. And now what have you and Mr Fox done to that book? Reduced it to a monument of the folly of Archbishop Ussher, who dated the creation of the world at four thousand and four, B.C., and of my stupidity in assuming that he had proved his case. My book is nonsense from beginning to end. How could I, who have calculated that God deals in millions of miles of infinite space, be such an utter fool as to limit eternity, which has neither beginning nor end, to a few thousand years? But this man Fox, without education, without calculation, without even a schoolboy's algebra, knew this when I, who was born one of the greatest mathematicians in the world, drudged over my silly book for months, and could not see what was staring me in the face.

JAMES. Well, why howl about it? Bring out another edition and confess that your Protestant mathematics are a delusion and a snare, and your Protestant archbishops impostors.

NEWTON. You do not know the worst, sir. I have another book in hand: one which should place me in line with Kepler, Copernicus, and Galileo as a master astronomer, and as the completer of their celestial systems. Can you tell me why the heavenly bodies in their eternal motion do not move in straight lines, but always in ellipses?

CHARLES. I understand that this is an unsolved problem of science. I certainly cannot solve it.

NEWTON. I have solved it by the discovery of a force in nature which I call gravitation. I have accounted for all the celestial movements by it. And now comes this painter, this ignorant dauber who, were it to save his soul—if he has a soul—could not work out the simplest equation, or as much as conceive an infinite series of numbers! this fellow substitutes for my first law of motion—straight line motion— motion in a curve.

JAMES. So bang goes your second volume of Protestant philosophy! Squashed under Barbara's outlines.

BARBARA. I will not have my outlines discussed by men. I am not a heathen goddess: I am a Christian lady. Charles always encourages infidels and libertines to blaspheme. And now he encourages them to insult me. I will not bear it.

CHARLES. Do not be an idiot, Barbara: Mr Kneller is paying you the greatest compliment in taking you for a model of the universe. The choice would seem to be between a universe of Barbara's curves and a universe of straight lines seduced from their straightness by some purely mathematical attraction. The facts seem to be on the side of the painter. But in a matter of this kind can I, as founder of the Royal Society, rank the painter as a higher authority than the philosopher?

KNELLER. Your Majesty: the world must learn from its artists because God made the world as an artist. Your philosophers steal all their boasted discoveries from the artists; and then pretend they have deduced them from figures which they call equations, invented for that dishonest purpose. This man talks of Copernicus, who pretended to discover that the earth goes round the sun instead of the sun going round the earth. Sir: Copernicus was a painter before he became an astronomer. He found astronomy easier. But his discovery was made by the great Italian painter Leonardo, born twentyone years before him, who told all his intimates that the earth is a moon of the sun.

NEWTON. Did he prove it?

KNELLER. Man: artists do not prove things. They do not need to. They KNOW them.

NEWTON. This is false. Your notion of a spherical universe is borrowed from the heathen Ptolemy, from all the magicians who believed that the only perfect figure is the circle.

KNELLER. Just what such blockheads would believe. The circle is a dead thing like a straight line: no living hand can draw it: you make it by twirling a pair of dividers. Take a sugar loaf and cut it slantwise, and you will get hyperbolas and parabolas, ellipses and ovals, which Leonardo himself could not draw, but which any fool can make with a knife and a lump of sugar. I believe in none of these mechanical forms. The line drawn by the artist's hand, the line that flows, that strikes, that speaks, that reveals! that is the line that shews the divine handiwork.

CHARLES. So you, too, are a philosopher, Mr Kneller!

KNELLER. Sir: when a man has the gift of a painter, that qualification is so magical that you cannot think of him as anything else. Who thinks of Leonardo as an engineer? of Michael Angelo as an inventor or a sonneteer? of me as a scholar and a philosopher? These things are all in our day's work: they come to us without thinking. They are trifles beside our great labor of creation and interpretation.

JAMES. I had a boatswain once in my flagship who thought he knew everything.

FOX. Perhaps he did. Divine grace takes many strange forms. I smell it in this painter. I have met it in common sailors like your boatswain. The cobbler thinks there is nothing like leather—

NELL. Not when you make it into breeches instead of boots, George.

BARBARA. Be decent, woman. One does not mention such garments in well-bred society.

NELL. Orange girls and players and such like poor folk think nothing of mentioning them. They have to mend them, and sometimes to make them; so they have an honest knowledge of them, and are not ashamed like fine ladies who have only a dishonest knowledge of them.

CHARLES. Be quiet, Nelly: you are making Barbara blush.

NELL. Thats more than you have ever been able to do, Rowley darling.

BARBARA. It is well for you that you have all these men to protect you, mistress. Someday when I catch you alone I'll make you wish you had ten pairs of leather breeches on you.

CHARLES. Come come! no quarrelling.

NELL. She began it, Rowley darling.

CHARLES. No matter who began it, no quarrelling, I command.

LOUISE. Charles: the men have been quarrelling all the morning. Does your command apply to them too?

CHARLES. Their quarrels are interesting, Louise.

NELL. Are they? They bore me to distraction.

CHARLES. Much blood has been shed for them; and much more will be after we are gone.

BARBARA. Oh, do not preach, Charles. Leave that to this person who is dressed partly in leather. It is his profession:

64

it is not yours.

CHARLES. The Protestants will not let me do anything else, my dear. But come! Mr Newton has asked us to leave his house many times. And we must not forget that he never asked us to come into it. But I have a duty to fulfil before we go. I must reconcile him with Mr Kneller, who must paint his portrait to hang in the rooms of the Royal Society.

KNELLER. It is natural that your Majesty should desire a work of mine for the Society. And this man's head is unusual, as one would expect from his being a philosopher: that is, half an idiot. I trust your Majesty was pleased with my sketch of Her Grace of Cleveland.

BARBARA. Your filthy caricature of Her Grace of Cleveland is under your feet. You are walking on it.

KNELLER [*picking up a fragment and turning it over to identify it*] Has the King torn up a work of mine? I leave the country this afternoon.

CHARLES. I would much sooner have torn up Magna Carta. Her Grace tore it up herself.

KNELLER. It is a strange fact, your Majesty, that no living man or woman can endure his or her portrait if it tells all the truth about them.

BARBARA. You lie, you miserable dauber. When our dear Peter Lilly, who has just died, painted me as I really am, did I destroy his portrait? But he was a great painter; and you are fit only to whitewash unmentionable places.

CHARLES. Her Grace's beauty is still so famous that we are all tired of it. She is the handsomest woman in England. She is also the stupidest. Nelly is the wittiest: she is also the kindest. Louise is the loveliest and cleverest. She is also a lady. I should like to have portraits of all three as they are now, not as Lilly painted them.

LOUISE. No, Charles: I do not want to have the whole truth about me handed down to posterity.

NELL. Same here. I prefer the orange girl.

KNELLER. I see I shall not succeed in England as a painter. My master Rembrandt did not think a woman worth painting until she was seventy.

NELL. Well, you shall paint me when I am seventy. In

65

the theatre the young ones are beginning to call me Auntie! When they call me Old Mar Gwyn I shall be ready for you; and I shall look my very best then.

CHARLES. What about your portrait, Mr Fox? You have been silent too long.

FOX. I am dumbfounded by this strange and ungodly talk. To you it may seem mere gossip; but to me it is plain that this painter claims that his hand is the hand of God.

KNELLER. And whose hand is it if not the hand of God? You need hands to scratch your heads and carry food to your mouths. That is all your hands mean to you. But the hand that can draw the images of God and reveal the soul in them, and is inspired to do this and nothing else even if he starves and is cast off by his father and all his family for it: is not his hand the hand used by God, who, being a spirit without body, parts or passions, has no hands?

FOX. So the men of the steeplehouse say; but they lie. Has not God a passion for creation? Is He not all passion of that divine nature?

KNELLER. Sir: I do not know who you are; but I will paint your portrait.

CHARLES. Bravo! We are getting on. How about your portrait, Mr Newton?

NEWTON. Not by a man who lives in a curved universe. He would distort my features.

LOUISE. Perhaps gravitation would distort them equally, Mr Newton.

CHARLES. That is very intelligent of you, Louise.

BARBARA. It takes some intelligence to be both a French spy and a bluestocking. I thank heaven for my stupidity, as you call it.

CHARLES. Barbara: must I throw you downstairs?

LOUISE. In France they call me the English spy. But this is the first time I have been called a bluestocking. All I meant was that Mr Kneller and Mr Newton seem to mean exactly the same thing; only one calls it beauty and the other gravitation; so they need not quarrel. The portrait will be the same both ways.

NEWTON. Can he measure beauty?

66

KNELLER. No. I can paint a woman's beauty; but I cannot measure it in a pint pot. Beauty is immeasurable.

NEWTON. I can measure gravitation. Nothing exists until it is measured. Fine words are nothing. Do you expect me to go to the Royal Society and tell them that the orbits of a planet are curved because painters think them prettier so? How much are they curved? This man cannot tell you. I can. Where will they be six months hence? He cannot tell you. I can. All he has to say is that the earth is a moon of the sun and that the line of beauty is a curve. Can he measure the path of the moon? Can he draw the curve?

KNELLER. I can draw your portrait. Can you draw mine?

NEWTON. Yes, with a camera obscura; and if I could find a chemical salt sensitive to light I could fix it. Some day portraits will be made at the street corners for sixpence apiece.

KNELLER. A looking glass will make your portrait for nothing. It makes the duchess's portrait fifty times a day.

BARBARA. It does not. I dont look at myself in the glass fifty times a day. Charles never passes one without looking at himself. I have watched him.

CHARLES. It rebukes my vanity every time, Barbara. I am an ugly fellow; yet I always think of myself as an Adonis.

LOUISE. You are not so ugly as you think, Charles. You were an ugly baby; and your wicked mother told you so. You have never got over it. But when I was sent to England to captivate you with my baby face, it was you who captivated me with your seventy inches and your good looks.

BARBARA. Ay, flatter him, flatter him: he loves it.

CHARLES. I cannot bear this. The subject is to be dropped.

LOUISE. But, Charles—

CHARLES. No, no, No. Not a word more. The King commands it.

Dead silence. They sit as if in church, except Fox, who chafes at the silence.

FOX. In the presence of this earthly king all you great nobles become dumb flunkeys. What will you be when the

67

King of Kings calls you from your graves to answer for your lives?

NELL. Trust you, George, to put in a cheerful word. Rowley darling: may we all stop being dumb flunkeys and be human beings again?

CHARLES. Mr Rowley apologizes for his lapse into royalty. Only, the King's person is not to be discussed.

LOUISE. But, Charles, I love you when you put on your royalty. My king, Louis Quatorze, le grand monarque, le roi soleil, never puts off his royalty for a moment even in the most ridiculous circumstances.

BARBARA. Yes; and he looks like a well-to-do grocer, and will never look like anything else.

LOUISE. You would not dare to say so at Versailles, or even to think so. He is always great; and his greatness makes us great also. But it is true that he is not six feet high, and that the grand manner is not quite natural to him. Charles can do it so much better when he chooses. Charles: why dont you choose?

CHARLES. I prefer to keep the crown and the grand manner up my sleeve until I need them. Louis and I played together when we were boys. We know each other too well to be pleasant company; so I take care to keep out of his way. Besides, Louise, when I make you all great you become terrible bores. I like Nelly because nothing can make a courtier of her. Do you know why?

BARBARA. Because the orange girl has the gutter in her blood.

CHARLES. Not at all. Tell her the reason, Nell.

NELL. I dont know it, Rowley darling. I never was an orange girl; but I have the gutter in my blood all right. I think I have everything in my blood; for when I am on the stage I can be anything you please, orange girl or queen. Or even a man. But I dont know the reason why. So you can tell it to her, Rowley darling, if you know it.

CHARLES. It is because in the theatre you are a queen. I tell you the world is full of kings and queens and their little courts. Here is Pastor Fox, a king in his meeting house, though his meetings are against the law. Here is Mr Newton, a king in the new Royal Society. Here is Godfrey Kneller: a king among painters. I can make you duchesses and your sons dukes; but who would be mere dukes or duchesses if they could be kings and queens?

NELL. Dukes will be six a penny if you make all Barbara's sons dukes.

BARBARA. Oh! My sons have gentle blood in their veins, not gutter dirt.

CHARLES. For shame, Nelly! It was illbred of you to reproach her Grace for the most amiable side of her character.

NELL. I beg pardon. God forgive me, I am no better myself.

BARBARA. No better! You impudent slut.

NELL. Well, no worse, if you like. One little duke is enough for me.

LOUISE. Change the subject, Charles. What you were saying about little kings and queens being everywhere was very true. You are very spiritual.

BARBARA. Ha ha! Ha ha ha! He spiritual!

LOUISE. Clever, you call it. I am always in trouble with my English. And Charles is too lazy to learn French properly, though he lived in France so long.

BARBARA. If you mean clever, he is as clever as fifty foxes.

FOX. He may be fifty times as clever as I; but so are many of the blackest villains. Value him rather for his flashes of the inner light? Did he not stop the butchering of the regicides on the ground that if he punished them they could never punish themselves? That was what made me his loyal subject.

BARBARA. I did not mean fifty of you: I meant real foxes. He is so clever that he can always make me seem stupid when it suits him: that is, when I want anything he wont give me. He is as stingy as a miser.

CHARLES. You are like a dairymaid: you think there is no end to a king's money. Here is my Nelly, who is more careful of my money than she is of her own. Well, when I am dying, and all the rest of you are forgotten, my last thought

69

will be of Nelly.

NELL. Rowley darling: dont make me cry. I am not the only one. Louise is very thoughtful about money.

BARBARA. Yes: she knows exactly how much he has: she gets it for him from the King of France.

LOUISE. This subject of conversation is in the worst possible taste. Charles: be a king again; and forbid it.

CHARLES. Nobody but Barbara would have introduced it. I forbid it absolutely.

Mrs Basham returns.

MRS BASHAM. Mr Newton: dinner is served.

BARBARA. You should address yourself to His Majesty. Where are your manners, woman?

MRS BASHAM. In this house Mr Newton comes first. Come along quick, all of you; or your victuals will be cold.

NEWTON [*rising*] Mr Kneller: will you take her Grace of Cleveland, as you are interested in her curves?

BARBARA [*violently*] No. I am the senior duchess: it is my right to be taken in by the King.

CHARLES [*rising and resignedly giving her his arm*] The Duke of York will follow with the junior duchess. Happy man!

All rise, except Fox.

BARBARA. Brute! [*She tries to disengage herself*].

CHARLES [*holding her fast*] You are on the King's arm. Behave yourself. [*He takes her out forcibly*].

MRS BASHAM. Now, your Highness. Now, Madam Carwell.

JAMES [*taking Louise*] You have remembered, I hope, that Madam Carwell is a Catholic?

MRS BASHAM. Yes: there will be enough cod for the two of you.

LOUISE. Provided Charles does not get at it first. Let us hurry. [*She hurries James out*].

MRS BASHAM. Will you take the player woman, Mr Kneller?

NELL. No no. The player woman goes with her dear old Fox. [*She swoops on the Quaker and drags him along*] George: today you will dine with publicans and sinners. You will say grace for them.

FOX. You remind me that where my Master went I must follow. [*They go out*].

MRS BASHAM. There is no one left for you to take in, Mr Kneller. Mr Newton must take me in and come last.

KNELLER. I will go home. I cannot eat in this house of straight lines.

MRS BASHAM. You will do nothing of the sort, Mr Kneller. There is a cover laid for you; and the King expects you.

NEWTON. The lines are not straight, Mr Kneller. Gravitation bends them. And at bottom I know no more about gravitation than you do about beauty.

KNELLER. To you the universe is nothing but a clock that an almighty clockmaker has wound up and set going for all eternity.

NEWTON. Shall I tell you a secret, Mr Beautymonger? The clock does not keep time. If it did there would be no further need for the Clockmaker. He is wiser than to leave us to our foolish selves in that fashion. When He made a confusion of tongues to prevent the Tower of Babel from reaching to heaven He also contrived a confusion of time to prevent us from doing wholly without Him. The sidereal clock, the clock of the universe, goes wrong. He has to correct it from time to time. Can you, who know everything because you and God are both artists, tell me what is amiss with the perihelion of Mercury?

KNELLER. The what?

NEWTON. The perihelion of Mercury.

KNELLER. I do not know what it is.

NEWTON. I do. But I do not know what is amiss with it. Not until the world finds this out can it do without the Clockmaker in the heavens who can set the hands back or forward, and move the stars with a touch of His almighty finger as He watches over us in the heavens.

KNELLER. In the heavens! In your universe there is no heaven. You have abolished the sky.

NEWTON. Ignoramus: there may be stars beyond our vision bigger than the whole solar system. When I have

71

perfected my telescope it will give you your choice of a hundred heavens.

MRS BASHAM. Mr Kneller: your dinner will be cold; and you will be late for grace. I cannot have any more of this ungodly talk. Down with you to your dinner at once.

KNELLER. In this house, you said, Mr Newton comes first. But you take good care that he comes last. The mistress of this and every other house is she who cooks the dinner. [*He goes out*].

MRS BASHAM [*taking Newton out*] Thats a funny fellow, sir. But you really should not begin talking about the stars to people just as they are going away quietly. It is a habit that is growing on you. What do they know or care about the perry healing of Mercury that interests you so much? We shall never get these people out of the house if— [*They pass out of hearing*].

There is peace in the deserted room.

ACT II

THE *boudoir of Catherine of Braganza, Charles's queen, in his not too palatial quarters in New-market late in the afternoon on the same day. A prie-dieu, and the pictures, which are all devotional, are signs of the queen's piety. Charles, in slippers and breeches, shirt and cravat, wrapped in an Indian silk dressing gown, is asleep on a couch. His coat and boots are on the carpet where he has thrown them. His hat and wig are on a chair with his tall walking stick. The door, opening on a staircase landing, is near the head of the couch, between it and the prie-dieu. There is a clock in the room.*

Catherine, aged 42, enters. She contemplates her husband and the untidiness he has made. With a Portuguese shake of the head (about six times) she sets to work to put the room in order by taking up the boots and putting them tidily at the foot of the couch. She then takes out the coat and hangs it on the rail of the landing. Returning, she purposely closes the door with a bang sufficient to wake Charles.

CHARLES. How long have I been asleep?

CATHERINE. I not know. Why leave you your things about all over my room? I have to put them away like a chambermaid.

CHARLES. Why not send for Chiffinch? It is his business to look after my clothes.

CATHERINE. I not wish to be troubled with Chiffinch when we are alone.

CHARLES [*rising*] Belovéd: you should make me put away my clothes myself. Why should you do chamber-maid's work for me? [*His "beloved" always has three syllables*].

CATHERINE. I not like to see you without your wig. But I am your wife and must put up with it.

CHARLES [*getting up*] I am your husband; and I count it a great privilege. [*He kisses her*].

CATHERINE. Yes yes; but why choose you my boudoir for your siesta?

CHARLES. Here in our Newmarket lodging it is the only place where the women cannot come after me.

73

CATHERINE. A wife is some use then, after all.

CHARLES. There is nobody like a wife.

CATHERINE. I hear that Cleveland has come back from Paris. Did you send for her?

CHARLES. Send for her! I had as soon send for the divvle. I finished with Barbara long ago.

CATHERINE. How often have you told me that you are finished with all women! Yet Portsmouth keeps her hold on you, and Nellie the player. And now Cleveland comes back.

CHARLES. Beloved: you do not understand. These women do not keep their hold on me: I keep my hold on them. I have a bit of news for you about Louise. What do you think I caught her at this morning?

CATHERINE. I had rather not guess.

CHARLES. Buying a love potion. That was for me. I do not make love to her enough, it seems. I hold her because she is intelligent and ladylike and keeps me in touch with France and the French court, to say nothing of the money I have to extract from Louis through her.

CATHERINE. And Nelly? She can play the fine lady; but is she one?

CHARLES. Nelly is a good creature; and she amuses me. You know, beloved, one gets tired of court ladies and their conversation, always the same.

CATHERINE. And you really did not send for Cleveland to come back?

CHARLES. Beloved: when I was young I thought that there was only one unbearable sort of woman: the one that could think of nothing but her soul and its salvation. But in Barbara I found something worse: a woman who thought of nothing but her body and its satisfaction, which meant men and money. For both, Barbara is insatiable. Grab, grab, grab. When one is done with Barbara's body—a very fine body, I admit—what is there left?

CATHERINE. And you are done with Barbara's body?

CHARLES. Beloved: I am done with all bodies. They are all alike: all cats are grey in the dark. It is the souls and the brains that are different. In the end one learns to leave the body out. And then Barbara is packed off to Paris, and is not

asked back by me, though I have no doubt there is some man
in the case.

CATHERINE. Why spend you so much time with me here
—so much more than you used to?

CHARLES. Beloved: do I plague you? I am off.

He makes for the door: she runs to it and bars his egress.

CATHERINE. No: that is not what I meant. Go back and
sit down.

*Charles obediently goes back to the couch, where they sit
side by side.*

CHARLES. And what did you mean, beloved?

CATHERINE. You spend too much time away from court.
Your brother is stealing the court away from you. When he
is here his rooms are crowded: yours are empty.

CHARLES. I thank heaven for it. The older I grow, the
less I can endure that most tiresome of all animals, the courtier. Even a dissolute court, as they say mine is—I suppose
they mean a court where bawdy stories are told out loud instead of whispered—is more tedious than a respectable one.
They repeat themselves and repeat themselves endlessly.
And I am just as bad with my old stories about my flight
after the battle of Worcester. I told the same one twice over
within an hour last Tuesday. This morning Barbara called
me an old wreck.

CATHERINE [*flaming up*] She dared! Send her to the
Tower and let her rot there.

CHARLES. She is not so important as that, beloved. Nor
am I. And we must forgive our enemies when we can afford
to.

CATHERINE. I forgive my enemies, as you well know,
Charles. It is my duty as a Catholic and a Christian. But it is
not my duty to forgive your enemies. And you never forgive mine.

CHARLES. An excellent family arrangement for a royal
pair. We can exchange our revenges and remain good Christians. But Barbara may be right. When a king is shunned,
and his heir is courted, his death is not far off.

CATHERINE. You must not say things like that: I not
can bear it. You are stronger in your mind than ever; and

nobody can keep up with you walking.

CHARLES. Nevertheless, beloved, I shall drop before you do. What will happen to you then? that is what troubles me. When I am dead you must go back to Portugal, where your brother the king will take care of you. You will never be safe here, because you are a Catholic queen.

CATHERINE. I not think I shall care what becomes of me when you are gone. But James is a Catholic. When he is king what have I to fear? Or do you believe your son Monmouth will prevent him from succeeding you and become a Protestant king?

CHARLES. No. He will try, poor boy; but Jamie will kill him. He is his mother's son; and his mother was nothing. Then the Protestants will kill Jamie; and the Dutch lad will see his chance and take it. He will be king: a Protestant king. So you must make for Portugal.

CATHERINE. But such things not could happen. Why are you, who are afraid of nothing else, so afraid of the Protestants?

CHARLES. They killed my great grandmother. They killed my father. They would kill you if I were not a little too clever for them: they are trying hard enough, damn them! They are great killers, these Protestants. Jamie has just one chance. They may call in Orange Billy before they kill him; and then it will hardly be decent for Billy to kill his wife's father. But they will get rid of Jamie somehow; so you must make for home the moment I have kissed you goodbye for the last time.

CATHERINE [*almost in tears*] you not must talk of it— [*She breaks down*].

CHARLES [*caressing her*] Beloved: you will only lose the worst of husbands.

CATHERINE. That is a lie: if anyone else said it I would kill her. You are the very best husband that ever lived.

CHARLES [*laughing*] Oh! Oh! Oh! The merry monarch! Beloved: can anything I can ever do make up to you for my unfaithfulness?

CATHERINE. People think of nothing but that, as if that were the whole of life. What care I about your women? your

76

concubines? your handmaidens? the servants of your common pleasures? They have set me free to be something more to you than they are or can ever be. You have never been really unfaithful to me.

CHARLES. Yes, once, with the woman whose image as Britannia is on every British penny, and will perhaps stay there to all eternity. And on my honor nothing came of that: I never touched her. But she had some magic that scattered my wits: she made me listen for a moment to those who were always pressing me to divorce my patient wife and take a Protestant queen. But I could never have done it, though I was furious when she ran away from me and married Richmond.

CATHERINE. Oh, I know, I know: it was the only time I ever was jealous. Well, I forgive you: why should a great man like you be satisfied with a little thing like me?

CHARLES. Stop. I cannot bear that. I am not a great man; and neither are you a little woman. You have more brains and character than all the rest of the court put together.

CATHERINE. I am nothing except what you have made me. What did I know when I came here? Only what the nuns teach a Portuguese princess in their convent.

CHARLES. And what more had I to teach you except what I learnt when I was running away from the battle of Worcester? And when I had learnt that much there was an end of me as a king. I knew too much.

CATHERINE. With what you have taught me I shall govern Portugal if I return to it?

CHARLES. I have no doubt of it, beloved; but whether that will make you any happier I have my doubts. I wish you could govern the English for me.

CATHERINE. No one can govern the English: that is why they will never come to any good. In Portugal there is the holy Church: we know what we believe; and we all believe the same things. But here the Church itself is a heresy; and there are a thousand other heresies: almost as many heresies as there are people. And if you ask any of them what his sect believes he does not know: all he can say is that the men of the other sects should be hanged and their women

77

whipped through the town at the cart's tail. But they are all against the true Church. I do not understand the English; and I do not want to govern them.

CHARLES. You are Portuguese. I am Italian, French, Scottish, hardly at all English. When I want to know how the great lump of my subjects will take anything I tell it to Barbara. Then I tell it to Chiffinch. Then I tell it to Jamie. When I have the responses of Barbara, Chiffinch, and Jamie, I know how Tom, Dick and Harry will take it. And it is never as I take it.

CATHERINE. In Portugal we not have this strange notion that Tom, Dick and Harry matter. What do they know about government?

CHARLES. Nothing; but they hate it. And nobody teaches them how necessary it is. Instead, when we teach them anything we teach them grammar and dead languages. What is the result? Protestantism and parliaments instead of citizenship.

CATHERINE. In Portugal, God be praised, there are no Protestants and no parliaments.

CHARLES. Parliaments are the very divvle. Old Noll began by thinking the world of parliaments. Well, he tried every sort of parliament, finishing with a veritable reign of the saints. And in the end he had to turn them all out of doors, neck and crop, and govern through his major-generals. And when Noll died they went back to their parliament and made such a mess of it that they had to send for me.

CATHERINE. Suppose there had been no you?

CHARLES. There is always somebody. In every nation there must be the makings of a capable council and a capable king three or four times over, if only we knew how to pick them. Nobody has found out how to do it: that is why the world is so vilely governed.

CATHERINE. But if the rulers are of noble birth—

CHARLES. You mean if they are the sons of their fathers. What good is that?

CATHERINE. You are king because you are the son of your father. And you are the best of kings.

78

"IN KING CHARLES'S GOLDEN DAYS"

CHARLES. Thank you. And your brother Alfonso was king of Portugal because he was the son of his father. Was he also the best of kings?

CATHERINE. Oh, he was dreadful. He was barely fit to be a stable boy; but my brother Pedro took his crown and locked him up; and Pedro also is my father's son.

CHARLES. Just so: six of one and half a dozen of the other. Heredity is no use. Learning Latin is no use: Jack Churchill, who is an ignoramus, is worth fifty scholars. If Orange Billy dies and one of my nieces succeeds him Jack will be King of England.

CATHERINE. Perhaps the Church should select the king —or the queen.

CHARLES. The Church has failed over and over again to select a decent Pope. Alexander Borgia was a jolly fellow; and I am the last man alive to throw stones at him; but he was not a model Pope.

CATHERINE. My father was a great king. He fought the Spaniards and set Portugal free from their yoke. And it was the people who chose him and made him do it. I have sometimes wondered whether the people should not choose their king.

CHARLES. Not the English people. They would choose Titus Oates. No, beloved: the riddle of how to choose a ruler is still unanswered; and it is the riddle of civilization. I tell you again there are in England, or in any other country, the makings of half a dozen decent kings and councils; but they are mostly in prison. If we only knew how to pick them out and label them, then the people could have their choice out of the half dozen. It may end that way, but not until we have learnt how to pick the people who are fit to be chosen before they are chosen. And even then the picked ones will be just those whom the people will not choose. Who is it that said that no nation can bear being well governed for more than three years? Old Noll found that out. Why am I a popular king? Because I am a lazy fellow. I enjoy myself and let the people see me doing it, and leave things as they are, though things as they are will not bear thinking of by those who know what they are. That is what

79

the people like. It is what they would do if they were kings.

CATHERINE. You are not lazy: I wish you were: I should see more of you. You take a great deal too much exercise: you walk and walk and nobody can keep up with you; you are always gardening or sailing or building and talking to gardeners and sailors and shipwrights and bricklayers and masons and people like that, neglecting the court. That is how your brother gathers the court round him and takes it away from you.

CHARLES. Let him. There is nothing to be learnt at court except that a courtier's life is not a happy one. The gardeners and the watermen, the shipwrights and bricklayers and carpenters and masons, are happier and far far more contented. It is the worst of luck to be born a king. Give me a skilled trade and eight or ten shillings a week, and you and I, beloved, would pig along more happily than we have ever been able to do as our majesties.

CATHERINE. I not want to pig along. I was born to rule; and if the worst comes to the worst and I have to go back to my own country I shall shew the world that I can rule, and that I am not the ninny I am made to look like here.

CHARLES. Why dont you do it, beloved? I am not worth staying with.

CATHERINE. I am torn ten different ways. I know that I should make you divorce me and marry a young Protestant wife who would bring you a son to inherit the crown and save all this killing of Monmouth and James and the handing over of your kingdom to the Hollander. I am tempted to do it because then I should return to my own beautiful country and smell the Tagus instead of the dirty Thames, and rule Portugal as my mother used to rule over the head of my worthless brother. I should be somebody then. But I cannot bring myself to leave you: not for all the thrones in the world. And my religion forbids me to put a Protestant on the throne of England when the rightful heir to it is a good Catholic.

CHARLES. You shall not, beloved. I will have no other widow but you.

CATHERINE. Ah! you can coax me so easily.

"IN KING CHARLES'S GOLDEN DAYS"

CHARLES. I treated you very badly when I was a young man because young men have low tastes and think only of themselves. Besides, odsfish! we could not talk to one-another. The English they taught you in Portugal was a tongue that never was spoke on land or sea; and my Portuguese made you laugh. We must forget our foolish youth: we are grown-up now.

CATHERINE. Happy man! You forget so easily. But think of the difference in our fortunes! All your hopes of being a king were cut off: you were an exile, an outcast, a fugitive. Yet your kingdom dropped into your mouth at last; and you have been a king since you were old enough to use your power. But I! My mother was determined from my birth that I should be a queen: a great queen: Queen of England. Well, she had her way: we were married; and they call me queen. But have I ever reigned? Am I not as much an exile and an outcast as ever you were? I am not Catherine of England: I am Catherine of Bragança: a foreign woman with a funny name that they cannot pronounce. Yet I have the blood of rulers in my veins and the brains of rulers in my head.

CHARLES. They are no use here: the English will not be ruled; and there is nothing they hate like brains. For brains and religion you must go to Scotland; and Scotland is the most damnable country on earth: never shall I forget the life they led me there with their brains and their religion when they made me their boy king to spite Old Noll. I sometimes think religion and brains are the curse of the world. No, beloved, England for me, with all its absurdities!

CATHERINE. There can be only one true religion; and England has fifty.

CHARLES. Well, the more the merrier, if only they could let one another live. But they will not do even that.

CATHERINE. Have you no conscience?

CHARLES. I have; and a very troublesome one too. I would give a dukedom to any doctor that would cure me of it. But somehow it is not a conscience of the standard British pattern.

CATHERINE. That is only your witty nonsense. Our consciences, which come from God, must be all the same.

CHARLES. They are not. Do you think God so stupid that he could invent only one sort of conscience?

CATHERINE [*shocked*] What a dreadful thing to say! I must not listen to you.

CHARLES. No two consciences are the same. No two love affairs are the same. No two marriages are the same. No two illnesses are the same. No two children are the same. No two human beings are the same. What is right for one is wrong for the other. Yet they cannot live together without laws; and a law is something that obliges them all to do the same thing.

CATHERINE. It may be so in England. But in Portugal the Holy Church makes all Catholics the same. My mother ruled them though she was a Spaniard. Why should I not do what my mother did?

CHARLES. Why not, indeed? I daresay you will do it very well, beloved. The Portuguese can believe in a Church and obey a king. The English robbed the Church and destroyed it: if a priest celebrates Mass anywhere in England outside your private chapel he is hanged for it. My great grandmother was a Catholic queen: rather than let her succeed to the throne they chopped her head off. My father was a Protestant king: they chopped his head off for trying to govern them and asking the Midlands to pay for the navy. While the Portuguese were fighting the Spaniards the English were fighting oneanother. You can do nothing with the English. How often have I told you that I am no real king: that the utmost I can do is to keep my crown on my head and my head on my shoulders. How often have you asked me to do some big thing like joining your Church, or some little thing like pardoning a priest or a Quaker condemned to some cruel punishment! And you have found that outside the court, where my smiles and my frowns count for everything, I have no power. The perjured scoundrel, Titus Oates, steeped in unmentionable vices, is lodged in my palace with a pension. If I could have my way he would be lodged on the gallows. There is a preacher named Bunyan who has written a book about the Christian life that is being

read, they tell me, all the world over; and I could not re-
lease him from Bedford Gaol, where he rotted for years.
The world will remember Oates and Bunyan; and I shall be
The Merry Monarch. No: give me English birds and Eng-
lish trees, English dogs and Irish horses, English rivers and
English ships; but English men! No, NO, NO.

CATHERINE. And Englishwomen?

CHARLES. Ah! there you have me, beloved. One cannot
do without women: at least I cannot. But having to manage
rascals like Buckingham and Shaftesbury, and dodgers like
Halifax, is far worse than having to manage Barbara and
Louise.

CATHERINE. Is there really any difference? Shaftesbury
is trying to have me beheaded on Tower Hill on a charge of
plotting to poison you sworn to by Titus Oates. Barbara is
quite ready to support him in that.

CHARLES. No, beloved. The object of having you beheaded is to enable me to marry a Protestant wife and have
a Protestant heir. I have pointed out to Barbara that the
Protestant wife would not be so kind to her as you are, and
would have her out of the kingdom before she could say
Jack Robinson. So now she has thrown over Shaftesbury;
and when I have thrown him over, as I shall know how to
do presently, there will be an end of him. But he will be
succeeded by some stupider rascal, or, worse still, some
stupid fellow who is not a rascal. The clever rascals are all
for sale; but the honest dunderheads are the very divvle.

CATHERINE. I wish you were not so clever.

CHARLES. Beloved: you could not do without my cleverness. That is why you must go back to Portugal when I am
gone.

CATHERINE. But it makes your mind twist about so. You
are so clever that you think you can do without religion. If
only I could win you to the Church I should die perfectly
happy; and so would you.

CHARLES. Well, I promise you I will not die a Protestant. You must see to that when the hour strikes for me: the
last hour. So my very belovedest will die happy; and that
is all I care about. [*Caressing her*] Does that satisfy you?

83

"IN KING CHARLES'S GOLDEN DAYS"

CATHERINE. If only I could believe it.

CHARLES. You mean I am the king whose word no man relies on.

CATHERINE. No: you are not that sort of king for me. But will it be a real conversion? I think you would turn Turk to please me.

CHARLES. Faith I believe I would. But there is more in it than that. It is not that I have too little religion in me for the Church: I have too much, like a queer fellow I talked with this morning. [*The clock strikes five*]. Odsfish! I have a Council meeting. I must go. [*He throws off his dressing gown*]. My boots! What has become of my boots?

CATHERINE. There are your boots. And wait until I make you decent.

Whilst he pulls his boots on, she fetches his coat and valets him into it. He snatches up his hat and stick and puts the hat on.

CATHERINE. No no: you have forgotten your wig. [*She takes his hat off and fetches the wig*]. Fancy your going into the Council Chamber like that! Nobody would take you for King Charles the Second without that wig. Now. [*She puts the wig on him; then the hat. A few final pats and pulls complete his toilet*]. Now you look every inch a king. [*Making him a formal curtsey*] Your Majesty's visit has made me very happy. Long live the King!

CHARLES. May the Queen live for ever!

He throws up his arm in a gallant salute and stalks out. She rises and throws herself on her knees at her prie-dieu.

FANNY'S FIRST PLAY

AN EASY PLAY FOR A LITTLE THEATRE

By Xxxxxxx Xxxx

Written in 1911

First Performed London 1911

PREFACE TO FANNY'S FIRST PLAY

FANNY'S FIRST PLAY, being but a potboiler, needs no preface. But its lesson is not, I am sorry to say, unneeded. Mere morality, or the substitution of custom for conscience, was once accounted a shameful and cynical thing: people talked of right and wrong, of honor and dishonor, of sin and grace, of salvation and damnation, not of morality and immorality. The word morality, if we met it in the Bible, would surprise us as much as the word telephone or motor car. Nowadays we do not seem to know that there is any other test of conduct except morality; and the result is that the young had better have their souls awakened by disgrace, capture by the police, and a month's hard labor, than drift along from their cradles to their graves doing what other people do for no other reason than that other people do it, and knowing nothing of good and evil, of courage and cowardice, or indeed anything but how to keep hunger and concupiscence and fashionable dressing within the bounds of good taste except when their excesses can be concealed. Is it any wonder that I am driven to offer to young people in our suburbs the desperate advice: Do something that will get you into trouble? But please do not suppose that I defend a state of things which makes such advice the best that can be given under the circumstances, or that I do not know how difficult it is to find out a way of getting into trouble that will combine loss of respectability with integrity of self-respect and reasonable consideration for other peoples' feelings and interests on every point except their dread of losing their own respectability. But when there's a will there's a way. I hate to see dead people walking about: it is unnatural. And our respectable middle class people are all as dead as mutton. Out of the mouth of Mrs Knox I have delivered on them the judgment of her God.

The critics whom I have lampooned in the induction to this play under the names of Trotter, Vaughan, and Gunn will forgive me: in fact Mr Trotter forgave me beforehand, and assisted the make-up by which Mr Claude King so successfully simulated his personal appearance. The critics whom I did not introduce were somewhat hurt, as I should have been myself under the same circumstances; but I had not room for them all; so I can only apologize and assure them that I meant no disrespect.

The concealment of the authorship, if a *secret de Polichinelle* can be said to involve concealment, was a necessary part of the play. In so far as it was effectual, it operated as a measure of relief to those critics and playgoers who are so obsessed by my strained legendary reputation that they approach my plays in a condition which is really one of derangement, and are quite unable to conceive a play of mine as anything but a trap baited with paradoxes, and designed to compass their ethical perversion and intellectual confusion. If it were possible, I should put forward all my plays anonymously, or hire some less disturbing person, as Bacon is said to have hired Shakespear, to father my plays for me.

THIS PROLOGUE, "TO BE SUBSTITUTED FOR THE INDUCTION WHEN THE PLAY ALONE IS PERFORMED", WAS WRITTEN BY SHAW FOR CHARLES MACDONA IN 1916.

THE Actress who plays the part of Margaret Knox comes before the curtain dressed as Fanny O'Dowda, and addresses the audience.

We're going to act a play. I shall be in it. [*Applause*]
Thank you for that applause. But—just a minute—
Would you mind very much if I explained to you
What wouldn't otherwise be very plain to you
That is, why—though the play's won worldwide fame—
The author's given it such a funny name!
Fanny's First Play! Its catching. Lots of pence in it.
But at first sight there doesn't seem much sense in it;
But dont make up your minds there isn't any:
It's really Fanny's play; and I am Fanny.
I wrote the play. It was my very first.
(I had to write it or I should have burst:
I couldn't help it). Now, from what youve read of it,
You know, perhaps, that all the critics said of it
That, though my first might fairly good be reckoned,
Heaven forbid that I should write a second!
That was a nasty one: they thought it witty
But I felt nothing for the fools but pity;
For stalls and pit to praise my play united;
And now I'll tell you how I came to write it.
    In childhood's sunny days, I, by an aunt of mine,
    Was taken—prematurely—to the pantomime.
From that time forth, each evening I would be at her:
"Take me again, dear Auntie, to the theatre":
Twas thus I first on Shakespear's golden nage struck.
The natural result was, I got stage struck.
I loved the playhouse: after my first bout of it,
I dared my family to keep me out of it.
I went and went and went, until alas!

FANNY'S FIRST PLAY

Something most unexpected came to pass.
I loved the actors; copied all their ways;
But oh! I got so tired of the plays.
Always the same—what they call oversexed:
You always know just what is coming next:
The husband and the lover and the wife,
Not one of them a bit like real life.
At first I liked them. All my soul was stored with them:
But in a year or so I got quite bored with them.
Just think! in real life what is it touches us?
Stories about ourselves, not about duchesses.
If we all live by honest business, such as is
The backbone of this town, why not insist
On plays that shew at least that we exist,
Instead of these continual appealings
To millionaires, as if we had no feelings!
Why are stage lovers' speeches drowned by coughs?
Because we're tired of their all being toffs.
Though too much business maynt be any fun
Its better anyhow than having none.
Remember good Sam Richardson. Said he,
"I keep my shop, sirs; and my shop keeps me".
You havnt read Sam's novels: theyre too long;
But in the love scenes Sam could come out strong.
To me the thing's as plain as a church steeple:
We must have business plays for business people.
As to the titled heroine, I'd banish her;
But when I hinted at it to the manager,
He said "To put the duchess on the shelf,
Just write a play and act in it yourself".

Ladies and gentlemen; I all but kissed him:
In fact I threw a kiss—like that—but missed him.
I wrote the play: Fanny's First, at your service.
You'll see me act in it. Oh, I'm so nervous.
You wont expect me in the first act, will you?
But in the second I shall simply thrrrill you.

90

ALTERNATE PROLOGUE

The third you must especially attend to.
If you dont like my part, oh, please pretend to.
You see, unless you think it rather funny
You wont feel youve had value for your money.
I really must break off: its downright wrong
Making all this up as I go along:
Besides, Ive got to change, I look too rowdy.
Business folk like their daughters to be dowdy.
I'll make myself so plain, youll all despise me,
I'm sure not one of you will recognize me.
But beauty's nothing: common people love it;
But youre not common people: youre above it.
I knew you were. You all look quite resigned.
Well, since youve been so very very kind,
My good looks shall not be too much diminished.
Thank you for hearing me. [*to the prompter, roughly, as
she retires through the curtain*] Ring up. Ive finished.

FANNY'S FIRST PLAY

INDUCTION

THE end of a saloon in an old-fashioned country house (Florence Towers, the property of Count O'Dowda), has been curtained off to form a stage for a private theatrical performance. A footman in grandiose Spanish livery enters before the curtain, on its O.P. side.

FOOTMAN [announcing] Mr Cecil Savoyard. [Cecil Savoyard comes in: a middle-aged man in evening dress and a fur-lined overcoat. He is surprised to find nobody to receive him. So is the Footman]. Oh, beg pardon, sir: I thought the Count was here. He was when I took up your name. He must have gone through the stage into the library. This way, sir. [He moves towards the division in the middle of the curtains].

SAVOYARD. Half a mo. [The Footman stops]. When does the play begin? Half-past eight?

FOOTMAN. Nine, sir.

SAVOYARD. Oh, good. Well, will you telephone to my wife at the George that it's not until nine?

FOOTMAN. Right, sir. Mrs Cecil Savoyard, sir?

SAVOYARD. No: Mrs William Tinkler. Dont forget.

THE FOOTMAN. Mrs Tinkler, sir. Right, sir. [The Count comes in through the curtains]. Here is the Count, sir. [Announcing] Mr Cecil Savoyard, sir. [He withdraws].

COUNT O'DOWDA [A handsome man of fifty, dressed with studied elegance a hundred years out of date, advancing cordially to shake hands with his visitor] Pray excuse me, Mr Savoyard. I suddenly recollected that all the bookcases in the library were locked—in fact theyve never been opened since we came from Venice—and as our literary guests will probably use the library a good deal, I just ran in to unlock everything.

SAVOYARD. Oh, you mean the dramatic critics. M'yes. I suppose theres a smoking room?

THE COUNT. My study is available. An old-fashioned house, you understand. Wont you sit down, Mr Savoyard?

SAVOYARD. Thanks. [They sit. Savoyard, looking at his host's obsolete costume, continues] I had no idea you were going

93

to appear in the piece yourself.

THE COUNT. I am not. I wear this costume because—well, perhaps I had better explain the position, if it interests you.

SAVOYARD. Certainly.

THE COUNT. Well, you see, Mr Savoyard, I'm rather a stranger in your world. I am not, I hope, a modern man in any sense of the word. I'm not really an Englishman: my family is Irish: Ive lived all my life in Italy—in Venice mostly—my very title is a foreign one: I am a Count of the Holy Roman Empire.

SAVOYARD. Where's that?

THE COUNT. At present, nowhere, except as a memory and an ideal. [*Savoyard inclines his head respectfully to the ideal*]. But I am by no means an idealogue. I am not content with beautiful dreams: I want beautiful realities.

SAVOYARD. Hear, hear! I'm all with you there—when you can get them.

THE COUNT. Why not get them? The difficulty is not that there are no beautiful realities, Mr Savoyard: the difficulty is that so few of us know them when we see them. We have inherited from the past a vast treasure of beauty—of imperishable masterpieces of poetry, of painting, of sculpture, of architecture, of music, of exquisite fashions in dress, in furniture, in domestic decoration. We can contemplate these treasures. We can reproduce many of them. We can buy a few inimitable originals. We can shut out the nineteenth century—

SAVOYARD [*correcting him*] The twentieth.

THE COUNT. To me the century I shut out will always be the nineteenth century, just as your national anthem will always be God Save the Queen, no matter how many kings may succeed. I found England befouled with industrialism: well, I did what Byron did: I simply refused to live in it. You remember Byron's words: "I am sure my bones would not rest in an English grave, or my clay mix with the earth of that country. I believe the thought would drive me mad
94

on my deathbed could I suppose that any of my friends would be base enough to convey my carcase back to her soil. I would not even feed her worms if I could help it."

SAVOYARD. Did Byron say that?

THE COUNT. He did, sir.

SAVOYARD. It dont sound like him. I saw a good deal of him at one time.

THE COUNT. You! But how is that possible? You are too young.

SAVOYARD. I was quite a lad, of course. But I had a job in the original production of Our Boys.

THE COUNT. My dear sir, not that Byron. Lord Byron, the poet.

SAVOYARD. Oh, I beg your pardon. I thought you were talking of the Byron. So you prefer living abroad?

THE COUNT. I find England ugly and Philistine. Well, I dont live in it. I find modern houses ugly. I dont live in them: I have a palace on the grand canal. I find modern clothes prosaic. I dont wear them, except, of course, in the street. My ears are offended by the Cockney twang: I keep out of hearing of it and speak and listen to Italian. I find Beethoven's music coarse and restless, and Wagner's senseless and detestable. I do not listen to them: I listen to Cimarosa, to Pergolesi, to Gluck and Mozart. Nothing simpler, sir.

SAVOYARD. It's all right when you can afford it.

THE COUNT. Afford it! My dear Mr Savoyard, if you are a man with a sense of beauty you can make an earthly paradise for yourself in Venice on £1500 a year, whilst our wretched vulgar industrial millionaires are spending twenty thousand on the amusements of billiard markers. I assure you I am a poor man according to modern ideas. But I have never had anything less than the very best that life has produced. It is my good fortune to have a beautiful and lovable daughter; and that girl, sir, has never seen an ugly sight or heard an ugly sound that I could spare her; and she has certainly never worn an ugly dress or tasted coarse food or

95

bad wine in her life. She has lived in a palace; and her perambulator was a gondola. Now you know the sort of people we are, Mr Savoyard. You can imagine how we feel here.

SAVOYARD. Rather out of it, eh?

THE COUNT. Out of it, sir! Out of what?

SAVOYARD. Well, out of everything.

THE COUNT. Out of soot and fog and mud and east wind; out of vulgarity and ugliness, hypocrisy and greed, superstition and stupidity. Out of all this, and in the sunshine, in the enchanted region of which great artists alone have had the secret, in the sacred footsteps of Byron, of Shelley, of the Brownings, of Turner and Ruskin. Dont you envy me, Mr Savoyard?

SAVOYARD. Some of us must live in England, you know, just to keep the place going. Besides—though, mind you, I dont say it isnt all right from the high art point of view and all that—three weeks of it would drive me melancholy mad. However, I'm glad you told me, because it explains why it is you dont seem to know your way about much in England. I hope, by the way, that everything has given satisfaction to your daughter.

THE COUNT. She seems quite satisfied. She tells me that the actors you sent down are perfectly suited to their parts, and very nice people to work with. I understand she had some difficulties at the first rehearsals with the gentleman you call the producer, because he hadnt read the play; but the moment he found out what it was all about everything went smoothly.

SAVOYARD. Havnt you seen the rehearsals?

THE COUNT. Oh no. I havnt been allowed even to meet any of the company. All I can tell you is that the hero is a Frenchman [*Savoyard is rather scandalized*]: I asked her not to have an English hero. That is all I know. [*Ruefully*] I havnt been consulted even about the costumes, though there, I think, I could have been some use.

SAVOYARD [*puzzled*] But there arnt any costumes.

THE COUNT [*seriously shocked*] What! No costumes! Do

you mean to say it is a modern play?

SAVOYARD. I dont know: I didnt read it. I handed it to Billy Burjoyce—the producer, you know—and left it to him to select the company and so on. But I should have had to order the costumes if there had been any. There wernt.

THE COUNT [*smiling as he recovers from his alarm*] I understand. She has taken the costumes into her own hands. She is an expert in beautiful costumes. I venture to promise you, Mr Savoyard, that what you are about to see will be like a Louis Quatorze ballet painted by Watteau. The heroine will be an exquisite Columbine, her lover a dainty Harlequin, her father a picturesque Pantaloon, and the valet who hoodwinks the father and brings about the happiness of the lovers a grotesque but perfectly tasteful Punchinello or Mascarille or Sganarelle.

SAVOYARD. I see. That makes three men; and the clown and policeman will make five. Thats why you wanted five men in the company.

THE COUNT. My dear sir, you dont suppose I mean that vulgar, ugly, silly, senseless, malicious and destructive thing the harlequinade of a nineteenth century English Christmas pantomime! What was it after all but a stupid attempt to imitate the success made by the genius of Grimaldi a hundred years ago? My daughter does not know of the existence of such a thing. I refer to the graceful and charming fantasies of the Italian and French stages of the seventeenth and eighteenth centuries.

SAVOYARD. Oh, I beg pardon. I quite agree that harlequinades are rot. Theyve been dropped at all smart theatres. But from what Billy Burjoyce told me I got the idea that your daughter knew her way about here, and had seen a lot of plays. He had no idea she'd been away in Venice all the time.

THE COUNT. Oh, she has not been. I should have explained that two years ago my daughter left me to complete her education at Cambridge. Cambridge was my own University; and though of course there were no women there in

97

my time, I felt confident that if the atmosphere of the eight‑ eenth century still existed anywhere in England, it would be at Cambridge. About three months ago she wrote to me and asked whether I wished to give her a present on her next birthday. Of course I said yes; and she then astonished and delighted me by telling me that she had written a play, and that the present she wanted was a private performance of it with real actors and real critics.

SAVOYARD. Yes: thats what staggered me. It was easy enough to engage a company for a private performance: it's done often enough. But the notion of having critics was new. I hardly knew how to set about it. They dont expect private engagements; and so they have no agents. Besides, I didnt know what to offer them. I knew that they were cheaper than actors, because they get long engagements: forty years sometimes; but thats no rule for a single job. Then theres such a lot of them: on first nights they run away with all your stalls: you cant find a decent place for your own mother. It would have cost a fortune to bring the lot.

THE COUNT. Of course I never dreamt of having them all. Only a few first-rate representative men.

SAVOYARD. Just so. All you want is a few sample opinions. Out of a hundred notices you wont find more than four at the outside that say anything different. Well, Ive got just the right four for you. And what do you think it has cost me?

THE COUNT [shrugging his shoulders] I cannot guess.

SAVOYARD. Ten guineas, and expenses. I had to give Flawner Bannal ten. He wouldnt come for less; and he asked fifty. I had to give it, because if we hadnt had him we might just as well have had nobody at all.

THE COUNT. But what about the others, if Mr Flannel—

SAVOYARD [shocked] Flawner Bannal.

THE COUNT.—if Mr Bannal got the whole ten?

SAVOYARD. Oh, I managed that. As this is a high-class sort of thing, the first man I went for was Trotter.

THE COUNT. Oh indeed. I am very glad you have secured Mr Trotter. I have read his Playful Impressions.

98

SAVOYARD. Well, I was rather in a funk about him. He's not exactly what I call approachable; and he was a bit stand-off at first. But when I explained and told him your daughter—

THE COUNT [*interrupting in alarm*] You did not say that the play was by her, I hope?

SAVOYARD. No: thats been kept a dead secret. I just said your daughter has asked for a real play with a real author and a real critic and all the rest of it. The moment I mentioned the daughter I had him. He has a daughter of his own. Wouldnt hear of payment! Offered to come just to please her! Quite human. I was surprised.

THE COUNT. Extremely kind of him.

SAVOYARD. Then I went to Vaughan, because he does music as well as the drama; and you said you thought there would be music. I told him Trotter would feel lonely without him; so he promised like a bird. Then I thought youd like one of the latest sort: the chaps that go for the newest things and swear theyre oldfashioned. So I nailed Gilbert Gunn. The four will give you a representative team. By the way [*looking at his watch*] theyll be here presently.

THE COUNT. Before they come, Mr Savoyard, could you give me any hints about them that would help me to make a little conversation with them? I am, as you said, rather out of it in England; and I might unwittingly say something tactless.

SAVOYARD. Well, let me see. As you dont like English people, I dont know that youll get on with Trotter, because he's thoroughly English: never happy except when he's in Paris, and speaks French so unnecessarily well that everybody there spots him as an Englishman the moment he opens his mouth. Very witty and all that. Pretends to turn up his nose at the theatre and says people make too much fuss about art [*the Count is extremely indignant*]. But thats only his modesty, because art is his own line, you understand. Mind you dont chaff him about Aristotle.

THE COUNT. Why should I chaff him about Aristotle?

99

SAVOYARD. Well, I dont know; but it's one of the recognized ways of chaffing him. However, youll get on with him all right: he's a man of the world and a man of sense. The one youll have to be careful about is Vaughan.

THE COUNT. In what way, may I ask?

SAVOYARD. Well, Vaughan has no sense of humor; and if you joke with him he'll think youre insulting him on purpose. Mind: it's not that he doesnt see a joke: he does; and it hurts him. A comedy scene makes him sore all over: he goes away black and blue, and pitches into the play for all he's worth.

THE COUNT. But surely that is a very serious defect in a man of his profession?

SAVOYARD. Yes it is, and no mistake. But Vaughan is honest, and dont care a brass farthing what he says, or whether it pleases anybody or not; and you must have one man of that sort to say the things that nobody else will say.

THE COUNT. It seems to me to carry the principle of division of labor too far, this keeping of the honesty and the other qualities in separate compartments. What is Mr Gunn's speciality, if I may ask?

SAVOYARD. Gunn is one of the Intellectuals.

THE COUNT. But arnt they all Intellectuals?

SAVOYARD. Lord! no: heaven forbid! You must be careful what you say about that: I shouldnt like anyone to call me an Intellectual: I dont think any Englishman would! They dont count really, you know; but still it's rather the thing to have them. Gunn is one of the young Intellectuals: he writes plays himself. He's useful because he pitches into the older Intellectuals who are standing in his way. But you may take it from me that none of these chaps really matter. Flawner Bannal's your man. Bannal really represents the British playgoer. When he likes a thing, you may take your oath there are a hundred thousand people in London thatll like it if they can only be got to know about it. Besides, Bannal's knowledge of the theatre is an inside knowledge. We know him; and he knows us. He knows the ropes: he knows his way about: he knows what he's talking about.

THE COUNT [*with a little sigh*] Age and experience, I suppose?

SAVOYARD. Age! I should put him at twenty at the very
outside, myself. It's not an old man's job after all, is it?
Bannal may not ride the literary high horse like Trotter and
the rest; but I'd take his opinion before any other in London.
He's the man in the street; and thats what you want.

THE COUNT. I am almost sorry you didnt give the gentleman his full terms. I should not have grudged the fifty
guineas for a sound opinion. He may feel shabbily treated.

SAVOYARD. Well, let him. It was a bit of side, his asking
fifty. After all, what is he? Only a pressman. Jolly good
business for him to earn ten guineas: he's done the same
job often enough for half a quid, I expect.

*Fanny O'Dowda comes precipitately through the curtains,
excited and nervous. A girl of nineteen in a dress synchronous
with her father's.*

FANNY. Papa, papa, the critics have come. And one of
them has a cocked hat and sword like a—[*she notices Savoyard*] Oh, I beg your pardon.

THE COUNT. This is Mr Savoyard, your impresario, my
dear.

FANNY [*shaking hands*] How do you do?

SAVOYARD. Pleased to meet you, Miss O'Dowda. The
cocked hat is all right. Trotter is a member of the new
Academic Committee. He induced them to go in for a uniform like the French Academy; and I asked him to wear it.

THE FOOTMAN [*announcing*] Mr Trotter, Mr Vaughan,
Mr Gunn, Mr Flawner Bannal.

*The four critics enter. Trotter wears a diplomatic dress, with
sword and three-cornered hat. His age is about 50. Vaughan is
40. Gunn is 30. Flawner Bannal is 20 and is quite unlike the
others, who can be classed at sight as professional men whilst
Bannal is obviously an unemployable of the business class picking
up a living by an obtuse courage which gives him cheerfulness,
conviviality, and bounce, and is helped out positively by a slight*

*turn for writing, and negatively by a comfortable ignorance and
lack of intuition which hides from him all the dangers and dis-
graces that keep men of finer perception in check. The Count
approaches them hospitably.*

SAVOYARD. Count O'Dowda, gentlemen. Mr Trotter.

TROTTER [*looking at the Count's costume*] Have I the pleasure of meeting a *confrère?*

THE COUNT. No, sir: I have no right to my costume except the right of a lover of the arts to dress myself handsomely. You are most welcome, Mr Trotter. [*Trotter bows
in the French manner*].

SAVOYARD. Mr Vaughan.

THE COUNT. How do you do, Mr Vaughan?

VAUGHAN. Quite well, thanks.

SAVOYARD. Mr Gunn.

THE COUNT. Delighted to make your acquaintance, Mr
Gunn.

GUNN. Very pleased.

SAVOYARD. Mr Flawner Bannal.

THE COUNT. Very kind of you to come, Mr Bannal.

BANNAL. Dont mention it.

THE COUNT. Gentlemen, my daughter. [*They all bow*].
We are very greatly indebted to you, gentlemen, for so
kindly indulging her whim. [*The dressing bell sounds. The
Count looks at his watch*]. Ah! The dressing bell, gentlemen.
As our play begins at nine, I have had to put forward the
dinner hour a little. May I shew you to your rooms? [*He
goes out, followed by all the men, except Trotter, who, going
last, is detained by Fanny*].

FANNY. Mr Trotter: I want to say something to you
about this play.

TROTTER. No: thats forbidden. You must not attempt
to *souffler* the critic.

FANNY. Oh, I would not for the world try to influence
your opinion.

TROTTER. But you do: you are influencing me very
shockingly. You invite me to this charming house, where

102

I'm about to enjoy a charming dinner. And just before the dinner I'm taken aside by a charming young lady to be talked to about the play. How can you expect me to be impartial? God forbid that I should set up to be a judge, or do more than record an impression; but my impressions can be influenced; and in this case voure influencing them shamelessly all the time.

FANNY. Dont make me more nervous than I am already, Mr Trotter. If you knew how I feel!

TROTTER. Naturally: your first party: your first appearance in England as hostess. But youre doing it beautifully. Dont be afraid. Every *nuance* is perfect.

FANNY. It's so kind of you to say so, Mr Trotter. But that isnt whats the matter. The truth is, this play is going to give my father a dreadful shock.

TROTTER. Nothing unusual in that, I'm sorry to say. Half the young ladies in London spend their evenings making their fathers take them to plays that are not fit for elderly people to see.

FANNY. Oh, I know all about that; but you cant understand what it means to Papa. Youre not so innocent as he is.

TROTTER [*remonstrating*] My dear young lady—

FANNY. I dont mean morally innocent: everybody who reads your articles knows youre as innocent as a lamb.

TROTTER. What!

FANNY. Yes, Mr Trotter: Ive seen a good deal of life since I came to England; and I assure you that to me youre a mere baby: a dear, good, well-meaning, delightful, witty, charming baby; but still just a wee lamb in a world of wolves. Cambridge is not what it was in my father's time.

TROTTER. Well, I must say!

FANNY. Just so. Thats one of our classifications in the Cambridge Fabian Society.

TROTTER. Classifications? I dont understand.

FANNY. We classify our aunts into different sorts. And one of the sorts is the "I m u s t says."

TROTTER. I withdraw "I must say." I substitute "Blame

my cats!" No: I substitute "Blame my kittens!" Observe, Miss O'Dowda: kittens. I say again in the teeth of the whole Cambridge Fabian Society, kittens. Impertinent little kittens. Blame them. Smack them. I guess what is on your conscience. This play to which you have lured me is one of those in which members of Fabian Societies instruct their grandmothers in the art of milking ducks. And you are afraid it will shock your father. Well, I hope it will. And if he consults me about it I shall recommend him to smack you soundly and pack you off to bed.

FANNY. Thats one of your prettiest literary attitudes, Mr Trotter; but it doesnt take me in. You see, I'm much more conscious of what you really are than you are yourself, because weve discussed you thoroughly at Cambridge; and youve never discussed yourself, have you?

TROTTER. I—

FANNY. Of course you havnt; so you see it's no good Trottering at me.

TROTTER. Trottering!

FANNY. Thats what we call it at Cambridge.

TROTTER. If it were not so obviously a stage *cliché*, I should say Damn Cambridge. As it is, I blame my kittens. And now let me warn you. If youre going to be a charming healthy young English girl, you may coax me. If youre going to be an unsexed Cambridge Fabian virago, I'll treat you as my intellectual equal, as I would treat a man.

FANNY [*adoringly*] But how few men are your intellectual equals, Mr Trotter!

TROTTER. I'm getting the worst of this.

FANNY. Oh no. Why do you say that?

TROTTER. May I remind you that the dinner-bell will ring presently?

FANNY. What does it matter? We're both ready. I havnt told you yet what I want you to do for me.

TROTTER. Nor have you particularly predisposed me to do it, except out of pure magnanimity. What is it?

FANNY. I dont mind this play shocking my father morally.

It's good for him to be shocked morally. It's all that the young can do for the old, to shock them and keep them up to date. But I know that this play will shock him artistically; and that terrifies me. No moral consideration could make a breach between us: he would forgive me for anything of that kind sooner or later; but he never gives way on a point of art. I darent let him know that I love Beethoven and Wagner; and as to Strauss, if he heard three bars of Elektra, it'd part us for ever. Now what I want you to do is this. If he's very angry—if he hates the play, because it's a modern play—will you tell him that it's not my fault; that its style and construction, and so forth, are considered the very highest art nowadays: that the author wrote it in the proper way for repertory theatres of the most superior kind—you know the kind of plays I mean?

TROTTER [*emphatically*] I think I know the sort of entertainments you mean. But please do not beg a vital question by calling them plays. I dont pretend to be an authority; but I have at least established the fact that these productions, whatever else they may be, are certainly not plays.

FANNY. The authors dont say they are.

TROTTER [*warmly*] I am aware that one author, who is, I blush to say, a personal friend of mine, resorts freely to the dastardly subterfuge of calling them conversations, discussions, and so forth, with the express object of evading criticism. But I'm not to be disarmed by such tricks. I say they are not plays. Dialogues, if you will. Exhibitions of character, perhaps: especially the character of the author. Fictions, possibly, though a little decent reticence as to introducing actual persons, and thus violating the sanctity of private life, might not be amiss. But plays, no. I say NO. Not plays. If you will not concede this point I cant continue our conversation. I take this seriously. It's a matter of principle. I must ask you, Miss O'Dowda, before we go a step further, Do you or do you not claim that these works are plays?

FANNY. I assure you I dont.

TROTTER. Not in any sense of the word?

FANNY. Not in any sense of the word. I loathe plays.

TROTTER [*disappointed*] That last remark destroys all the value of your admission. You admire these— these theatrical nondescripts? You enjoy them?

FANNY. Dont you?

TROTTER. Of course I do. Do you take me for a fool? Do you suppose I prefer popular melodramas? Have I not written most appreciative notices of them? But I say theyre not plays. Theyre not plays. I cant consent to remain in this house another minute if anything remotely resembling them is to be foisted on me as a play.

FANNY. I fully admit that theyre not plays. I only want you to tell my father that plays are not plays nowadays— not in your sense of the word.

TROTTER. Ah, there you go again! In my sense of the word! You believe that my criticism is merely a personal impression; that—

FANNY. You always said it was.

TROTTER. Pardon me: not on this point. If you had been classically educated—

FANNY. But I have.

TROTTER. Pooh! Cambridge! If you had been educated at Oxford, you would know that the definition of a play has been settled exactly and scientifically for two thousand two hundred and sixty years. When I say that these entertainments are not plays, I dont mean in my sense of the word, but in the sense given to it for all time by the immortal Stagirite.

FANNY. Who is the Stagirite?

TROTTER [*shocked*] You dont know who the Stagirite was!

FANNY. Sorry. Never heard of him.

TROTTER. And this is Cambridge education! Well, my dear young lady, I'm delighted to find theres something you dont know; and I shant spoil you by dispelling an ignorance which, in my opinion, is highly becoming to your age and sex. So we'll leave it at that.

FANNY. But you will promise to tell my father that lots of people write plays just like this one—that I havnt selected it out of mere heartlessness?

TROTTER. I cant possibly tell you what I shall say to your father about the play until Ive seen the play. But I'll tell you what I shall say to him about you. I shall say that youre a very foolish young lady; that youve got into a very questionable set; and that the sooner he takes you away from Cambridge and its Fabian Society, the better.

FANNY. It's so funny to hear you pretending to be a heavy father. In Cambridge we regard you as a *bel esprit*, a wit, an Irresponsible, a Parisian Immoralist, *très chic*.

TROTTER. I!

FANNY. Theres quite a Trotter set.

TROTTER. Well, upon my word!

FANNY. They go in for adventures and call you Aramis.

TROTTER. They wouldnt dare!

FANNY. You always make such delicious fun of the serious people. Your *insouciance*—

TROTTER [*frantic*] Stop talking French to me: it's not a proper language for a young girl. Great heavens! how is it possible that a few innocent pleasantries should be so frightfully misunderstood? Ive tried all my life to be sincere and simple, to be unassuming and kindly. Ive lived a blameless life. Ive supported the Censorship in the face of ridicule and insult. And now I'm told that I'm a centre of Immoralism! of Modern Minxism! a trifler with the most sacred subjects! a Nietzschean!! perhaps a Shavian!!!

FANNY. Do you mean you are really on the serious side, Mr Trotter?

TROTTER. Of course I'm on the serious side. How dare you ask me such a question?

FANNY. Then why dont you play for it?

TROTTER. I do play for it—short, of course, of making myself ridiculous.

FANNY. What! not make yourself ridiculous for the sake of a good cause! Oh, Mr Trotter! Thats *vieux jeu*.

TROTTER [*shouting at her*] Dont talk French. I will not allow it.

FANNY. But this dread of ridicule is so frightfully out of date. The Cambridge Fabian Society—

TROTTER. I forbid you to mention the Fabian Society to me.

FANNY. Its motto is "You cannot learn to skate without making yourself ridiculous."

TROTTER. Skate! What has that to do with it?

FANNY. Thats not all. It goes on, "The ice of life is slippery."

TROTTER. Ice of life indeed! You should be eating penny ices and enjoying yourself. I wont hear another word.

The Count returns.

THE COUNT. We're all waiting in the drawing room, my dear. Have you been detaining Mr Trotter all this time?

TROTTER. I'm so sorry. I must have just a little brush up: I—[*He hurries out*].

THE COUNT. My dear, you should be in the drawing room. You should not have kept him here.

FANNY. I know. Dont scold me: I had something important to say to him.

THE COUNT. I shall ask him to take you in to dinner.

FANNY. Yes, papa. Oh, I hope it will go off well.

THE COUNT. Yes, love, of course it will. Come along.

FANNY. Just one thing, papa, while we're alone. Who was the Stagirite?

THE COUNT. The Stagirite! Do you mean to say you dont know?

FANNY. Havnt the least notion.

THE COUNT. The Stagirite was Aristotle. By the way, dont mention him to Mr Trotter.

They go to the dining room.

THE PLAY

ACT I

IN the dining room of a house in Denmark Hill, an elderly lady sits at breakfast reading the newspaper. Her chair is at the end of the oblong dining table furthest from the fire. There is an empty chair at the other end. The fireplace is behind this chair; and the door is next the fireplace, between it and the corner. An armchair stands beside the coal-scuttle. In the middle of the back wall is the sideboard, parallel to the table. The rest of the furniture is mostly dining-room chairs, ranged against the walls, and including a baby rocking-chair on the lady's side of the room. The lady is a placid person. Her husband, Mr Robin Gilbey, not at all placid, bursts violently into the room with a letter in his hand.

GILBEY [grinding his teeth] This is a nice thing. This is a b—

MRS GILBEY [cutting him short] Leave it at that, please. Whatever it is, bad language wont make it better.

GILBEY [bitterly] Yes, put me in the wrong as usual. Take your boy's part against me. [He flings himself into the empty chair opposite her].

MRS GILBEY. When he does anything right, he's your son. When he does anything wrong he's mine. Have you any news of him?

GILBEY. Ive a good mind not to tell you.

MRS GILBEY. Then dont. I suppose he's been found. Thats a comfort, at all events.

GILBEY. No, he hasnt been found. The boy may be at the bottom of the river for all you care. [Too agitated to sit quietly, he rises and paces the room distractedly].

MRS GILBEY. Then what have you got in your hand?

GILBEY. Ive a letter from the Monsignor Grenfell. From New York. Dropping us. Cutting us. [Turning fiercely on her] Thats a nice thing, isnt it?

MRS GILBEY. What for?

GILBEY [flinging away towards his chair] How do I know what for?

109

MRS GILBEY. What does he say?

GILBEY [*sitting down and grumblingly adjusting his spectacles*] This is what he says. "My dear Mr Gilbey: The news about Bobby had to follow me across the Atlantic: it did not reach me until to-day. I am afraid he is incorrigible. My brother, as you may imagine, feels that this last escapade has gone beyond the bounds; and I think, myself, that Bobby ought to be made to feel that such scrapes involve a certain degree of reprobation." "As you may imagine!" And we know no more about it than the babe unborn.

MRS GILBEY. What else does he say?

GILBEY. "I think my brother must have been just a little to blame himself; so, between ourselves, I shall, with due and impressive formality, forgive Bobby later on; but for the present I think it had better be understood that he is in disgrace, and that we are no longer on visiting terms. As ever, yours sincerely." [*His agitation masters him again*] Thats a nice slap in the face to get from a man in his position! This is what your son has brought on me.

MRS GILBEY. Well, I think it's rather a nice letter. He as good as tells you he's only letting on to be offended for Bobby's good.

GILBEY. Oh, very well: have the letter framed and hang it up over the mantelpiece as a testimonial.

MRS GILBEY. Dont talk nonsense, Rob. You ought to be thankful to know that the boy is alive after his disappearing like that for nearly a week.

GILBEY. Nearly a week! A fortnight, you mean. Wheres your feelings, woman! It was fourteen days yesterday.

MRS GILBEY. Oh, dont call it fourteen days, Rob, as if the boy was in prison.

GILBEY. How do you know he's not in prison? It's got on my nerves so, that I'd believe even that.

MRS GILBEY. Dont talk silly, Rob. Bobby might get into a scrape like any other lad; but he'd never do anything low.

Juggins, the footman, comes in with a card on a salver. He is a rather low-spirited man of thirty-five or more, of good ap-

pearance and address, and iron self-command.

JUGGINS [*presenting the salver to Mr Gilbey*] Lady wishes to see Mr Bobby's parents, sir.

GILBEY [*pointing to Mrs Gilbey*] Theres Mr Bobby's parent. I disown him.

JUGGINS. Yes, sir. [*He presents the salver to Mrs Gilbey*].

MRS GILBEY. You mustnt mind what your master says, Juggins: he doesnt mean it. [*She takes the card and reads it*]. Well, I never!

GILBEY. Whats up now?

MRS GILBEY [*reading*] "Miss D. Delaney. Darling Dora." Just like that—in brackets. What sort of person, Juggins?

GILBEY. Whats her address?

MRS GILBEY. The West Circular Road. Is that a respectable address, Juggins?

JUGGINS. A great many most respectable people live in the West Circular Road, madam; but the address is not a guarantee of respectability.

GILBEY. So it's come to that with him, has it?

MRS GILBEY. Dont jump to conclusions, Rob. How do you know? [*To Juggins*] Is she a lady, Juggins? You know what I mean.

JUGGINS. In the sense in which you are using the word, no, madam.

MRS GILBEY. I'd better try what I can get out of her. [*To Juggins*] Shew her up. You dont mind, do you, Rob?

GILBEY. So long as you dont flounce out and leave me alone with her. [*He rises and plants himself on the hearth-rug*].

Juggins goes out.

MRS GILBEY. I wonder what she wants, Rob?

GILBEY. If she wants money, she shant have it. Not a farthing. A nice thing, everybody seeing her on our doorstep! If it wasnt that she may tell us something about the lad, I'd have Juggins put the hussy into the street.

JUGGINS [*returning and announcing*] Miss Delaney. [*He waits for express orders before placing a chair for this visitor*].

Miss Delaney comes in. She is a young lady of hilarious dis-

position, very tolerable good looks, and killing clothes. She is so affable and confidential that it is very difficult to keep her at a distance by any process short of flinging her out of the house.

DORA [*plunging at once into privileged intimacy and into the middle of the room*] How d'ye do, both. I'm a friend of Bobby's. He told me all about you once, in a moment of confidence. Of course he never let on who he was at the police court.

GILBEY. Police court?

MRS GILBEY [*looking apprehensively at Juggins*]. Tch—! Juggins: a chair.

DORA. Oh, Ive let it out, have I! [*Contemplating Juggins approvingly as he places a chair for her between the table and the sideboard*] But he's the right sort: I can see that. [*Button-holing him*] You wont let on downstairs, old man, will you?

JUGGINS. The family can rely on my absolute discretion. [*He withdraws*].

DORA [*sitting down genteelly*] I dont know what youll say to me: you know I really have no right to come here; but then what was I to do? You know Holy Joe, Bobby's tutor, dont you? But of course you do.

GILBEY [*with dignity*] I know Mr Joseph Grenfell, the brother of Monsignor Grenfell, if it is of him you are speaking.

DORA [*wide-eyed and much amused*] No!!! You dont tell me that old geezer has a brother a Monsignor! And youre Catholics! And I never knew it, though Ive known Bobby ever so long! But of course the last thing you find out about a person is their religion, isnt it?

MRS GILBEY. We're not Catholics. But when the Samuelses got an Archdeacon's son to form their boy's mind, Mr Gilbey thought Bobby ought to have a chance too. And the Monsignor is a customer. Mr Gilbey consulted him about Bobby; and he recommended a brother of his that was more sinned against than sinning.

GILBEY [*on tenterhooks*] She dont want to hear about that, Maria. [*To Dora*] Whats your business?

DORA. I'm afraid it was all my fault.

GILBEY. What was all your fault? I'm half distracted. I dont know what has happened to the boy: he's been lost these fourteen days—

MRS GILBEY. A fortnight, Rob.

GILBEY.—and not a word have we heard of him since.

MRS GILBEY. Dont fuss, Rob.

GILBEY [yelling] I will fuss. Youve no feeling. You dont care what becomes of the lad. [He sits down savagely].

DORA [soothingly] Youve been anxious about him. Of course. How thoughtless of me not to begin by telling you he's quite safe. Indeed he's in the safest place in the world, as one may say: safe under lock and key.

GILBEY [horrified, pitiable] Oh my—[his breath fails him]. Do you mean that when he was in the police court he was in the dock? Oh, Maria! Oh, great Lord! What has he done? What has he got for it? [Desperate] Will you tell me or will you see me go mad on my own carpet?

DORA [sweetly] Yes, old dear—

MRS GILBEY [starting at the familiarity] Well!

DORA [continuing] I'll tell you; but dont you worry: he's all right. I came out myself this morning: there was such a crowd! and a band! they thought I was a suffragette: only fancy! You see it was like this. Holy Joe got talking about how he'd been a champion sprinter at college.

MRS GILBEY. A what?

DORA. A sprinter. He said he was the fastest hundred yards runner in England. We were all in the old cowshed that night.

MRS GILBEY. What old cowshed?

GILBEY [groaning] Oh, get on. Get on.

DORA. Oh, of course you wouldnt know. How silly of me! It's a rather go-ahead sort of music hall in Stepney. We call it the old cowshed.

MRS GILBEY. Does Mr Grenfell take Bobby to music halls?

DORA. No: Bobby takes him. But Holy Joe likes it: fairly

laps it up like a kitten, poor old dear. Well, Bobby says to me, "Darling—"

MRS GILBEY [*placidly*] Why does he call you darling?

DORA. Oh, everybody calls me darling: it's a sort of name Ive got. Darling Dora, you know. Well, he says, "Darling, if you can get Holy Joe to sprint a hundred yards, I'll stand you that squiffer with the gold keys."

MRS GILBEY. Does he call his tutor Holy Joe to his face?

Gilbey clutches at his hair in his impatience.

DORA. Well, what would he call him? After all, Holy Joe is Holy Joe; and boys will be boys.

MRS GILBEY. Whats a squiffer?

DORA. Oh, of course: excuse my vulgarity: a concertina. Theres one in a shop in Green Street, ivory inlaid, with gold keys and Russia leather bellows; and Bobby knew I hankered after it; but he couldnt afford it, poor lad, though I knew he just longed to give it to me.

GILBEY. Maria: if you keep interrupting with silly questions, I shall go out of my senses. Heres the boy in gaol and me disgraced for ever; and all you care to know is what a squiffer is.

DORA. Well, remember it has gold keys. The man wouldnt take a penny less than £15 for it. It was a presentation one.

GILBEY [*shouting at her*] Wheres my son? Whats happened to my son? Will you tell me that, and stop cackling about your squiffer?

DORA. Oh, aint we impatient! Well, it does you credit, old dear. And you neednt fuss: theres no disgrace. Bobby behaved like a perfect gentleman. Besides, it was all my fault. I'll own it: I took too much champagne. I was not what you might call drunk; but I was bright, and a little beyond myself; and—I'll confess it—I wanted to shew off before Bobby, because he was a bit taken by a woman on the stage; and she was pretending to be game for anything. You see youve brought Bobby up too strict; and when he gets loose theres no holding him. He does enjoy life more than any lad

114

I ever met.

GILBEY. Never you mind how he's been brought up: thats my business. Tell me how he's been brought down: thats yours.

MRS GILBEY. Oh, dont be rude to the lady, Rob.

DORA. I'm coming to it, old dear: dont you be so headstrong. Well, it was a beautiful moonlight night; and we couldnt get a cab on the nod; so we started to walk, very jolly, you know: arm in arm, and dancing along, singing and all that. When we came into Jamaica Square, there was a young copper on point duty at the corner. I says to Bob: "Dearie boy: is it a bargain about the squiffer if I make Joe sprint for you?" "Anything you like, darling," says he: "I love you." I put on my best company manners and stepped up to the copper. "If you please, sir," says I, "can you direct me to Carrickmines Square?" I was so genteel, and talked so sweet, that he fell to it like a bird. "I never heard of any such Square in these parts," he says. "Then," says I, "what a very silly little officer you must be!"; and I gave his helmet a chuck behind that knocked it over his eyes, and did a bunk.

MRS GILBEY. Did a what?

DORA. A bunk. Holy Joe did one too all right: he sprinted faster than he ever did in college, I bet, the old dear. He got clean off, too. Just as he was overtaking me half-way down the square, we heard the whistle; and at the sound of it he drew away like a streak of lightning; and that was the last I saw of him. I was copped in the Dock Road myself: rotten luck, wasnt it? I tried the innocent and genteel and all the rest; but Bobby's hat done me in.

GILBEY. And what happened to the boy?

DORA. Only fancy! he stopped to laugh at the copper! He thought the copper would see the joke, poor lamb. He was arguing about it when the two that took me came along to find out what the whistle was for, and brought me with them. Of course I swore I'd never seen him before in my life; but there he was in my hat and I in his. The cops were very spiteful and laid it on for all they were worth: drunk and disorderly and assaulting the police and all that. I got fourteen days without the option, because you see—well, the fact is, I'd done it before, and been warned. Bobby was a first offender and had the option; but the dear boy had no money left and wouldnt give you away by telling his name; and anyhow he couldnt have brought himself to buy himself off and leave me there; so he's doing his month. Well, it was two forty shillingses; and Ive only twenty-eight shillings in the world. If I pawn my clothes I shant be able to earn any more. So I cant pay the fine and get him out; but if youll stand £3 I'll stand one; and thatll do it. If youd like to be very kind and nice you could pay the lot; but I cant deny that it was my fault; so I wont press you.

GILBEY [*heart-broken*] My son in gaol!

DORA. Oh, cheer up, old dear: it wont hurt him: look at me after fourteen days of it: I'm all the better for being kept a bit quiet. You mustnt let it prey on your mind.

GILBEY. The disgrace of it will kill me. And it will leave a mark on him to the end of his life.

DORA. Not a bit of it. Dont you be afraid: Ive educated Bobby a bit: he's not the mollycoddle he was when you had him in hand.

MRS GILBEY. Indeed Bobby is not a mollycoddle. They wanted him to go in for singlestick at the Young Men's Christian Association; but, of course, I couldnt allow that: he might have had his eye knocked out.

GILBEY [*to Dora, angrily*] Listen here, you.

DORA. Oh, aint we cross!

GILBEY. I want none of your gaiety here. This is a respectable household. Youve gone and got my poor innocent boy in trouble. It's the like of you thats the ruin of the like of him.

DORA. So you always say, you old dears. But you know better. Bobby came to me: I didnt come to him.

GILBEY. Would he have gone if you hadnt been there for him to go to? Tell me that. You know why he went to you, I suppose.

DORA [*charitably*] It was dull for him at home, poor lad, wasnt it?

MRS GILBEY. Oh no. I'm at home on first Thursdays. And we have the Knoxes to dinner every Friday. Margaret Knox and Bobby are as good as engaged. Mr Knox is my husband's partner. Mrs Knox is very religious; but she's quite cheerful. We dine with them on Tuesdays. So thats two evenings pleasure every week.

GILBEY [*almost in tears*] We done what we could for the boy. Short of letting him go into temptations of all sorts, he can do what he likes. What more does he want?

DORA. Well, old dear, he wants me; and thats about the long and short of it. And I must say youre not very nice to me about it. Ive talked to him like a mother, and tried my best to keep him straight; but I dont deny I like a bit of fun myself; and we both get a bit giddy when we're lighthearted. Him and me is a pair, I'm afraid.

GILBEY. Dont talk foolishness, girl. How could you and he be a pair, you being what you are, and he brought up as he has been with the example of a religious woman like Mrs Knox before his eyes? I cant understand how he could bring himself to be seen in the street with you. [*Pitying himself*] I havnt deserved this. Ive done my duty as a father. Ive kept him sheltered. [*Angry with her*] Creatures like you that take advantage of a child's innocence ought to be whipped through the streets.

DORA. Well, whatever I may be, I'm too much the lady to lose my temper; and I dont think Bobby would like me to tell you what I think of you; for when I start giving people a bit of my mind I sometimes use language thats beneath me. But I tell you once for all I must have the money to get Bobby out; and if you wont fork out, I'll hunt up Holy Joe. He might get it off his brother, the Monsignor.

GILBEY. You mind your own concerns. My solicitor will do what is right. I'll not have you paying my son's fine as if you were anything to him.

DORA. Thats right. Youll get him out today, wont you?

GILBEY. It's likely I'd leave my boy in prison, isnt it?

DORA. I'd like to know when theyll let him out.

GILBEY. You would, would you? Youre going to meet him at the prison door.

DORA. Well, dont you think any woman would that had the feelings of a lady?

GILBEY [*bitterly*] Oh yes: I know. Here! I must buy the lad's salvation, I suppose. How much will you take to clear out and let him go?

DORA [*pitying him: quite nice about it*] What good would that do, old dear? There are others, you know.

GILBEY. Thats true. I must send the boy himself away.

DORA. Where to?

GILBEY. Anywhere, so long as he's out of the reach of you and your like.

DORA. Then I'm afraid youll have to send him out of the world, old dear. I'm sorry for you: I really am, though you mightnt believe it; and I think your feelings do you real credit. But I cant give him up just to let him fall into the hands of people I couldnt trust, can I?

GILBEY [*beside himself, rising*] Wheres the police? Wheres the Government? Wheres the Church? Wheres respectability and right reason? Whats the good of them if I have to stand here and see you put my son in your pocket as if he was a chattel slave, and you hardly out of gaol as a common drunk and disorderly? Whats the world coming to?

DORA. It is a lottery, isnt it, old dear?

Mr Gilbey rushes from the room, distracted.

MRS GILBEY [*unruffled*] Where did you buy that white lace? I want some to match a collaret of my own; and I cant get it at Perry and John's.

DORA. Knagg and Pantle's: one and fourpence. It's machine hand-made.

MRS GIBLEY. I never give more than one and tuppence. But I suppose youre extravagant by nature. My sister Martha was just like that. Pay anything she was asked.

DORA. Whats tuppence to you, Mrs Bobby, after all?

MRS GILBEY [*correcting her*] Mrs Gilbey.

DORA. Of course, Mrs Gilbey. I am silly.

MRS GILBEY. Bobby must have looked funny in your hat. Why did you change hats with him?

DORA. I dont know. One does, you know.

MRS GILBEY. I never did. The things people do! I cant understand them. Bobby never told me he was keeping company with you. His own mother!

DORA [*overcome*] Excuse me: I cant help smiling.

Juggins enters.

JUGGINS. Mr Gilbey has gone to Wormwood Scrubbs, madam.

MRS GILBEY. Have you ever been in a police court, Juggins?

JUGGINS. Yes, madam.

MRS GILBEY [*rather shocked*] I hope you had not been exceeding, Juggins.

JUGGINS. Yes, madam, I had. I exceeded the legal limit.

MRS GILBEY. Oh, that! Why do they give a woman a fortnight for wearing a man's hat, and a man a month for wearing hers?

JUGGINS. I didnt know that they did, madam.

MRS GILBEY. It doesnt seem justice, does it, Juggins?

JUGGINS. No, madam.

MRS GILBEY [*to Dora, rising*] Well, goodbye. [*Shaking her hand*] So pleased to have made your acquaintance.

DORA [*standing up*] Dont mention it. I'm sure it's most kind of you to receive me at all.

MRS GILBEY. I must go off now and order lunch. [*She trots to the door*]. What was it you called the concertina?

DORA. A squiffer, dear.

MRS GILBEY [*thoughtfully*] A squiffer, of course. How funny! [*She goes out*].

DORA [*exploding into ecstasies of mirth*] Oh my! isnt she an old love? How do you keep your face straight?

JUGGINS. It is what I am paid for.

DORA [*confidentially*] Listen here, dear boy. Your name

isnt Juggins. Nobody's name is Juggins.

JUGGINS. My orders are, Miss Delaney, that you are not to be here when Mr Gilbey returns from Wormwood Scrubbs.

DORA. That means telling me to mind my own business, doesnt it? Well, I'm off. Tootle Loo, Charlie Darling. [*She kisses her hand to him and goes*].

ACT II

ON the afternoon of the same day, Mrs Knox is writing notes in her drawing room, at a writing-table which stands against the wall. Anyone placed so as to see Mrs Knox's left profile, will have the door on the right and the window on the left, both further away than Mrs Knox, whose back is presented to an obsolete upright piano at the opposite side of the room. The sofa is near the piano. There is a small table in the middle of the room, with some gilt-edged books and albums on it, and chairs near it.

Mr Knox comes in almost furtively, a troubled man of fifty, thinner, harder, and uglier than his partner, Gilbey, Gilbey being a soft stoutish man with white hair and thin smooth skin, whilst Knox has coarse black hair, and blue jaws which no diligence in shaving can whiten. Mrs Knox is a plain woman, dressed without regard to fashion, with thoughtful eyes and thoughtful ways that make an atmosphere of peace and some solemnity. She is surprised to see her husband at home during business hours.

MRS KNOX. What brings you home at this hour? Have you heard anything?

KNOX. No. Have you?

MRS KNOX. No. Whats the matter?

KNOX [sitting down on the sofa] I believe Gilbey has found out.

MRS KNOX. What makes you think that?

KNOX. Well, I dont know: I didnt like to tell you: you have enough to worry you without that; but Gilbey's been very queer ever since it happened. I cant keep my mind on business as I ought; and I was depending on him. But he's worse than me. He's not looking after anything; and he keeps out of my way. His manner's not natural. He hasnt asked us to dinner; and he's never said a word about our not asking him to dinner, after all these years when weve dined every week as regular as clockwork. It looks to me as if Gilbey's trying to drop me socially. Well, why should he do that if he hasnt heard?

MRS KNOX. I wonder! Bobby hasnt been near us either:

thats what I cant make out.

KNOX. Oh, thats nothing. I told him Margaret was down in Cornwall with her aunt.

MRS KNOX [*reproachfully*] Jo! [*She takes her handkerchief from the writing-table and cries a little*].

KNOX. Well, I got to tell lies, aint I? You wont. Somebody's got to tell em.

MRS KNOX [*putting away her handkerchief*] It only ends in our not knowing what to believe. Mrs Gilbey told me Bobby was in Brighton for the sea air. Theres something queer about that. Gilbey would never let the boy loose by himself among the temptations of a gay place like Brighton without his tutor; and I saw the tutor in Kensington High Street the very day she told me.

KNOX. If the Gilbeys have found out, it's all over between Bobby and Margaret, and all over between us and them.

MRS KNOX. It's all over between us and everybody. When a girl runs away from home like that, people know what to think of her and her parents.

KNOX. She had a happy, respectable home—everything—

MRS KNOX [*interrupting him*] Theres no use going over it all again, Jo. If a girl hasnt happiness in herself, she wont be happy anywhere. Youd better go back to the shop and try to keep your mind off it.

KNOX [*rising restlessly*] I cant. I keep fancying everybody knows it and is sniggering about it. I'm at peace nowhere but here. It's a comfort to be with you. It's a torment to be with other people.

MRS KNOX [*going to him and drawing her arm through his*] There, Jo, there! I'm sure I'd have you here always if I could. But it cant be. God's work must go on from day to day, no matter what comes. We must face our trouble and bear it.

KNOX [*wandering to the window arm in arm with her*] Just look at the people in the street, going up and down as if nothing had happened. It seems unnatural, as if they all knew and didnt care.

MRS KNOX. If they knew, Jo, thered be a crowd round the house looking up at us. You shouldnt keep thinking about it.

KNOX. I know I shouldnt. You have your religion, Amelia; and I'm sure I'm glad it comforts you. But it doesnt come to me that way. Ive worked hard to get a position and be respectable. Ive turned many a girl out of the shop for being half an hour late at night; and heres my own daughter gone for a fortnight without word or sign, except a telegram to say she's not dead and that we're not to worry about her.

MRS KNOX [*suddenly pointing to the street*] Jo, look!

KNOX. Margaret! With a man!

MRS KNOX. Run down. Jo, quick. Catch her: save her.

KNOX [*lingering*] She's shaking hands with him: she's coming across to the door.

MRS KNOX [*energetically*] Do as I tell you. Catch the man before he's out of sight.

Knox rushes from the room. Mrs Knox looks anxiously and excitedly from the window. Then she throws up the sash and leans out. Margaret Knox comes in, flustered and annoyed. She is a strong, springy girl of eighteen, with large nostrils, an audacious chin, and a gaily resolute manner, even peremptory on occasions like the present, when she is annoyed.

MARGARET. Mother. Mother.

Mrs Knox draws in her head and confronts her daughter.

MRS KNOX [*sternly*] Well, miss?

MARGARET. Oh, mother, do go out and stop father making a scene in the street. He rushed at him and said "Youre the man who took away my daughter" loud enough for all the people to hear. Everybody stopped. We shall have a crowd round the house. Do do something to stop him.

Knox returns with a good-looking young marine officer.

MARGARET. Oh, Monsieur Duvallet, I'm so sorry—so ashamed. Mother: this is Monsieur Duvallet, who has been extremely kind to me. Monsieur Duvallet: my mother.

123

[*Duvallet bows*].

KNOX. A Frenchman! It only needed this.

MARGARET [*much annoyed*] Father: do please be commonly civil to a gentleman who has been of the greatest service to me. What will he think of us?

DUVALLET [*debonair*] But it's very natural. I understand Mr Knox's feelings perfectly. [*He speaks English better than Knox, having learnt it on both sides of the Atlantic*].

KNOX. If Ive made any mistake I'm ready to apologize. But I want to know where my daughter has been for the last fortnight.

DUVALLET. She has been, I assure you, in a particularly safe place.

KNOX. Will you tell me what place? I can judge for myself how safe it was.

MARGARET. Holloway Gaol. Was that safe enough?

KNOX AND MRS KNOX. Holloway Gaol!

KNOX. Youve joined the Suffragets!

MARGARET. No. I wish I had. I could have had the same experience in better company. Please sit down, Monsieur Duvallet. [*She sits between the table and the sofa. Mrs Knox, overwhelmed, sits at the other side of the table. Knox remains standing in the middle of the room*].

DUVALLET [*sitting down on the sofa*] It was nothing. An adventure. Nothing.

MARGARET [*obdurately*] Drunk and assaulting the police! Forty shillings or a month!

MRS KNOX. Margaret! Who accused you of such a thing?

MARGARET. The policeman I assaulted.

KNOX. You mean to say that you did it!

MARGARET. I did. I had that satisfaction at all events. I knocked two of his teeth out.

KNOX. And you sit there coolly and tell me this!

MARGARET. Well, where do you want me to sit? Whats the use of saying things like that?

KNOX. My daughter in Holloway Gaol!

MARGARET. All the women in Holloway are somebody's

124

daughters. Really, father, you must make up your mind to it. If you had sat in that cell for fourteen days making up your mind to it, you would understand that I'm not in the humor to be gaped at while youre trying to persuade yourself that it can't be real. These things really do happen to real people every day; and you read about them in the papers and think it's all right. Well, theyve happened to me: thats all.

KNOX [*feeble-forcible*] But they shouldnt have happened to you. Dont you know that?

MARGARET. They shouldnt happen to anybody, I suppose. But they do. [*Rising impatiently*] And really I'd rather go out and assault another policeman and go back to Holloway than keep talking round and round it like this. If youre going to turn me out of the house, turn me out: the sooner I go the better.

DUVALLET [*rising quickly*] That is impossible, mademoiselle. Your father has his position to consider. To turn his daughter out of doors would ruin him socially.

KNOX. Oh, youve put her up to that, have you? And where did you come in, may I ask?

DUVALLET. I came in at your invitation—at your amiable insistence, in fact, not at my own. But you need have no anxiety on my account. I was concerned in the regrettable incident which led to your daughter's incarceration. I got a fortnight without the option of a fine on the ridiculous ground that I ought to have struck the policeman with my fist. I should have done so with pleasure had I known; but, as it was, I struck him on the ear with my boot—a magnificent *moulinet*, I must say—and was informed that I had been guilty of an act of cowardice, but that for the sake of the *entente cordiale* I should be dealt with leniently. Yet Miss Knox, who used her fist, got a month, but with the option of a fine. I did not know this until I was released, when my first act was to pay the forty shillings. And here we are.

MRS KNOX. You ought to pay the gentleman the fine, Jo.

KNOX [*reddening*] Oh, certainly. [*He takes out some money*].

DUVALLET. Oh please! it does not matter. [*Knox hands him two sovereigns*]. If you insist—[*he pockets them*]. Thank you.

MARGARET. I'm ever so much obliged to you, Monsieur Duvallet.

DUVALLET. Can I be of any further assistance, mademoiselle?

MARGARET. I think you had better leave us to fight it out, if you dont mind.

DUVALLET. Perfectly. Madame [*bow*]—Mademoiselle [*bow*]—Monsieur [*bow*]—[*He goes out*].

MRS KNOX. Dont ring, Jo. See the gentleman out yourself.

Knox hastily sees Duvallet out. Mother and daughter sit looking forlornly at one another without saying a word. Mrs Knox slowly sits down. Margaret follows her example. They look at one another again. Mr Knox returns.

KNOX [*shortly and sternly*] Amelia: this is your job. [*To Margaret*] I leave you to your mother. I shall have my own say in the matter when I hear what you have to say to her. [*He goes out, solemn and offended*].

MARGARET [*with a bitter little laugh*] Just what the Suffraget said to me in Holloway. He throws the job on you.

MRS KNOX [*reproachfully*] Margaret!

MARGARET. You know it's true.

MRS KNOX. Margaret: if youre going to be hardened about it, theres no use my saying anything.

MARGARET. I'm not hardened, mother. But I cant talk nonsense about it. You see, it's all real to me. Ive suffered it. Ive been shoved and bullied. Ive had my arms twisted. Ive been made scream with pain in other ways. Ive been flung into a filthy cell with a lot of other poor wretches as if I were a sack of coals being emptied into a cellar. And the only difference between me and the others was that I hit back. Yes I did. And I did worse. I wasnt ladylike. I cursed. I called names. I heard words that I didnt even know that I knew, coming out of my mouth just as if somebody else had

126

spoken them. The policeman repeated them in court. The magistrate said he could hardly believe it. The policeman held out his hand with his two teeth in it that I knocked out. I said it was all right; that I had heard myself using those words quite distinctly; and that I had taken the good conduct prize for three years running at school. The poor old gentleman put me back for the missionary to find out who I was, and to ascertain the state of my mind. I wouldnt tell, of course, for your sakes at home here; and I wouldnt say I was sorry, or apologize to the policeman, or compensate him or anything of that sort. I wasnt sorry. The one thing that gave me any satisfaction was getting in that smack on his mouth; and I said so. So the missionary reported that I seemed hardened and that no doubt I would tell who I was after a day in prison. Then I was sentenced. So now you see I'm not a bit the sort of girl you thought me. I'm not a bit the sort of girl I thought myself. And I dont know what sort of person you really are, or what sort of person father really is. I wonder what he would say or do if he had an angry brute of a policeman twisting his arm with one hand and rushing him along by the nape of his neck with the other. He couldnt whirl his leg like a windmill and knock a policeman down by a glorious kick on the helmet. Oh, if theyd all fought as we two fought we'd have beaten them.

MRS KNOX. But how did it all begin?

MARGARET. Oh, I dont know. It was boat-race night, they said.

MRS KNOX. Boat-race night! But what had you to do with the boat race? You went to the great Salvation Festival at the Albert Hall with your aunt. She put you into the bus that passes the door. What made you get out of the bus?

MARGARET. I dont know. The meeting got on my nerves, somehow. It was the singing, I suppose: you know I love singing a good swinging hymn; and I felt it was ridiculous to go home in the bus after we had been singing so wonderfully about climbing up the golden stairs to heaven. I wanted more music—more happiness—more life. I wanted some

127

comrade who felt as I did. I felt exalted: it seemed mean to be afraid of anything: after all, what could anyone do to me against my will? I suppose I was a little mad: at all events, I got out of the bus at Piccadilly Circus, because there was a lot of light and excitement there. I walked to Leicester Square; and went into a great theatre.

MRS KNOX [*horrified*] A theatre!

MARGARET. Yes. Lots of other women were going in alone. I had to pay five shillings.

MRS KNOX [*aghast*] Five shillings!

MARGARET [*apologetically*] It w a s a lot. It was very stuffy; and I didnt like the people much, because they didnt seem to be enjoying themselves; but the stage was splendid and the music lovely. I saw that Frenchman, Monsieur Duvallet, standing against a barrier, smoking a cigarette. He seemed quite happy; and he was nice and sailorlike. I went and stood beside him, hoping he would speak to me.

MRS KNOX [*gasps*] Margaret!

MARGARET [*continuing*] He did, just as if he had known me for years. We got on together like old friends. He asked me would I have some champagne; and I said it would cost too much, but that I would give anything for a dance. I longed to join the people on the stage and dance with them: one of them was the most beautiful dancer I ever saw. He told me he had come there to see her, and that when it was over we could go somewhere where there was dancing. So we went to a place where there was a band in a gallery and the floor cleared for dancing. Very few people danced: the women only wanted to shew off their dresses; but we danced and danced until a lot of them joined in. We got quite reckless; and we had champagne after all. I never enjoyed anything so much. But at last it got spoilt by the Oxford and Cambridge students up for the Boat race. They got drunk; and they began to smash things; and the police came in. Then it was quite horrible. The students fought with the police; and the police suddenly got quite brutal, and began to throw everybody downstairs. They attacked the women, who were not doing anything, and treated them just as roughly as they had treated the students. Duvallet got indignant and remonstrated with a policeman, who was shoving a woman though she was going quietly as fast as she could. The policeman flung the woman through the door and then turned on Duvallet. It was then that Duvallet swung his leg like a windmill and knocked the policeman down. And then three policemen rushed at him and carried him out by the arms and legs face downwards. Two more attacked me and gave me a shove to the door. That quite maddened me. I just got in one good bang on the mouth of one of them. All the rest was dreadful. I was rushed through the streets to the police station. They kicked me with their knees; they twisted my arms; they taunted and insulted me; they called me vile names; and I told them what I thought of them, and provoked them to do their worst. Theres one good thing about being hard hurt: it makes you sleep. I slept in that filthy cell with all the other drunks sounder than I should have slept at home. I cant describe how I felt next morning: it was hideous; but the police were quite jolly; and everybody said it was a bit of English fun, and talked about last year's boat-race night when it had been a great deal worse. I was black and blue and sick and wretched. But the strange thing was that I wasnt sorry; and I'm not sorry. And I dont feel that I did anything wrong, really. [*She rises and stretches her arms with a large liberating breath*] Now that it's all over I'm rather proud of it; though I know now that I'm not a lady; but whether thats because we're only shopkeepers, or because nobody's really a lady except when theyre treated like ladies, I dont know. [*She throws herself into a corner of the sofa*].

MRS KNOX [*lost in wonder*] But how could you bring yourself to do it, Margaret? I'm not blaming you: I only want to know. How could you bring yourself to do it?

MARGARET. I cant tell you. I dont understand it myself. The prayer meeting set me free, somehow. I should never have done it if it were not for the prayer meeting.

129

MRS KNOX [*deeply horrified*] Oh, dont say such a thing as that. I know that prayer can set us free; though you could never understand me when I told you so; but it sets us free for good, not for evil.

MARGARET. Then I suppose what I did was not evil; or else I was set free for evil as well as good. As father says, you cant have anything both ways at once. When I was at home and at school I was what you call good; but I wasnt free. And when I got free I was what most people would call not good. But I see no harm in what I did; though I see plenty in what other people did to me.

MRS KNOX. I hope you dont think yourself a heroine of romance.

MARGARET. Oh no. [*She sits down again at the table*]. I'm a heroine of reality, if you call me a heroine at all. And reality is pretty brutal, pretty filthy, when you come to grips with it. Yet it's glorious all the same. It's so real and satisfactory.

MRS KNOX. I dont like this spirit in you, Margaret. I dont like your talking to me in that tone.

MARGARET. It's no use, mother. I dont care for you and papa any the less; but I shall never get back to the old way of talking again. Ive made a sort of descent into hell—

MRS KNOX. Margaret! Such a word!

MARGARET. You should have heard all the words that were flying round that night. You should mix a little with people who dont know any other words. But when I said that about a descent into hell I was not swearing. I was in earnest, like a preacher.

MRS KNOX. A preacher utters them in a reverent tone of voice.

MARGARET. I know: the tone that shews they dont mean anything real to him. They usent to mean anything real to me. Now hell is as real to me as a turnip; and I suppose I shall always speak of it like that. Anyhow, Ive been there; and it seems to me now that nothing is worth doing but redeeming people from it.

MRS KNOX. They are redeemed already if they choose to

believe it.

MARGARET. Whats the use of that if they dont choose to believe it? You dont believe it yourself, or you wouldnt pay policemen to twist their arms. Whats the good of pretending? Thats all our respectability is, pretending, pretending, pretending. Thank heaven Ive had it knocked out of me once for all!

MRS KNOX [*greatly agitated*] Margaret: dont talk like that. I cant bear to hear you talking wickedly. I can bear to hear the children of this world talking vainly and foolishly in the language of this world. But when I hear you justifying your wickedness in the words of grace, it's too horrible: it sounds like the devil making fun of religion. Ive tried to bring you up to learn the happiness of religion. Ive waited for you to find out that happiness is within ourselves and doesnt come from outward pleasures. Ive prayed oftener than you think that you might be enlightened. But if all my hopes and all my prayers are to come to this, that you mix up my very words and thoughts with the promptings of the devil, then I dont know what I shall do: I dont indeed: itll kill me.

MARGARET. You shouldnt have prayed for me to be enlightened if you didnt want me to be enlightened. If the truth were known, I suspect we all want our prayers to be answered only by halves: the agreeable halves. Your prayer didnt get answered by halves, mother. Youve got more than you bargained for in the way of enlightenment. I shall never be the same again. I shall never speak in the old way again. Ive been set free from this silly little hole of a house and all its pretences. I know now that I am stronger than you and papa. I havnt found that happiness of yours that is within yourself; but Ive found strength. For good or evil I am set free; and none of the things that used to hold me can hold me now.

Knox comes back, unable to bear his suspense.

KNOX. How long more are you going to keep me waiting, Amelia? Do you think I'm made of iron? Whats the girl

131

done? What are we going to do?

MRS KNOX. She's beyond my control, Jo, and beyond yours. I cant even pray for her now; for I dont know rightly what to pray for.

KNOX. Dont talk nonsense, woman: is this a time for praying? Does anybody k n o w? Thats what we have to consider now. If only we can keep it dark, I dont care for anything else.

MARGARET. Dont hope for that, father. Mind: I'll tell everybody. It ought to be told: it must be told.

KNOX. Hold your tongue, you young hussy; or go out of my house this instant.

MARGARET. I'm quite ready. [*She takes her hat and turns to the door*].

KNOX [*throwing himself in front of it*] Here! where are you going?

MRS KNOX [*rising*] You mustnt turn her out, Jo! I'll go with her if she goes.

KNOX. Who wants to turn her out? But is she going to ruin us? To let everybody know of her disgrace and shame? To tear me down from the position Ive made for myself and you by forty years hard struggling?

MARGARET. Yes: I'm going to tear it all down. It stands between us and everything. I'll tell everybody.

KNOX. Magsy, my child: dont bring down your father's hairs with sorrow to the grave. Theres only one thing I care about in the world: to keep this dark. I'm your father. I ask you here on my knees—in the dust, so to speak—not to let it out.

MARGARET. I'll tell everybody.

Knox collapses in despair. Mrs Knox tries to pray and cannot. Margaret stands inflexible.

ACT III

AGAIN in the Gilbeys' dining room. Afternoon. The table is not laid: it is draped in its ordinary cloth, with pen and ink, an exercise-book, and school-books on it. Bobby Gilbey is in the armchair, crouching over the fire, reading an illustrated paper. He is a pretty youth, of very suburban gentility, strong and manly enough by nature, but untrained and unsatisfactory, his parents having imagined that domestic restriction is what they call "bringing up." He has learnt nothing from it except a habit of evading it by deceit.

He gets up to ring the bell; then resumes his crouch. Juggins answers the bell.

BOBBY. Juggins.

JUGGINS. Sir?

BOBBY [morosely sarcastic] Sir be blowed!

JUGGINS [cheerfully] Not at all, sir.

BOBBY. I'm a gaol-bird: youre a respectable man.

JUGGINS. That doesnt matter, sir. Your father pays me to call you sir; and as I take the money, I keep my part of the bargain.

BOBBY. Would you call me sir if you wernt paid to do it?

JUGGINS. No, sir.

BOBBY. Ive been talking to Dora about you.

JUGGINS. Indeed, sir?

BOBBY. Yes. Dora says your name cant be Juggins, and that you have the manners of a gentleman. I always thought you hadnt any manners. Anyhow, your manners are different from the manners of a gentleman in my set.

JUGGINS. They would be, sir.

BOBBY. You dont feel disposed to be communicative on the subject of Dora's notion, I suppose.

JUGGINS. No, sir.

BOBBY [throwing his paper on the floor and lifting his knees over the arm of the chair so as to turn towards the footman] It was part of your bargain that you were to valet me a bit, wasnt it?

JUGGINS. Yes, sir.

BOBBY. Well, can you tell me the proper way to get out of an engagement to a girl without getting into a row for breach of promise?

JUGGINS. No, sir. You cant get out of an engagement without being sued for breach of promise if the lady wishes to be paid for her disappointment.

BOBBY. But it wouldnt be for her happiness to marry me when I dont really care for her.

JUGGINS. Women dont always marry for happiness, sir. They often marry because they wish to be married women and not old maids.

BOBBY. Then what I am to do?

JUGGINS. Marry her, sir, or take the consequences.

BOBBY [*jumping up*] Well, I wont marry her: thats flat. What would you do if you were in my place?

JUGGINS. I should tell the young lady that I found I couldnt fulfil my engagement.

BOBBY. But youd have to make some excuse, you know. I want to give it a gentlemanly turn: to say I'm not worthy of her, or something like that.

JUGGINS. That is not a gentlemanly turn, sir. Quite the contrary.

BOBBY. I dont see that at all. Do you mean that it's not exactly true?

JUGGINS. Not at all, sir.

BOBBY. I can say that no other girl can ever be to me what she's been. That would be quite true, because our circumstances have been rather exceptional; and she'll imagine I mean I'm fonder of her than I can ever be of anyone else. You see, Juggins, a gentleman has to think of a girl's feelings.

JUGGINS. If you wish to spare her feelings, sir, you can marry her. If you hurt her feelings by refusing, you had better not try to get credit for considerateness at the same time by pretending to spare them. She wont like it. And it will start an argument, of which you will get the worse.

BOBBY. But, you know, I'm not really worthy of her.

JUGGINS. Probably she never supposed you were, sir.

BOBBY. Oh, I say, Juggins, you are a pessimist.

JUGGINS [*preparing to go*] Anything else, sir?

BOBBY [*querulously*] You havnt been much use. [*He wanders disconsolately across the room*]. You generally put me up to the correct way of doing things.

JUGGINS. I assure you, sir, theres no correct way of jilting. It's not correct in itself.

BOBBY [*hopefully*] I'll tell you what. I'll say I cant hold her to an engagement with a man whos been in quod. Thatll do it. [*He seats himself on the table, relieved and confident*].

JUGGINS. Very dangerous, sir. No woman will deny herself the romantic luxury of self-sacrifice and forgiveness when they take the form of doing something agreeable. She's almost sure to say that your misfortune will draw her closer to you.

BOBBY. What a nuisance! I dont know what to do. You know, Juggins, your cool simple-minded way of doing it wouldnt go down in Denmark Hill.

JUGGINS. I daresay not, sir. No doubt youd prefer to make it look like an act of self-sacrifice for her sake on your part, or provoke her to break the engagement herself. Both plans have been tried repeatedly, but never with success, as far as my knowledge goes.

BOBBY. You have a devilish cool way of laying down the law. You know, in my class you have to wrap up things a bit. Denmark Hill isnt Camberwell, you know.

JUGGINS. I have noticed, sir, that Denmark Hill thinks that the higher you go in the social scale, the less sincerity is allowed, and that only tramps and riff-raff are quite sincere. Thats a mistake. Tramps are often shameless; but theyre never sincere. Swells—if I may use that convenient name for the upper classes—play much more with their cards on the table. If you tell the young lady that you want to jilt her, and she calls you a pig, the tone of the transaction may leave much to be desired; but itll be less Camber-wellian than if you say youre not worthy.

BOBBY. Oh, I cant make you understand, Juggins. The girl isnt a scullery-maid. I want to do it delicately.

JUGGINS. A mistake, sir, believe me, if you are not a born artist in that line.—Beg pardon, sir, I think I heard the bell. [*He goes out*].

Bobby, much perplexed, shoves his hands into his pockets, and comes off the table, staring disconsolately straight before him; then he goes reluctantly to his books, and sits down to write. Juggins returns.

JUGGINS [*announcing*] Miss Knox.

Margaret comes in. Juggins withdraws.

MARGARET. Still grinding away for that Society of Arts examination, Bobby? Youll never pass.

BOBBY [*rising*] No: I was just writing to you.

MARGARET. What about?

BOBBY. Oh, nothing. At least— How are you?

MARGARET [*passing round the other end of the table and putting down on it a copy of Lloyd's Weekly and her purse-bag*] Quite well, thank you. How did you enjoy Brighton?

BOBBY. Brighton! I wasnt at— Oh yes, of course. Oh, pretty well. Is your aunt all right?

MARGARET. My aunt! I suppose so. I havent seen her for a month.

BOBBY. I thought you were down staying with her.

MARGARET. Oh! was that what they told you?

BOBBY. Yes. Why? Wernt you really?

MARGARET. No. Ive something to tell you. Sit down and lets be comfortable.

She sits on the edge of the table. He sits beside her, and puts his arm wearily round her waist.

MARGARET. You neednt do that if you dont like, Bobby. Suppose we get off duty for the day, just to see what it's like.

BOBBY. Off duty? What do you mean?

MARGARET. You know very well what I mean. Bobby: did you ever care one little scrap for me in that sort of way?

Dont funk answering: *I* dont care a bit for you—that way.

BOBBY [*removing his arm rather huffily*] I beg your pardon, I'm sure. I thought you did.

MARGARET. Well, did you? Come! Dont be mean. Ive owned up. You can put it all on me if you like; but I dont believe you care any more than I do.

BOBBY. You mean weve been shoved into it rather by the pars and mars.

MARGARET. Yes.

BOBBY. Well, it's not that I dont care for you: in fact, no girl can ever be to me exactly what you are; but weve been brought up so much together that it feels more like brother and sister than—well, than the other thing, doesnt it?

MARGARET. Just so. How did you find out the difference?

BOBBY [*blushing*] Oh, I say!

MARGARET. I found out from a Frenchman.

BOBBY. Oh, I say! [*He comes off the table in his consternation*].

MARGARET. Did you learn it from a Frenchwoman? You know you must have learnt if from somebody.

BOBBY. Not a Frenchwoman. She's quite a nice woman. But she's been rather unfortunate. The daughter of a clergyman.

MARGARET [*startled*] Oh, Bobby! That sort of woman!

BOBBY. What sort of woman?

MARGARET. You dont believe she's really a clergyman's daughter, do you, you silly boy? It's a stock joke.

BOBBY. Do you mean to say you dont believe me?

MARGARET. No: I mean to say I dont believe her.

BOBBY [*curious and interested, resuming his seat on the table beside her*] What do you know about her? What do you know about all this sort of thing?

MARGARET. What sort of thing, Bobby?

BOBBY. Well, about life.

MARGARET. Ive lived a lot since I saw you last. I wasnt at my aunt's. All that time that you were in Brighton, I mean.

BOBBY. I wasnt at Brighton, Meg. I'd better tell you: youre bound to find out sooner or later. [*He begins his confession humbly, avoiding her gaze*]. Meg: it's rather awful: youll think me no end of a beast. Ive been in prison.

MARGARET. You!

BOBBY. Yes, me. For being drunk and assaulting the police.

MARGARET. Do you mean to say that you—oh! this is a let-down for me. [*She comes off the table and drops, disconsolate, into a chair at the end of it furthest from the hearth*].

BOBBY. Of course I couldnt hold you to our engagement after that. I was writing to you to break it off. [*He also descends from the table and makes slowly for the hearth*]. You must think me an utter rotter.

MARGARET. Oh, has e v e r y b o d y been in prison for being drunk and assaulting the police? How long were you in?

BOBBY. A fortnight.

MARGARET. Thats what I was in for.

BOBBY. What are you talking about? In where?

MARGARET. In quod.

BOBBY. But I'm serious: I'm not rotting. Really and truly—

MARGARET. What did you do to the copper?

BOBBY. Nothing, absolutely nothing. He exaggerated grossly. I only laughed at him.

MARGARET [*jumping up, triumphant*] Ive beaten you hollow. I knocked out two of his teeth. Ive got one of them. He sold it to me for ten shillings.

BOBBY. Now please do stop fooling, Meg. I tell you I'm not rotting. [*He sits down in the armchair, rather sulkily*].

MARGARET [*taking up the copy of Lloyd's Weekly and going to him*] And I tell you I'm not either. Look! Heres a report of it. The daily papers are no good; but the Sunday papers are splendid. [*She sits on the arm of the chair*]. See! [*Reading*]: "Hardened at Eighteen. A quietly dressed, respectable-looking girl who refuses her name"—thats me.

BOBBY [*pausing a moment in his perusal*] Do you mean to

138

say that you went on the loose out of pure devilment?

MARGARET. I did no harm. I went to see a lovely dance. I picked up a nice man and went to have a dance myself. I cant imagine anything more innocent and more happy. All the bad part was done by other people: they did it out of pure devilment if you like. Anyhow, here we are, two gaol-birds, Bobby, disgraced forever. Isnt it a relief?

BOBBY [*rising stiffly*] But you know, it's not the same for a girl. A man may do things a woman maynt. [*He stands on the hearthrug with his back to the fire*].

MARGARET. Are you scandalized, Bobby?

BOBBY. Well, you cant expect me to approve of it, can you, Meg? I never thought you were that sort of girl.

MARGARET [*rising indignantly*] I'm not. You mustnt pretend to think that *I'm* a clergyman's daughter, Bobby.

BOBBY. I wish you wouldnt chaff about that. Dont forget the row you got into for letting out that you admired Juggins [*she turns her back on him quickly*]—a footman! And what about the Frenchman?

MARGARET [*facing him again*] I know nothing about the Frenchman except that he's a very nice fellow and can swing his leg round like the hand of a clock and knock a policeman down with it. He was in Wormwood Scrubbs with you. I was in Holloway.

BOBBY. It's all very well to make light of it, Meg; but this is a bit thick, you know.

MARGARET. Do you feel you couldnt marry a woman whos been in prison?

BOBBY [*hastily*] No. I never said that. It might even give a woman a greater claim on a man. Any girl, if she were thoughtless and a bit on, perhaps, might get into a scrape. Anyone who really understood her character could see there was no harm in it. But youre not the larky sort. At least you usent to be.

MARGARET. I'm not; and I never will be. [*She walks straight up to him*]. I didnt do it for a lark, Bob: I did it out of the very depths of my nature. I did it because I'm that sort of person. I did it in one of my religious fits. I'm hardened at eighteen, as they say. So what about the match, now?

BOBBY. Well, I dont think you can fairly hold me to it, Meg. Of course it would be ridiculous for me to set up to be shocked, or anything of that sort. I cant afford to throw stones at anybody; and I dont pretend to. I can understand a lark; I can forgive a slip; as long as it is understood that it is only a lark or a slip. But to go on the loose on principle; to talk about religion in connection with it; to—to—well, Meg, I do find that a bit thick, I must say. I hope youre not in earnest when you talk that way.

MARGARET. Bobby: youre no good. No good to me, anyhow.

BOBBY [huffed] I'm sorry, Miss Knox.

MARGARET. Goodbye, Mr Gilbey. [She turns on her heel and goes to the other end of the table]. I suppose you wont introduce me to the clergyman's daughter.

BOBBY. I dont think she'd like it. There are limits, after all. [He sits down at the table, as if to resume work at his books: a hint to her to go].

MARGARET [on her way to the door] Ring the bell, Bobby; and tell Juggins to shew me out.

BOBBY [reddening] I'm not a cad, Meg.

MARGARET [coming to the table] Then do something nice to prevent us feeling mean about this afterwards. Youd better kiss me. You neednt ever do it again.

BOBBY. If I'm no good, I dont see what fun it would be for you.

MARGARET. Oh, it'd be no fun. If I wanted what you call fun, I should ask the Frenchman to kiss me—or Juggins.

BOBBY [rising and retreating to the hearth] Oh, dont be disgusting, Meg. Dont be low.

MARGARET [determinedly, preparing to use force] Now, I'll make you kiss me, just to punish you. [She seizes his wrist; pulls him off his balance; and gets her arm round his neck].

BOBBY. No. Stop. Leave go, will you.

140

Juggins appears at the door.

JUGGINS. Miss Delaney, Sir. [*Dora comes in. Juggins goes out. Margaret hastily releases Bobby, and goes to the other side of the room*].

DORA [*through the door, to the departing Juggins*] Well, you are a Juggins to shew me up when theres company. [*To Margaret and Bobby*] It's all right, dear: all right, old man: I'll wait in Juggins's pantry til youre disengaged.

MARGARET. Dont you know me?

DORA [*coming to the middle of the room and looking at her very attentively*] Why, it's never No. 406!

MARGARET. Yes it is.

DORA. Well, I should never have known you out of the uniform. How did you get out? You were doing a month, werent you?

MARGARET. My bloke paid the fine the day he got out himself.

DORA. A real gentleman! [*Pointing to Bobby, who is staring open-mouthed*] Look at him! He cant take it in.

BOBBY. I suppose you made her acquaintance in prison, Meg. But when it comes to talking about blokes and all that—well!

MARGARET. Oh, Ive learnt the language; and I like it. It's another barrier broken down.

BOBBY. It's not so much the language, Meg. But I think [*he looks at Dora and stops*].

MARGARET [*suddenly dangerous*] What do you think, Bobby?

DORA. He thinks you oughtnt to be so free with me dearie. It does him credit: he always was a gentleman, you know.

MARGARET. Does him credit! To insult you like that! Bobby: say that that wasnt what you meant.

BOBBY. I didnt say it was.

MARGARET. Well, deny that it was.

BOBBY. No. I wouldnt have said it in front of Dora; but I do think it's not quite the same thing my knowing her and you knowing her.

DORA. Of course it isnt, old man. [*To Margaret*] I'll just trot off and come back in half an hour. You two can make it up together. I'm really not fit company for you, dearie: I couldnt live up to you. [*She turns to go*].

MARGARET. Stop. Do you believe he could live up to me?

DORA. Well, I'll never say anything to stand between a girl and a respectable marriage, or to stop a decent lad from settling himself. I have a conscience; though I maynt be as particular as some.

MARGARET. You seem to me to be a very decent sort; and Bobby's behaving like a skunk.

BOBBY [*much ruffled*] Nice language that!

DORA. Well, dearie, men have to do some awfully mean things to keep up their respectability. But you cant blame them for that, can you? Ive met Bobby walking with his mother; and of course he cut me dead. I wont pretend I liked it; but what could he do, poor dear?

MARGARET. And now he wants me to cut you dead to keep him in countenance. Well, I shant: not if my whole family were there. But I'll cut him dead if he doesnt treat you properly. [*To Bobby, with a threatening move in his direction*] I'll educate you, you young beast.

BOBBY [*furious, meeting her half way*] Who are you calling a young beast?

MARGARET. You.

DORA [*peacemaking*] Now, dearies!

BOBBY. If you dont take care, youll get your fat head jolly well clouted.

MARGARET. If you dont take care, the policeman's tooth will be the beginning of a collection.

DORA. Now, loveys, be good.

Bobby, lost to all sense of adult dignity, puts out his tongue at Margaret. Margaret, equally furious, catches his protended countenance a box on the cheek. He hurls himself on her. They wrestle.

BOBBY. Cat! I'll teach you.

MARGARET. Pig! Beast! [*She forces him backwards on the table*]. Now where are you?

DORA [*calling*] Juggins, Juggins. Theyll murder one another.

JUGGINS [*throwing open the door, and announcing*] Monsieur Duvallet.

Duvallet enters. Sudden cessation of hostilities, and dead silence. The combatants separate by the whole width of the room. Juggins withdraws.

DUVALLET. I fear I derange you.

MARGARET. Not at all. Bobby: you really are a beast: Monsieur Duvallet will think I'm always fighting.

DUVALLET. Practising jujitsu or the new Iceland wrestling. Admirable, Miss Knox. The athletic young Englishwoman is an example to all Europe. [*Indicating Bobby*] Your instructor, no doubt. Monsieur—[*he bows*].

BOBBY [*bowing awkwardly*] How d'y' do?

MARGARET [*to Bobby*] I'm so sorry, Bobby: I asked Monsieur Duvallet to call for me here; and I forgot to tell you. [*Introducing*] Monsieur Duvallet: Miss Four hundred and seven. Mr Bobby Gibley. [*Duvallet bows*]. I really dont know how to explain our relationships. Bobby and I are like brother and sister.

DUVALLET. Perfectly. I noticed it.

MARGARET. Bobby and Miss—Miss—

DORA. Delaney, dear. [*To Duvallet, bewitchingly*] Darling Dora, to real friends.

MARGARET. Bobby and Dora are— are— well, not brother and sister.

DUVALLET [*with redoubled comprehension*] PERfectly.

MARGARET. Bobby has spent the last fortnight in prison. You dont mind, do you?

DUVALLET. No, naturally. *I* have spent the last fortnight in prison.

The conversation drops. Margaret renews it with an effort.

MARGARET. Dora has spent the last fortnight in prison.

DUVALLET. Quite so. I felicitate Mademoiselle on her

143

enlargement.

DORA. *Trop merci*, as they say in Boulogne. No call to be stiff with one another, have we?

Juggins comes in.

JUGGINS. Beg pardon, sir. Mr and Mrs Gilbey are coming up the street

DORA. Let me absquatulate [*making for the door*].

JUGGINS. If you wish to leave without being seen, you had better step into my pantry and leave afterwards.

DORA. Righto! [*She bursts into song*]

Hide me in the meat safe til the cop goes by.

Hum the dear old music as his step draws nigh.

[*She goes out on tiptoe*].

MARGARET. I wont stay here if she has to hide. I'll keep her company in the pantry. [*She follows Dora*].

BOBBY. Lets all go. We cant have any fun with the Mar here. I say, Juggins: you can give us tea in the pantry, cant you?

JUGGINS. Certainly, sir.

BOBBY. Right. Say nothing to my mother. You dont mind, Mr Doovalley, do you?

DUVALLET. I shall be charmed.

BOBBY. Right you are. Come along. [*At the door*] Oh, by the way, Juggins, fetch down that concertina from my room, will you?

JUGGINS. Yes, sir. [*Bobby goes out. Duvallet follows him to the door*]. You understand, sir, that Miss Knox is a lady absolutely *comme il faut*?

DUVALLET. Perfectly. But the other?

JUGGINS. The other, sir, may be both charitably and accurately described in your native idiom as a daughter of joy.

DUVALLET. It is what I thought. These English domestic interiors are very interesting. [*He goes out, followed by Juggins*].

Presently Mr and Mrs Gilbey come in. They take their accustomed places: he on the hearthrug, she at the colder end of the table.

MRS GILBEY. Did you smell scent in the hall, Rob?

GILBEY. No, I didnt. And I dont want to smell it. Dont you go looking for trouble, Maria.

MRS GILBEY [*snuffing up the perfumed atmosphere*] She's been here. [*Gilbey rings the bell*]. What are you ringing for? Are you going to ask?

GILBEY. No, I'm not going to ask. Juggins said this morning he wanted to speak to me. If he likes to tell me, let him; but I'm not going to ask; and dont you either. [*Juggins appears at the door*]. You said you wanted to say something to me.

JUGGINS. When it would be convenient to you, sir.

GILBEY. Well, what is it?

MRS GILBEY. Oh, Juggins, we're expecting Mr and Mrs Knox to tea.

GILBEY. He knows that. [*He sits down. Then, to Juggins*] What is it?

JUGGINS [*advancing to the middle of the table*] Would it inconvenience you, sir, if I were to give you a month's notice?

GILBEY [*taken aback*] What! Why? Aint you satisfied?

JUGGINS. Perfectly, sir. It is not that I want to better myself, I assure you.

GILBEY. Well, what do you want to leave for, then? Do you want to worse yourself?

JUGGINS. No, sir. Ive been well treated in your most comfortable establishment; and I should be greatly distressed if you or Mrs Gilbey were to interpret my notice as an expression of dissatisfaction.

GILBEY [*paternally*] Now you listen to me, Juggins. I'm an older man than you. Dont you throw out dirty water til you get in fresh. Dont get too big for your boots. Youre like all servants nowadays: you think youve only to hold up your finger to get the pick of half a dozen jobs. But you wont be treated everywhere as youre treated here. In bed every night before eleven; hardly a ring at the door except on Mrs Gilbey's day once a month; and no other man-

145

servant to interfere with you. It may be a bit quiet perhaps; but youre past the age of adventure. Take my advice: think over it. You suit me; and I'm prepared to make it suit you if youre dissatisfied—in reason, you know.

JUGGINS. I realize my advantages, sir; but Ive private reasons—

GILBEY [*cutting him short angrily and retiring to the hearth-rug in dudgeon*] Oh, I know. Very well: go. The sooner the better.

MRS GILBEY. Oh, not until we're suited. He must stay his month.

GILBEY [*sarcastic*] Do you want to lose him his character, Maria? Do you think I dont see what it is? We're prison folk now. Weve been in the police court. [*To Juggins*] Well, I suppose you know your own business best. I take your notice: you can go when your month is up, or sooner, if you like.

JUGGINS. Believe me, sir—

GILBEY. Thats enough: I dont want any excuses. I dont blame you. You can go downstairs now, if youve nothing else to trouble me about.

JUGGINS. I really cant leave it at that, sir. I assure you Ive no objection to young Mr Gilbey's going to prison. You may do six months yourself, sir, and welcome, without a word of remonstrance from me. I'm leaving solely because my brother, who has suffered a bereavement, and feels lonely, begs me to spend a few months with him until he gets over it.

GILBEY. And is he to keep you all that time? or are you to spend your savings in comforting him? Have some sense, man: how can you afford such things?

JUGGINS. My brother can afford to keep me, sir. The truth is, he objects to my being in service.

GILBEY. Is that any reason why you should be dependent on him? Dont do it, Juggins: pay your own way like an honest lad; and dont eat your brother's bread while youre able to earn your own.

JUGGINS. There is sound sense in that, sir. But unfortunately it is a tradition in my family that the younger brothers should spunge to a considerable extent on the eldest.

GILBEY. Then the sooner that tradition is broken, the better, my man.

JUGGINS. A Radical sentiment, sir. But an excellent one.

GILBEY. Radical! What do you mean? Dont you begin to take liberties, Juggins, now that you know we're loth to part with you. Your brother isnt a duke, you know.

JUGGINS. Unfortunately, he is, sir.

GILBEY } *together* { What!
MRS GILBEY } *together* { Juggins!

JUGGINS. Excuse me, sir: the bell. [*He goes out*].

GILBEY [*overwhelmed*] Maria: did you understand him to say his brother was a duke?

MRS GILBEY. Fancy his condescending! Perhaps if youd offer to raise his wages and treat him as one of the family he'd stay.

GILBEY. And have my own servant above me! Not me. Whats the world coming to? Heres Bobby and—

JUGGINS [*entering and announcing*] Mr and Mrs Knox.

The Knoxes come in. Juggins takes two chairs from the wall and places them at the table, between the host and hostess. Then he withdraws.

MRS GILBEY [*to Mrs Knox*] How are you, dear?

MRS KNOX. Nicely, thank you. Good evening, Mr Gilbey. [*They shake hands; and she takes the chair nearest Mrs Gilbey. Mr Knox takes the other chair*].

GILBEY [*sitting down*] I was just saying, Knox, What is the world coming to?

KNOX [*appealing to his wife*] What was I saying myself only this morning?

MRS KNOX. This is a strange time. I was never one to talk about the end of the world; but look at the things that have happened!

KNOX. Earthquakes!

GILBEY. San Francisco!

MRS GILBEY. Jamaica!

KNOX. Martinique!

GILBEY. Messina!

MRS GILBEY. The plague in China!

MRS KNOX. The floods in France!

GILBEY. My Bobby in Wormwood Scrubbs!

KNOX. Margaret in Holloway!

GILBEY. And now my footman tells me his brother's a duke!

KNOX. }{No!
MRS KNOX.}{Whats that?

GILBEY. Just before he let you in. A duke! Here has everything been respectable from the beginning of the world, as you may say, to the present day; and all of a sudden everything is turned upside down.

MRS KNOX. It's like in the book of Revelations. But I do say that when people have happiness within themselves, all the earthquakes, all the floods, and all the prisons in the world cant make them really unhappy.

KNOX. It isnt alone the curious things that are happening, but the unnatural way people are taking them. Why, theres Margaret been in prison, and she hasnt time to go to all the invitations she's had from people that never asked her before.

GILBEY. I never knew we could live without being respectable.

MRS GILBEY. Oh, Rob, what a thing to say! Who says we're not respectable?

GILBEY. Well, it's not what I call respectable to have your children in and out of jail.

KNOX. Oh come, Gilbey! we're not tramps because weve had, as it were, an accident.

GILBEY. It's no use, Knox: look it in the face. Did I ever tell you my father drank?

KNOX. No. But I knew it. Simmons told me.

GILBEY. Yes: he never could keep his mouth quiet: he told me your aunt was a kleptomaniac.

MRS KNOX. It wasnt true, Mr Gilbey. She used to pick up

148

handkerchiefs if she saw them lying about: but you might trust her with untold silver.

GILBEY. My Uncle Phil was a teetotaler. My father used to say to me: Rob, he says, dont you ever have a weakness. If you find one getting a hold on you, make a merit of it, he says. Your Uncle Phil doesnt like spirits; and he makes a merit of it, and is chairman of the Blue Ribbon Committee. I do like spirits; and I make a merit of it, and I'm the King Cockatoo of the Convivial Cockatoos. Never put yourself in the wrong, he says. I used to boast about what a good boy Bobby was. Now I swank about what a dog he is; and it pleases people just as well. What a world it is!

KNOX. It turned my blood cold at first to hear Margaret telling people about Holloway; but it goes down better than her singing used to.

MRS KNOX. I never thought she sang right after all those lessons we paid for.

GILBEY. Lord, Knox, it was lucky you and me got let in together. I tell you straight, if it hadnt been for Bobby's disgrace, I'd have broke up the firm.

KNOX. I shouldnt have blamed you: I'd have done the same only for Margaret. Too much straitlacedness narrows a man's mind. Talking of that, what about those hygienic corset advertisements that Vines & Jackson want us to put in the window? I told Vines they werent decent and we couldnt shew them in our shop. I was pretty high with him. But what am I to say to him now if he comes and throws this business in our teeth?

GILBEY. Oh, put em in. We may as well go it a bit now.

MRS GILBEY. Youve been going it quite far enough, Rob. [*To Mrs Knox*] He wont get up in the mornings now: he that was always out of bed at seven to the tick!

MRS KNOX. You hear that, Jo? [*To Mrs Gilbey*] He's taken to whisky and soda. A pint a week! And the beer the same as before!

KNOX. Oh, dont preach, old girl.

MRS KNOX [*to Mrs Gilbey*] Thats a new name he's got for

me. [*To Knox*] I tell you, Jo, this doesnt sit well on you. You may call it preaching if you like; but it's the truth for all that. I say that if youve happiness within yourself, you dont need to seek it outside, spending money on drink and theatres and bad company, and being miserable after all. You can sit at home and be happy; and you can work and be happy. If you have that in you, the spirit will set you free to do what you want and guide you to do right. But if you havnt got it, then youd best be respectable and stick to the ways that are marked out for you; for youve nothing else to keep you straight.

KNOX [*angrily*] And is a man never to have a bit of fun? See whats come of it with your daughter! She was to be content with your happiness that youre always talking about; and how did the spirit guide her? To a month's hard for being drunk and assaulting the police. Did *I* ever assault the police?

MRS KNOX. You wouldnt have the courage. I dont blame the girl.

MRS GILBEY. ⎫ Oh, Maria! What are you saying?
GILBEY.   ⎭ What! And you so pious!

MRS KNOX. She went where the spirit guided her. And what harm there was in it she knew nothing about.

GILBEY. Oh, come, Mrs Knox! Girls are not so innocent as all that.

MRS KNOX. I dont say she was ignorant. But I do say that she didnt know what we know: I mean the way certain temptations get a sudden hold that no goodness nor self-control is any use against. She was saved from that, and had a rough lesson too; and I say it was no earthly protection that did that. But dont think, you two men, that youll be protected if you make what she did an excuse to go and do as y o u d like to do if it wasnt for the fear of losing your characters. The spirit wont guide you, because it isnt in you; and it never has been: not in either of you.

GILBEY [*with ironic humility*] I'm sure I'm obliged to you for your good opinion, Mrs Knox.

MRS KNOX. Well, I will say for you, Mr Gilbey, that youre better than my man here. He's a bitter hard heathen, is my Jo, God help me! [*She begins to cry quietly*].

KNOX. Now, dont take on like that, Amelia. You know I always gave in to you that you were right about religion. But one of us had to think of other things, or we'd have starved, we and the child.

MRS KNOX. How do you know youd have starved? All the other things might have been added unto you.

GILBEY. Come, Mrs Knox, dont tell me Knox is a sinner. I know better. I'm sure youd be the first to be sorry if anything was to happen to him.

KNOX [*bitterly to his wife*] Youve always had some grudge against me; and nobody but yourself can understand what it is.

MRS KNOX. I wanted a man who had that happiness within himself. You made me think you had it; but it was nothing but being in love with me.

MRS GILBEY. And do you blame him for that?

MRS KNOX. I blame nobody. But let him not think he can walk by his own light. I tell him that if he gives up being respectable he'll go right down to the bottom of the hill. He has no powers inside himself to keep him steady; so let him cling to the powers outside him.

KNOX [*rising angrily*] Who wants to give up being respectable? All this for a pint of whisky that lasted a week! How long would it have lasted Simmons, I wonder?

MRS KNOX [*gently*] Oh, well, say no more, Jo. I wont plague you about it. [*He sits down*]. You never did understand; and you never will. Hardly anybody understands: even Margaret didnt til she went to prison. She does now; and I shall have a companion in the house after all these lonely years.

KNOX [*beginning to cry*] I did all I could to make you happy. I never said a harsh word to you.

GILBEY [*rising indignantly*] What right have you to treat a man like that? an honest respectable husband? as if he were

151

dirt under your feet?

KNOX. Let her alone, Gilbey. [*Gilbey sits down, but mutinously*].

MRS KNOX. Well, you gave me all you could, Jo; and if it wasnt what I wanted, that wasnt your fault. But I'd rather have you as you were than since you took to whisky and soda.

KNOX. I dont want any whisky and soda. I'll take the pledge if you like.

MRS KNOX. No: you shall have your beer because you like it. The whisky was only brag. And if you and me are to remain friends, Mr Gilbey, youll get up tomorrow morning at seven.

GILBEY [*defiantly*] Damme if I will! There!

MRS KNOX [*with gentle pity*] How do you know, Mr Gilbey, what youll do tomorrow morning?

GILBEY. Why shouldnt I know? Are we children not to be let do what we like, and our own sons and daughters kicking their heels all over the place? [*To Knox*] I was never one to interfere between man and wife, Knox; but if Maria started ordering me about like that—

MRS GILBEY. Now dont be naughty, Rob. You know you mustnt set yourself up against religion?

GILBEY. Whos setting himself up against religion?

MRS KNOX. It doesnt matter whether you set yourself up against it or not, Mr Gilbey. If it sets itself up against you, youll have to go the appointed way: it's no use quarrelling about it with me that am as great a sinner as yourself.

GILBEY. Oh, indeed! And who told you I was a sinner?

MRS GILBEY. Now, Rob, you know we are all sinners. What else is religion?

GILBEY. I say nothing against religion. I suppose we're all sinners, in a manner of speaking; but I dont like to have it thrown at me as if I'd really done anything.

MRS GILBEY. Mrs Knox is speaking for your good, Rob.

GILBEY. Well, I dont like to be spoken to for my good. Would anybody like it?

MRS KNOX. Dont take offence where none is meant, Mr Gilbey. Talk about something else. No good ever comes of arguing about such things among the like of us.

KNOX. The like of us! Are you throwing it in our teeth that your people were in the wholesale and thought Knox and Gilbey wasnt good enough for you?

MRS KNOX. No, Jo: you know I'm not. What better were my people than yours, for all their pride? But Ive noticed it all my life: we're ignorant. We dont really know whats right and whats wrong. We're all right as long as things go on the way they always did. We bring our children up just as we were brought up; and we go to church or chapel just as our parents did; and we say what everybody says; and it goes on all right until something out of the way happens: theres a family quarrel, or one of the children goes wrong, or a father takes to drink, or an aunt goes mad, or one of us finds ourselves doing something we never thought we'd want to do. And then you know what happens: complaints and quarrels and huff and offence and bad language and bad temper and regular bewilderment as if Satan possessed us all. We find out then that with all our respectability and piety, weve no real religion and no way of telling right from wrong. Weve nothing but our habits; and when theyre upset, where are we? Just like Peter in the storm trying to walk on the water and finding he couldnt.

MRS GILBEY [*piously*] Aye! He found out, didnt he?

GILBEY [*reverently*] I never denied that youve a great intellect, Mrs Knox—

MRS KNOX. Oh, get along with you, Gilbey, if you begin talking about my intellect. Give us some tea, Maria. Ive said my say; and I'm sure I beg the company's pardon for being so long about it, and so disagreeable.

MRS GILBEY. Ring, Rob. [*Gilbey rings*]. Stop. Juggins will think we're ringing for him.

GILBEY [*appalled*] It's too late. I rang before I thought of it.

MRS GILBEY. Step down and apologize, Rob.

KNOX. Is it him that you said was brother to a—

Juggins comes in with the tea-tray. All rise. He takes the tray to Mrs Gilbey.

GILBEY. I didnt mean to ask you to do this, Mr Juggins. I wasnt thinking when I rang.

MRS GILBEY [*trying to take the tray from him*] Let me, Juggins.

JUGGINS. Please sit down, madam. Allow me to discharge my duties just as usual, sir. I assure you that is the correct thing. [*They sit down, ill at ease, whilst he places the tray on the table. He then goes out for the curate*].

KNOX [*lowering his voice*] Is this all right, Gilbey? Anybody may be the son of a duke, you know. Is he legitimate?

GILBEY. Good Lord! I never thought of that.

Juggins returns with the cakes. They regard him with suspicion.

GILBEY [*whispering to Knox*] You ask him.

KNOX [*to Juggins*] Just a word with you, my man. Was your mother married to your father?

JUGGINS. I believe so, sir. I cant say from personal knowledge. It was before my time.

GILBEY. Well but look here you know—[*he hesitates*].

JUGGINS. Yes, sir?

KNOX. I know whatll clinch it, Gilbey. You leave it to me. [*To Juggins*] Was your mother the duchess?

JUGGINS. Yes, sir. Quite correct, sir, I assure you. [*To Mrs Gilbey*] That is the milk, madam. [*She has mistaken the jugs*]. This is the water.

They stare at him in pitiable embarrassment.

MRS KNOX. What did I tell you? Heres something out of the common happening with a servant; and we none of us know how to behave.

JUGGINS. It's quite simple, madam. I'm a footman, and should be treated as a footman. [*He proceeds calmly with his duties, handing round cups of tea as Mrs Knox fills them*].

Shrieks of laughter from below stairs reach the ears of the company.

154

MRS GILBEY. Whats that noise? Is Master Bobby at home? I heard his laugh.

MRS KNOX. I'm sure I heard Margaret's.

GILBEY. Not a bit of it. It was that woman.

JUGGINS. I can explain, sir. I must ask you to excuse the liberty; but I'm entertaining a small party to tea in my pantry.

MRS GILBEY. But youre not entertaining Master Bobby?

JUGGINS. Yes, madam.

GILBEY. Whos with him?

JUGGINS. Miss Knox, sir.

GILBEY. Miss Knox! Are you sure? Is there anyone else?

JUGGINS. Only a French marine officer, sir, and—er—Miss Delaney. [*He places Gilbey's tea on the table before him*]. The lady that called about Master Bobby, sir.

KNOX. Do you mean to say theyre having a party all to themselves downstairs, and we having a party up here and knowing nothing about it?

JUGGINS. Yes, sir. I have to do a good deal of entertaining in the pantry for Master Bobby, sir.

GILBEY. Well, this is a nice state of things!

KNOX. Whats the meaning of it? What do they do it for?

JUGGINS. To enjoy themselves, sir, I should think.

MRS GILBEY. Enjoy themselves! Did ever anybody hear of such a thing?

GILBEY. Knox's daughter shewn into my pantry!

KNOX. Margaret mixing with a Frenchman and a foot-man—[*Suddenly realizing that the footman is offering him cake*] She doesnt know about—about His Grace, you know.

MRS GILBEY. Perhaps she does. Does she, Mr Juggins?

JUGGINS. The other lady suspects me, madam. They call me Rudolph, or the Long Lost Heir.

MRS GILBEY. It's a much nicer name than Juggins. I think I'll call you by it, if you dont mind.

JUGGINS. Not at all, madam.

Roars of merriment from below.

GILBEY. Go and tell them to stop laughing. What right

have they to make a noise like that?

JUGGINS. I asked them not to laugh so loudly, sir. But the French gentleman always sets them off again.

KNOX. Do you mean to tell me that my daughter laughs at a Frenchman's jokes?

GILBEY. We all know what French jokes are.

JUGGINS. Believe me: you do not, sir. The noise this afternoon has all been because the Frenchman said that the cat had whooping cough.

MRS GILBEY [*laughing heartily*] Well, I never!

GILBEY. Dont be a fool, Maria. Look here, Knox: we cant let this go on. People cant be allowed to behave like this.

KNOX. Just what I say.

A concertina adds its music to the revelry.

MRS GILBEY [*excited*] Thats the squiffer. He's bought it for her.

GILBEY. Well, of all the scandalous—[*Redoubled laughter from below*].

KNOX. I'll put a stop to this. [*He goes out to the landing and shouts*] Margaret! [*Sudden dead silence*]. Margaret, I say!

MARGARET'S VOICE. Yes, father. Shall we all come up? We're dying to.

KNOX. Come up and be ashamed of yourselves, behaving like wild Indians.

DORA'S VOICE [*screaming*] Oh! oh! oh! Dont, Bobby. Now—Oh! [*In headlong flight she dashes into and right across the room, breathless, and slightly abashed by the company*]. I beg your pardon, Mrs Gilbey, for coming in like that; but whenever I go upstairs in front of Bobby, he pretends it's a cat biting my ankles; and I just must scream.

Bobby and Margaret enter rather more shyly, but evidently in high spirits. Bobby places himself near his father, on the hearthrug, and presently slips down into the armchair.

MARGARET. How do you do, Mrs Gilbey? [*She puts herself behind her mother*].

Duvallet comes in behaving himself perfectly. Knox follows.

MARGARET. Oh—let me introduce. My friend Lieuten-

156

ant Duvallet. Mrs Gilbey. Mr Gilbey.

Duvallet bows and sits down on Mr Knox's left, Juggins placing a chair for him.

DORA. Now, Bobby: introduce me: theres a dear.

BOBBY [*a little nervous about it; but trying to keep up his spirits*] Miss Delaney: Mr and Mrs Knox. [*Knox, as he resumes his seat, acknowledges the introduction suspiciously. Mrs Knox bows gravely, looking keenly at Dora and taking her measure without prejudice*].

DORA. Pleased to meet you. [*Juggins places the baby rocking-chair for her on Gilbey's right, opposite the Knoxes*]. Thank you. [*She sits*]. Bobby's given me the squiffer. Do you know what theyve been doing downstairs? Youd never guess. Theyve been trying to teach me table manners. The Lieutenant and Rudolph say I'm a regular pig. I'm sure I never knew there was anything wrong with me. But live and learn. [*To Gilbey*] Eh, old dear?

JUGGINS. Old dear is not correct, Miss Delaney. [*He retires to the end of the sideboard nearest the door*].

DORA. Oh get out! I must call a man something. He doesnt mind: do you, Charlie?

MRS GILBEY. His name isnt Charlie.

DORA. Excuse me. I call everybody Charlie.

JUGGINS. You mustnt.

DORA. Oh, if I were to mind you, I should have to hold my tongue altogether; and then how sorry youd be! Lord, how I do run on! Dont mind me, Mrs Gilbey.

KNOX. What I want to know is, whats to be the end of this? It's not for me to interfere between you and your son, Gilbey: he knows his own intentions best, no doubt, and perhaps has told them to you. But Ive my daughter to look after; and it's my duty as a parent to have a clear understanding about her. No good is ever done by beating about the bush. I ask Lieutenant—well, I dont speak French; and I cant pronounce the name—

MARGARET. Mr Duvallet, father.

KNOX. I ask Mr Doovalley what his intentions are.

MARGARET. Oh father: how can you?

DUVALLET. I'm afraid my knowledge of English is not enough to understand. Intentions? How?

MARGARET. He wants to know will you marry me.

MRS GILBEY. ⎱ What a thing to say!

KNOX. ⎱ Silence, miss.

DORA. ⎰ Well, thats straight, aint it?

DUVALLET. But I am married already. I have two daughters.

KNOX [*rising, virtuously indignant*] You sit there after carrying on with my daughter, and tell me coolly youre married.

MARGARET. Papa: you really must not tell people that they sit there. [*He sits down again sulkily*].

DUVALLET. Pardon. Carrying on? What does that mean?

MARGARET. It means—

KNOX [*violently*] Hold your tongue, you shameless young hussy. Dont you dare say what it means.

DUVALLET [*shrugging his shoulders*] What does it mean, Rudolph?

MRS KNOX. If it's not proper for her to say, it's not proper for a man to say, either. Mr Doovalley: youre a married man with daughters. Would you let them go about with a stranger, as you are to us, without wanting to know whether he intended to behave honorably?

DUVALLET. Ah, madam, my daughters are French girls. That is very different. It would not be correct for a French girl to go about alone and speak to men as English and American girls do. That is why I so immensely admire the English people. You are so free—so unprejudiced—your women are so brave and frank—their minds are so—how do you say?—wholesome. I intend to have my daughters educated in England. Nowhere else in the world but in England could I have met at a Variety Theatre a charming young lady of perfect respectability, and enjoyed a dance with her at a public dancing saloon. And where else are women trained to box and knock out the teeth of policemen as a protest against injustice and violence? [*Rising, with immense élan*] Your daughter, madam, is superb. Your country is a model to the rest of Europe. If you were a Frenchman, stifled in prudery, hypocrisy, and the tyranny of the family and the home, you would understand how an enlightened Frenchman admires and envies your freedom, your broadmindedness, and the fact that home life can hardly be said to exist in England. You have made an end of the despotism of the parent; the family council is unknown to you; everywhere in these islands one can enjoy the exhilarating, the soul-liberating spectacle of men quarrelling with their brothers, defying their fathers, refusing to speak to their mothers. In France we are not men: we are only sons—grown-up children. Here one is a human being—an end in himself. Oh, Mrs Knox, if only your military genius were equal to your moral genius—if that conquest of Europe by France which inaugurated the new age after the Revolution had only been an English conquest, how much more enlightened the world would have been now! We, alas, can only fight. France is unconquerable. We impose our narrow ideas, our prejudices, our obsolete institutions, our insufferable pedantry on the world by brute force—by that stupid quality of military heroism which shews how little we have evolved from the savage: nay, from the beast. We can charge like bulls; we can spring on our foes like gamecocks; when we are overpowered by treason, we can die fighting like rats. And we are foolish enough to be proud of it! Why should we be? Does the bull progress? Can you civilize the gamecock? Is there any future for the rat? We never fight intelligently: when we lose battles, it is because we have not sense enough to know when we are beaten. At Waterloo, had we known when we were beaten, we should have retreated; tried another plan; and won the battle. But no: we were too pigheaded to admit that there is anything impossible to a Frenchman: we were quite satisfied when our Marshals had six horses shot under them, and our stupid old grognards died fighting rather than surrender like reasonable beings. Think of your great Wellington: think of his inspiring words, when the lady asked him whether British soldiers ever ran away. "All soldiers run away, madam," he said; "but if there are supports for them to fall back on it does not matter." Think of your illustrious Nelson, always beaten on land, always victorious at sea, where his men could not run away. Y o u are not dazzled and misled by false ideals of patriotic enthusiasm: your honest and sensible statesmen demand for England a two-power standard, even a three-power standard, frankly admitting that it is wise to fight three to one: whilst we, fools and braggarts as we are, declare that every Frenchman is a host in himself, and that when one Frenchman attacks three Englishmen he is guilty of an act of cowardice comparable to that of the man who strikes a woman. It is folly: it is nonsense: a Frenchman is not really stronger than a German, than an Italian, even than an Englishman. Sir: if all Frenchwomen were like your daughter—if all Frenchmen had the good sense, the power of seeing things as they really are, the calm judgment, the open mind, the philosophic grasp, the foresight and true courage, which are so natural to you as an Englishman that you are hardly conscious of possessing them, France would become the greatest nation in the world.

MARGARET. Three cheers for old England! [*She shakes hands with him warmly*].

BOBBY. Hurra-a-ay! And so say all of us.

Duvallet, having responded to Margaret's handshake with enthusiasm, kisses Juggins on both cheeks, and sinks into his chair, wiping his perspiring brow.

GILBEY. Well, this sort of talk is above me. Can you make anything out of it, Knox?

KNOX. The long and short of it seems to be that he cant lawfully marry my daughter, as he ought after going to prison with her.

DORA. I'm ready to marry Bobby, if that will be any satisfaction.

GILBEY. No you dont. Not if I know it.

MRS KNOX. He ought to, Mr Gilbey.

GILBEY. Well, if thats your religion, Amelia Knox, I want no more of it. Would you invite them to your house if he married her?

MRS KNOX. He ought to marry her whether or no.

BOBBY. I feel I ought to, Mrs Knox.

GILBEY. Hold your tongue. Mind your own business.

BOBBY [*wildly*] If I'm not let marry her, I'll do something downright disgraceful. I'll enlist as a soldier.

JUGGINS [*sternly*] That is not a disgrace, sir.

BOBBY. Not for you, perhaps. But youre only a footman. I'm a gentleman.

MRS GILBEY. Dont dare to speak disrespectfully to Mr Rudolph, Bobby. For shame!

JUGGINS [*coming forward to the middle of the table*] It is not gentlemanly to regard the service of your country as disgraceful. It is gentlemanly to marry the lady you make love to.

GILBEY [*aghast*] My boy is to marry this woman and be a social outcast!

JUGGINS. Your boy and Miss Delaney will be inexorably condemned by respectful society to spend the rest of their days in precisely the sort of company they seem to like best and be most at home in.

KNOX. And my daughter? Whos to marry my daughter?

JUGGINS. Your daughter, sir, will probably marry the man she makes up her mind to marry. She is a lady of very determined character.

KNOX. Yes: if he'd have her with her character gone. But who would? Youre the brother of a duke. Would—

BOBBY. ⎫⎧Whats that?
MARGARET. ⎪⎪Juggins a duke!
DUVALLET. ⎬⎨*Comment!*
DORA. ⎭⎩What did I tell you?

KNOX. Yes: the brother of a duke: thats what he is. [*To Juggins*] Well, would y o u marry her?

JUGGINS. I was about to propose that solution of your

problem, Mr Knox.

MRS GILBEY.⎫ ⎧Well, I never!
KNOX.　　 ⎬ ⎨D'ye mean it?
MRS KNOX. ⎭ ⎩Marry Margaret!

JUGGINS [*continuing*] As an idle younger son, unable to support myself, or even to remain in the Guards in competition with the grandsons of American millionaires, I could not have aspired to Miss Knox's hand. But as a sober, honest, and industrious domestic servant, who has, I trust, given satisfaction to his employer [*he bows to Mr Gilbey*] I feel I am a man with a character. It is for Miss Knox to decide.

MARGARET. I got into a frightful row once for admiring you, Rudolph.

JUGGINS. I should have got into an equally frightful row myself, Miss, had I betrayed my admiration for you. I looked forward to those weekly dinners.

MRS KNOX. But why did a gentleman like you stoop to be a footman?

DORA. He stooped to conquer.

MARGARET. Shut up, Dora: I want to hear.

JUGGINS. I will explain; but only Mrs Knox will understand. I once insulted a servant. Rashly; for he was a sincere Christian. He rebuked me for trifling with a girl of his own class. I told him to remember what he was, and to whom he was speaking. He said God would remember. I discharged him on the spot.

GILBEY. Very properly.

KNOX. What right had he to mention such a thing to you?

MRS GILBEY. What are servants coming to?

MRS KNOX. Did it come true, what he said?

JUGGINS. It stuck like a poisoned arrow. It rankled for months. Then I gave in. I apprenticed myself to an old butler of ours who kept a hotel. He taught me my present business, and got me a place as footman with Mr Gilbey. If ever I meet that man again I shall be able to look him in the face.

MRS KNOX. Margaret: it's not on account of the duke:

dukes are vanities. But take my advice; and take him.

MARGARET [*slipping her arm through his*] I have loved Juggins since the first day I beheld him. I felt instinctively he had been in the Guards. May he walk out with me. Mr Gilbey?

KNOX. Dont be vulgar, girl. Remember your new position. [*To Juggins*] I suppose youre serious about this, Mr —Mr Rudolph?

JUGGINS. I propose, with your permission, to begin keeping company this afternoon, if Mrs Gilbey can spare me.

GILBEY [*in a gust of envy, to Bobby*] Itll be long enough before y o u l l marry the sister of a duke, you young good-for-nothing.

DORA. Dont fret, old dear. Rudolph will teach me high-class manners. I call it quite a happy ending: dont you, lieutenant?

DUVALLET. In France it would be impossible. But here— ah [*kissing his hand*] la belle Angleterre!

EPILOGUE

BEFORE *the curtain. The Count, dazed and agitated, hurries to the 4 critics, as they rise, bored and weary, from their seats.*

THE COUNT. Gentlemen: do not speak to me. I implore you to withhold your opinion. I am not strong enough to bear it. I could never have believed it. Is this a play? Is this in any sense of the word, Art? Is it agreeable? Can it conceivably do good to any human being? Is it delicate? Do such people really exist? Excuse me, gentlemen: I speak from a wounded heart. There are private reasons for my discomposure. This play implies obscure, unjust, unkind reproaches and menaces to all of us who are parents.

TROTTER. Pooh! you take it too seriously. After all, the thing has amusing passages. Dismiss the rest as impertinence.

THE COUNT. Mr Trotter: it is easy for you to play the pococurantist. [*Trotter, amazed, repeats the first three syllables in his throat, making a noise like a pheasant*]. You see hundreds of plays every year. But to me, who have never seen anything of this kind before, the effect of this play is terribly disquieting. Sir: if it had been what people call an immoral play, I shouldnt have minded a bit. [*Vaughan is shocked*]. Love beautifies every romance and justifies every audacity. [*Bannal assents gravely*]. But there are reticences which everybody should respect. There are decencies too subtle to be put into words, without which human society would be unbearable. People could not talk to one another as those people talk. No child could speak to its parent: no girl could speak to a youth: no human creature could tear down the veils—[*Appealing to Vaughan, who is on his left flank, with Gunn between them*] Could they, sir?

VAUGHAN. Well, I dont see that.

THE COUNT. You dont see it! dont feel it! [*To Gunn*] Sir: I appeal to you.

GUNN [*with studied weariness*] It seems to me the most ordinary sort of old-fashioned Ibsenite drivel.

164

FANNY'S FIRST PLAY

THE COUNT [*turning to Trotter, who is on his right, between him and Bannal*] Mr Trotter: will y o u tell me that y o u are not amazed, outraged, revolted, wounded in your deepest and holiest feelings by every word of this play, every tone, every implication; that you did not sit there shrinking in every fibre at the thought of what might come next?

TROTTER. Not a bit. Any clever modern girl could turn out that kind of thing by the yard.

THE COUNT. Then sir, tomorrow I start for Venice, never to return. I must believe what you tell me. I perceive that you are not agitated, not surprised, not concerned; that my own horror (yes, gentlemen, horror—horror of the very soul) appears unaccountable to you, ludicrous, absurd, even to you, Mr Trotter, who are little younger than myself. Sir: if young people spoke to me like that, I should die of shame: I could not face it. I must go back. The world has passed me by and left me. Accept the apologies of an elderly and no doubt ridiculous admirer of the art of a bygone day, when there was still some beauty in the world and some delicate grace in family life. But I promised my daughter your opinion; and I must keep my word. Gentlemen: you are the choice and master spirits of this age: you walk through it without bewilderment and face its strange products without dismay. Pray deliver your verdict. Mr Bannal: you know that it is the custom at a Court Martial for the youngest officer present to deliver his judgment first, so that he may not be influenced by the authority of his elders. You are the youngest. What is your opinion of the play?

BANNAL. Well, whos it by?

THE COUNT. That is a secret for the present.

BANNAL. You dont expect me to know what to say about a play when I dont know who the author is, do you?

THE COUNT. Why not?

BANNAL. Why not! Why not! ! Suppose you had to write about a play by Pinero and one by Jones! Would you say exactly the same thing about them?

THE COUNT. I presume not.

BANNAL. Then how could you write about them until you knew which was Pinero and which was Jones? Besides, what sort of play is this? thats what I want to know. Is it a comedy or a tragedy? Is it a farce or a melodrama? Is it repertory theatre tosh, or really straight paying stuff?

GUNN. Cant you tell from seeing it?

BANNAL. I can see it all right enough; but how am I to know how to take it? Is it serious, or is it spoof? If the author knows what his play is, let him tell us what it is. If he doesnt, he cant complain if I dont know either. *I'm* not the author.

THE COUNT. But is it a good play, Mr Bannal? Thats a simple question.

BANNAL. Simple enough when you know. If it's by a good author, it's a good play, naturally. That stands to reason. Who is the author? Tell me that; and I'll place the play for you to a hair's breadth.

THE COUNT. I'm sorry I'm not at liberty to divulge the author's name. The author desires that the play should be judged on its merits.

BANNAL. But what merits can it have except the author's merits? Who would you say it's by, Gunn?

GUNN. Well, who do you think? Here you have a rotten old-fashioned domestic melodrama acted by the usual stage puppets. The hero's a naval lieutenant. All melodramatic heroes are naval lieutenants. The heroine gets into trouble by defying the law (if she didnt get into trouble, thered be no drama) and plays for sympathy all the time as hard as she can. Her good old pious mother turns on her cruel father when he's going to put her out of the house, and says she'll go too. Then theres the comic relief: the comic shopkeeper, the comic shopkeeper's wife, the comic footman who turns out to be a duke in disguise, and the young scapegrace who gives the author his excuse for dragging in a fast young woman. All as old and stale as a fried fish shop on a winter morning.

THE COUNT. But—

GUNN [*interrupting him*] I know what youre going to say, Count. Youre going to say that the whole thing seems to you to be quite new and unusual and original. The naval lieutenant is a Frenchman who cracks up the English and runs down the French: the hackneyed old Shaw touch. The characters are second-rate middle class, instead of being dukes and millionaires. The heroine gets kicked through the mud: real mud. Theres no plot. All the old stage conventions and puppets without the old ingenuity and the old enjoyment. And a feeble air of intellectual pretentiousness kept up all through to persuade you that if the author hasnt written a good play it's because he's too clever to stoop to anything so commonplace. And you three experienced men have sat through all this, and cant tell me who wrote it! Why, the play bears the author's signature in every line.

BANNAL. Who?

GUNN. Granville-Barker, of course. Why, old Gilbey is straight out of The Madras House.

BANNAL. Poor old Barker!

VAUGHAN. Utter nonsense! Cant you see the difference in style?

BANNAL. No.

VAUGHAN [*contemptuously*] Do you know what style is?

BANNAL. Well, I suppose youd call Trotter's uniform style. But it's not my style—since you ask me.

VAUGHAN. To me it's perfectly plain who wrote that play. To begin with, it's intensely disagreeable. Therefore it's not by Barrie, in spite of the footman, whos cribbed from The Admirable Crichton. He was an earl, you may remember. You notice, too, the author's offensive habit of saying silly things that have no real sense in them when you come to examine them, just to set all the fools in the house giggling. Then what does it all come to? An attempt to expose the supposed hypocrisy of the Puritan middle class in England: people just as good as the author, anyhow. With, of course, the inevitable improper female: Mrs Tanqueray, Iris, and so forth. Well, if you cant recognize the

167

author of that, youve mistaken your profession: thats all I
have to say.

BANNAL. Why are you so down on Pinero? and what
about that touch that Gunn spotted? the Frenchman's long
speech. I believe it's Shaw.

GUNN. Rubbish!

VAUGHAN. Rot! You may put that idea out of your head,
Bannal. Poor as this play is, theres the note of passion in it.
You feel somehow that beneath all the assumed levity of
that poor waif and stray, she really loves Bobby and will be
a good wife to him. Now Ive repeatedly proved that Shaw is
physiologically incapable of the note of passion.

BANNAL. Yes, I know. Intellect without emotion. Thats
right. I always say that myself. A giant brain, if you ask me;
but no heart.

GUNN. Oh, shut up, Bannal. This crude medieval psychology of heart and brain—Shakespear would have called
it liver and wits—is really schoolboyish. Surely weve had
enough of second-hand Schopenhauer. Even such a played-
out old back number as Ibsen would have been ashamed of
it. Heart and brain, indeed!

VAUGHAN. You have neither one nor the other, Gunn.
Youre dekkadent.

GUNN. Decadent! How I love that early Victorian word!

VAUGHAN. Well, at all events, you cant deny that the
characters in this play are quite distinguishable from one
another. That proves it's not by Shaw, because all Shaw's
characters are himself: mere puppets stuck up to spout
Shaw. It's only the actors that make them seem different.

BANNAL. There can be no doubt of that: everybody
knows it. But Shaw doesnt write his plays as plays. All he
wants to do is to insult everybody all round and set us talking about him.

TROTTER [wearily] And naturally, here we are all talking
about him. For heaven's sake, let us change the subject.

VAUGHAN. Still, my articles about Shaw—

GUNN. Oh, stow it, Vaughan. Drop it. What Ive always

told you about Shaw is—

BANNAL. There you go, Shaw, Shaw, Shaw! Do chuck it. If you want to know my opinion about Shaw—

TROTTER ⎫
VAUGHAN ⎬ [*yelling*] ⎧ No, please, we dont.
GUNN ⎭ ⎨ Shut your head, Bannal.
⎩ Oh do drop it.

The deafened Count puts his fingers in his ears and flies from the centre of the group to its outskirts, behind Vaughan.

BANNAL [*sulkily*] Oh, very well. Sorry I spoke, I'm sure.

TROTTER ⎫ ⎫ Shaw—
VAUGHAN ⎬ [*beginning again simultaneously*] ⎬ Shaw—
GUNN ⎭ ⎭ Shaw—

They are cut short by the entry of Fanny through the curtains. She is almost in tears.

FANNY [*coming between Trotter and Gunn*] I'm so sorry, gentlemen. And it was such a success when I read it to the Cambridge Fabian Society!

TROTTER. Miss O'Dowda: I was about to tell these gentlemen what I guessed before the curtain rose: that you are the author of the play. [*General amazement and consternation*].

FANNY. And you all think it beastly. You hate it. You think I'm a conceited idiot, and that I shall never be able to write anything decent.

She is almost weeping. A wave of sympathy carries away the critics.

VAUGHAN. No, no. Why, I was just saying that it must have been written by Pinero. Didnt I, Gunn?

FANNY [*enormously flattered*] Really?

TROTTER. I thought Pinero was much too popular for the Cambridge Fabian Society.

FANNY. Oh yes, of course; but still— Oh, did you really say that, Mr Vaughan?

GUNN. I owe you an apology, Miss O'Dowda. I said it was by Barker.

FANNY [*radiant*] Granville-Barker! Oh, you couldnt really have thought it so fine as that.

169

BANNAL. *I* said Bernard Shaw.

FANNY. Oh, of course it would be a little like Bernard Shaw. The Fabian touch, you know.

BANNAL [*coming to her encouragingly*] A jolly good little play, Miss O'Dowda. Mind: I dont say it's like one of Shakespear's—Hamlet or The Lady of Lyons, you know —but still, a firstrate little bit of work. [*He shakes her hand*].

GUNN [*following Bannal's example*] I also, Miss O'Dowda. Capital. Charming. [*He shakes hands*].

VAUGHAN [*with maudlin solemnity*] Only be true to yourself, Miss O'Dowda. Keep serious. Give up making silly jokes. Sustain the note of passion. And youll do great things.

FANNY. You think I have a future?

TROTTER. You have a past, Miss O'Dowda.

FANNY [*looking apprehensively at her father*] Sh-sh-sh!

THE COUNT. A past! What do you mean, Mr Trotter?

TROTTER [*to Fanny*] You cant deceive me. That bit about the police was real. Youre a Suffraget, Miss O'Dowda. You were on that Deputation.

THE COUNT. Fanny: is this true?

FANNY. It is. I did a month with Lady Constance Lytton; and I'm prouder of it than I ever was of anything or ever shall be again.

TROTTER. Is that any reason why you should stuff naughty plays down my throat?

FANNY. Yes: itll teach you what it feels like to be forcibly fed.

THE COUNT. She will never return to Venice. I feel now as I felt when the Campanile fell.

Savoyard comes in through the curtains.

SAVOYARD [*to the Count*] Would you mind coming to say a word of congratulation to the company? Theyre rather upset at having had no curtain call.

THE COUNT. Certainly, certainly. I'm afraid Ive been rather remiss. Let us go on the stage, gentlemen.

The curtains are drawn, revealing the last scene of the play and the actors on the stage. The Count, Savoyard, the critics, and

FANNY'S FIRST PLAY

Fanny join them, shaking hands and congratulating.

THE COUNT. Whatever we may think of the play, gentle-men, I'm sure you will agree with me that there can be only one opinion about the acting.

THE CRITICS. Hear, hear! [*They start the applause*].

AYOT ST LAWRENCE, *March* 1911.

THE MILLIONAIRESS

A JONSONIAN COMEDY IN FOUR ACTS

Written in 1935

First Performed (in German) Vienna 1936

PREFACE ON BOSSES

THOUGH this play of The Millionairess does not pretend to be anything more than a comedy of humorous and curious contemporary characters such as Ben Jonson might write were he alive now, yet it raises a question that has troubled human life and moulded human society since the creation.

The law is equal before all of us; but we are not all equal before the law. Virtually there is one law for the rich and another for the poor, one law for the cunning and another for the simple, one law for the forceful and another for the feeble, one law for the ignorant and another for the learned, one law for the brave and another for the timid, and within family limits one law for the parent and no law at all for the child.

In the humblest cabin that contains a family you may find a *maitresse femme* who rules in the household by a sort of divine right. She may rule amiably by being able to think more quickly and see further than the others, or she may be a tyrant ruling violently by intensity of will and ruthless egotism. She may be a grandmother and she may be a girl. But the others find they are unable to resist her. Often of course the domestic tyrant is a man; but the phenomenon is not so remarkable in his case, as he is by convention the master and lawgiver of the hearthstone.

In every business street you will find a shopkeeper who is always in difficulties and ends his business adventures in the bankruptcy court. Hard by you will find another shopkeeper, with no greater advantages to start with, or possibly less, who makes larger and larger profits, and inspires more and more confidence in his banker, until he ends as the millionaire head of a giant multiple shop.

How does the captain of a pirate ship obtain his position and maintain his authority over a crew of scoundrels who are all, like himself, outside the law? How does an obscure village priest, the son of humble fisherfolk, come to wear the triple crown and sit in the papal chair? How

175

do common soldiers become Kings, Shahs, and Dictators? Why does a hereditary peer find that he is a nonentity in a grand house organized and ruled by his butler?

Questions like these force themselves on us so continually and ruthlessly that many turn in despair from Socialism and political reform on the ground that to abolish all the institutional tyrannies would only deliver the country helplessly into the hands of the born bosses. A king, a prelate, a squire, a capitalist, a justice of the peace may be a good kind Christian soul, owing his position, as most of us do, to being the son of his father; but a born boss is one who rides roughshod over us by some mysterious power that separates him from our species and makes us fear him: that is, hate him.

What is to be done with that section of the possessors of specific talents whose talent is for moneymaking? History and daily experience teach us that if the world does not devise some plan of ruling them, they will rule the world. Now it is not desirable that they should rule the world; for the secret of moneymaking is to care for nothing else and to work at nothing else; and as the world's welfare depends on operations by which no individual can make money, whilst its ruin by war and drink and disease and drugs and debauchery is enormously profitable to moneymakers, the supremacy of the moneymaker is the destruction of the State. A society which depends on the incentive of private profit is doomed.

And what about ambitious people who possess commanding business ability or military genius or both? They are irresistible unless they are restrained by law; for ordinary individuals are helpless in their hands. Are they to be the masters of society or its servants?

What should the nineteenth century have done in its youth with Rothschild and Napoleon? What is the United States to do with its money kings and bosses? What are we to do with ours? How is the mediocre private citizen to hold his own with the able bullies and masterful women who establish family despotisms, school despotisms, office despotisms, religious despotisms in their little circles all over the country? Our boasted political liberties are a mockery to the subjects of such despotisms. They may work well when the despot is benevolent; but they are worse than any political tyranny in the selfish cases.

It is much more difficult to attack a personal despotism than an institutional one. Monarchs can be abolished: they have been abolished in all directions during the last century and a half, with the result, however, of sometimes replacing a personally amiable and harmless monarch, reigning under strict constitutional and traditional restraints, by energetic dictators and presidents who, having made hay of constitutions and traditions, are under no restraints at all. A hereditary monarch, on the throne because he is the son of his father, may be a normal person, amenable to reasonable advice from his councils, and exercising no authority except that conferred on him (or her) by the Constitution. Behead him, as we beheaded our Charles, or the French their Louis, and the born despot Cromwell or Napoleon (I purposely avoid glaring contemporary examples because I am not quite sure where they will be by the time this book is published) takes his place. The same mysterious personal force that makes the household tyrant, the school tyrant, the office tyrant, the brigand chief and the pirate captain, brings the born boss to the top by a gravitation that ordinary people cannot resist.

The successful usurpers of thrones are not the worst cases. The political usurper may be an infernal scoundrel, ruthless in murder, treachery, and torture; but once his ambition is achieved and he has to rule a nation, the magnitude and difficulty of his job, and the knowledge that if he makes a mess of it he will fall as suddenly as he has risen, will civilize him with a ruthlessness greater than his own. When Henry IV usurped the English crown he certainly did not intend to die of political overwork; but that is what happened to him. No political ruler could possibly be as wickedly selfish and cruel as the tyrant of a private house. Queen Elizabeth was a *maîtresse femme;* but she could have had her own way much more completely as landlady of the Mermaid Tavern than she had as sovereign of England. Because Nero and Paul I of Russia could not be made to understand this, they were killed like mad dogs by their own courtiers. But our petty fireside tyrants are not killed. Christina of Sweden would not have had to abdicate if her realm had been a ten-roomed villa. Had Catherine II reigned over her husband only, she need not nor could not have had him murdered; but as Tsarina she was forced to liquidate poor Peter very much against her own easy good nature, which prevented her from scolding her maids properly.

Modern Liberal democracy claims unlimited opportunities for tyranny: qualification for rule by heredity and class narrows it and puts it in harness and blinkers. Especially does such democracy favor money rule. It is in fact not democracy at all, but unashamed plutocracy. And as the meanest creature can become rich if he devotes his life to it, and the people with wider and more generous interests become or remain poor with equal certainty, plutocracy is the very devil socially, because it creates a sort of Gresham law by which the baser human currency drives out the nobler coinage. This is quite different from the survival of the fittest in the contests of character and talent which are independent of money. If Moses is the only tribesman capable of making a code of laws, he inevitably becomes Lawgiver to all the tribes, and, equally inevitably, is forced to add to what he can understand of divine law a series of secular regulations designed to maintain his personal authority. If he finds that it is useless to expect the tribesmen to obey his laws as a matter of common sense, he must persuade them that his inspiration is the result of direct and miraculous communication with their deity. Moses and Mahomet and Joseph Smith the Mormon had to plead divine revelations to get them out of temporary and personal difficulties as well as out of eternal and impersonal ones. As long as an individual of their calibre remains the indispensable man (or woman) doing things that the common man can neither do without nor do for himself, he will be, up to a point, the master of the common man in spite of all the democratic fudge that may be advanced to the contrary.

Of course there are limits. He cannot go to the lengths at which the common man will believe him to be insane or impious: when measures of that complexion are necessary, as they very often are, he must either conceal them or mask them as follies of the sort the common man thinks splendid. If the ruler thinks it well to begin a world war he must persuade his people that it is a war to end war, and that the people he wants them to kill are diabolical scoundrels; and if he is forced to suspend hostilities for a while, and does so by a treaty which contains the seeds of half a dozen new wars and is impossible enough in its conditions to make its violation certain, he must create a general belief that it is a charter of eternal peace and a monument of retributive justice.

In this way the most honest ruler becomes a tyrant and a fabricator of legends and falsehoods, not out of any devilment in himself, but because those whom he rules do not understand his business, and, if they did, would not sacrifice their own immediate interests to the permanent interests of the nation or the world. In short, a ruler must not only make laws, and rule from day to day: he must, by school instruction and printed propaganda, create and maintain an artificial mentality which will endorse his proceedings and obey his authority. This mentality becomes what we call Conservatism; and the revolt against it when it is abused oppressively or becomes obsolete as social conditions change, is classed as sedition, and reviled as Radicalism, Anarchism, Bolshevism, or what you please.

When a mentality is created and a code imposed, the born ruler, the Moses or Lenin, is no longer indispensable: routine government by dunderheads becomes possible and in fact preferable as long as the routine is fairly appropriate to the current phase of social development. The assumption of the more advanced spirits that revolutionists are always right is as questionable as the conservative assumption that they are always wrong. The industrious dunderhead who always does what was done last time because he is incapable of conceiving anything better, makes the best routineer. This explains the enormous part played by dunderheads as such in the history of all nations, provoking repeated explanations of surprise at the littleness of the wisdom with which the world is governed.

But what of the ambitious usurper? the person who has a capacity for kingship but has no kingdom and must therefore acquire a readymade one which is getting along in its own way very well without him? It cannot be contended with any plausibility that William the Conqueror was indispensable in England: he wanted England and grabbed it. He did this by virtue of his personal qualities, entirely against the will of the people of England, who, as far as they were politically conscious at all, would have greatly preferred Harold. But William had all the qualities that make an individual irresistible: the physical strength and ferocity of a king of beasts, the political genius of a king of men, the strategic cunning and tactical gumption of a military genius; and nothing that France or England could say or do prevailed against him. What are we to do with such people?

When an established political routine breaks down and produces political chaos, a combination of personal ambition with military genius and political capacity in a single individual gives that individual his opportunity. Napoleon, if he had been born a century earlier, would have had no more chance of becoming emperor of the French than Marshal Saxe had of supplanting Louis XV. In spite of the French Revolution, he was a very ordinary snob in his eighteenth-century social outlook. His assumption of the imperial diadem, his ridiculous attempt to establish the little Buonaparte family on all the thrones under his control, his remanufacture of a titular aristocracy to make a court for himself, his silly insistence on imperial etiquette when he was a dethroned and moribund prisoner in St Helena, shew that, for all his genius, he was and always had been behind the times. But he was for a time irresistible because, though he could fight battles on academic lines only, and was on that point a routineer soldier, he could play the war game on the established procedure so superbly that all the armies of Europe crumpled up before him. It was easy for anti-Bonapartist writers, from Taine to Mr H. G. Wells, to disparage him as a mere cad; but Goethe, who could face facts, and on occasion rub them in, said simply "You shake your chains in vain." Unfortunately for himself and Europe Napoleon was fundamentally a commonplace human fool. In spite of his early failure in the east he made a frightful draft on the manhood of France for his march to Moscow, only to hurry back leaving his legions dead in the snow, and thereafter go from disaster to disaster. Bernadotte, the lawyer's son who enlisted as a common soldier and ended unconquered on the throne of Sweden (his descendants still hold it), made a far better job of his affairs. When for the first time Napoleon came up against a really original commander at Waterloo, he still made all the textbook moves he had learnt at the military academy, and did not know when he was beaten until it was too late to do anything but run away. Instead of making for America at all hazards he threw himself on the magnanimity of the Prince Regent, who obviously could not have spared him even if he had wanted to. His attempt to wedge himself and his upstart family into the old dynasties by his divorce and his Austrian marriage ended in making him a notorious cuckold. But the vulgarer fool and the paltrier snob you prove Napoleon to have been, the more alarming becomes the fact that this shabby-genteel Corsican subaltern (and

a very unsatisfactory subaltern at that) dominated Europe
for years, and placed on his own head the crown of Char-
lemagne. Is there really nothing to be done with such men
but submit to them until, having risen by their specialities,
they ruin themselves by their vulgarities?

It was easy for Napoleon to make a better job of restoring order after the French Revolution than Sieyès, who
tried to do it by writing paper constitutions, or than a
plucky bully like Barras, who cared for nothing except
feathering his own nest. Any tidy and public spirited person could have done as much with the necessary prestige.
Napoleon got that prestige by feeding the popular appetite
for military glory. He could not create that natural appetite; but he could feed it by victories; and he could use all
the devices of journalism and pageantry and patriotic
braggadocio to make La Gloire glorious. And all this because, like William the Conqueror, he had the group of
talents that make a successful general and democratic
ruler. Had not the French Revolution so completely
failed to produce a tolerable government to replace the
monarchy it overthrew, and thereby reduced itself to desperation, Napoleon would have been only a famous general like Saxe or Wellington or Marlborough, who under
similar circumstances could and indeed must have become
kings if they had been ungovernable enough to desire it.
Only the other day a man without any of the social advantages of these commanders made himself Shah of Iran.

Julius Cæsar and Cromwell also mounted on the débris
of collapsing political systems; and both of them refused
crowns. But no crown could have added to the power their
military capacity gave them. Cæsar bribed enormously; but
there were richer men than he in Rome to play that game.
Only, they could not have won the battle of Pharsalia.
Cromwell proved invincible in the field—such as it was.

It is not, however, these much hackneyed historical
figures that trouble us now. Pharsalias and Dunbars and
Waterloos are things of the past: battles nowadays last sev-

erals months and then peter out on barbed wire under the
fire of machine guns. Suppose Ludendorff had been a
Napoleon, and Haig a Marlborough, Wellington, and
Cromwell rolled into one, what more could they have done
than either declare modern war impossible or else keep
throwing masses of infantry in the old fashion against
slaughtering machinery like pigs in Chicago? Napoleon's
booklearnt tactics and the columns that won so many battles
for him would have no more chance nowadays than the
ragged Irish pikemen on Vinegar Hill; and Wellington's
thin red line and his squares would have vanished in the
fumes of T.N.T. on the Somme. "The Nelson touch"
landed a section of the British fleet at the bottom of the
Dardanelles. And yet this war, which, if it did not end
civilized war (perhaps it did, by the way, though the War
Office may not yet have realized it) at least made an end
of the supremacy of the glory virtuoso who can play brilliant variations on the battle of Hastings, has been followed
by such a group of upstart autocrats as the world has ceased
to suppose possible. Mussolini, Hitler, Kemal and Riza
Khan began in the ranks, and have no Marengos to their
credit; yet there they are at the top!

Here again the circumstances gave the men their
opportunity. Neither Mussolini nor Hitler could have
achieved their present personal supremacy when I was born
in the middle of the nineteenth century, because the prevailing mentality of that deluded time was still hopefully
parliamentary. Democracy was a dream, an idea. Everything would be well when all men had votes. Everything would be better than well when all women had
votes. There was a great fear of public opinion because
it was a dumb phantom which every statesman could identify with his own conscience and dread as the Nemesis of
unscrupulous ambition. That was the golden age of democracy: the phantom was a real and beneficent force. Many
delusions are. In those days even our Conservative rulers
agreed that we were a liberty loving people: that, for in-

stance, Englishmen would never tolerate compulsory military service as the slaves of foreign despots did.

It was part of the democratic dream that Parliament was an instrument for carrying out the wishes of the voters, absurdly called its constituents. And as, in the nineteenth century, it was still believed that British individual liberty forbad Parliament to do anything that it could possibly leave to private enterprise, Parliament was able to keep up its reputation by simply maintaining an effective police force and enforcing private contracts. Even Factory Acts and laws against adulteration and sweating were jealously resisted as interferences with the liberty of free Britons. If there was anything wrong, the remedy was an extension of the franchise. Like Hamlet, we lived on the chameleon's dish "air, promise crammed."

But you cannot create a mentality out of promises without having to face occasional demands for their materialization. The Treasury Bench was up for auction at every election, the bidding being in promises. The political parties, finding it much less troublesome to give the people votes than to carry out reforms, at last established adult suffrage.

The result was a colossal disappointment and disillusion. The phantom of Democracy, *alias* Public Opinion, which, acting as an artificial political conscience, had restrained Gladstone and Disraeli, vanished. The later parliamentary leaders soon learnt from experience that they might with perfect impunity tell the nation one thing on Tuesday and the opposite on Friday without anyone noticing the discrepancy. The donkey had overtaken the carrots at last; and instead of eating them he allowed them to be snatched away from him by any confidence trickster who told him to look up into the sky.

The diplomatists immediately indulged themselves with a prodigiously expensive war, after which the capitalist system, which had undertaken to find employment for everybody at subsistence wages, and which, though it

184

had never fulfilled that undertaking, had at least found employment for enough of them to leave the rest too few to be dangerous, defaulted in respect of unprecedented millions of unemployed, who had to be bought off by doles administered with a meanness and cruelty which revived all the infamies of the Poor Law of a century ago (the days of Oliver Twist) and could not be administered in any kinder way without weakening the willingness of its recipients to prefer even the poorliest paid job to its humiliations.

The only way of escape was for the Government to organize the labor of the unemployed for the supply of their own needs. But Parliament not only could not do this, but could and did prevent its being done. In vain did the voters use their votes to place a Labor Government, with a Cabinet of Socialists, on the Treasury Bench. Parliament took these men, who had been intransigent Socialists and revolutionists all their lives, and reduced them to a condition of political helplessness in which they were indistinguishable except by name from the most reactionary members of the House of Lords or the military clubs. A Socialist Prime Minister, after trying for years to get the parliamentary car into gear for a move forward, and finding that though it would work easily and smoothly in neutral the only gear that would engage was the reverse gear (popularly called "the axe" because it could do nothing but cut down wages), first formed what he called a national government by a coalition of all parties, and then, having proved by this experiment that it did not make the smallest difference whether members of the Cabinet were the reddest of Bolsheviks or the bluest of Tories, made things easier by handing over his premiership to a colleague who, being a Conservative, and popular and amiable into the bargain, could steal a horse where a Socialist dare not look over a hedge. The voters rejected him at the next election; but he retained his membership of the Cabinet precisely as if he had been triumphantly returned.

THE MILLIONAIRESS

Bismarck could have done no more.

These events, helped by the terrific moral shock of the war, and the subsequent exposure of the patriotic lying by which the workers of Europe had been provoked to slaughter one another, made an end of the nineteenth century democratic mentality. Parliament fell into contempt; ballot papers were less esteemed than toilet papers; the men from the trenches had no patience with the liberties that had not saved them from being driven like sheep to the shambles.

Of this change our parliamentarians and journalists had no suspicion. Creatures of habit, they went on as if nothing had occurred since Queen Victoria's death except a couple of extensions of the franchise and an epochmaking revolution in Russia which they poohpooed as a transient outburst of hooliganism fomented by a few bloodthirsty scoundrels, exactly as the American revolution and the French revolution had been poohpooed when they, too, were contemporary.

Here was clearly a big opportunity for a man psychologist enough to grasp the situation and bold enough to act on it. Such a man was Mussolini. He had become known as a journalist by championing the demobilized soldiers, who, after suffering all the horrors of the war, had returned to find that the men who had been kept at home in the factories comfortably earning good wages, had seized those factories according to the Syndicalist doctrine of "workers' control", and were wrecking them in their helpless ignorance of business. As one indignant master-Fascist said to me "They were listening to speeches round red flags and leaving the cows unmilked."

The demobilized fell on the Syndicalists with sticks and stones. Some, more merciful, only dosed them with castor oil. They carried Mussolini to Rome with a rush. This gave him the chance of making an irreparable mistake and spending the next fifteen years in prison. It seemed just the occasion for a grand appeal for liberty, for democ-

186

racy, for a parliament in which the people were supreme: in short, for nineteenth century resurrection pie. Mussolini did not make that mistake. With inspired precision he denounced Liberty as a putrefying corpse. He declared that what people needed was not liberty but discipline, the sterner the better. He said that he would not tolerate Oppositions: he called for action and silence. The people, instead of being shocked like good Liberals, rose to him. He was able to organize a special constabulary who wore black shirts and applied the necessary coercion.

Such improvised bodies attracted young men of military tastes and old soldiers, inevitably including a percentage of ruffians and Sadists. This fringe of undesirables soon committed outrages and a couple of murders, whereupon all the Liberal newspapers in Europe shrieked with horror as if nothing else was happening in Italy. Mussolini refused to be turned aside from his work like a parliamentary man to discuss "incidents." All he said was "I take the responsibility for everything that has happened." When the Italian Liberals joined in the shrieking he seized the shriekers and transported them to the Lipari Isles. Parliament, openly flouted, chastised, and humiliated, could do nothing. The people were delighted; for that was just how they wanted to see Parliament treated. The doctrinaires of liberty fled to France and England, preferring them to Lipari, and wrote eloquent letters to the papers demanding whether every vestige of freedom, freedom of speech, freedom of the press, freedom of Parliament, was to be trampled under the heel of a ruthless dictator merely because the Italian trains were running punctually and travellers in Italy could depend on their luggage not being stolen without actually sitting on it. The English editors gave them plenty of space, and wrote sympathetic articles paraphrasing John Stuart Mill's Essay on Liberty. Mussolini, now Il Duce, never even looked round: he was busy sweeping up the elected municipalities, and replacing them with efficient commissioners of his own choice, who had to do their job or get out. The editors had finally to accord him a sort of Pragmatic Sanction by an admission that his plan worked better than the old plan; but they were still blind to the fact staring them in the face that Il Duce, knowing what the people wanted and giving it to them, was responding to the real democratic urge whilst the cold tealeaves of the nineteenth century were making them sick. It was evident that Mussolini was master of Italy as far as such mastership is possible; but what was not evident to Englishmen who had had their necks twisted the other way from their childhood was that even when he deliberately spat in the face of the League of Nations at Corfu, and defiantly asked the Powers whether they had anything to say about it, he was delighting his own people by the spectacle of a great Italian bullying the world, and getting away with it triumphantly. Parliaments are supposed to have their fingers always on the people's pulse and to respond to its slightest throb. Mussolini proved that parliaments have not the slightest notion of how the people are feeling, and that he, being a good psychologist and a man of the people himself to boot, was a true organ of democracy.

I, being a bit of a psychologist myself, also understood the situation, and was immediately denounced by the refugees and their champions as an anti-democrat, a hero worshipper of tyrants, and all the rest of it.

Hitler's case was different; but he had one quality in common with Il Duce: he knew what the victorious Allies would fight for and what they would only bluster about. They had already been forced to recognize that their demands for plunder had gone far beyond Germany's utmost resources. But there remained the clauses of the Versailles treaty by which Germany was to be kept in a condition of permanent, decisive, and humiliating military inferiority to the other Powers, and especially to France. Hitler was political psychologist enough to know that the time had arrived when it would be quite impossible for the Allies to begin the war over again to enforce these clauses. He saw his opportunity and took it. He violated the clauses, and declared that he was going to go on violating them until a fully re-armed Germany was on equal terms with the victors. He did not soften his defiance by any word of argument or diplomacy. He knew that his attitude was safe and sure of success; and he took care to make it as defiant as that of Ajax challenging the lightning. The Powers had either to renew the war or tear up the impossible clauses with a good grace. But they could not grasp the situation, and went on nagging pitifully about the wickedness of breaking a treaty. Hitler said that if they mentioned that subject again Germany would withdraw from the League of Nations and cut the Powers dead. He bullied and snubbed as the man who understands a situation can always bully and snub the nincompoops who are only whining about it. He at once became a popular idol, and had the regular executive forces so completely devoted to him that he was able to disband the brownshirted constabulary he had organized on the Mussolini model. He met the conventional democratic challenge by plebiscites of ninety per cent in his favor. The myopia of the Powers had put him in a position so far stronger than Mussolini's that he was able to kill seventy-seven of his most dangerous opponents at a blow and then justify himself completely before an assembly fully as representative as the British Parliament, the climax being his appointment as absolute dictator in Germany for life, a stretch of Cæsarism no nineteenth century Hohenzollern would have dreamt of demanding.

Hitler was able to go further than Mussolini because he had a defeated, plundered, humiliated nation to rescue and restore, whereas Mussolini had only an irritated but victorious one. He carried out a persecution of the Jews which went to the scandalous length of outlawing, plundering, and exiling Albert Einstein, a much greater man than any politician, but great in such a manner that he was quite above the heads of the masses and therefore so utterly powerless economically and militarily that he depended for his very existence on the culture and conscience of the rulers of the earth. Hitler's throwing Einstein to the Anti-semite wolves was an appalling breach of cultural faith. It raised the question which is the root question of this pref-ace: to wit, what safeguard have the weaponless great against the great who have myrmidons at their call? It is the most frightful betrayal of civilization for the rulers who monopolize physical force to withhold their protection from the pioneers in thought. Granted that they are some-times forced to do it because intellectual advances may present themselves as quackery, sedition, obscenity, or blas-phemy, and always present themselves as heresies. Had Einstein been formally prosecuted and sentenced by the German National Socialist State, as Galileo was prosecuted by the Church, for shaking the whole framework of estab-lished physical science by denying the infallibility of New-ton, introducing fantastic factors into mathematics, de-stroying human faith in absolute measurement, and play-ing an incomprehensible trick with the sacred velocity of light, quite a strong case could have been made out by the public prosecutor. But to set the police on him because he was a Jew could be justified only on the ground that the Jews are the natural enemies of the rest of the human race, and that as a state of perpetual war necessarily exists be-tween them any Gentile has the same reason for killing any Jew at sight as the Roman soldier had for killing Archimedes.

Now no doubt Jews are most obnoxious creatures. Any competent historian or psycho-analyst can bring a mass of incontrovertible evidence to prove that it would have been better for the world if the Jews had never existed. But I, as an Irishman, can, with patriotic relish, demonstrate the same of the English. Also of the Irish. If Herr Hitler would only consult the French and British newspapers and magazines of the latter half of 1914, he would learn that the Germans are a race of savage idolaters, murderers, liars, and fiends whose assumption of the human form is thinner than that of the wolf in Little Red Riding Hood.

We all live in glass houses. Is it wise to throw stones at the Jews? Is it wise to throw stones at all?

Herr Hitler is not only an Antisemite, but a believer in the possibility and desirability of a pure bred German race. I should like to ask him why. All Germans are not Mozarts, not even Mendelssohns and Meyerbeers, both of whom, by the way, though exceptionally desirable Germans, were Jews. Surely the average German can be improved. I am told that children bred from Irish colleens and Chinese laundrymen are far superior to inbred Irish or Chinese. Herr Hitler is not a typical German. I should not be at all surprised if it were discovered that his very mixed blood (all our bloods today are hopelessly mixed) got fortified somewhere in the past by that of King David. He cannot get over the fact that the lost tribes of Israel expose us all to the suspicion (sometimes, as in Abyssinia, to the boast) that we are those lost tribes, or at least that we must have absorbed them.

One of my guesses in this matter is that Herr Hitler in his youth was fascinated by Houston Chamberlain's Foundations of the XIX Century, an interesting book which at the time of its appearance I recommended everybody to read. Its ethnology was not wholly imaginary. A smattering of Mendelism is all that one needs to know that the eternal fusion of races does not always blend them. The Jews will often throw up an apparently purebred Hittite or a pure-bred Philistine. The Germans throw up out-and-out blond beasts side by side with dark Saturnine types like the Führer himself. I am a blond, much less an antique Roman than a Dane. One of my sisters was a brunette: the other had hair of a flaming red seen only in the Scottish Highlands, to which my ancestry has been traced. All these types with which writers like Chamberlain play: the Teutons and Latins, the Apollonians and Dionysians, the Nordics and Southics, the Dominants and Recessives, have existed and keep cropping up as individuals, and exciting antipathies or affinities quite often enough to give substance to theories about them; but the notion that they can be segregated as races or species is bosh. We have nations with national characteristics (rapidly fading, by the way), national languages, and national customs. But they deteriorate without cross fertilization; and if Herr Hitler could put a stop to cross fertilization in Germany and produce a population of brainless Bismarcks Germany would be subjugated by crossfertilized aliens, possibly by cosmopolitan Jews. There is more difference between a Catholic Bavarian and a Lutheran Prussian, between a tall fair Saxon and a stocky Baltic Celt, than there is between a Frankfort Jew and a Frankfort Gentile. Even in Africa, where pink emigrants struggle with brown and black natives for possession of the land, and our Jamaican miscegenation shocks public sentiment, the sun sterilizes the pinks to such an extent that Cabinet ministers call for more emigration to maintain the pink population. They do not yet venture to suggest that the pinks had better darken their skins with a mixture Bantu or Zulu blood; but that conclusion is obvious. In New Zealand, in Hawaii, there are pure-bred pinks and yellows; but there are hardly any pure-bred Maories or South Sea Islanders left. In Africa the intelligent pink native is a Fusionist as between Dutch and British stock. The intelligent Jew is a Fusionist as between Jew and Gentile stock, even when he is also a bit of a Zionist. Only the stupidest or craziest ultra-Nationalists believe that people corralled within the same political frontier are all exactly alike, and that they improve by continuous inbreeding.

Now Herr Hitler is not a stupid German. I therefore urge upon him that his Antisemitism and national exclusiveness must be pathological: a craze, a complex, a bee in his bonnet, a hole in his armor, a hitch in his statesmanship, one of those lesions which sometimes prove fatal. As it has no logical connection with Fascism or National Socialism, and has no effect on them except to bring them into disrepute, I doubt whether it can survive its momentary usefulness as an excuse for plundering raids and *coups d'état* against inconvenient Liberals or Marxists. A persecution is always a man hunt; and man hunting is not only a very horrible sport but socially a dangerous one, as it revives a primitive instinct incompatible with civilization: indeed civilization rests fundamentally on the compact that it shall be dropped.

And here comes the risk we run when we allow a dominant individual to become a despot. There is a story told of a pious man who was sustained through a lifetime of crushing misfortune by his steady belief that if he fought the good fight to the end he would at last stand in the presence of his God. In due course he died, and presented himself at the gates of heaven for his reward. St Peter, who was for some reason much worried, hastily admitted him and bade him go and enjoy himself. But the good man said that he did not want to enjoy himself: he wanted to stand in the presence of God. St Peter tried to evade the claim, dwelling on the other delights of heaven, coaxing, bullying, arguing. All in vain: he could not shake the claimant and could not deny his right. He sent for St Paul, who was as worried and as evasive as his colleague; but he also failed to induce the newcomer to forgo his promised privilege. At last they took him by the arms and led him to a mighty cathedral, where, entering by the west door, he saw the Ancient of Days seated in silent majesty on a throne in the choir. He sprang forward to prostrate himself at the divine feet, but was held back firmly by the apostles. "Be quiet" said St Paul. "He has gone mad; and we dont know what to do." "Dont tell anybody" added St Peter. And there the story ends.

But that is not how the story ends on earth. Make any common fellow an autocrat and at once you have the Beggar on Horseback riding to the devil. Even when, as the son of his father, he has been trained from infancy to behave well in harness and blinkers, he may go as mad sadistically as a Roman emperor or a Russian Tsar. But that is only the extreme case. Uncommon people, promoted on their merits, are by no means wholly exempt from megalomania. Morris's simple and profound saying that "no man is good enough to be another man's master" holds good unless both master and man regard themselves as equally the fellow servants of God in States where God still reigns, or, in States where God is dead, as the subjects and agents of a political constitution applying humane principles which neither of them may violate. In that case autocrats are no longer autocrats. Failing any such religious or political creed all autocrats go more or less mad. That is a plain fact of political pathology.

Judged in this light our present predicament is lamentable. We no longer believe in the old "sanctions" (as they are called nowadays) of heaven and hell; and except in Russia there is not in force a single political constitution that enables and enjoins the citizen to earn his own living as a matter of elementary honesty, or that does not exalt vast personal riches and the organization of slaughter and conquest above all other conditions and activities. The financier and the soldier are the cocks of the walk; and democracy means that their parasites and worshippers carry all before them.

Thus when so many other tyrannies have been swept away by simple Liberalism, the tyranny of the talented individuals will remain. Again I ask what are we to do with them in self-defence? Mere liquidation would be disastrous, because at present only about five per cent of the population are capable of making decisions of any importance; and without many daily decisions civilization would go to pieces. The problem is how to make sure that the decisions shall be made in the general interest and not solely in the immediate personal interest of the decider. It was argued by our classical political economists that there is a divine harmony between these two interests of

194

such a nature that if every decider does the best for himself the result will also be the best for everybody. In spite of a century of bitter experience of the adoption of these excuses for laziness in politics, shameless selfishness in industry, and glorification of idle uselessness in the face of the degrading misery of the masses, they are still taught in our universities, and, what is worse, broadcast by university professors by wireless, as authentic political economy instead of what they really are: that is, the special pleading put forward in defence of the speculators, exploiters, and parasitic property owners in whose grossly antisocial interests the country is misgoverned. Since Karl Marx and Friedrich Engels exposed the horrible condition of the working classes that underlies the pursepride and snobbery of the upper middle classes and the prestige of the landed gentry and peerage there has been no substantial excuse for believing in the alleged harmony of interests. Nothing more diabolical can be conceived than the destiny of a civilization in which the material sources of the people's subsistence are privately owned by a handful of persons taught from childhood that every penny they can extort from the propertyless is an addition to the prosperity of their country and an enrichment of the world at large.

But private property is not the subject of my demonstration in The Millionairess. Private property can be communized. Capitalists and landlords can be pressed into the service of the community, or, if they are idle or incorrigibly recalcitrant, handed over to the police. Under such circumstances the speculator would find his occupation gone. With him would disappear the routine exploiter. But the decider, the dominator, the organizer, the tactician, the mesmerizer would remain; and if they were still educated as ladies and gentlemen are educated today, and consequently had the same sort of consciences and ambitions, they would, if they had anything like our present proletariat to deal with, re-establish industrial anarchy and heritable private property in land with all their disastrous consequences and Gadarene destiny. And their rule, being that of able persons and not of nincompoops born with silver spoons in their mouths, would at first produce some striking improvements in the working of the public services, including the elimination of dud dignitaries and the general bracing up of plodders and slackers. But when dominators die, and are succeeded by persons who can only work a routine, a relapse is inevitable; and the destruction by the dominators of the organizations by which citizens defend themselves against oppression (trade unions, for example) may be found to leave society less organized than it was before the hand of the master had risen from the dust to which it has returned. For it is obvious that a business organized for control by an exceptionally omnipotent and omniscient head will go to pieces when that head is replaced by a commonplace numskull. We need not go back to Richard Cromwell or the Duke of Reichstadt to illustrate this. It is occurring every day in commercial business.

Now the remedy lies, not in the extermination of all dominators and deciders, but on the contrary in their multiplication to what may be called their natural minority limit, which will destroy their present scarcity value. But we must also eliminate the mass of ignorance, weakness, and timidity which force them to treat fools according to their folly. Armies, fanatical sects and mobs, and the blackshirts complained of today by their black and blue victims, have consisted hitherto mostly of people who should not exist in civilized society. Titus Oates and Lord George Gordon owed their vogue to the London mob. There should not have been any London mob. The soldiers of Marlborough and Wellington were never-do-wells, mental defectives, and laborers with the minds and habits of serfs. Military geniuses could hunt with such products more easily than with a pack of hounds. Our public school and university education equips armies of this kind with appropriate staffs of officers. When both are extinct

196

we shall be able to breathe more freely.

Let us therefore assume that the soldier and his officer as we know them, the Orange and Papist rioters of Belfast, the Moslem and Hindu irreconcilables of the east and the Ku-Klux-Klans and lynching mobs of the west, have passed away as the less dangerous prehistoric monsters have passed, and that all men and women are meeting on equal terms as far as circumstances and education are concerned. Let us suppose that no man can starve or flog his fellows into obeying him, or force upon them the alternative of risking their lives for him in battle or being shot at dawn. Let us take for granted armies intelligent enough to present their officers at any moment with the alternative of organizing a return home or being superseded out of hand. Let us narrow the case to the mysterious precedence into which certain people get pushed even when they lack ambition and are far too intelligent to believe that eminence and its responsibilities are luxuries. To be "greatest among you" is a distinction dearly bought at the price of being "servant to all the rest." Plato was quite right in taking reluctance to govern as a leading symptom of supreme fitness for it. But if we insisted on this qualification in all cases, we should find ourselves as short of governors as the churches would be if they insisted on all their parish priests or rectors being saints. A great deal of the directing and organizing work of the world will still have to be done by energetic and capable careerists who are by no means void of vulgar ambition, and very little troubled by the responsibilities that attend on power. When I said that Napoleon was fundamentally a fool and a snob I did not mean for a moment to question his extraordinary capacity as a ruler of men. If we compare him with his valet-secretary Bourrienne we find that there were no external circumstances to prevent Bourrienne becoming the emperor and Napoleon the valet. They quarrelled and parted with an exchange of epithets unprintable in polite English. Bourrienne was as much a Man of Destiny as Buonaparte. But

it was his destiny to be ruled and Buonaparte's to rule;
and so Buonaparte became Napoleon Bonaparte, First Con-
sul and Emperor, as inevitably as Bourrienne remained a
speculator, litterateur and diplomatist. I am not forgetting that Bourrienne saw Napoleon come and go, and had
a much more comfortable and finally a more successful
career than his quondam master; but the point is that
Napoleon was master whilst their personal relations lasted.
And please note that Napoleon did not and could not
impose on Bourrienne and Talleyrand, nor even on the
more cultivated of his marshals (all planetary Napoleons)
as he could and did on the soldiery and peasantry. They
turned against him very promptly when his fortunes
changed and he could no longer be of any use to them.

Now if a ruler can command men only as long as he is
efficient and successful his rule is neither a tyranny nor a
calamity: it is a very valuable asset. But suppose the nation
is made up for the most part of people too ignorant to understand efficient government, and taught, as far as they
are taught at all, to measure greatness by pageantry and
the wholesale slaughter called military glory. It was this
ignorance and idolatry that first exalted Napoleon and
then smashed him. From Toulon to Austerlitz Napoleon
did what good he did by stealth, and had no occasion to
"blush to find it fame," as nobody gave him the least
credit for anything but killing. When the glory turned to
shame on the road back from Moscow his good works
availed him nothing, and the way was open to St Helena.
Catherine of Russia, when she was faced with a revolt
against the misery of her people, said, not "Let us relieve
their misery by appropriate reforms," but "Let us give
them a little war to amuse them." Every tottering regime
tries to rally its subjects to its support in the last resort by a
war. It was not only the last card of Napoleon III before
he lost the game: it played a considerable part in the capitalist support of Hohenzollern sabre rattling which made
the desperate onslaught of Germany in 1914 possible. Pa-
198

triotism, roused to boiling point by an enemy at the gate, is not only the last refuge of a scoundrel in Dr. Johnson's sense, it is far more dangerously the everyday resort of capitalism and feudalism as a red herring across the scent of Communism. Under such circumstances it is fortunate that war on the modern scale is so completely beyond the capacity of private capitalism that, as in 1915, it forces the belligerents into national factory production, public discipline, and rational distribution: in short, into Socialism. Not only did national factories spring up like mushrooms, but the private factories had to be brought up to the mark by public control of prices and dictation of scientific business methods, involving such an exposure of the obsolescence and inefficiency of profitmongering methods that it took years of reckless lying from Press and platform to make the silly public believe the contrary. For war is like the seven magic bullets which the devil has ready to sell for a human soul. Six of them may hit the glorymonger's mark very triumphantly; but the seventh plays some unexpected and unintended trick that upsets the gunman's apple cart. It seemed an astute stroke of German imperial tactics to send Lenin safely through Germany to Russia so that he might make trouble for the Tsar. But the bullet was a number seven: it killed the Tsar very efficiently; but it came back like a boomerang and laid the Hohenzollerns beside the Romanoffs.

Pageantry will lose its black magic when it becomes a local popular amusement; so that the countryside may come to know it from behind the scenes, when, though it will still please, it will no longer impose. For mere iconoclasm is a mistake: the Roundhead folly (really a Thickhead one) of destroying the power of the pageant by forbidding all theatrical displays and dressings-up, and making everybody wear ugly clothes, ended in the flamboyant profligacy of the Restoration; and the attempt to enforce the second commandment by smashing the images soon smashed the second commandment. Give away the secret

199

that the dressed-up performers are only amateurs, and the images works of art, and the dupes and worshippers will become undeluded connoisseurs.

Unfortunately it is easier to produce a nation of artistic than of political connoisseurs. Our schools and universities do not concern themselves with fine art, which they despise as an unmanly pursuit. It is possible for a young gentleman to go through the whole education mill of preparatory school, public school, and university with the highest academic honors without knowing the difference between a chanty and a symphony, a tavern sign and a portrait by Titian, a ballad by Macaulay and a stanza by Keats. But at least he is free to find out all this for himself if he has a fancy that way.

Not so in political science. Not so in religion. In these subjects he is proselytized from the beginning in the interests of established institutions so effectually that he remains all his life firmly convinced that his greatest contemporaries are rascally and venal agitators, villainous blasphemers, or at best seditious cads. He will listen to noodles' orations, read pompous leading articles, and worship the bloodthirsty tribal idols of Noah and Samuel with a gravity and sincerity that would make him infinitely pitiable if they did not also make him infinitely dangerous. He will feed his mind on empty phrases as Nebuchadnezzar fed his body on grass; and any boss who has mastered these phrases can become his dictator, his despot, his evangelist, and in effect his god-emperor.

Clearly we shall be bossridden in one form or another as long as education means being put through this process, or the best imitation of it that our children's parents can afford. The remedy is another Reformation, now long and perilously overdue, in the direction and instruction of our children's minds politically and religiously. We should begin well to the left of Russia, which is still encumbered with nineteenth century superstitions. Communism is the fairy godmother who can transform Bosses into "servants to all the rest"; but only a creed of Creative Evolution can set the souls of the people free. Then the dominator will still find himself face to face with subordinates who can do nothing without him; but that will not give him the inside grip. A late rich shipowner, engaged in a quarrel with his workmen in which he assumed that I was on their side, rashly asked me what his men could do without him. Naturally I asked him what he could do without them, hoping to open his eyes to the fact that apart from the property rights he had bought or borrowed he was as dependent on them as they on him. But I fear I impressed him most by adding, quite untruly, that no gentleman would have asked that question.

Save for my allusion to the persecution and exile of Einstein I have not said a word here about the miserable plight of the great men neglected, insulted, starved, and occasionally put to death, sometimes horribly, by the little ones. Their case is helpless because nothing can defend them against the might of overwhelming numbers unless and until they develop the Vril imagined by Bulwer-Lytton which will enable one person to destroy a multitude, and thereby make us more particular than we are at present about the sort of persons we produce. I am confining myself to the power wielded by the moneymakers and military geniuses in political life and by the dominant personalities in private life. Lytton's Vril was a fiction only in respect of its being available for everybody, and therefore an infallible preventive of any attempt at oppression. For that individuals here and there possess a power of domination which others are unable to resist is undeniable; and since this power is as yet nameless we may as well call it Vril as anything else. It is the final reality of inequality. It is easy to equalize the dominators with the commonplacers economically: you just give one of them half-a-crown and the other two-and-sixpence. Nelson was paid no more than any other naval captain or admiral; and the poverty of Mozart or Marx was worse than the voluntary holy pov-

erty of the great heads of the religious orders. Dominators
and dominated are already equalized before the law: shall
not I, a playwright of Shakesperean eminence, be hanged
if I commit a murder precisely as if I were the most illiterate call boy? Politically we all have at least the symbol
of equality in our votes, useless as they are to us under political and economic institutions made to encourage William the Conqueror to slay Harold and exploit Hodge.
But, I repeat, when all these perfectly feasible equaliza-
tions are made real, there still remains Epifania, shorn of
her millions and unable to replace them, but still as dominant as Saint Joan, Saint Clare, and Saint Teresa. The
most complete Communism and Democracy can only give
her her chance far more effectively than any feudal or capitalist society.

And this, I take it, is one of the highest claims of Communism and Democracy to our consideration, and the explanation of the apparently paradoxical fact that it is always the greatest spirits, from Jesus to Lenin, from St
Thomas More to William Morris, who are communists
and democrats, and always the commonplace people who
weary us with their blitherings about the impossibility of
equality when they are at a loss for any better excuse for
keeping other people in the kitchen and themselves in the
drawing room. I say cheerfully to the dominators "By all
means dominate: it is up to us to so order our institutions
that you shall not oppress us, nor bequeath any of your
precedence to your commonplace children." For when ambition and greed and mere brainless energy have been dis-
abled, the way will be clear for inspiration and aspiration
to save us from the fatheaded stagnation of the accursed
Victorian snobbery which is bringing us to the verge of
ruin.

MALVERN,
  28th August 1935.

THE MILLIONAIRESS

ACT I

MR JULIUS SAGAMORE, *a smart young solicitor, is in his office in Lincoln's Inn Fields. It is a fine morning in May. The room, an old panelled one, is so arranged that Mr Sagamore, whom we see sitting under the window in profile with his back to it and his left side presented to us, is fenced off by his writing table from excessive intimacy with emotional clients or possible assault by violent or insane ones. The door is on his right towards the farther end of the room. The faces of the clients are thus illuminated by the window whilst his own countenance is in shadow. The fireplace, of Adams design, is in the wall facing him. It is surmounted by a dingy portrait of a judge. In the wall on his right, near the corner farthest from him, is the door, with a cleft pediment enshrining a bust of some other judge. The rest of this wall is occupied by shelves of calf-bound law books. The wall behind Mr Sagamore has the big window as aforesaid, and beside it a stand of black tin boxes inscribed with clients' names.*

So far, the place proclaims the eighteenth century; but as the year is 1935, and Mr Sagamore has no taste for dust and mould, and requires a room which suggests opulence, and in which lady clients will look their best, everything is well dusted and polished; the green carpet is new, rich, and thick; and the half dozen chairs, four of which are ranged under the bookshelves, are Chippendales of the very latest fake. Of the other two one is occupied by himself, and the other stands half way between his table and the fireplace for the accommodation of his clients.

The telephone, on the table at his elbow, rings.

SAGAMORE [*listening*] Yes? . . . [*Impressed*] Oh! Send her up at once.

A tragic looking woman, athletically built and expensively dressed, storms into the room. He rises obsequiously.

THE LADY. Are you Julius Sagamore, the worthless

203

nephew of my late solicitor Pontifex Sagamore?

SAGAMORE. I do not advertize myself as worthless; but Pontifex Sagamore was my uncle; and I have returned from Australia to succeed to as much of his business as I can persuade his clients to trust me with.

THE LADY. I have heard him speak of you; and I naturally concluded that as you had been packed off to Australia you must be worthless. But it does not matter, as my business is very simple. I desire to make my will, leaving everything I possess to my husband. You can hardly go wrong about that, I suppose.

SAGAMORE. I shall do my best. Pray sit down.

THE LADY. No: I am restless. I shall sit down when I feel tired.

SAGAMORE. As you please. Before I draw up the will it will be necessary for me to know who your husband is.

THE LADY. My husband is a fool and a blackguard. You will state that fact in the will. You will add that it was his conduct that drove me to commit suicide.

SAGAMORE. But you have not committed suicide.

THE LADY. I shall have, when the will is signed.

SAGAMORE. Of course, quite so: stupid of me. And his name?

THE LADY. His name is Alastair Fitzfassenden.

SAGAMORE. What! The amateur tennis champion and heavy weight boxer?

THE LADY. Do you know him?

SAGAMORE. Every morning we swim together at the club.

THE LADY. The acquaintance does you little credit.

SAGAMORE. I had better tell you that he and I are great friends, Mrs Fitzfassen—

THE LADY. Do not call me by his detestable name. Put me in your books as Epifania Ognisanti di Parerga.

SAGAMORE [*bowing*] Oh! I am indeed honored. Pray be seated.

EPIFANIA. Sit down yourself; and dont fuss.

THE MILLIONAIRESS

SAGAMORE. If you prefer it, certainly. [*He sits*]. Your father was a very wonderful man, madam.

EPIFANIA. My father was the greatest man in the world. And he died a pauper. I shall never forgive the world for that.

SAGAMORE. A pauper! You amaze me. It was reported that he left you, his only child, thirty millions.

EPIFANIA. Well, what was thirty millions to him? He lost a hundred and fifty millions. He had promised to leave me two hundred millions. I was left with a beggarly thirty. It broke his heart.

SAGAMORE. Still, an income of a million and a half—

EPIFANIA. Man: you forget the death duties. I have barely seven hundred thousand a year. Do you know what that means to a woman brought up on an income of seven figures? The humiliation of it!

SAGAMORE. You take away my breath, madam.

EPIFANIA. As I am about to take my own breath away, I have no time to attend to yours.

SAGAMORE. Oh, the suicide! I had forgotten that.

EPIFANIA. Had you indeed? Well, will you please give your mind to it for a moment, and draw up a will for me to sign, leaving everything to Alastair.

SAGAMORE. To humiliate him?

EPIFANIA. No. To ruin him. To destroy him. To make him a beggar on horseback so that he may ride to the devil. Money goes to his head. I have seen it at work on him.

SAGAMORE. I also have seen that happen. But you cannot be sure. He might marry some sensible woman.

EPIFANIA. You are right. Make it a condition of the inheritance that within a month from my funeral he marries a low female named Polly Seedystockings.

SAGAMORE [*making a note of it*] A funny name.

EPIFANIA. Her real name is Patricia Smith. But her letters to Alastair are signed Polly Seedystockings, as a hint, I suppose, that she wants him to buy her another dozen.

SAGAMORE [*taking another sheet of paper and writing*]

205

I should like to know Polly.

EPIFANIA. Pray why?

SAGAMORE [*talking as he writes*] Well, if Alastair prefers her to you she must be indeed worth knowing. I shall certainly make him introduce me.

EPIFANIA. You are hardly tactful, Julius Sagamore.

SAGAMORE. That will not matter when you have taken this [*he hands her what he has written*].

EPIFANIA. Whats this?

SAGAMORE. For the suicide. You will have to sign the chemist's book for the cyanide. Say it is for a wasp's nest. The tartaric acid is harmless: the chemist will think you want it to make lemonade. Put the two separately in just enough water to dissolve them. When you mix the two solutions the tartaric and potash will combine and make tartrate of potash. This, being insoluble, will be precipitated to the bottom of the glass; and the supermatant fluid will be pure hydrocyanic acid, one sip of which will kill you like a thunderbolt.

EPIFANIA [*fingering the prescription rather disconcertedly*] You seem to take my death very coolly, Mr Sagamore.

SAGAMORE. I am used to it.

EPIFANIA. Do you mean to tell me that you have so many clients driven to despair that you keep a prescription for them?

SAGAMORE. I do. It's infallible.

EPIFANIA. You are sure that they have all died painlessly and instantaneously?

SAGAMORE. No. They are all alive.

EPIFANIA. Alive! The prescription is a harmless fraud!

SAGAMORE. No. It's a deadly poison. But they dont take it.

EPIFANIA. Why?

SAGAMORE. I dont know. But they never do.

EPIFANIA. I will. And I hope you will be hanged for giving it to me.

SAGAMORE. I am only acting as your solicitor. You say you are going to commit suicide; and you come to me for advice. I do my best for you, so that you can die without wasting a lot of gas or jumping into the Serpentine. Six and eightpence I shall charge your executors.

EPIFANIA. For advising me how to kill myself!

SAGAMORE. Not today. Tomorrow.

EPIFANIA. Why put it off until tomorrow?

SAGAMORE. Well, it will do as well tomorrow as today. And something amusing may happen this evening. Or even tomorrow evening. Theres no hurry.

EPIFANIA. You are a brute, a beast, and a pig. My life is nothing to you: you do not even ask what has driven me to this. You make money out of the death of your clients.

SAGAMORE. I do. There will be a lot of business connected with your death. Alastair is sure to come to me to settle your affairs.

EPIFANIA. And you expect me to kill myself to make money for you?

SAGAMORE. Well, it is you who have raised my expectations, madam.

EPIFANIA. O God, listen to this man! Has it ever occurred to you that when a woman's life is wrecked she needs a little sympathy and not a bottle of poison?

SAGAMORE. I really cant sympathize with suicide. It doesnt appeal to me, somehow. Still, if it has to be done, it had better be done promptly and scientifically.

EPIFANIA. You dont even ask what Alastair has done to me?

SAGAMORE. It wont matter what he has done to you when you are dead. Why bother about it?

EPIFANIA. You are an unmitigated hog, Julius Sagamore.

SAGAMORE. Why worry about me? The prescription will cure everything.

EPIFANIA. Damn your prescription. There! [*She tears it up and throws the pieces in his face*].

207

THE MILLIONAIRESS

SAGAMORE [*beaming*] It's infallible. And now that you have blown off steam, suppose you sit down and tell me all about it.

EPIFANIA. You call the outcry of an anguished heart blowing off steam, do you?

SAGAMORE. Well, what else would you call it?

EPIFANIA. You are not a man: you are a rhinoceros. You are also a fool.

SAGAMORE. I am only a solicitor.

EPIFANIA. You are a rotten solicitor. You are not a gentleman. You insult me in my distress. You back up my husband against me. You have no decency, no understanding. You are a fish with the soul of a blackbeetle. Do you hear?

SAGAMORE. Yes: I hear. And I congratulate myself on the number of actions for libel I shall have to defend if you do me the honor of making me your solicitor.

EPIFANIA. You are wrong. I never utter a libel. My father instructed me most carefully in the law of libel. If I questioned your solvency, that would be a libel. If I suggested that you are unfaithful to your wife, that would be a libel. But if I call you a rhinoceros—which you are: a most unmitigated rhinoceros—that is only vulgar abuse. I take good care to confine myself to vulgar abuse; and I have never had an action for libel taken against me. Is that the law, or is it not?

SAGAMORE. I really dont know. I will look it up in my law books.

EPIFANIA. You need not. I instruct you that it is the law. My father always had to instruct his lawyers in the law whenever he did anything except what everybody was doing every day. Solicitors know nothing of law: they are only good at practice, as they call it. My father was a great man: every day of his life he did things that nobody else ever dreamt of doing. I am not, perhaps, a great woman; but I am his daughter; and as such I am an unusual woman. You will take the law from me and do exactly what I tell you to do.

SAGAMORE. That will simplify our relations considerably, madam.

EPIFANIA. And remember this. I have no sense of humor. I will not be laughed at.

SAGAMORE. I should not dream of laughing at a client with an income of three quarters of a million.

EPIFANIA. Have you a sense of humor?

SAGAMORE. I try to keep it in check; but I am afraid I have a little. You appeal to it, somehow.

EPIFANIA. Then I tell you in cold blood, after the most careful consideration of my words, that you are a heartless blackguard. My distress, my disgrace, my humiliation, the horrible mess and failure I have made of my life seem to you merely funny. If it were not that my father warned me never to employ a solicitor who had no sense of humor I would walk out of this office and deprive you of a client whose business may prove a fortune to you.

SAGAMORE. But, my dear lady, I dont know anything about your distress, your disgrace, the mess you have made of your life and all the rest of it. How can I laugh at things I dont know? If I am laughing—and am I really laughing?—I assure you I am laughing, not at your misfortunes, but at you.

EPIFANIA. Indeed? Am I so comic a figure in my misery?

SAGAMORE. But what is your misery? Do, pray, sit down.

EPIFANIA. You seem to have one idea in your head, and that is to get your clients to sit down. Well, to oblige you. [*She sits down with a flounce. The back of the chair snaps off short with a loud crack. She springs up*]. Oh, I cannot even sit down in a chair without wrecking it. There is a curse on me.

SAGAMORE [*collapses on the table, shaking with uncontrollable laughter*]!!!!!

EPIFANIA. Ay: laugh, laugh, laugh. Fool! Clown!

SAGAMORE [*rising resolutely and fetching another chair*

from the wall] My best faked Chippendale gone. It cost me four guineas. [*Placing the chair for her*] Now will you please sit down as gently as you can, and stop calling me names? Then, if you wish, you can tell me what on earth is the matter. [*He picks up the broken-off back of the chair and puts it on the table*].

EPIFANIA [*sitting down with dignity*] The breaking of that chair has calmed and relieved me, somehow. I feel as if I had broken your neck, as I wanted to. Now listen to me. [*He comes to her and looks down gravely at her*]. And dont stand over me like that. Sit down on what is left of your sham Chippendale.

SAGAMORE. Certainly [*he sits*]. Now go ahead.

EPIFANIA. My father was the greatest man in the world. I was his only child. His one dread was that I should make a foolish marriage, and lose the little money he was able to leave me.

SAGAMORE. The thirty millions. Precisely.

EPIFANIA. Dont interrupt me. He made me promise that whenever a man asked me to marry him I should impose a condition on my consent.

SAGAMORE [*attentive*] So? What condition?

EPIFANIA. I was to give him one hundred and fifty pounds, and tell him that if within six months he had turned that hundred and fifty pounds into fifty thousand, I was his. If not, I was never to see him again. I saw the wisdom of this. Nobody but my father could have thought of such a real, infallible, unsentimental test. I gave him my sacred promise that I would carry it out faithfully.

SAGAMORE. And you broke that promise. I see.

EPIFANIA. What do you mean—broke that promise?

SAGAMORE. Well, you married Alastair. Now Alastair is a dear good fellow—one of the best in his way—but you are not going to persuade me that he made fifty thousand pounds in six months with a capital of one hundred and fifty.

EPIFANIA. He did. Wise as my father was, he sometimes forgot the wise things he said five minutes after he said them. He warned me that ninety per cent of our self-made millionaires are criminals who have taken a five hundred to one chance and got away with it by pure luck. Well, Alastair was that sort of criminal.

SAGAMORE. No no: not a criminal. That is not like Alastair. A fool, perhaps, in business. But not a criminal.

EPIFANIA. Like all solicitors you think you know more about my husband than I do. Well, I tell you that Alastair came back to me after six months probation with fifty thousand pounds in his pocket instead of the penal servitude he richly deserved. That man's luck is extraordinary. He always wins. He wins at tennis. He wins at boxing. He won me, the richest heiress in England.

SAGAMORE. But you were a consenting party. If not, why did you put him to the test? Why did you give him the hundred and fifty to try his luck with?

EPIFANIA. Boxing.

SAGAMORE. Boxing?

EPIFANIA. My father held that women should be able to defend themselves against male brutality. He had me taught to box. I became a boxing fan and went to all the championship fights. I saw Alastair win the amateur heavy weight. He has a solar plexus punch that nothing can withstand.

SAGAMORE. And you married a man because he had a superlative solar plexus punch!

EPIFANIA. Well, he was handsome. He stripped well, unlike many handsome men. I am not insusceptible to sex appeal, very far from it.

SAGAMORE [*hastily*] Oh quite, quite: you need not go into details.

EPIFANIA. I will if I like. It is your business as a solicitor to know the details. I made a very common mistake. I thought that this irresistible athlete would be an ardent lover. He was nothing of the kind. All his ardor was in his fists. Never shall I forget the day—it was during our honeymoon—when his coldness infuriated me to such a degree that I went for him with my fists. He knocked me out with that abominable punch in the first exchange. Have you ever been knocked out by a punch in the solar plexus?

SAGAMORE. No, thank heaven. I am not a pugilist.

EPIFANIA. It does not put you to sleep like a punch on the jaw. When he saw my face distorted with agony and my body writhing on the floor, he was horrified. He said he did it automatically—that he always countered that way, by instinct. But that does not prevent him from threatening to do it again whenever I lose my temper.

SAGAMORE [troubled] I could not have believed it of Alastair.

EPIFANIA. Pooh! I asked for it. It helps me to control my temper. It is one of his few redeeming points. For there he is effective: he is in earnest: he is doing the right thing. I almost respected him for it.

SAGAMORE. But what is it all about then? Why do you want to get rid of him?

EPIFANIA. I want to get rid of myself. I want to punish myself for making a mess of my life and marrying an imbecile. I, Epifania Ognisanti di Parerga, saw myself as the most wonderful woman in England marrying the most wonderful man. And I was only a goose marrying a buck rabbit. What was there for me but death? And now you have put me off it with your fooling; and I dont know what I want. That is a horrible state of mind. I am a woman who must always want something and always get it.

SAGAMORE. An acquisitive woman. Precisely. How splendid! [The telephone rings. He rises]. Excuse me. [He goes to the table and listens] Yes? . . . [Hastily] One moment. Hold the line. [To Epifania] Your husband is downstairs, with a woman. They want to see me.

EPIFANIA [rising] That woman! Have them up at once.

THE MILLIONAIRESS

SAGAMORE. But can I depend on you to control yourself?

EPIFANIA. You can depend on Alastair's fists. I must have a look at Seedystockings. Have them up, I tell you.

SAGAMORE [*into the telephone*] Send Mr Fitzfassenden and the lady up.

EPIFANIA. We shall see now the sort of woman for whom he has deserted ME!

SAGAMORE. I am thrilled. I expect something marvellous.

EPIFANIA. Dont be a fool. Expect something utterly common.

Alastair Fitzfassenden and Patricia Smith come in. He is a splendid athlete, with most of his brains in his muscles. She is a pleasant quiet little woman of the self-supporting type. She makes placidly for the table, leaving Alastair to deal with his wife.

ALASTAIR. Eppy! What are you doing here? [*To Sagamore*] Why didnt you tell me?

EPIFANIA. Introduce the female.

PATRICIA. Patricia Smith is my name, Mrs Fitzfassenden.

EPIFANIA. That is not how you sign your letters, I think.

ALASTAIR. Look here, Eppy. Dont begin making a row—

EPIFANIA. I was not speaking to you. I was speaking to the woman.

ALASTAIR [*losing his temper*] You have no right to call her a woman.

PATRICIA. Now, now, Ally: you promised me—

EPIFANIA. Promised you! What right had he to promise you? How dare he promise you? How dare you make him promise you?

ALASTAIR. I wont have Polly insulted.

213

SAGAMORE [*goodhumoredly*] You dont mind, Miss Smith, do you?

PATRICIA [*unconcerned*] Oh, I dont mind. My sister goes on just like that.

EPIFANIA. Your sister! You presume to compare your sister to me!

PATRICIA. Only when she goes off at the deep end. You mustnt mind me: theres nothing like letting yourself go if you are built that way. Introduce me to the gentleman, Ally.

ALASTAIR. Oh, I forgot. Julius Sagamore, my solicitor. An old pal. Miss Smith.

EPIFANIA. Alias Polly Seedystockings.

PATRICIA. Thats only my pet name, Mr Sagamore. Smith is the patronymic, as dear wise old father says.

EPIFANIA. She sets up a wise father! This is the last straw.

SAGAMORE. Do sit down, Miss Smith, wont you? [*He goes to fetch a chair from the wall*].

PATRICIA [*contemplating the wrecked chair*] Hallo! Whats happened to the chair?

EPIFANIA. *I* have happened to the chair. Let it be a warning to you.

Sagamore places the chair for Patricia next the table. Alastair shoves the broken chair back out of the way with his foot; fetches another from the wall, and is about to sit on it next Patricia when Epifania sits on it and motions him to her own chair, so that she is seated between the two, Patricia on her left, Alastair on her right. Sagamore goes back to his official place at the table.

PATRICIA. You see, Mr Sagamore, it's like this, Alastair—

EPIFANIA. You need not explain. I have explained everything to Mr Sagamore. And you will please have the decency in his presence and in mine to speak of my husband as Mr Fitzfassenden. His Christian name is no business of yours.

THE MILLIONAIRESS

ALASTAIR [*angry*] Of course, Eppy, if you wont let anybody speak—

EPIFANIA. I am not preventing you nor anybody from speaking. If you have anything to say for yourself, say it.

PATRICIA. I am sorry. But it's such a long name. In my little circle everyone calls him just Ally.

EPIFANIA [*her teeth on edge*] You hear this, Mr. Sagamore! My husband is called "Ally" by these third rate people! What right have they to speak of him at all? Am I to endure this?

PATRICIA [*soothingly*] Yes: we know you have to put up with a lot, deary;—

EPIFANIA [*stamping*] Deary!!!

PATRICIA [*continuing*]—but thats what the world is like.

EPIFANIA. The world is like that to people who are like that. Your world is not my world. Every woman has her own world within her own soul. Listen to me, Mr Sagamore. I married this man. I admitted him to my world, the world which my imagination had peopled with heroes and saints. Never before had a real man been permitted to enter it. I took him to be hero, saint, lover all in one. What he really was you can see for yourself.

ALASTAIR [*jumping up with his fists clenched and his face red*] I am damned if I stand this.

EPIFANIA [*rising and facing him in the pose of a martyr*] Yes: strike me. Shew her your knock-out punch. Let her see how you treat women.

ALASTAIR [*baffled*] Damn! [*He sits down again*].

PATRICIA. Dont get rattled, Ally: you will only put yourself in the wrong before Mr Sagamore. I think youd better go home and leave me to have it out with her.

EPIFANIA. Will you have the goodness not to speak of me as "her"? I am Mrs Fitzfassenden. I am not a pronoun. [*She resumes her seat haughtily*].

PATRICIA. Sorry; but your name is such a tongue-twister. Mr Sagamore: dont you think Ally had better

215

go? It's not right that we should sit here arguing about him to his face. Besides, he's worn out: he's hardly slept all night.

EPIFANIA. How do you know that, pray?

PATRICIA. Never mind how I know it. I do.

ALASTAIR. It was quite innocent; but where could I go to when you drove me out of the house by your tantrums?

EPIFANIA [*most unexpectedly amused*] You went to her?

ALASTAIR. I went to Miss Smith: she's not a pronoun, you know. I went where I could find peace and kindness, to my good sweet darling Polly. So there!

EPIFANIA. I have no sense of humor; but this strikes me as irresistibly funny. You actually left ME to spend the night in the arms of Miss Seedystockings!

ALASTAIR. No, I tell you. It was quite innocent.

EPIFANIA [*to Patricia*] Was he in your arms or was he not?

PATRICIA. Well, yes, of course he was for a while. But not in the way you mean.

EPIFANIA. Then he is even a more sexless fish than I took him for. But really a man capable of flouncing out of the house when I was on the point of pardoning him and giving him a night of legitimate bliss would be capable of any imbecility.

ALASTAIR. Pardoning me! Pardoning me for what? What had I done when you flew out at me?

EPIFANIA. I did not fly out at you. I have never lost my dignity even under the most insufferable wrongs.

ALASTAIR. You hadnt any wrongs. You drove me out of the house—

EPIFANIA. I did not. I never meant you to go. It was abominably selfish of you. You had your Seedystockings to go to; but I had nobody. Adrian was out of town.

SAGAMORE. Adrian! This is a new complication. Who is Adrian?

PATRICIA. Adrian is Mrs Fitzfassenden's Sunday husband, Mr Sagamore.

EPIFANIA. My what, did you say?

PATRICIA. Your Sunday husband. You understand. What Mr Adrian Blenderbland is to you, as it were. What Ally is to me.

SAGAMORE. I dont quite follow. What is Mr Blenderbland to you, Mrs Fitzfassenden, if I may ask?

EPIFANIA. Well, he is a gentleman with whom I discuss subjects that are beyond my husband's mental grasp, which is extremely limited.

ALASTAIR. A chap that sets up to be an intellectual because his father was a publisher! He makes up to Eppy and pretends to be in love with her because she has a good cook; but I tell her he cares for nothing but his food. He always calls at mealtimes. A bellygod, I call him. And I am expected to put up with him. But if I as much as look at Polly! Oh my!

EPIFANIA. The cases are quite different. Adrian worships the ground I tread on: that is quite true. But if you think that Seedystockings worships the ground you tread on, you flatter yourself grossly. She endures you and pets you because you buy stockings for her, and no doubt anything else she may be short of.

PATRICIA. Well, I never contradict anyone, because it only makes trouble. And I am afraid I do cost him a good deal; for he likes me to have nice things that I cant afford.

ALASTAIR [*affectionately*] No, Polly: you dont. Youre as good as gold. I'm always pressing things on you that you wont take. Youre a jolly sight more careful of my money than I am myself.

EPIFANIA. How touching! You are the Sunday wife, I suppose.

PATRICIA. No: I should say that you are the Sunday wife, Mrs Fitzfassenden. It's I that have to look after his clothes and make him get his hair cut.

EPIFANIA. Surely the creature is intelligent enough to do at least that much for himself.

PATRICIA. You dont understand men: they get interested in other things and neglect themselves unless they have a woman to look after them. You see, Mr Sagamore, it's like this. There are two sorts of people in the world: the people anyone can live with and the people that no one can live with. The people that no one can live with may be very goodlooking and vital and splendid and temperamental and romantic and all that; and they can make a man or woman happy for half an hour when they are pleased with themselves and disposed to be agreeable; but if you try to live with them they just eat up your whole life running after them or quarrelling or attending to them one way or another: you cant call your soul your own. As Sunday husbands and wives, just to have a good tearing bit of lovemaking with, or a blazing row, or mostly one on top of the other, once a month or so, theyre all right. But as everyday partners theyre just impossible.

EPIFANIA. So I am the Sunday wife. [*To Patricia, scornfully*] And what are you, pray?

PATRICIA. Well, I am the angel in the house, if you follow me.

ALASTAIR [*blubbering*] You are, dear: you are.

EPIFANIA [*to Patricia*] You are his doormat: thats what you are.

PATRICIA. Doormats are very useful things if you want the house kept tidy, dear.

The telephone rings. Sagamore attends to it.

SAGAMORE. Yes? . . . Did you say Blenderbland?

EPIFANIA. Adrian! How did he know I was here?

SAGAMORE. Ask the gentleman to wait. [*He hangs up the receiver*]. Perhaps you can tell me something about him, Mrs Fitzfassenden. Is he the chairman of Blenderbland's Literary Pennyworths?

EPIFANIA. No. That is his father, who created the business. Adrian is on the board; but he has no business ability. He is on fifteen boards of directors on the strength of his father's reputation, and has never, as far as I know, coniributed an idea to any of them.

ALASTAIR. Be fair to him, Eppy. No man in London knows how to order a dinner better. Thats what keeps him at the top in the city.

SAGAMORE. Thank you: I think I have his measure sufficiently. Shall I have him up?

EPIFANIA. Certainly. I want to know what he is doing here.

ALASTAIR. I dont mind. You understand, of course, that I am not supposed to know anything of his relations with my wife, whatever they may be.

EPIFANIA. They are perfectly innocent, so far. I am not quite convinced that I love Adrian. He makes himself agreeable: that is all.

SAGAMORE [*into the telephone*] Send Mr Blenderbland up. [*He hangs up the instrument*].

ALASTAIR [*to Patricia*] You will now see the blighter who has cut me out with Eppy.

PATRICIA. I cant imagine any man cutting you out with any woman, dear.

EPIFANIA. Will you be good enough to restrain your endearments when he comes in?

Adrian Blenderbland, an imposing man in the prime of life, bearded in the Victorian literary fashion, rather handsome, and well dressed, comes in. Sagamore rises. Adrian is startled when he sees the company, but recovers his aplomb at once, and advances smiling.

ADRIAN. Hallo! Where have we all come from? Good morning, Mrs Fitzfassenden. How do, Alastair? Mr Sagamore, I presume. I did not know you were engaged.

SAGAMORE. Your arrival is quite opportune, sir. Will you have the goodness to sit down? [*He takes a chair from the wall and places it at the table, on his own right and Patricia's left*].

ADRIAN [*sitting down*] Thank you. I hope I am not interrupting this lady.

PATRICIA. Not at all. Dont mind me.

219

SAGAMORE [*introducing*] Miss Smith, an intimate friend of Mr Fitzfassenden.

PATRICIA. Pleased to meet you, I'm sure.

Adrian bows to her; then turns to Sagamore.

ADRIAN. The fact is, Mrs Fitzfassenden mentioned your name to me in conversation as her choice of a new solicitor. So I thought I could not place myself in better hands.

SAGAMORE [*bowing*] Thank you, sir. But—excuse me —had you not a solicitor of your own?

ADRIAN. My dear Mr Sagamore: never be content with a single opinion. When I feel ill I always consult at least half a dozen doctors. The variety of their advice and prescriptions convinces me that I had better cure myself. When a legal point arises I consult six solicitors, with much the same—

EPIFANIA. Adrian: I have no sense of humor; and you know how it annoys me when you talk the sort of nonsense that is supposed to be funny. Did you come here to consult Mr Sagamore about me?

ADRIAN. I did. But of course I expected to find him alone.

PATRICIA. And here we are, the whole caboodle.

EPIFANIA. I was speaking to Mr Blenderbland, not to you. And I am not a member of your caboodle, as you call it.

PATRICIA. Sorry, dear. It was only a reminder that I was listening.

SAGAMORE. Has the matter on which you wish to consult me any reference to Mr Fitzfassenden's family circle?

ADRIAN. It has.

SAGAMORE. Is it of such a nature that sooner or later it will have to be discussed with all the adult members of that circle?

ADRIAN. Well, yes: I suppose so. But hadnt we better talk it over a little in private first?

EPIFANIA. You shall do nothing of the sort. I will not

have my affairs discussed by anybody in public or in private. They concern myself alone.

ADRIAN. May I not discuss my own affairs?

EPIFANIA. Not with my solicitor. I will not have it.

ALASTAIR. Now she is off at the deep end again. We may as well go home.

EPIFANIA [restlessly rising] Oh, the deep end! the deep end! What is life if it is not lived at the deep end? Alastair: you are a tadpole. [She seizes his head and ruffles his hair as she passes him].

ALASTAIR. Dont do that. [He tries to smooth his hair].

EPIFANIA [to Patricia] Smooth it for him, angel in the house.

PATRICIA [moving to Epifania's chair and doing so] You shouldnt make a sight of him like that.

SAGAMORE. Mr Fitzfassenden: why did you marry Mrs Fitzfassenden?

EPIFANIA. Why!!! Does that require any explanation? I have told you why I married him.

ALASTAIR. Well, though you mightnt think it, she can be frightfully fascinating when she really wants to be.

EPIFANIA. Why might he not think it? What do you mean?

ALASTAIR. He knows what I mean.

EPIFANIA. Some silly joke, I suppose.

ADRIAN. Dont be absurd, Fitzfassenden. Your wife is the most adorable woman on earth.

EPIFANIA. Not here, Adrian. If you are going to talk like that, take me away to some place where we can be alone.

ALASTAIR. Do, for heaven's sake, before she drives us all crazy.

SAGAMORE. Steady! steady! I hardly know where I am. You are all consulting me; but none of you has given me any instructions. Had you not better all be divorced?

EPIFANIA. What is the creature to live on? He has nothing: he would have had to become a professional boxer

221

or tennis player if his uncle had not pushed him into an insurance office, where he was perfectly useless.

ALASTAIR. Look here, Eppy: Sagamore doesnt want to hear all this.

EPIFANIA. He does. He shall. Be silent. When Alastair proposed to me—he was too great an idiot to comprehend his own audacity—I kept my promise to my father. I handed him a cheque for a hundred and fifty pounds. "Make that into fifty thousand within six months" I said "and I am yours."

ADRIAN. You never told me this.

EPIFANIA. Why should I? It is a revolting story.

ALASTAIR. What is there revolting about it? Did I make good or did I not? Did I go through hell to get that money and win you or did I not?

ADRIAN [amazed] Do I understand you to say, Alastair, that you made fifty thousand pounds in six months?

ALASTAIR. Why not?

EPIFANIA. You may well look incredulous, Adrian. But he did. Yes: this imbecile made fifty thousand pounds and won Epifania Ognisanti di Parerga for his bride. You will not believe me when I tell you that the possession of all that money, and the consciousness of having made it himself, gave him a sort of greatness. I am impulsive: I kept my word and married him instantly. Then, too late, I found out how he had made it.

ALASTAIR. Well, how did I make it? By my own brains.

EPIFANIA. Brains! By your own folly, your ignorance, your criminal instincts, and the luck that attends the half-witted. You won my hand, for which all Europe was on its knees to me. What you deserved was five years penal servitude.

ALASTAIR. Five years! Fifteen, more likely. That was what I risked for you. And what did I get by it? Life with you was worse than any penal servitude.

EPIFANIA. It would have been heaven to you if Nature had fitted you for such a companionship as mine. But what was it for me? No man had been good enough for me. I was like a princess in a fairy tale offering all men alive my hand and fortune if they could turn my hundred and fifty pound cheque into fifty thousand within six months. Able men, brilliant men, younger sons of the noblest families either refused the test or failed. Why? Because they were too honest or too proud. This thing succeeded; and I found myself tied for life to an insect.

ALASTAIR. You may say what you like; but you were just as much in love with me as I was with you.

EPIFANIA. Well, you were young; you were well shaped; your lawn tennis was outstanding; you were a magnificent boxer; and I was excited by physical contact with you.

SAGAMORE. Is it necessary to be so very explicit, Mrs Fitzfassenden?

EPIFANIA. Julius Sagamore: you may be made of sawdust; but I am made of flesh and blood. Alastair is physically attractive: that is my sole excuse for having married him. Will you have the face to pretend that he has any mental charm?

ADRIAN. But how did he make the fifty thousand pounds? Was it on the Stock Exchange?

EPIFANIA. Nonsense! the creature does not know the difference between a cumulative preference and a deferred ordinary. He would not know even how to begin.

ADRIAN. But how did he begin? My bank balance at present is somewhere about a hundred and fifty. I should very much like to know how to make it up to fifty thousand. You are so rich, Epifania, that every decent man who approaches you feels like a needy adventurer. You dont know how a man to whom a hundred pounds is a considerable sum feels in the arms of a woman to whom a million is mere pin money.

EPIFANIA. Nor do you know what it feels like to be in the arms of a man and know that you could buy him up twenty times over and never miss the price.

ADRIAN. If I give you my hundred and fifty pounds, will you invest it for me?

EPIFANIA. It is not worth investing. You cannot make money on the Stock Exchange until your weekly account is at least seventy thousand. Do not meddle with money, Adrian: you do not understand it. I will give you all you need.

ADRIAN. No, thank you: I should lose my self-respect. I prefer the poor man's luxury of paying for your cabs and flowers and theatre tickets and lunches at the Ritz, and lending you all the little sums you have occasion for when we are together.

The rest all stare at this light on Epifania's habits.

EPIFANIA. It is quite true: I never have any pocket money: I must owe you millions in odd five pound notes. I will tell my bankers that you want a thousand on account.

ADRIAN. But I dont. I love lending you fivers. Only, as they run through my comparatively slender resources at an appalling rate, I should honestly like a few lessons from Alastair in the art of turning hundreds into tens of thousands.

EPIFANIA. His example would be useless to you, Adrian, because Alastair is one of Nature's marvels; and there is nothing marvellous about you except your appetite. Listen. On each of his birthdays his aunt had presented him with a gramophone record of the singing of the celebrated tenor Enrico Caruso. Now it so happens that Nature, is one of her most unaccountable caprices, has endowed Alastair with a startlingly loud singing voice of almost supernatural range. He can sing high notes never before attained by mortal man. He found that he could imitate gramophone records with the greatest facility; and he became convinced that he could make a fortune as an operatic tenor. The first use he made of my money was to give fifty pounds to the manager of some trumpery little opera company which was then on its last legs in the suburbs to allow him to appear for one night in one of Caruso's most popular roles. He actually took me to hear his performance.

ALASTAIR. It wasnt my fault. I can sing Caruso's head off. It was a plot. The regular tenor of the company: a swine that could hardly reach B flat without breaking his neck, paid a lot of blackguards to go into the gallery and boo me.

EPIFANIA. My dear Alastair, the simple truth is that Nature, when she endowed you with your amazing voice, unfortunately omitted to provide you with a musical ear. You can bellow loudly enough to drown ten thousand bulls; but you are always at least a quarter tone sharp or flat as the case may be. I laughed until I fell on the floor of my box in screaming hysterics. The audience hooted and booed; but they could not make themselves heard above your roaring. At last the chorus dragged you off the stage; and the regular tenor finished the performance only to find that the manager had absconded with my fifty pounds and left the whole company penniless. The prima donna was deaf in the left ear, into which you had sung with all your force. I had to pay all their salaries and send them home.

ALASTAIR. I tell you it was a plot. Why shouldnt people like my singing? I can sing louder than any tenor on the stage. I can sing higher.

EPIFANIA. Alastair: you cannot resist a plot when the whole world is a party to it.

ADRIAN. Still, this does not explain how Alastair made the fifty thousand pounds.

EPIFANIA. I leave him to tell that disgraceful tale himself. I believe he is proud of it. [*She sits down disdainfully in the vacant chair*].

ALASTAIR. Well, it worked out all right. But it was a near thing, I tell you. What I did was this. I had a hundred pounds left after the opera stunt. I met an American. I told him I was crazy about a woman who wouldnt marry me unless I made fifty thousand in six months, and that I had only a hundred pounds in the world. He jumped up and said "Why, man alive, if you have a hundred you can open a bank account and get a cheque book." I said "What good is a cheque book?" He said "Are we partners, fifty fifty?" So I said yes: what else could I say? That very day we started in. We lodged the money and got a book of a hundred cheques. We took a theatre. We engaged a first rate cast. We got a play. We got a splendid production: the scenery was lovely: the girls were lovely: the principal woman was an angry-eyed creature with a queer foreign voice and a Hollywood accent, just the sort the public loves. We never asked the price of anything: we just went in up to our necks for thousands and thousands.

ADRIAN. But how did you pay for all these things?

ALASTAIR. With our cheques, of course. Didnt I tell you we had a cheque book?

ADRIAN. But when the hundred was gone the cheques must have been dishonored.

ALASTAIR. Not one of them. We kited them all. But it was a heartbreaking job.

ADRIAN. I dont understand. What does kiting mean?

SAGAMORE. It is quite simple. You pay for something with a cheque after the banks have closed for the day: if on Saturday or just before a bank holiday all the better. Say the cheque is for a hundred pounds and you have not a penny at the bank. You must then induce a friend or a hotel manager to cash another cheque for one hundred pounds for you. That provides for the previous cheque; but it obliges you, on pain of eighteen months hard labour, to induce another friend or hotel manager to cash another cheque for you for two hundred pounds. And so you go on spending and kiting from hundreds to thousands and from risks of eighteen months imprisonment to five years, ten years, fourteen years even.

ALASTAIR. If you think that was an easy job, just try it

yourself: thats all. I dream of it sometimes: it's my worst nightmare. Why, my partner and I never saw that theatre! never saw that play! until the first night: we were signing cheques and kiting them all the time. Of course it was easier after a while, because as we paid our way all right we found it easier to get credit; and the biggest expenses didnt come until after the play was produced and the money was coming in. I could have done it for half the money; but the American could only keep himself up to the excitement of it by paying twice as much as we needed for everything and shoving shares in it on people for nothing but talk. But it didnt matter when the money began to come in. My! how it did come in! The whole town went mad about the angry-eyed woman. It rained money in bucketsful. It went to my head like drink. It went to the American's head. It went to the head of the American's American friends. They bought all the rights: the film rights, the translation rights, the touring rights, all sorts of rights that I never knew existed, and began selling them to one another until everybody in London and New York and Hollywood had a rake-off on them. Then the American bought all the rights back for five hundred thousand dollars, and sold them to an American syndicate for a million. It took six more Americans to do it; and every one of them had to have a rake-off; but all I wanted was fifty thousand pounds; and I cleared out with that and came swanking back to claim Eppy's hand. She thought I was great. I was great: the money made me great: I tell you I was drunk with it: I was another man. You may believe it or not as you like; but my hats were really too small for me.

EPIFANIA. It is quite true. The creature was not used to money; and it transfigured him. I, poor innocent, had no suspicion that money could work such miracles; for I had possessed millions in my cradle; and it meant no more to me than the air I breathed.

SAGAMORE. But just now, when I suggested a divorce,

you asked how he was to live. What has become of the fifty thousand pounds?

EPIFANIA. He lost it all in three weeks. He bought a circus with it. He thought everything he touched would turn into gold. I had to liquidate that circus a month later. He was about to turn the wild beasts loose and run away when I intervened. I was down four hundred and thirty pounds sixteen and sevenpence by the transaction.

ALASTAIR. Was it my fault? The elephant got influenza. The Ministry of Health closed me down and wouldnt let me move on because the animals might carry foot-and-mouth disease.

EPIFANIA. At all events, the net result was that instead of his being fifty thousand pounds to the good I was four hundred and thirty pounds to the bad. Instead of bringing me the revenues of a prince and a hero he cost me the allowance of a worm. And now he has the audacity to ask for a divorce.

ALASTAIR. No I dont. It was Sagamore who suggested that. How can I afford to let you divorce me? As your husband I enjoy a good deal of social consideration; and the tradesmen give me unlimited credit.

EPIFANIA. For stockings, among other things.

PATRICIA. Oh [*she weeps*]! Does she pay for them, Ally?

ALASTAIR. Never mind, dear: I have shewn that I can make money when I am put to it; and I will make it again and buy you all the stockings you need out of my own earnings. [*He rises and goes behind her chair to take her cheeks in his hands*]. There, darling: dont cry.

EPIFANIA. There! They think they are married already!

SAGAMORE. But the matter is not in your hands, Mr Fitzfassenden. Mrs Fitzfassenden can divorce you whether you like it or not. The evidence is that on a recent occasion you left your wife and took refuge in the arms of Miss Smith. The Court will give Mrs. Fitzfassenden a decree on that.

PATRICIA [*consoled and plucky*] Well, let it. I can support Alastair until he has time to make another fortune. You all think him a fool; but he's a dear good boy; and it just disgusts me the way you all turn against him, and the way his wife treats him as if he were dirt under her feet. What would she be without her money, I'd like to know?

EPIFANIA. Nobody is anybody without money, Seedystockings. My dear old father taught me that. "Stick to your money" he said "and all the other things shall be added unto you." He said it was in the Bible. I have never verified the quotation; but I have never forgotten it. I have stuck to my money; and I shall continue to stick to it. Rich as I am, I can hardly forgive Alastair for letting me down by four hundred and thirty pounds.

ALASTAIR. Sixteen and sevenpence! Stingy beast. But I will pay it.

PATRICIA. You shall, dear. I will sell out my insurance and give it to you.

EPIFANIA. May I have that in writing, Miss Smith?

ALASTAIR. Oh, you ought to be ashamed of yourself, you greedy pig. It was your own fault. Why did you let the elephant go for thirty pounds? He cost two hundred.

SAGAMORE. Do not let us wander from the point.

EPIFANIA. What is the point, pray?

SAGAMORE. The point is that you can obtain a divorce if you wish.

EPIFANIA. I dont wish. Do you think I am going to be dragged through the divorce court and have my picture in the papers with that thing? To have the story of my infatuation told in headlines in every rag in London! Besides, it is convenient to be married. It is respectable. It keeps other men off. It gives me a freedom that I could not enjoy as a single woman. I have become accustomed to a husband. No: decidedly I will not divorce Alastair—at least until I can find a substitute whom I really want.

PATRICIA. You couldnt divorce him unless he chose to

let you. Alastair's too much the gentleman to mention it; but you know very well that your own behavior hasnt been so very nunlike that you dare have it shewn up in court.

EPIFANIA. Alastair was the first man I ever loved; and I hope he will not be the last. But legal difficulties do not exist for people with money. At all events, as Alastair cannot afford to divorce me, and I have no intention of divorcing him, the question does not arise. What o'clock is it?

ALASTAIR. I really think, Eppy, you might buy a wrist watch. I have told you so over and over again.

EPIFANIA. Why should I go to the expense of buying a wrist watch when everyone else has one; and I have nothing to do but ask? I have not carried a watch since I lost the key of my father's old repeater.

PATRICIA. It is ten minutes past twelve.

EPIFANIA. Gracious! I have missed my lesson. How annoying!

ALASTAIR. Your lesson? What are you learning now, may I ask?

EPIFANIA. All-in wrestling. When you next indulge in your favorite sport of wife beating, look out for a surprise. What did I come here for, Mr Sagamore?

SAGAMORE. To give me instructions about your will.

ALASTAIR. She makes a new will every time she loses her temper, Sagamore. Jolly good business for you.

EPIFANIA. Do be quiet, Alastair. You forget the dignity of your position as my husband. Mr. Sagamore: I have changed my mind about my will. And I shall overlook your attempt to poison me.

SAGAMORE. Thank you.

EPIFANIA. What do I owe you for this abortive consultation?

SAGAMORE. Thirteen and fourpence, if you please.

EPIFANIA. I do not carry money about with me. Adrian: can you lend me thirteen and fourpence?

ADRIAN [*Puts his hand in his pocket*]——

EPIFANIA. Stop. Mr Sagamore: you had better be my

family solicitor and send me your bill at the end of the year.

ALASTAIR. Send a County Court summons with it, Sagamore; or you may go whistle for your money.

EPIFANIA. Do hold your tongue, Alastair. Of course I always wait for a summons. It is a simple precaution against paying bills sent in twice over.

SAGAMORE. Quite, Mrs Fitzfassenden. An excellent rule.

EPIFANIA. You are a man of sense, Mr Sagamore. And now I must have some fresh air: this orgy of domesticity has made the room stuffy. Come along, Adrian: we'll drive out into the country somewhere, and lunch there. I know the quaintest little place up the river. Goodbye, Mr Sagamore. Goodbye, Seedy: take care of Alastair for me. His good looks will give you a pleasing sensation down your spine. [*She goes out*].

SAGAMORE [*as Adrian is following her out*] By the way, Mr. Blenderbland, what did you come for?

ADRIAN. I totally forget. I dont feel equal to any more this morning. [*He goes out without further salutations*].

SAGAMORE [*to Alastair*] Your wife is a most extraordinary lady.

ALASTAIR [*utters a stifled howl*]!

PATRICIA. He cant find words for her, poor dear.

SAGAMORE. And now, Mr Fitzfassenden, may I ask what you came to consult me about?

ALASTAIR. I dont know. After ten minutes of Eppy I never do know whether I am standing on my head or my heels.

PATRICIA. It was about a separation. Pull yourself together a bit, dear.

ALASTAIR. Separation! You might as well try to separate yourself from a hurricane. [*He becomes sententious*]. Listen to me, Sagamore. I am one of those unfortunate people—you must know a lot of them—I daresay many of them have sat in this chair and talked to you as I am now talking to you—

SAGAMORE [*after waiting in vain for a completion of the sentence*] Yes? You were saying—?

PATRICIA. Dont wander, Ally. Tell Mr Sagamore what sort of people.

ALASTAIR. The people that have bitten off more than they can chew. The ordinary chaps that have married extraordinary women. The commonplace women that have married extraordinary men. They all thought it was a splendid catch for them. Take my advice, Sagamore: marry in your own class. Dont misunderstand me: I dont mean rank or money. What I mean—what I mean—

PATRICIA [*coming to the rescue*] What he means is that people who marry should think about the same things and like the same things. They shouldnt be over one-another's heads, if you follow me.

SAGAMORE. Perfectly. May I take it that Alastair made that mistake, and that later on (too late, unfortunately) he discovered in you a—shall I say a soul mate?

ALASTAIR. No: that sounds silly. Literary, you know.

PATRICIA. More of a mind mate, I should call it.

SAGAMORE. Precisely. Thank you. A mind mate with whom he could be thoroughly comfortable.

ALASTAIR [*grasping Sagamore's hand fervently*] Thank you, Sagamore: you are a real friend. Youve got it exactly. Think over it for us. Come on, Seedy darling: we mustnt waste a busy man's time.

He goes out, leaving Patricia and Sagamore alone together. She rises and goes to the table.

PATRICIA. Mr. Sagamore: youll stand by us, wont you? Youll save Ally from that awful woman. Youll save him for me.

SAGAMORE. I'm afraid I cant control her, Miss Smith. Whats worse, I'm afraid she can control me. It's not only that I cant afford to offend so rich a client. It's that her will paralyzes mine. It's a sort of genius some people have.

PATRICIA. Dont you be afraid of her, Mr Sagamore.

232

She has a genius for making money. It's in her family. Money comes to her. But I have my little bit of genius too; and she cant paralyze me.

SAGAMORE. And what have you a genius for, Miss Smith, if I may ask?

PATRICIA. For making people happy. Unhappy people come to me just as money comes to her.

SAGAMORE [*shaking his head*] I cant think that your will is stronger than hers, Miss Smith.

PATRICIA. It isnt, Mr Sagamore. I have no will at all. But I get what I want, somehow. Youll see.

ALASTAIR [*outside, shouting*] Seedy! Come on!

PATRICIA. Coming, darling. [*To Sagamore*] Goodbye, Mr Sagamore [*they shake hands quickly. She hurries to the door*]. Youll see. [*She goes out*].

SAGAMORE [*to himself*] I think I shall wait and see.

He resumes his morning's work.

ACT II

A DISMAL old coffee room in an ancient riverside inn. An immense and hideous sideboard of the murkiest mahogany stretches across the end wall. Above it hang, picture-wise, two signboards, nearly black with age: one shewing the arms of the lord of the manor, and the other a sow standing upright and playing a flageolet. Underneath the sow is inscribed in tall letters THE PIG & WHISTLE. Between these works of art is a glass case containing an enormous stuffed fish, certainly not less than a century old.

At right angles to the sideboard, and extending nearly the whole length of the room, are two separate long tables, laid for lunch for about a dozen people each. The chairs, too close together, are plain wooden ones, hard and uncomfortable. The cutlery is cheap kitchen ware, with rickety silver cruets and salt cellars to keep up appearances. The table cloths are coarse, and are not fresh from the laundry.

The walls are covered with an ugly Victorian paper which may have begun as a design of dull purple wreaths on a dark yellow background, but is now a flyblown muck of no describable color, but crushingly depressing. There is no carpet. The door, which stands wide open and has COFFEE ROOM inscribed on it, is to the right of anyone contemplating the sideboard from the opposite end of the room. Next the door an old fashioned hatstand flattens itself against the wall; and on it hangs the hat and light overcoat of Mr Adrian Blenderbland.

He, with Epifania, is seated at the end of the table farthest from the door. They have just finished a meal. The cheese and biscuits are still on the table. She looks interested and happy. He is in the worst of tempers.

EPIFANIA. How jolly!

ADRIAN [looking round disparagingly] I must be a very attractive man.

EPIFANIA [opening her eyes wide] Indeed! Not that I am denying it; but what has it to do with what I have just said?

234

THE MILLIONAIRESS

ADRIAN. You said "How jolly!" I look round at this rotten old inn trying to pretend that it's a riverside hotel. We have just had a horrible meal of tomato tea called soup, the remains of Sunday's joint, sprouts, potatoes, apple tart and stale American synthetic cheese. If you can suffer this and say "How jolly!" there must be some irresistible attraction present; and I can see nothing that is not utterly repulsive except myself.

EPIFANIA. Dont you like these dear old-world places? I do.

ADRIAN. I dont. They ought all to be rooted up, pulled down, burnt to the ground. Your flat on the Embankment in London cost more to furnish than this place did to build from the cellar to the roof. You can get a decent lunch there, perfectly served, by a word through the telephone. Your luxurious car will whisk you out to one of a dozen first rate hotels in lovely scenery. And yet you choose this filthy old inn and say "How jolly!" What is the use of being a millionairess on such terms?

EPIFANIA. Psha! When I was first let loose on the world with unlimited money, how long do you think it took me to get tired of shopping and sick of the luxuries you think so much of? About a fortnight. My father, when he had a hundred millions, travelled third class and never spent more than ten shillings a day on himself except when he was entertaining people who were useful to him. Why should he? He couldnt eat more than anyone else. He couldnt drink more than anyone else. He couldnt wear more than anyone else. Neither can I.

ADRIAN. Then why do you love money and hate spending it?

EPIFANIA. Because money is power. Money is security. Money is freedom. It's the difference between living on the slope of a volcano and being safe in the garden of the Hesperides. And there is the continual pleasure of making more of it, which is quite easy if you have plenty to start with. I can turn a million into two million much more

235

easily than a poor woman can turn five pounds into ten, even if she could get the five pounds to begin with. It turns itself, in fact.

ADRIAN. To me money is a vulgar bore and a soul destroying worry. I need it, of course; but I dont like it. I never think of it when I can possibly help it.

EPIFANIA. If you dont think about money what do you think about? Women?

ADRIAN. Yes, of course; but not exclusively.

EPIFANIA. Food?

ADRIAN. Well, I am not always thinking about my food; but I am rather particular about it. I confess I looked forward to a better lunch than [*indicating the table*] that.

EPIFANIA. Oho! So that is what has put you out of temper, is it?

ADRIAN [*annoyed*] I am not out of temper, I hope. But you promised me a very special treat. You said you had found out the most wonderful place on the river, where we could be ourselves and have a delicious cottage meal in primitive happiness. Where is the charm of this dismal hole? Have you ever eaten a viler lunch? There is not even a private sitting room: anybody can walk in here at any moment. We should have been much more comfortable at Richmond or Maidenhead. And I believe it is raining.

EPIFANIA. Is that my fault?

ADRIAN. It completes your notion of a happy day up the river. Why is it that the people who know how to enjoy themselves never have any money, and the people who have money never know how to enjoy themselves?

EPIFANIA. You are not making yourself agreeable, Adrian.

ADRIAN. You are not entertaining me very munificently, Epifania. For heaven's sake let us get into the car and drive about the country. It is much more luxurious than this hideous coffee room, and more private.

EPIFANIA. I am tired of my car.

ADRIAN. I am not. I wish I could afford one like it.

EPIFANIA. I thought you would enjoy sitting in this crazy out-of-way place talking to me. But I find you are a spoilt old bachelor: you care about nothing but your food and your little comforts. You are worse than Alastair; for he at least could talk about boxing and tennis.

ADRIAN. And you can talk about nothing but money.

EPIFANIA. And you think money uninteresting! Oh, you should have known my father!

ADRIAN. I am very glad I did not.

EPIFANIA [*suddenly dangerous*] Whats that you say?

ADRIAN. My dear Epifania, if we are to remain friends, I may as well be quite frank with you. Everything you have told me about your father convinces me that though he was no doubt an affectionate parent and amiable enough to explain your rather tiresome father fixation, as Dr Freud would call it, he must have been quite the most appalling bore that ever devastated even a Rotary club.

EPIFANIA. My father! You dare think such things of my father! You infinite nothingness! My father made a hundred and fifty millions. You never made even half a million.

ADRIAN. My good girl, your father never made anything. I have not the slightest notion of how he contrived to get a legal claim on so much of what other people made; but I do know that he lost four fifths of it by being far enough behind the times to buy up the properties of the Russian nobility in the belief that England would squash the Soviet revolution in three weeks or so. Could anyone have made a stupider mistake? Not I, fool as you think me. In short, Epifania, the world would not have been a penny the poorer if your father had never existed. You see that, dont you?

EPIFANIA [*springing up and squaring at him*] I see red. Stand up, you cur. Put up your hands. Put them up.

ADRIAN [*rising in some consternation, but not fully recognizing his peril*] Epifania: it's no use losing your temper—

EPIFANIA [*delivering a straight left to his chin*] Take that for calling my father a bore. [*Following it up with a savage punch with her right*] Take that for saying he never made anything.

ADRIAN [*writhing on the floor*] Help! Police! Murder! [*He is unable to rise; but he rolls and scrambles to the door gasping piteously*].

EPIFANIA [*sending him through the door with a mule kick*] Rotter! Bounder! Stinker! [*She snatches his hat and coat from the stand and throws them after him whilst he is heard falling downstairs*].

ADRIAN [*piteously*] Help! Help!

EPIFANIA. You brute! You have killed me. [*She totters to the nearest chair and sinks into it, scattering the crockery as she clutches the table with her outstretched arms and sprawls on it in convulsions*].

A serious looking middleaged Egyptian gentleman in an old black frock coat and tarboosh, speaking English too well to be mistaken for a native, hurries in.

THE EGYPTIAN [*peremptorily*] Whats the matter? What is going on here?

EPIFANIA [*raising her head slowly and gazing at him*] Who the devil are you?

THE EGYPTIAN. I am an Egyptian doctor. I hear a great disturbance. I hasten to ascertain the cause. I find you here in convulsions. Can I help?

EPIFANIA. I am dying.

THE DOCTOR. Nonsense! You can swear. The fit has subsided. You can sit up now: you are quite well. Good afternoon.

EPIFANIA. Stop. I am not quite well: I am on the point of death. I need a doctor. I am a rich woman.

THE DOCTOR. In that case you will have no difficulty in finding an English doctor. Is there anyone else who needs my help? I was upstairs. The noise was of somebody falling downstairs. He may have broken some bones. [*He goes out promptly*].

THE MILLIONAIRESS

EPIFANIA [*struggling to her feet and calling after him*] Never mind him: if he has broken every bone in his body it is no more than he deserves. Come back instantly. I want you. Come back. Come back.

THE DOCTOR [*returning*] The landlord is taking the gentleman to the Cottage Hospital in your car.

EPIFANIA. In my car! I will not permit it. Let them get an ambulance.

THE DOCTOR. The car has gone. You should be very glad that it is being so useful.

EPIFANIA. It is your business to doctor me, not to lecture me.

THE DOCTOR. I am not your doctor: I am not in general practice. I keep a clinic for penniless Mahometan refugees; and I work in the hospital. I cannot attend to you.

EPIFANIA. You can attend to me. You must attend to me. Are you going to leave me here to die?

THE DOCTOR. You are not dying. Not yet, at least. Your own doctor will attend to you.

EPIFANIA. You are my own doctor. I tell you I am a rich woman: doctors' fees are nothing to me: charge me what you please. But you must and shall attend to me. You are abominably rude; but you inspire confidence as a doctor.

THE DOCTOR. If I attended all those in whom I inspire confidence I should be worn out in a week. I have to reserve myself for poor and useful people.

EPIFANIA. Then you are either a fool or a Bolshevik.

THE DOCTOR. I am nothing but a servant of Allah.

EPIFANIA. You are not: you are my doctor: do you hear? I am a sick woman: you cannot abandon me to die in this wretched place.

THE DOCTOR. I see no symptoms of any sickness about you. Are you in pain?

EPIFANIA. Yes. Horrible pain.

THE DOCTOR. Where?

EPIFANIA. Dont cross-examine me as if you didnt believe me. I must have sprained my knuckles and my wrist on that beast's chin.

THE DOCTOR. Which hand?

EPIFANIA [*presenting her left*] This, of course.

THE DOCTOR [*taking her hand in a businesslike way, and pulling and turning the fingers and wrist*] Nothing whatever the matter.

EPIFANIA. How do you know? It's my hand, not yours.

THE DOCTOR. You would scream the house down if your wrist were sprained. You are shamming—lying. Why? Is it to make yourself interesting?

EPIFANIA. Make myself interesting! Man: I am interesting.

THE DOCTOR. Not in the least, medically. Are you interesting in any other way?

EPIFANIA. I am the most interesting woman in England. I am Epifania Ognisanti di Parerga.

THE DOCTOR. Never heard of her. Italian aristocrat, I presume.

EPIFANIA. Aristocrat! Do you take me for a fool? My ancestors were moneylenders to all Europe five hundred years ago: we are now bankers to all the world.

THE DOCTOR. Jewess, eh?

EPIFANIA. Christian, to the last drop of my blood. Jews throw half their money away on charities and fancies like Zionism. The stupidest di Parerga can just walk round the cleverest Jew when it comes to moneymaking. We are the only real aristocracy in the world: the aristocracy of money.

THE DOCTOR. The plutocracy, in fact.

EPIFANIA. If you like. I am a plutocrat of the plutocrats.

THE DOCTOR. Well, that is a disease for which I do not prescribe. The only known cure is a revolution; but the mortality rate is high; and sometimes, if it is the wrong sort of revolution, it intensifies the disease. I can do nothing for you. I must go back to my work. Good morning.

EPIFANIA [*holding him*] But this is your work. What

240

else have you to do?

THE DOCTOR. There is a good deal to be done in the world besides attending rich imaginary invalids.

EPIFANIA. But if you are well paid?

THE DOCTOR. I make the little money I need by work which I venture to think more important.

EPIFANIA [*throwing him away and moving about distractedly*] You are a pig and a beast and a Bolshevik. It is the most abominable thing of you to leave me here in my distress. My car is gone. I have no money. I never carry money about.

THE DOCTOR. I have none to carry. Your car will return presently. You can borrow money from your chauffeur.

EPIFANIA. You are an unmitigated hippopotamus. You are a Bashibazouk. I might have known it from your ridiculous tarboosh. You should take it off in my presence. [*She snatches it from his head and holds it behind her back*]. At least have the manners to stay with me until my chauffeur comes back.

The motor horn is heard honking.

THE DOCTOR. He has come back.

EPIFANIA. Damn! Cant you wait until he has had his tea and a cigarette?

THE DOCTOR. No. Be good enough to give me back my fez.

EPIFANIA. I wanted to see what you looked like without it. [*She puts it tenderly on his head*]. Listen to me. You are having an adventure. Have you no romance in you? Havent you even common curiosity? Dont you want to know why I threw that beast downstairs? Dont you want to throw your wretched work to the devil for once and have an afternoon on the river with an interesting and attractive woman?

THE DOCTOR. Women are neither interesting nor attractive to me except when they are ill. I know too much about them, inside and out. You are perfectly well.

241

EPIFANIA. Liar. Nobody is perfectly well, nor ever has been, nor ever will be. [*She sits down, sulking*].

THE DOCTOR. That is true. You must have brains of a sort. [*He sits down opposite to her*]. I remember when I began as a young surgeon I killed several patients by my operations because I had been taught that I must go on cutting until there was nothing left but perfectly healthy tissue. As there is no such thing as perfectly healthy tissue I should have cut my patients entirely away if the nurse had not stopped me before they died on the table. They died after they left the hospital; but as they were carried away from the table alive I was able to claim a successful operation. Are you married?

EPIFANIA. Yes. But you need not be afraid. My husband is openly unfaithful to me and cannot take you into court if you make love to me. I can divorce him if necessary.

THE DOCTOR. And the man you threw downstairs: who was he? One does not throw one's husband downstairs. Did he make love to you?

EPIFANIA. No. He insulted my father's memory because he was disappointed with his lunch here. When I think of my father all ordinary men seem to me the merest trash. You are not an ordinary man. I should like to see some more of you. Now that you have asked me confidential questions about my family, and I have answered them, you can no longer pretend that you are not my family doctor. So that is settled.

THE DOCTOR. A father fixation, did you say?

EPIFANIA [*nods*]!

THE DOCTOR. And an excess of money?

EPIFANIA. Only a beggarly thirty millions.

THE DOCTOR. A psychological curiosity. I will consider it.

EPIFANIA. Consider it! You will feel honored, gratified, delighted.

THE DOCTOR. I see. Enormous self-confidence. Reckless audacity. Insane egotism. Apparently sexless.

EPIFANIA. Sexless! Who told you that I am sexless?

THE DOCTOR. You talk to me as if you were a man. There is no mystery, no separateness, no sacredness about men to you. A man to you is only a male of your species.

EPIFANIA. My species indeed! Men are a different and very inferior species. Five minutes conversation with my husband will convince you that he and I do not belong to the same species. But there are some great men, like my father. And there are some good doctors, like you.

THE DOCTOR. Thank you. What does your regular doctor say about you?

EPIFANIA. I have no regular doctor. If I had I should have an operation a week until there was nothing left of me or of my bank balance. I shall not expect you to maul me about with a stethoscope, if that is what you are afraid of. I have the lungs of a whale and the digestion of an ostrich. I have a clockwork inside. I sleep eight hours like a log. When I want anything I lose my head so completely about it that I always get it.

THE DOCTOR. What things do you want mostly?

EPIFANIA. Everything. Anything. Like a lightning flash. And then there is no stopping me.

THE DOCTOR. Everything and anything is nothing.

EPIFANIA. Five minutes ago I wanted you. Now I have got you.

THE DOCTOR. Come! You cannot bluff a doctor. You may want the sun and the moon and the stars; but you cannot get them.

EPIFANIA. That is why I take good care not to want them. I want only what I can get.

THE DOCTOR. Good. A practical intellect. And what do you want at present, for instance?

EPIFANIA. That is the devil of it. There is nothing one can get except more money.

THE DOCTOR. What about more men?

EPIFANIA. More Alastairs! More Blenderblands!

THE MILLIONAIRESS

Those are not deep wants. At present I want a motor launch.

THE DOCTOR. There is no such thing in this little place.

EPIFANIA. Tell the landlord to stop the first one that comes along and buy it.

THE DOCTOR. Tcha! People will not sell their boats like that.

EPIFANIA. Have you ever tried?

THE DOCTOR. No.

EPIFANIA. I have. When I need a car or a motor boat or a launch or anything like that I buy straight off the road or off the river or out of the harbor. These things cost thousands when they are new; but next day you cannot get fifty pounds for them. Offer £300 for any of them, and the owner dare not refuse: he knows he will never get such an offer again.

THE DOCTOR. Aha! You are a psychologist. This is very interesting.

EPIFANIA. Nonsense! I know how to buy and sell, if that is what you mean.

THE DOCTOR. That is how good psychologists make money.

EPIFANIA. Have you made any?

THE DOCTOR. No. I do not care for money: I care for knowledge.

EPIFANIA. Knowledge is no use without money. Are you married?

THE DOCTOR. I am married to Science. One wife is enough for me, though by my religion I am allowed four.

EPIFANIA. Four! What do you mean?

THE DOCTOR. I am what you call a Mahometan.

EPIFANIA. Well, you will have to be content with two wives if you marry me.

THE DOCTOR. Oh! Is there any question of that between us?

EPIFANIA. Yes. I want to marry you.

THE DOCTOR. Nothing doing, lady. Science is my bride.

THE MILLIONAIRESS

EPIFANIA. You can have Science as well: I shall not be jealous of her. But I made a solemn promise to my father on his deathbed—

THE DOCTOR [*interrupting*] Stop. I had better tell you that I made a solemn promise to my mother on her deathbed.

EPIFANIA. What!!!

THE DOCTOR. My mother was a very wise woman. She made me swear to her that if any woman wanted to marry me, and I felt tempted, I would hand the woman two hundred piastres and tell her that unless she would go out into the world with nothing but that and the clothes she stood in, and earn her living alone and unaided for six months, I would never speak to her again.

EPIFANIA. And if she stood the test?

THE DOCTOR. Then I must marry her even if she were the ugliest devil on earth.

EPIFANIA. And you dare ask me—me, Epifania Ognisanti di Parerga! to submit myself to this test—to any test!

THE DOCTOR. I swore. I have a mother fixation. Allah has willed it so. I cannot help myself.

EPIFANIA. What was your mother?

THE DOCTOR. A washerwoman. A widow. She brought up eleven children. I was the youngest, the Benjamin. The other ten are honest working folk. With their help she made me a man of learning. It was her ambition to have a son who could read and write. She prayed to Allah; and he endowed me with the necessary talent.

EPIFANIA. And you think I will allow myself to be beaten by an old washerwoman?

THE DOCTOR. I am afraid so. You could never pass the test.

EPIFANIA. Indeed! And my father's test for a husband worthy of me?

THE DOCTOR. Oh! The husband is to be tested too! That never occurred to me.

EPIFANIA. Nor to your mother either, it seems. Well,

245

you know better now. I am to give you a hundred and fifty pounds. In six months you are to increase it to fifty thousand. How is that for a test.

THE DOCTOR. Quite conclusive. At the end of the six months I shall not have a penny of it left, praise be to Allah.

EPIFANIA. You confess yourself beaten?

THE DOCTOR. Absolutely. Completely.

EPIFANIA. And you think I am beaten too.

THE DOCTOR. Hopelessly. You do not know what homeless poverty is; and Allah the Compassionate will take care that you never do.

EPIFANIA. How much is two hundred piastres?

THE DOCTOR. At the rate of exchange contemplated by my mother, about thirtyfive shillings.

EPIFANIA. Hand it over.

THE DOCTOR. Unfortunately my mother forgot to provide for this contingency. I have not got thirtyfive shillings. I must borrow them from you.

EPIFANIA. I have not a penny on me. No matter: I will borrow it from the chauffeur. He will lend you a hundred and fifty pounds on my account if you dare ask him. Goodbye for six months. [*She goes out*].

THE DOCTOR. There is no might and no majesty save in Thee, O Allah; but, oh! most Great and Glorious, is this another of Thy terrible jokes?

ACT III

A BASEMENT *in the Commercial Road. An elderly man, anxious, poor, and ratlike, sits at a table with his wife. He is poring over his accounts. She, on his left, is sewing buttons on a coat, working very fast. There is a pile of coats on the table to her right waiting to have buttons sewn on, and another to her left which she has finished. The table is draped down to the ground with an old cloth. Some daylight comes in down the stone stairs; but does not extend to the side where the couple sit, which is lighted by a small electric bulb on a wire. Between the stairs and the table a dirty old patched curtain hangs in front of an opening into a farther compartment.*

A bell tinkles. The woman instantly stops sewing and conceals the piles of coats under the table. Epifania, her dress covered by an old waterproof, and wearing an elaborately damaged hat, comes down the stairs. She looks at the pair; then looks round her; then goes to the curtain and looks through. The old man makes a dash to prevent her, but is too late. He snatches the curtain from her and bars her passage.

THE MAN. What do you want? What are you doing here?

EPIFANIA. I want employment. A woman told me I should find it here. I am destitute.

THE MAN. Thats not the way to get employment: poking your nose into places that dont concern you. Get out. There are no women employed here.

EPIFANIA. You lie. There are six women working in there. Who employs them?

THE MAN. Is that the way to talk to me? You think a lot of yourself, dont you? What do you take me for?

EPIFANIA. A worm.

THE MAN [*making a violent demonstration*]!!

EPIFANIA. Take care. I can use my fists. I can shoot, if necessary.

THE WOMAN [*hurrying to the man and holding him*]

247

Take care, Joe. She's an inspector. Look at her shoes.

EPIFANIA. I am not an inspector. And what is the matter with my shoes, pray?

THE WOMAN [*respectfully*] Well maam, could a woman looking for work at tuppence hapeny an hour afford a west end shoe like that? I assure you we dont employ any women here. We're only caretakers.

EPIFANIA. But I saw six women—

THE MAN [*throwing open the curtain*] Where? Not a soul. Search the whole bloody basement.

THE WOMAN. Hush, hush, Joe: dont speak to the lady like that. You see, maam: theres not a soul.

EPIFANIA. Theres a smell. You have given them a signal to hide. You are breaking the law. Give me some work or I will send a postcard to the Home Office.

THE MAN. Look here, lady. Cant we arrange this? What good will it do you to get me into trouble and shut up my little shop?

EPIFANIA. What good will it do me to say nothing?

THE MAN. Well, what about half a crown a week?

EPIFANIA. I cannot live on half a crown a week.

THE MAN. You can if you look round a bit. There are others, you know.

EPIFANIA. Give me the address of the others. If I am to live by blackmail I must have an extended practice.

THE MAN. Well, if I have to pay I dont see why the others shouldnt too. Will you take half a crown? [*He holds up half a crown*]. Look here! Look at it! Listen to it! [*He rings it on the table.*] It's yours, and another every Wednesday if you keep the inspector off me.

EPIFANIA. It's no use ringing half crowns at me: I am accustomed to them. And I feel convinced that you will pay five shillings if I insist.

THE WOMAN. Oh, maam, have some feeling for us. You dont know the struggle we have to live.

THE MAN [*roughly*] Here: we're not beggars. I'll pay what the business can afford and not a penny more. You seem to know that it can afford five shillings. Well, if you know that, you know that it cant afford any more. Take your five shillings and be damned to you. [*He flings two half crowns on the table*].

THE WOMAN. Oh, Joe, dont be so hasty.

THE MAN. You shut up. You think you can beg a shilling or two off; but you cant. I can size up a tough lot without looking at her shoes. She's got us; and she knows she's got us.

EPIFANIA. I do not like this blackmailing business. Of course if I must I must; but can you not give me some manual work?

THE MAN. You want to get a little deeper into our business, dont you?

EPIFANIA. I am as deep as I can go already. You are employing six women in there. The thing in the corner is a gas engine: that makes you a workshop under the Act. Except that the sanitary arrangements are probably abominable, there is nothing more for me to know. I have you in the hollow of my hand. Give me some work that I can live by or I will have you cleared out like a wasp's nest.

THE MAN. I have a good mind to clear out now and take some place where you wont find me so easy. I am used to changing my address.

EPIFANIA. That is the best card in your hand. You have some business ability. Tell me why you cannot give me work to live by just as you give it, I suppose, to the women I saw in there.

THE MAN. I dont like the people I employ to know too much.

EPIFANIA. I see. They might call in the inspector.

THE MAN. Call in the inspector! What sort of fool are you? They dread the inspector more than I do.

EPIFANIA. Why? Dont they want to be protected?

THE WOMAN. The inspector wouldnt protect them, maam: he'd only shut up the place and take away their job from them. If they thought youd be so cruel as to report them theyd go down on their knees to you to spare them.

THE MAN. You that know such a lot ought to know that a business like this cant afford any luxuries. It's a cheap labor business. As long as I get women to work for their natural wage, I can get along; but no luxuries, mind you. No trade union wages. No sanitary arrangements as you call them. No limewashings every six months. No separate rooms to eat in. No fencing in of dangerous machinery or the like of that: not that I care; for I have nothing but the old gas engine that wouldnt hurt a fly, though it brings me under the blasted Workshop Act as you spotted all right. I have no big machinery; but I have to undersell those that have it. If I put up my prices by a farthing theyd set their machinery going and drop me. You might as well ask me to pay trade union wages as do all that the inspector wants: I should be out of business in a week.

EPIFANIA. And what is a woman's natural wage?

THE MAN. Tuppence hapeny an hour for twelve hours a day.

EPIFANIA. Slavery!

THE WOMAN. Oh no, maam: nobody could call that slavery. A good worker can make from twelve to fifteen shillings a week at it, week in and week out.

THE MAN. Isnt it what the Government paid at the beginning of the war when all the women were called on to do their bit? Do you expect me to pay more than the British Government?

THE WOMAN. I assure you it's the regular and proper wage and always has been, maam.

THE MAN. Like five per cent at the Bank of England it is. This is a respectable business, whatever your inspectors may say.

EPIFANIA. Can a woman live on twelve shillings a week?

THE MAN. Of course she can. Whats to prevent her?

THE WOMAN. Why, maam, when I was a girl in a

match factory I had five shillings a week; and it was a god-send to my mother. And a girl who had no family of her own could always find a family to take her in for four and sixpence, and treat her better than if she had been in her father's house.

THE MAN. I can find you a family what'll do it today, in spite of all the damned doles and wages boards that have upset everything and given girls ideas above their station without giving them the means to pamper themselves.

EPIFANIA. Well, I will work even for that, to prove that I can work and support myself. So give me work and have done talking.

THE MAN. Who started talking? You or I?

EPIFANIA. I did. I thank you for the information you have given me: it has been instructive and to the point. Is that a sufficient apology? And now to work, to work. I am in a hurry to get to work.

THE MAN. Well, what work can you do?

THE WOMAN. Can you sew? Can you make button-holes?

EPIFANIA. Certainly not. I dont call that work.

THE MAN. Well, what sort of work are you looking for?

EPIFANIA. Brain work.

THE MAN. She's dotty!

EPIFANIA. Your work. Managing work. Planning work. Driving work. Let me see what you make here. Tell me how you dispose of it.

THE MAN [*to his wife*] You had better get on with your work. Let her see it. [*To Epifania, whilst the woman pulls out the pile of coats from under the table and sits down resignedly to her sewing*] And when youve quite satisfied your curiosity, perhaps youll take that five shillings and go.

EPIFANIA. Why? Dont you find my arrival a pleasant sort of adventure in this den?

THE MAN. I never heard the like of your cheek, not

251

from nobody. [*He sits down to his accounts*].

EPIFANIA [*to the woman, indicating the pile of coats*] What do you do with these when they are finished?

THE WOMAN [*going on with her work*] The man comes with his lorry and takes them away.

EPIFANIA. Does he pay you for them?

THE WOMAN. Oh no. He gives us a receipt for them. Mr Superflew pays us for the receipts at the end of the week.

EPIFANIA. And what does Mr Superflew do with the coats?

THE WOMAN. He takes them to the wholesaler that supplies him with the cloth. The lorry brings us the cloth when it takes away the finished clothes.

EPIFANIA. Why dont you deal directly with the wholesalers?

THE WOMAN. Oh no: that wouldnt be right. We dont know who they are; and Mr Superflew does. Besides, we couldnt afford a lorry.

EPIFANIA. Does Mr Superflew own the lorry?

THE WOMAN. Oh no: that wouldnt be right. He hires it by the hour from Bolton's.

EPIFANIA. Is the driver always the same man?

THE WOMAN. Yes, of course: always old Tim Good-enough.

EPIFANIA [*to the man*] Write those names for me: Superflew, Bolton's, Goodenough.

THE MAN. Here! I'm not your clerk, you know.

EPIFANIA. You will be, soon. Do as I tell you.

THE MAN. Well of all the cheek—! [*He obeys*].

EPIFANIA. When Goodenough comes round next, tell him to tell Bolton's that he has found somebody who will buy the lorry for fourteen pounds. Tell him that if he can induce Bolton's to part from it at that figure you will give him a pound for himself and engage him at half a crown advance on his present wages to drive it just the same old round to the same places. He knows the wholesalers. Mr

Superflew is superfluous. We shall collect not only our own stuff but that of all the other sweaters.

THE MAN. Sweaters! Who are you calling sweaters?

EPIFANIA. Man, know thyself. You sweat yourself; you sweat your wife; you sweat those women in there; you live on sweat.

THE MAN. Thats no way to talk about it. It isnt civil. I pay the right wages, same as everybody pays. I give employment that the like of them couldnt make for themselves.

EPIFANIA. You are sensitive about it. I am not. I am going to sweat Mr Superflew out of existence. I am going to sweat Mr Timothy Goodenough instead of allowing Mr Superflew to sweat him.

THE MAN. See here. Does this business belong to me or to you?

EPIFANIA. We shall see. Dare you buy the lorry?

THE MAN. Wheres the money to come from?

EPIFANIA. Where does all money come from? From the bank.

THE MAN. You got to put it there first, havnt you?

EPIFANIA. Not in the least. Other people put it there; and the bank lends it to you if it thinks you know how to extend your business.

THE WOMAN [terrified] Oh, Joe, dont trust your money in a bank. No good ever comes out of banks for the likes of us. Dont let her tempt you, Joe.

EPIFANIA. When had you last a holiday?

THE WOMAN. Me! A holiday! We cant afford holidays. I had one on Armistice Day, eighteen years ago.

EPIFANIA. Then it cost a world war and the slaughter of twenty millions of your fellow creatures to give you one holiday in your lifetime. I can do better for you than that.

THE WOMAN. We dont understand that sort of talk here. Weve no time for it. Will you please take our little present and go away?

THE MILLIONAIRESS

The bell tinkles.

THE MAN [*rising*] Thats Tim, for the clothes.

EPIFANIA [*masterfully*] Sit down. I will deal with Tim.

She goes out. The man, after a moment of irresolution, sits down helplessly.

THE WOMAN [*crying*] Oh, Joe, dont listen to her: dont let her meddle with us. That woman would spend our little savings in a week, and leave us to slave to the end of our days to make it up again. I cant go on slaving for ever: we're neither of us as young as we were.

THE MAN [*sullen*] What sort of wife are you for a man? You take the pluck out of me every time. Dont I see other men swanking round and throwing money about that they get out of the banks? In and out of banks they are, all day. What do they do but smoke cigars and drink champagne? A five pound note is to them what a penny is to me. Why shouldnt I try their game instead of slaving here for pence and hapence?

THE WOMAN. Cause you dont understand it, Joe. We know our own ways; and though we're poor our ways have never let us down; and they never will if we stick to them. And who would speak to us? who would know us or give us a helping hand in hard times if we began doing things that nobody else does? How would you like to walk down Commercial Road and get nothing but black looks from all your friends and be refused a week's credit in the shops? Joe: Ive gone on in our natural ways all these years without a word of complaint; and I can go on long enough still to make us comfortable when we're too old to see what I'm sewing or you to count the pence. But if youre going to risk everything and put our money in a bank and change our ways I cant go on: I cant go on: itll kill me. Go up and stop her, Joe. Dont let her talk: just put her out. Be a man, darling: dont be afraid of her. Dont break my heart and ruin yourself. Oh, dont sit there dithering: you dont know what she may be doing. Oh! oh! oh! [*She can say no*

254

more for sobbing].

THE MAN [*rising, but not very resolutely*] There!
there! Hold your noise: I'm not going to let her interfere
with us. I'll put her out all right. [*He goes to the stairs.
Epifania comes down*]. Now, missis: lets have an understanding.

EPIFANIA. No understanding is necessary. Tim is sure
that Bolton's will take ten pounds for the lorry. Tim is my
devoted slave. Make that poor woman stop howling if you
can. I am going now. There is not enough work here for
me: I can do it all in half a day every week. I shall take a
job as scullery maid at a hotel to fill up my time. But first
I must go round to the address Tim has given me and
arrange that we send them our stuff direct and collect just
as Superflew did. When I have arranged everything with
them I will come back and arrange everything for you.
Meanwhile, carry on as usual. Good morning. [*She goes
out*].

THE MAN [*stupefied*] It seems to me like a sort of
dream. What could I do?

THE WOMAN [*who has stopped crying on hearing Epifania's allusion to her*] Do what she tells us, Joe. We're
like children—[*She begins crying again softly*].

There is nothing more to be said.

ACT IV

THE coffee room of *The Pig & Whistle, now trans-mogrified into the lounge of The Cardinal's Hat, a very attractive riverside hotel. The long tables are gone, replaced by several teatables with luxurious chairs round them. The old sideboard, the stuffed fish, the signboards are no more: instead there is an elegant double writing desk for two sitters, divided by stationery cases and electric lamps with dainty shades. Near it is a table with all the illustrated papers and magazines to hand. Farther down the room, towards the side next the door, there is a long well cushioned seat, capable of accommodating three persons. With three chairs at the other side it forms a fireside circle. The old hatstand has gone to its grave with the sideboard. The newly painted walls present an attractive color scheme. The floor is parquetted and liberally supplied with oriental rugs. All the appurtenances of a brand new first class hotel lounge are in evidence.*

Alastair, in boating flannels, is sprawling happily on the long seat, reading an illustrated magazine. Patricia, in her gladdest summer rags, is knitting in the middle chair opposite, full of quiet enjoyment.

It is a fine summer afternoon; and the general effect is that of a bank holiday paradise.

ALASTAIR. I say, Seedy, isnt this jolly?

PATRICIA. Yes, darling: it's lovely.

ALASTAIR. Nothing beats a fine week-end on the river. A pull on the water in the morning to give one a good stretch and a good appetite. A good lunch, and then a good laze. What more can any man desire on earth?

PATRICIA. You row so beautifully, Ally. I love to see you sculling. And punting too. You look so well standing up in the punt.

ALASTAIR. It's the quiet of it, the blessed quiet. You are so quiet: I'm never afraid of your kicking up a row about nothing. The river is so smooth. I dont know which is more comforting, you or the river, when I think of my-

256

self shooting Niagara three or four times a day at home.

PATRICIA. Dont think of it, darling. It isnt home: this is home.

ALASTAIR. Yes, dear: youre right: this is what home ought to be, though it's only a hotel.

PATRICIA. Well, what more could anyone ask but a nice hotel? All the housekeeping done for us: no trouble with the servants: no rates nor taxes. I have never had any peace except in a hotel. But perhaps a man doesnt feel that way.

The manager of the hotel, a young man, smartly dressed, enters. He carries the hotel register, which he opens and places on the newspaper table. He then comes obsequiously to his two guests.

MANAGER [*between them*] Good afternoon, sir. I hope you find everything here to your liking.

ALASTAIR. Yes, thanks. But what have you done to the old place? When I was here last, a year ago, it was a common pub called The Pig and Whistle.

THE MANAGER. It was so until quite lately, sir. My father kept The Pig and Whistle. So did his forefathers right back to the reign of William the Conqueror. Cardinal Wolsey stopped once for an hour at The Pig and Whistle when his mule cast a shoe and had to go to the blacksmith's. I assure you my forefathers thought a lot of themselves. But they were uneducated men, and ruined the old place by trying to improve it by getting rid of the old things in it. It was on its last legs when you saw it, sir. I was ashamed of it.

ALASTAIR. Well, you have made a first rate job of it now.

THE MANAGER. Oh, it was not my doing, sir: I am only the manager. You would hardly believe it if I were to tell you the story of it. Much more romantic, to my mind, than the old tale about Wolsey. But I mustnt disturb you talking. You will let me know if theres anything I can do to make you quite comfortable.

PATRICIA. I should like to know about the old Pig if

257

it's romantic. If you can spare the time, of course.

THE MANAGER. I am at your service, madam, always.

ALASTAIR. Fire ahead, old man.

THE MANAGER. Well, madam, one day a woman came here and asked for a job as a scullery maid. My poor old father hadnt the nerve to turn her out: he said she might just try for a day or two. So she started in. She washed two dishes and broke six. My poor old mother was furious: she thought the world of her dishes. She had no suspicion, poor soul, that they were ugly and common and old and cheap and altogether out of date. She said that as the girl had broken them she should pay for them if she had to stay for a month and have the price stopped out of her wages. Off went the girl to Reading and came back with a load of crockery that made my mother cry: she said we should be disgraced for ever if we served a meal on such old fashioned things. But the very next day an American lady with a boating party bought them right off the table for three times what they cost; and my poor mother never dared say another word. The scullery maid took things into her own hands in a way we could never have done. It was cruel for us; but we couldnt deny that she was always right.

PATRICIA. Cruel! What was there cruel in getting nice crockery for you?

THE MANAGER. Oh, it wasnt only that, madam: that part of it was easy and pleasant enough. You see all she had to do with the old crockery was to break it and throw the bits into the dustbin. But what was the matter with the old Pig and Whistle was not the old thick plates that took away your appetite. It was the old people it had gathered about itself that were past their work and had never been up to much according to modern ideas. They had to be thrown into the street to wander about for a few days and then go into the workhouse. There was the bar that was served by father and mother: she dressed up to the nines, as she thought, poor old dear, never dreaming that the

world was a day older than when she was married. The
scullery maid told them the truth about themselves; and
it just cut them to pieces; for it was the truth; and I
couldnt deny it. The old man had to give in, because he
had raised money on his freehold and was at his wits' end
to pay the mortgage interest. The next thing we knew,
the girl had paid off the mortgage and got the whip hand
of us completely. "It's time for you two to sell your freehold and retire: you are doing no good here" she said.

PATRICIA. But that was dreadful, to root them up like
that.

THE MANAGER. It was hard; but it was the truth. We
should have had the brokers in sooner or later if we had
gone on. Business is business; and theres no room for sentiment in it. And then, think of the good she did. My
parents would never have got the price for the freehold
that she gave them. Here was I, ashamed of the place,
tied to the old Pig and Whistle by my feeling for my
parents, with no prospects. Now the house is a credit to the
neighborhood and gives more employment than the poor
old Pig did in its best days; and I am the manager of it
with a salary and a percentage beyond anything I could
have dreamt of.

ALASTAIR. Then she didnt chuck you, old man.

THE MANAGER. No, sir. You see, though I could never
have made the change myself, I was intelligent enough to
see that she was right. I backed her up all through. I have
such faith in that woman, sir, that if she told me to burn
down the hotel tonight I'd do it without a moment's hesitation. When she puts her finger on a thing it turns into
gold every time. The bank would remind my father if he
overdrew by five pounds; but the manager keeps pressing
overdrafts on her: it makes him miserable when she has a
penny to her credit. A wonderful woman, sir: one day a
scullery maid, and the next the proprietress of a first class
hotel.

PATRICIA. And are the old people satisfied and happy?

259

THE MANAGER. Well, no: the change was too much for them at their age. My father had a stroke and wont last long, I'm afraid. And my mother has gone a bit silly. Still, it was best for them; and they have all the comforts they care for.

ALASTAIR. Well, thats a very moving tale: more so than you think, old boy, because I happen to know a woman of that stamp. By the way, I telegraphed for a friend of mine to come and spend the week-end with us here: a Mr Sagamore. I suppose you can find a room for him.

THE MANAGER. That will be quite all right, sir, thank you.

PATRICIA. Have you many people in the house this week-end?

THE MANAGER. Less than usual, madam. We have an Egyptian doctor who takes his meals here: a very learned man I should think: very quiet: not a word to anybody. Then there is another gentleman, an invalid, only just discharged from the Cottage Hospital. The Egyptian doctor recommended our chef to him; and he takes his meals here too. And that is all, madam, unless some fresh visitors arrive.

ALASTAIR. Well, we must put up with them.

THE MANAGER. By the way, sir, I am sorry to trouble you; but you came up this morning without signing the register. I have brought it up. Would you be so good? [*He fetches the register from the table and presents it to Alastair with his fountain pen*].

ALASTAIR [*sitting up and taking it on his knees*] Oh, I am sorry: I forgot. [*He signs*]. There you are. [*He puts up his legs again*].

THE MANAGER. Thanks very much, sir. [*He glances at the register before shutting it. The signature surprises him*]. Oh, indeed, sir! We are honored.

ALASTAIR. Anything wrong?

THE MANAGER. Oh no, sir, nothing wrong: quite the contrary. Mr and Mrs Fitzfassenden. The name is so un-

THE MILLIONAIRESS

usual. Have I the honor of entertaining the celebrated—

ALASTAIR [*interrupting*] Yes: it's all right: I am the tennis champion and the boxing champion and all the rest of it; but I am here for a holiday and I dont want to hear anything more about it.

THE MANAGER [*shutting the book*] I quite understand, sir. I should not have said anything if it were not that the proprietress of this hotel, the lady I told you of, is a Mrs Fitzfassenden.

ALASTAIR [*rising with a yell*] What! Let me out of this. Pack up, Seedy. My bill, please, instantly.

THE MANAGER. Certainly, sir. But may I say that she is not on the premises at present and that I do not expect her this week-end.

PATRICIA. Dont fuss, darling. Weve a perfect right to be in her hotel if we pay our way just like anybody else.

ALASTAIR. Very well: have it your own way. But my week-end is spoilt.

THE MANAGER. Depend on it, she wont come, sir. She is getting tired of paying us unexpected visits now that she knows she can depend on me. [*He goes out, but immediately looks in again to say*] Your friend Mr Sagamore, sir, coming up with the invalid gentleman. [*He holds the door open for Sagamore and Adrian, who come in. Then he goes out, taking the register with him*].

Adrian, who comes first, limps badly on two walking sticks; and his head is bandaged. He is disagreeably surprised at seeing Fitzfassenden and Patricia.

ADRIAN. Alastair! Miss Smith! What does this mean, Sagamore? You never told me who you were bringing me to see: you said two friends. Alastair: I assure you I did not know you were here. Sagamore said some friends who would be glad to see me.

PATRICIA. Well, we are glad to see you, Mr Blenderbland. Wont you sit down?

ALASTAIR. But whats happened to you, old chap? What on earth have you done to yourself?

261

THE MILLIONAIRESS

ADRIAN [*exasperated*] Everyone asks me what I have done to myself. I havnt done anything to myself. I suppose you mean this and this [*he indicated his injuries*]. Well, they are what your wife has done to me. That is why Sagamore should not have brought me here.

ALASTAIR. I say: I am frightfully sorry, old chap.

PATRICIA [*rising solicitously*] Do sit down, Mr Blenderbland. Rest yourself on that couch. [*Arranging cushions*] Dear! dear!

ALASTAIR. Eppy is like that, you know.

ADRIAN. Yes: I know now. But I ought not to be here: Sagamore should not have brought me here.

PATRICIA. But why not? I assure you we're delighted to see you. We dont mind what Mrs Fitzfassenden does.

ADRIAN. But I do. You are most kind; but I cannot claim the privilege of a friend and at the same time be the plaintiff in an action for assault and battery.

ALASTAIR. Yes you can, old chap. The situation is not new. The victims always come to us for sympathy. Make yourself comfortable.

ADRIAN [*reluctantly sitting down and disposing his damaged limbs along the couch*] Well, it's most kind of you; and I really cant stand any longer. But I dont understand why Sagamore should have played such a trick on me. And, of course, on you too.

Patricia returns to her chair, and resumes her knitting.

SAGAMORE [*taking a chair next Patricia on her left*] Well, the truth of the matter is that Blenderbland wont be reasonable; and I thought you two might help me to bring him to his senses.

ADRIAN [*obstinately*] It's no use, Sagamore. Two thousand five hundred. And costs. Not a penny less.

SAGAMORE. Too much. Ridiculous. A jury might give five hundred if there was a clear disablement from earning, or if the defendant had done something really womanly, like throwing vitriol. But you are only a sleeping partner in the firm your father founded: you dont really earn your income. Besides, hang it all! a man accusing a woman of assault!

ALASTAIR. Why didnt you give her a punch in the solar plexus?

ADRIAN. Strike a woman! Impossible.

ALASTAIR. Rot! If a woman starts fighting she must take what she gets and deserves.

PATRICIA. Look at the marks she's left on you, Mr. Blenderbland! You shouldnt have put up with it: it only encourages her.

ALASTAIR. Search me for marks: you wont find any. Youd have found a big mark on her the first time she tried it on me. There was no second time.

ADRIAN. Unfortunately I have neither your muscle nor your knowledge of how to punch. But I will take lessons when I get well. And she shall pay for them. Two thousand five hundred. And medical expenses. And costs.

SAGAMORE. And cab fare to the Cottage Hospital, I suppose.

ADRIAN. No: I went in her own car. But now you remind me, I tipped the chauffeur. Now dont misunderstand me. It is not the money. But I wont be beaten by a woman. It's a point of honor: of self-respect.

SAGAMORE. Yes; but how do you arrive at the figure? Why is your honor and self-respect worth two thousand five hundred pounds and not two thousand five hundred millions?

ADRIAN. My brother got two thousand five hundred from the railway company when an electric truck butted into him on the platform at Paddington. I will not let Epifania off with less. It was an unprovoked, brutal, cowardly assault.

SAGAMORE. Was it quite unprovoked? You will not get a jury to swallow that without a peck of salt?

ADRIAN. I have told you over and over again that it was absolutely unprovoked. But the concussion from which I suffered obliterated all consciousness of what happened immediately before the assault: the last thing I can recollect was a quite ordinary conversation about her father's money.

SAGAMORE. So much the worse for you. She can accuse you of anything she likes. And remember: no man can get damages out of a British jury unless he goes into court as a moral man.

ADRIAN. Do you suggest that I am not a moral man?

SAGAMORE. No; but Mrs Fitzfassenden's counsel will if you take her into court.

ADRIAN. Stuff! Would any jury believe that she and I were lovers on the strength of a sprained ankle, a dislocated knee, and a lump on my head the size of an ostrich's egg?

SAGAMORE. The best of evidence against you. It's only lovers that have lovers' quarrels. And suppose she pleads self-defence against a criminal assault!

ADRIAN. She dare not swear to such a lie.

SAGAMORE. How do you know it's a lie? You don't know what happened at the end. You had concussion of the brain.

ADRIAN. Yes: after the assault.

SAGAMORE. But it obliterated your consciousness of what happened before the assault. How do you know what you did in those moments?

ADRIAN. Look here. Are you my solicitor or hers?

SAGAMORE. Fate seems to have made me the solicitor of everybody in this case. If I am forced to throw up either her case or yours, I must throw up yours. How can I afford to lose a client with such an income and such a temper? Her tantrums are worth two or three thousand a year to any solicitor.

ADRIAN. Very well, Sagamore. You see my condition: you know that right and justice are on my side. I shall not forget this.

The manager enters, looking very serious.

THE MANAGER [*to Alastair*] I am extremely sorry, sir. Mrs Fitzfassenden is downstairs with the Egyptian doctor.

I really did not expect her.

EPIFANIA [*dashing into the room and addressing herself fiercely to the manager*] You have allowed my husband to bring a woman to my hotel and register her in my name. You are fired. [*She is behind the couch and does not see Adrian. Sagamore rises*].

THE MANAGER. I am sorry, madam: I did not know that the gentleman was your husband. However, you are always right. Do you wish me to go at once or to carry on until you have replaced me?

EPIFANIA. I do not wish you to go at all: you are re-engaged. Throw them both out, instantly.

ALASTAIR. Ha ha ha!

SAGAMORE. Your manager cannot throw Alastair out: Alastair can throw all of us out, if it comes to that. As to Miss Smith, this is a licensed house; and she has as much right to be here as you or I.

EPIFANIA. I will set fire to the hotel if necessary. [*She sees Adrian*]. Hallo! What is this? Adrian here too! What has happened to your head? What are those sticks for? [*To the manager*] Send the doctor here at once. [*To Adrian*] Have you hurt yourself?

The manager hurries out, glad to escape from the mêlée.

ADRIAN. Hurt myself! Hurt myself!!!

EPIFANIA. Has he been run over?

ADRIAN. This woman has half killed me; and she asks have I hurt myself! I fell down the whole flight of stairs. My ankle was sprained. My knee was twisted. The small bone of my leg was broken. I ricked my spine. I had to give them a subscription at the Cottage Hospital, where your man took me. I had to go from there to a nursing home: twelve guineas a week. I had to call in three Harley Street surgeons; and none of them knew anything about dislocated knees: they wanted to cut my knee open to see what was the matter with it. I had to take it to a bonesetter; and he charged me fifty guineas.

EPIFANIA. Well, why did you not walk downstairs properly? Were you drunk?

ADRIAN [*suffocating*] I—

SAGAMORE [*cutting in quickly*] He declares that his injuries were inflicted by you when you last met, Mrs Fitzfassenden.

EPIFANIA. By me! Am I a prizefighter? Am I a coalheaver?

ADRIAN. Both.

SAGAMORE. Do you deny that you assaulted him?

EPIFANIA. Of course I deny it. Anything more monstrous I never heard. What happened was that he insulted my father grossly, without the slightest provocation, at a moment when I had every reason to expect the utmost tenderness from him. The blood rushed to my head: the next thing I remember is that I was lying across the table, trembling, dying. The doctor who found me can tell you what my condition was.

ADRIAN. I dont care what your condition was. What condition did your chauffeur find me in?

SAGAMORE. Then neither of you has the least notion of how this affair ended.

ADRIAN. I have medical evidence.

EPIFANIA. So have I.

ADRIAN. Well, we shall see. I am not going to be talked out of my case.

EPIFANIA. What do you mean by your case?

SAGAMORE. He is taking an action against you.

EPIFANIA. An action! Very well: you know my invariable rule. Fight him to the last ditch, no matter what it costs. Take him to the House of Lords if necessary. We shall see whose purse will hold out longest. I will not be blackmailed.

ADRIAN. You think your father's money places you above the law?

EPIFANIA [*flushing*] Again!

She raises her fists. Alastair seizes her from behind and

whirls her away towards Sagamore; then places himself on guard between her and the couch, balancing his fist warningly.

ALASTAIR. Now! now! now! None of that. Toko, my girl, toko.

SAGAMORE. Toko! What is toko?

ALASTAIR. She knows. Toko is an infallible medicine for calming the nerves. A punch in the solar plexus and a day in bed: thats toko.

EPIFANIA. You are my witness, Mr Sagamore, how I go in fear of my husband's brutal violence. He is stronger than I am: he can batter me, torture me, kill me. It is the last argument of the lower nature against the higher. My innocence is helpless. Do your worst. [*She sits down in Sagamore's chair with great dignity*]

ALASTAIR. Quite safe now, ladies and gentlemen. [*He picks up his illustrated paper, and retires with it to one of the remoter tea-tables, where he sits down to read as quietly as may be*].

ADRIAN [*to Epifania*] Now you know what I felt. It serves you right.

EPIFANIA. Yes: go on. Insult me. Threaten me. Blackmail me. You can all do it with impunity now.

SAGAMORE [*behind her chair*] Dont take it that way, Mrs Fitzfassenden. There is no question of blackmailing or insulting you. I only want to settle this business of Mr Blenderbland's injuries before we go into the matrimonial question.

EPIFANIA. I want to hear no more of Mr Blenderbland and his ridiculous injuries.

SAGAMORE. Do be a little reasonable, Mrs Fitzfassenden. How are we to discuss the compensation due to Mr Blenderbland without mentioning his injuries?

EPIFANIA. There is no compensation due to Mr Blenderbland. He deserved what he got, whatever that was.

SAGAMORE. But he will take an action against you.

EPIFANIA. Take one against him first.

THE MILLIONAIRESS

SAGAMORE. What for?

EPIFANIA. For anything; only dont bother me about it. Claim twenty thousand pounds damages. I tell you I will not be blackmailed.

ADRIAN. Neither will I. I am entitled to compensation and I mean to have it.

SAGAMORE [*coming between them*] Steady! steady! please. I cannot advise either of you to go to law; but quite seriously, Mrs Fitzfassenden, Mr Blenderbland is entitled to some compensation. You can afford it.

EPIFANIA. Mr Sagamore: a woman as rich as I am cannot afford anything. I have to fight to keep every penny I possess. Every beggar, every blackmailer, every swindler, every charity, every testimonial, every political cause, every league and brotherhood and sisterhood, every church and chapel, every institution of every kind on earth is busy from morning to night trying to bleed me to death. If I weaken for a moment, if I let a farthing go, I shall be destitute by the end of the month. I subscribe a guinea a year to the Income Tax Payers' Defence League; but that is all: absolutely all. My standing instructions to you are to defend every action and to forestall every claim for damages by a counterclaim for ten times the amount. That is the only way in which I can write across the sky "Hands off My Money."

SAGAMORE. You see, Mr Blenderbland, it's no use. You must withdraw your threat of an action.

ADRIAN. I wont.

SAGAMORE. You will. You must. Mrs Fitzfassenden: he can do nothing against you. Let me make an appeal on his behalf ad misericordiam.

EPIFANIA [*impatiently*] Oh, we are wasting time; and I have more important business to settle. Give him a ten pound note and have done with it.

ADRIAN. A ten pound note!!!

SAGAMORE [*remonstrant*] Oh, Mrs Fitzfassenden!

EPIFANIA. Yes: a ten pound note. No man can refuse

268

a ten pound note if you crackle it under his nose.

SAGAMORE. But he wants two thousand five hundred.

EPIFANIA [*rising stupefied*] Two thou—[*She gasps*].

ADRIAN. Not a penny less.

EPIFANIA [*going past Sagamore to the couch*] Adrian, my child, I have underrated you. Your cheek, your gluttony, your obstinacy impose respect on me. I threw a half baked gentleman downstairs; and my chauffeur picked him up on the mat a magnificently complete Skunk.

ADRIAN [*furious*] Five thousand for that, Sagamore: do you hear?

SAGAMORE. Please! please! Do keep your temper.

ADRIAN. Keep your own temper. Has she lamed you for life? Has she raised a bump on your head? Has she called you a skunk?

SAGAMORE. No; but she may at any moment.

EPIFANIA [*flinging her arms round him with a whoop of delight*] Ha ha! Ha ha! My Sagamore! My treasure! Shall I give him five thousand on condition that he turns it into a million in six months?

ADRIAN. I will do what I like with it. I will have it unconditionally.

SAGAMORE [*extricating himself gently from Epifania's hug*] Mr Blenderbland: it is a mistake to go into court in the character of a man who has been called a skunk. It makes the jury see you in that light from the start. It is also very difficult for a plaintiff to get sympathy in the character of a man who has been thrashed by a woman. If Mrs Fitzfassenden had stabbed you, or shot you, or poisoned you, that would have been quite in order: your dignity would not have been compromised. But Mrs Fitzfassenden knows better. She knows the privileges of her sex to a hair's breadth and never oversteps them. She would come into court beautifully dressed and looking her best. No woman can be more ladylike—more feminine—when it is her cue to play the perfect lady. Long before we can get the case into the lists the bump on your head will *have* subsided; your broken bone will have set; and the color will have come back to your cheeks. Unless you can provoke Mrs Fitzfassenden to assault you again the day before the trial—and she is far too clever for that—the chances are a million to one against you.

ALASTAIR [*rising and coming from the other end of the room*] That is so, Blenderbland. You havent a dog's chance. Next time you see her fist coming in your direction, duck and counter. If you dont get that satisfaction you wont get any. [*He sits down next Patricia, on her right*].

PATRICIA. Yes, Mr Blenderbland: Alastair's right. Ask her nicely, and perhaps she'll pay your expenses.

ADRIAN [*sitting up and taking his head in his hands, shaken, almost lachrymose*] Is there any justice for a man against a woman?

SAGAMORE [*sitting beside him to console him*] Believe me: no. Not against a millionairess.

EPIFANIA. And what justice is there for a millionairess, I should like to know?

SAGAMORE. In the courts—

EPIFANIA. I am not thinking of the courts: there is little justice there for anybody. My millions are in themselves an injustice. I speak of the justice of heaven.

ALASTAIR. Oh Lord! Now we're for it. [*He deliberately puts his arm round Patricia's waist*].

EPIFANIA. Alastair: how can you jeer at me? Is it just that I, because I am a millionairess, cannot keep my husband, cannot keep even a lover, cannot keep anything but my money? There you sit before my very eyes, snuggling up to that insignificant little nothingness who cannot afford to pay for her own stockings; and you are happy and she is happy. [*She turns to Adrian*] Here is this suit of clothes on two sticks. What does it contain?

ADRIAN [*broken*] Let me alone, will you?

EPIFANIA. Something that once resembled a man, something that liked lending me five pound notes and never asked me to repay them. Why? Kindness to me?

Love of me? No: the swank of a poor man lending to a millionairess. In my divine wrath I smashed him as a child smashes a disappointing toy; and when he was beaten down to his real self I found I was not a woman to him but a bank account with a good cook.

PATRICIA. Thats all very fine, deary; but the truth is that no one can live with you.

EPIFANIA. And anyone can live with you. And apparently you can live with anybody.

ALASTAIR. What Seedy says is God's truth. Nobody could live with you.

EPIFANIA. But why? Why? Why?

SAGAMORE. Do be reasonable, Mrs Fitzfassenden. Can one live with a tornado? with an earthquake? with an avalanche?

EPIFANIA. Yes. Thousands of people live on the slopes of volcanoes, in the track of avalanches, on land thrown up only yesterday by earthquakes. But with a millionairess who can rise to her destiny and wield the power her money gives her, no. Well, be it so. I shall sit in my lonely house, and be myself, and pile up millions until I find a man good enough to be to me what Alastair is to Seedystockings.

PATRICIA. Well, I hope you wont have to wait too long.

EPIFANIA. I never wait. I march on; and when I come upon the things I need I grab them. I grabbed your Alastair. I find that he does not suit me: he beats me—

ALASTAIR. In self-defence. I never raised a hand to you except in self-defence.

EPIFANIA. Yes: you are like the great European Powers: you never fight except in self-defence. But you are two stone heavier than I; and I cannot keep my head at infighting as you can. You do not suit. I throw you to Greedy-Seedy-Stockings: you can punch her to your heart's content. Mr Sagamore: arrange the divorce. Cruelty and adultery.

PATRICIA. But I dont like this: it's not fair to Alastair. Why is he to be divorced instead of you?

THE MILLIONAIRESS

EPIFANIA. Mr Sagamore: take an action against Patricia Smith for alienating my husband's affections. Damages twenty thousand pounds.

PATRICIA. Oh! Is such a thing possible, Mr Sagamore?

SAGAMORE. I am afraid it is, Miss Smith. Quite possible.

PATRICIA. Well, my dear old father used to say that in the law courts there is only one way to beat the people who have unlimited money; and that is to have no money at all. You cant get twenty thousand out of me. And call it vanity if you will; but I should rather like the world to know that in my little way I was able to take the best and dearest man in England from the richest woman.

EPIFANIA. Damn your dear old father!

ALASTAIR [laughing boisterously] Ha ha! One for you, Eppy. [He kisses Patricia].

SAGAMORE [smiling] I am afraid the laugh is with old Mr Smith, Mrs Fitzfassenden. Where there is nothing, the king loses his rights.

EPIFANIA. Oh, I can bear no more of this. I will not have my life dragged down to planes of vulgarity on which I cannot breathe. I will live in utter loneliness and keep myself sacred until I find the right man—the man who can stand with me on the utmost heights and not lose his head—the mate created for me in heaven. He must be somewhere.

THE DOCTOR [appearing at the door] The manager says I am wanted here. Who wants me?

EPIFANIA. I want you. Come here [she stretches out her hand to him imperiously].

THE DOCTOR [coming to her and feeling her pulse] Something wrong with your blood pressure, eh? [Amazed] Ooooh!! I have never felt such a pulse. It is like a slow sledge hammer.

EPIFANIA. Well, is my pulse my fault?

THE DOCTOR. No. It is the will of Allah. All our pulses are part of the will of Allah.

ALASTAIR. Look here, you know, Doc: that wont go

down in this country. We dont believe in Allah.

THE DOCTOR. That does not disconcert Allah in the least, my friend. The pulse beats still, slow, strong. [*To Epifania*] You are a terrible woman; but I love your pulse. I have never felt anything like it before.

PATRICIA. Well, just fancy that! He loves her pulse.

THE DOCTOR. I am a doctor. Women as you fancy them are nothing to me but bundles of ailments. But the life! the pulse! is the heartbeat of Allah, save in Whom there is no majesty and no might. [*He drops her hand*].

EPIFANIA. My pulse will never change: this is the love I crave for. I will marry you. Mr Sagamore: see about a special licence the moment you have got rid of Alastair.

THE DOCTOR. It is not possible. We are bound by our vows.

EPIFANIA. Well, have I not passed your mother's test? You shall have an accountant's certificate. I learned in the first half hour of my search for employment that the living wage for a single woman is five shillings a week. Before the end of the week I had made enough to support me for a hundred years. I did it honestly and legitimately. I explained the way in which it was done.

THE DOCTOR. It was not the way of Allah, the Merciful, the Compassionate. Had you added a farthing an hour to the wages of those sweated women, that wicked business would have crashed on your head. You sold it to the man Superflew for the last penny of his savings; and the women still slave for him at one piastre an hour.

EPIFANIA. You cannot change the market price of labor: not Allah himself can do that. But I came to this hotel as a scullery maid: the most incompetent scullery maid that ever broke a dinner service. I am now its owner; and there is no tuppence-hapeny an hour here.

THE DOCTOR. The hotel looks well in photographs; and the wages you pay would be a fortune to a laborer on the Nile. But what of the old people whose natural home this place had become? the old man with his paralytic stroke? the old woman gone mad? the cast out creatures in the workhouse? Was not this preying on the poverty of the poor? Shall I, the servant of Allah, live on such gains? Shall I, the healer, the helper, the guardian of life and the counsellor of health, unite with the exploiter of misery?

EPIFANIA. I have to take the world as I find it.

THE DOCTOR. The wrath of Allah shall overtake those who leave the world no better than they found it.

EPIFANIA. I think Allah loves those who make money.

SAGAMORE. All the evidence is that way, certainly.

THE DOCTOR. I do not see it so. I see that riches are a curse; poverty is a curse; only in the service of Allah is there justice, righteousness, and happiness. But all this talk is idle. This lady has easily fulfilled the condition imposed by my mother. But I have not fulfilled the condition imposed by the lady's father.

EPIFANIA. You need not trouble about that. The six months have not expired. I will shew you how to turn your hundred and fifty pounds into fifty thousand.

THE DOCTOR. You cannot. It is gone.

EPIFANIA. Oh, you cannot have spent it all: you who live like a mouse. There must be some of it left.

THE DOCTOR. Not a penny. Not a piastre. Allah—

EPIFANIA. Oh, bother Allah! What did you do with it?

THE DOCTOR. Allah is never bothered. On that afternoon when you left me to earn your own living I called upon the Merciful, the Compassionate, to reveal to me whether you were not one of the strokes of his infinite humor. Then I sat down and took up a newspaper. And behold! a paragraph headed Wills and Bequests. I read a name that I cannot remember: Mrs Somebody of Clapham Park, one hundred and twentytwo thousand pounds. She had never done anything but live in Clapham Park; and she left £122,000. But what was the next name? It was that of the teacher who changed my whole life and gave me a new soul by opening the world of science to me. I was his assistant for four years. He used to make his own apparatus for his experiments; and one day he needed a filament of metal that would resist a temperature that melted platinum like sealing wax.

EPIFANIA. Buy his patent for me if it has not been snapped up.

THE DOCTOR. He never took out a patent. He believed that knowledge is no man's property. And he had neither time nor money to waste in patent offices. Millions have been made out of that discovery of his by people who care nothing about science and everything about money. He left four hundred pounds and a widow: the good woman who had been a second mother to me. A shilling a day for her at most: not even one piastre an hour.

EPIFANIA. That comes of marrying an incompetent dreamer. Are you going to beg for her? I warn you I am tired of destitute widows. I should be a beggar myself if I took them all on my shoulders.

THE DOCTOR. Have no fear. The Merciful, the Compassionate heard the prayer of the widow. Listen. I once cured a Prime Minister when he imagined himself to be ill. I went to him and told him that it was the will of Allah that the widow should have a civil list pension. She received it: a hundred pounds a year. I went to the great Metallurgical Trust which exploits his discovery, and told them that her poverty was a scandal in the face of Allah. They were rich and generous: they made a special issue of founders' shares for her, worth three hundred a year to her. They called it letting her in on the ground floor. May her prayers win them favor from Him save in whom there is no might and no majesty! But all this took time. The illness, the nurse, the funeral, the disposal of the laboratory, the change to a cheaper lodging, had left her without a penny, though no doctor and no lawyer took a farthing, and the shopkeepers were patient; for the spirit of Allah worked more strongly upon them than on the British Treasury, which clamored for its little death duty.

Between the death and the pensions there was a gap exactly one hundred and fifty pounds wide. He who is just and exact supplied that sum by your chauffeur's hands and by mine. It rejoiced my heart as money had never rejoiced it before. But instead of coming to you with fifty thousand pounds I am in arrear with my bill for my daily bread in your hotel, and am expecting every day to be told by your manager that this cannot go on: I must settle.

ALASTAIR. Well, old man, you may not have done a lot for yourself; but you have done damned well for the widow. And you have escaped Eppy. She wont marry you with your pockets empty.

EPIFANIA. Pray why? Fifty thousand pounds must have been made out of that discovery ten times over. The doctor, in putting my money into the widow's necessary expenses, may be said to have made a retrospective investment in the discovery. And he has shewn the greatest ability in the affair: has he not, Mr Sagamore?

SAGAMORE. Unquestionably. He has bowled out the Prime Minister. He has bowled out the Imperial Metallurgical Trust. He has settled the widow's affairs to perfection.

THE DOCTOR. But not my own affairs. I am in debt for my food.

EPIFANIA. Well, if you come to that, *I* am in debt for my food. I got a letter this morning from my purveyors to say that I have paid them nothing for two years, and unless I let them have something on account they will be obliged to resort to the premises.

THE DOCTOR. What does that mean?

EPIFANIA. Sell my furniture.

THE DOCTOR. You cannot sell mine, I am afraid. I have hardly any.

BLENDERBLAND. If you have a stick she will sell it. She is the meanest woman in England.

EPIFANIA. That is why I am also the richest. Mr Sagamore: my mind is made up: I will marry this doctor. Ascertain his name and make the necessary arrangements.

BLENDERBLAND. You take care, doctor. She is unfaithful to her husband in wanting to marry you. She flirted with me: took me down the river and made me believe I was to be Alastair's successor before ever she saw you. See what she has done to me! She will do it to you when the next man takes her fancy.

THE DOCTOR [to Epifania] What have you to say to that?

EPIFANIA. You must learn to take chances in this world. This disappointed philanderer tries to frighten you with my unfaithfulness. He has never been married: I have. And I tell you that in the very happiest marriages not a day passes without a thousand moments of unfaithfulness. You begin by thinking you have only one husband: you find you have a dozen. There is a creature you hate and despise and are tied to for life; and before breakfast is over the fool says something nice and becomes a man whom you admire and love; and between these extremes there are a thousand degrees with a different man and woman at each of them. A wife is all women to one man: she is everything that is devilish: the thorn in his flesh, the jealous termagant, the detective dogging all his movements, the nagger, the scolder, the worrier. He has only to tell her an affectionate lie and she is his comfort, his helper, at best his greatest treasure, at worst his troublesome but beloved child. All wives are all these women in one, all husbands all these men in one. What do the unmarried know of this infinitely dangerous heart tearing everchanging life of adventure that we call marriage? Face it as you would face a dangerous operation: have you not performed hundreds of them?

THE DOCTOR. Of a surety there is no wit and no wisdom like that of a woman ensnaring the mate chosen for her by Allah. Yet I am very well as I am. Why should I change? I shall be very happy as an old bachelor.

EPIFANIA [flinging out her wrist at him] Can you feel

my pulse every day as an old bachelor?

THE DOCTOR [*taking her wrist and mechanically taking out his watch at the same time*] Ah! I had forgotten the pulse. One, two, three: it is irresistible: it is a pulse in a hundred thousand. I love it: I cannot give it up.

BLENDERBLAND. You will regret it to the last day of your life.

EPIFANIA. Mr Sagamore: you have your instructions.

SAGAMORE [*bows*]!

PATRICIA. Congratulations, darling.

THE INTERLUDE AT THE PLAYHOUSE

Written in 1907

Only Performance London 1907

Written for a gala theatrical occasion so that Winifred Emery, actress
wife of the Theatre's manager, could appear at the opening
of the new Playhouse

THE INTERLUDE AT THE PLAYHOUSE

*O*PENING *night. Brilliant first-night audience assembled. Conclusion of overture. In each programme a slip has been distributed, stating that before the play begins the Manager will address a few words to the audience.*

The float is turned up. Lights down in auditorium.
Expectancy. Silence.

The act drop is swung back. Evidently somebody is coming forward to make a speech.

Enter before the curtain the Manager's wife, with one of the programme slips in her hand.

THE MANAGER'S WIFE. Ladies and gentlemen. [*She hesitates, overcome with nervousness; then plunges ahead*]. About this speech—you know—this little slip in your programmes—it says that Edwin—I mean Mr. Goldsmith—I am so frightfully nervous—I—[*she begins tearing up the slip carefully into very small pieces*] I have to get this finished before he comes up from his dressing-room, because he doesn't know what I'm doing. If he *did*—! Well, what I want to say is—of course, I am saying it very badly because I never could speak in public; but the fact is, neither can Edwin. Excuse my calling him Edwin; I know I should speak of him as Mr. Goldsmith; but—but—perhaps I had better explain that we are married; and the force of habit is so strong—er—yes, isn't it? You see, it's like this. At least, what I wanted to say is—is—is—er—. A little applause would encourage me, perhaps, if you don't mind. Thank you. Of course, it's so ridiculous to be nervous like this, among friends, isn't it? But I have had such a dreadful week at home over this speech of Edwin's. He gets so angry with me when I tell him that he can't make speeches, and that nobody wants him to make one! I only wanted to encourage him; but he is *so* irritable when he has to build a theatre! Of course, you wouldn't think so, seeing him act; but you don't know what he is at home. Well, dear ladies and gentlemen, will

you be very nice and kind to him when he is speaking, and
if he is nervous, don't notice it? And please don't make any
noise; the least sound upsets him and puts his speech out
of his head. It is really a very good speech; he has not let
me see the manuscript, and he thinks I know nothing about
it; but I have heard him make it four times in his sleep.
He does it very well when he is asleep—quite like an
orator; but unfortunately he is awake now, and in a fearful state of nerves. I felt I must come out and ask you to
be kind to him—after all, we are old friends, aren't we?
[*Applause*] Oh, thank you, thank you; that is your
promise to me to be kind to him. Now I will run away.
Please don't tell him I dared to do this. [*Going*] And,
please, please, not the least noise. If a hairpin drops, all is
lost. [*Coming back to centre*] Oh, and Mr. Conductor,
would you be so very good, when he comes to the pathetic
part, to give him a little slow music. Something affecting,
you know.

CONDUCTOR. Certainly, Mrs. Goldsmith, certainly.

THE MANAGER'S WIFE. Thank you. You know, it is
one of the great sorrows of his life that the managers will
not give him an engagement in melodrama. Not that he
likes melodrama; but he says that the slow music is such
a support on the stage; and he needs all the support he
can get tonight, poor fellow! The—

A CARPENTER [*from the side, putting his head round
the edge of the curtain*] Tsst! ma'am, tsst!

THE MANAGER'S WIFE. Eh? What's the matter?

THE CARPENTER. The governor's dressed and coming
up, ma'am.

THE MANAGER'S WIFE. Oh! [*To the audience*] Not a
word. [*She hurries off, with her finger on her lips*].

*The warning for the band sounds. "Auld Lang Syne"
is softly played. The curtain rises, and discovers a reading
table, with an elaborate, triple-decked folding desk on it.
A thick manuscript of unbound sheets is on the desk. A
tumbler and decanter, with water, and two candles, shaded*

282

THE INTERLUDE AT THE PLAYHOUSE

from the audience, are on the table. Right of table, a chair, in which the Manager's Wife is seated. Another chair, empty, left on table. At the desk stands the Manager, ghastly pale. Applause. When silence is restored, he makes two or three visible efforts to speak.

THE MANAGER'S WIFE [*aside*] Courage, dear.

THE MANAGER [*smiling with effort*] Oh, quite so, quite so. Don't be frightened, dearest. I am quite self-possessed. It would be very silly for me to—er—there is no occasion for nervousness—I—er—quite accustomed to public life —er—ahem! [*He opens the manuscript, raises his head, and takes breath*]. Er— [*He flattens the manuscript out with his hand, affecting the ease and large gesture of an orator. The desk collapses with an appalling clatter. He collapses, shaking with nervousness, into the chair*].

THE MANAGER'S WIFE [*running to him solicitously*] Never mind, dear; it was only the desk. Come, come now. You're better now, aren't you? The audience is waiting.

THE MANAGER. I thought it was the station.

THE MANAGER'S WIFE. There's no station there now, dear; it's quite safe. [*Replacing the MS. on the desk*] There! That's right. [*She sits down and composes herself to listen*].

THE MANAGER [*beginning his speech*] Dear friends— I wish I could call you ladies and gentlemen—

THE MANAGER'S WIFE. Hm! Hm! Hm!

THE MANAGER. What's the matter?

THE MANAGER'S WIFE [*prompting him*] Ladies and gentlemen, I wish I could call you dear friends.

THE MANAGER. Well, what did I say?

THE MANAGER'S WIFE. You said it the other way about. No matter. Go on. They will understand.

THE MANAGER. Well, what difference does it make? [*Testily*] How am I to make a speech if I am to be interrupted in this way? [*To the audience*] Excuse my poor wife, ladies and gentlemen. She is naturally a little nervous to-night. You will overlook a woman's weakness. [*To his*

THE INTERLUDE AT THE PLAYHOUSE

wife] Compose yourself, my dear. Ahem! [*He returns to the MS.*]. The piece of land on which our theatre is built is mentioned in Domesday Book; and you will be glad to hear that I have succeeded in tracing its history almost year by year for the 800 years that have elapsed since that book—perhaps the most interesting of all English books—was written. That history I now propose to impart to you. Angelina, I really cannot make a speech if you look at your watch. If you think I am going on too long, say so.

THE MANAGER'S WIFE. Not at all, dear. But our friends may not be so fond of history as you are.

THE MANAGER. Why not? I am surprised at you, Angelina. Do you suppose that this is an ordinary frivolous audience of mere playgoers? You are behind the times. Look at our friend Tree, making a fortune out of Roman history! Look at the Court Theatre: they listen to this sort of thing for three hours at a stretch there. Look at the Royal Institution, the Statistical Society, the House of Commons! Are we less scholarly, less cultured, less serious than the audiences there? I say nothing of my own humble powers; but *am* I less entertaining than an average Cabinet Minister? You show great ignorance of the times we live in, Angelina; and if my speech bores you, that only shows that you are not in the movement. I am determined that this theatre shall be in the movement.

THE MANAGER'S WIFE. Well, all I can tell you is that if you don't get a little more movement into your speech, there won't be time for Pickles.

THE MANAGER. That does not matter. We can omit Pickles if necessary. I have played Pickles before. If you suppose I am burning to play Pickles again you are very much mistaken. If the true nature of my talent were understood I should be playing Hamlet. Ask the audience whether they would not like to see me play Hamlet. [*Enthusiastic assent*]. There! You ask me why I don't play Hamlet instead of Pickles.

THE MANAGER'S WIFE. I never asked you anything of

284

the kind.

THE MANAGER. Please don't contradict me, Angelina—at least not in public. I say you ask me why I don't play Hamlet instead of Pickles. Well, the reason is that anybody can play Hamlet, but it takes me to play Pickles. I leave Hamlet to those who can provide no livelier form of entertainment. [*Resolutely returning to the MS.*] I am now going back to the year eleven hundred.

THE STAGE MANAGER [*coming on in desperation*] No, sir, you can't go back all that way; you promised me you would be done in ten minutes. I've got to set for the first act.

THE MANAGER. Well, is it my fault? My wife won't let me speak. I have not been able to get in a word edgeways. [*Coaxing*] Come, there's a dear, good chap; just let me have another twenty minutes or so. The audience *wants* to hear my speech. You wouldn't disappoint them, would you?

THE STAGE MANAGER [*going*] Well, it's as you please, sir; not as I please. Only don't blame me if the audience loses its last train and comes back to sleep in the theatre, that's all. [*He goes off with the air of a man who is prepared for the worst*].

During the conversation with the Stage Manager, the Manager's Wife, unobserved by her husband, steals the manuscript; replaces the last two leaves of it on the desk; puts the rest on her chair, and sits down on it.

THE MANAGER. That man is hopelessly frivolous; I really must get a more cultured staff. [*To the audience*] Ladies and gentlemen, I'm extremely sorry for these unfortunate interruptions and delays; you can see that they are not my fault. [*Returning to the desk*] Ahem! Er—hallo! I am getting along faster than I thought. I shall not keep you much longer now. [*Resuming his oration*] Ladies and gentlemen, I have dealt with our little playhouse in its historical aspect. I have dealt with it in its political aspect, in its financial aspect, in its artistic aspect,

THE INTERLUDE AT THE PLAYHOUSE

in its social aspect, in its County Council aspect, in its biological and psychological aspects. You have listened to me with patience and sympathy. You have followed my arguments with intelligence, and accepted my conclusions with indulgence. I have explained to you why I have given our new theatre its pleasant old name; why I selected "Pickles" as the opening piece. I have told you of our future plans, of the engagements we have made, the pieces we intend to produce, the policy we are resolved to pursue. [*With graver emphasis*] There remains only one word more. [*With pathos*] If that word has a personal note in it you will forgive me. [*With deeper pathos*] If the note is a deeper and tenderer one than I usually venture to sound on the stage, I hope you will not think it out of what I believe is called my line. [*With emotion*] Ladies and gentlemen, it is now more than twenty years since I and my dear wife—[*Violins tremolando; flute solo, "Auld Lang Syne"*] What's that noise? Stop. What do you mean by this?

The band is silent.

THE MANAGER'S WIFE. They are only supporting you, Edwin. Nothing could be more appropriate.

THE MANAGER. Supporting me! They have emptied my soul of all its welling pathos. I never heard anything so ridiculous. Just as I was going to pile it on about *you*, too.

THE MANAGER'S WIFE. Go on, dear. The audience was just getting interested.

THE MANAGER. So was I. And then the band starts on me. Is this Drury Lane or is it the Playhouse? Now, I haven't the heart to go on.

THE MANAGER'S WIFE. Oh, please do. You were getting on so nicely.

THE MANAGER. Of course I was. I had just got everybody into a thoroughly serious frame of mind, and then the silly band sets everybody laughing—just like the latest

286

fashion in tragedy. All my trouble gone for nothing! There's nothing left of my speech now; it might as well be the Education Bill.

THE MANAGER'S WIFE. But you must finish it, dear.

THE MANAGER. I won't. Finish it yourself.

Exit in high dudgeon.

THE MANAGER'S WIFE [*rising and coming C*] Ladies and gentlemen. Perhaps I had better finish it. You see, what my husband and I have been trying to do is a very difficult thing. We have some friends here—some old and valued friends—some young ones, too, we hope, but we also have for the first time in this house of ours the great public. We dare not call ourselves the friends of the public. We are only its servants; and, like all servants, we are very much afraid of seeming disrespectful if we allow ourselves to be too familiar; and we are most at our ease when we are doing our work. We rather dread occasions like these, when we are allowed, and even expected, to step out of our place, and speak in our own persons of our own affairs—even for a moment, perhaps, *very* discretely, of our own feelings. Well, what can we do? We recite a little verse; we make a little speech; we are shy; in the end we put ourselves out of countenance, put you out of countenance, and strain your attitude of kindness and welcome until it becomes an attitude of wishing that it was all over. Well, we resolved not to do that to-night if we could help it. After all, you know how glad we are to see you, for you have the advantage of us; you can do without us; we cannot do without you. I will not say that

The drama's laws the drama's patrons give,

And we who live to please must please to live,

because that is not true; and it never has been true. The drama's laws have a higher source than your caprice or ours; and in in this playhouse of ours we will not please you except on terms honourable to ourselves and to you. But on those terms we hope that you may spend many pleasant hours here, and we as many hard-working ones, as at our old home in the Haymarket. And now may I run away and tell Edwin that his speech has been a great success after all, and that you are quite ready for Pickles? [*Assent and applause*]. Thank you. [*Exit*]

PRESS CUTTINGS

A TOPICAL SKETCH COMPILED FROM
THE EDITORIAL AND CORRESPONDENCE COLUMNS OF
THE DAILY PAPERS DURING THE WOMAN'S WAR IN 1909

Written in 1909

First Performed London 1909

See Preface: Trifles and Tomfooleries (*Volume IV*, *page 721*)

By direction of the Lord Chamberlain the General and the Prime Minister in this play must in all public performances of it be addressed and described as General Bones and Mr Johnson, and by no means as General Mitchener and Mr Balsquith. The allusions to commoner persons are allowed to stand as they are.

General Mitchener, by the way, is not the late Lord Kitchener, but an earlier and more highly connected commander. Balsquith (Balfour-Asquith) is obviously neither of these statesmen, and cannot in the course of nature be both.

PRESS CUTTINGS

*T*HE *forenoon of the first of April, three years hence.*
General Mitchener is at his writing-table in the War
Office, opening letters. On his left is the fireplace, with
a fire burning. On his right, against the opposite wall, is a stand-
ing desk with an office stool. The door is in the wall behind him,
half way between the table and the desk. The table is not quite in
the middle of the room: it is nearer to the hearthrug than to the
desk. There is a chair at each end of it for persons having business
with the General. There is a telephone on the table.

Long silence.

A VOICE FROM THE STREET. Votes for Women!

The General starts convulsively; snatches a revolver from a
drawer; and listens in an agony of apprehension. Nothing hap-
pens. He puts the revolver back, ashamed; wipes his brow; and
resumes his work. He is startled afresh by the entry of an Orderly.
This Orderly is an unsoldierly, slovenly, discontented young man.

MITCHENER. Oh, it's only you. Well?

THE ORDERLY. Another one, sir. She's chained herself.

MITCHENER. Chained herself? How? To what? Weve
taken away the railings and everything that a chain can be
passed through.

THE ORDERLY. We forgot the door-scraper, sir. She lay
down on the flags and got the chain through before she
started hollerin. She's lyin there now; and she downfaces us
that youve got the key of the padlock in a letter in a buff
envelope, and that youll see her when you open it.

MITCHENER. She's mad. Have the scraper dug up and let
her go home with it hanging round her neck.

THE ORDERLY. There is a buff envelope there, sir.

MITCHENER. Youre all afraid of these women. [*He picks*
the letter up] It does seem to have a key in it. [*He opens the*
letter; takes out a key and a note; and reads] "Dear Mitch"—
Well, I'm dashed!

THE ORDERLY. Yes, sir.

MITCHENER. What do you mean by Yes, sir?

THE ORDERLY. Well, you said you was dashed, sir; and

291

you did look—if youll excuse my saying it, sir—well, you looked it.

MITCHENER [*who has been reading the letter, and is too astonished to attend to the Orderly's reply*] This is a letter from the Prime Minister asking me to release the woman with this key if she padlocks herself, and to have her shewn up and see her at once.

THE ORDERLY [*tremulously*] Dont do it, governor.

MITCHENER [*angrily*] How often have I ordered you not to address me as governor? Remember that you are a soldier and not a vulgar civilian. Remember also that when a man enters the army he leaves fear behind him. Heres the key. Unlock her and shew her up.

THE ORDERLY. Me unlock her! I dursent. Lord knows what she'd do to me.

MITCHENER [*pepperily, rising*] Obey your orders instantly, sir; and dont presume to argue. Even if she kills you, it is your duty to die for your country. Right about face. March.

The Orderly goes out, trembling.

THE VOICE OUTSIDE. Votes for Women! Votes for Women! Votes for Women!

MITCHENER [*mimicking her*] Votes for Women! Votes for Women! Votes for Women! [*In his natural voice*] Votes for children! Votes for babies! Votes for monkeys! [*He posts himself on the hearthrug and awaits the enemy*].

THE ORDERLY [*outside*] In you go. [*He pushes a panting Suffraget into the room*] The person, sir. [*He withdraws*].

The Suffraget takes off her tailor-made skirt and reveals a pair of fashionable trousers.

MITCHENER [*horrified*] Stop, madam. What are you doing? you must not undress in my presence. I protest. Not even your letter from the Prime Minister—

THE SUFFRAGET. My dear Mitchener: I am the Prime Minister. [*He takes off his hat and cloak; throws them on the desk; and confronts the General in the ordinary costume of a Cabinet Minister*].

292

MITCHENER. Good heavens! Balsquith!

BALSQUITH [*throwing himself into Mitchener's chair*] Yes: it is indeed Balsquith. It has come to this: that the only way the Prime Minister of England can get from Downing Street to the War Office is by assuming this disguise; shrieking "VOTES FOR WOMEN"; and chaining himself to your doorscraper. They were at the corner in force. They cheered me. Bellachristina herself was there. She shook my hand and told me to say I was a vegetarian, as the diet was better in Holloway for vegetarians.

MITCHENER. Why didnt you telephone?

BALSQUITH. They tap the telephone. Every switchboard in London is in their hands, or in those of their young men.

MITCHENER. Where on earth did you get the dress? I hope it's not a French dress!

BALSQUITH. Great heavens, no. We're not allowed even to put on our gloves with French chalk. Everything's labelled "Made in Camberwell."

MITCHENER. As a Tariff Reformer, I must say Quite right. [*Balsquith has a strong controversial impulse and is evidently going to dispute this profession of faith*]. No matter. Dont argue. What have you come for?

BALSQUITH. Sandstone has resigned.

MITCHENER [*amazed*] Old Red resigned!

BALSQUITH. Resigned.

MITCHENER. But how? Why? Oh, impossible! the proclamation of martial law last Tuesday made Sandstone virtually Dictator in the metropolis; and to resign now is flat desertion.

BALSQUITH. Yes, yes, my dear Mitchener: I know all that as well as you do: I argued with him until I was black in the face, and he so red about the neck that if I had gone on he would have burst. He is furious because we have abandoned his plan.

MITCHENER. But you accepted it unconditionally.

BALSQUITH. Yes, before we knew what it was. It was unworkable, you know.

293

MITCHENER. I dont know. Why is it unworkable?

BALSQUITH. I mean the part about drawing a cordon round Westminster at a distance of two miles, and turning all women out of it.

MITCHENER. A masterpiece of strategy. Let me explain. The Suffragets are a very small body; but they are numerous enough to be troublesome—even dangerous—when they are all concentrated in one place—say in Parliament Square. But by making a two-mile radius and pushing them beyond it, you scatter their attack over a circular line twelve miles long. Just what Wellington would have done.

BALSQUITH. But the women wont go.

MITCHENER. Nonsense: they must go.

BALSQUITH. They wont.

MITCHENER. What does Sandstone say?

BALSQUITH. He says: Shoot them down.

MITCHENER. Of course.

BALSQUITH. Youre not serious?

MITCHENER. I'm perfectly serious.

BALSQUITH. But you cant shoot them down! Women, you know!

MITCHENER [straddling confidently] Yes you can. Strange as it may seem to you as a civilian, Balsquith, if you point a rifle at a woman and fire it, she will drop exactly as a man drops.

BALSQUITH. But suppose your own daughters—Helen and Georgina—

MITCHENER. My daughters would not dream of disobeying the proclamation. [As an afterthought] At least Helen wouldnt.

BALSQUITH. But Georgina?

MITCHENER. Georgina would if she knew she'd be shot if she didnt. Thats how the thing would work. Military methods are really the most merciful in the end. You keep sending these misguided women to Holloway and killing them slowly and inhumanly by ruining their health; and it does no good: they go on worse than ever. Shoot a few,

294

promptly and humanely; and there will be an end at once of all resistance and of all the suffering that resistance entails.

BALSQUITH. But public opinion would never stand it.

MITCHENER [*walking about and laying down the law*] Theres no such thing as public opinion.

BALSQUITH. No such thing as public opinion!!

MITCHENER. Absolutely no such thing. There are certain persons who entertain certain opinions. Well, shoot them down. When you have shot them down, there are no longer any persons entertaining those opinions alive; consequently there is no longer any more of the public opinion you are so much afraid of. Grasp that fact, my dear Balsquith; and you have grasped the secret of government. Public opinion is mind. Mind is inseparable from matter. Shoot down the matter and you kill the mind.

BALSQUITH. But hang it all—

MITCHENER [*intolerantly*] No I wont hang it all. It's no use coming to me and talking about public opinion. You have put yourself into the hands of the army; and you are committed to military methods. And the basis of all military methods is that when people wont do what theyre told to do, you shoot them down.

BALSQUITH. Oh yes; it's all jolly fine for you and Old Red. You dont depend on votes for your places. What do you suppose would happen at the next election?

MITCHENER. Have no next election. Bring in a Bill at once repealing all the Reform Acts and vesting the Government in a properly trained magistracy responsible only to a Council of War. It answers perfectly in India. If anyone objects, shoot him down.

BALSQUITH. But none of the members of my party would be on the Council of War. Neither should I. Do you expect us to vote for making ourselves nobodies?

MITCHENER. Youll have to, sooner or later, or the Socialists will make nobodies of the lot of you by collaring every penny you possess. Do you suppose this damned democracy can be allowed to go on now that the mob is beginning to take it seriously and using its power to lay hands on property? Parliament must abolish itself. The Irish parliament voted for its own extinction. The English parliament will do the same if the same means are taken to persuade it.

BALSQUITH. That would cost a lot of money.

MITCHENER. Not money necessarily. Bribe them with titles.

BALSQUITH. Do you think we dare?

MITCHENER [*scornfully*] Dare! Dare! What is life but daring, man? "To dare, to dare, and again to dare—"

FEMALE VOICE IN THE STREET. Votes for Women! [*Mitchener, revolver in hand, rushes to the door and locks it. Balsquith hides under the table*]. Votes for Women!

A shot is heard.

BALSQUITH [*emerging in the greatest alarm*] Good heavens, you havnt given orders to fire on them: have you?

MITCHENER. No; but it's a sentinel's duty to fire on anyone who persists in attempting to pass without giving the word.

BALSQUITH [*wiping his brow*] This military business is really awful.

MITCHENER. Be calm, Balsquith. These things must happen: they save bloodshed in the long run, believe me. Ive seen plenty of it; and I know.

BALSQUITH. I havnt; and I dont know. I wish those guns didnt make such a devil of a noise. We must adopt Maxim's Silencer for the army rifles if we're going to shoot women. I really couldnt stand hearing it. [*Someone outside tries to open the door and then knocks*]. Whats that?

MITCHENER. Who's there?

THE ORDERLY. It's only me, governor. It's all right.

MITCHENER [*unlocking the door and admitting the Orderly, who comes between them*] What was it?

THE ORDERLY. Suffraget, sir.

BALSQUITH. Did the sentry shoot her?

THE ORDERLY. No, sir: she shot the sentry.

BALSQUITH [*relieved*] Oh: is that all?

MITCHENER [*most indignantly*] All! A civilian shoots down one of His Majesty's soldiers on duty; and the Prime Minister of England asks, Is that all?!!! Have you no regard for the sanctity of human life?

BALSQUITH [*much relieved*] Well, getting shot is what a soldier is for. Besides, he doesnt vote.

MITCHENER. Neither do the Suffragets.

BALSQUITH. Their husbands do. [*To the Orderly*] Did she kill him?

THE ORDERLY. No, sir. He got a stinger on his trousers, sir; but it didnt penetrate. He lost his temper a bit and put down his gun and clouted her head for her. So she said he was no gentleman; and we let her go, thinking she'd had enough, sir.

MITCHENER [*groaning*] Clouted her head! These women are making the army as lawless as themselves. Clouted her head indeed! A purely civil procedure.

THE ORDERLY. Any orders, sir?

MITCHENER. No. Yes. No. Yes: send everybody who took part in this disgraceful scene to the guard-room. No. I'll address the men on the subject after lunch. Parade them for that purpose: full kit. Dont grin at me, sir. Right about face. March.

The Orderly obeys and goes out.

BALSQUITH [*taking Mitchener affectionately by the arm and walking him persuasively to and fro*] And now, Mitchener, will you come to the rescue of the Government and take the command that Old Red has thrown up?

MITCHENER. How can I? You know that the people are devoted heart and soul to Sandstone. He is only bringing you "on the knee," as we say in the army. Could any other living man have persuaded the British nation to accept universal compulsory military service as he did last year? Why, even the Church refused exemption. He is supreme —omnipotent.

BALSQUITH. He w a s, a year ago. But ever since your book of reminiscences went into two more editions than his, and the rush for it led to the wrecking of the Times Book Club, you have become to all intents and purposes his senior. He lost ground by saying that the wrecking was got up by the booksellers. It shewed jealousy; and the public felt it.

MITCHENER. But I cracked him up in my book—you see I could do no less after the handsome way he cracked me up in his—and I cant go back on it now. [*Breaking loose from Balsquith*] No: it's no use, Balsquith: he can dictate his terms to you.

BALSQUITH. Not a bit of it. That affair of the curate—

MITCHENER [*impatiently*] Oh, damn that curate. I ve heard of nothing but that wretched mutineer for a fortnight past. He's not a curate: whilst he's serving in the army he's a private soldier and nothing else. I really havnt time to discuss him further. I'm busy. Good morning. [*He sits down at his table and takes up his letters*].

BALSQUITH [*near the door*] I'm sorry you take that tone, Mitchener. Since you do take it, let me tell you frankly that I think Lieutenant Chubbs-Jenkinson shewed a great want of consideration for the Government in giving an unreasonable and unpopular order, and bringing compulsory military service into disrepute.

MITCHENER. No order is unreasonable; and all orders are unpopular.

BALSQUITH. When the leader of the Labor Party appealed to me and to the House last year not to throw away all the liberties of Englishmen by accepting compulsory military service without full civil rights for the soldier—

MITCHENER. Rot.

BALSQUITH. —I said that no British officer would be capable of abusing the authority with which it was absolutely necessary to invest him.

MITCHENER. Quite right.

BALSQUITH. That carried the House;—

MITCHENER. Naturally.

BALSQUITH. —and the feeling was that the Labor Party were soulless cads.

MITCHENER. So they are.

BALSQUITH. And now comes this unmannerly young whelp Chubbs-Jenkinson, the only son of what they call a soda king, and orders a curate to lick his boots. And when the curate punches his head, you first sentence him to be shot; and then make a great show of clemency by commuting it to a flogging. What did you expect the curate to do?

MITCHENER [*throwing down his pen and his letters and jumping up to confront Balsquith*] His duty was perfectly simple. He should have obeyed the order; and then laid his complaint against the officer in proper form. He would have received the fullest satisfaction.

BALSQUITH. What satisfaction?

MITCHENER. Chubbs-Jenkinson would have been reprimanded. In fact, he w a s reprimanded. Besides, the man was thoroughly insubordinate. You cant deny that the very first thing he did when they took him down after flogging him was to walk up to Chubbs-Jenkinson and break his jaw. That shewed there was no use flogging him; so now he will get two years' hard labor; and serve him right!

BALSQUITH. I bet you a guinea he wont get even a week. I bet you another that Chubbs-Jenkinson apologizes abjectly. You evidently havnt heard the news.

MITCHENER. What news?

BALSQUITH. It turns out that the curate is well connected. [*Mitchener staggers at the shock. He reels into his chair and buries his face in his hands over the blotter*]. He has three aunts in the peerage; Lady Richmond's one of them [*Mitchener punctuates these announcements with heartrending groans*]; and they all adore him. The invitations for six garden parties and fourteen dances have been cancelled for all the subalterns in Chubbs's regiment. [*Mitchener attempts to shoot himself*].

BALSQUITH [*seizing the pistol*] No: your country needs you, Mitchener.

MITCHENER [*putting down the pistol*] For my country's sake. [*Balsquith, reassured, sits down*]. But what an infernal young fool Chubbs-Jenkinson is, not to know the standing of his man better! Why didnt he know? It was his business to know. He ought to be flogged.

BALSQUITH. Probably he will be, by the other subalterns.

MITCHENER. I hope so. Anyhow, out he goes. Out of the army. He or I.

BALSQUITH. Steady, steady. His father has subscribed a million to the party funds. We owe him a peerage.

MITCHENER. I dont care.

BALSQUITH. I do. How do you think parties are kept up? Not by the subscriptions of the local associations, I hope. They dont pay for the gas at the meetings.

MITCHENER. Man: can you not be serious? Here are we, face to face with Lady Richmond's grave displeasure; and you talk to me about gas and subscriptions. Her own nephew!!!!!

BALSQUITH [gloomily] It's unfortunate. He was at Oxford with Bobby Bessborough.

MITCHENER. Worse and worse. What shall we do?

A VOICE IN THE STREET. Votes for Women! Votes for Women!

A terrific explosion shakes the building. They take no notice.

MITCHENER [breaking down] You dont know what this means to me, Balsquith. I love the army. I love my country.

BALSQUITH. It certainly is rather awkward.

The Orderly comes in.

MITCHENER [angrily] What is it? How dare you interrupt us like this?

THE ORDERLY. Didnt you hear the explosion, sir?

MITCHENER. Explosion. What explosion? No: I heard no explosion: I have something more serious to attend to than explosions. Great heavens! Lady Richmond's nephew has been treated like any common laborer; and while England is reeling under the shock, a private walks in and asks me if I heard an explosion.

BALSQUITH. By the way, what was the explosion?

THE ORDERLY. Only a sort of bombshell, sir.

BALSQUITH. Bombshell!

THE ORDERLY. A pasteboard one, sir. Full of papers with Votes for Women in red letters. Fired into the yard from the roof of the Alliance Office.

MITCHENER. Pooh! Go away. GO away.

The Orderly, bewildered, goes out.

BALSQUITH. Mitchener: you can save the country yet. Put on your full dress uniform and your medals and orders and so forth. Get a guard of honor—something showy— horse guards or something of that sort; and call on the old girl—

MITCHENER. The old girl?

BALSQUITH. Well, Lady Richmond. Apologize to her. Ask her leave to accept the command. Tell her that youve made the curate your adjutant or your aide-de-camp or whatever is the proper thing. By the way, what can you make him?

MITCHENER. I might make him my chaplain. I dont see why I shouldnt have a chaplain on my staff. He shewed a very proper spirit in punching that young cub's head. I should have done the same myself.

BALSQUITH. Then Ive your promise to take command if Lady Richmond consents?

MITCHENER. On condition that I have a free hand. No nonsense about public opinion or democracy.

BALSQUITH. As far as possible, I think I may say yes.

MITCHENER [*rising intolerantly and going to the hearthrug*] That wont do for me. Dont be weak-kneed, Balsquith. You know perfectly well that the real government of this country is and always must be the government of the masses by the classes. You know that democracy is damned nonsense, and that no class stands less of it than the working class. You know that we are already discussing the steps that will have to be taken if the country should ever be face to face with the possibility of a Labor majority in Parliament. You know that in that case we should disfranchise the mob, and if they made a fuss, shoot them down. You know that if we need public opinion to support us, we can get any quantity of it manufactured in our papers by poor devils of journalists who will sell their souls for five shillings. You know—

BALSQUITH. Stop. Stop, I say. I dont know. That is the difference between your job and mine, Mitchener. After twenty years in the army a man thinks he knows everything. After twenty months in the Cabinet he knows that he knows nothing.

MITCHENER. We learn from history—

BALSQUITH. We learn from history that men never learn anything from history. That's not my own: it's Hegel.

MITCHENER. Who's Hegel?

BALSQUITH. Dead. A German philosopher. [*He half rises, but recollects something and sits down again*]. Oh, confound it: that reminds me. The Germans have laid down four more Dreadnoughts.

MITCHENER. Then you must lay down twelve.

BALSQUITH. Oh yes: it's easy to say that; but think of what theyll cost.

MITCHENER. Think of what it would cost to be invaded by Germany and forced to pay an indemnity of five hundred millions.

BALSQUITH. But you said that if you got compulsory military service there would be an end of the danger of invasion.

MITCHENER. On the contrary, my dear fellow, it increases the danger tenfold, because it increases German jealousy of our military supremacy.

BALSQUITH. After all, why should the Germans invade us?

MITCHENER. Why shouldnt they? What else has their army to do? What else are they building a navy for?

BALSQUITH. Well, we never think of invading Germany.

MITCHENER. Yes, we do. I have thought of nothing else for the last ten years. Say what you will, Balsquith, the Germans have never recognized, and until they get a stern lesson they never will recognize, the plain fact that the interests of the British Empire are paramount, and that the command of the sea belongs by nature to England.

BALSQUITH. But if they wont recognize it, what can I do?

MITCHENER. Shoot them down.

BALSQUITH. I cant shoot them down.

MITCHENER. Yes you can. You dont realize it; but if you fire a rifle into a German he drops just as surely as a rabbit does.

BALSQUITH. But dash it all, man, a rabbit hasnt got a rifle and a German has. Suppose he shoots you down.

MITCHENER. Excuse me, Balsquith; but that consideration is what we call cowardice in the army. A soldier always assumes that he is going to shoot, not to be shot.

BALSQUITH [*jumping up and walking about sulkily*] Oh come! I like to hear you military people talking of cowardice. Why, you spend your lives in an ecstasy of terror of imaginary invasions. I dont believe you ever go to bed without looking under it for a burglar.

MITCHENER [*calmly*] A very sensible precaution, Balsquith. I always take it; and, in consequence, Ive never been burgled.

BALSQUITH. Neither have I. Anyhow, dont you taunt me with cowardice. [*He posts himself on the hearthrug beside Mitchener, on his left*]. I never look under my bed for a burglar. I'm not always looking under the nation's bed for an invader. And if it comes to fighting, I'm quite willing to fight without being three to one.

MITCHENER. These are the romantic ravings of a Jingo civilian, Balsquith. At least youll not deny that the absolute command of the sea is essential to our security.

BALSQUITH. The absolute command of the sea is essential to the security of the principality of Monaco. But Monaco isnt going to get it.

MITCHENER. And consequently Monaco enjoys no security. What a frightful thing! How do the inhabitants sleep with the possibility of invasion, of bombardment, continually present to their minds? Would you have our English slumbers broken in the same way? Are we also to live without security?

BALSQUITH [*dogmatically*] Yes. Theres no such thing as security in the world; and there never can be as long as men are mortal. England will be secure when England is dead, just as the streets of London will be safe when theres no longer a man in her streets to be run over or a vehicle to run over him. When you military chaps ask for security you are crying for the moon.

MITCHENER [*very seriously*] Let me tell you, Balsquith, that in these days of aeroplanes and Zeppelin airships the question of the moon is becoming one of the greatest importance. It will be reached at no very distant date. Can you, as an Englishman, tamely contemplate the possibility of having to live under a German moon? The British flag must be planted there at all hazards.

BALSQUITH. My dear Mitchener, the moon is outside practical politics. I'd swop it for a coaling-station tomorrow with Germany or any other Power sufficiently military in its way of thinking to attach any importance to it.

MITCHENER [*losing his temper*] You are the friend of every country but your own.

BALSQUITH. Say nobody's enemy but my own. It sounds nicer. You really neednt be so horribly afraid of the other countries. Theyre all in the same fix as we are. I'm much more interested in the death-rate in Lambeth than in the German fleet.

MITCHENER. You darent say that in Lambeth.

BALSQUITH. I'll say it the day after you publish your scheme for invading Germany and repealing all the Reform Acts.

The Orderly comes in.

MITCHENER. What do you want?

THE ORDERLY. I dont want anything, governor, thank you. The secretary and president of the Anti-Suffraget League says they had an appointment with the Prime Minister, and that theyve been sent on here from Downing Street.

BALSQUITH [*going to the table*] Quite right. I forgot them.

[*To Mitchener*] Would you mind my seeing them here? I feel extraordinarily grateful to these women for standing by us and facing the Suffragets, especially as they are naturally the gentler and timider sort of women. [*The Orderly moans*]. Did you say anything?

THE ORDERLY. No, sir.

BALSQUITH. Did you catch their names?

THE ORDERLY. Yes, sir. The president is Lady Corinthia Fanshawe; and the secretary is Mrs Banger.

MITCHENER [*abruptly*] Mrs what?

THE ORDERLY. Mrs Banger.

BALSQUITH. Curious that quiet people always seem to have violent names.

THE ORDERLY. Not much quiet about her, sir.

MITCHENER [*outraged*] Attention! Speak when youre spoken to. Hold your tongue when youre not. Right about face. March. [*The Orderly obeys*]. Thats the way to keep these chaps up to the mark. [*The Orderly returns*]. Back again! What do you mean by this mutiny?

THE ORDERLY. What am I to say to the ladies, sir?

BALSQUITH. You dont mind my seeing them somewhere, do you?

MITCHENER. Not at all. Bring them in to see me when youve done with them. I understand that Lady Corinthia is a very fascinating woman. Who is she, by the way?

BALSQUITH. Daughter of Lord Broadstairs, the automatic turbine man. Gave quarter of a million to the party funds. She's musical and romantic and all that—dont hunt: hates politics: stops in town all the year round: one never sees her except at the opera and at musical at-homes and so forth.

MITCHENER. What a life! [*To the Orderly*] Where are the ladies?

THE ORDERLY. In No. 17, sir.

MITCHENER. Shew Mr Balsquith there; and send Mrs Farrell here.

THE ORDERLY [*calling into the corridor*] Mrs Farrell! [*To

305

Balsquith] This way, sir. [*He goes out with Balsquith*].

Mrs Farrell, a lean, highly respectable Irish charwoman of about fifty, comes in.

MITCHENER. Mrs Farrell: Ive a very important visit to pay: I shall want my full dress uniform and all my medals and orders and my presentation sword. There was a time when the British Army contained men capable of discharging these duties for their commanding officer. Those days are over. The compulsorily enlisted soldier runs to a woman for everything. I'm therefore reluctantly obliged to trouble you.

MRS FARRELL. Your meddles n ordhers n the crooked sword widh the ivory handle n your full dress uniform is in the waxworks in the Chamber o Military Glory over in the place they used to call the Banquetin Hall. I told you youd be sorry for sendin them away; and you told me to mind me own business. Youre wiser now.

MITCHENER. I am. I had not at that time discovered that you were the only person in the whole military establishment of this capital who could be trusted to remember where anything was, or to understand an order and obey it.

MRS FARRELL. It's no good flattherin me. I'm too old.

MITCHENER. Not at all, Mrs Farrell. How is your daughter?

MRS FARRELL. Which daughter?

MITCHENER. The one who has made such a gratifying success in the Music Halls.

MRS FARRELL. Theres no Music Halls nowadays: theyre Variety Theatres. She's got an offer of marriage from a young jook.

MITCHENER. Is it possible? What did you do?

MRS FARRELL. I told his mother on him.

MITCHENER. Oh! What did she say?

MRS FARRELL. She was as pleased as Punch. Thank Heaven, she says, he's got somebody thatll be able to keep him when the supertax is put up to twenty shillings in the pound.

306

MITCHENER. But your daughter herself? What did she say?

MRS FARRELL. Accepted him, of course. What else would a young fool like her do? He inthrojooced her to the Poet Laureate, thinkin she'd inspire him.

MITCHENER. Did she?

MRS FARRELL. Faith, I dunna. All I know is she walked up to him as bold as brass n said, "Write me a sketch, dear." Afther all the throuble Ive took with that child's manners she's no more notion how to behave herself than a pig. Youll have to wear General Sandstone's uniform: it's the only one in the place, because he wont lend it to the shows.

MITCHENER. But Sandstone's clothes wont fit me.

MRS FARRELL [unmoved] Then youll have to fit them. Why shouldnt they fitchya as well as they fitted General Blake at the Mansion House?

MITCHENER. They didnt fit him. He looked a frightful guy.

MRS FARRELL. Well, you must do the best you can with them. You cant exhibit your clothes and wear them too.

MITCHENER. And the public thinks the lot of a commanding officer a happy one! Oh, if they could only see the seamy side of it. [He returns to his table to resume work].

MRS FARRELL. If they could only see the seamy side o General Sandstone's uniform, where his flask rubs agen the buckle of his braces, theyd tell him he ought to get a new one. Let alone the way he swears at me.

MITCHENER. When a man has risked his life on eight battlefields, Mrs Farrell, he has given sufficient proof of his self-control to be excused a little strong language.

MRS FARRELL. Would you put up with bad language from me because Ive risked me life eight times in childbed?

MITCHENER. My dear Mrs Farrell, you surely would not compare a risk of that harmless domestic kind to the fearful risks of the battlefield.

MRS FARRELL. I wouldnt compare risks run to bear livin people into the world to risks run to blow dhem out of it. A mother's risk is jooty: a soldier's is nothin but divilmint.

MITCHENER [*nettled*] Let me tell you, Mrs Farrell, that if the men did not fight, the women would have to fight themselves. We spare you that at all events.

MRS FARRELL. You cant help yourselves. If three-quarters of you was killed we could replace you with the help of the other quarter. If three-quarters of us was killed how many people would there be in England in another generation? If it wasnt for that, the men'd put the fightin on us just as they put all the other dhrudgery. What would you do if we was all kilt? Would you go to bed and have twins?

MITCHENER. Really, Mrs Farrell, you must discuss these questions with a medical man. You make be blush, positively.

MRS FARRELL [*grumbling to herself*] A good job too. If I could have made Farrell blush I wouldnt have had to risk me life so often. You n your risks n your bravery n your self-conthrol indeed! "Why dont you conthrol yourself?" I sez to Farrell. "It's agen me religion," he sez.

MITCHENER [*plaintively*] Mrs Farrell: youre a woman of very powerful mind. I'm not qualified to argue these delicate matters with you. I ask you to spare me, and to be good enough to take these clothes to Mr Balsquith when the ladies leave.

The Orderly comes in.

THE ORDERLY. Lady Corinthia Fanshawe and Mrs Banger want to see you, sir. Mr Balsquith told me to tell you.

MRS FARRELL. Theyve come about the vote. I dont know whether it's dhem dhat want it or dhem dhat doesnt want it: anyhow, theyre all alike when they get into a state about it. [*She goes out, having gathered Balsquith's Suffraget disguise from the desk*].

MITCHENER. Is Mr Balsquith not with them.

THE ORDERLY. No, sir. Couldnt stand Mrs Banger, I expect. Fair caution she is. [*Chuckling*] Couldnt help larfin when I sor im op it.

MITCHENER [*highly incensed*] How dare you indulge in this unseemly mirth in the presence of your commanding

308

officer? Have you no sense of a soldier's duty?

THE ORDERLY [*sadly*] I'm afraid I shant ever get the ang of it, sir. You see, my father has a tidy little barber's business down off Shoreditch; and I was brought up to be chatty and easy-like with everybody. I tell you, when I drew the number in the conscription it gev my old mother the needle and it gev me the ump. I should take it very kind, sir, if youd let me off the drill and let me shave you instead. Youd appreciate my qualities then: you would indeed, sir. I shant never do myself jastice at soljerin, sir. I cant bring myself to think of it as proper work for a man with an active mind, as you might say, sir. Arf of it's only ousemaidin; and tother arf is dress-up and make-believe.

MITCHENER. Stuff, sir. It's the easiest life in the world. Once you learn your drill, all you have to do is to hold your tongue and obey your orders.

THE ORDERLY. But I do assure you, sir, arf the time theyre the wrong orders; and I get into trouble when I obey them. The sergeant's orders is all right; but the officers dont know what theyre talkin about. Why, the orses knows better sometimes. "Fours," says Lieutenant Trevor at the gate of Bucknam Palace only this mornin when we was on dooty for a State visit to the Coal Trust. I was fourth man like in the first file; and when I started the orse eld back; and the sergeant was on to me straight. Threes, you bally fool, e whispers. An e was on to me again about it when we come back, and called me a fathead, e did. What am I to do, I says: the lieutenant's orders was fours, I says. I'll shew you who's lieutenant here, e says. In future you attend to my orders and not to iz, e says: what does e know about it? e says. You didnt give me any orders, I says. Couldnt you see for yourself there wasnt room for fours, e says: why cant you think? General Mitchener tells me I'm not to think, but to obey orders, I says. Is Mitchener your sergeant or am I? e says in his bullyin way. You are, I says. Well, e says, you got to do what your sergeant tells you: thats discipline, e says. And what am I to do for the General? I says. Youre to

309

let him talk, e says: thats what e's for.

MITCHENER [*groaning*] It is impossible for the human mind to conceive anything more dreadful than this. Youre a disgrace to the service.

THE ORDERLY [*deeply wounded*] The service is a disgrace to me. When my mother's people pass me in the street with this uniform on, I ardly know which way to look. There never was a soldier in my family before.

MITCHENER. There never was anything else in mine, sir.

THE ORDERLY. My mother's second cousin was one of the Parkinsons o Stepney. [*Almost in tears*] What do you know of the feelings of a respectable family in the middle station of life? I cant bear to be looked down on as a common soldier. Why cant my father be let buy my discharge? Youve done away with the soldier's right to ave his discharge bought for him by his relations. The country didnt know you were going to do that or it'd never ave stood it. Is an Englishman to be made a mockery like this?

MITCHENER. Silence. Attention. Right about face. March.

THE ORDERLY [*retiring to the standing desk and bedewing it with passionate tears*] Oh that I should have lived to be spoke to as if I was the lowest of the low! Me! that has shaved a City o London alderman wiv me own and.

MITCHENER. Poltroon. Crybaby. Well, better disgrace yourself here than disgrace your country on the field of battle.

THE ORDERLY [*angrily coming to the table*] Who's going to disgrace his country on the field of battle? It's not fightin I object to: it's soljerin. Shew me a German and I'll ave a go at him as fast as you or any man. But to ave me time wasted like this, an be stuck in a sentry-box at a street corner for an ornament to be stared at; and to be told "right about face: march," if I speak as one man to another: that aint pluck: that aint fightin: that aint patriotism: it's bein made a bloomin sheep of.

MITCHENER. A sheep has many valuable military qualities. Emulate them, dont disparage them.

THE ORDERLY. Oh, wots the good of talkin to you? If I wasnt a poor soldier I could punch your ed for forty shillins or a month. But because youre my commandin officer you deprive me of my right to a magistrate, and make a compliment of giving me two years ard stead o shootin me. Why cant you take your chance the same as any civilian does?

MITCHENER [rising majestically] I search the pages of history in vain for a parallel to such a speech made by a private to a General. But for the coherence of your remarks I should conclude that you were drunk. As it is, you must be mad. You shall be placed under restraint at once. Call the guard.

THE ORDERLY. Call your grandmother. If you take one man off the doors the place'll be full of Suffragets before you can wink.

MITCHENER. Then arrest yourself; and off with you to the guard-room.

THE ORDERLY. What am I to arrest myself for?

MITCHENER. Thats nothing to you. You have your orders: obey them. Do you hear? Right about face. March.

THE ORDERLY. How would you feel if you was told to right-about-face and march as if you was a door-mat?

MITCHENER. I should feel as if my country had spoken through the voice of my officer. I should feel proud and honored to be able to serve my country by obeying its commands. No thought of self, no vulgar preoccupation with my own petty vanity, could touch my mind at such a moment. To me my officer would not be a mere man: he would be for the moment—whatever his personal frailties—the incarnation of our national destiny.

THE ORDERLY. What I'm saying to you is the voice of old England a jolly sight more than all this rot that you get out of books. I'd rather be spoke to by a sergeant than by you. He tells me to go to hell when I challenges him to argue it out like a man. It aint polite; but it's English. What you say aint anything at all. You dont act on it yourself. You dont believe in it. Youd punch my head if I tried it on you; and

serve me right. And look here. Heres another point for you
to argue—

MITCHENER [*with a shriek of protest*] No—

Mrs Banger comes in followed by Lady Corinthia Fanshawe.
Mrs Banger is a masculine woman of forty with a powerful
voice and great physical strength. Lady Corinthia, who is also
over thirty, is beautiful and romantic.

MRS BANGER [*throwing the door open decisively and march-*
ing straight to Mitchener] Pray how much longer is the Anti-
Suffraget League to be kept waiting? [*She passes him con-*
temptuously and sits down with impressive confidence in the chair
next the fireplace. Lady Corinthia takes the chair on the opposite
side of the table with equal aplomb].

MITCHENER. I'm extremely sorry. You really do not know
what I have to put up with. This imbecile, incompetent,
unsoldierly disgrace to the uniform he should never have
been allowed to put on, ought to have shewn you in fifteen
minutes ago.

THE ORDERLY. All I said was—

MITCHENER. Not another word. Attention. Right about
face. March. [*The Orderly sits down doggedly*]. Get out of the
room this instant, you fool; or I'll kick you out.

THE ORDERLY [*civilly*] I dont mind that, sir. It's human.
It's English. Why couldnt you have said it before? [*He*
goes out].

MITCHENER. Take no notice, I beg: these scenes are of
daily occurrence now that we have compulsory service under
the command of the halfpenny papers. Pray sit down.

LADY CORINTHIA
AND MRS BANGER } [*rising*] { Thank you. [*They sit down*
again].

MITCHENER [*sitting down with a slight chuckle of satisfac-*
tion] And now, ladies, to what am I indebted—

MRS BANGER. Let me introduce us. I am Rosa Carmina
Banger: Mrs Banger, organizing secretary of the Anti-
Suffraget League. This is Lady Corinthia Fanshawe, the
president of the League, known in musical circles—*I* am
not musical—as the Richmond Park nightingale. A soprano.

I am myself said to be almost a baritone; but I do not profess to understand these distinctions.

MITCHENER [*murmuring politely*] Most happy, I'm sure.

MRS BANGER. We have come to tell you plainly that the Anti-Suffragets are going to fight.

MITCHENER [*gallantly*] Oh, pray leave that to the men, Mrs Banger.

LADY CORINTHIA. We can no longer trust the men.

MRS BANGER. They have shewn neither the strength, the courage, nor the determination which are needed to combat women like the Suffragets.

LADY CORINTHIA. Nature is too strong for the combatants.

MRS BANGER. Physical struggles between persons of opposite sexes are unseemly.

LADY CORINTHIA. Demoralizing.

MRS BANGER. Insincere.

LADY CORINTHIA. They are merely embraces in disguise.

MRS BANGER. No such suspicion can attach to combats in which the antagonists are of the same sex.

LADY CORINTHIA. The Anti-Suffragets have resolved to take the field.

MRS BANGER. They will enforce the order of General Sandstone for the removal of all women from the two-mile radius—that is, all women except themselves.

MITCHENER. I am sorry to have to inform you, madam, that the Government has given up that project, and that General Sandstone has resigned in consequence.

MRS BANGER. That does not concern us in the least. We approve of the project and will see that it is carried out. We have spent a good deal of money arming ourselves; and we are not going to have that money thrown away through the pusillanimity of a Cabinet of males.

MITCHENER. Arming yourselves! But, my dear ladies, under the latest proclamation women are strictly forbidden to carry chains, padlocks, tracts on the franchise, or weapons of any description.

LADY CORINTHIA [*producing an ivory-handled revolver and*

313

pointing it at his nose] You little know your countrywomen, General Mitchener.

MITCHENER [*without flinching*] Madam: it is my duty to take possession of that weapon in accordance with the proclamation. Be good enough to put it down.

MRS BANGER [*producing an XVIII century horse pistol*] Is it your duty to take possession of this also?

MITCHENER. That, madam, is not a weapon: it is a curiosity. If you would be kind enough to place it in some museum instead of pointing it at my head, I should be obliged to you.

MRS BANGER. This pistol, sir, was carried at Waterloo by my grandmother.

MITCHENER. I presume you mean your grandfather.

MRS BANGER. You presume unwarrantably.

LADY CORINTHIA. Mrs Banger's grandmother commanded a canteen at that celebrated battle.

MRS BANGER. Who my grandfather was is a point that has never been quite clearly settled. I put my trust, not in my ancestors, but in my good sword, which is at my lodgings.

MITCHENER. Your sword!

MRS BANGER. The sword with which I slew five Egyptians with my own hand at Kassassin, where I served as a trooper.

MITCHENER. Lord bless me! But was your sex never discovered?

MRS BANGER. It was never even suspected. I had a comrade—a gentleman ranker—whom they called Fanny. They never called me Fanny.

LADY CORINTHIA. The Suffragets have turned the whole woman movement on to the wrong track. They ask for a vote.

MRS BANGER. What use is a vote? Men have the vote.

LADY CORINTHIA. And men are slaves.

MRS BANGER. What women need is the right to military service. Give me a well-mounted regiment of women with sabres, opposed to a regiment of men with votes. We shall see which will go down before the other. No: we have had enough of these gentle pretty creatures who merely talk and cross-examine ministers in police courts, and go to prison like sheep, and suffer and sacrifice themselves. This question must be solved by blood and iron, as was well said by Bismarck, whom I have reason to believe was a woman in disguise.

MITCHENER. Bismarck a woman!

MRS BANGER. All the really strong men of history have been disguised women.

MITCHENER [*remonstrating*] My dear lady!

MRS BANGER. How can you tell? You never knew that the hero of the charge at Kassassin was a woman: yet she was: it was I, Rosa Carmina Banger. Would Napoleon have been so brutal to women, think you, had he been a man?

MITCHENER. Oh, come, come! Really! Surely female rulers have often shewn all the feminine weaknesses. Queen Elizabeth, for instance. Her vanity, her levity—

MRS BANGER. Nobody who has studied the history of Queen Elizabeth can doubt for a moment that she was a disguised man.

LADY CORINTHIA [*admiring Mrs Banger*] Isnt she splendid!

MRS BANGER [*rising with a large gesture*] This very afternoon I shall cast off this hampering skirt for ever; mount my charger; and with my good sabre lead the Anti-Suffragets to victory. [*She strides to the other side of the room, snorting*].

MITCHENER. But I cant allow anything of the sort, madam. I shall stand no such ridiculous nonsense. I'm perfectly determined to put my foot down—

LADY CORINTHIA. Dont be hysterical, General.

MITCHENER. Hysterical!

MRS BANGER. Do you think we are to be stopped by these childish exhibitions of temper? They are useless; and your tears and entreaties—a man's last resource—will avail you just as little. I sweep them away, just as I sweep your plans of campaign "made in Germany"—

MITCHENER [*flying into a transport of rage*] How dare you

315

repeat that infamous slander! [*He rings the bell violently*]. If this is the alternative to votes for women, I shall advocate giving every woman in the country six votes. [*The Orderly comes in*]. Remove that woman. See that she leaves the building at once.

The Orderly forlornly contemplates the iron front presented by Mrs Banger.

THE ORDERLY [*propitiatorily*] Would you av the feelin art to step out, madam?

MRS BANGER. You are a soldier. Obey your orders. Put me out. If I got such an order I should not hesitate.

THE ORDERLY [*to Mitchener*] Would you mind lendin me a and, Guvner?

LADY CORINTHIA [*raising her revolver*] I shall be obliged to shoot you if you stir, General.

MRS BANGER [*To the Orderly*] When you are ordered to put a person out you should do it like this. [*She hurls him from the room. He is heard falling headlong downstairs and crashing through a glass door*]. I shall now wait on General Sandstone. If he shews any sign of weakness, he shall share that poor wretch's fate. [*She goes out*].

LADY CORINTHIA. Isnt she magnificent?

MITCHENER. Thank heaven she's gone. And now, my dear lady, is it necessary to keep that loaded pistol to my nose all through our conversation?

LADY CORINTHIA. It's not loaded. It's heavy enough, goodness knows, without putting bullets in it.

MITCHENER [*triumphantly snatching his revolver from the drawer*] Then I am master of the situation. This is loaded. Ha, ha!

LADY CORINTHIA. But since we are not really going to shoot one another, what difference can it possibly make?

MITCHENER [*putting his pistol down on the table*] True. Quite true. I recognize there the practical good sense that has prevented you from falling into the snares of the Suffragets.

LADY CORINTHIA. The Suffragets, General, are the dupes

of dowdies. A really attractive and clever woman—

MITCHENER [*gallantly*] Yourself, for instance.

LADY CORINTHIA [*snatching up his revolver*] Another step and you are a dead man.

MITCHENER [*amazed*] My dear lady!

LADY CORINTHIA. I am not your dear lady. You are not the first man who has concluded that because I am devoted to music and can reach F in alt with the greatest facility— Patti never got above E flat—I am marked out as the prey of every libertine. You think I am like the thousands of weak women whom you have ruined—

MITCHENER. I solemnly protest—

LADY CORINTHIA. Oh, I know what you officers are. To you a woman's honor is nothing, and the idle pleasure of the moment is everything.

MITCHENER. This is perfectly ridiculous. I never ruined anyone in my life.

LADY CORINTHIA. Never! Are you in earnest?

MITCHENER. Certainly I am in earnest. Most indignantly in earnest.

LADY CORINTHIA [*throwing down the pistol contemptuously*] Then you have no temperament: you are not an artist. You have no soul for music.

MITCHENER. Ive subscribed to the regimental band all my life. I bought two sarrusophones for it out of my own pocket. When I sang Tosti's Goodbye for Ever at Knightsbridge in 1880 the whole regiment wept. You are too young to remember that.

LADY CORINTHIA. Your advances are useless. I—

MITCHENER. Confound it, madam, can you not receive an innocent compliment without suspecting me of dishonorable intentions?

LADY CORINTHIA. Love—real love—makes all intentions honorable. But you could never understand that.

MITCHENER. I'll not submit to the vulgar penny-novelette notion that an officer is less honorable than a civilian in his relations with women. While I live I'll raise my voice—

LADY CORINTHIA. Tush!

MITCHENER. What do you mean by tush?

LADY CORINTHIA. You cant raise your voice above its natural compass. What sort of voice have you?

MITCHENER. A tenor. What sort had you?

LADY CORINTHIA. Had! I have it still. I tell you I am the highest living soprano. [*Scornfully*] What was your highest note, pray?

MITCHENER. B flat—once—in 1879. I was drunk at the time.

LADY CORINTHIA [*gazing at him almost tenderly*] Though you may not believe me, I find you are more interesting when you talk about music than when you are endeavoring to betray a woman who has trusted you by remaining alone with you in your apartment.

MITCHENER [*springing up and fuming away to the fireplace*] Those repeated insults to a man of blameless life are as disgraceful to you as they are undeserved by me, Lady Corinthia. Such suspicions invite the conduct they impute. [*She raises the pistol*]. You need not be alarmed: I am only going to leave the room.

LADY CORINTHIA. Fish.

MITCHENER. Fish! This is worse than tush. Why fish?

LADY CORINTHIA. Yes, fish: cold-blooded fish.

MITCHENER. Dash it all, madam, do you want me to make advances to you?

LADY CORINTHIA. I have not the slightest intention of yielding to them; but to make them would be a tribute to romance. What is life without romance?

MITCHENER [*making a movement towards her*] I tell you—

LADY CORINTHIA. Stop. No nearer. No vulgar sensuousness. If you must adore, adore at a distance.

MITCHENER. This is worse than Mrs Banger. I shall ask that estimable woman to come back.

LADY CORINTHIA. Poor Mrs Banger! Do not for a moment suppose, General Mitchener, that Mrs Banger represents my views on the suffrage question. Mrs Banger is a man in petticoats. I am every inch a woman; but I find it convenient to work with her.

MITCHENER. Do you find the combination comfortable?

LADY CORINTHIA. I do not wear combinations, General: [*with dignity*] they are unwomanly.

MITCHENER [*throwing himself despairingly into the chair next the hearthrug*] I shall go mad. I never for a moment dreamt of alluding to anything of the sort.

LADY CORINTHIA. There is no need to blush and become self-conscious at the mention of underclothing. You are extremely vulgar, General.

MITCHENER. Lady Corinthia: you have my pistol. Will you have the goodness to blow my brains out? I should prefer it to any other effort to follow the gyrations of the weathercock you no doubt call your mind. If you refuse, then I warn you that youll not get another word out of me— not if we sit here until doomsday.

LADY CORINTHIA. I dont want you to talk. I want you to listen. You do not understand my views on the question of the suffrage. [*She rises to make a speech*]. I must preface my remarks by reminding you that the Suffraget movement is essentially a dowdy movement. The Suffragets are not all dowdies; but they are mainly supported by dowdies. Now I am not a dowdy. Oh, no compliments—

MITCHENER. I did not utter a sound.

LADY CORINTHIA [*smiling*] It is easy to read your thoughts. I am one of those women who are accustomed to rule the world through men. Man is ruled by beauty, by charm. The men who are not have no influence. The Salic Law, which forbade women to occupy a throne, is founded on the fact that when a woman is on the throne the country is ruled by men, and therefore ruled badly; whereas when a man is on the throne the country is ruled by women, and therefore ruled well. The Suffragets would degrade women from being rulers to being voters, mere politicians, the drudges of the caucus and the polling booth. We should lose our influence completely under such a state of affairs. The New

Zealand women have the vote. What is the result? No poet
ever makes a New Zealand woman his heroine. One might
as well be romantic about New Zealand mutton. Look at the
Suffragets themselves. The only ones who are popular are
the pretty ones, who flirt with mobs as ordinary women flirt
with officers.

MITCHENER. Then I understand you to hold that the
country should be governed by the women after all.

LADY CORINTHIA. Not by all the women. By certain
women. I had almost said by one woman. By the women
who have charm—who have artistic talent—who wield a
legitimate, a refining influence over the men. [*She sits down
gracefully, smiling, and arranging her draperies with conscious
elegance*].

MITCHENER. In short, madam, you think that if you give
the vote to the man, you give the power to the woman who
can get round the man.

LADY CORINTHIA. That is not a very delicate way of putting it; but I suppose that is how you would express what
I mean.

MITCHENER. Perhaps youve never had any experience of
garrison life. If you had, youd have noticed that the sort of
woman who's clever at getting round men is sometimes
rather a bad lot.

LADY CORINTHIA. What do you mean by a bad lot?

MITCHENER. I mean a woman who would play the very
devil if the other women didnt keep her in pretty strict
order. I dont approve of democracy, because it's rot; and
I'm against giving the vote to women, because I'm not
accustomed to it, and therefore am able to see with an unprejudiced eye what infernal nonsense it is. But I tell you
plainly, Lady Corinthia, that there is one game that I dislike
more than either democracy or votes for women; and that is
the game of Antony and Cleopatra. If I must be ruled by
women, let me have decent women, and not—well, not the
other sort.

LADY CORINTHIA. You have a coarse mind, General

Mitchener.

MITCHENER. So has Mrs Banger. And, by George! I prefer Mrs Banger to you!

LADY CORINTHIA [*bounding to her feet*] You prefer Mrs Banger to me!!!

MITCHENER. I do. You said yourself she was splendid.

LADY CORINTHIA. You are no true man. You are one of those unsexed creatures who have no joy in life, no sense of beauty, no high notes.

MITCHENER. No doubt I am, madam. As a matter of fact, I am not clever at discussing public questions, because, as an English gentleman, I was not brought up to use my brains. But occasionally, after a number of remarks which are perhaps sometimes rather idiotic, I get certain convictions. Thanks to you, I have now got a conviction that this woman question is not a question of lovely and accomplished females, but of dowdies. The average Englishwoman is a dowdy and never has half a chance of becoming anything else. She hasnt any charm; and she has no high notes, except when she's giving her husband a piece of her mind, or calling down the street for one of the children.

LADY CORINTHIA. How disgusting!

MITCHENER. Somebody must do the dowdy work! If we had to choose between pitching all the dowdies into the Thames and pitching all the lovely and accomplished women, the lovely ones would have to go.

LADY CORINTHIA. And if you had to do without Wagner's music or do without your breakfast, you would do without Wagner. Pray does that make eggs and bacon more precious than music, or the butcher and baker better than the poet and philosopher? The scullery may be more necessary to our bare existence than the cathedral. Even humbler apartments might make the same claim. But which is the more essential to the higher life?

MITCHENER. Your arguments are so devilishly ingenious that I feel convinced you got them out of some confounded book. Mine—such as they are—are my own. I imagine it's something like this. There is an old saying that if you take care of the pence, the pounds will take care of themselves. Well, perhaps if we take care of the dowdies and the butchers and the bakers, the beauties and the bigwigs will take care of themselves. [*Rising and facing her determinedly*] Anyhow, I dont want to have things arranged for me by Wagner. I'm not Wagner. How does h e know where the shoe pinches m e? How do y o u know where the shoe pinches your washerwoman? you and your high F in alt! How are you to know when you havnt made her comfortable unless she has a vote? Do you want her to come and break your windows?

LADY CORINTHIA. Am I to understand that General Mitchener is a Democrat and a Suffraget?

MITCHENER. Yes: you have converted me—you and Mrs Banger.

LADY CORINTHIA. Farewell, creature. [*Balsquith enters hurriedly*]. Mr Balsquith: I am going to wait on General Sandstone. He, at least, is an officer and a gentleman. [*She sails out*].

BALSQUITH. Mitchener: the game is up.

MITCHENER. What do you mean?

BALSQUITH. The strain is too much for the Cabinet. The old Liberal and Unionist Free Traders declare that if they are defeated on their resolution to invite tenders from private contractors for carrying on the Army and Navy, they will go solid for votes for women as the only means of restoring the liberties of the country which we have destroyed by compulsory military service.

MITCHENER. Infernal impudence!

BALSQUITH. The Labor Party is taking the same line. They say the men got the Factory Acts by hiding behind the women's petticoats, and that they will get votes for the army in the same way.

MITCHENER. Balsquith: we must not yield to clamor. I have just told that woman that I am at last convinced—

BALSQUITH [*joyfully*] —that the Suffragets must be supported?

MITCHENER. No: that the Anti-Suffragets must be put down at all hazards.

BALSQUITH. Same thing.

MITCHENER. No. For you now tell me that the Labor Party demands votes for women. That makes it impossible to give them, because it would be yielding to clamor. The one condition on which we can consent to grant anything in this country is that nobody shall presume to ask for it.

BALSQUITH [*earnestly*] Mitchener: it's no use. You cant have the conveniences of Democracy without its occasional inconveniences.

MITCHENER. What are its conveniences, I should like to know?

BALSQUITH. Well, when you tell people that they are the real rulers and they can do what they like, nine times out of ten they say "All right: tell us what to do." But it happens sometimes that they get an idea of their own; and then of course youre landed.

MITCHENER. Sh—

BALSQUITH [*desperately shouting him down*] No: it's no use telling me to shoot them down: I'm not going to do it. After all, I dont suppose votes for women will make much difference. It hasnt in the other countries in which it has been tried.

MITCHENER. I never supposed it would make a n y difference. What I cant stand is giving in to that Pankhurst lot. Hang it all, Balsquith, it seems only yesterday that we put them in quad for a month. I said at the time that it ought to have been ten years. If my advice had been taken this wouldnt have happened. It's a consolation to me that events are proving how thoroughly right I was.

The Orderly rushes in.

THE ORDERLY. Look 'ere, sir: Mrs Banger's locked the door of General Sandstone's room on the inside; an' she's sittin on his ed til he signs a proclamation for women to serve in the army.

MITCHENER. Put your shoulder to the door and burst it open.

THE ORDERLY. It's only in story books that doors burst open as easy as that. Besides, I'm only too thankful to av a locked door between me and Mrs B.; and so is all the rest of us.

MITCHENER. Cowards. Balsquith: to the rescue! [*He dashes out*].

BALSQUITH [*ambling calmly to the hearth*] This is the business of the Serjeant-at-Arms rather than of the leader of the House. Theres no use in my tackling Mrs Banger: she would only sit on my head too.

THE ORDERLY. You take my tip, Mr Balsquith. Give the women the vote and give the army civil rights; and av done with it.

Mitchener returns and comes between them.

MITCHENER. Balsquith: prepare to hear the worst.

BALSQUITH. Sandstone is no more?

MITCHENER. On the contrary, he is particularly lively. He has softened Mrs Banger by a proposal of marriage in which he appears to be perfectly in earnest. He says he has met his ideal at last, a really soldierly woman. She will sit on his head for the rest of his life; and the British Army is now to all intents and purposes commanded by Mrs Banger. When I remonstrated with Sandstone she positively shouted "Right about face. March" at me in the most offensive tone. If she hadnt been a woman I should have punched her head. I precious nearly punched Sandstone's. The horrors of martial law administered by Mrs Banger are too terrible to be faced. I demand civil rights for the army.

THE ORDERLY [*chuckling*] Wot oh, General! Wot oh!

MITCHENER. Hold your tongue. [*He goes to the door and calls*] Mrs Farrell! [*He returns, and again addresses the Orderly*]. Civil rights dont mean the right to be uncivil. [*Pleased with his own wit*] Almost a pun. Ha ha!

MRS FARRELL [*entering*] Whats the matther now? [*She comes to the table*].

MITCHENER [*to the Orderly*] I have private business with Mrs Farrell. Outside, you infernal blackguard.

THE ORDERLY [*arguing, as usual*] Well, I didnt ask to—
[*Mitchener seizes him by the nape; marches him out; slams the
door; and comes solemnly to Mrs Farrell*].

MITCHENER. Excuse the abruptness of this communication, Mrs Farrell; but I know only one woman in the country whose practical ability and force of character can maintain her husband in competition with the husband of Mrs
Banger. I have the honor to propose for your hand.

MRS FARRELL. D'ye mean you want to marry me?

MITCHENER. I do.

MRS FARRELL. No thank you. I'd have to work for you
just the same; only I shouldnt get any wages for it.

BALSQUITH. That will be remedied when women get the
vote. Ive had to promise that.

MITCHENER [*winningly*] Mrs Farrell: you have been charwoman here now ever since I took up my duties. Have you
really never, in your more romantic moments, cast a favorable eye on my person?

MRS FARRELL. Ive been too busy casting an unfavorable
eye on your cloze an on the litther you make with your
papers.

MITCHENER [*wounded*] Am I to understand that you refuse me?

MRS FARRELL. Just wait a bit. [*She takes Mitchener's chair
and rings up the telephone*] Double three oh seven Elephant.

MITCHENER. I trust youre not ringing for the police, Mrs
Farrell. I assure you I'm perfectly sane.

MRS FARRELL [*into the telephone*] Is that you, Eliza? [*She
listens for the answer*]. Not out o bed yet! Go and pull her out
be the heels, the lazy sthreel; an tell her her mother wants to
speak to her very particularly about General Mitchener.
[*To Mitchener*] Dont you be afeard: I know youre sane
enough when youre not talkin about the Germans. [*Into the
telephone*] Is that you, Eliza? [*She listens for the answer*].
D'ye remember me givin you a clout on the side of the head
for tellin me that if I only knew how to play me cards I could
marry any General on the staff instead o disgracin you be

bein a charwoman? [*She listens for the answer*]. Well, I can have General Mitchener without playin any cards at all. What d'ye think I ought to say? [*She listens*]. Well, I'm no chicken meself. [*To Mitchener*] How old are you?

MITCHENER [*with an effort*] Fifty-two.

MRS FARRELL [*into the telephone*] He says he's fifty-two. [*She listens; then, to Mitchener*] She says youre down in *Who's Who* as sixty-one.

MITCHENER. Damn *Who's Who*!

MRS FARRELL [*into the telephone*] Anyhow I wouldnt let that stand in the way. [*She listens*]. If I really w h a t? [*She listens*]. I cant hear you. If I really w h a t? [*She listens*]. Who druv him? I never said a word to— Eh? [*She listens*]. Oh, love him. Arra, dont be a fool, child. [*To Mitchener*] She wants to know do I really love you. [*Into the telephone*] It's likely indeed I'd frighten the man off with any such nonsense at my age. What? [*She listens*]. Well, thats just what I was thinkin.

MITCHENER. May I ask what you were thinking, Mrs Farrell? This suspense is awful.

MRS FARRELL. I was thinkin that praps the Duchess might like her daughter-in-law's mother to be a General's lady betther than to be a charwoman. [*Into the telephone*] Waitle youre married yourself, me fine lady: youll find out that every woman's a charwoman from the day she's married. [*She listens*]. Then you think I might take him? [*She listens*]. G'lang, you young scald: if I had you here I'd teach you manners. [*She listens*]. Thats enough now. Back wid you to bed; and be thankful I'm not there to put me slipper across you. [*She rings off*]. The impudence! [*To Mitchener*] Bless you, me childher, may you be happy, she says. [*To Balsquith, going to his side of the room*] Give dear old Mitch me love, she says.

The Orderly opens the door, ushering in Lady Corinthia.

THE ORDERLY. Lady Corinthia Fanshawe to speak to you, sir.

LADY CORINTHIA. General Mitchener: your designs on

Mrs Banger are defeated. She is engaged to General Sandstone. Do you still prefer her to me?

MRS FARRELL. He's out o the hunt. He's engaged to me.

The Orderly, overcome by this news, reels from the door to the standing desk and clutches the stool to save himself from collapsing.

MITCHENER. And extremely proud of it, Lady Corinthia.

LADY CORINTHIA [*contemptuously*] She suits you exactly. [*Coming to Balsquith*] Mr Balsquith: you, at least, are not a Philistine.

BALSQUITH. No, Lady Corinthia; but I'm a confirmed bachelor. I dont want a wife; but I want an Egeria.

MRS FARRELL. More shame for you!

LADY CORINTHIA. Silence, woman. The position and functions of a wife may suit your gross nature. An Egeria is exactly what I desire to be. [*To Balsquith*] Can you play accompaniments?

BALSQUITH. Melodies only, I regret to say. With one finger. But my brother, who is a very obliging fellow, and not unlike me personally, is acquainted with three chords, with which he manages to accompany most of the comic songs of the day.

LADY CORINTHIA. I do not sing comic songs. Neither will you when I am your Egeria. You must come to my musical at-home this afternoon. I will allow you to sit at my feet.

BALSQUITH [*doing so*] That is my ideal of romantic happiness. It commits me exactly as far as I desire to venture. Thank you.

THE ORDERLY. Wot price me, General? Wont you celebrate your engagement by doin somethin for me? Maynt I be promoted to be a sergeant?

MITCHENER. Youre too utterly incompetent to discharge the duties of a sergeant. You are only fit to be a lieutenant. I shall recommend you for a commission.

THE ORDERLY. Hooray! The Parkinsons o Stepney'll be proud to have me call on em now. I'll go and tell the sergeant what I think of him. Hooray! [*He rushes out*].

327

MRS FARRELL [*going to the door and calling after him*] You might have the manners to shut the door afther you. [*She shuts it and comes between Mitchener and Lady Corinthia*].

MITCHENER. Poor wretch! the day after civil rights are conceded to the army he and Chubbs-Jenkinson will be found incapable of maintaining discipline. They will be sacked and replaced by really capable men. Mrs Farrell: as we are engaged, and I am anxious to do the correct thing in every way, I am quite willing to kiss you if you wish it.

MRS FARRELL. Youd only feel like a fool; and so would I.

MITCHENER. You are really the most sensible woman. Ive made an extremely wise choice. [*He kisses her hand*].

LADY CORINTHIA [*to Balsquith*] You may kiss my hand, if you wish.

BALSQUITH [*cautiously*] I think we had better not commit ourselves too far. Let us change a subject which threatens to become embarrassing. [*To Mitchener*] The moral of the occasion for you, Mitchener, appears to be that youve got to give up treating soldiers as if they were schoolboys.

MITCHENER. The moral for you, Balsquith, is that youve got to give up treating women as if they were angels. Ha ha!

MRS FARRELL. It's a mercy youve found one another out at last. Thats enough now.

OVERRULED

A DEMONSTRATION

Written in 1912

First Performed London 1912

PREFACE TO OVERRULED

THE ALLEVIATIONS OF MONOGAMY

THIS piece is not an argument for or against polygamy. It is a clinical study of how the thing actually occurs among quite ordinary people, innocent of all unconventional views concerning it. The enormous majority of cases in real life are those of people in that position. Those who deliberately and conscientiously profess what are oddly called advanced views by those others who believe them to be retrograde, are often, and indeed mostly, the last people in the world to engage in unconventional adventures of any kind, not only because they have neither time nor disposition for them, but because the friction set up between the individual and the community by the expression of unusual views of any sort is quite enough hindrance to the heretic without being complicated by personal scandals. Thus the theoretic libertine is usually a person of blameless family life, whilst the practical libertine is mercilessly severe on all other libertines, and excessively conventional in professions of social principle.

What is more, these professions are not hypocritical: they are for the most part quite sincere. The common libertine, like the drunkard, succumbs to a temptation which he does not defend, and against which he warns others with an earnestness proportionate to the intensity of his own remorse. He (or she) may be a liar and a humbug, pretending to be better than the detected libertines, and clamoring for their condign punishment; but this is mere self-defence. No reasonable person expects the burglar to confess his pursuits, or to refrain from joining in the cry of Stop Thief when the police get on the track of another burglar. If society chooses to penalize candor, it has itself to thank if its attack is countered by falsehood. The clamorous virtue of the libertine is therefore no more hypocritical than the plea of Not Guilty which is allowed to every criminal. But one result is that the theorists who write most sincerely and favorably about polygamy know least about it; and the practitioners who know most about it keep their knowledge very jealously to themselves. Which is hardly fair to the practice.

INACCESSIBILITY OF THE FACTS

Also, it is impossible to estimate its prevalence. A practice to which nobody confesses may be both universal and unsuspected, just as a virtue which everybody is expected, under heavy penalties, to claim, may have no existence. It is often assumed—indeed it is the official assumption of the Churches and the divorce courts—that a gentleman and a lady cannot be alone together innocently. And that is manifest blazing nonsense, though many women have been stoned to death in the east, and divorced in the west, on the strength of it. On the other hand, the innocent and conventional people who regard gallant adventures as crimes of so horrible a nature that only the most depraved and desperate characters engage in them or would listen to advances in that direction without raising an alarm with the noisiest indignation, are clearly examples of the fact that most sections of society do not know how the other sections live. Industry is the most effective check on gallantry. Women may, as Napoleon said, be the occupation of the idle man just as men are the preoccupation of the idle woman; but the mass of mankind is too busy and too poor for the long and expensive sieges which the professed libertine lays to virtue. Still, wherever there is idleness or even a reasonable supply of elegant leisure there is a good deal of coquetry and philandering. It is so much pleasanter to dance on the edge of a precipice than to go over it that leisured society is full of people who spend a great part of their lives in flirtation, and conceal nothing but the humiliating secret that they have never gone any further. For there is no pleasing people in the matter of reputation in this department: every insult is a flattery: every testimonial is a disparagement: Joseph is despised and promoted, Potiphar's wife admired and condemned: in short, you are never on solid ground until you get away from the subject altogether. There is a continual and irreconcilable conflict between the natural and conven-

332

tional sides of the case, between spontaneous human relations between independent men and women on the one hand and the property relation between husband and wife on the other, not to mention the confusion under the common name of love of a generous natural attraction and interest with the murderous jealousy that fastens on and clings to its mate (especially a hated mate) as a tiger fastens on a carcase. And the confusion is natural; for these extremes are extremes of the same passion; and most cases lie somewhere on the scale between them, and are so complicated by ordinary likes and dislikes, by incidental wounds to vanity or gratifications of it, and by class feeling, that A will be jealous of B and not of C, and will tolerate infidelities on the part of D whilst being furiously angry when they are committed by E.

THE CONVENTION OF JEALOUSY

That jealousy is independent of sex is shewn by its intensity in children, and by the fact that very jealous people are jealous of everybody without regard to relationship or sex, and cannot bear to hear the person they "love" speak favorably of anyone under any circumstances (many women, for instance, are much more jealous of their husbands' mothers and sisters than of unrelated women whom they suspect him of fancying); but it is seldom possible to disentangle the two passions in practice. Besides, jealousy is an inculcated passion, forced by society on people in whom it would not occur spontaneously. In Brieux's Bourgeois aux Champs, the benevolent hero finds himself detested by the neighboring peasants and farmers, not because he preserves game, and sets mantraps for poachers, and defends his legal rights over his land to the extremest point of unsocial savagery, but because, being an amiable and public-spirited person, he refuses to do all this, and thereby offends and disparages the sense of property in his neighbors. The same thing is true of matrimonial jealousy: the man who does not at least pretend to feel it, and behave as badly as if he really felt it, is despised and insulted; and many a man has shot or stabbed a friend or been shot or stabbed by him in a duel,

333

or disgraced himself and ruined his own wife in a divorce scandal, against his conscience, against his instinct, and to the destruction of his home, solely because Society conspired to drive him to keep its own lower morality in countenance in this miserable and undignified manner.

Morality is confused in such matters. In an elegant plutocracy, a jealous husband is regarded as a boor. Among the tradesmen who supply that plutocracy with its meals, a husband who is not jealous, and refrains from assailing his rival with his fists, is regarded as a ridiculous, contemptible, and cowardly cuckold. And the laboring class is divided into the respectable section which takes the tradesman's view, and the disreputable section which enjoys the license of the plutocracy without its money: creeping below the law as its exemplars prance above it; cutting down all expenses of respectability and even decency; and frankly accepting squalor and disrepute as the price of anarchic self-indulgence. The conflict between Malvolio and Sir Toby, between the marquis and the bourgeois, the cavalier and the puritan, the ascetic and the voluptuary, goes on continually, and goes on not only between class and class and individual and individual, but in the selfsame breast in a series of reactions and revulsions in which the irresistible becomes the unbearable, and the unbearable the irresistible, until none of us can say what our characters really are in this respect.

THE MISSING DATA OF A SCIENTIFIC NATURAL HISTORY OF MARRIAGE

Of one thing I am persuaded: we shall never attain to a reasonably healthy public opinion on sex questions until we offer, as the data for that opinion, our actual conduct and our real thoughts instead of a moral fiction which we agree to call virtuous conduct, and which we then—and here comes in the mischief—pretend is our conduct and our thoughts. If the result were that we all believed one another to be better than we really are, there would be something to be said for it; but the actual result appears to be a monstrous exaggeration of the power and continuity of sexual passion. The whole world shares the fate of Lucrezia Borgia, who, though she seems on investigation to have been quite a suitable wife for a modern British Bishop, has been invested by the popular historical imagination with all the extravagances of a Messalina or a Cenci. Writers of belles lettres who are rash enough to admit that their whole life is not one constant preoccupation with adored members of the opposite sex, and who even countenance La Rochefoucauld's remark that very few people would ever imagine themselves in love if they had never read anything about it, are gravely declared to be abnormal or physically defective by critics of crushing unadventurousness and domestication. French authors of saintly temperament are forced to include in their retinue countesses of ardent complexion with whom they are supposed to live in sin. Sentimental controversies on the subject are endless; but they are useless, because nobody tells the truth. Rousseau did it by an extraordinary effort, aided by a superhuman faculty for human natural history; but the result was curiously disconcerting because, though the facts were so conventionally shocking that people felt that they ought to matter a great deal, they actually mattered very little. And even at that everybody pretends not to believe him.

ARTIFICIAL RETRIBUTION

The worst of this is that busybodies with perhaps rather more than a normal taste for mischief are continually trying to make negligible things matter as much in fact as they do in convention by deliberately inflicting injuries—sometimes atrocious injuries—on the parties concerned. Few people have any knowledge of the savage punishments that are legally inflicted for aberrations and absurdities to which no sanely instructed community would call any attention. We create an artificial morality, and consequently an artificial conscience, by manufacturing disastrous consequences for events which, left to themselves, would do very little harm (sometimes not any) and be forgotten in a few days.

But the artificial morality is not therefore to be condemned offhand. In many cases it may save mischief instead of making it: for example, though the hanging of a murderer is the duplication of a murder, yet it may be less murderous than leaving the matter to be settled by blood feud or vendetta. As long as human nature insists on revenge, the official organization and satisfaction of revenge by the State may be also its minimization. The mischief begins when the official revenge persists after the passion it satisfies has died out of the race. Stoning a woman to death in the east because she has ventured to marry again after being deserted by her husband may be more merciful than allowing her to be mobbed to death; but the official stoning or burning of an adulteress in the west would be an atrocity, because few of us hate an adulteress to the extent of desiring such a penalty, or of being prepared to take the law into our own hands if it were withheld. Now what applies to this extreme case applies also in due degree to the other cases. Offenses in which sex is concerned are often needlessly magnified by penalties, ranging from various forms of social ostracism to long sentences of penal servitude, which would be seen to be monstrously disproportionate to the real feeling against them if the removal of both the penalties and the taboo on their discussion made it possible for us to ascertain their real prevalence and estimation. Fortunately there is one outlet for the truth. We are permitted to discuss in jest what we may not discuss in earnest. A serious comedy about sex is taboo: a farcical comedy is privileged.

THE FAVORITE SUBJECT OF FARCICAL COMEDY

The little piece which follows this preface accordingly takes the form of a farcical comedy, because it is a contribution to the very extensive dramatic literature which takes as its special department the gallantries of married people. The stage has been preoccupied by such affairs for centuries, not only in the jesting vein of Restoration Comedy and Palais Royal farce, but in the more tragically turned adulteries of the Parisian school which dominated the stage until

PREFACE TO OVERRULED

Ibsen put them out of countenance and relegated them to their proper place as articles of commerce. Their continued vogue in that department maintains the tradition that adultery is the dramatic subject *par excellence*, and indeed that a play that is not about adultery is not a play at all. I was considered a heresiarch of the most extravagant kind when I expressed my opinion, at the outset of my career as a playwright, that adultery is the dullest of themes on the stage, and that from Francesca and Paolo down to the latest guilty couple of the school of Dumas *fils*, the romantic adulterers have all been intolerable bores.

THE PSEUDO SEX PLAY

Later on, I had occasion to point out to the defenders of sex as the proper theme of drama, that though they were right in ranking sex as an intensely interesting subject, they were wrong in assuming that sex is an indispensable motive in popular plays. The plays of Molière are, like the novels of the Victorian epoch or Don Quixote, as nearly sexless as anything not absolutely inhuman can be; and some of Shakespear's plays are sexually on a par with the census: they contain women as well as men, and that is all. This had to be admitted; but it was still assumed that the plays of the nineteenth century Paris school are, in contrast with the sexless masterpieces, saturated with sex; and this I strenuously denied. A play about the convention that a man should fight a duel or come to fisticuffs with his wife's lover if she has one, or the convention that he should strangle her like Othello, or turn her out of the house and never see her or allow her to see her children again, or the convention that she should never be spoken to again by any decent person and should finally drown herself, or the convention that persons involved in scenes of recrimination or confession by these conventions should call each other certain abusive names and describe their conduct as guilty and frail and so on: all these may provide material for very effective plays; but such plays are not dramatic studies of sex: one might as well say that Romeo and Juliet is a dramatic study

337

of pharmacy because the catastrophe is brought about through an apothecary. Duels are not sex; divorce cases are not sex; the Trade Unionism of married women is not sex. Only the most insignificant fraction of the gallantries of married people produce any of the conventional results; and plays occupied wholly with the conventional results are therefore utterly unsatisfying as sex plays, however interesting they may be as plays of intrigue and plot puzzles.

The world is finding this out rapidly. The Sunday papers, which in the days when they appealed almost exclusively to the lower middle class were crammed with police intelligence, and more especially with divorce and murder cases, now lay no stress on them; and police papers which confined themselves entirely to such matters, and were once eagerly read, have perished through the essential dulness of their topics. And yet the interest in sex is stronger than ever: in fact, the literature that has driven out the journalism of the divorce courts is a literature occupied with sex to an extent and with an intimacy and frankness that would have seemed utterly impossible to Thackeray or Dickens if they had been told that the change would complete itself within fifty years of their own time.

ART AND MORALITY

It is ridiculous to say, as inconsiderate amateurs of the arts do, that art has nothing to do with morality. What is true is that the artist's business is not that of the policeman; and that such factitious consequences and put-up jobs as divorces and executions and the detective operations that lead up to them are no essential part of life, though, like poisons and buttered slides and red-hot pokers, they provide material for plenty of thrilling or amusing stories suited to people who are incapable of any interest in psychology. But the fine artist must keep the policeman out of his studies of sex and studies of crime. It is by clinging nervously to the policeman that most of the pseudo sex plays convince me that the writers have either never had any serious personal experience of their ostensible subject, or else have never

338

conceived it possible that the stage dare present the phenomena of sex as they appear in nature.

THE LIMITS OF STAGE PRESENTATION

But the stage presents much more shocking phenomena
than those of sex. There is, of course, a sense in which you
cannot present sex on the stage, just as you cannot present
murder. Macbeth must no more really kill Duncan than he
must himself be really slain by Macduff. But the feelings of
a murderer can be expressed in a certain artistic convention;
and a carefully prearranged sword exercise can be gone
through with sufficient pretence of earnestness to be accepted by the willing imaginations of the younger spectators
as a desperate combat.

The tragedy of love has been presented on the stage in
the same way. In Tristan and Isolde, the curtain does not,
as in Romeo and Juliet, rise with the lark: the whole night
of love is played before the spectators. The lovers do not
discuss marriage in an elegantly sentimental way: they utter
the visions and feelings that come to lovers at the supreme
moments of their love, totally forgetting that there are such
things in the world as husbands and lawyers and duelling
codes and theories of sin and notions of propriety and all
the other irrelevancies which provide hackneyed and blood-
less material for our so-called plays of passion.

PRUDERIES OF THE FRENCH STAGE

To all stage presentations there are limits. If Macduff
were to stab Macbeth, the spectacle would be intolerable;
and even the pretence which we allow on our stage is ridicu-
lously destructive to the illusion of the scene. Yet pugilists
and gladiators will actually fight and kill in public without
shame, even as a spectacle for money. But no sober couple
of lovers of any delicacy could endure to be watched. We in
England, accustomed to consider the French stage much
more licentious than the British, are always surprised and
puzzled when we learn, as we may do any day if we come
within reach of such information, that French actors are
often scandalized by what they consider the indecency of

339

the English stage, and that French actresses who desire a greater license in appealing to the sexual instincts than the French stage allows them, learn English and establish themselves on the English stage. The German and Russian stages are in the same relation to the French and, perhaps more or less, all the Latin stages. The reason is that, partly from a want of respect for the theatre, partly from a sort of respect for art in general which moves them to accord moral privileges to artists, partly from the very objectionable tradition that the realm of art is Alsatia and the contemplation of works of art a holiday from the burden of virtue, partly because French prudery does not attach itself to the same points of behavior as British prudery, and has a different code of the mentionable and the unmentionable, and for many other reasons, the French tolerate plays which are never performed in England until they have been spoiled by a process of bowdlerization; yet French taste is more fastidious than ours as to the exhibition and treatment on the stage of the physical incidents of sex. On the French stage a kiss is as obvious a convention as the thrust under the arm by which Macduff runs Macbeth through. It is even a purposely unconvincing convention: the actors rather insisting that it shall be impossible for any spectator to mistake a stage kiss for a real one. In England, on the contrary, realism is carried to the point at which nobody except the two performers can perceive that the caress is not genuine. And here the English stage is certainly in the right; for whatever question there arises as to what incidents are proper for representation on the stage or not, my experience as a playgoer leaves me in no doubt that once it is decided to represent an incident, it will be offensive, no matter whether it be a prayer or a kiss, unless it is presented with a convincing appearance of sincerity.

OUR DISILLUSIVE SCENERY

For example, the main objection to the use of illusive scenery (in most modern plays scenery is not illusive: everything visible is as real as in your drawing room at home) is that it is unconvincing; whilst the imaginary scenery with which the audience transfigures a platform or tribune like the Elizabethan stage or the Greek stage used by Sophocles, is quite convincing. In fact, the more scenery you have the less illusion you produce. The wise playwright, when he cannot get absolute reality of presentation, goes to the other extreme, and aims at atmosphere and suggestion of mood rather than at direct simulative illusion. The theatre, as I first knew it, was a place of wings and flats which destroyed both atmosphere and illusion. This was tolerated, and even intensely enjoyed, but not in the least because nothing better was possible; for all the devices employed in the productions of Mr Granville Barker or Max Reinhardt or the Moscow Art Theatre were equally available for Colley Cibber and Garrick, except the intensity of our artificial light. When Garrick played Richard III in slashed trunk hose and plumes, it was not because he believed that the Plantagenets dressed like that, or because the costumiers could not have made him a XV century dress as easily as a nondescript combination of the state robes of George III with such scraps of older fashions as seemed to playgoers for some reason to be romantic. The charm of the theatre in those days was its makebelieve. It has that charm still, not only for the amateurs, who are happiest when they are most unnatural and impossible and absurd, but for audiences as well. I have seen performances of my own plays which were to me far wilder burlesques than Sheridan's Critic or Buckingham's Rehearsal; yet they have produced sincere laughter and tears such as the most finished metropolitan productions have failed to elicit. Fielding was entirely right when he represented Partridge as enjoying intensely the performance of the king in Hamlet because anybody could see that the king was an actor, and resenting Garrick's Hamlet because it might have been a real man. Yet we have only to look at the portraits of Garrick to see that his performances would nowadays seem almost as extravagantly stagey as his costumes. In our day Calvé's intensely real Carmen never pleased the

mob as much as the obvious fancy ball masquerading of
suburban young ladies in the same character.

HOLDING THE MIRROR UP TO NATURE

Theatrical art begins as the holding up to Nature of a
distorting mirror. In this phase it pleases people who are
childish enough to believe that they can see what they look
like and what they are when they look at a true mirror.
Naturally they think that a true mirror can teach them nothing. Only by giving them back some monstrous image
can the mirror amuse them or terrify them. It is not until
they grow up to the point at which they learn that they know
very little about themselves, and that they do not see themselves in a true mirror as other people see them, that they become consumed with curiosity as to what they really are like,
and begin to demand that the stage shall be a mirror of such
accuracy and intensity of illumination that they shall be able
to get glimpses of their real selves in it, and also learn a little
how they appear to other people.

For audiences of this highly developed class, sex can no
longer be ignored or conventionalized or distorted by the
playwright who makes the mirror. The old sentimental extravagances and the old grossnesses are of no further use to
him. Don Giovanni and Zerlina are not gross: Tristan and
Isolde are not extravagant or sentimental. They say and do
nothing that you cannot bear to hear and see; and yet they
give you, the one pair briefly and slightly, and the other fully
and deeply, what passes in the minds of lovers. The love de-
picted may be that of a philosophic adventurer tempting an
ignorant country girl, or of a tragically serious poet en-
tangled with a woman of noble capacity in a passion which
has become for them the reality of the whole universe. No
matter: the thing is dramatized and dramatized directly,
not talked about as something that happened before the
curtain rose, or that will happen after it falls.

FARCICAL COMEDY SHIRKING ITS SUBJECT

Now if all this can be done in the key of tragedy and
philosophic comedy, it can, I have always contended, be

done in the key of farcical comedy; and Overruled is a trifling experiment in that manner. Conventional farcical comedies are always finally tedious because the heart of them, the inevitable conjugal infidelity, is always evaded. Even its consequences are evaded. Mr Granville Barker has pointed out rightly that if the third acts of our farcical comedies dared to describe the consequences that would follow from the first and second in real life, they would end as squalid tragedies; and in my opinion they would be greatly improved thereby even as entertainments; for I have never seen a three-act farcical comedy without being bored and tired by the third act, and observing that the rest of the audience were in the same condition, though they were not vigilantly introspective enough to find that out, and were apt to blame one another, especially the husbands and wives, for their crossness. But it is happily by no means true that conjugal infidelities always produce tragic consequences, or that they need produce even the unhappiness which they often do produce. Besides, the more momentous the consequences, the more interesting become the impulses and imaginations and reasonings, if any, of the people who disregard them. If I had an opportunity of conversing with the ghost of an executed murderer, I have no doubt he would begin to tell me eagerly about his trial, with the names of the distinguished ladies and gentlemen who honored him with their presence on that occasion, and then about his execution. All of which would bore me exceedingly. I should say, "My dear sir: such manufactured ceremonies do not interest me in the least. I know how a man is tried, and how he is hanged. I should have had you killed in a much less disgusting, hypocritical, and unfriendly manner if the matter had been in my hands. What I want to know about is the murder. How did you feel when you committed it? Why did you do it? What did you say to yourself about it? If, like most murderers, you had not been hanged, would you have committed other murders? Did you really dislike the victim, or did you want his money, or did you murder a person whom you did

343

not dislike, and from whose death you had nothing to gain, merely for the sake of murdering? If so, can you describe the charm to me? Does it come upon you periodically; or is it chronic? Has curiosity anything to do with it?" I would ply him with all manner of questions to find out what murder is really like; and I should not be satisfied until I had realized that I, too, might commit a murder, or else that there is some specific quality present in a murderer and lacking in me. And, if so, what that quality is.

In just the same way, I want the unfaithful husband or the unfaithful wife in a farcical comedy not to bother me with their divorce cases or the stratagems they employ to avoid a divorce case, but to tell me how and why married couples are unfaithful. I dont want to hear the lies they tell one another to conceal what they have done, but the truths they tell one another when they have to face what they have done without concealment or excuse. No doubt prudent and considerate people conceal such adventures, when they can, from those who are most likely to be wounded by them; but it is not to be presumed that, when found out, they necessarily disgrace themselves by irritating lies and transparent subterfuges.

My playlet, which I offer as a model to all future writers of farcical comedy, may now, I hope, be read without shock. I may just add that Mr Sibthorpe Juno's view that morality demands, not that we should behave morally (an impossibility to our sinful nature) but that we shall not attempt to defend our immoralities, is a standard view in England, and was advanced in all seriousness by an earnest and distinguished British moralist shortly after the first performance of Overruled. My objection to that aspect of the doctrine of original sin is that no necessary and inevitable operation of human nature can reasonably be regarded as sinful at all, and that a morality which assumes the contrary is an absurd morality, and can be kept in countenance only by hypocrisy. When people were ashamed of sanitary problems, and refused to face them, leaving them to solve themselves clandestinely in dirt and secrecy, the solution arrived at was the Black Death. A similar policy as to sex problems has solved itself by an even worse plague than the Black Death; and the remedy for that is not salvarsan, but sound moral hygiene, the first foundation of which is the discontinuance of our habit of telling not only the comparatively harmless lies that we know we ought not to tell, but the ruinous lies that we foolishly think we ought to tell.

OVERRULED

A LADY *and gentleman are sitting together on a chester-field in a retired corner of the lounge of a seaside hotel. It is a summer night: the French window behind them stands open. The terrace without overlooks a moonlit harbor. The lounge is dark. The chesterfield, upholstered in silver grey, and the two figures on it in evening dress, catch the light from an arc lamp somewhere; but the walls, covered with a dark green paper, are in gloom. There are two stray chairs, one on each side. On the gentleman's right, behind him up near the window, is an unused fireplace. Opposite it on the lady's left is a door. The gentleman is on the lady's right.*

The lady is very attractive, with a musical voice and soft appealing manners. She is young: that is, one feels sure that she is under thirty-five and over twenty-four. The gentleman does not look much older. He is rather handsome, and has ventured as far in the direction of poetic dandyism in the arrangement of his hair as any man who is not a professional artist can afford to in England. He is obviously very much in love with the lady, and is, in fact, yielding to an irresistible impulse to throw his arms round her.

THE LADY. Dont—oh dont be horrid. Please, Mr Lunn [*she rises from the lounge and retreats behind it*]! Promise me you wont be horrid.

GREGORY LUNN. I'm not being horrid, Mrs Juno. I'm not going to be horrid. I love you: thats all. I'm extraordinarily happy.

MRS JUNO. You will really be good?

GREGORY. I'll be whatever you wish me to be. I tell you I love you. I love loving you. I dont want to be tired and sorry, as I should be if I were to be horrid. I dont want you to be tired and sorry. Do come and sit down again.

MRS JUNO [*coming back to her seat*] Youre sure you dont want anything you oughtnt to?

GREGORY. Quite sure. I only want you [*she recoils*]. Dont be alarmed: I like wanting you. As long as I have a want, I have a reason for living. Satisfaction is death.

347

MRS JUNO. Yes; but the impulse to commit suicide is sometimes irresistible.

GREGORY. Not with you.

MRS JUNO. What!

GREGORY. Oh, it sounds uncomplimentary; but it isnt really. Do you know why half the couples who find themselves situated as we are now behave horridly?

MRS JUNO. Because they cant help it if they let things go too far.

GREGORY. Not a bit of it. It's because they have nothing else to do, and no other way of entertaining each other. You dont know what it is to be alone with a woman who has little beauty and less conversation. What is a man to do? She cant talk interestingly; and if he talks that way himself she doesnt understand him. He cant look at her: if he does, he only finds out that she isnt beautiful. Before the end of five minutes they are both hideously bored. Theres only one thing that can save the situation; and thats what you call being horrid. With a beautiful, witty, kind woman, theres no time for such follies. It's so delightful to look at her, to listen to her voice, to hear all she has to say, that nothing else happens. That is why the woman who is supposed to have a thousand lovers seldom has one; whilst the stupid, graceless animals of women have dozens.

MRS JUNO. I wonder! It's quite true that when one feels in danger one talks like mad to stave it off, even when one doesnt quite want to stave it off.

GREGORY. One never does quite want to stave it off. Danger is delicious. But death isnt. We court the danger; but the real delight is in escaping, after all.

MRS JUNO. I dont think we'll talk about it any more. Danger is all very well when you do escape; but sometimes one doesnt. I tell you frankly I dont feel as safe as you do— if you really do.

GREGORY. But surely you can do as you please without injuring anyone, Mrs Juno. That is the whole secret of your extraordinary charm for me.

MRS JUNO. I dont understand.

GREGORY. Well, I hardly know how to begin to explain. But the root of the matter is that I am what people call a good man.

MRS JUNO. I thought so until you began making love to me.

GREGORY. But you knew I loved you all along.

MRS JUNO. Yes, of course; but I depended on you not to tell me so; because I thought you were good. Your blurting it out spoilt it. And it was wicked besides.

GREGORY. Not at all. You see, it's a great many years since Ive been able to allow myself to fall in love. I know lots of charming women; but the worst of it is, theyre all married. Women dont become charming, to my taste, until theyre fully developed; and by that time, if theyre really nice, theyre snapped up and married. And then, because I am a good man, I have to place a limit to my regard for them. I may be fortunate enough to gain friendship and even very warm affection from them; but my loyalty to their husbands and their hearths and their happiness obliges me to draw a line and not overstep it. Of course I value such affectionate regard very highly indeed. I am surrounded with women who are most dear to me. But every one of them has a post sticking up, if I may put it that way, with the inscription: Trespassers Will Be Prosecuted. How we all loathe that notice! In every lovely garden, in every dell full of primroses, on every fair hillside, we meet that confounded board; and there is always a gamekeeper round the corner. But what is that to the horror of meeting it on every beautiful woman, and knowing that there is a husband round the corner? I have had this accursed board standing between me and every dear and desirable woman until I thought I had lost the power of letting myself fall really and wholeheartedly in love.

MRS JUNO. Wasnt there a widow?

GREGORY. No. Widows are extraordinarily scarce in modern society. Husbands live longer than they used to; and even when they do die, their widows have a string of

349

names down for their next.

MRS JUNO. Well, what about the young girls?

GREGORY. Oh, who cares for young girls? Theyre unsympathetic. Theyre beginners. They dont attract me. I'm afraid of them.

MRS JUNO. Thats the correct thing to say to a woman of my age. But it doesnt explain why you seem to have put your scruples in your pocket when you met me.

GREGORY. Surely thats quite clear. I—

MRS JUNO. No: please dont explain. I dont want to know. I take your word for it. Besides, it doesnt matter now. Our voyage is over; and tomorrow I start for the north to my poor father's place.

GREGORY [surprised] Your poor father! I thought he was alive.

MRS JUNO. So he is. What made you think he wasnt?

GREGORY. You said your poor father.

MRS JUNO. Oh, thats a trick of mine. Rather a silly trick, I suppose; but theres something pathetic to me about men: I find myself calling them poor So-and-So when theres nothing whatever the matter with them.

GREGORY [who has listened in growing alarm] But—I— is?—wa—? Oh Lord!

MRS JUNO. Whats the matter?

GREGORY. Nothing.

MRS JUNO. Nothing! [Rising anxiously] Nonsense: youre ill.

GREGORY. No. It was something about your late husband—

MRS JUNO. My late husband! What do you mean? [Clutching him, horror-stricken] Dont tell me he's dead.

GREGORY [rising, equally appalled] Dont tell me he's alive.

MRS JUNO. Oh, dont frighten me like this. Of course he's alive—unless youve heard anything.

GREGORY. The first day we met—on the boat—you spoke to me of your poor dear husband.

MRS JUNO [releasing him, quite reassured] Is that all?

GREGORY. Well, afterwards you called him poor Tops. Always poor Tops, or poor dear Tops. What could I think?

MRS JUNO [*sitting down again*] I wish you hadnt given me such a shock about him; for I havnt been treating him at all well. Neither have you.

GREGORY [*relapsing into his seat, overwhelmed*] And you mean to tell me youre not a widow!

MRS JUNO. Gracious, no! I'm not in black.

GREGORY. Then I have been behaving like a blackguard! I have broken my promise to my mother. I shall never have an easy conscience again.

MRS JUNO. I'm sorry. I thought you knew.

GREGORY. You thought I was a libertine?

MRS JUNO. No: of course I shouldnt have spoken to you if I had thought that. I thought you liked me, but that you knew, and would be good.

GREGORY [*stretching his hands towards her breast*] I thought the burden of being good had fallen from my soul at last. I saw nothing there but a bosom to rest on: the bosom of a lovely woman of whom I could dream without guilt. What do I see now?

MRS JUNO. Just what you saw before.

GREGORY [*despairingly*] No, no.

MRS JUNO. What else?

GREGORY. Trespassers Will Be Prosecuted: Trespassers Will Be Prosecuted.

MRS JUNO. They wont if they hold their tongues. Dont be such a coward. My husband wont eat you.

GREGORY. I'm not afraid of your husband. I'm afraid of my conscience.

MRS JUNO [*losing patience*] Well! I dont consider myself at all a badly behaved woman; for nothing has passed between us that was not perfectly nice and friendly; but really! to hear a grown-up man talking about promises to his mother!—

GREGORY [*interrupting her*] Yes, yes: I know all about that. It's not romantic: it's not Don Juan: it's not advanced;

351

but we feel it all the same. It's far deeper in our blood and bones than all the romantic stuff. My father got into a scandal once: that was why my mother made me promise never to make love to a married woman. And now Ive done it I cant feel honest. Dont pretend to despise me or laugh at me. You feel it too. You said just now that your own conscience was uneasy when you thought of your husband. What must it be when you think of my wife?

MRS JUNO [*rising aghast*] Your wife!!! You dont dare sit there and tell me coolly that youre a married man!

GREGORY. I never led you to believe I was unmarried.

MRS JUNO. Oh! You never gave me the faintest hint that you had a wife.

GREGORY. I did indeed. I discussed things with you that only married people really understand.

MRS JUNO. Oh!!

GREGORY. I thought it the most delicate way of letting you know.

MRS JUNO. Well, you are a daisy, I must say. I suppose thats vulgar; but really! really! You and your goodness! However, now weve found one another out theres only one thing to be done. Will you please go?

GREGORY [*rising slowly*] I ought to go.

MRS JUNO. Well, go.

GREGORY. Yes. Er—[*he tries to go*] I—I somehow cant. [*He sits down again helplessly*] My conscience is active: my will is paralyzed. This is really dreadful. Would you mind ringing the bell and asking them to throw me out? You ought to, you know.

MRS JUNO. What! make a scandal in the face of the whole hotel! Certainly not. Dont be a fool.

GREGORY. Yes; but I cant go.

MRS JUNO. Then I can. Goodbye.

GREGORY [*clinging to her hand*] Can you really?

MRS JUNO. Of course I—[*she wavers*] Oh dear! [*They contemplate one another helplessly*]. I cant. [*She sinks on the lounge, hand in hand with him*].

GREGORY. For heaven's sake pull yourself together. It's a question of self-control.

MRS JUNO [*dragging her hand away and retreating to the end of the chesterfield*] No: it's a question of distance. Self-control is all very well two or three yards off, or on a ship, with everybody looking on. Dont come any nearer.

GREGORY. This is a ghastly business. I want to go away; and I cant.

MRS JUNO. I think you ought to go [*he makes an effort; and she adds quickly*] but if you try to I shall grab you round the neck and disgrace myself. I implore you to sit still and be nice.

GREGORY. I implore you to run away. I believe I can trust myself to let you go for your own sake. But it will break my heart.

MRS JUNO. I dont want to break your heart. I cant bear to think of your sitting here alone. I cant bear to think of sitting alone myself somewhere else. It's so senseless—so ridiculous—when we might be so happy. I dont want to be wicked, or coarse. But I like you very much; and I do want to be affectionate and human.

GREGORY. I ought to draw a line.

MRS JUNO. So you shall, dear. Tell me: do you really like me? I dont mean l o v e me: you might love the housemaid—

GREGORY [*vehemently*] No!

MRS JUNO. Oh yes you might; and what does that matter, anyhow? Are you really fond of me? Are we friends—comrades? Would you be sorry if I died?

GREGORY [*shrinking*] Oh dont.

MRS JUNO. Or was it the usual aimless man's lark: a mere shipboard flirtation?

GREGORY. Oh no, no; nothing half so bad, so vulgar, so wrong. I assure you I only meant to be agreeable. It grew on me before I noticed it.

MRS JUNO. And you were glad to let it grow?

GREGORY. I let it grow because the board was not up.

MRS JUNO. Bother the board! I am just as fond of Sibthorpe as—

GREGORY. Sibthorpe!

MRS JUNO. Sibthorpe is my husband's Christian name. I oughtnt to call him Tops to you now.

GREGORY [*chuckling*] It sounded like something to drink. But I have no right to laugh at him. My Christian name is Gregory, which sounds like a powder.

MRS JUNO [*chilled*] That is so like a man! I offer you my heart's warmest friendliest feeling; and you think of nothing but a silly joke. A quip like that makes you forget me.

GREGORY. Forget you! Oh, if only I could!

MRS JUNO. If you could, would you?

GREGORY [*burying his shamed face in his hands*] No: I'd die first. Oh, I hate myself.

MRS JUNO. I glory in myself. It's so jolly to be reckless. Can a man be reckless, I wonder?

GREGORY [*straightening himself desperately*] No. I'm not reckless. I know what I'm doing: my conscience is awake. Oh, where is the intoxication of love? the delirium? the madness that makes a man think the world well lost for the woman he adores? I dont think anything of the sort: I see that it's not worth it: I know that it's wrong: I have never in my life been cooler, more businesslike.

MRS JUNO [*opening her arms to him*] But you cant resist me.

GREGORY. I must. I ought. [*Throwing himself into her arms*]. Oh my darling, my treasure, we shall be sorry for this.

MRS JUNO. We can forgive ourselves. Could we forgive ourselves if we let this moment slip?

GREGORY. I protest to the last. I'm against this. I have been pushed over a precipice. I'm innocent. This wild joy, this exquisite tenderness, this ascent into heaven can thrill me to the uttermost fibre of my heart [*with a gesture of ecstasy she hides her face on his shoulder*]; but it cant subdue my mind or corrupt my conscience, which still shouts to the skies that I'm not a willing party to this outrageous conduct. I repudiate the bliss with which you are filling me.

MRS JUNO. Never mind your conscience. Tell me how happy you are.

GREGORY. No: I recall you to your duty. But oh, I will give you my life with both hands if you can tell me that you feel for me one millionth part of what I feel for you now.

MRS JUNO. Oh yes, yes. Be satisfied with that. Ask for no more. Let me go.

GREGORY. I cant. I have no will. Something stronger than either of us is in command here. Nothing on earth or in heaven can part us now. You know that, dont you?

MRS JUNO. Oh, dont make me say it. Of course I know. Nothing—not life nor death nor shame nor anything can part us.

A MATTER-OF-FACT MALE VOICE IN THE CORRIDOR. All right. This must be it.

The two recover with a violent start; release one another; and spring back to opposite sides of the lounge.

GREGORY. That did it.

MRS JUNO [*in a thrilling whisper*] Sh-sh-sh! That was my husband's voice.

GREGORY. Impossible: it's only our guilty fancy.

A WOMAN'S VOICE. This is the way to the lounge. I know it.

GREGORY. Great Heaven! we're both mad. Thats my wife's voice.

MRS JUNO. Ridiculous! Oh, we're dreaming it all. We— [*the door opens; and Sibthorpe Juno appears in the roseate glow of the corridor (which happens to be papered in pink) with Mrs Lunn, like Tannhäuser in the hill of Venus. He is a fussily energetic little man, who gives himself an air of gallantry by greasing the points of his moustaches and dressing very carefully. She is a tall, imposing, handsome, languid woman, with flashing dark eyes and long lashes. They make for the chesterfield, not noticing the two palpitating figures blotted against the walls in the gloom on either side. The figures flit away noiselessly through the window and disappear*].

JUNO [*officiously*] Ah: here we are. [*He leads the way to the*

355

sofa]. Sit down: I'm sure youre tired. [*She sits*]. Thats right. [*He sits beside her on her left*]. Hullo! [*he rises*] this sofa's quite warm.

MRS LUNN [*bored*] Is it? I dont notice it. I expect the sun's been on it.

JUNO. I felt it quite distinctly: I'm more thinly clad than you. [*He sits down again, and proceeds, with a sigh of satisfaction*]. What a relief to get off the ship and have a private room! Thats the worst of a ship. Youre under observation all the time.

MRS LUNN. But why not?

JUNO. Well, of course theres no reason: at least I suppose not. But, you know, part of the romance of a journey is that a man keeps imagining that something might happen; and he cant do that if there are a lot of people about and it simply cant happen.

MRS LUNN. Mr Juno: romance is all very well on board ship; but when your foot touches the soil of England theres an end of it.

JUNO. No: believe me, thats a foreigner's mistake: we are the most romantic people in the world, we English. Why, my very presence here is a romance.

MRS LUNN [*faintly ironical*] Indeed?

JUNO. Yes. Youve guessed, of course, that I'm a married man.

MRS LUNN. Oh, thats all right. I'm a married woman.

JUNO. Thank Heaven for that! To my English mind, passion is not real passion without guilt. I am a red-blooded man, Mrs Lunn: I cant help it. The tragedy of my life is that I married, when quite young, a woman whom I couldnt help being very fond of. I longed for a guilty passion—for the real thing—the wicked thing; and yet I couldnt care twopence for any other woman when my wife was about. Year after year went by: I felt my youth slipping away without ever having had a romance in my life; for marriage is all very well; but it isnt romance. Theres nothing wrong in it, you see.

356

MRS LUNN. Poor man! How you must have suffered!

JUNO. No: that was what was so tame about it. I wanted to suffer. You get so sick of being happily married. It's always the happy marriages that break up. At last my wife and I agreed that we ought to take a holiday.

MRS LUNN. Hadnt you holidays every year?

JUNO. Oh, the seaside and so on! Thats not what we meant. We meant a holiday from one another.

MRS LUNN. How very odd!

JUNO. She said it was an excellent idea; that domestic felicity was making us perfectly idiotic; that she wanted a holiday too. So we agreed to go round the world in opposite directions. I started for Suez on the day she sailed for New York.

MRS LUNN [*suddenly becoming attentive*] Thats precisely what Gregory and I did. Now I wonder did he want a holiday from me! What he said was that he wanted the delight of meeting me after a long absence.

JUNO. Could anything be more romantic than that? Would anyone else than an Englishman have thought of it? I daresay my temperament seems tame to your boiling southern blood—

MRS LUNN. My what!

JUNO. Your southern blood. Dont you remember how you told me, that night in the saloon when I sang "Farewell and adieu to you dear Spanish ladies," that you were by birth a lady of Spain? Your splendid Andalusian beauty speaks for itself.

MRS LUNN. Stuff! I was born in Gibraltar. My father was Captain Jenkins. In the artillery.

JUNO [*ardently*] It is climate and not race that determines the temperament. The fiery sun of Spain blazed on your cradle; and it rocked to the roar of British cannon.

MRS LUNN. What eloquence! It reminds me of my husband when he was in love—before we were married. Are you in love?

JUNO. Yes; and with the same woman.

357

MRS LUNN. Well, of course, I didnt suppose you were in love with two women.

JUNO. I dont think you quite understand. I meant that I am in love with you.

MRS LUNN [*relapsing into deepest boredom*] Oh, that! Men do fall in love with me. They all seem to think me a creature with volcanic passions: I'm sure I dont know why; for all the volcanic women I know are plain little creatures with sandy hair. I dont consider human volcanoes respectable. And I'm so tired of the subject! Our house is always full of women who are in love with my husband and men who are in love with me. We encourage it because it's pleasant to have company.

JUNO. And is your husband as insensible as yourself?

MRS LUNN. Oh, Gregory's not insensible: very far from it; but I am the only woman in the world for him.

JUNO. But you? Are you really as insensible as you say you are?

MRS LUNN. I never said anything of the kind. I'm not at all insensible by nature; but (I dont know whether youve noticed it) I am what people call rather a fine figure of a woman.

JUNO [*passionately*] Noticed it! Oh, Mrs Lunn! Have I been able to notice anything else since we met?

MRS LUNN. There you go, like all the rest of them! I ask you, how do you expect a woman to keep up what you call her sensibility when this sort of thing has happened to her about three times a week ever since she was seventeen? It used to upset me and terrify me at first. Then I got rather a taste for it. It came to a climax with Gregory: that was why I married him. Then it became a mild lark, hardly worth the trouble. After that I found it valuable once or twice as a spinal tonic when I was run down; but now it's an unmitigated bore. I dont mind your declaration: I daresay it gives you a certain pleasure to make it. I quite understand that you adore me; but (if you dont mind) I'd rather you didnt keep on saying so.

JUNO. Is there then no hope for me?

MRS LUNN. Oh, yes. Gregory has an idea that married women keep lists of the men theyll marry if they become widows. I'll put your name down, if that will satisfy you.

JUNO. Is the list a long one?

MRS LUNN. Do you mean the real list? Not the one I shew to Gregory: there are hundreds of names on that; but the little private list that he'd better not see?

JUNO. Oh, will you really put me on that? Say you will.

MRS LUNN. Well, perhaps I will. [*He kisses her hand*]. Now dont begin abusing the privilege.

JUNO. May I call you by your Christian name?

MRS LUNN. No: it's too long. You cant go about calling a woman Seraphita.

JUNO [*ecstatically*] Seraphita!

MRS LUNN. I used to be called Sally at home; but when I married a man named Lunn, of course that became ridiculous. Thats my one little pet joke. Call me Mrs Lunn for short. And change the subject, or I shall go to sleep.

JUNO. I cant change the subject. For me there is no other subject. Why else have you put me on your list?

MRS LUNN. Because youre a solicitor. Gregory's a solicitor. I'm accustomed to my husband being a solicitor and telling me things he oughtnt to tell anybody.

JUNO [*ruefully*] Is that all? Oh, I cant believe that the voice of love has ever thoroughly awakened you.

MRS LUNN. No: it sends me to sleep. [*Juno appeals against this by an amorous demonstration*]. It's no use, Mr Juno: I'm hopelessly respectable: the Jenkinses always were. Dont you realize that unless most women were like that, the world couldnt go on as it does?

JUNO [*darkly*] You think it goes on respectably; but I can tell you as a solicitor—

MRS LUNN. Stuff! of course all the disreputable people who get into trouble go to you, just as all the sick people go to the doctors; but most people never go to a solicitor.

JUNO [*rising, with a growing sense of injury*] Look here,

359

OVERRULED

Mrs Lunn: do you think a man's heart is a potato? or a turnip? or a ball of knitting wool? that you can throw it away like this?

MRS LUNN. I dont throw away balls of knitting wool. A man's heart seems to me much like a sponge: it sops up dirty water as well as clean.

JUNO. I have never been treated like this in my life. Here am I, a married man, with a most attractive wife: a wife I adore, and who adores me, and has never as much as looked at any other man since we were married. I come and throw all this at your feet. I! I, a solicitor! braving the risk of your husband putting me into the divorce court and making me a beggar and an outcast! I do this for your sake. And you go on as if I were making no sacrifice: as if I had told you it's a fine evening, or asked you to have a cup of tea. It's not human. It's not right. Love has its rights as well as respectability [*he sits down again, aloof and sulky*].

MRS LUNN. Nonsense! Here! heres a flower [*she gives him one*]. Go and dream over it until you feel hungry. Nothing brings people to their senses like hunger.

JUNO [*contemplating the flower without rapture*] What good's this?

MRS LUNN [*snatching it from him*] Oh! you dont love me a bit.

JUNO. Yes I do. Or at least I did. But I'm an Englishman; and I think you ought to respect the conventions of English life.

MRS JUNO. But I am respecting them; and youre not.

JUNO. Pardon me. I may be doing wrong; but I'm doing it in a proper and customary manner. You may be doing right; but youre doing it in an unusual and questionable manner. I am not prepared to put up with that. I can stand being badly treated: I'm no baby, and can take care of myself with anybody. And of course I can stand being well treated. But the one thing I cant stand is being unexpectedly treated. It's outside my scheme of life. So come now! youve got to behave naturally and straightforwardly with me. You

360

can leave husband and child, home, friends, and country, for my sake, and come with me to some southern isle—or say South America—where we can be all in all to one another. Or you can tell your husband and let him jolly well punch my head if he can. But I'm damned if I'm going to stand any eccentricity. It's not respectable.

GREGORY [*coming in from the terrace and advancing with dignity to his wife's end of the chesterfield*] Will you have the goodness, sir, in addressing this lady, to keep your temper and refrain from using profane language?

MRS LUNN [*rising, delighted*] Gregory! Darling [*she enfolds him in a copious embrace*]!

JUNO [*rising*] You make love to another man to my face!

MRS LUNN. Why, he's my husband.

JUNO. That takes away the last rag of excuse for such conduct. A nice world it would be if married people were to carry on their endearments before everybody!

GREGORY. This is ridiculous. What the devil business is it of yours what passes between my wife and myself? Youre not her husband, are you?

JUNO. Not at present; but I'm on the list. I'm her prospective husband: youre only her actual one. I'm the anticipation: youre the disappointment.

MRS LUNN. Oh, my Gregory is not a disappointment. [*Fondly*] Are you, dear?

GREGORY. You just wait, my pet. I'll settle this chap for you. [*He disengages himself from her embrace, and faces Juno. She sits down placidly*]. You call me a disappointment, do you? Well, I suppose every husband's a disappointment. What about yourself? Dont try to look like an unmarried man. I happen to know the lady you disappointed. I travelled in the same ship with her; and—

JUNO. And you fell in love with her.

GREGORY [*taken aback*] Who told you that?

JUNO. Aha! you confess it. Well, if you want to know, nobody told me. Everybody falls in love with my wife.

GREGORY. And do you fall in love with everybody's wife?

361

JUNO. Certainly not. Only with yours.

MRS LUNN. But whats the good of saying that, Mr Juno? I'm married to him; and theres an end of it.

JUNO. Not at all. You can get a divorce.

MRS LUNN. What for?

JUNO. For his misconduct with my wife.

GREGORY [*deeply indignant*] How dare you, sir, asperse the character of that sweet lady? a lady whom I have taken under my protection.

JUNO. Protection!

MRS JUNO [*returning hastily*] Really you must be more careful what you say about me, Mr Lunn.

JUNO. My precious! [*He embraces her*]. Pardon this betrayal of feeling; but Ive not seen my wife for several weeks; and she is very dear to me.

GREGORY. I call this cheek. Who is making love to his own wife before people now, pray?

MRS LUNN. Wont you introduce me to your wife, Mr Juno?

MRS JUNO. How do you do? [*They shake hands; and Mrs Juno sits down beside Mrs Lunn, on her left*].

MRS LUNN. I'm so glad to find you do credit to Gregory's taste. I'm naturally rather particular about the women he falls in love with.

JUNO [*sternly*] This is no way to take your husband's unfaithfulness. [*To Lunn*] You ought to teach your wife better. Wheres her feelings? It's scandalous.

GREGORY. What about your own conduct, pray?

JUNO. I dont defend it; and theres an end of the matter.

GREGORY. Well, upon my soul! What difference does your not defending it make?

JUNO. A fundamental difference. To serious people I may appear wicked. I dont defend myself: I am wicked, though not bad at heart. To thoughtless people I may even appear comic. Well, laugh at me: I have given myself away. But Mrs Lunn seems to have no opinion at all about me. She doesnt seem to know whether I'm wicked or comic. She

362

OVERRULED

doesnt seem to care. She has no moral sense. I say it's not right. I repeat, I have sinned; and I'm prepared to suffer.

MRS JUNO. Have you really sinned, Tops?

MRS LUNN [*blandly*] I dont remember your sinning. I have a shocking bad memory for trifles; but I think I should remember that—if you mean me.

JUNO [*raging*] Trifles! I have fallen in love with a monster.

GREGORY. Dont you dare call my wife a monster.

MRS JUNO [*rising quickly and coming between them*] Please dont lose your temper, Mr Lunn: I wont have my Tops bullied.

GREGORY. Well, then, let him not brag about sinning with my wife. [*He turns impulsively to his wife; makes her rise; and takes her proudly on his arm*]. What pretension has he to any such honor?

JUNO. I sinned in intention. [*Mrs Juno abandons him and resumes her seat, chilled*]. I'm as guilty as if I had actually sinned. And I insist on being treated as a sinner, and not walked over as if I'd done nothing, by your wife or any other man.

MRS LUNN. Tush! [*She sits down again contemptuously*].

JUNO [*furious*] I wont be belittled.

MRS LUNN [*to Mrs Juno*] I hope youll come and stay with us now that you and Gregory are such friends, Mrs Juno.

JUNO. This insane magnanimity—

MRS LUNN. Dont you think youve said enough, Mr Juno? This is a matter for two women to settle. Wont you take a stroll on the beach with my Gregory while we talk it over. Gregory is a splendid listener.

JUNO. I dont think any good can come of a conversation between Mr Lunn and myself. We can hardly be expected to improve one another's morals. [*He passes behind the chesterfield to Mrs Lunn's end; seizes a chair; deliberately pushes it between Gregory and Mrs Lunn; and sits down with folded arms, resolved not to budge*].

GREGORY. Oh! Indeed! Oh, all right. If you come to that

OVERRULED

—[*he crosses to Mrs Juno; plants a chair by her side; and sits down with equal determination*].

JUNO. Now we are both equally guilty.

GREGORY. Pardon me. I'm not guilty.

JUNO. In intention. Dont quibble. You were guilty in intention, as I was.

GREGORY. No. I should rather describe myself as being guilty in fact, but not in intention.

JUNO	*rising and*	What!
MRS JUNO	*exclaiming*	No, really—
MRS LUNN	*simultaneously*	Gregory!

GREGORY. Yes: I maintain that I am responsible for my intentions only, and not for reflex actions over which I have no control. [*Mrs Juno sits down, ashamed*]. I promised my mother that I would never tell a lie, and that I would never make love to a married woman. I never have told a lie—

MRS LUNN [*remonstrating*] Gregory! [*She sits down again*].

GREGORY. I say never. On many occasions I have resorted to prevarication; but on great occasions I have always told the truth. I regard this as a great occasion; and I wont be intimidated into breaking my promise. I solemnly declare that I did not know until this evening that Mrs Juno was married. She will bear me out when I say that from that moment my intentions were strictly and resolutely honorable; though my conduct, which I could not control and am therefore not responsible for, was disgraceful—or would have been had this gentleman not walked in and begun making love to my wife under my very nose.

JUNO [*flinging himself back into his chair*] Well, I like this!

MRS LUNN. Really, darling, theres no use in the pot calling the kettle black.

GREGORY. When you say darling, may I ask which of us you are addressing?

MRS LUNN. I really dont know. I'm getting hopelessly confused.

JUNO. Why dont you let my wife say something? I dont think she ought to be thrust into the background like this.

364

MRS LUNN. I'm sorry, I'm sure. Please excuse me, dear.

MRS JUNO [*thoughtfully*] I dont know what to say. I must think over it. I have always been rather severe on this sort of thing; but when it came to the point I didnt behave as I thought I should behave. I didnt intend to be wicked; but somehow or other, Nature, or whatever you choose to call it, didnt take much notice of my intentions. [*Gregory instinctively seeks her hand and presses it*]. And I really did think, Tops, that I was the only woman in the world for you.

JUNO [*cheerfully*] Oh, thats all right, my precious. Mrs Lunn thought she was the only woman in the world for him.

GREGORY [*reflectively*] So she is, in a sort of way.

JUNO [*flaring up*] And so is my wife. Dont you set up to be a better husband than I am; for youre not. Ive owned I'm wrong. You havnt.

MRS LUNN. Are you sorry, Gregory?

GREGORY [*perplexed*] Sorry?

MRS LUNN. Yes, sorry. I think it's time for you to say youre sorry, and to make friends with Mr Juno before we all dine together.

GREGORY. Seraphita: I promised my mother—

MRS JUNO [*involuntarily*] Oh, bother your mother! [*Recovering herself*] I beg your pardon.

GREGORY. A promise is a promise. I cant tell a deliberate lie. I know I ought to be sorry; but the flat fact is that I'm not sorry. I find that in this business, somehow or other, there is a disastrous separation between my moral principles and my conduct.

JUNO. Theres nothing disastrous about it. It doesnt matter about your conduct if your principles are all right.

GREGORY. Bosh! It doesnt matter about your principles if your conduct is all right.

JUNO. But your conduct isnt all right; and my principles are.

GREGORY. Whats the good of your principles being right if they wont work?

JUNO. They will work, sir, if you exercise self-sacrifice.

365

GREGORY. Oh yes: if, if, if. You know jolly well that self-sacrifice doesnt work either when you really want a thing. How much have you sacrificed yourself, pray?

MRS LUNN. Oh, a great deal, Gregory. Dont be rude. Mr Juno is a very nice man: he has been most attentive to me on the voyage.

GREGORY. And Mrs Juno's a very nice woman. She oughtnt to be; but she is.

JUNO. Why oughtnt she to be a nice woman, pray?

GREGORY. I mean she oughtnt to be nice to me. And you oughtnt to be nice to my wife. And your wife oughtnt to like me. And my wife oughtnt to like you. And if they do, they oughtnt to go on liking us. And I oughtnt to like your wife; and you oughtnt to like mine; and if we do, we oughtnt to go on liking them. But we do, all of us. We oughtnt; but we do.

JUNO. But, my dear boy, if we admit we are in the wrong wheres the harm of it? We're not perfect; but as long as we keep the ideal before us—

GREGORY. How?

JUNO. By admitting we're wrong.

MRS LUNN [*springing up, out of patience, and pacing round the lounge intolerantly*] Well, really, I must have my dinner. These two men, with their morality, and their promises to their mothers, and their admissions that they were wrong, and their sinning and suffering, and their going on at one another as if it meant anything, or as if it mattered, are getting on my nerves. [*Stooping over the back of the chesterfield to address Mrs Juno*]. If you will be so very good, my dear, as to take my sentimental husband off my hands occasionally, I shall be more than obliged to you: I'm sure you can stand more male sentimentality than I can. [*Sweeping away to the fireplace*] I, on my part, will do my best to amuse your excellent husband when you find him tiresome.

JUNO. I call this polyandry.

MRS LUNN. I wish you wouldnt call innocent things by offensive names, Mr Juno. What do you call your own conduct?

366

JUNO [*rising*] I tell you I have admitted—

GREGORY ⎫   ⎧ Whats the good of keeping on at that?

MRS JUNO ⎬ *together* ⎨ Oh, not that again, please.

MRS LUNN ⎭   ⎩ Tops: I'll scream if you say that again.

JUNO. Oh, well, if you wont listen to me—! [*He sits down again*].

MRS JUNO. What is the position now exactly? [*Mrs Lunn shrugs her shoulders and gives up the conundrum. Gregory looks at Juno. Juno turns away his head huffily*]. I mean, what are we going to do?

MRS LUNN. What would you advise, Mr Juno?

JUNO. I should advise you to divorce your husband.

MRS LUNN. You want me to drag your wife into court and disgrace her?

JUNO. No: I forgot that. Excuse me; but for the moment I thought I was married to you.

GREGORY. I think we had better let bygones be bygones. [*To Mrs Juno, very tenderly*] You will forgive me, wont you? Why should you let a moment's forgetfulness embitter all our future life?

MRS JUNO. But it's Mrs Lunn who has to forgive you.

GREGORY. Oh, dash it, I forgot. This is getting ridiculous.

MRS LUNN. I'm getting hungry.

MRS JUNO. Do you really mind, Mrs Lunn?

MRS LUNN. My dear Mrs Juno, Gregory is one of those terribly uxorious men who ought to have ten wives. If any really nice woman will take him off my hands for a day or two occasionally, I shall be greatly obliged to her.

GREGORY. Seraphita: you cut me to the soul [*he weeps*].

MRS LUNN. Serve you right! Youd think it quite proper if it cut me to the soul.

MRS JUNO. Am I to take Sibthorpe off your hands too, Mrs Lunn?

JUNO [*rising*] Do you suppose I'll allow this?

367

MRS JUNO. Youve admitted that youve done wrong, Tops. Whats the use of your allowing or not allowing after that?

JUNO. I do not admit that I have done wrong. I admit that what I did was wrong.

GREGORY. Can you explain the distinction?

JUNO. It's quite plain to anyone but an imbecile. If you tell me Ive done something wrong you insult me. But if you say that something that I did is wrong you simply raise a question of morals. I tell you flatly if you say I did anything wrong you will have to fight me. In fact I think we ought to fight anyhow. I dont particularly want to; but I feel that England expects us to.

GREGORY. I wont fight. If you beat me my wife would share my humiliation. If I beat you, she would sympathize with you and loathe me for my brutality.

MRS LUNN. Not to mention that as we are human beings and not reindeer or barndoor fowl, if two men presumed to fight for us we couldnt decently ever speak to either of them again.

GREGORY. Besides, neither of us could beat the other, as we neither of us know how to fight. We should only blacken each other's eyes and make fools of ourselves.

JUNO. I dont admit that. Every Englishman can use his fists.

GREGORY. Youre an Englishman. Can you use yours?

JUNO. I presume so: I never tried.

MRS JUNO. You never told me you couldnt fight, Tops. I thought you were an accomplished boxer.

JUNO. My precious: I never gave you any ground for such a belief.

MRS JUNO. You always talked as if it were a matter of course. You spoke with the greatest contempt of men who didnt kick other men downstairs.

JUNO. Well, I cant kick Mr Lunn downstairs. We're on the ground floor.

MRS JUNO. You could throw him into the harbor.

GREGORY. Do you want me to be thrown into the harbor?

MRS JUNO. No: I only want to shew Tops that he's making a ghastly fool of himself.

GREGORY [*rising and prowling disgustedly between the chesterfield and the windows*] We're all making fools of ourselves.

JUNO [*following him*] Well, if we're not to fight, I must insist at least on your never speaking to my wife again.

GREGORY. Does my speaking to your wife do you any harm?

JUNO. No. But it's the proper course to take. [*Emphatically*] We must behave with some sort of decency.

MRS LUNN. And are you never going to speak to me again, Mr Juno?

JUNO. I'm prepared to promise never to do so. I think your husband has a right to demand that. Then if I speak to you after, it will not be his fault. It will be a breach of my promise; and I shall not attempt to defend my conduct.

GREGORY [*facing him*] I shall talk to your wife as often as she'll let me.

MRS JUNO. I have no objection to your speaking to me, Mr Lunn.

JUNO. Then I shall take steps.

GREGORY. What steps?

JUNO. Steps. Measures. Proceedings. Such steps as may seem advisable.

MRS LUNN [*to Mrs Juno*] Can your husband afford a scandal, Mrs Juno?

MRS JUNO. No.

MRS LUNN. Neither can mine.

GREGORY. Mrs Juno: I'm very sorry I let you in for all this. I dont know how it is that we contrive to make feelings like ours, which seem to me to be beautiful and sacred feelings, and which lead to such interesting and exciting adventures, end in vulgar squabbles and degrading scenes.

JUNO. I decline to admit that my conduct has been vulgar or degrading.

369

OVERRULED

GREGORY. I promised—

JUNO. Look here, old chap: I dont say a word against your mother; and I'm sorry she's dead; but really, you know, most women are mothers; and they all die some time or other; yet that doesnt make them infallible authorities on morals, does it?

GREGORY. I was about to say so myself. Let me add that if you do things merely because you think some other fool expects you to do them, and he expects you to do them because he thinks you expect him to expect you to do them, it will end in everybody doing what nobody wants to do, which is in my opinion a silly state of things.

JUNO. Lunn: I love your wife; and thats all about it.

GREGORY. Juno: I love yours. What then?

JUNO. Clearly she must never see you again.

MRS JUNO. Why not?

JUNO. Why not! My love: I'm surprised at you.

MRS JUNO. Am I to speak only to men who dislike me?

JUNO. Yes: I think that is, properly speaking, a married woman's duty.

MRS JUNO. Then I wont do it: thats flat. I like to be liked. I like to be loved. I want everyone round me to love me. I dont want to meet or speak to anyone who doesnt like me.

JUNO. But, my precious, this is the most horrible immorality.

MRS LUNN. I dont intend to give up meeting you, Mr Juno. You amuse me very much. I dont like being loved: it bores me. But I do like to be amused.

JUNO. I hope we shall meet very often. But I hope also we shall not defend our conduct.

MRS JUNO [rising] This is unendurable. Weve all been flirting. Need we go on footling about it?

JUNO [huffily] I dont know what you call footling—

MRS JUNO [cutting him short] You do. Youre footling. Mr Lunn is footling. Cant we admit that we're human and have done with it?

JUNO. I have admitted it all along. I—

MRS JUNO [*almost screaming*] Then stop footling.

The dinner gong sounds.

MRS LUNN [*rising*] Thank heaven! Lets go into dinner. Gregory: take in Mrs Juno.

GREGORY. But surely I ought to take in our guest, and not my own wife.

MRS LUNN. Well, Mrs Juno is not your wife, is she?

GREGORY. Oh, of course: I beg your pardon. I'm hopelessly confused. [*He offers his arm to Mrs Juno, rather apprehensively*].

MRS JUNO. You seem quite afraid of me [*she takes his arm*].

GREGORY. I am. I simply adore you. [*They go out together; and as they pass through the door he turns and says in a ringing voice to the other couple*] I have said to Mrs Juno that I simply adore her. [*He takes her out defiantly*].

MRS LUNN [*calling after him*] Yes, dear. She's a darling. [*To Juno*] Now, Sibthorpe.

JUNO [*giving her his arm gallantly*] You have called me Sibthorpe! Thank you. I think Lunn's conduct fully justifies me in allowing you to do it.

MRS LUNN. Yes: I think you may let yourself go now.

JUNO. Seraphita: I worship you beyond expression.

MRS LUNN. Sibthorpe: you amuse me beyond description. Come. [*They go in to dinner together*].

JITTA'S ATONEMENT

BY SIEGFRIED TREBITSCH, ENGLISH VERSION BY
G. BERNARD SHAW

Written in 1922

First Performed Washington 1923

TRANSLATOR'S NOTE

SIEGFRIED TREBITSCH, a well-known Austrian novelist and playwright, was born in Vienna on the 21st December 1869. The list of his original works includes eight novels and volumes of stories, and six or seven plays, including Frau Gitta's Sühne, of which the present work is a translation. I have to stress the word original, because, with a devotion extraordinary in the case of a writer with a successful career open to him as an original writer, he has undertaken and carried out the heavy additional task of translating and introducing to the German-speaking public and to the German theatre the entire body of my own works, both literary and theatrical.

This enterprise is the more remarkable because it was begun at a time when my position in the English theatre was one not of good repute, but of infamy. I was rated in the theatrical world of London as an absurd pamphleteer, who had been allowed to display his ignorance of the rudiments of stage technique, and his hopeless incapacity for representing human nature dramatically or otherwise, in a few performances at coterie theatres quite outside recognized theatrical commerce. Trebitsch knew better. He also knew English. He was quite unknown to me when he appeared one day at my house and asked to see me with a view to his becoming my interpreter and apostle in Central Europe. I attempted to dodge his visit by asking my wife to see him and to explain politely that a proposal to translate could be entertained only when made by the responsible manager of a theatre with a view to immediate production. The evasion failed ignominiously. My wife came to me and said that the young gentleman, though he seemed a very nice young gentleman, had swept aside her excuse with explosive contempt, and would take no denial. If I was to get rid of him (which she already regarded as doubtful policy) I must go down and do it myself. I came down; and the result was that the young gentleman carried the citadel by storm as successfully as he had carried the outworks. I did what I could to dissuade him from what seemed a desperate undertaking; but his faith in my destiny was invincible. I surrendered at discretion; and the result was that I presently found myself a successful and respected playwright in the German language whilst the English critics were still explaining laboriously that my plays were not plays, and urging me, in the kindest spirit, to cease my vain efforts to enter a profession for which Nature had utterly unfitted me. In the last decade of the nineteenth century I was deriving a substantial income as a playwright from America and Central Europe. Not until the middle of the first decade of the twentieth could I have lived by my theatrical earnings in London. Today I have only to lift up my finger to attract a hundred translators. When Trebitsch volunteered for the job, the hundred would have fled from my invitation as one man.

It is not for me to say how far English drama is indebted to Herr Trebitsch for its present prestige abroad. It *is* for me to say that my personal debt to him is incalculable. When the horrible catastrophe of the war had torn Anglo-German relations to fragments, and only the fools who would not heed Mr Lloyd George's warning to "stop snarling" could doubt the vital European necessity for mending them, I could do no less than take advantage of the fact that Trebitsch has written plays of his own, to translate one of them from German into English for the man who has translated so many plays from English into German.

There were technical difficulties: how great I never realized until I took the job in hand. At first I was preoccupied with a quite minor matter. I can neither claim knowledge of the German language nor plead ignorance of it. I am like most literary persons: I have spent several holidays in Germany (mostly in Bayreuth), and have just managed to ask my way, and get what I wanted in the shops and railway stations, without the aid of an interpreter. The proverbial bits of Goethe and Wagner and Nietzsche are familiar to me; and when a German writes to me I can generally make out what he wants provided he uses the

TRANSLATOR'S NOTE

Latin and not the Gothic script. And that is all. When I opened the pages of Frau Gitta's Sühne, I was driven to the dictionary, only to discover that Trebitsch apparently does not use words that are in the dictionary. It was not by any process known to men of learning, but rather by some telepathic method of absorption, that I managed at last to divine, infer, guess, and co-invent the story of Gitta, or Jitta, as I have had to spell her to avert having her name pronounced with a hard G. Trebitsch is amiable enough to say that I have succeeded wonderfully; but even a very bad translation may be a wonderful feat for a translator who does not know the language.

However, when it comes to translating a play the mere translation is only the tiniest fraction of the business. I soon found that a literal translation would fail completely to convey the play to an Anglo-American audience. It was necessary to translate the audience as well as the play: that is, to translate Vienna into London and New York. And this involved translating one theatrical epoch into another. Vienna is still romantic in the manner of Verdi's operas, and modern in the manner of De Maupassant and Baudelaire. And as the conqueror always acquires some of the qualities of the conquered, even now that he no longer eats him, there is a touch of the east in Vienna, not only brought by the winds along the Danube, but left by the Turks when Sobieski drove them back from the gates. Add to this that Vienna has never weaned itself from the sweet milk of eighteenth-century art, when even woe was a luxury, and the heroine could not die in gloom too deep to please the audience. When natural history (sometimes ambiguously called realism) is banished from the theatre, cruelty, horror and death become painless there, and even luxurious, because nobody believes in them. The most frightful torments may be heaped on the heroine until she dies of poison or a broken heart: the villain may, like the wicked Count in Il Trovatore, live only to *centuplicar la morte* of the hero in *mille atroci spasimi*, and the hero himself may not know a moment

377

of happiness or security until misfortune dogs him to his death; yet no one will turn a hair: the more dreadful it all is the better it is liked, because romance can never come home to reality. To preserve this delicious anæsthesia there must be no bringing down to earth of the business by the disillusioning touch of comedy.

In England and America nowadays, such romance is privileged only in Italian Opera, and is not tolerated without the music. The Anglo-American audience wants a happy ending because it wants a credible ending, and therefore cannot bear an utterly unhappy one. It is true, as the late St John Hankin pointed out and illustrated by his Plays With Happy Endings, that the conventional happy ending is often as unhappy and disastrous as the marriages which foolish magistrates and police-court missionaries force on young people who have been no better than they ought to be. But the fact remains that in proportion as a play succeeds in producing an illusion of real life, it must dispense with the frantic agonies and despairs and poisonings and butcheries of the romantic theatre. Consequently, if you take a play written under the tyranny of a romantic audience and present it without modification to a comparatively matter-of-fact audience, it will miss its mark, and may even miss fire altogether.

To avert this result in the case of Frau Gitta's Sühne, I have taken advantage of the fortunate circumstance that in real life the consequences of conjugal infidelity are seldom either so serious as they are assumed to be in romantic tragedy or so trivial as in farcical comedy. I may as well confess at once that in the original play Jitta lives miserably ever after, and that her husband bears malice, and presents a character-study much subtler and more elusive than you will gather from my frankly comedic British version of him. Also Trebitsch, being a German poet, has a certain melancholic delicacy which escapes my comparatively barbarous and hilarious occidental touch. I could not help suggesting, by a few translator's treacheries here and there, that the ill-

378

assorted pair settle down on reasonable human terms, and find life bearable after all.

Trebitsch goes so far as to say "You have made my last act almost a comedy"; but he is too amiable to reproach me, and tolerates my variations, which affect, not the story itself, but only the key in which it ends. Though the assumptions of the audience as to what will happen after the fall of the curtain will be more cheerful in England and America than they were in Vienna, the action of the play remains unaltered. Nevertheless those who can should read the original, to the idiosyncratic literary quality of which I have been shamefully unable to do justice.

Frau Gitta's Sühne was first performed at the great Burgtheater of Vienna on the 3rd February 1920.

Jitta's Atonement was performed for the first time at the Grand Theatre, Fulham, London, on the 3rd February 1925, with Violet Vanbrugh in the title part.

It was performed for the first time in America at the Shubert Theatre, New York City, on the 6th January 1923, when Jitta was played by Bertha Kalich.

379

JITTA'S ATONEMENT

ACT I

1920. *The drawing room in a flat in Vienna. It is fashionably decorated and elegantly furnished, but not homelike, as there are no books nor personal belongings nor household odds and ends lying about. The two photogravure reproductions of pictures on the walls, symmetrically placed at equal distances from the door, are of the refinedly aphrodisiac character considered de rigueur in hotels. But the place is not quite like a hotel sitting room; because there is very little furniture: only two seats, a couch, and a small table with a glass flower-vase and a mirror on it.*

It is an oblong room; and from the point of view of anyone looking towards the corner the long wall on the right has in the middle of it the door leading to the entrance hall; and the short wall on the left has an open door close to the corner through which a bed with rose-colored hangings is partly visible. In the same wall further forward from the same point of view is the fireplace.

The couch is in the corner, parallel to the longer wall, not quite close against it. A comfortable upholstered stool, really a chair without a back, is at the foot of the couch. This stool has a cushion on it which evidently belongs to the couch. The other seat, a chair with arms, is almost in the middle of the room, but nearer to the fireplace than to the door. The table stands near the corner of the fireplace.

It is almost dark.

Mrs Billiter, an elderly housekeeper, has something of the same undomesticated air as the room. Her hair, though not aggressively dyed, is still rather younger than her face. She is well dressed, like a hotel manageress. She opens the door, letting in some electric light from the hall. She has a silver tray in her hands, with a siphon, two tumblers, and a bottle on it. She switches on the light at the door, and crosses the room to the table, where she puts down the tray. She looks round the room to see whether it is tidy. She goes to the stool; takes the cushion from it; and puts it in its proper place on the couch.

Somebody rings at the outer door of the flat. Mrs Billiter goes out to open it.

JITTA'S ATONEMENT

A GIRL'S VOICE [*the accent is not that of a lady*] Gentleman ordered these. Suppose it's all right, isnt it?

MRS BILLITER'S VOICE. Yes. Just bring them in, and put them in the vase for me, will you?

Mrs Billiter returns, followed by a girl from the florist's shop, carrying a handsome present of flowers.

MRS BILLITER [*pointing to the vase*] There. I'll fetch some water.

She goes into the bedroom and switches on the light there. The roseate hangings of the bed appear to great advantage. The flower girl, on her way to the vase, stops fascinated.

Mrs Billiter returns with a jug from the bedroom washstand: a very pretty jug in rose color and gold.

The flower girl puts the roses into the vase; and Mrs Billiter fills it with water.

Mrs Billiter takes the jug back into the bedroom; and the girl steals after her to the door and peeps enviously in.

Mrs Billiter returns, putting out the bedroom light as she does so, and finds the girl at the door.

THE FLOWER GIRL. Just right for two, aint it?

MRS BILLITER [*incensed*] What do you mean, with your "Just right for two"?

THE FLOWER GIRL [*grinning*] Oh, it's nothing to me. But I know.

MRS BILLITER. You know too much, you do. Are they paid for?

THE FLOWER GIRL. Oh yes: thats quite all right. [*She grins again, shewing no sign of going*].

MRS BILLITER [*peremptorily*] Well? What are you waiting for? And what are you grinning at?

THE FLOWER GIRL. Aint the gentleman here? He promised to leave me something.

MRS BILLITER [*impatiently groping in her purse and extracting a tip*] Thats how they give themselves away, offering tips when they have no call to. [*She gives her some money*]. There! Now, out you go. I'm busy.

THE FLOWER GIRL [*sarcastic*] Sorry, I'm sure. Thanks

awfully. [*She goes to the door, but stops on hearing the outer door opened by a latch-key from without*]. Oh, here i s the gentleman.

The gentleman enters. The girl ogles him. He recognizes her, and makes a gesture towards his pocket.

MRS BILLITER [*very decisively*] Thats all right, sir: she's had what you promised. [*To the girl, sternly*] Good evening to you. [*She sails to the door so formidably that the girl, after an ineffectual grimace, has to go*].

The moment the gentleman is left alone he shews signs of severe physical suffering. His ascent of the stairs has brought on an attack of angina pectoris. He makes his way to the stool, and collapses on it, struggling with the paroxysm. Mrs Billiter returns.

MRS BILLITER [*running to him*] Oh dear, oh dear, has it come on again, sir?

THE GENTLEMAN [*a little better*] It's all right now, Mrs Billiter. I took the stairs too fast. I rush at them without thinking. [*He rises, and tries to take off his overcoat. She helps him*]. Thank you, Mrs Billiter. I—I—I— [*gasping*] Just a moment. Whew! [*As the coat comes off he plunges to the armchair, and sinks into it*].

MRS BILLITER. How often have I begged you never to walk upstairs but always to take the lift? And now see the state you are in!

THE GENTLEMAN. Dont look at me: it will only distress you. Angina pectoris is a horrible thing; but it passes off soon. You can do nothing, thank you.

MRS BILLITER [*taking his hat and coat out into the vestibule*] Dear! dear! dear!

Rather dazed by the attack, he sits up, straightening his collar and coat rather irresolutely, and looking very careworn indeed. He is well dressed, on the verge of fifty, going grey, very distinguished in appearance and kindly in manner.

MRS BILLITER [*returning*] Why will you never take the lift, sir? It isnt as if anyone in this house knew you. And for that matter you meet people on the stairs as well as in the lift.

THE GENTLEMAN. I know; but I mustnt let the liftmen see me coming here too often. People talk, even when they have to live by holding their tongues.

MRS BILLITER [*reproachfully*] Oh, sir!

THE GENTLEMAN [*quickly saving the situation*] Except you, Mrs Billiter. You are an exception to all the rules.

MRS BILLITER. It's you who are the exception, sir. I wish all the other gentlemen that keep rooms here on the quiet to enjoy themselves were like you. There are people and people in this world; and I know a gentleman when I see him. And I feel sure your lady is a real lady, and always the same lady; though of course I take care never to see her.

THE GENTLEMAN. Thats very kind of you, Mrs Billiter. [*He rises to go to the table*].

MRS BILLITER [*stopping him*] Now do sit quiet a moment, sir. What was it you wanted?

THE GENTLEMAN. A mouthful of soda water.

MRS BILLITER. There: I'll get it for you. Sit down. [*He does so. She goes to the table and fills a glass from the siphon*]. If you would only let me put a drop of brandy in it?

THE GENTLEMAN [*shaking his head decisively*] It would probably kill me. I know. I am a doctor. [*He takes the glass from her*]. Thank you. [*He drinks*].

MRS BILLITER. You are not right yet. I can see it in your face.

THE GENTLEMAN [*hands her back the glass a little abruptly, and pulls himself together*] !!!

MRS BILLITER. There! I shouldnt have said that. [*She replaces the glass on the table, snubbed*].

THE GENTLEMAN. Not at all: I know how anxious you are about me, and how kindly you mean it. But I am all right now; and I—I [*he takes out his watch and looks at it*] I am expecting somebody.

MRS BILLITER [*taking the hint*] Yes, sir: I'm going. [*She crosses the room to the door, but turns for a moment appealingly before going out*]. But you will take the lift next time, sir, wont you? If anything were to happen to you—not that I think anything like that, of course; but—

THE GENTLEMAN. Of course not, Mrs Billiter. Still—[*he

shrugs his shoulders] !

MRS BILLITER. Yes, sir. And then what could I do but send for the police?

THE GENTLEMAN. Quite so, quite so. If I come again I will take the lift. I promise.

MRS BILLITER. Thank you, sir. Thank you kindly. [*She goes out, closing the door very softly behind her*].

The gentleman, left alone, rises and goes to the table, where he takes up the mirror and looks at his wrinkles and his blanching hair. He shakes his head and puts the mirror down. Then he takes out a cigaret; puts it between his lips; takes out a match, and is about to strike it when the bell rings twice. His face lights up; he throws the match and the cigaret into the fire; and goes out eagerly to admit the visitor, leaving the door of the room open. Immediately afterwards a veiled lady hurries in like a hunted creature. He follows her; shuts the door; and comes to her in the middle of the room. They embrace.

THE GENTLEMAN [*affectionately*] Why do you always look as if you were running away, and had just stumbled into my arms by chance?

THE LADY. I always feel as if my husband were lying in wait for me at the next turn.

THE GENTLEMAN. Well, suppose he were! You are not afraid of poor Alfred, are you? At home you are a perfect tyrant to him.

JITTA. I should have no courage if he caught me. Besides, if we are found out there will be an end of everything.

BRUNO. I almost wish we were found out.

JITTA. Why?

BRUNO. It would force us to stand by one another, and come out openly before all the world with our love.

JITTA [*embracing him impulsively*] Shall we?

BRUNO. There is my wife. Always my wife.

JITTA [*recoiling from him impatiently, and throwing her cloak on the couch*] Oh yes: Agnes. Always Agnes, Agnes, Agnes.

BRUNO. She has done nothing to deserve our betrayal of

her: she has sacrificed her life to me. I cant face what she would suffer.

JITTA. Has she sacrificed more for you than you for her? It is not the thought of Agnes that holds me back. But the scandal would ruin you. [*She takes off her hat, and puts it on the table*].

BRUNO [*with sudden energy*] I want to be ruined. Oh, the life of a University professor. His respectability kills his mind. His wife's respectability kills her soul. They both become mere shells of their former selves: going through life in grooves, on rails like tramcars, envying the tinkers and gipsies. If it were not for Agnes I should commit some disgraceful offence to free myself.

JITTA. I am afraid disgrace would not mend matters. I could not bear yours.

BRUNO. Nor I yours. We are in the net.

JITTA. Not here, Bruno. We have broken through the net into our dreamland. [*Now that her hat and veil are off Jitta is revealed as one of those attractively refined women whose wistfully sensitive unsmiling mouths and tragic eyes not only make imaginative men fancy unfathomable depths in their natures, and something undefinably sad and splendid in their destinies, but actually force this conception on the women themselves, however commonplace their characters and circumstances may be. Jitta is nothing more extraordinary than the wife of a college don, and has done nothing more heroic than fall in love with another and more poetic don (also married); but to her lover and herself her life is as dignified and beautiful as her face, and their relations as nobly tragic as her eyes. So, as we are all a little like that, let us share their dream for a moment whilst she continues, sitting down beside him*] You must brush off the bits of the broken net. [*Tracing on his brow*] There is a thread of it here, and here, and straight down here. [*She kisses his brow*]. No: they are not gone yet.

BRUNO. It is not the net. I can leave that behind when I come here into the dreamland. These last few months have been wonderful. But they have been terrible.

JITTA. Yes: wonderful and terrible. But they have been real, real. Life in the net is never real: it is all acting.

BRUNO. That is true. But there is something still more real than the dream.

JITTA. What is that?

BRUNO. The awakening.

JITTA. For me there will be no awakening.

BRUNO. There is always the tap at the door in the morning. The tap with bony knuckles. The caller.

JITTA. Death! Oh, why will you always harp on that? Death is nothing. Life with love is everything. Think, Bruno. We are here alone. There is nothing between us and happiness except the courage to grasp it. Can you never be happy?

BRUNO. Can any mortal be happy?

JITTA [*suddenly prosaic and impatient*] Yes: Alfred can. A glass of wine and a cigar can make Alfred happy. A vote of thanks can make Alfred happy. A cheque for £25 can make him happy. But I cannot make you happy.

BRUNO. Dearest love: you can, you do make me inexpressibly happy. So happy, that every time you go away from me, and I stand listening to your footsteps dying away in the distance—I always listen to them to catch the last sound of you—I am stabbed with a fear that I have held you in my arms for the last time. But when we have been parted for days, and I am here waiting for you and thinking the moments endless until you come, and at last I hear your ring, I suddenly become like a freshman just up from school. [*She laughs, smoothing his grey hair*]. Yes: I know; but grey as I am, I am still a hobbledehoy: just a student waiting for his girl at the corner of the street where her shop is.

JITTA [*moved*] And do you think it is any different with me? All day I long to be with you, to say a thousand things to you! And when at last— [*she finishes the sentence by a caress*]! When you are away from me, I plod through my housework, and just count the days until—until this [*she again presses him in her arms, and draws him down beside her*

387

on the couch].

BRUNO. If only I were young! Then I could really begin a new life with you instead of merely thinking and dreaming about it.

JITTA. I like it better as it is. I dont want to see you every day and become a commonplace with you, Bruno.

BRUNO. But are you content with these heartbreaking stolen hours? I'd risk you becoming a commonplace: I want you to be a commonplace for me; but I daresay I should bore you.

JITTA [*sighing blissfully*] The happiness of these stolen hours is so delicious that it makes up to me for everything I have to endure between times. And who knows what would happen if I were to break up your home and shatter your career? Are you sure we should not be too tired out, too broken by the effort, to enjoy our rest? One has to be young to do such things, Bruno: young enough to be able to forget.

BRUNO. [*sadly*] You are right. Our love looks well only by candlelight. It wont stand daylight.

JITTA [*refusing to be discouraged*] Daylight is for your work, for your great book that is to be the crown of your career. But here in the candlelight you belong to me, and to me only.

BRUNO [*quickly*] Oh, not here alone. Do you think that my wife and my daughter put you quite out of my head when I am at home? They never do: you are everywhere. But what must it be for you? I often reproach myself—

JITTA [*softly*] You mustnt do that. I am not unhappy, Bruno. I was at first: I hardly dared go home and face Alfred's inquisitive eyes. But he saw nothing: his self-conceit is impenetrable. His cheerful grin killed my conscience. I hold up my head now everywhere: I am proud of belonging to you. When one is really happy, one is ruthless and shameless.

BRUNO. Jitta: do you know that you belonged to me before we ever saw one another?

JITTA. Yes. We were destined—

BRUNO. I dont mean that. I mean that we actually belonged to one another p h y s i c a l l y. I mean that my daughter —born before we knew one another—is your daughter.

JITTA. Edith! What do you mean, Bruno? You have the strangest fancies.

BRUNO. This is not a fancy, Jitta. It is a hard scientific fact: I worked out its theoretic possibility before Edith was born—before I ever set eyes on you. It strikes me dumb with wonder when I think how it has worked out between us. The daughter of my wife, my child and hers, not yours, resembles you, aye, loves you more than she loves her own mother, though she may not know it.

JITTA [*thoughtfully*] Strange. And I love your Edith as only a childless woman can love the child of the man she has interested and saved. I am not clever enough to share the rest of your science with you; but this I believe and accept. But how can such a miracle come about?

BRUNO [*mystically*] Men do not yet realize that no prophetic aspiration of theirs can fall utterly without fruit if its roots lie deep enough in their innermost conviction.

JITTA. Bruno: that must be right. It is an inspiration. It takes hold of my heart with both hands. You really are great.

BRUNO. Not at all: it is not new: everybody knows it nowadays in the rough. But it has never been worked out scientifically far enough to explain this miracle of Edith and you. Well, I am working it out; and there is somebody else working at it with me.

JITTA [*jealous*] Somebody else!

BRUNO. You would never guess who.

JITTA. I do not want to guess. I do not care.

BRUNO. Think of the most hardened materialist you know: the very last man you could imagine lending himself to such a mystical speculation!

JITTA [*relieved*] Oh, a man! The most hopeless materialist I know is my husband; and I do not want to be reminded of him just now.

BRUNO. But it is your husband I mean. I have converted

him.

JITTA. Oh, impossible. He would never believe a thing like that. Dont let Alfred deceive you, Bruno. He is only playing with your belief because he feels sure of discovering some grossly material explanation of it, and making you ridiculous. He does not believe it as you believe it.

BRUNO [*brightly*] I do not say he does: I do not say he can. Alfred is clever; but he is not me—or rather, not us two: two in one.

JITTA. Darling!

BRUNO. All the same, he is burning with ambition to have his name connected with a new departure in science. As he has failed to do it in physics he is willing to do it in psychology rather than not do it at all.

JITTA [*scornfully*] At your expense?

BRUNO. Not altogether, dearest. He really has given me some quite handy curve diagrams for my lectures. He knows everything: what he lacks is a sense of the significance of what he knows. I am really sorry for him, and should like to help him.

JITTA. You can help him without letting him rob you of your ideas.

BRUNO. It is not he who is robbing me of my ideas: it is I who am robbing him of his wife; and the less he is conscious of his loss the meaner thief am I. I feel that through and through. [*He kisses her hand passionately*]. I have taken a priceless treasure from him. I must make amends somehow: I must pay my debt. That sense of obligation is in my very bones.

JITTA [*looking hard at him*] Why have I never felt this sense of obligation to your wife? Have I no conscience? or have you too much?

BRUNO. It is not the same. You do not feel that you have taken anything from Agnes: you feel that she has taken something from you.

JITTA. I know that I have a divine right to you. And I know that she has not.

BRUNO. There are other rights beside divine rights. If I had never come into your life, you would perhaps have come to some sort of understanding with Alfred; and he would have found some sort of happiness in possessing you.

JITTA. He has all the happiness he is capable of.

BRUNO. We have no right to say so. I have taken you from him.

JITTA. You have not taken me from him. I belonged to myself: and I gave you myself.

BRUNO. I have betrayed his trust.

JITTA. As I have betrayed your wife's trust.

BRUNO. That is quite different. Your relations with Agnes are mere society relations, conventional and superficial. But I am your husband's comrade: we were chums at school: we were at college together: we are professional colleagues. He knows me intimately; and if he were not such a confoundedly bad psychologist he would know that Nature meant you to be my wife. It is a stroke of luck for us that he knows nothing —if indeed it is only luck, and not his subconscious knowledge that he must not let himself know. Yes: he not only does not know: he will not know: he refuses to know. And that refusal, because it is unconscious, binds my sense of honor as if he spared us knowingly.

JITTA [changing her tone, and trying to soothe and coax him] Darling: you are tormenting yourself for nothing. Let me see whether I can cure you of all these scruples and fancies. They are only spooks. [She draws him towards the bedroom]. Come.

BRUNO. No, not yet. [He gets away from her by standing up. She shrinks a little, wounded]. I am telling you this once for all; so that I may never have to speak of it again. God knows it is not to involve you in my struggles with myself, nor to whitewash myself, that I am spending our priceless moments like this. I am as impatient as you are: I long for you beyond all expression. But there is something you must do for me. Something you can understand only when you know the rights of it.

JITTA [*repelled and anxious*] But what is it?

BRUNO [*pulling himself together*] I want to speak to you about my book. I have something very important to say to you about it.

JITTA [*a little disappointed*] Bruno: cant that wait a little? You know how I value your work; but we have so little time left this evening—

BRUNO [*resolutely*] It is just because I have so little time left that I dare not put this off any longer. You know the value of my book. Well, you must take charge of it.

JITTA. You need not trouble about that, Bruno: it will make your name famous without my help.

BRUNO [*looking hard at her, and forcing the emphasis of his words to the utmost*] Not my name. His name.

JITTA. God of Heaven! whose name?

BRUNO. Your husband's.

JITTA [*springing up*] Alfred's!

BRUNO. Listen to me. The book is finished: the typed copy will be found in my desk. And the title-page reads "Fetters of the Feminine Psyche, by Professor Alfred Lenkheim."

JITTA. Bruno! You are mad.

BRUNO. I burnt the original manuscript yesterday: there is not a word of it in my handwriting left to prove that I am the author. They will find a book by your husband among my things: that is all. [*She is about to protest*]. Promise me that you will leave this secret buried in my grave.

JITTA [*beside herself*] But why? Why? Why?

BRUNO [*seizing her hands, but now pleading like a lover*] It is my deepest wish. It is my most urgent prayer to you, Jitta.

JITTA [*gasping*] You ask me to do that! to promise you this unheard-of thing! This man who has no soul; who has been guilty of everything to me that a man can be guilty of to a woman except the infidelity that I would welcome with delight to excuse my own (he is not man enough for that): the fruit of your life's work is to drop into his mouth! And I am to be your accomplice in such a crime! No. I cannot.

392

Never.

BRUNO [*soothing her*] I know how hard it is for you, darling. That is why I have not been able to bring myself to tell you until today. But I know you will not fail me.

JITTA. Dont say that, Bruno, as if it settled everything. I cannot act like a madwoman. Give me a reason.

BRUNO. I will. Listen. A book by a dead man is an orphan. Orphans sometimes die when they are not adopted. Mendel's masterpiece lay dead for thirty-five years while the fame of the living Darwin spread over the world. If Alfred adopts my orphan it will not perish; for Alfred's wife will adopt it too.

JITTA. Oh, Bruno, Bruno, how can you? That is so clever, so damnably clever. Has it come to mere cleverness between us?

BRUNO. I asked for a promise. You asked for a reason.

JITTA. But I am thinking of your fame—

BRUNO [*snapping his fingers*] Psha! That for my fame! What does it matter from whose hands the new generation will take the torch to carry on the great race of science? The truth will be as true with Alfred's name tacked on to it as Bruno's.

JITTA [*impatiently*] Oh yes, yes: I know all that. It sounds like a sentence from your annual address to your students. It's not true, Bruno: I feel it. It is not human. There is something else at the back of your mind.

BRUNO. No—except this. When I finally and irrevocably sealed my resolution yesterday by burning the manuscript, there came to me a moment of extraordinary exaltation in which I saw this sacrifice as my atonement to Alfred. It is the price at which I buy his wife from him; and now at last I can take my happiness with both hands, free in my conscience, right in my heart, in all honor as well as in all affection to the very end. [*He clasps her to his breast*].

JITTA [*still wondering at him*] You throw the greatest achievement of your life to him like a bone to a dog; and then feel you have made us two one. [*Breaking away from*

393

him] No, no, Bruno: you are asking too much. You know that I love you as my man, without a thought of your greatness and your work; but all the same your work, your greatness, are a part of you; and I love every bit of you, your body, your soul, your reputation, your work, everything that would not exist if you did not exist. All that is my treasure and my pride. When you take a handful of it and throw it into the mud, you make me so much the poorer. Have you thought of that?

BRUNO. When two people stand to one another as we stand, the children born from their intercourse are not always children of flesh and blood, but inspirations, intuitions, convictions that they cannot discard without unfaithfulness. This is such an inspiration. Will you be unfaithful to it?

JITTA. Bruno: you want to play at Providence. Alfred is far too conceited to let anyone play Providence to him. If he refuses, what then?

BRUNO. He will not refuse. I have thought all that out. Why should he refuse to father a book which he already regards as half his own? He believes that I could never have written it without him. And you know how ambitious he is. I can depend on Alfred absolutely. Can I depend on you?

JITTA [*half beaten*] Who knows? I cannot depend on myself. This sacrifice is no child born of our intercourse, Bruno: you may be its father; but I am not its mother. I shall be its stepmother; and I shall hate it as no stepmother ever hated before. But the book is yours; and I have no rights over it: it must take the course you desire. I cannot go further than that. When you ask me to bind myself by a solemn vow, I— [*shuddering*] no, no: it is inhuman: a mockery, an impossibility.

BRUNO. I know I am putting your love to the cruellest test; but oh, Jitta, Jitta, do not fail me.

JITTA. So be it. [*He snatches her hands and kisses them*]. I promise you that if I survive the day that takes you from me, I will hide the truth as you demand, and take all the ghastly consequences just as you are mad enough to mean them.

394

Are you satisfied now?

BRUNO [*clasping her convulsively to him and hardly able to speak*] I—I—thanks, thanks. My love.

JITTA [*extricating herself quickly from his embrace*] But if God wishes to be good to me he will never let me live to keep my promise.

BRUNO. I could not have pained you like this if I had the smallest doubt that I shall go first and go soon.

JITTA. Dont say that. Oh, do let us forget Death for one moment.

BRUNO. Death is nothing: if I could be sure that I should die tonight I should be unspeakably glad; for I should not have to strike you the bitterest blow of all.

JITTA. Bruno! Another blow!

BRUNO. Yes, another. My strength is going from me; and I need it all to force myself not to play the coward.

JITTA. How?

BRUNO. By leaving you today without daring to tell you that I do not intend to meet you again.

JITTA [*struck to the heart*] Not meet me again! Leave me!

BRUNO [*with deliberate emphasis*] This must be the last time. [*Rising, with a sudden fanciful recklessness*] Come: let it be the best. Let it be so full of happiness that we can say "It is enough: farewell."

JITTA. You are going to give me up! You can bring yourself to do that!

BRUNO. Nonsense! I shall never give you up. But it would be a crime to let you meet me here again at such a risk.

JITTA. How is the risk greater now than it has always been?

BRUNO. It was only a risk of being caught here with a live man. That was nothing: only a secret that three can keep. What about the risk of being found with a dead one?

JITTA [*about to shriek*] !

BRUNO [*covering her mouth with his hand*] Hush—sh! [*She looks affrightedly at him: he looks gravely and significantly at her*]. It is all up with me, dearest. I could not stop work-

395

ing; and my heart—

JITTA [*with agonizing anxiety*] Is it worse?

BRUNO [*with a ghost of a laugh*] Worse! It has gone all to pieces. I had no right to let you come this evening. I have put off telling you too long; but when I climbed those terrible stairs just now, I knew. You would have to give your name to the police. Our relations would be shouted through the streets and posted on the newspaper bills if you were found here with a—with a [*he cannot say it, and indicates, by a gesture, the figure of a dead man lying on the floor*].

JITTA [*flinching at the image, but steadfast in her thought*] Have no fear, Bruno. Why did you not tell me sooner what was troubling you? I could have relieved your mind. I have known all along that you were ill; and my only fear was that that [*she repeats his gesture*] might happen when you were alone instead of in my arms. Does that sound as if I cared what would become of me without you?

BRUNO. But I care, dearest. That is why I am resolved on our parting before this crazy tired old clock [*he taps his left breast*] runs down and stops ticking for good and all.

JITTA. Never. There is only one thing that can part me from you; and that is not the stopping of the clock, but of your love for me. No other danger exists for me; and no forethought of ours can protect us against that if it comes. [*Abandoning herself to her passion*] All the more reason why we must make the most of our love while it is within our reach. I love you: I love you: we are alive, not dead: you are living with my life as well as your own: your blood surges to mix with mine: you cannot die while I hold you fast. All the rest is an uneasy dream that means nothing: this is love; and love is life made irresistible.

BRUNO [*carried away*] Life: yes: this is life, and this [*he kisses her eyes*], and this [*he kisses her lips*]. What a fool I was with my iron resolutions! one throb of your breast, one touch of your lips; and where are they? Nothing matters but Jitta, Jitta, Jitta [*he kisses her again and again*]. I am neither weak nor afraid now; and I promise you to live a hundred years.

JITTA. All the unhappinesses are forgotten: they never existed. [*She turns him round and draws him towards the bedroom*] Come.

BRUNO [*beside himself*] You trust me; and I must betray you. You thought me a young man; and I let you think so. But you shall not be deceived. You have made me as young as I seemed to you. [*He seizes her round the hips, and lifts her up exultantly*].

JITTA [*terrified*] Oh God, no: take care, Bruno: take care.

BRUNO [*setting her down gaily*] Bah! Do I love you?

JITTA. Yes, yes. You love me. I love you. Come.

BRUNO [*pushing her towards the bedroom door*] Quick, quick.

JITTA [*running into the bedroom*] Yes, yes, yes.

BRUNO [*with a grim change of countenance*] Poor Jitta! That lift broke the mainspring. [*He staggers against the door frame; clutches at the wall to save himself; strikes the electric light out by chance; reels back into the middle of the room; and drops dead*].

JITTA [*running in: she has begun to undress*] What is the matter? Where are you? [*She stumbles against the body*]. Oh God! [*She switches on the light*] Bruno. [*She rushes to him and kneels by him*]. Bruno: speak to me if you can: is it your heart again? What can I do for you? Shall I try to lift you?

She tries to raise him by his shoulders; but they are too heavy. She puts her hands round his neck and pulls it up from the floor; but the back of his head remains hanging and his jaw drops. With a gasp of horror she replaces the head and closes the open mouth. Then she scrambles to her feet and runs to the other door, calling breathlessly and voicelessly Mrs Billiter, Mrs Billiter. *She opens the door, and regaining her voice, cries* Mrs— *She checks herself, suddenly remembering the consequences to herself of being found with the body. She closes the door quickly and noiselessly. She tries to think, her strained senses shewing in her eyes. Her fingers clutch for a moment at her half-naked breast as she thinks of her disordered appearance. She dashes into the bedroom, and reappears almost immediately with her blouse on,*

397

arranging it with nervous hands. She puts on her hat and mantle anyhow. As she turns to rush to the door the hat falls off. With a little cry of misery she takes the hat-pins from the hat and pins it properly to her hair; then she looks at herself in the mirror and shakes her mantle straight. She turns, and is hurrying to the door when she finds the body in her way. A flush of remorse comes over her. She turns impulsively to the vase; takes out a handful of roses; and is stooping to lay them on his breast when she realizes that a man who drops dead cannot scatter flowers on himself. She shakes her head and puts the roses back; puts her hands distractedly to her head in an anguish of perplexity, feeling that she must not leave him without some ceremony of love. There is only one thing that comes into her mind that will not compromise her. She goes to him, and cannot touch him or kiss him; but she makes the sign of the cross over him; kisses her hand; crosses herself; and hurries out, closing the door very softly behind her.

A WEEK has elapsed. Bruno is buried, and his death from natural causes duly certified. Jitta has taken refuge in an illness, and is keeping her bed. Her husband, Professor Alfred Lenkheim, is sitting in his study after lunch with young Dr Fessler, who is engaged to Bruno's daughter Edith. Alfred lacks the distinction and heroic touch of Bruno; but prosaic as he certainly is, he is saved from being common, if not from being a little comic, by the stamp put upon him as a man of learning by his university training and his professorial Chair. His age is between forty and fifty. Fessler is just an ordinary nice-looking young doctor.

The room has two doors: one, in the middle of the wall behind the two men, opening on the corridor; the other, on their left, leading to an inner room. The window faces the inner door from the opposite side; and there is a window-seat before it. At right angles to this window-seat, further up the room, is a sofa. There are two tables: one a writing-table on the side near the window, at which the professor is sitting, and the other a round table on the side near the inner door. There is a chair at it with its back to the wall in which the entrance door is, and another, in which Dr Fessler is sitting, between it and the writing-table. The walls are crowded with book-shelves; and the writing-table is heaped with examination papers and manuscripts.

LENKHEIM. Whats the matter? Going asleep at your age! You were not called up last night, were you?

FESSLER. No. But, by Jimminy, Lenkheim, I have gone through a lot this last week.

LENKHEIM. How?

FESSLER. Just consider. Imagine having to console Bruno's widow when I'm engaged to his daughter!

LENKHEIM. Why not?

FESSLER. Because theyre at daggers drawn. Every word that soothes old Agnes is an outrage to Edith.

LENKHEIM. Why? Whats wrong between them?

FESSLER. Oh, Mrs Haldenstedt is old-fashioned. She keeps up the convention that because Edith is a young unmarried woman she cant possibly understand about her father's death; and Edith has to pretend to be in the dark. But of course she knows as well as you or I; and it maddens her to have to hold her tongue and be treated like a child when all her feelings are boiling over about it. She was very fond of her father.

LENKHEIM. I knew the mother and daughter never got on very well together—jealousy, I suppose, as usual—but I thought this awful business would have brought them together.

FESSLER. Not a bit. It has set them more against one another than ever.

LENKHEIM. I suppose theyve no notion who the woman was?

FESSLER. None. She will never be found out unless she comes forward herself.

LENKHEIM. She wont do that. Why should she give herself away?

FESSLER. Women do, sometimes, God knows why! But meanwhile, poor Mrs Haldenstedt is most frightfully cut up. There she is, distracted by all sorts of surmises and suspicions, not knowing what to think, asking herself every minute whether he went on the loose and died in a vulgar street adventure, or whether there was somebody all along whom she never suspected, making her marriage a mockery. We are all as much in the dark as she is; for there never was a word against him: he seemed the correctest, most domesticated of men. That is, unless you know anything. You were so intimate with him, you know.

LENKHEIM. Was I really intimate with him? Certainly we were friends at college; and we kept it up afterwards. But he never told me much about himself.

FESSLER. He was not that sort of man. But he trusted nobody in the world as he trusted you: the widow is dead certain of that. By the way, she asked me to prepare you for a visit she is going to pay you.

LENKHEIM. Why should you prepare me?

FESSLER. Well, she is going to ask you to act as his scientific and literary executor.

LENKHEIM [*pleasantly surprised and suddenly self-conscious*] Really! Of course I shall be delighted. I may tell you that in my own will I made him my literary executor. Who would have thought that he would peg out first?

FESSLER. But didnt you know that he was ill?

LENKHEIM. Oh, I knew about his heart and so forth. But many a patient with heart disease lives to bury his doctor. As a matter of fact his case was not a very serious one. His heart would not have stood racing up two or three flights of stairs. But does any man of his age race upstairs? A very strong emotion or excitement might have killed him; but a settled married man with a wife and a grown-up daughter suffers more from too little excitement than from too much. What emotions has a domesticated man of science to fear after forty?

FESSLER. Then why did he die?

LENKHEIM. Just so: why did he die? He wouldnt have died if he had been leading the quiet life we all gave him credit for. What sort of life did he really lead? That is the question.

FESSLER. Isnt it shocking that such a man should die under such—such—well, such shady circumstances?

LENKHEIM. Shady! I should call them disgraceful. Yes, my dear boy, we must face it: he came to a disgraceful end. An operatic tenor, or even a literary man, might be forgiven for dying in an adventure of that kind. But a man of science! Unfortunate, to say the least: most unfortunate.

FESSLER. At all events, since it was his luck to die in the dark, we are not called on to light the candle, are we?

LENKHEIM. We are not; but what about the police? And what about his wife?

FESSLER. They havnt the ghost of a clue.

LENKHEIM. It wont upset or delay your engagement, I hope. Not that I could blame you if you broke it off. Still—

FESSLER. *I* break it off! Good gracious, no!

LENKHEIM. I'm glad of that. Of course you must keep it up to Edith that there was nothing wrong.

FESSLER. But she wont have it that there was nothing wrong.

LENKHEIM. What!

FESSLER. You see, she adored her father. She sees him with a halo round his head; and nothing that he could do would be wrong for her. She has always felt that her mother could not live up to him; and she is persuading herself that this unknown woman was some wonderful person who made him as happy as she thinks he deserved to be.

LENKHEIM. Thats funny. Very funny. Does she suspect anybody?

FESSLER. I dont know. I cant see through her; and the worst of it is, she can see through me. She will find out what I think.

LENKHEIM. Which is?

FESSLER. Well, just what you think. And when she finds out what that is, heaven help me!

LENKHEIM. She wont find out. All that a young girl sees in a death is the romance of it: the vulgar reality does not exist for her. What an eye-opener for us who know better! [*Sententiously*] And yet, whatever view we may take of the affair, we must admit that these moral problems are very difficult: in fact, insoluble. Is there any man who can say that he has never been in a position in which sudden death would have been extremely embarrassing?

FESSLER. I suppose not. [*Naïvely*] By the way, that reminds me that I forgot to ask how Mrs Lenkheim is.

LENKHEIM. Oh, Jitta is getting over it. She hopes to be able to get up for a couple of hours today. Just in a dressing-gown, you know, to sit about a bit.

FESSLER. Oh, good. Well, I must be off to the hospital. [*He rises*]. Tell her I asked after her.

LENKHEIM [*rising*] I will. How soon do you think I may expect the Haldenstedts?

402

FESSLER. Any time now, I should think. The old girl wont be easy until she has seen you.

Lenkheim goes out for a moment through the inner door. Jitta comes in, languid, and dressed as Lenkheim has described.

JITTA. Oh, so glad youve come, Doctor. [*She shakes hands with Fessler*]. Have you seen the Haldenstedts? I was so sorry not to be able to call on them. I have been really too ill. I hope they know that.

FESSLER [*with affectionate deference*] They thoroughly understand that. You must take the greatest care of yourself.

JITTA. You are not running away, are you?

FESSLER. I must. I have to be at the hospital; and I am late already.

JITTA. Come again soon, Doctor.

FESSLER. I hope to find you quite well then, dear lady.

He kisses her hand, and goes out. When he has gone, Lenkheim returns, full of excitement and curiosity.

LENKHEIM. Jitta: old Agnes is coming to see us. Bruno has made me his literary executor. That is what she is coming about.

JITTA. Has she recovered enough to bear discussing it with you?

LENKHEIM. She must. The world doesnt stand still when people die. I wonder what we shall find in his papers!

JITTA [*going white*] Has she found anything?

LENKHEIM. Yes: didnt I tell you? He has made me his scientific and literary executor.

JITTA. I mean about—about—

LENKHEIM. About his death? Absolutely nothing: Fessler has just told me so.

JITTA [*sitting down at the table, reassured*] Poor Fessler!

LENKHEIM [*resuming his seat at his writing-table*] Yes, poor chap: he is rather in a fright about Edith.

JITTA. Why?

LENKHEIM. He is afraid that her grief for her father will kill her feeling for him; so youd better take Edith in hand: you know how she clings to you. She is like her father in

403

that: h e clung to you.

JITTA. To me!

LENKHEIM. Yes: you know very well he did. If I had died you would have been up before this, I expect.

JITTA. Alfred: if you begin nagging I shall have to go back to bed.

LENKHEIM. Who's nagging? [*She rises. He jumps up apprehensively*]. There now: for God's sake dont make a scene about nothing. All I meant was that if he ever told anything to anybody he would have told it to you. [*She sits down again*]. Jitta: have you really no suspicion?

JITTA. Of what?

LENKHEIM. Who the woman was.

JITTA. How could he tell anyone who she was? It would have been dishonorable to betray her.

LENKHEIM. Men do tell, all the same. They dont tell the newspapers; but they tell other women.

JITTA. I object to be classed with "other women."

LENKHEIM. Oh well, it's no use talking to you if you will be so touchy. I didnt suggest that he told you: you brought that in yourself. All that was in my mind was that as you were so much in and out of his house you must have met her one time or another if she was the wife of any of his friends. It usually is a friend's wife.

JITTA [*with affected listlessness*] Is it?

LENKHEIM. Well, it stands to reason, doesnt it? Unless it's a chance woman from the streets.

JITTA [*wincing*] I suppose so.

LENKHEIM. Did he never talk to you about love, or anything of that sort?

JITTA. The last time we were at the theatre he discussed the play with me. It was a play about love.

LENKHEIM. Well, what else would a play be about? Thats no clue. I wonder was she a patient of his?

JITTA. Does it matter? Need we gossip about it?

LENKHEIM [*impatiently*] Dont be so superior. I like gossip. Everybody likes gossip. You like it yourself as well as anybody. If she was a patient that would account for his being so reserved about her.

JITTA. Alfred: you are unbearable. I will go back to bed.

She rises and makes for the door, but is checked by the entrance of Agnes Haldenstedt and her daughter, both in deep mourning. Agnes carries a small dispatch case. She is not really much older than Jitta; but she has retired so completely from the competition of women in attractiveness, and accepted so fully her lot as a good bourgeoise with a home to keep and a family to manage on a slender income that she is set down as much older and less distinguished socially. Her sense of duty has kept her upright; and her uprightness has given her a certain authority, as of a person of some consequence. She has been deeply wounded by the circumstances of her husband's death, and is stiff and suspicious in her manner.

Her daughter is young and ingenuous, with a strong character. A passion of grief for her father has set her on fire with pride and a sense of being ready for any sacrifice.

The conversation which ensues is solemn, artificial, and constrained. They condole with one another in low tones and unnaturally bookish sentences. Jitta has to draw the girl to her, and kiss her on the brow. Alfred leads Mrs Haldenstedt to the sofa. When she sits down, he sits on the window-seat near her. Jitta leads Edith to the chair she has just vacated, and goes to the sofa, where she seats herself on the widow's left.

All these movements are ridiculous; yet the mourning worn by the two visitors makes them seem, if not natural, at least becoming.

LENKHEIM [*in hollow tones*] May I say again, dear Mrs Haldenstedt, how deeply I—

JITTA [*gushing*] At last, dearest Mrs Haldenstedt, I am able to tell you what I felt when I lay helpless, unable to pay the last respects to our dear lost friend. [*As she sits down, she seizes the hands of Mrs Haldenstedt, giving her no opportunity of refusing the attention*]. But in my sick room I was with you in spirit. Indeed I have never been closer to you and poor Edith than in that moment when I had to ask my husband

405

to tell you what it cost me to stay away.

AGNES [*not at all disposed to allow Jitta so prominent a share in her grief, but conventionally resorting to her handkerchief*] Thank you. I'm sure it's very kind of you.

LENKHEIM [*clearing his throat and sniffing*] Under such a sudden blow, what can we say? We are all struck dumb. We all share your grief.

AGNES. When people are sick, and we can sacrifice ourselves completely to the duty of nursing them: when they can lean on us to the very last, then, when the parting comes, there is some consolation in the thought that we have done all in our power. But an end like this, so sudden, so dreadful—[*she breaks down*].

LENKHEIM [*making the best of it*] Still, I am not sure that a lingering death really spares the feelings of the survivors. Death often tortures its victims before it strikes the final blow. In your case, dear Mrs Haldenstedt, there was at least no torture.

AGNES [*staring at him*] No torture! What has the future for me but the torture of a widow's grief?

EDITH [*unsympathetic*] It has the honor of father's name. Is that nothing?

LENKHEIM [*effusively*] Which I will help you both to uphold, my dear Edith, believe me.

AGNES. He knew he could depend on you. I have a packet of papers marked "Professor Lenkheim's property: to be given into his own hands": that is why I have come today instead of waiting for Mrs Lenkheim to call.

LENKHEIM. Dear fellow: how conscientious of him! such papers as he had of mine were of no consequence. Shall we have a little quiet talk all to ourselves, in here? [*He rises and crosses the room, inviting her, by a gesture, to come with him through the door opposite the window*].

AGNES [*pausing between Jitta and Edith*] I wanted to come alone; but Edith insisted on coming with me.

LENKHEIM. She was quite right. She is now your only support.

EDITH [*proudly*] Thank you, Professor. I wish you could persuade my mother that I could do much more for her if she would tell me all her troubles. I am no longer a child. There is nothing now that cannot be spoken of quite frankly before me.

AGNES [*with a weary smile*] Of course not, dear. But there are things it is better not to know. I know them; and I only wish I could change places with you.

Emphasizing this with an emphatic nod at Edith, she goes into the next room. Lenkheim follows her.

JITTA [*throwing off her false manner, whilst retaining the patronizing suavity of an older woman to a younger one, holds out her hands to Edith with genuine sympathy*] Come, darling. [*Edith comes to her and takes her hands*]. Sit here, close to me. [*She makes room for her on the sofa beside her. Edith sits down on her left, and looks gratefully and longingly into her eyes*]. Do you remember when we were last here together? Your father brought you. He was radiant with joy and pride in you. We were all so happy.

EDITH [*thoughtfully*] How long was that ago?

JITTA. Barely three weeks.

EDITH. It seems an age. I was a child then. I can hardly remember how I felt. It is as if I had been asleep.

JITTA. Your father's death has awakened you: you are looking at life for the first time.

EDITH. I have been looking at death for the first time.

JITTA. My poor child! But dont lose courage. Life lies before you: it will make up to you for many sorrows. You will get over it, Edith.

EDITH. Why should I get over it? I dont want to get over it. Do you suppose I feel disgraced?

JITTA. Oh no, no: of course not. But such a grief as this always makes us feel that we have come to the end of everything: that nothing can ever be the same again. Yet next day we find ourselves at the beginning of everything instead.

EDITH [*impatient*] You need not speak to me like that. You know very well that what is the matter is not merely the loss of a father: a thing that happens to everybody sooner or later.

JITTA [*taken aback*] Edith, dear—

EDITH [*downright and indignant*] Why do you treat me as if I were a little girl, as my mother does? I did not expect it from you. Oh, I am so tired of all this humbug. I turned to you because I hoped you would understand me, and let me open my heart to you like a friend.

JITTA. My dear: I will be an elder sister to you—

EDITH [*fiercely*] I said a friend.

JITTA [*surrendering*] Oh, you are terrible. I will be everything you want, if I can. But why are you angry with me? I really meant what I said. Life has a great deal to offer you: dont forget that you are going to be married. I believe you can trust your man. He adored your father. He will regard you as a sacred legacy.

EDITH. Thats curious. He used that word himself the day we buried poor papa. But I dont intend to be taken as a legacy, sacred or not.

JITTA. Edith: he feels your loss as deeply as you do yourself. Some of us perhaps feel it more deeply, because we have more experience of men, and know how much better what he was than you are yet old enough to know.

EDITH [*rising and pacing restlessly across the room*] Oh, these commonplaces! How you keep throwing them at me! None of us know what my father was: he was thrown away among us. [*Turning on Jitta*] Why did he not die with us? Why had he no last word for us? I was nothing to him: none of us were anything to him.

JITTA. You know, dear, that you are unjust to him when you say so.

EDITH. Unjust! unjust! what has that to do with it? Why did he not come to us for help, for nursing, for care?

JITTA. He was too considerate to let you know how ill he was.

EDITH. He told everyone else. We were left in the dark.

JITTA. No, no. No one knew it except himself.

EDITH [*passionately*] My mother wont speak to me about it; but I know very well what she is thinking. They whisper all day at home. I see it in the eyes of the visitors; and it makes me furious. I never want to see anyone cry again as my mother cried that night when they brought him home. It wasnt only grief: there was a bitterness in her that had nothing to do with grief or love. I have often felt in my soul that papa never found in his home what he needed and longed for. There were moments when I somehow got beyond myself and became another person; perhaps the woman I am growing into; and he was so responsive to that flash of something different in me, so grateful for it, that I saw quite plainly how he was longing for something else, something more, than we were giving him. We were not good enough for him. [*She throws herself into the chair beside the round table, sobbing*].

JITTA [*rising and going to her*] Dearest: dont cry like that.

EDITH. It nearly killed me to see him sitting there, as he often did, staring right through me without seeing me, and sighing as he drew his hand across his eyes and through his hair.

JITTA. Dear child: you must not worry yourself because he sometimes looked straight at you and did not see you. Just think. He was a doctor: he knew his danger better than anyone. When a man finds himself condemned to death, his thoughts and feelings must be overwhelming. Well, if you were looking at the sea in a storm or at the heavens opening above it, would you see a tiny figure on the shore, even if it were your own child?

EDITH [*rising in a girlish rapture*] Thank you for that: it is beautiful, and quite true. [*She closes her eyes, silent for a moment, and a little breathless. Jitta smiles, and sits down in the writing-table chair*]. And now, wont you help me to find out the secret of his death?

JITTA. What secret?

EDITH. Who is the woman in whose arms my father died?

JITTA [*startled*] So that is what you think! Poor child!

409

EDITH [*angry*] I do not think it: I know it. You know it. Please let us have no more of the poor child business: it does not impose on me. How am I to find her?

JITTA [*remonstrating*] Edith, Edith, what could you say to her, even if you found her?

EDITH. Only that I love her.

JITTA. Love her! What for?

EDITH. For making my father happy. [*Restless again, pacing up and down*]. Oh, if you knew how infamously all those people who call on us misunderstand him. They insult my mother by condoling with her on her husband's unfaithfulness. They insult God by declaring that my father threw himself into the gutter, and was justly punished for it.

JITTA [*springing up*] What! They dare say such brutal things!

EDITH. Oh, not in those words: they are too polite to speak as horribly as they think; but I know. And my mother encourages them. She actually likes to feel that some unheard-of disgrace has fallen on her. She thinks it makes her interesting and revenges her. She positively wallows in it.

JITTA [*shocked*] Edith!

EDITH. Oh, it is the right word for it: why should I not use it? She never thinks of his sorrows: only of her own.

JITTA [*taking her arm persuasively*] My dear: you mustnt go on like this. Come: let me talk to you quietly. [*She draws her back to the sofa, and makes her sit down again*]. If you loved your mother as you loved your father, you would be kinder to her. You think of him as a man whose wife has failed him. Dont forget that she is a woman whose husband failed her.

EDITH. How did he fail her? If she had been worthy of him—

JITTA. Yes, yes, dear; but she was not worthy of him. Or stop: no: we have no right to say that.

EDITH. We have a right to say that she was not the right woman for him.

JITTA. Yes; but dont forget that that means that he was not the right man for her. He was her superior if you like;

but that only made it worse for her. His superiority must often have wounded her self-respect; and as any weakness of his flattered it, she perhaps likes to think that he was not quite perfect, and even that he treated her badly.

EDITH. You think that an excuse for her! I call it abominable.

JITTA. Dont be impossible, dear. Abominable or not, it explains her readiness to believe the worst. You must not blame her because your faith in him is greater, and your consolation nobler. Remember: he did not betray you as he betrayed her. For he did betray her; and so did that woman. Tell yourself that, Edith, whenever you feel tempted to hate your mother. Promise me you will.

EDITH. I will never tell myself such a silly lie. I will take my father's memory and good name out of my mother's hands, and out of the hands of her tittle-tattling friends. I will make the world see him as he was, and as I loved him, not as she sees him, and as she hates him.

JITTA. The world will see him with its own eyes, dear, not with yours. All you can do is to save his memory from being blackened by that odious thing, a family quarrel. Come! promise me to stop worrying about your mother?

EDITH. I am not worrying about her: I am worrying about the woman my father loved. I cannot help it: she is always in my mind. Why was she not with him when they found him? Why did she run away like a criminal?

JITTA. Perhaps she is asking herself those questions every day in her shame and misery. Oh, Edith, we dont know what meannesses we are capable of until we are tried. The dread of a public scandal—of having to face a policeman prying into the most sacred and secret places in her soul—will drive a woman to anything. Remember: she had not only to save herself from the scandal, but his memory as well.

EDITH. No, no, no. She did not save him. She left him under the stigma of having died in the arms of some vile creature. I know in my soul that she was not that. The world would forgive him if it knew that she is what I know she must be if he loved her. Oh, why does she not defy all the silly world for his sake, and say "It was I."

JITTA. You ask too much from her. She may have been capable of great things when he was alive and at her side. What is the poor wretch now but a broken-hearted lonely coward?

EDITH. She is not broken-hearted: my father never broke any woman's heart. I loved him; and that makes even his death a glory to me. If she is lonely why does she not come to me? She shall come to me. We shall cure one another's loneliness, we two. Where is she to cry her heart out if not in my arms?

JITTA. No: she slunk away into the darkness. Let her be. She can bleed to death in her hiding-place.

EDITH. She shall not: she will be drawn to me: you will see. Remember that I have no longer any place at home. I cannot live with people who cannot feel about my father as I do; and there is only one such person in the world.

JITTA. That woman?

EDITH. Yes. I will give her every right over me that the woman who returned my father's love should have over his daughter: the right I deny to my mother. I swear it.

JITTA. How serious you are, Edith! But what will your mother say, and the man you are engaged to?

EDITH. My mother would never understand: I take nothing from her that she is capable of missing. As to the man who says he loves me, and asks me to share my whole life with him, if he cannot understand me and support me in this he will never have me for a wife. I can do without any man if I can find the woman to whom I am bound for ever and ever. You will help me to find her, will you not?

JITTA [*deeply moved, drawing Edith to her*] Oh, darling, darling, if only I could! If only I dared!

Lenkheim throws the door open: he is returning with Agnes. Jitta and Edith move asunder and rise hastily. Agnes comes in, drying her eyes with her handkerchief. Lenkheim follows her solemnly with her dispatch case in his hand.

412

EDITH [*stamping*] Oh, bother! Always at the wrong moment. Always spoiling everything. [*She turns impatiently to the window, and stands with her back to them, fuming*].

AGNES [*to Alfred*] Thank God I found strength for this. It is a great relief to me. But I am dead tired: I must go home. [*To Edith*] Come, child.

JITTA. Wont you sit down and rest for a moment?

AGNES. Thank you; but I shall be better at home. And I have so many accounts to settle.

LENKHEIM. Ah, yes, yes: of course you have. Well, if you must go, you must. And you may depend on me not to keep you waiting too long before I go to work on the scientific papers.

JITTA. I hope to be allowed to go out again in a day or two. May I come to see you if the doctor says I may?

AGNES. Do, of course. I shall expect you. [*To Lenkheim*] You will forgive me, wont you, all the trouble I am giving you? It has done me so much good to unburden myself to a real friend.

LENKHEIM. You have had a cruel experience, dear Mrs Haldenstedt; but we must all resign ourselves to our trials.

AGNES. Yes: I suppose that is a great consolation.

EDITH. My consolation is that nobody dares console me.

ALFRED [*pompously*] Proud words; and how true! how true! [*Unctuously, as he shakes her hand*] Goodbye, dear lady, good-bye.

AGNES. Goodbye. [*To Edith, laughing a little maliciously*] Since you are so strong, child, just give me your arm.

JITTA [*shaking hands*] Goodbye.

Edith goes out with her mother leaning heavily on her. Jitta goes out with them.

LENKHEIM [*relieved at being rid of the widow*] Ouf! [*He carries the dispatch case to his writing-table, and sits down to examine its contents. He is in no hurry. It contains nothing but the manuscript of a biggish book. He leans lazily back with his legs stretched, and turns over the cover without looking at it. He reads a bit, and makes a wry face. He disagrees intensely and*

413

contemptuously with every passage he reads, abandoning each with sniffs and pishes, only to be still more disgusted with the next.

Jitta returns; sees what he is doing; and halts between him and the round table, silently watching him.

Finally he gives the book up as hopeless; shuts up the pages; and stares at the mass of manuscript as if wondering what he is to do with such trash. Suddenly his expression changes. His eyes bulge in amazement.

ALFRED [*after a stifled exclamation*] Jitta! Jitta! [*He turns, half rising, and sees her*]. Oh, youre there.

JITTA. What is the matter? [*knowing only too well, and very angry at his contemptuous air, but pretending to be listless and languid*].

LENKHEIM [*shewing her the manuscript*] Look at this!

JITTA. Well?

LENKHEIM. Look at the title.

JITTA [*reading*] "Fetters of the Feminine Psyche." Is that the book you worked on with him?

LENKHEIM. I! Certainly not: he wrote it all himself: I only gave him his facts. Read the next line.

JITTA [*reading*] "By Alfred Lenkheim." I suppose he meant you to finish it.

LENKHEIM [*turning over to the end*] But it is finished. Look. Was he mad? Did he suppose I would condescend to put my name to another man's work? I have some reputation of my own to fall back on, thank God. There is something behind this.

JITTA. I suppose he wished to leave you something valuable as a keepsake. You were his friend.

LENKHEIM [*scornfully*] A keepsake! Dont talk nonsense, Jitta: a man does not give away his biggest work as if it were his diamond pin, unless he is afraid to put his own name to it. But if he thinks he is going to put mine to his trash he is greatly mistaken.

JITTA [*boiling with rage, pointing to the manuscript*] He has sacrificed his immortality for your benefit.

414

LENKHEIM [*angrily*] Rot. Why should he? Nobody who can create sacrifices his creation. [*He throws the manuscript on the table*]. Not that he ever pretended to think much of the book.

JITTA [*indignantly*] He thought the world of it. It was his greatest pride.

LENKHEIM [*turning on her, a suspicion flashing on him*] How do you know?

JITTA [*checking herself, feeling that her temper has betrayed her*] He often spoke to me about this book, and about the hopes he had built on it.

LENKHEIM. To you! What do you know about psychiatry? Why should he sacrifice his reputation to add to mine? quite unnecessarily.

JITTA. The whim of an invalid, I suppose.

LENKHEIM [*out of patience*] Whim! He throws away his one chance of notoriety; and you call that a whim. Do you take me for a fool?

JITTA. Dont shout, Alfred, please.

ALFRED [*subsiding a little*] I'm not shouting: I'm asking you to talk sense. You say he spoke to you about this. What did he tell you?

JITTA. Of course I knew too little of the work you and he were doing together to be able to help or understand much. [*Decisively*] But in any case you must carry out his wishes.

LENKHEIM. What wishes?

JITTA. You must accept what he has left you.

LENKHEIM. Why must I?

JITTA. It was his last wish: we have no choice.

LENKHEIM. We! Me, you mean. What have you to do with it?

JITTA. Well, you if you like.

LENKHEIM. It's not me youre thinking of. Funny, the way women run after a dead man if only he dies romantically! Anyhow this thing is impossible. I wont do it.

JITTA. Why?

LENKHEIM. Because it would be nothing short of swind-

415

ling the scientific world to pass off his stuff on it as mine: thats why. And now, what the deuce am I to say to old Agnes? [*Grumbling*] Such an unreasonable thing to ask me to do! Such an ungrateful thing!

JITTA. Was it ungrateful to give you the whole credit when you were only his collaborator?

LENKHEIM. Collaborator! What are you talking about? He knew as well as I did that I was only waiting for the publication of his idiotic theory to tear it to pieces. You dont suppose I believe in it, do you?

JITTA. Then perhaps that was what he wanted to prevent.

LENKHEIM. Jitta: you are simply drivelling. Bruno was too jolly conceited to be afraid of me. Dont be childish.

JITTA [*irritably*] I am like yourself: I am only trying to guess why he did it.

LENKHEIM. Just so. Why did he do it? Where is the sense in it? I believe you know, Jitta.

JITTA. Really, Alfred—! I must go back to bed.

LENKHEIM. You havnt been up an hour.

JITTA. But I am dead tired.

LENKHEIM. You cant be as tired as all that. What do you want to run away for?

JITTA. Have you forgotten that I am ill? I can hardly stand. I must lie down.

ALFRED. Well, lie on the sofa.

JITTA. Dont be brutal, Alfred.

LENKHEIM. Bosh! You are hiding something from me: I havnt experimented with psycho-analysis for nothing. I notice that this crazy thing that bothers me doesnt bother you. You understand it: you couldnt take it so quietly if you didnt.

JITTA. I take it without shouting, if that is what you mean.

LENKHEIM. What did he say to you about the book and about his hopes? Why did you never say a word about them to me?

JITTA. I never thought about it.

LENKHEIM. If you had never thought about it you would have talked to me about it.

JITTA. I suppose I did not think it worth mentioning.

LENKHEIM. Psha! Would a man who told you all that not tell you plenty of other things? That love affair, now—?

JITTA [*shrinking*] Oh, Alfred!

LENKHEIM. Oh, stuff! Who was the woman? You know all about her: I can see it in your eyes. [*He takes her by the shoulders and turns her face to face*]. Aha! You know who she was. You know all about it.

JITTA [*rising indignantly and letting herself go*] You are mad, and grossly rude.

LENKHEIM [*rising also*] I have had enough of being humbugged. Who was she?

JITTA [*closes her lips obstinately*]!

LENKHEIM. Was he so much to you that you will not give the other woman away, even to me, your husband? Were those his orders?

JITTA [*exhausted*] I have no orders. I go my own way [*she attempts to leave the room*].

LENKHEIM [*intercepting her*] You shant run away. If you dont tell me who she is, I will—I will—[*he makes a threatening gesture, not very convincingly*].

JITTA. Take care, Alfred. Your cunning is only a fool's cunning after all. The answer to your question is staring you in the face. Thank your stars you are too stupid to see it.

LENKHEIM. Am I? We shall see. Before you leave this room I will find out the part you have played in this dirty business.

JITTA [*starting as from the lash of a whip*] Dirty! Oh, never was anything purer, holier, nobler.

LENKHEIM [*screaming*] Ah! It was you! There was no other woman: it was you, you. He bought you from me, for that [*he bangs his fist on the manuscript*]. The damned thief! [*He collapses into his chair at the table, clasping his head in his hands*].

JITTA [*sitting down wearily on the sofa*] Leave the dead in

417

peace. If you cannot hold your tongue, abuse me. I am alive, and can feel it.

LENKHEIM [*miserably*] You dont even deny it!

JITTA. No. Are you surprised? You lost me long ago.

LENKHEIM. My fault, of course. You worthless devil: what do you expect me to think of you?

JITTA. You can think what you like, Alfred. I dont grudge you that melancholy satisfaction.

LENKHEIM. Have you no conscience, no shame?

JITTA. Do you want me to make a scene for you, Alfred? I am sorry: I am too tired.

LENKHEIM. If I had him here—

JITTA. Threaten him to your heart's content. He is dead.

ALFRED. Yes; but I am very much alive. Dont forget that.

JITTA. Not so very much alive, Alfred.

ALFRED. Yah [*gnashes his teeth with rage*]!

JITTA. However, what I enjoyed I shall have to pay for. I know that.

LENKHEIM. You and he were lovers?

JITTA [*proudly*] Yes: you have found the right word at last. Lovers.

LENKHEIM [*whining pitiably*] And you could live in the house with me, and take my care and my nursing and my money, and even—[*He looks at her and chokes*]. How long has this affair been going on?

JITTA. Our love has lasted three years.

LENKHEIM. Love! Love in the sort of house he was found dead in!

JITTA. Love wherever we were. And wherever we were was paradise. Does that give you any idea of his greatness?

LENKHEIM. Of your meanness, more likely. Dont try to stuff me with big words: they only shew that you wont confess your caddishness even to yourself.

JITTA [*rising*] Oh, please! I cut a pretty contemptible figure—

LENKHEIM [*triumphing*] You do. You do.

JITTA [*continuing*]—beside him.

418

LENKHEIM [*rising, goaded beyond endurance: threatening her*] You take care, do you hear?

JITTA [*wringing her hands*] My place was at his side. They should have had to tear me away from him by force. Yes; and I will tell you something more. The last beat of his heart would have broken mine if I had been any good. But I am no good; and here I am, as you see me. Oh, you are quite right. I have no right to be in any decent house [*she turns to the door*].

LENKHEIM. Stop: where are you going?

JITTA. I dont know. Into the streets, I suppose.

LENKHEIM. Oh, damn your heroics! You shant leave this room until you have told me everything.

JITTA [*bitterly*] Dont you know enough already?

LENKHEIM [*pointing to the manuscript*] What does that title-page mean?

JITTA. You know. You have said what it means.

LENKHEIM. I want to know what he said.

JITTA. That you are to be the father to his orphaned book. That the fame it will bring you will make amends to you—for me.

LENKHEIM. The blackguard! Not content with stealing you from me, he must dictate the rest of my life to me, as if I were a child.

JITTA. Yes: compared to him you are a child. He has provided for you.

LENKHEIM. Ha! And were you equally kind and thoughtful for his wife, eh?

JITTA [*earnestly*] Alfred: it was too strong for us.

LENKHEIM. What was too strong for you?

JITTA. Love. You dont understand love. Have you anything else to say to me?

LENKHEIM. No. [*He turns his back on her, and goes sulkily to the window*].

JITTA. Goodbye. [*She tries to go, but suddenly becomes weak, and reels against the head of the sofa*]. Alfred.

LENKHEIM. Whats the matter? [*He runs to her; and gets*

419

her safely seated].

JITTA. Dont mind, Alfred. I shall be better soon: it is passing.

LENKHEIM [*turning brusquely from her like an angry child*] I am not sympathizing with you. It serves you right. [*He sits down at the round table, with his elbows on it, muttering and sulking*]. Treated me disgracefully. Disgracefully.

JITTA [*sighs wearily*]!!

LENKHEIM [*unaggressively*] Jitta?

Her name and the change in his tone give her a shock. She turns and looks searchingly at him.

LENKHEIM [*recovering his self-control by a rather broken effort*]. This is no use. I have come to my senses. I—I will take it quietly and reasonably.

JITTA. I am glad you can: I wish I could.

LENKHEIM [*shaking his head*] But we cant leave it like this, can we?

JITTA. What can we do, Alfred?

LENKHEIM. You have done me harm enough. Do you want to ruin me as well?

JITTA. It is I who am ruined, as you call it, is it not? The sin is mine: I will pay the penalty by myself. Your life is only beginning: with that book you have a future. I have only a past. I will take it and myself out of your life. [*She rises*].

LENKHEIM [*out of patience, jumping up*] Look here: since you wont talk sense and be commonly civil to me, I'm going to assert myself. You cant settle an affair like this by looking like a martyr and walking out into the street. You must learn to consider other people a little. If you have no regard for me, at least remember that Agnes and Edith have a future, and have a right not to have it spoiled. For their sake I am prepared to endure your presence in my house.

JITTA [*with faint surprise and some irony*] You can bring yourself to that? You can still bear to look at me?

LENKHEIM. Make no mistake: all is over between you and me. For ever. I mean it.

JITTA. So do I.

LENKHEIM. Very well: be it so. But that does not mean that we need separate. People can live miles apart under the same roof. That is how you will have to live with me. If you have a spark of decent feeling left, you will not force a public scandal on me.

JITTA. Does it matter?

LENKHEIM. Does it matter! Are you utterly selfish? Dont you understand that if this miserable break-up of our marriage becomes known it will break up that poor woman's widowhood as well?

JITTA. Does she matter so much?

LENKHEIM [*playing his ace*] Well, what about Edith? Doesnt she matter? Do you suppose Fessler can afford to marry her if you drag her family through the mud?

JITTA [*staggered*] Oh! I was not thinking, Alfred. Give me until tomorrow to think it over. I can bear no more today. I can hardly stand.

LENKHEIM. You can stand as well as I can. [*She immediately sits down obstinately at the writing-table*]. Very well; but stand or sit, you dont leave this room until you give me your word to stay.

JITTA. With you?

LENKHEIM. Yes, with me. It is I who will have to pay the housekeeping bills. But dont be afraid: I am done with you, except before company. Not one word will I ever speak to you again when we are alone together.

JITTA. Oh, Alfred, you will tell me so ten times a day. Dont let us talk nonsense.

LENKHEIM. You will see. Not one word. Not a sound. I tell you I am done with you; and I wish I had never met you.

JITTA. It sounds too good to be true, Alfred.

LENKHEIM. Psha!

JITTA. But that part of it rests with yourself. [*Determinedly*] And now for my conditions.

LENKHEIM. Your conditions! Yours!!! You dare talk to me of conditions!

JITTA. You are in my hands, Alfred; and you know it. I

can give the whole scandal away if you defy me. I will not be unkind; but if I am to keep up appearances, you must keep them up too. If I am to pretend to be a good woman, you must pretend to be a great man.

LENKHEIM. Pretend!

JITTA. Oh, be a great man by all means, Alfred, if you can. But you must pretend in any case.

LENKHEIM. How?

JITTA. You will pretend to be the author of that great book. That will be your share of the sham of our life together.

LENKHEIM. But I tell you I dont believe a word of the silly thing.

JITTA. Of course not. If you had the genius to believe it, you would have had the genius to write it.

LENKHEIM [*goaded*] I—

JITTA [*continuing calmly*] You cannot believe it, just as I cannot believe that you will never speak to me again;—

LENKHEIM. I never will.

JITTA [*still ignoring his protests*] —but you will come to believe every word of the silly thing, as you call it, when it makes Lenkheim as famous as Einstein.

LENKHEIM [*startled by the name*] Einstein! You are tempting me, you devil.

JITTA. You envied Einstein, Alfred. Well, all that you envied him for is within your reach. Stretch out your hand, and take it.

LENKHEIM. And you envied Einstein's wife, did you? I see. Why could not your stupid husband give you a triumphant tour through Europe? Why should you not shake hands with all the kings, and dine with all the presidents, and have gala nights at the Opera? To get all that you will be my accomplice in a fraud, eh? Since you cannot have a good time with him you will have one with me.

JITTA [*round-eyed for a moment at this new light on her conduct*] How clever of you, Alfred! You have found a reason you can really believe in. I should never have thought of it; but you are welcome to it if only you will father his book.

LENKHEIM [*desperately perplexed: yielding*] But, Jitta: I dont really believe that. It's not like you: you are not clever enough, not ambitious enough. What is your real reason?

JITTA [*decisively*] He wished it: that is enough for me. He knew better than either of us what is best for us.

LENKHEIM. Did he indeed, confound him!

JITTA. He did indeed, Alfred; and I forbid you to confound him.

LENKHEIM. Well, if I do—and mind: I dont say I will—I—

JITTA. Yes?

LENKHEIM. I will think it over.

JITTA. Just so, Alfred. Goodnight. [*She goes out, tranquilly convinced that she will have her own way*].

LENKHEIM [*rushing to the door in a last effort to assert himself, and shouting after her*] If you think— [*He peters out; thrusts his hands desperately into his pockets like a cleaned-out gambler; trots back irresolutely to his writing-table; takes up the MS.; stares at it for a moment; and reads slowly*] "By Professor Alfred Lenkheim, Doctor of Philosophy in the University of Vienna." Well, I'm dashed!

ACT III

MRS HALDENSTEDT *is in her sitting-room with Alfred and Fessler, all three very busy going through the papers of her late husband. She is feverishly reading letters, and tearing them up and throwing them into the waste-paper basket as they prove one after another to be of no interest. Her sighs and exclamations of disappointment and impatience are getting on the nerves of Alfred, who is trying to read a manuscript. He flinches at the sharp sounds made by her violent tearing of the letters. Fessler, who is sorting some papers which he has already gone through, is sympathetic, and looks pityingly at the widow from time to time.*

The room is lighted by a large bay window, with a window-seat under it. The table heaped with papers is in this bay; and Mrs Haldenstedt sits at the head of it with her back to the light, and Alfred and Fessler at the sides of it to her right and left respectively. The corner of the room behind them on their right is cut off by a double door leading to the study. Another door leading to the corridor of the flat is in the diagonally opposite corner, and is consequently before them on their left. On their right between the window and the study door, a console stands against the wall, with flowers on it, and above it a convex mirror. On the same side of the room, a couch.

LENKHEIM [*unable to bear the noise any longer*] Do you mind my taking these manuscripts into the study and examining them there? They require a certain degree of quiet concentration.

AGNES. I am so sorry. Bruno always said that it was like trying to work in a shooting gallery when I cleared up his papers and tore up useless letters. But if you dont tear them what is there to prevent the servants and everyone else from reading them?

ALFRED. Just so. But why not leave the work to us? Why worry? Cant you trust us?

AGNES. Oh, Professor, how can you ask me that? Of course I can trust you.

LENKHEIM [*nodding*] Good. Then do trust us. [*He goes*

424

into the study, and shuts the door behind him].

AGNES [*alone with Fessler, letting herself droop*] I have gone through this last batch of letters three times over in the hope of finding some clue. But it's no use: theres nothing.

FESSLER. You mustnt worry.

AGNES [*sitting up sharply*] Have you ever lost anyone you really cared for?

FESSLER. Well, my poor dear father!

AGNES. I'm not talking about poor dear fathers or poor dear anybodies. Bruno was none of your poor dears: he was three quarters of my life, even if half of it was being his slave and his household drudge. All the same, I cant spend my whole life doing nothing but grieving, can I?

FESSLER. Just so. Of course not.

AGNES. Life goes on, doesnt it? Housekeeping goes on: the future has to be thought for as well as the past. All my business and responsibilities and duties go on just as if nothing had happened.

FESSLER. I'm so glad you have recovered enough to be able to look at it in that way.

AGNES. Doctor Fessler: a widow is not an invalid; and it doesnt help her to be treated as one when the first shock is over.

FESSLER. Quite so. Quite so.

AGNES. I am going to talk to you very seriously.

FESSLER. Of course. Of course.

AGNES. And you are going to talk to me seriously, I hope.

FESSLER [*surprised*] But certainly, my dear Mrs Haldenstedt.

AGNES. Yes; but that doesnt mean saying "Certainly" and "Of course" and "Quite so: quite so" to everything I say, as if you were soothing a baby.

FESSLER [*protesting*] But I assure you I—

AGNES [*gripping his hand on the table*] Tell me the honest truth. Did you consider Bruno a clever man?

FESSLER [*amazed*] Mrs Haldenstedt!!!

AGNES. Do you think he had anything to say more than

425

any of the rest of the professors? [*Stopping him as he opens his mouth for a fresh protest*] Now if you dont, please dont begin to excuse yourself and spare my feelings. Ive had enough of having my feelings spared: I want the truth.

FESSLER [*whole-heartedly*] My dear Mrs Haldenstedt: he was a g r e a t man. His psychological doctrine was a revelation. It was the beginning of a new epoch in science.

AGNES. So I have always understood. I know he thought so himself.

FESSLER [*indignant*] Oh no: he was the most modest of men. I am sure he never said so.

AGNES. Do you think a man's wife knows nothing about his thoughts except what he tells?

FESSLER. I am quite sure he did not know half his own greatness.

AGNES. Then will you tell me what has become of it all? You and Professor Lenkheim have gone through his papers with me. Have we come across one word that could not have been written by an elementary schoolmaster?

FESSLER [*shaken a little*] Well, everything he wrote, even about trifles, has his peculiar touch.

AGNES. Everything he wrote is in his own handwriting, of course, if you mean that. But can you pick out from all that heap one single bit of paper which you could shew to a stranger and expect him to say "The man that wrote this must have been as great as Einstein"?

FESSLER. Well, not exactly Einstein, perhaps. But— [*he stops*].

AGNES. But what? Suppose he had left you a safe full of diamonds, and when you opened the safe it was empty!

FESSLER. Oh, you exaggerate!

AGNES [*rising, out of patience*] Doctor Fessler: if you can take neither me nor my husband's affairs seriously, I think you had better leave both alone.

FESSLER [*rising, greatly surprised*] Have I offended you?

AGNES [*disarmed by his naïve sincerity*] No, no. Never mind. Never mind. You are too young. You are not used to

women. [*Sitting down again*] Sit down, wont you? I will talk
to Professor Lenkheim about it. He will understand.

FESSLER [*standing stiffly, being now really offended*] By all
means, Mrs Haldenstedt, though I really do not see what
he can say more than I can.

AGNES. There! You are offended. But if you had been
neglected as I have been for months past, while my husband
spent hours and hours and hours in his study, writing, writing, writing, using up paper until it cost as much as the
butter and eggs, you would want to know what had become
of it all.

FESSLER [*sitting down again with a gesture of apology*] True.
I should have thought of that.

AGNES. I never complained, because I thought it was a
book that would make him famous and bring him in money.
Well, is that heap of old letters and bills and prescriptions
all that came of it? Dont tell me: there is a book somewhere;
and I want to know where it is. Did he go mad and destroy
it? If not, who took it from him? Did that woman?

FESSLER. Good gracious, Mrs Haldenstedt!

AGNES. Oh, this dreadful ending to all our happiness! It
spoils everything that was nice in our lives. When the first
and best of it was over and we settled down, troubles came
I know; but I had my memories, and could sit and think of
them. Now they are all poisoned for me.

FESSLER [*reflectively*] Dear Mrs Haldenstedt: may I speak
quite frankly to you?

AGNES. Why, I am begging and praying you to. But I
can get nothing out of you but sympathy, as if you were only
a visitor instead of going to marry my daughter.

FESSLER. You see, though your husband will be remembered as a great psychologist, he had to practise as a doctor
to make a living. Well, the wickedest and worst people have
to call in doctors just as often as respectable people; and a
doctor cant have them coming to his own house where his
wife and daughter are. He has to keep a consulting room
somewhere where they can come. The landlady said he

427

rented the room to see his friends in occasionally. I daresay the women he saw there were common women; but how do you know that they were not his patients?

AGNES. Dont deceive yourself; and dont try to deceive me. Whatever I may have said when I was upset, I knew very well all along that Bruno never went with common women from the streets. The landlady said it was always the same woman, and that she was a lady. When she ran away she took that book with her: you mark my words. [*She rises and goes moodily to the console*].

They are interrupted by Lenkheim, who opens the door of the study and trots in flourishing a manuscript.

LENKHEIM. See here!

AGNES. The book!

LENKHEIM. I have just found an unfinished lecture on varieties of sleep.

AGNES [*disappointed*] Only a lecture! [*Taking the manuscript*] Why, it's only six pages. And what can it mean? There is only one sort of sleep.

LENKHEIM. Not at all. He says that hardly any two people sleep in the same way. Every case is an individual one. You must read it, Fessler.

FESSLER [*eagerly*] How interesting! May I look? [*Taking it from Mrs Haldenstedt*] Thank you. I'll read it in the study. [*To Alfred*] Mrs Haldenstedt wants to speak to you. [*He hurries into the study*].

AGNES [*shaking her head*] You see, Professor, it doesnt account for anything.

LENKHEIM. What doesnt?

AGNES. The lecture about sleep. He could have written it in one evening. Thats not the book that he said might be my best insurance policy. It was part of his provision for me. He would never have given it to another woman. If she has it, she stole it. [*She sits down on the couch*].

LENKHEIM. You are still worrying about that woman. I shouldnt if I were you. [*He takes his former chair, drawing it from the table to the couch*].

AGNES. I shall worry about her until I find out who she is. And I will find her out some day.

LENKHEIM. If it is any comfort to you, you may take my word for it that with all his professional engagements it was utterly impossible for him to have given much of his time to any woman.

AGNES. What comfort is there in that? One hour is enough for a man. Then he can sit alone at his desk, thinking he is writing some great scientific work, when all the time he is thinking of her, living the hour over again, and looking forward to the next one, right in his wife's face.

LENKHEIM [*very uncomfortable*] Mrs Haldenstedt: do you suspect anybody?

AGNES. I cant see anything clearly. I thought I knew everybody that it could possibly be; but there's nobody. All I know is what he liked and what he wanted, and how easily he could get it by lifting up his little finger. Oh, I know exactly how he deceived us.

LENKHEIM [*rising, startled*] Us!

AGNES. Well, me and Edith, of course.

LENKHEIM [*sitting down, relieved*] Oh! Just so.

AGNES. She wasnt what you think she was, Professor: she was one of us. And I say that when a man has a wife and children and a home and a good position, he should think twice before asking any respectable woman to meet him in such a room in such a house. It was fit neither for him nor for her.

LENKHEIM [*drawing a little closer to her*] Dear lady: may I ask you a very indiscreet question? I shall not be in the least offended if you refuse to answer it.

AGNES. What is it?

LENKHEIM. Was your marriage a happy one?

AGNES. I always thought it was, at least until the last few years. Then there was a sudden change. Up to that time he was full of interest in his home, in Edith's education, in our plans, our money, the chance of our being able to move into a better house, the furniture and pictures, in everything.

429

Then he seemed to get beyond us somehow.

LENKHEIM. What were the symptoms?

AGNES. Well, he was sometimes very irritable, though he used to be a perfect lamb. I thought it was only his health; for of course neither of us was growing younger. I know better now. Oh, what a fool I was! But that is how things happen. They go on from year to year under your very nose, staring you in the face; and you never notice, never think, because your mind is off the track. And then suddenly your eyes are opened with a bang; and you could kill yourself for having been so blind. If I could only find out who she was! [*She rises restlessly*].

LENKHEIM. Mrs Haldenstedt: take my advice: give it up. What is the use of tormenting yourself? You will have no peace until you put that woman out of your head.

AGNES. I dont want peace. I want to find her out.

LENKHEIM [*rising*] But suppose you do find her. What then? Think of the scandal. Believe me, it's better not to know. You could not hurt her without hurting yourself and Edith worse.

AGNES. I dont want to make a scandal; and I dont want to hurt her: I want to find out from her what sort of life Bruno was really leading, and what has become of all that work he did.

LENKHEIM. But the lecture on varieties of sleep—

AGNES. Stuff! I know the variety of sleep he learnt from her. [*Looking at him queerly*] Why do you want to prevent me from finding her out?

LENKHEIM [*meeting her eye with imposing firmness*] Solely for your own sake, Mrs Haldenstedt. How could it possibly affect me? Banish this abandoned female from your mind; and trust to Time. Time is the great healer. Time will restore your happiness.

AGNES. Well, Time works wonders, they say. But it will never comfort me until I know for certain that the happiness he had with me was the right sort of happiness, and the happiness he had with the other woman the wrong sort. How do I know that she wasnt a cleverer woman than I am? I dont care that [*snapping her fingers*] how young she is, or how pretty she is: Time will bring her to my level in those ways soon enough. But I'm not clever at the things he was clever at. I dont understand science nor care about it. If I have to keep the house spick and span I cant always keep myself spick and span; and I know he was particular about such things. Thats where she might have cut me out. She might easily have persuaded him that she was the right woman for him, and that I was the wrong one.

LENKHEIM. No, no. You were an excellent wife to him, Mrs Haldenstedt; and he knew it.

AGNES. I dont say I wasnt. But she hadnt to keep the house for him. She had nothing to do but please him. And if she was clever into the bargain, what chance had I?

Edith comes in from the corridor.

EDITH. Good morning, Professor.

LENKHEIM [*relieved by the interruption*] Good morning. Will you excuse me, Mrs Haldenstedt: I have a few words to say to Fessler before Jitta comes.

AGNES. You have been so good. I will think over your advice: indeed I will.

LENKHEIM [*encouragingly*] Do. [*He waves his hand to Edith, and goes into the study, leaving the mother and daughter alone together*].

AGNES [*looking after him bitterly as she goes back to her place at the table*] It's easy for him to talk.

EDITH [*wandering about restlessly between the table and the console*] Why do you listen to him? Why do you run to strangers when you want to talk about father? Why should our being mother and daughter keep us so far apart?

AGNES. What a thing to say, child.

EDITH [*going to her*] Of course if you dont want me, mother, I dont want to force myself on you.

AGNES [*dutifully, without real feeling*] Well, of course, darling, I want you.

EDITH [*irritated*] No, not of course, not in the way

431

you think. Has it occurred to you that it is rather hard on me to be left entirely to myself when things are so serious with us?

AGNES. I dont know what you have to complain of. You used to trust me to know what was right for you, and now you have suddenly turned on me. Surely, child, nobody can be a better judge of what is best for you than your own mother. Here I am, worried to death almost; and you making it worse for me by setting yourself against me.

EDITH. I am not setting myself against you, mother. What I am setting myself against is being expected to go through life blindfold, or pretending to be blindfold. I am to be a good little child, and not know anything nor feel anything that little children ought not to know and feel, just when I, as a woman, most want the companionship of another woman to whom I can pour out my feelings and my sorrow on equal terms.

AGNES. I cant understand you, child; and I wont have you talking to me like that.

EDITH. I often wonder whether you have ever understood anybody. Perhaps you did not understand father.

AGNES. You dare—

EDITH [continuing impetuously] Oh, I know very well how tidy you kept his house for him, just as I keep my room. You did your duty: nobody can blame you. But was his house a home for him, as his heart made it a home for me?

AGNES. You are simply silly, child. Your grief and your crazy love for your father have turned your head. I wonder what you would say if you really knew.

EDITH [scornfully] If I really knew! Do you suppose any girl of my age nowadays does not know more than you were ever taught?

AGNES [shrieking] What?

EDITH. I know, as well as you do, where my father died, and how he died.

Mrs Haldenstedt covers her eyes in horror. Fessler, opening the study door, appears on the threshold.

JITTA'S ATONEMENT

AGNES. Oh, how dreadful! This will kill me. [*To Edith, rising*] Oh, now I know what you are. Just as bad as your father! Just as bad as your father!

FESSLER. What on earth is the matter?

AGNES. Dont ask me. Oh, this is beyond everything. Let me go [*she rushes from the room*].

FESSLER. What have you done?

EDITH [*cooly*] Told her I knew. I had to.

FESSLER [*closing the door, and coming softly to Edith*] My dear: you have dragged the poor woman down from her little heaven.

EDITH. My father's wife might have had a heaven on earth; but that poor woman, as you call her, did not know even how to begin.

FESSLER. Your grief is carrying you too far. Try not to be unjust to her.

EDITH. I am not unjust. It is my father who needs justice.

FESSLER. It is not much use, is it, giving justice to the dead and withholding it from the living?

EDITH. You need not lecture me: I am on my guard.

FESSLER. Against what?

EDITH. Against sharing my father's fate.

FESSLER [*terrified*] Dying!

EDITH. No. Living in utter loneliness.

FESSLER. Oh, that! How you frightened me! But you know, dear, you mustnt worry too much about your father. It's a sort of hypochondria; and it may make you really ill.

EDITH [*scornfully*] Yes, I know. What cant be cured must be endured; so let us get away from this unfortunate affair and fall back into the current of everyday life. That is what you want me to do. But I cannot do it. He was everything to me: I cannot describe what I feel: it is as if I were a branch broken off from him, a limb torn out of him, as if I were bleeding to death of the wound that killed him. As I see him now he is quite different from what he seemed to me when he was alive, and much greater. I think of him imprisoned in these walls, longing for his proper happiness, and then

433

finding too late the woman who was his real destiny.

FESSLER. Ah yes: destiny! destiny! He had to fulfil his destiny, I suppose.

EDITH. He did not fulfil it. Life fulfils destiny, not death.

FESSLER [*prosaically*] Well, you know, death is a sort of destiny as well. If you are right, and he really was lonely here owing to your mother being incompatible and all that, then I quite agree it was a mercy he hit on somebody who could understand him and comfort him. Still, you must be careful not to idealize a person you dont know. You see, everybody is an ideal person to us until we meet them; and then, undoubtedly, some of the gilt comes off the gingerbread. I am so desperately afraid that if you find her out, she will prove a horrible disappointment to you.

EDITH. Never fear. I know my father too well. [*Turning fiercely on him*] But that you can think so little of him as to believe what other people are whispering about him: yes, and about her: you! who have worked with him and had all his confidence! that digs a gulf between us.

FESSLER. Oh dont say that. You cant mean it, Edith. I love you. I have the truest respect for your father.

EDITH. Then how can you belittle him so?

FESSLER. My dear, I am a man; and I know more about men's ways than you do. A man is a very mixed sort of animal. Ask any experienced man, and he will tell you that there is a certain side to human nature that must just be ruled out in judging people's characters. Even the best men are subject to aberrations, or at least commonnesses, in their relations with women, just as they will eat rotten cheese, and half-putrid partridges that are really only fit for pigs.

EDITH. You are not making it any better by saying such disgusting things.

FESSLER. Yes: but you want the truth, dont you? You know very well that Goethe was a great man; but the fine ladies of Weimar were shocked by his marriage. Rousseau was a great man; but his Teresa married a groom after his death.

EDITH. My father was a gentleman. He was worlds above Rousseau in refinement, and even above Goethe.

FESSLER. Well, I could say something more; but I suppose I mustnt.

EDITH. What more can you say? Is it something more against my father?

FESSLER. Not exactly against him; but still—

EDITH. Well, still?

FESSLER. He married your mother.

EDITH [*staggered*] Oh! How mean of you to throw that in his face! Why do you not point out what is so clear to any unprejudiced mind, that a man who made a mistake like that once would be the last person in the world to make the same mistake again?

FESSLER [*with placid obstinacy*] Because I am sorry to say, my dear, that men's lives consist mostly of their making the same mistake over and over again. I see a lot of that as a doctor. Look at your mother: she knows that if she eats prawns and cucumbers she will have a wretched night; but she never can resist them. I knew a man who was married three times; and every one of his wives drank.

EDITH. The more you say, the more I see that we shall never understand one another, and that you will never feel about my father as I do. I could not have believed you could be so coarse. Nobody in this house understands me, neither my mother nor you nor anybody.

FESSLER. But if you want people to understand you, you must be reasonable. I often used to have to say that to your father. You take after him, you know.

EDITH. If I do I must take care not to make the mistake in marrying that he made. Doctor Fessler: I am sorry; but I cannot be your wife.

FESSLER. I dont mind that so much for the present if only you wont call me Doctor Fessler. It's ridiculous. You dont expect me to call you Miss Haldenstedt, do you?

EDITH. Yes I do.

FESSLER. Then I wont. You see, I dont know how long

435

this mood of yours will last.

EDITH. Life is short: dont waste any more of yours on me. I shall not go back from what I have said.

FESSLER. Neither shall I. I can wait.

EDITH. I cannot prevent your waiting. Everybody seems to think they know my own mind better than I do myself. I can only tell you one thing. I have one object in life now, and one only.

FESSLER. And what is that, if I may ask?

EDITH. To find the woman who made my father happy, and to force you to confess that she is high heavens above your Goethe's Christiane, and your Rousseau's Teresa, and—you neednt remind me—above my own mother.

FESSLER. Well, I hope you may, darling. Does that please you?

Jitta comes in from the corridor. Fessler pulls himself together into his best professional bedside manner. Edith rushes to Jitta and embraces her.

EDITH. Oh, how good of you to come! How glad I am to see you!

JITTA. Is your mother at home?

EDITH. Yes: do you want her? I will send her [*she runs out*].

JITTA [*coming to Fessler in the middle of the room*] What is the matter with the child?

FESSLER. She is still fearfully upset. She is having a hard fight of it here.

JITTA [*looking at him with quick sympathy*] You are not looking very happy yourself, Doctor.

FESSLER. She has broken it off [*he narrowly misses a sob*].

JITTA. Oh, that mustnt be. Why, it was for your sake that I opened her eyes a little about her father.

FESSLER. I am afraid it had rather the opposite effect.

JITTA. I hope not. Tell me: does my husband know of this new turn?

FESSLER. Not yet. Perhaps you had better tell him. I dont know that I can go on working here every day if Edith sticks

436

to it.

JITTA. Don't give in too soon, Doctor.

FESSLER. I am pretending not to—to her. But I am really afraid she may be in earnest.

JITTA. Is there nothing I can do?

FESSLER. It's very good of you, Mrs Lenkheim. But I must see this thing through myself, thank you. And now I must be off. [*He goes past her towards the door*].

JITTA [*shaking his hand*] Goodbye, Doctor. Dont despise my help.

FESSLER. Oh no, Mrs Lenkheim; but—

Mrs Haldenstedt comes in.

AGNES [*still distracted*] Oh, what is this that Edith tells me, Doctor?

FESSLER. We wont discuss it now, Mrs Haldenstedt. You had better talk it over with Mrs Lenkheim. Goodbye. Goodbye, Mrs Lenkheim. [*He bows to them and goes out*].

AGNES. Sit down, wont you? [*Jitta sits on the couch. Agnes sits down woefully beside her*]. He's gone; and Heaven knows whether he will ever come back. This is a marked house: everybody deserts it. Who knows how soon I shall be left alone here to haunt the place like my own shadow? I shall sit alone, going over and over that dreadful time in my imagination, with no relief but just thinking how I can catch that wretch that stole from me my right to be beside my husband when he died.

JITTA. She did not intend that. You may forgive her that, at least.

AGNES. Oh, you mustnt think it's mere spite and revenge. It's that I really loved Bruno to the last as I loved him from the first. He was all I had that I cared about. I am not like a man, to begin all over again with a new love: I shall never get away from it or get over it. Day by day all those years we lived together; sat at the same table; took it in turns to rock the cradle or take the child in our hands to pet it; and then he goes off to another woman without a word or a thought for me. [*Crying*] I didnt deserve it: I didnt indeed.

JITTA. There, dear, there! Dont torture yourself. After all, if he had died in your arms, you would still have had to grieve for him. It might even have broken your heart.

AGNES. Oh, if only it had! I could think of him then without bitterness and shame.

JITTA. Try to forgive him for the sake of the old days when you were young together. What does it matter what foolish things we old people do?

AGNES. I cant forgive him. Not while I am in the dark about her. Listen to me, Mrs Lenkheim. If I thought it was only her body that took him, I wouldnt care a straw. I have had thoughts myself about our young men at the college sports: only fancies of course; and I wouldnt have indulged them for the world; but a man might. What I cant bear is the thought that she might have been somebody like you.

JITTA [*startled*] Like me!

AGNES. Yes; for he thought a great deal of you; and if you had been that sort of woman, I might have been jealous of you. You are clever in his way; and you could understand him when he was talking right above my head. You could talk about his work to him. I couldnt.

JITTA. Oh no, Mrs Haldenstedt: I knew better than that. Nothing annoys a man more than a woman who talks to him about his business and pretends to understand it. Do you know what Bruno always talked to me about? what it always came round to, no matter what subject he started with?

AGNES. What?

JITTA. You.

AGNES. Me!

JITTA. Yes, you, you, you, you. Do you know, I sometimes wanted to shake him for not taking a little more interest in me occasionally? His conscience was never easy about you. You had done everything for him; and he had taken it all and gone on with his scientific work: the work that did not pay, when he might have been making a fashionable practice for himself and leaving you comfortably off.

AGNES [*beginning to cry*] But I never grudged it to him. I

438

wanted him to be great. I wasnt really as good a wife as I might have been. I worried him about things that he neednt have known anything about. It's in my nature: I cant help it.

JITTA. It was not in his nature to blame you for that. He understood. He was frightfully faithful to you. You possessed all his thoughts: you dominated his destiny: you haunted him. What right had you to take a great man like that all to yourself? I wanted a little bit of Bruno; but you stood always in the way. Marriage is a very wonderful thing. It held him as nothing else could hold him.

AGNES. But the other woman?

JITTA. Oh, the other woman! Need you make such a fuss about her? You dont even know whether she was not a patient who had to conceal the fact that she was consulting a doctor. There are such people, you know. But suppose she was what you think! Would a woman who had any serious relations with him have coolly walked off and left him to die? A pet dog would not have done such a thing. They would have found it at his side.

AGNES [*excitedly*] You think then that though he forgot what was due to himself, he didnt forget what was due to me? that when he went into that disgraceful place with another woman he was only making a convenience of her? that it was a mere chance that she was there to close his eyes, like a chambermaid in a hotel?

JITTA. She did not close his eyes. She stole away from his side after coldbloodedly covering up her tracks. Could you have done that?

AGNES. I never thought of that. Of course: of course. Yes: that shewed what she was, didnt it?

JITTA. What does it matter what she was? She came out of the dark, and went back into the dark. Leave her there, as she left him.

AGNES [*shaking her head*] I cant imagine how women can bring themselves to behave so. What sort of women must they be? She must have known that he could never have cared for her.

439

JITTA. You dont know how she got him there. But I know that if he really opened his heart to her, he talked to her about you.

AGNES [*smiling*] Well, I am sure, Mrs Lenkheim, this talk has made the most wonderful difference to me. You dont know how much good you have done me. It only shews how little we can trust our own feelings and our own judgment when such troubles come to us. The weight you have taken off my mind! you cant imagine.

JITTA. Have I? Then I have done what I came to do. [*She rises*].

AGNES [*holding her*] Oh, dont go yet. You know, it's very funny how one's mind works.

JITTA [*sitting down again*] How?

AGNES [*slowly and almost roguishly*] I'm so grateful to you, that I'm afraid of offending you if I tell you. But I am sure you will only laugh.

JITTA [*with a melancholy smile*] We both need a good laugh, dont we?

AGNES. Have you ever found that you have been all along thinking something that never came into your head for a single moment?

JITTA. That sounds a little difficult. I am afraid I dont quite follow.

AGNES. Of course you dont: it's too silly. But do you know that the moment you took that weight off my mind, and gave me back my peace and happiness—

JITTA [*murmurs*] I am so glad that I did.

AGNES [*nodding gratefully, and continuing*] Well, that very moment I knew that I had been believing all along—but I dont think I ought to say it; only it's so funny.

JITTA. What?

AGNES. Why, that YOU were the woman. [*She begins to chuckle*].

JITTA. No!!!

AGNES. Yes I did.

JITTA. But really?

AGNES. Really and truly.

JITTA [*beginning to laugh hysterically*] How funny!

AGNES [*her chuckles now culminating in hearty laughter*] Isnt it? Youre not angry, are you? Oh dear—[*laughing more than ever*].

JITTA. Oh no: of course not.

Jitta has a paroxysm of agonizing laughter; and Agnes accompanies her without a suspicion that she is not enjoying the joke in good faith. Jitta at last recovers her self-control with a desperate effort.

JITTA. Dont make me laugh any more: I am afraid I shall go into hysterics. I am still very far from well.

AGNES. It's such a shame to laugh at all at such a time. But for the life of me I couldnt help it.

JITTA [*looking hard at her*] You know, Mrs Haldenstedt, I was very v e r y fond of him.

AGNES. I am sure you were, darling; and I shouldnt have minded a bit if it had been you: in fact I'm half disappointed that it wasnt, you have been such an angel to me. Isnt it funny, the things that come into our heads? But it's wicked of me to make you talk and laugh so much, and you so ill. Youre very pale, dear. Can I get you anything?

JITTA. If I might just lie down here for awhile. I—

AGNES [*rising to make room for Jitta to recline*] Yes, yes: of course you shall, dear. Make yourself comfortable.

JITTA. I dont want to go without seeing Edith.

AGNES [*taken aback*] Oh!

JITTA. What is it?

AGNES. I forgot all about Edith. Who is to tell her? She sees her father like a saint in a picture; and I could never put it to her in the wonderful way you put it to me. If only you would be so good as to tell her for me. Would you mind?

JITTA. Not in the least. Edith is like a child of my own to me: it would be the greatest happiness to me if I could set her mind at rest as you are good enough to think I have set yours.

AGNES. You have: indeed and indeed you have. I am sure

what we owe you, with your dear husband coming here every day to set the papers in order, and you being more than an angel to me in spite of your illness, words can never say. Just lie quiet where you are; and I will send Edith to you. Oh, you h a v e made me happy, dear! [*She goes out into the corridor*].

Jitta, left alone, begins to laugh again hysterically, and is dissolving into convulsive sobs when she makes a great effort; springs up from the sofa; dashes the tears from her eyes with a proud gesture; goes to the glass; and has just made herself presentable when Edith appears. Her eyes are wide open and her expression one of joyful surprise and relief. She runs eagerly to Jitta.

EDITH. What on earth have you done to mother? She is laughing. She is positively singing. Either you are a witch, or she has gone mad.

JITTA. Are you angry with her for daring to sing in this house of mourning? Or angry with me for making her sing?

EDITH. Oh no: it's rather a relief. But it's very odd. How did you do it?

JITTA. She made me laugh before I made her sing. You mustnt be shocked, dear. There is always a sort of reaction: Nature must have a relief from any feeling, no matter how deep and sincere it is. Have you ever seen a soldier's funeral?

EDITH. No. Why?

JITTA. They play the Dead March as they go to the grave; but they play the merriest tunes they know on their way back.

EDITH. How unfeeling!

JITTA. Yes; but how natural! Your mother would have gone mad if she had gone on as she was for another week. I am not sure that I should not have gone mad myself if she had not made me laugh. [*Taking Edith by the shoulders and looking straight at her*] And now what I want to know is how I am to make y o u laugh. For y o u will go mad if you do not get back into everyday life again.

EDITH [*backing to the table, and half sitting against its edge*]

442

Yes: I know. This house has been a sort of madhouse since my father died. We havnt spoken naturally, nor walked naturally, nor breathed naturally, nor thought naturally, because we were all so determined to feel naturally. Somehow, my mother's laughing and singing has made nonsense of it all suddenly.

JITTA. Then you are happy again? If so, I may as well go home.

EDITH. Happy! Oh no. But I am done with hypocrisy and conventionality; and that is such a relief that I seem happy by contrast. I suppose it is a sort of happiness to be able to give myself up at last wholly to my sorrow.

JITTA [*sitting down in Lenkheim's chair*] Which sorrow? The old sorrow that God made for you, or the new one that you have made for yourself?

EDITH [*straightening up*] I dont know what you mean.

JITTA. Doctor Fessler says you have jilted him.

EDITH. Did he call it jilting him?

JITTA. No. I call it that.

EDITH. But you cant think that. Do you know what he said?

JITTA. No. Anything very dreadful?

EDITH. He believes that my father died in the arms of a common woman of the streets.

JITTA. And he thinks your father must have been as worthless as the woman he died with. I see.

EDITH. Not at all. That is what is so dreadful. He thinks it makes no difference. He adores my father as much as he ever did; but he thinks you have to leave all that out when you are judging men. He thinks a woman doesnt matter. I cant forgive him for that. I couldnt marry a man unless he felt exactly as I do about my father.

JITTA. Is that reasonable, dear? How could poor Doctor Fessler feel as you feel? you! your father's daughter!

EDITH. Oh, of course I know that. I dont expect him to feel the same affection. But if he thought my father could go with low women—if he did not know for certain, as I

443

know, that the woman my father loved must have been one of the best and noblest of women, I would rather die than let him touch me.

JITTA. My dear: how can he know for certain? You do not know for certain yourself.

EDITH. I know I cant prove it. But I am certain. And I will devote my life to proving it.

JITTA. How?

EDITH. I will find the woman: that is how. I have thought and thought about it. I know that she cannot be very far off. I know that her grief and desolation must be as great as mine: greater. I know she will love me because I am his daughter. And I know that she will be somebody worthy of him.

JITTA. Edith, Edith, how sentimental you are!

EDITH [*fiercely*] You call my feeling sentimentality! Are you going to disappoint me too?

JITTA [*sternly*] You must learn to expect disappointments. How do you know that if you found this woman she would not disappoint you? It is easy to imagine wonderful women worthy of your father's love. But the real person always kills the imagined person.

EDITH. He said that once.

JITTA. Well, is it not true? Can you think of any real woman among your acquaintances that you could bear to think of as that woman—even the best of them?

EDITH. You cant put me off that way. I tell you I know. There is some woman who was real to my father; and he loved her. I shall love her when she is real to me. Besides, I have a queer sense that I know her quite as well as a real person; that she is here within reach of my hands if only I could recollect. I—I sometimes wonder does everybody know? does my mother know?

JITTA [*quickly*] Your mother does not know. Your mother could never understand.

EDITH. Jitta: do you know?

JITTA. Yes.

EDITH. Jitta!!!

JITTA. Yes. I know that poor criminal. I know what has become of her. I know what she did. I know what she has suffered ever since.

EDITH. But how do you know? Oh, tell me. You must tell me now.

JITTA. When you are excited like that your voice is his voice. Oh, the agony of hearing it, and the happiness! You bring him to life again for me.

EDITH. Then it was—

JITTA. Only me, dear.

EDITH [*flinging herself into Jitta's arms*] Only you! Who better could it be? Of course it was you. I knew it all along, only I couldnt recollect. Oh, darling! Dont you want a daughter? Here I am. His daughter.

JITTA. Dearest, yes. You have been a daughter to me ever since I knew him. But we must be very careful, very discreet. You see, you are very young.

EDITH. Oh, dont begin that. I dont want that sort of mother.

JITTA. I know. But I mustnt take your devotion—it is devotion, isnt it?—

EDITH. Oh yes, yes.

JITTA. I mustnt take it under false pretences. Above all, you must not throw away your engagement because your lover does not feel about me as you do. He is right about me, you know: I am not a good woman. Have you quite forgotten that *I* have a husband, and that for your father's sake I was unfaithful to him?

EDITH [*naïvely*] Oh, but Alfred is such a chump!

JITTA [*a little shocked*] Edith!

EDITH. And papa was such a wonderful man! Nobody could blame you.

JITTA. I assure you a great many people would blame me so much that they would never speak to me again if they knew.

EDITH. More shame for them! Do such people matter?

JITTA. They do, dear. I am afraid they are the only

445

people who do matter in this wretched world. So you mustnt tell them. You mustnt tell anybody.

EDITH [*slowly*] I suppose not.

JITTA. Did you intend to tell everybody?

EDITH. No, of course not: I am not such a fool as that. But I did think that if I told Doctor Fessler he might see that he was wrong.

JITTA. And you might forgive him. Very well: I give you leave to tell him. But you understand that if you tell him you must marry him; for you mustnt tell anyone except your husband.

EDITH. You want me to marry him?

JITTA. I do.

EDITH. Then I'll telephone him. I suppose that will do. I am so happy now that it doesnt matter tuppence whom I marry. [*Lenkheim opens the study door and is coming in when Edith, not hearing him, goes on*] I'd marry anyone to please you. I'd even marry Alfred.

LENKHEIM. Thank you. [*The two women spring up in dismay*]. Thats very kind of you, Edith, and very kind of Jitta to include me in the number of husbands she has apparently been offering you. But I have no intention of divorcing her at present.

EDITH [*not knowing what else to say*] It wasnt that. Mrs Lenkheim never offered you to me.

JITTA. Go off to the telephone, dear, and make it up with your man. I will make it up for you with Alfred.

LENKHEIM. Do, Edith. [*He crosses the room to the other door, and opens it for her with sardonic politeness*].

EDITH [*to Lenkheim, after kissing Jitta rather defiantly*] Mrs Lenkheim did not say a single unkind word about you. I did. [*She nods mockingly in his face and goes out*].

LENKHEIM. Have you told her?

JITTA [*her bored manner with her husband contrasting strongly with her warm interest in Edith*] She guessed. She knew. It is no use keeping secrets when they will not keep themselves. I have made her happy: that is all I care about.

446

[*She goes listlessly to the window-seat, and sits there looking out, with her shoulder turned to him*].

LENKHEIM. And have you told the old woman? Have you made her happy?

JITTA. I have made her happy. But I did not tell her. The strange thing is that she guesses it too; but she will never know it. She doesnt want to know it. Edith did. That makes all the difference. I have made them both happy. I wish someone could make me happy.

LENKHEIM. As I unfortunately am only your husband, I suppose there is no use my trying.

JITTA [*turning her face to him with open contempt*] You!

LENKHEIM. Funny, isnt it?

JITTA [*rising*] Dont be insufferable. You owe it to your position as an injured husband never to speak to me when we are alone and there are no appearances to be kept up. You swore not to. And you have been talking to me ever since, except when there was somebody else present to talk to.

LENKHEIM. Make no mistake, Jitta: when I swore that, I meant it.

JITTA [*ironically*] So it appears.

LENKHEIM. When you swore to be faithful to me, you meant it, didnt you?

JITTA [*interrupting him curtly*] You need not remind me of that again. I have not denied it. I have not excused myself. But I do not intend to have it thrown in my teeth every time we meet. [*She turns away from him determinedly, and sits down in the chair between the table and the door*].

LENKHEIM. Very well, then, dont you start reminding me every time we meet that I swore to do a good many things that I find I cant do. Is that a bargain?

JITTA [*a little ashamed, feeling that she has allowed herself to descend to his level*] Yes. I beg your pardon. I should not have said it. But please remember that you can hurt me more than I can hurt you, because you have done nothing wrong. You are within your rights: you are above reproach: you have the superior position morally: no taunts of mine can

447

degrade you as your reproaches can degrade me. [*Tragically*] I am a miserable creature. I betrayed you to please myself. I deserted him in his extremity to save myself. Please leave me to my disgrace. Nothing that you can say or think can add to the contempt I feel for myself.

LENKHEIM [*chuckling a little*] How you enjoy being miserable, Jitta!

JITTA. Enjoy!!

LENKHEIM. You just revel in it. You think yourself such a jolly romantic figure. You think that everything that happens to you is extraordinarily interesting because it happens to you. And you think that everything that happens to me is quite uninteresting because it hasnt happened to you. But what has happened to you has happened to lots of women—except, of course, the way it ended. And even that was an accident that might have happened to anyone.

JITTA. No doubt. Unfortunately, I did not behave as any decent woman would.

LENKHEIM. That is just where you are mistaken, darling. When you were brought to the point and put to the proof, you didnt behave romantically: you behaved very sensibly. You kept your head, and did just the right thing. You saved your reputation and my reputation. You prevented a horrible scandal. You have managed to make his wife and daughter happy. And yet you think you are ashamed of yourself because you were not found stretched on his dead body, with the limelight streaming on your white face, and the band playing slow music.

JITTA. Oh, what a nature you have, Alfred! You are prosaic to the core.

LENKHEIM [*grinning*] If you had only been clever enough to take me in, your success would have been complete. It wouldnt have been difficult. I always took you in when I had an adventure.

JITTA [*rising, very unpleasantly surprised, and not a little furious*] You! You have had adventures since we were married? You have deceived me?

LENKHEIM. Now dont begin imagining that I am a Don Juan. To be precise, I have kissed other women twice. I was drunk both times. And I had a serious affair with your dear friend Thelma Petersen. That lasted until she and her husband went back to Norway.

JITTA. Oh, how disgraceful! And you call her my friend!

LENKHEIM. I call Bruno Haldenstedt my friend. So you see I am not your moral superior. I thought it might restore your happiness a little to know that.

JITTA. Alfred: I will never speak to you nor cross the threshold of your house again.

LENKHEIM [*more amused than ever*] Except when you call to tell me so. When you let out about Haldenstedt I felt just as you feel now. Tomorrow you will think better of it, as I have thought better of it.

JITTA [*more dignified than ever*] If you imagine that any relations that could exist between Mrs Petersen and yourself were in the least like my relations with Bruno, you only shew for the thousandth time how incapable you are of understanding either him or me.

LENKHEIM. I'm afraid you dont understand either Thelma or me as sympathetically as I could wish. Thelma was a very superior woman, let me tell you. If my taste did not lie in the direction of superior women I shouldnt have married you.

JITTA. I will not have it, Alfred. I will not be dragged down to your level.

LENKHEIM. Five minutes ago you were amusing yourself by pretending that you were beneath contempt.

JITTA. So I am, on my own plane, and on his. But not on yours.

LENKHEIM. I dont believe theres a woman alive who doesnt look on herself as a special creation, and consider her husband an inferior and common sort of animal.

JITTA. You forget that I did not think of Bruno in that way.

LENKHEIM. Yes; but then he wasnt your husband. Thel-

449

ma thought me a much finer fellow than Petersen.

JITTA [*exasperated*] If you mention that woman to me again, I will break my promise to you, and walk straight out of your house before all the world.

LENKHEIM. That will only make us quits, because, as it happens, I am going to break my promise to you.

JITTA. How?

LENKHEIM. About the book. I have read it.

JITTA. Well?

LENKHEIM. Well, I'll be hanged if I put my name to it. In the first place nobody would believe I had ever written it. In the second, it's the most utter tommy-rot that was ever put forward as a serious contribution to psychology. Why, it flatly contradicts everything I have been teaching for years past, and everything I was taught myself.

JITTA [*intensely angry*] Does that prove it to be tommy-rot, or does it prove that you are an idiot?

LENKHEIM. I may be an idiot; but my idiocy is the accepted idiocy taught in the University at which I am a professor; and his idiocy is not taught anywhere. Do you forget that I have to earn bread for the household, and that your own money hardly pays for your dresses? This book would ruin us both.

JITTA. It is a sacred trust; and I swore to him that it should be fulfilled.

LENKHEIM. *I* didnt. And the old woman has just told me that he said the book was to be her insurance policy. No doubt I am Bruno's inferior; but I draw the line at helping him to rob his widow for my own profit.

JITTA. Then you refuse to carry out his intentions?

LENKHEIM. I cant carry out his intentions.

JITTA. You mean you wont.

LENKHEIM. I mean what I say. When he left me this book of his, he did so on the understanding that I was to know nothing of his relations with you. He hadnt quite such a low opinion of me as to suppose that I would take it as the price of my wife. Well, whose fault is it that I know all about it?

Who let the secret out? You did.

JITTA [*collapsing into his chair*] Oh, how shamefully I have betrayed him at every step! How despicable I am!

LENKHEIM [*sympathetically*] Not a bit of it, dear. You have just said yourself that if secrets dont keep themselves, nobody can keep them. This secret wouldnt keep itself. Come! stop crying. If only you would be content to be a woman for a moment, and not a heroine! And oh Lord! if you only had the smallest sense of humor!

JITTA [*passionately*] You cant even try to console me without sneering at me. Do you know what Edith called you?

LENKHEIM. No. You can tell me if it will relieve your feelings.

JITTA. She said you were a chump; and so you are.

LENKHEIM. All husbands are chumps, dear, after the first month or so. Jolly good thing for their wives too, sometimes.

JITTA. What are you going to do with that book?

LENKHEIM. If I had any regard for his reputation I should burn it at our domestic hearth.

JITTA [*recovering her dignity; rising; and speaking with tranquil conviction*] You shall not do that, Alfred.

LENKHEIM. Perhaps not; but it would serve you right if I did.

JITTA. It would not serve Edith right. Besides, his work, his reputation, his greatness—for whatever you may say I know that that book is the greatest that ever was written—belong not only to humanity, but to her. And I love her as if she were my own daughter. I have no other child.

LENKHEIM [*wincing a little*] My fault, I suppose. Oh, you can be nasty when you want to, Jitta.

JITTA. Oh, no, no. Will you never understand?

LENKHEIM. Probably not, being only a chump. Be a little amiable, Jitta: I havnt been so very hard on you, have I?

JITTA [*insisting*] You will not destroy the book? You will edit it? You will do everything for it that you could for a book of your own?

LENKHEIM. Well, if—

JITTA'S ATONEMENT

Fessler and Edith come in arm-in-arm, followed by Mrs Haldenstedt.

EDITH. Here he is. Kiss him.

FESSLER [*hastily*] Tchut! [*Taking Jitta's hand, and kissing it*] I owe you my life's happiness, Mrs Lenkheim.

AGNES. I am sure we all owe you the happiness of our lives. You are our good angel: indeed you are. Oh, you are a lucky man, Mr Lenkheim, to have such a wife.

JITTA [*striking in before he can reply*] I have one more piece of news for you, Mrs Haldenstedt. Alfred has found your husband's book. It is a masterpiece. He will edit it. He will do everything he could do for it if it were his own book.

FESSLER [*triumphant*] Splendid!

AGNES [*overjoyed*] Oh, think of that! Edith [*she kisses Edith*]! Doctor [*she kisses the doctor*]! Professor [*she kisses Lenkheim*]! Didnt I say she was our good angel?

LENKHEIM. And now, may I take my good angel home?

AGNES [*to Jitta*] Oh, must you go, dear?

JITTA [*sweetly, to Agnes*] Yes, dear. [*Threateningly to Alfred*] Come home. [*She goes to the door*].

LENKHEIM [*cheerily, as he shakes hands with everybody*] Goodbye.

ALL [*shaking hands*] Goodbye. Goodbye. Goodbye.

JITTA [*sternly*] Alfred: come home.

LENKHEIM [*hastily obeying*] Yes, dear.

AGNES [*as the door closes sharply behind them*] She's too good for him.

FARFETCHED FABLES

Written during 1949 and 1950

First Performed London 1950

PREFACE

AS I have now entered my 93rd year, my fans must not expect from me more than a few crumbs dropped from the literary loaves I distributed in my prime, plus a few speculations as to what may happen in the next million light years that are troubling me in the queer second wind that follows second childhood.

Being unable to put everything in the heavens above and on the earth beneath into every page I write, as some of my correspondents seem to expect, I have had to leave some scraps and shavings out; and now I gather up a few of them and present them in the childish form of Farfetched Fables. Philosophic treatises, however precise and lucid, are thrown away on readers who can enjoy and sometimes even understand parables, fairy tales, novels, poems, and prophecies. Proverbs are more memorable than catechisms and creeds. Fictions like The Prodigal Son, The Good Samaritan, The Pilgrim's Progress, and Gulliver's Travels, stick in minds impervious to the Epistles of Paul, the sermons of Bunyan, and the wisecracks of Koheleth and Ecclesiasticus. Hard workers who devour my plays cannot all tackle my prefaces without falling asleep almost at once.

The Panjandrums of literature will no doubt continue to assume that whoever can read anything can read everything, and that whoever can add two and two, bet on a horse, or play whist or bridge, can take in the tensor calculus. I know better, and can only hope that a batch of childish fables may stick in some heads that my graver performances overshoot.

THE NEW PSYCHOBIOLOGY

Nowadays biology is taking a new turn in my direction. What I called metabiology when I wrote The Doctor's Dilemma has made a step towards reality as psychobiology. The medical profession has split violently into psychotherapists and old-fashioned pill and bottle prescribers backed by surgeons practising on our living bodies as flesh plumbers and carpenters. When these surgeons find a tumor or a cancer they just cut it out. When your digestion or excretion goes wrong the bottlemen dose you with hydrochloric acid or chalk-and-opium ("the old mixture") as the case may

be. When these treatments fail, or when they are imprac-
ticable, they tell you sympathetically that you must die; and
die you do, unless you cure yourself or are cured by a disciple of Mrs Eddy practising Christian Science.

The more intelligent, observant, and open-minded
apothecaries and Sawbones, wakened up by an extraordinarily indelicate adventurer named Sigmund Freud, and
by the able Scotch doctor Scott Haldane (J. B. S. Haldane's
father), become more and more sceptical of the dogma that
a healthy body insures a healthy mind (*mens sana in corpore
sano*) and more and more inclined to believe that an unhealthy body is the result of a diseased mind. As I write, a
treatise on Mental Abnormality by Dr Millais Culpin has
just been published. It would have been impossible when I
wrote The Doctor's Dilemma. In spite of its author's efforts
to be impartial, it is convincing and converting as to his
evident belief that the old mechanistic surgery and *materia
medica* cost many lives.

AM I A PATHOLOGICAL CASE?

This leads my restlessly speculative mind further than
Dr Culpin has ventured. Is literary genius a disease? Shakespear, Walter Scott, Alexandre Dumas, myself: are we all
mental cases? Are we simply incorrigible liars? Are players
impostors and hypocrites? Were the Bible Christians right
when they disowned Bunyan because the incidents he described had never occurred nor the characters of whom he
told such circumstantial tales ever existed? He pleaded that
Jesus had taught by parables; but this made matters worse;
for the Bibliolators never doubted that the Prodigal Son
and the Good Samaritan were historical personages whose
adventures had actually occurred. To them Bunyan's plea,
classing the parables with Esop's Fables and the stories of
Reynard the Fox, was a blasphemy. The first Freudians
used to recite a string of words to their patients, asking what
they suggested, and studying the reaction, until they
wormed their way into the sufferer's sub-conscious mind,
and unveiled some forgotten trouble that had been worrying him and upsetting his health. By bringing it to light
they cured the patient.

FARFETCHED FABLES

When this Freudian technique was tried on me it failed because the words suggested always something fictitious. On the salt marshes of Norfolk I had been struck by the fact that when the horses stood round timidly at a distance, a handsome and intelligent donkey came and conversed with me after its fashion. I still have the photograph I took of this interesting acquaintance. The word Ass would have recalled this experience to any normal person. But when it was put to me, I immediately said Dogberry. I was once shewn the dagger with which Major Sirr killed Lord Edward Fitzgerald; but the word dagger got nothing from me but Macbeth. Highway or stile produced Autolycus, Interpreter the Pilgrim's Progress, blacksmith Joe Gargery. I was living in an imaginary world. Deeply as I was interested in politics, Hamlet and Falstaff were more alive to me than any living politician or even any relative. Can I then be given credit for common sanity? Can I make any effective excuse except Bunyan's excuse, which is no excuse at all? If I plead that I am only doing what More and Bunyan, Dickens and Wells did I do not exonerate myself: I convict them.

All I can plead is that as events as they actually occur mean no more than a passing crowd to a policeman on point duty, they must be arranged in some comprehensible order as stories. Without this there can be no history, no morality, no social conscience. Thus the historian, the story teller, the playwright and his actors, the poet, the mathematician, and the philosopher, are functionaries without whom civilization would not be possible. I conclude that I was born a story teller because one was needed. I am therefore not a disease but a social necessity.

DIVINE PROVIDENCE

Providence, which I call The Life Force, when not defeated by the imperfection of its mortal instruments, always takes care that the necessary functionaries are born specialized for their job. When no specialization beyond that of common mental ability is needed, millions of "hands" (correctly so called industrially) are born. But as they are helpless without skilled craftsmen and mechanics, without directors and deciders, without legislators and thinkers, these also are provided in the required numbers. Chaucer and Shakespear, Dante and Michael Angelo, Goethe and Ibsen, Newton and Einstein, Adam Smith and Karl Marx arrive only once at intervals of hundreds of years, whilst carpenters and tailors, stockbrokers and parsons, industrialists and traders are all forthcoming in thousands as fast as they are needed.

I present myself there as an instrument of the Life Force, writing by what is called inspiration; but as the Life Force proceeds experimentally by Trial-and-Error, and never achieves a 100 per cent success, I may be one of its complete failures, and certainly fall very short not only of perfection but of the Force's former highest achievements. For instance I am much less mentally gifted than, say, Leibniz, and can only have been needed because, as he was so gifted as to be unintelligible to the mob, it remained for some simpler soul like myself to translate his nomads and his universal substance, as he called the Life Force, into fables which, however farfetched, can at least interest, amuse, and perhaps enlighten those capable of such entertainment, but baffled by Leibniz's algebraic symbols and his philosophic jargon.

Here I must warn you that you can make no greater mistake in your social thinking than to assume, as too many do, that persons with the rarest mental gifts or specific talents are in any other respect superior beings. The Life Force, when it gives some needed extraordinary quality to some individual, does not bother about his or her morals. It may even, when some feat is required which a human being can perform only after drinking a pint of brandy, make him a dipsomaniac, like Edmund Kean, Robson, and Dickens on his last American tour. Or, needing a woman capable of bearing first rate children, it may endow her with enchanting sexual attraction yet leave her destitute of the qualities that make married life with her bearable. Apparently its aim is always the attainment of power over circumstances and matter through science, and is to this extent benevolent;

but outside this bias it is quite unscrupulous, and lets its agents be equally so. Geniuses are often spendthrifts, drunkards, libertines, liars, dishonest in money matters, backsliders of all sorts, whilst many simple credulous souls are models of integrity and piety, high in the calendar of saints.

MENTAL CAPACITY DIFFERS AND DIVIDES

When reading what follows it must not be forgotten that though we differ widely in practical ability and mental scope, the same basic income, or ration, or minimum wage, or national dividend, or whatever the newspapers call it for the moment, will suffice for mayor and scavenger, for admiral and cabin boy, for judge and executioner, for field marshal and drummer boy, for sexton and archbishop, bank manager and bank porter, sister of charity and prison wardress, and who not. What is more, they are all equally indispensable. An industrial magnate once wrote asking me did I realize that his army of laborers would be destitute and helpless without him. I replied that if he did not realize that without them he would be a nobody he was no gentleman. This closed the correspondence.

Equality of income is an obvious corollary. Yes; but how much income? A national dividend of, say, thirteen shillings a week per family, which was the share agricultural laborers got in the nineteenth century, kept them alive for thirty years or so, but left no surplus for education and culture: in short, for civilization. Now without cultured homes civilization is impossible. Without culture possible in every home democratic civilization is impossible, because equality of opportunity is impossible. The present combination of class culture and general savagery produces civil war, called class war, until strikes, lock-outs, and police batons are succeeded by shot and shell. Then the final destruction of civilization is threatened.

Consequently the basic income to be aimed at must be sufficient to establish culture in every home, and wages must be levelled up, not down, to this quota by increased production. When the quota is achieved, arithmetical inequality will no longer matter; for the eugenic test is general inter-

459

marriageability; and though the difference between £5 a week and £50 makes the recipients practically exogamous, millionaires could not marry at all if they scorned brides from homes with £5000 a year. There is no harm in a few people having some spare money, called capital, to experiment with; for the basic income will keep them in the normal grooves.

So much for the economics of the situation produced by differences in mental capacity! Having dealt with it in former writings, I mention it here only for new readers saturated with the common notion that income ought to vary with mental capacity, personal talent, and business ability. Such equations are wildly impossible, and having nothing to do with the insane misdistribution of national income produced by nineteenth century plutocracy. And so I pass on to political ethics.

Most of us so far are ungovernable by abstract thought. Our inborn sense of right and wrong, of grace and sin, must be embodied for us in a supernatural ruler of the universe: omnipotent, omniscient, all wise, all benevolent. In ancient Greece this was called making the word flesh, because the Greeks did not then discriminate between thought and the words that expressed it. The Bible translators have Englished it too literally as the word made flesh.

But as the minds of the masses could not get beyond their trades and their localities, their God could not be omnipresent; and a host of minor gods sprang up. The Greeks added to Zeus and Chronos vocational deities: Vulcan the blacksmith, Athene (Minerva) the thinker, Diana the huntress, Aphrodite (Venus) the sexmistress. They reappear in Christianity as Peter the fisherman, Luke the painter, Joseph the carpenter, Saint Cecilia the musician, and the rest.

But this also was too wide a classification for the very simple souls, who carried the localization of their gods to the extent of claiming exclusive property for their own city in each saint, and waging civil war in the name of the black image of the Blessed Virgin in their parish church against the worshippers of her white image in the next village.

FARFETCHED FABLES
SATANIC SOLUTION OF THE PROBLEM
OF EVIL

A difficulty was raised by the fact that evil was in the world as well as good, and often triumphed over the good. Consequently there must be a devil as well as a divinity: Poochlihoochli as well as Hoochlipoochli, Ahriman as well as Ormudz, Lucifer Beelzebub and Apollyon as well as the Holy Trinity, the Scarlet Woman as well as Our Lady: in short as many demons as saints.

At first, however, this setting up against God of a rival deity with a contrary ideology was resented as a Manichean heresy, because plague pestilence and famine, battle murder and sudden death, were not regarded with horror as the work of Shelley's Almighty Fiend, but with awe as evidence of the terrible greatness of God, the fear of him being placed to his credit as the beginning of wisdom. The invention of Satan is a heroic advance on Jahvism. It is an attempt to solve the Problem of Evil, and at least faces the fact that evil *is* evil.

Thus the world, as we imagine it, is crowded with anthropomorphic supernatural beings of whose existence there is no scientific proof. None the less, without such belief the human race cannot be civilized and governed, though the ten per cent or so of persons mentally capable of civilizing and governing are mostly too clever to be imposed on by fairy tales, and in any case have to deal with hard facts as well as fancies and fictions.

MENDACITY COMPULSORY IN KINGCRAFT
AND PRIESTCRAFT

This lands them in the quaintest moral dilemmas. It drives them to falsehoods, hypocrisies, and forgeries most distressing to their intellectual consciences. When the people demand miracles, worship relics, and will not obey any authority that does not supply them, the priest must create and nourish their faith by liquefying the blood of Saint Januarius, and saying Mass over a jawbone labelled as that of Saint Anthony of Padua. When the people believe that the earth is flat, immovable, and the centre of the universe, and Copernicus and Leonardo convince both Galileo the scientist and the Vatican that the earth is a planet of the sun, the Pope and the cardinals have to make Galileo recant and pretend that he believes what the people believe, because, if the Church admits that it has ever been mistaken, its whole authority will collapse, and civilization perish in anarchy. If Joshua could not make the sun stand still, there is a blunder in the Bible. When the Protestants blew the gaff to discredit the Vatican, and the secret could no longer be kept by forbidding Catholics to read the Bible, the people were not logical enough to draw subversive inferences. They swallowed the contradiction cheerfully.

Meanwhile the people had to be threatened with a posthumous eternity in a brimstone hell if they behaved in an uncivilized way. As burning brimstone could not hurt a spirit, they had to be assured that their bodies would be resurrected on a great Day of Judgment. But the official translators of the Bible in England were presently staggered by a passage in the Book of Job, in which that prophet declared that as worms would destroy his body, in the flesh he should not see God. Such a heresy, if published, would knock the keystone out of the arch of British civilization. There was nothing for it but to alter the word of God, making Job say that though worms would destroy his body yet in his flesh he should see God. The facts made this forgery necessary; but it was a forgery all the same.

A later difficulty was more easily got over. The apostles were Communists so Red that St Peter actually struck a man and his wife dead for keeping back money from the common stock. The translators could not pretend that St Peter was a disciple of the unborn Adam Smith rather than of Jesus; so they let the narrative stand, but taught that Ananias and Sapphira were executed for telling a lie and not for any economic misdemeanor. This view was impressed on me in my childhood. I now regard it as a much graver lie than that of Ananias.

"The lie" said Ferdinand Lassalle "is a European Power." He might, however, have added that it is none the worse when it does a necessary job; for I myself have been a faker of miracles. Let me tell one of my old stories over again.

FARFETCHED FABLES
G.B.S. MIRACLE FAKER

When I was a vestryman I had to check the accounts of the Public Health Committee. It was a simple process: I examined one in every ten or so of the receipted accounts and passed it whilst my fellow members did the same; and so enough of the accounts got checked to make their falsification too risky.

As it happened, one which I examined was for sulphur candles to disinfect houses in which cases of fever had occurred. I knew that experiments had proved that the fumes of burning sulphur had no such effect. Pathogenic bacilli like them and multiply on them.

I put the case to the Medical Officer of Health, and asked why the money of the ratepayers should be spent on a useless fumigant. He replied that the sulphur was not useless: it was necessary. But, I urged, the houses are not being disinfected at all. "Oh yes they are" he said. "How?" I persisted. "Soap and water and sunshine" he explained. "Then why sulphur?" "Because the strippers and cleaners will not venture into an infected house unless we make a horrible stink in it with burning sulphur."

I passed the account. It was precisely equivalent to liquefying the blood of Saint Januarius.

Some twenty years later I wrote a play called Saint Joan in which I made an archbishop explain that a miracle is an event that creates faith, even if it is faked for that end. Had I not been a vulgar vestryman as well as a famous playwright I should not have thought of that. All playwrights should know that had I not suspended my artistic activity to write political treatises and work on political committees long enough to have written twenty plays, the Shavian idiosyncrasy which fascinates some of them (or used to) and disgusts the Art For Art's Sake faction, would have missed half its value, such as it is.

PARENTAL DILEMMAS

The first and most intimate of the moral dilemmas that arise from differences in mental ability are not between classes and Churches, but in the daily work of bringing up children. The difference between Einstein and an average ploughman is less troublesome than the difference between

463

children at five, at ten, and at fifteen. At five the Church
catechism is only a paradigm: I learnt it at that age and
still remember its phrases; but it had no effect on my conduct. I got no farther with it critically than to wonder why
it obliged me, when asked what my name was, to reply that
it was N or M, which was not true.

What did affect my conduct was my nurse's threat that
if I was naughty or dirty the cock would come down the
chimney. I confidently recommended this formula to all
parents, nurses, and kindergarten teachers, as it effects its
purpose and then dies a natural death, fading from the mind
as the child grows out of it without leaving any psychic com-
plexes.

But the same cannot be said for more complicated
schemes of infant civilization. If they begin with Law's Serious Call, as many pious parents think they should, they
may be worse than no scheme at all. I knew a man whose
youth was made miserable by a dread of hell sedulously
inculcated from his infancy. His reaction against it carried
him into Socialism, whereupon he founded a Labor Church
in which all the meetings began by calling on the speakers
to pray: a demand which so took aback my Fabian colleagues
that one of them began with "Heavenly Father: unaccustomed as I have been many years to address you, I *etc. etc.*"
The Labor Church did not last; but the reaction did; and
the last I heard of its founder was that he was helping the
movement against Victorian prudery in a very practical way
as a Nudist photographer, the basis of that prudery being
the fact that the clothing, or rather upholstering, of Victorian women was much more aphrodisiac than their un-
adorned bodies.

As to the Socialist orator who parodied "Unaccustomed
as I am to public speaking," he died in the bosom of the
Roman Catholic Church.

I tell these anecdotes because they give an impression,
better than any abstract argument could, of the way in which
highly intelligent children of pious families, or of irreligious ones capable of nothing more intellectual than sport
and sex, reacted against their bringing-up. One day, at a

rehearsal of one of my plays, an actress who was a Roman Catholic consulted me in some distress because her adolescent son had become an atheist. I advised her not to worry; for as family religions have to be cast off as thoughtless habits before they can be replaced by genuine religious convictions, she might safely leave her son's case to God.

Edmund Gosse was the son of a Plymouth Brother, and was baptized by total immersion, of which he wrote a highly entertaining description in his book called Father and Son. The immersion had washed all the father's pious credulity out of the son. George Eliot, also piously brought up, began her reaction by translating Emil Strauss's Life of Jesus, which divested the worshipped Redeemer of supernatural attributes, and even questioned the sanity of his pretension to them.

THE ALL OR NOTHING COMPLEX

In those days we were all what I called Soot or Whitewash merchants, pilloried as All or Nothings in Ibsen's Brand. When one link in our mental chain snapped we did not pick up the sound links and join them, we threw the chain away as if all its links had snapped. If the story of Noah's Ark was a fable, if Joshua could not have delayed the sunset in the Valley of Ajalon, if the big fish could not have swallowed Jonah nor he survive in its belly, then nothing in the Bible was true. If Jehovah was a barbarous tribal idol, irreconcilable with the God of Micah, then there was no God at all, and the heavens were empty. On the other hand if Galileo, the man of science, knew better than Joshua, and Linneus and Darwin better than Moses, then everything that scientists said was true. Thus the credulity that believed in the Garden of Eden with its talking serpent, and in the speeches of Balaam's ass, was not cured. It was simply transferred to Herbert Spencer and John Stuart Mill. The transfer was often for the worse, as when baptism by water and the spirit, consecrating the baptized as a soldier and a servant of the Highest, was replaced by the poisonous rite of vaccination on evidence that could not have imposed on any competent statistician, and was picked up by Jenner from a dairy farmer and his milkmaids.

465

FARFETCHED FABLES
CATHOLICISM IMPRACTICABLE

The lesson of this is that a totally Catholic Church or Communist State is an impossible simplification of social organization. It is contrary to natural history. No Church can reconcile and associate in common worship a Jehovah's Witness with William Blake, who called Jehovah Old Nobodaddy. Napoleon, who pointed to the starry sky and asked "Who made all that?" did not kneel beside those who replied that it made itself, or retorted "We dont know: and neither do you." I, as a Creative Evolutionist, postulate a creative Life Force or Evolutionary Appetite seeking power over circumstances and mental development by the method of Trial and Error, making mistake after mistake, but still winning its finally irresistible way. Where in the world is there a Church that will receive me on such terms, or into which I could honestly consent to be received? There are Shaw Societies; but they are not Catholic Churches in pretence, much less in reality. And this is exactly as it should be, because, as human mental capacity varies from grade to grade, those who cannot find a creed which fits their grade have no established creed at all, and are ungovernable unless they are naturally amiable Vicars of Bray supporting any government that is for the moment established. There are hosts of such creedless voters, acting strongly as a conservative force, and usefully stabilizing government as such. But they make reforms very difficult sometimes.

THE TARES AND THE WHEAT

I therefore appreciate the wisdom of Jesus's warning to his missionaries that if they tore up the weeds they would tear up the wheat as well, meaning that if they tried to substitute his gospel for that of Moses instead of pouring the new wine into the old bottles (forgive the Biblical change of metaphor) nothing would be left of either Jesus or Moses. As I put it, the conversion of savagery to Christianity is the conversion of Christianity to savagery.

This is as true as ever. Not only are the immediate black converts of our missionaries inferior in character both to the unconverted and the born converted, but all the established religions in the world are deeply corrupted by the necessity

466

for adapting their original inspired philosophic creeds to the narrow intelligences of illiterate peasants and of children. Eight thousand years ago religion was carried to the utmost reach of the human mind by the Indian Jainists, who renounced idolatry and blood sacrifice long before Micah, and repudiated every pretence to know the will of God, forbidding even the mention of his name in the magnificent temples they built for their faith.

But go into a Jainist temple today: what do you find? Idols everywhere. Not even anthropomorphic idols but horse idols, cat odols, elephant idols and what not? The statues of the Jainist sages and saints, far from being contemplated as great seers, are worshipped as gods.

THE THIRTYNINE ARTICLES

For such examples it is not necessary to travel to Bombay. The articles of the Church of England begin with the fundamental truth that God has neither body, parts, nor passions, yet presently enjoin the acceptance as divine revelation of a document alleging that God exhibited his hind quarters to one of the prophets, and when he had resolved to destroy the human race as one of his mistakes, was induced to make an exception in the case of Noah and his family by a bribe of roast meat. Later articles instruct us to love our fellow-creatures, yet to obey an injunction to hold accursed all who do good works otherwise than in the name of Christ, such works being sinful. In one article it is at first assumed that the swallowing of a consecrated wafer is only the heathen rite of eating the god (transubstantiation) and as such abominable, and then that it is holy as a memorial of the last recorded supper of Jesus. No man can be ordained a minister of the Church of England unless he swears without any mental reservation that he believes these contradictions. I once held lightly that candidates of irresistible vocation might swear this blamelessly because they were under duress. But one day I was present at the induction of a rector. When the bishop asked the postulant to tell a flat lie which both of them knew to be a lie, and he told it without a blush, the impression made on me was so shocking that I have felt ever since that the Church of England must revise its articles at all hazards if it is to be credited with the intellectual honesty necessary to its influence and authority. Shake that authority, and churchgoing will be nothing more than parading in our best clothes every Sunday.

A HUNDRED RELIGIONS AND ONLY ONE SAUCE

As it is, Christianity has split into sects, persuasions, and Nonconformities in all directions. The Statesman's Year-Book has given up trying to list them. They range from Pillars of Fire, Jehovah's Witnesses, Plymouth Brothers, and Glasites, to Presbyterians, Methodists, Congregationalists, Baptists, Friends (Quakers), and Unitarians. Within the Established Church itself there are Ritualists, Anglo-Catholics who call their services Masses and never mention the Reformation, Laodicean Broad Churchmen, and Low Church Protestants. The Friends abhor ritual and dictated prayers, and repudiate cathedral services and Masses as playacting, whilst the Anglo-Catholics cannot think religiously without them. Presbyterians and Congregationalists differ from the clergy of the Established Church on the political issue of episcopal or lay Church government. The Unitarians reject the Trinity and deny deity to Jesus. Calvinists deny universal atonement, preached by our missionaries, who are practically all Independents.

Common to these irreconcilable faiths is the pretension that each is the true Catholic Church, and should hand over all whom it cannot convert to the State (the Secular Arm) to be exterminated for the crime of heresy by the cruellest possible methods, even to burning alive. This does not mean that all rulers who order such extermination are horribly cruel. "Bloody Mary" believed that heretics must be liquidated; but she was not responsible for the political circumstance that the secular criminal law was atrociously cruel, and that no other agency could effect the liquidation. Calvin agreed that Servetus must be killed; but he objected humanely to his being burned. Charles II, humane (indeed, as some think, too humane in his kindness to his dozen dogs and half dozen mistresses), could not question the necessity for punishing the Regicides with death; but he

loathed the butchering of them in the hideous manner ordained centuries earlier for the punishment of William
Wallace, and stopped it as soon as he dared. It was still un-
repealed during my own lifetime; and has only just (1948)
been repealed in Scotland.

So far I have not been imprisoned, as poorer men have
been in my time, for blasphemy or apostasy. I am not technically an apostate, as I have never been confirmed; and
my godparents are dead. But having torn some of the
Thirtynine Articles to rags, I should have been pilloried
and had my ears cropped had I lived in the days of the British Inquisition called the Star Chamber. Nowadays Non-
conformity and Agnosticism are far too powerful electorally
for such persecution. But the Blasphemy Laws are still
available and in use against obscure sceptics, whilst I suffer
nothing worse than incessant attempts to convert me. All
the religions and their sects, Christian or Moslem, Bud-
dhist or Shinto, Jain or Jew, call me to repentance, and ask
me for subscriptions. I am not so bigoted as to dismiss their
experiences as the inventions of liars and the fancies of
noodles. They are evidence like any other human evidence;
and they force me to the conclusion that every grade of
human intelligence can be civilized by providing it with
a frame of reference peculiar to its mental capacity, and
called a religion.

THE MARXIST CHURCH

The Marxist Church, called Cominform, is like all the
other Churches. Having ceased to believe in the beneficently
interfering and overruling God of Adam Smith and Voltaire, no less than in the vicarage of the Pope and his infallibility in council with the College of Cardinals, Cominform makes Karl Marx its Deity and the Kremlin his
Vatican. It worships his apostles at its conventicles and in
its chapels, with Das Kapital as its Bible and gospel, just as
Cobdenist Plutocracy used to make a Bible of Adam Smith's
Wealth of Nations with its gospel of The Economic Har-
monies and its policy of Free Trade.

I am myself much idolized. I receive almost daily letters from devout Shavians who believe that my income is

unlimited, my knowledge and wisdom infinite, my name a guarantee of success for any enterprise, my age that of Jesus at his death, and the entire Press at my command, especially The Times, of which I am assumed to be the proprietor.

If this is not idolatry the word has no meaning. The fact that I am ascertainably, and indeed conspicuously, only a superannuated (not supernatural) journalist and playwright does not shake the faith of my idolaters in the least. Facts count for nothing. I am told that I should be shot in Russia if I dared to pontificate against the Government there as I often do here, and that Freedom of the Press, the glory of England, does not and cannot exist under Communist tyranny.

SHOULD I BE SHOT IN RUSSIA?

As a matter of fact the Russian newspapers are full of complaints and grievances. There is a Government Department whose function it is to receive and deal with such complaints. Here in England I, an old journalist and agitator, know only too well that both platform and press are gagged by such an irresponsible tyranny of partisan newspaper proprietors and shamelessly mendacious advertizers, and by the law against seditious and blasphemous libel, that my speeches were never reported, and my letters and articles inserted only when I could combine what I believed and wanted to say with something that the paper wanted to have said, or when I could disguise it as an attractively readable art criticism, the queer result being that my reputation was made in Conservative papers whilst the Liberal, Radical, and Socialist editors dared not mention my name except in disparagement and repudiation. I owe more of my publicity to The Times than to any other daily newspaper. The same is true of my Fabian colleagues. The Webbs, now in Westminster Abbey, never could get into the British daily newspapers. In Russia, when Fabians were despised there as bourgeois Deviators, the Webbs were translated by Lenin.

As a playwright I was held up as an irreligious pornographer, and as such a public enemy, not to say a thoroughpaced cad, for many years by an irresponsible censorship which could not be challenged in parliament or elsewhere.

No such misfortune has happened to me in Russia.

What damns our foreign policy here is our ignorance of history of home affairs. In the imagination of our amateur politicians England is a Utopia in which everything and everybody is "free," and all other countries "police States." I, being Irish, know better.

To return to the inveteracy of idolatry. Ten years ago disciples of a rival celebrity were sending me portraits of an Austrian Messiah named Hitler, described by Mr Winston Churchill as a bloodthirsty guttersnipe, yet more fanatically deified in Germany than Horatio Bottomley in England.

One of the puzzles of history is whether Jesus, denounced by the ladies and gentlemen of his time as a Sabbath breaker, a gluttonous man, and a winebibber, and finally executed for rioting in the temple, really believed in his claim to be Messiah, or was forced to assume that character because he could not make converts on any other terms, just as Mahomet found that he could not govern the Arabs without inventing a very sensual paradise and a very disgusting hell to keep them in order. Whether he invented his conversations with the Archangel Gabriel, or, like Joan of Arc, really heard voices when he listened for the voice of God, we shall never know. I have just had a letter from a man who, having made repeated attempts to give up smoking and failed, until one day, walking through Hyde Park, he heard a Gospel preacher cry "Listen for the voice of God and it will come to you." This stuck in his mind. He listened, not piously but experimentally; and sure enough a voice said to him "Quit smoking: quit smoking." This time he quitted without the smallest difficulty.

COMPATIBILITIES

Differences of creed must be tolerated, analyzed, discussed, and as far as possible reconciled. My postulate of a provident and purposeful Life Force that proceeds by trial-and-error, and makes mistakes with the best intentions, is not in effect irreconcilable with belief in a supernatural benignant Providence at war with a malignant Satan. We cannot "make our souls" in the same assembly; but in the same building we can. Therefore if our cathedrals and churches are to be open to all faiths, as they in fact are, for contemplation and soul making, their different rituals must be performed at different hours, as they are at the Albert Hall in London, the Usher Hall in Edinburgh, the Free Trade hall in Manchester, the Montford Hall in Leicester, and wherever two or three gathered together may hear Messiah or the great Masses of Bach and Beethoven on Sunday or Monday, and watch a boxing show on Tuesday or Wednesday. The rituals differ, but not enough to provoke their votaries to burn one another at the stake or refuse to dine together on occasion. The sporting peer who becomes famous as the owner of a Derby winner meets the winner of a Nobel Prize without the least embarrassment; and I have never suffered the smallest discourtesy except once in a Manchester club, and then only because my criticisms of Shakespear stopped this side of idolatry.

It may seem that between a Roman Catholic who believes devoutly in Confession and a modern freethinking scientist there can be neither sympathy nor co-operation. Yet there is no essential difference between Confession and modern Psychotherapy. The post-Freudian psychoanalyst relieves his patient of the torments of guilt and shame by extracting a confession of their hidden cause. What else does the priest do in the confessional, though the result is called cure by one and absolution by the other? What I, a Freethinker, call the Life Force, my pious neighbors call Divine Providence: in some respects a better name for it. Bread and wine are changed into living tissue by swallowing and digestion. If this is not transubstantiation what *is* transubstantiation? I have described the surprise of a Fabian lecturer on being asked to open a political meeting with prayer. When I was invited to address the most important Secular Society in England I found that I had to supply the sermon in a ritual of hymns and lessons in all respects like a religious Sunday service except that the lessons were from Browning and the hymns were aspirations to "join the choir invisible." Later on, when I attended a church service in memory of my wife's sister, and was disposed to be moved by it, the lesson was the chapter from the Bible which describes how the Israelites in captivity were instructed by a deified Jonathan Wild to steal the jewelry of the Egyptians before their flight into the desert. The Leicester Atheists were in fact more pious than the Shropshire Anglicans.

BOHEMIAN ANARCHISM

The anarchy which the priests feared when they gagged Galileo actually came to pass much more widely than the epidemics which the Medical Officer of Health dreaded when he gagged me about the sulphur candles. In my early days as a Socialist lecturer I was once opposed by a speaker who had been an apostle of Robert Owen's New Moral World, the first version of British Socialism. His ground was that too many of his fellow apostles took the new moral world as an emancipation from all the obligations of the old moral world, and were dishonest and licentious. Prominent in my own generation of Marxists was one who, I believe, would have gone as a martyr to the scaffold or the stake rather than admit that God existed, or that Marx and Darwin were fallible. But when money or women were concerned, he was such a conscienceless rascal that he was finally blackballed by all the Socialist societies.

Do not misunderstand me. I am not stigmatizing all Owenites, Marxists, and Darwinists as immoral; but it must be borne in mind that all revolutionary and reform movements are recruited from those who are not good enough for the existing system as well as those who are too good for it. All such movements attract sinners as well as saints by giving them a prominence as platform orators and pamphleteers out of all proportion to their numbers and deserts. They justify their delinquencies as assertions of principle, and thus give Socialism a reputation for anarchism, irreligion, and sexual promiscuity which is association of ideas, not logic. No eminence in a specific department implies even ordinary ability in any other, nor does any specific personal depravity imply general depravity. I may fairly claim to be an adept in literature; but in dozens of other departments I am a duffer. I have often quoted a certain ex-Colonel who said to me "I know for certain that the Rector is the father

473

of his housemaid's illegitimate child; and after that you may tell me that the Bible is true: I shall not believe you." It does not follow that the Colonel was not a military genius, nor the Rector an eloquent preacher and efficient clergyman.

Nevertheless we cannot legislate for every individual separately, nor provide a special policeman to keep him (or her) in order. All civilized persons except certified lunatics and incorrigible criminals must for elementary purposes be held equally capable and responsible. Those who cannot read any book more abstruse than Esop's Fables, nor get beyond the multiplication table (if so far) in mathematics, can understand the Ten Commandments well enough to be legislated for in the mass.

SHAM DEMOCRACY

In the face of these hard facts most of the current interpretations of the word Democracy are dangerous nonsense. The fundamental notion that the voice of the people is the voice of God is a sample. What people? Were Solon and Sully, Voltaire and Adam Smith, Plato and Aristotle, Hobbes and Tom Paine and Marx, the people? Were Lord George Gordon, Titus Oates, and Horatio Bottomley the people? Were General Roberts and Henry Irving, nominated by Gallup poll as ideal rulers, the people? Am I the people? Was Ruskin? Were Moses, Jesus, Peter and Paul, Mahomet, Brigham Young? If their voices were all voices of God, God must be a very accomplished ventriloquist.

Democracy means government in the interest of everybody. It most emphatically does not mean government BY everybody. All recorded attempts at that have not only failed but rapidly developed into despotisms and tyrannies. The trade union secretary elected by everybody in his Union, the pirate captain whose crew can make him walk the plank at any moment, are the most absolute despots on earth. Cromwell tried government by a parliament of elected saints and had to turn it into the street as Bismarck turned the Frankfort Parliament in 1862. He tried an oligarchy of majors general, but finally had to make himself Lord Protector and govern despotically as much as it was

474

possible to govern Englishmen at all, which, as he bitterly complained, was not very much. Much or little, votes for everybody, politically called Adult Suffrage, always produces anarchy, which, being unbearable, produces by reaction overwhelming majorities in favor of Regressions called Restorations, or Napoleonic Emperors and South American dictator-presidents. Democratic government of the people by the people, professed ideologically nowadays by all Governments and Oppositions, has never for a moment existed.

Real democracy leaves wide open the question as to which method best secures it: monarchies, oligarchies, parliaments nominated or elected with or without proportional representation, restricted franchise, intervals between general elections, or other "checks and balances" devised to prevent glaring abuses of virtually irresponsible power. None of them has ever made Voltaire's *Monsieur Tout le Monde* master of the situation. Adult suffrage did not prevent two so-called world wars and a royal abdication on which the people were no more consulted than I was. Political adventurers and "tin Jesuses" rose like rockets to dictatorships and fell to earth like sticks, or were succeeded, as Napoleon was, by Bourbonic bosses. The Russian Bolsheviks, having invented the Soviet System, and brought their country to the verge of ruin and a little over by All or Nothing Catastrophism, were forced by the facts to make room in Bolshevism for more private enterprise than there is in England. The moment it did so, the basic difference between British and Russian economic policy vanished or crisscrossed. Lenin and Stalin had to cry *Laisser-faire* to all the enterprises not yet ripe for nationalization. The Labor Party in England nationalized as many industries as it could manage, and regulated private employers, controlled prices, rationed food and clothing, imposed purchase taxes on luxuries, and increased the bureaucracy both in numbers and power whilst jealously restricting official salaries more grudgingly with a view to equality of income than the Kremlin. Stalin's Russo-Fabian slogan, Socialism in a Single Country, is countered by Churchill's manifestos of Plu-

475

tocratic Capitalism Everywhere and Down with Communism, which is more than Trotsky claimed for international Marxism.

With all this staring them in the face, and no intention whatever of going back to turnpike roads, toll bridges, private detectives and prizefighters for police, sixpenny linkmen for municipal electric lighting, cadis under palm trees for judges, condottieri and privateers for national defence, profiteers for Exchequer Chancellors: in short, the substitution of private enterprise for the omnipresent Communism without which our civilization could not endure for a week, our politicians and partisans keep shouting their abhorrence of Communism as if their Parties were cannibal tribes fighting and eating one another instead of civilized men driven by sheer pressure of facts into sane co-operation.

THE POLITICAL TIME LAG

The worst features of our sham-democratic misgovernment are caused, not by incurable mental incapacity, but by an ignorance that is essentially mathematical. None of our politicians seems to know that political action, like all earthly action, must take place in a world of four dimensions, not three. The fourth dimension is that of Time. To ignore it is to be pre-Einstein, which is as out-of-date as to be pre-Marx. Fortunately it can be taught, just as the theories of rent and value can be taught; and those who learn it see that our British parliamentary system is far too slow for twentieth century social organization. The Soviet system in Russia outstrips it because, being faster, it is more immediately responsive to the continual need for reforms and adaptations to changing circumstances. It includes all the conventional democratic checks and safeguards against despotism now so illusory, and gives them as much effectiveness as their airy nature is capable of. Incidentally it gives Stalin the best right of any living statesman to the vacant Nobel peace prize, and our diplomatists the worst. This will shock our ignoramuses as a stupendous heresy and a mad paradox. Let us see.

When the horrors of unregulated selfish private enterprise forced both Conservatives and Cobdenists to devise

476

and pass the Factory Acts, it took the British Parliament a time lag of 50 years to make them effective. Home Rule for Ireland took thirty years to get through Parliament, and was decided after all by a sanguinary civil war.

In the simplest home affairs the time lag extends to centuries. For instance, the practice of earth burial, with its cemeteries crowding the living out by the dead, its poisonous slow putrefactions, its risk of burial alive, and its cost, should be forbidden and replaced by cremation. It was discussed 80 years ago when I was a boy. Yet not even the cremation of an Archbishop (Temple: one of our best) has overcome our dread of doing anything that everyone else is not yet doing, nor the bigoted opposition of the Churches which preach the Resurrection of The Body without considering that a body can be resurrected from dust and ashes as feasibly as from a heap of maggots. Our crematory gardens of rest are still countable only in dozens, and cremations only in thousands, even in big cities. In lesser towns the figure is zero.

ADULT SUFFRAGE IS MOBOCRACY

Adult Suffrage is supposed to be a substitute for civil war. The idea is that if two bodies of citizens differ on any public point they should not fight it out, but count heads and leave the decision to the majority. The snag in this is that as the majority is always against any change, and it takes at least thirty years to convert it, whilst only ten per cent or thereabouts of the population has sufficient mental capacity to foresee its necessity or desirability, a time lag is created during which the majority is always out-of-date. It would be more sensible to leave the decision to the minority if a qualified one could be selected and empanelled. Democratic government needs a Cabinet of Thinkers (Politbureau) as well as a Cabinet of Administrators (Commissars). Adult Suffrage can never supply this, especially in England, where intellect is hated and dreaded, not wholly without reason, as it is dangerous unless disciplined and politically educated; whilst acting and oratory, professional and amateur, are popular, and are the keys to success in elections.

477

FARFETCHED FABLES
THE MARXIST CLASS WAR

The conflict of economic interest between proprietors and proletarians was described by H. G. Wells as past and obsolete when it had in fact just flamed up in Spain from a bandying of strikes and lock-outs into raging sanguinary civil war, as it had already done in Russia, with the difference that in Russia the proletarians won, whereas in Spain they were utterly defeated through lack of competent ministers and commanders.

The struggle is confused by a cross conflict between feudal and plutocratic ideologies. The feudal proprietariat is all for well policed private property and *Laisser-faire*, the proletariat all for State industry with abolition of feudal privilege and replacement of private or "real" property by property on social conditions; so that a proprietor shall hold his land, his shares, his spare money (called capital) on the same terms as his umbrella: namely that he shall not use it to break his neighbor's head nor evict him from his country and homestead to make room for sheep or deer.

Both parties insist on the supreme necessity for increased production; but as the Plutocrats do all they can to sabotage State industry, and the Proletarians to sabotage private enterprise, the effect is to hinder production to the utmost and demonstrate the vanity of two-party government.

WHAT IS TO BE DONE?

I am asked every week what is my immediate practical remedy for all this. Also what is my solution of the riddle of the universe? When I reply that I dont know, and have no panacea, I am told that I am not constructive, implying that practical people are constructive and do know. If they are and do, why are we in our present perilous muddle?

I can only suggest certain definite and practicable experiments in social organization, on a provisional hypothesis or frame of reference (a necessary tool of thought) that will serve also as a credible religion. For nomenclatory purpose I may be called a Fabian Communist and Creative Evolutionist if I must have a label of some sort. At present I am stuck all over with labels like a tourist's trunk. I cannot call myself the Way and the Life, having only a ques-

478

tionable hypothesis or two to offer; but that is the heroic label that all Worldbetterers aspire to, and some have even dared to claim.

Some 30 years or so ago I wrote a play called As Far As Thought Can Reach. Perhaps I should have called it as far as my thought could reach; but I left this to be taken for granted.

POLITICAL MATHEMATICS

What we need desperately is an anthropometric slide-rule by which we can classify and select our rulers, most of whom are at present either rich nonentities, venal career-ists, or round pegs in square holes. Now it is no use my singing at the top of my voice that democracy is impossible without scientific anthropometry. I might as well be the Town Crier offering a reward for an imaginary lost dog. How are we to begin?

Sixty years ago Sidney Webb created a Progressive Party on the new County Councils by sending to all the candidates at the first election a catechism setting forth a program of Socialist reforms, and demanding whether they were in favor of them or not. As Nature abhors a vacuum the program flew into empty heads and won the election for them. This, as far as I know, was the first non-party test ever applied to membership of a public authority in England since benefit of clergy was legal, and the professions were closed to all but members of the Church of England. This at least provided some evidence as to whether the candidate could read, write, and even translate a little dog Latin. It was better than no test at all.

But it is now quite insufficient in view of the enormous increase of public functions involved by modern Socialism. We already have in our professional and university exam-inations virtual panels of persons tested and registered as qualified to exercise ruling functions as Astronomers Royal, Archbishops, Lord Chief Justices, and public schoolmasters. Even police constables are instructed. Yet for the ministers who are supported to direct and control them we have no guarantee that they can read or write, or could manage a baked potato stall successfully.

479

FARFETCHED FABLES

Now people who cannot manage baked potato stalls nor peddle bootlaces successfully cannot manage public departments manned with school-tested permanent executives. Consequently these executives constitute a bureaucracy, not a democracy. Elections do not touch them: the people have no choice. When they have passed the competitive examinations by which they are tested, they are there for life, practically irremovable. And so government goes on.

Unfortunately the tests tend to exclude born rulers. Knowledge of languages, dead and foreign, puts a Mezzofanti, useless as a legislator or administrator, above a Solon who knows no language but his own. It puts facility in doing set sums in algebra by rule of thumb above inborn mathematical comprehension by statesmen who cannot add up their washing bills accurately. Examinations by elderly men of youths are at least thirty years out of date: in economics, for instance, the candidate who has been taught that the latest views are those of Bastiat and Cobden, ignoring those of Cairnes and Mill, is successful, especially if he ranks those of Karl Marx as blasphemous, and history as ending with Macaulay. The questions that will be asked and the problems set at the examinations, with the answers and solutions that will be accepted by the elderly examiners, soon become known, enabling professional crammers to coach any sixth form schoolboy to pass in them to the exclusion of up-to-date candidates who are ploughed because they know better than their examiners, yet are as unconscious of their mental superiority as a baby is of the chemistry by which it performs the complicated chemical operation of digesting its food.

Evidently the present curriculum and method should be radically changed. When I say this, the reply is "Granted; but how?" Unfortunately I dont know; and neither does anyone else; but as somebody must make a beginning here are a few of the best suggestions I can think of.

RENT AND VALUE THE ASS'S BRIDGES

First, there is the economic Ass's Bridge: the theory of rent, and with it inextricably the theory of exchange value. Unless a postulant for first class honors in politics can write an essay shewing that he (or she) has completely mastered

480

these impartial physical and mathematical theories, the top
panel must be closed against him. This would plough Adam
Smith, Ricardo, Ruskin, and Marx; but they could read
up the subject and return to the charge. Stanley Jevons
would pass it, though after he had knocked out Ricardo and
the rest with his correct mathematical theory he taught that
a State parcel post is an impossibility. For when he returned
to England after serving in the Gold Escort in Australia,
and became a university professor, he taught anything and
everything the old examiners expected him to teach, and so
might have failed in a character test.

STATISTICS VITAL

The panel for health authorities should require a strin-
gent test in statistics. At present the most unbearable tyranny
is that of the State doctor who has been taught to prescribe
digitalis and immobilization, plus a diet of alcoholic stimu-
lants, for heart disease, and to amputate limbs and extirpate
tonsils as carpenters and plumbers deal with faulty chair
legs and leaking pipes. He may, like Jenner, be so ignorant
of the rudiments of statistics as to believe that the coincidence of a decrease in the number of deaths from a specific
disease following the introduction of an alleged prophylactic
proves that the prophylactic is infallible and that compulsion to use it will abolish the disease. Statisticians, checking
the figures by the comparisons they call controls, may prove
up to the hilt that the prophylactic not only fails to cure but
kills. When vaccination was made compulsory as a preventive of smallpox the controls were cholera, typhus, and
endemic fever: all three rampant when I was born. They
were wiped out by sanitation; whilst under compulsory vaccination, enforced by ruthless persecution, smallpox persisted and culminated in two appalling epidemics (1871
and 1881) which gave vaccination its deathblow, though its
ghost still walks because doctors are ignorant of statistics,
and, I must add, because it is lucrative, as it calls in the
doctor when the patient is not ill. In the army some thirty
inoculations are practically compulsory; and vaccination is
made a condition of admission to the United States and other
similarly deluded countries. The personal outrage involved

is so intolerable that it will not be in the least surprising if vaccination officers are resisted, not with facts and figures but with fists, if not pistols.

The remedy, however, is not to compel medical students to qualify as statisticians, but to establish a Ministry of Statistics with formidable powers of dealing with lying advertisements of panaceas, prophylactics, elixirs, immunizers, vaccines, antitoxins, vitamins, and professedly hygienic foods and drugs and drinks of all sorts. Such a public department should be manned not by chemists analyzing the advertized wares and determining their therapeutical value, but by mathematicians criticizing their statistical pretensions. As there is an enormous trade in such wares at present the opposition to such a Ministry will be lavishly financed; but the need for it is too urgent to allow any consideration to stand in its way; for the popular demand for miracles and deities has been transferred to "marvels of science" and doctors, by dupes who think they are emancipating themselves from what in their abysmal ignorance they call medieval barbarism when they are in fact exalting every laboratory vivisector and quack immunizer above Jesus and St James. Mrs Eddy, a much sounder hygienist than Jenner, Pasteur, Lister, and their disciples, had to call her doctrine Christian Science instead of calling the popular faith in pseudo-scientific quackery Anti-Christian Nonsense.

THE ESTHETIC TEST

The next test I propose may prove more surprising. For the top panel I would have postulants taken into a gallery of unlabelled reproductions of the famous pictures of the world, and asked how many of the painters they can name at sight, and whether they have anything to say about them, or are in any way interested in them. They should then be taken into a music room furnished with a piano, and asked to sing or whistle or hum or play as many of the leading themes of the symphonies, concertos, string quartets, and opera tunes of Mozart and Beethoven, and the Leitmotifs of Wagner, as they can remember. Their performances may be execrable; but that will not matter: the object is not to test their executive skill but to ascertain their knowledge of the best music and their interest in and enjoyment of it, if any.

I would have them taken then into a library stocked with the masterpieces of literature. They should be asked which of them they had ever read, and whether they read anything but newspapers and detective stories. If the answer be Yes, they can be invited to indicate the books they know.

I am quite aware of the possibility of misleading results. Dr Inge, an unquestionably top notcher, when he was Dean of St Paul's and had to deal with the music there, expressed a doubt whether the Almighty really enjoys "this perpetual serenading." William Morris, equally *honoris causa,* could not tolerate a piano in his house. When one was played in his hearing by his neighbors, he would throw up his window and roar curses at them.

But if Dr Inge had been brought up on Beethoven instead of on Jackson's Te Deum, he might have preferred Wagner to Plotinus; and Morris was deeply affected by medieval music, and quite right in loathing the modern steel grand piano of his day as a noisy nuisance. Still, some of the postulants will be tone deaf or color blind. Their comments may be none the less valuable as evidence of their mental capacity.

SUBCONSCIOUS CAPACITIES

More baffling at present are the cases in which the judges will be faced with apparently vacant minds, and met, not with an epigram of which no mediocrity would be capable, but with a blank "I dont know what you are talking about." This will not prove that the postulant is a nitwit: it will raise the question whether the question is beyond his mental powers or so far within them that he is unconscious of them. Ask anyone how water tastes, and you will get the reply of Pinero's Baron Croodle "Water is a doglike and revolting beverage" or simply "Water has no taste," or, intelligently, "Water has no taste for me, because it is always in my mouth." Ask an idle child what it is doing, and it will not claim that it is breathing and circulating its blood: it will say it is doing nothing. When we co-ordinate our two eyes to look at anything we do not notice that the images of every-

483

thing else within our range of vision are doubled. When we listen to an orchestra or an organ we are deaf to the accompanying thunder of beats, partials, and harmonics. Attention is a condition of consciousness. Without it we may miss many "self-evident truths." How then are we to distinguish between the unconscious genius and the idiot?

Again, I do not know; but we can at least call in the professional psychotherapists whose business it is to dig up the buried factors of the mind and bring them to light and consciousness. The technique of this therapy has developed since the days when, being asked what the word Ass suggested to me, I replied Dogberry and Balaam. It suggested, not facts and experiences, but fictions. Put the word Calculus to a surgeon and he will name the disease called stone, from which Newton suffered. Put it to a mathematician and he will cite the method of measurement Newton and Leibniz elaborated.

EXAMINATIONS AND SCHOOLMASTERS

I avoid calling the tests examinations because the word suggests the schoolmaster, the enemy of mankind at present, though when by the rarest chance he happens to be a born teacher, he is a priceless social treasure. I have met only one who accepted my challenge to say to his pupils "If I bore you you may go out and play." Set an average schoolmaster or schoolmarm to test for the panels, and the result will be a set of examination papers with such questions and problems as "Define the square root of minus one in Peano terms; and if an empty aeroplane travelling at supersonic speed takes a thousand light years to reach the nearest star, how long will it take a London motor bus keeping schedule time to travel from Millbank to Westminster Bridge with a full complement of passengers? Give the name, date, and locality of the birth of Beethoven's great grandmother's cousin's stepsister; and write a tonal fugue on the following theme. Give the family names of Domenichino and Titian; and write an essay not exceeding 32 words on their respective styles and influence on Renaissance art. Give the dates of six of Shakespear's plays, with the acreage occupied by (*a*) the Globe Theatre, (*b*) the Shoreditch Curtain the-

atre, and (*c*) the Blackfriars theatre. Estimate the age of
Ann Hathaway at her marriage with Shakespear. Enumer-
ate the discrepancies between the narratives of Homer,
Plutarch, Holinshed, and Shakespear. Was Bacon the author of Shakespear's plays (5000 words)?"

THE WRONG SORT OF MEMORY

And so on. The schoolmaster does not teach. He canes
or impositions or "keeps in" the pupils who cannot answer
pointless questions devised to catch them out. Such questions test memory, but secure victory in examinations for the
indiscriminate encyclopedic memory, which is the most dis-
abling of all memories. Universities are infested with ped-
ants who have all recorded history at their tongues' ends,
but can make no use of it except to disqualify examinees
with the priceless gift of forgetting all events that do not
matter. Were I to keep always in mind every experience
of my 93 years living and reading I should go mad. I am
often amazed when, having to refer to old papers filed away
and forgotten, I am reminded of transactions which I could
have sworn had never occurred, and meetings with notable
persons I have no recollection of having ever seen. But this
does not disconcert me. Kipling's "Lest we forget" is often
less urgent than "Lest we remember."

Certainly, those who forget everything are impossible
politically; and I have often wished I had the memory of
Macaulay or Sidney Webb, or the patience of my player
collaborators who have to memorize speeches I have myself
written but of which at rehearsal I cannot quote two words
correctly; but on the whole the people who remember
everything they ought to forget are, if given any authority,
more dangerous than those who forget some things they
had better remember. Dr Inge, commenting on the Irish
question, pointed out how difficult is the common government of a nation which never remembers and one which
never forgets.

Anyhow, we must keep schoolmasters away from the
panel tests. My own school experience has biased me on
this point. When the time came to teach me mathematics I
was taught simply nothing: I was set to explain Euclid's

485

FARFETCHED FABLES

diagrams and theorems without a word as to their use or history or nature. I found it so easy to pick this up in class that at the end of the half year I was expected to come out well in the examinations. I entirely disgraced myself because the questions did not pose the propositions but gave only their numbers, of which I could recollect only the first five and the one about the square of the hypothenuse.

The next step was algebra, again without a word of definition or explanation. I was simply expected to do the sums in Colenso's schoolbook.

Now an uninstructed child does not dissociate numbers or their symbols from the material objects it knows quite well how to count. To me a and b, when they meant numbers, were senseless unless they meant butter and eggs and a pound of cheese. I had enough mathematical faculty to infer that if $a = b$ and $b = c$, a must equal c. But I had wit enough to infer that if a quart of brandy equals three Bibles, and three Bibles the Apostles' Creed, the Creed is worth a quart of brandy, manifestly a *reductio ad absurdum*.

My schoolmaster was only the common enemy of me and my schoolfellows. In his presence I was forbidden to move, or to speak except in answer to his questions. Only by stealth could I relieve the torture of immobility by stealthily exchanging punches (called "the coward's blow") with the boy next me. Had my so-called teacher been my father, and I a child under six, I could have asked him questions, and had the matter explained to me. As it was, I did exactly what the Vatican felt everybody would do if Galileo picked a hole in the Bible. I concluded that mathematics are blazing nonsense, and thereafter made a fool of myself even in my twenties when I made the acquaintance of the editor of Biometrika, Karl Pearson, who maintained that no theory could be valid until it was proved mathematically. I threw in his teeth my conviction that his specialty was an absurdity. Instead of enlightening me he laughed (he had an engaging smile and was a most attractive man) and left me encouraged in my ignorance by my observation that though he was scrupulous and sceptical when counting and correlating, he was as credulous and careless as any ordinary mortal in selecting the facts to be counted. Not until Graham Wallas, a born teacher, enlightened me, did I understand mathematics and realize their enormous importance.

SOME RESULTS

Is it to be wondered at that with such school methods masquerading as education, millions of scholars pass to their graves unhonored and unsung whilst men and women totally illiterate or at most selftaught to read and write in their late teens, rise to eminence whilst "university engineers" are drugs in the labor market compared to those who go straight from their elementary schools to the factory, speaking slum English and signing with a mark. Experienced employers tell us they prefer uneducated workmen. Senior Wranglers and Double-Firsts and Ireland Scholars see no more than costermongers in the fact that a saving of 1 per cent per minute of time in writing English means 525,000 per cent per year, and that ten times that much could be saved by adding 15 letters to the alphabet. It took a world war to establish summer time after it had been contemptuously rejected by our pundits as a negligible fad. The fact that by adding two digits to our arithmetic tables we could make 16 figures do the work of twenty (a colossal saving of time for the world's bookkeeping) appeals no more to winners of the mathematical tripos than the infinitesimal calculus to a newly born infant. Political controversy is now (1949) raging on the nationalization of our industries; yet not one word is said nor a figure given as to its basic advantage in the fact that coal can be had in Sunderland for the trouble of picking it up from the sands at low tide, whilst in Whitehaven it has to be hewn out under the sea, miles from the pit head, or that land in the City of London fetches fabulous prices per square foot and twenty miles off will hardly support a goose on the common, thus making it impossible without nationalization to substitute cost-of-production prices, averaged over the whole country, for prices loaded with enormous rents for the proprietors of London land and Seaham mines, not equivalently surtaxed. Doctors and dental surgeons who excuse their high fees on the ground that they are working until

half past four in the afternoon earning rent for their landlords, and only the rest of the day for themselves and their
families, are so incapable of putting two and two together
politically that they vote like sheep for the landlords,
and denounce land municipalization as robbery. Had the
late famous President Franklin Roosevelt, a thoroughly
schooled gentleman-amateur Socialist, been taught the law
of rent, his first attempts at The New Deal would not have
failed so often. I could cite dozens of examples of how what
our Cabinet ministers call Democracy, and what I call
Mobocracy, places in authority would-be rulers who assure
us that they can govern England, plus the Commonwealth,
plus Western Europe, and finally the world, when as a
matter of fact they could not manage a village shop successfully.

CAPITAL ACCUMULATION

Capital is spare money saved by postponement of con-
sumption. To effect this in a private property system some
people must be made so rich that when they are satiated with
every purchasable luxury they have still a surplus which they
can invest without privation. In the nineteenth century this
arrangement was accepted as final and inevitable by able
and benevolent public men like Thomas de Quincey, Macaulay, Austin, Cobden, and Bright, until Karl Marx dealt
it a mortal blow by shewing from official records that its
delusive prosperity masked an abyss of plague, pestilence
and famine, battle, murder, compulsory prostitution, and
premature death. Ferdinand Lassalle in Germany had already demonstrated the injustice of its "iron law of wages."

ENGLAND'S SHAMEFACED LEADERSHIP

England was by no means silent on the subject. Marx's
invective, though it rivalled Jeremiah's, was pale beside
the fierce diatribes of Ruskin, who puzzled his readers by
describing himself as an old Tory and the Reddest of Red
Communists. Carlyle called our boasted commercial prosperity shooting Niagara, and dismissed Cobdenist Free
Trade as Godforsaken nonsense. The pious Conservative
Lord Shaftesbury and the Radical atheist demagogue Bradlaugh were at one in their agitation for Acts in restraint of

FARFETCHED FABLES

the prevalent ruthless exploitation of labor. Robert Owen had called for a New Moral world as loudly as any of our present post war Chadbands. It was he who made current the word Socialism as the alternative to Capitalist plutocracy. When the Russian Bolsheviks went ruinously wrong by ignoring "the inevitability of gradualness" and attempting a catastrophic transfer of industry and agriculture from private to public ownership, it was the Englishman Sidney Webb and his Fabians who corrected them and devised the new economic policy Lenin had to announce, and Stalin to put in practice. Thus Englishmen can claim to have been pioneers in the revolutionary development of political organization since Cobdenism conquered us.

Unfortunately, whenever English parties effect an advance, they are so ashamed of it that they immediately throw away all credit for it by protesting that they are respectable citizens who would never dream of changing anything, and shouting their abhorrence of all the wicked foreigners who are in effect taking their advice. And then they are surprised when their disciples, especially in Russia, regard them as enemies, and the Marxist Left wins more and more votes from them.

THE THREATENING FUTURE: HOMILIES NO USE

While the time lag lasts the future remains threatening. The problem of optimum wealth distribution, which Plutocracy, with its inherent class warfare, has hopelessly failed to solve, will not yield to the well-intentioned Utopian amateurs who infest our parliaments and parties, imagining that it can be solved by giving all of us according to our needs and balancing the account by taking from each of us according to our productive capacity. They might as well decree that we shall do unto others as we would have them do to us, or achieve the greatest good for the greatest number, or soothe our souls with exhortations to love oneanother. Homilies cut no ice in administrative councils: the literary talent and pulpit eloquence that has always been calling for a better world has never succeeded, though it has stolen credit for many changes forced on it by circumstances and

489

natural selection. The satirical humor of Aristophanes, the wisecracks of Confucius, the precepts of the Buddha, the parables of Jesus, the theses of Luther, the *jeux d'esprit* of Erasmus and Montaigne, the Utopias of More and Fourier and Wells, the allegories of Voltaire, Rousseau, and Bunyan, the polemics of Leibniz and Spinoza, the poems of Goethe, Shelley, and Byron, the manifesto of Marx and Engels, Mozart's Magic Flute and Beethoven's Ode to Joy, with the music dramas of Wagner, to say nothing of living seers of visions and dreamers of dreams: none of these esthetic feats have made Reformations or Revolutions; and most of them, as far as they have been thrown into the hands of the common people as the Protestant Reformation threw the Bible, have been followed by massacres, witch hunts, civil and international wars of religion, and all forms of persecution, from petty boycotts to legalized burnings at the stake and breakings on the wheel, highly popular as public entertainments. The nineteenth century, which believed itself to be the climax of civilization, of Liberty, Equality, and Fraternity, was convicted by Karl Marx of being the worst and wickedest on record; and the twentieth, not yet half through, has been ravaged by two so-called world wars culminating in the atrocity of the atomic bomb.

As long as atomic bomb manufacture remains a trade secret known to only one State, it will be the mainstay of Peace because all the States (including the one) will be afraid of it. When the secret is out atomic warfare will be barred as poison gas was in 1938–45; and war will be possible as before. How that may happen is the subject of the first two farfetched fables that follow.

Ayot Saint Lawrence,
    1948–9

FARFETCHED FABLES

FIRST FABLE

A PUBLIC *park on a fine summer afternoon. Chairs for hire scattered about the sward.*

A young woman of respectable appearance arrives and seats herself. A park attendant approaches her; takes two-pence from her; says "Kew," short for "Thankyou"; and gives her a ticket.

A well-dressed young man enters and takes the nearest chair. The attendant takes two-pence as before, and passes on.

YOUNG MAN. Excuse me. Would you rather I sat farther away?

YOUNG WOMAN. As you please. I dont care where you sit.

YOUNG MAN. I hope you dont think me intrusive?

YOUNG WOMAN. I am not thinking about you at all. But you may talk to me if you want to. I dont mind.

YOUNG MAN. Well, I certainly do want to talk to you. In fact that is why I took this chair.

YOUNG WOMAN. I thought so. Well, talk away. What have you to say to me?

YOUNG MAN. Ive never seen you before. But at first sight I find you irresistibly attractive.

YOUNG WOMAN. Lots of men do. What of it?

YOUNG MAN. Some women find me attractive. Are you married?

YOUNG WOMAN. No. Are you?

YOUNG MAN. No. Are you engaged?

YOUNG WOMAN. No. What is it to you whether I am engaged or not?

YOUNG MAN. Need you ask? Ive got into this conversation with a view to our possible marriage.

YOUNG WOMAN. Nothing doing. I'll not marry.

YOUNG MAN. It is odd that so many attractive women are unmarried. Dull ugly frumps never seem to have any difficulty in finding mates. Why wont you marry? I am available.

YOUNG WOMAN. My father was shot in the Great War

491

that now seems such a little one. My eldest brother was killed in Normandy when we were liberating France there. His wife and children were blown to bits by a bomb that wrecked the whole street they lived in. Do you think I'll bear children for that?

YOUNG MAN. They died for England. They made war to end war. Dont you admire bravery? Dont you love your country?

YOUNG WOMAN. What use is bravery now when any coward can launch an atomic bomb? Until men are wise and women civilized they had better not be born. At all events I shall not bring them into this wicked world to kill and be killed.

An excited middle-aged man comes along waving a newspaper and cheering.

M. A. M. Hurrah! Have you heard the news?

YOUNG MAN. No. Whats happened?

M. A. M. No more war. The United Nations have abolished it.

YOUNG MAN [*disparagingly*] Hmm! May I have a look at your paper?

M. A. M. Here it is in black and white. You may keep it. I'll buy another. Hurrah! hurrah!! hurrah!!!

He hands over the paper and rushes away, cheering.

YOUNG WOMAN. What does it say?

YOUNG MAN [*reading the headlines*] "THE WORLD AT PEACE AT LAST. WASHINGTON AGREES. MOSCOW AGREES. CHINA AGREES. THE WESTERN UNION AGREES. THE FEDERALISTS AGREE. THE COMMUNISTS AGREE. THE FASCISTS AGREE. ATOMIC BOMB MANUFACTURE MADE A CAPITAL CRIME. UNIVERSAL SECURITY GUARANTEED."

YOUNG WOMAN. Have the armies been disbanded? Have the military academies been closed? Has conscription been abolished?

YOUNG MAN. It doesnt say. Oh yes: here is a stop press paragraph. "ARMIES WILL IN FUTURE BE CALLED WORLD POLICE. NO MORE CONSCRIPTION." Hm!

YOUNG WOMAN. You dont seem pleased.

YOUNG MAN. I dont swallow all that rot about no more

war. Men will always fight even if they have nothing to fight with but their fists. And the women will egg them on.

YOUNG WOMAN. What does the leading article say?

YOUNG MAN [*turning to the leader page and quoting*] "Truce of God begins a new chapter in the history of the globe. The atomic bomb has reduced war to absurdity; for it threatens not only both victors and vanquished but the whole neutral world. We do not as yet know for certain that the bomb that disintegrated Hiroshima is not still at work disintegrating. The weather has been curiously unusual ever since. But no nation will ever venture on atomic warfare again."

YOUNG WOMAN. Do you believe that?

YOUNG MAN. Yes; but it wont stop war. In 1914 the Germans tried poison gas; and so did we. But the airmen who dropped it on the cities could not stay in the air for long; and when they had to come down they found the streets full of the gas, because poison gas is heavier than air and takes many days to disperse. So in the last war gas was not used; and atomic bombs wont be used in the next one.

YOUNG WOMAN. Oh! So you think there will be a next one.

YOUNG MAN. Of course there will, but not with atomic bombs. There is no satisfaction in seeing the world lit up by a blinding flash, and being burnt to dust before you have time to think about it, with every stick and stone for miles around falling and crumbling, all the drains and telephones and electrics torn up and flung into the air, and people who are too far off to be burnt die of radiation. Besides, bombs kill women. Killing men does not matter: the women can replace them; but kill the women and you kill the human race.

YOUNG WOMAN. That wont stop war. Somebody will discover a poison gas lighter than air! It may kill the inhabitants of a city; but it will leave the city standinig and in working order.

YOUNG MAN [*thoughtfully, letting the newspaper drop on his knees*] That is an idea.

YOUNG WOMAN. What idea?

493

YOUNG MAN. Yours. There is a lot of money in it. The Government gave £100,000 to the man who found out how to land our army in Normandy in 1945.

YOUNG WOMAN. Governments will pay millions for any new devilment, though they wont pay twopence for a washing machine. When a Jewish chemist found out how to make high explosive cheaply we made him a present of Jerusalem, which didnt belong to us.

YOUNG MAN [*hopefully*] Yes, by George! So we did.

YOUNG WOMAN. Well, what of it?

YOUNG MAN. I'm a chemist.

YOUNG WOMAN. Does that mean that you are in the atomic bomb business?

YOUNG MAN. No; but I'm on the staff in a chlorine gas factory. The atomic bomb people may be barking up the wrong tree.

YOUNG WOMAN [*rising wrathfully*] So that is what you are! One of these scientific devils who are destroying us! Well, you shall not sit next me again. Go where you belong: to hell. Good day to you.

She goes away.

YOUNG MAN [*still thoughtful*] Lighter than air, eh? [*Slower*] Ligh—ter—than—air?

The scene fades out.

SECOND FABLE

A ROOM *in the War Office in London. The Commander-in-Chief at work reading letters. A secretary opening them. The telephone rings. The secretary answers it.*

SEC. Yes? . . . [*To the C.-in-C.*] Lord Oldhand from the Foreign Office.

C.-IN-C. Shew him up; and get out.

SEC. He is shewing himself up. He must have heard—

Lord O. bursts in. The secretary hurries out.

OLDHAND. Ulsterbridge: have you heard the news?

C.-IN-C. Of course Ive heard the news. Here in the War Office we have to get the news in six minutes. At the Foreign Office six years is soon enough for you. Sit down.

OLDHAND [*seating himself*] Is this a time for your Irish jokes? What the devil are we to do? How much do you know?

C.-IN-C. Only that there is not one of God's creatures left alive in the Isle of Wight. I shall have to send every soldier in England to cremate the dead or throw them into the sea. The Home Office will have to find 88,454 civilians to dust the houses with vacuum cleaners and keep the banks and the telephone services and the wireless and water supplies and the lighting and the markets and all the rest of it going.

OLDHAND. Precisely. And all this is your fault.

C.-IN-C. Oldhand: you lie, categorically. How my fault?

OLDHAND. Do you forget that when that fellow who found out how to make volatile poison gas offered us his discovery it was you who turned him down?

C.-IN-C. That cockney blighter? He wanted a hundred thousand pounds for it. And the scientific authorities assured me that every penny spent on anything but atomic research would be wasted.

OLDHAND. Well, he sold it to the South African negro Hitler, Ketchewayo the Second, for a hundred and fifty thousand. Ketch could afford it: his backyard is chock full of diamonds. The fellow made a Declaration of Independence for Zululand with himself as emperor. Capetown, Natal, and Rhodesia went to war with him and involved us in it. That made it your job, didnt it?

C.-IN-C. Not a bit of it. Ketch is far too cunning to go to war with us. He did not go to war with anybody. He dropped his bombs on the Isle of Wight just to shew Capetown and the rest that the world was at his mercy. He selected the Isle of Wight because it's a safe distance from his own people, just as we selected Hiroshima in 1945. He thinks islands are out-of-the-way little places that dont matter to us. But he maintains that his relations with the Commonwealth are friendly; and as you have not declared war on him we are still technically at peace. That makes it your job, not mine, though as usual when there is anything to be done except what was done last time, I shall have to do it.

OLDHAND. You have a very important diplomatic point there, I admit; but it must stand over. Meanwhile let us put our heads together and get to work. The first practical step is to hang this traitor who has sold his accursed invention to the enemy.

C.-IN-C. What! Dont you know that he went to live in the Isle of Wight as the safest civilized place in the world, and is now lying dead there, killed by his own poison gas?

OLDHAND. Serve the scoundrel right! there is the hand of God in this. But your mistake in turning the fellow down was none the less a mistake because he is dead and you are alive—so far. You may be dead tomorrow.

C.-IN-C. So may you.

OLDHAND. Yes; and it will be your doing.

C.-IN-C. How was I to know that the gas was any good? I get dozens of such inventions every week, all guaranteed to make an end of war and establish heaven on earth. I'm a soldier, not a chemist. I have to go by what the scientific authorities tell me. Youre a diplomatist, not a laboratory bloke. Do you know what an isotype is? Do you know what a meson is? I dont: neither do you. What could you have done except what I did? kick the fellow out.

OLDHAND. Listen to me. I am, as you say, a diplomatist; and I think youll admit that I know my job after my fifteen years in the Foreign Office. You know your job too as a soldier: I dont question it. That gives us one great principle in common.

c.-in-c. And what is that, may I ask?

oldhand. It is to regard all our allies as Powers that may at any moment become our enemies. The public thinks it is the other way about; but we know better. We must be prepared for war before everything.

c.-in-c. We never are, thanks to the damned taxpayers who wont vote us the money. But of course I agree in principle. What then?

oldhand. I'll tell you what then. What sort of fellow was this volatile gas man? You interviewed him. What did you make of him?

c.-in-c. Oh, a middleclass cad through and through. Out for money and nothing else. Big money.

oldhand. Just so. Well, what security have we that after selling his invention to Ketchewayo in Africa he did not sell it over again in Europe? All he had to do was to hand over half a sheet of notepaper with a prescription on it and pocket another hundred and fifty thousand. Every State in Europe and America except ourselves may have it up its sleeve for all we know. The gas may come in at that window while we are talking.

c.-in-c. That is true: it may. Let us hope it wont.

oldhand. Hope wont help us if it does. Our first duty is at all cost to get hold of that receipt, and make the gas ourselves. When the other States know that we have plenty of it none of them will dare to start using it. Meanwhile—

c.-in-c. Meanwhile I have to provide gas masks for everybody in the country, and make wearing of them compulsory. I have to bury the dead; and I cant spare enough soldiers to do it. Youll have to buy a million vultures from Bombay to pick the bones of the dead before they stink us out. We must make every house in the country gas-proof, and rigidly enforce the closing of all windows. We must— [*he is interrupted by a siren alarm, followed by an artillery salvo*]. What the devil is that?

oldhand. Nothing. We have ordered a salute of five

497

guns to celebrate the hundred and first birthday of the President of the Board of Trade.

The siren screams again.

C.-IN-C. [*singing drowsily*]
> "Oh we dont want to lose you;
> But we think you ought to go."

He collapses, apparently into a deep sleep.

SHOUTS WITHOUT. Shut the windows! Shut the windows! Gas! Gas! *Another salvo.*

Oldhand rises and rushes toward the open window to shut it. He staggers, and can only clutch at the sill to steady himself.

OLDHAND [*with a vacant grin which develops into a smile of radiant happiness, sings*] "It's a long way to Tipperary—"

He falls dead.

THIRD FABLE

A PLEASANT *spot in the Isle of Wight. A building of steel and glass is inscribed* ANTHROPOMETRIC LABORATORY. *On the terrace before it a bench and chairs. Seated in conference are a middle-aged gentleman in a gay pullover and broadly striped nylon trousers, and two women: a comely matron in a purple academic gown, and a junior in short-skirted overall and blue slacks.*

A tourist comes along. His embroidered smock and trimmed beard proclaim the would-be artist. He stops on seeing the three, and produces a camera.

THE GIRL. Hello! What are you doing here?

THE TOURIST. Only hiking round the island. May I take a snapshot?

THE GIRL. You have no business to be here. You have no business to be on the Isle of Wight at all. Who let you land?

THE TOURIST. I came in my own boat. I landed on the beach. What harm am I doing?

THE GIRL. This is a colony of the Upper Ten. Anybodies are not allowed here.

THE TOURIST. I'm not an Anybody: I'm classed as a Mediocrity.

THE GIRL. Neither Mediocrities nor Anybodies are admitted. Go back to your boat; and clear out.

THE MATRON. Stop. You say you are classed as a Mediocrity. Did you pass with honors?

THE TOURIST. No. They were grossly unfair to me. I'm not a Mediocrity: I'm a genius.

THE MATRON. Indeed! Have you a job of any sort?

THE TOURIST. No. They offered me a job as hospital porter because I'm physically strong. How utterly beneath me! When I told them I am a genius and shewed them my drawings, they offered to make me a housepainter. I dont want to paint houses: my destiny is to paint temples in fresco.

THE GENTLEMAN [*amused*] Like Michael Angelo, eh?

THE TOURIST. Oh, I can do better work than Michael

499

Angelo. He is out of date. I am ultra-modern.

THE GENTLEMAN [*to the Matron*] The very man for us.

THE MATRON [*to the Tourist*] You are quite sure that you are a genius, are you?

THE TOURIST. Quite. I dont look like a bank clerk, do I?

THE MATRON. Well, we have no temples here for you to paint; but we can offer you a job that will enable you to support yourself and have enough leisure to paint what you like until the world recognizes your genius.

THE TOURIST. What sort of work will I have to do? I warn you I cant pass examinations; and I hate being regulated and disciplined. I must have perfect freedom.

THE MATRON. Anthropometric work is what we do here. Classifying men and women according to their abilities. Filling up their qualification certificates. Analyzing their secretions and reactions and so on. Quite easy laboratory work.

THE TOURIST. That will suit me down to the ground. I'm a first-rate judge of character.

THE MATRON. Splendid. Take this in to the office at the end of the passage on the right. You can have tea in the canteen when they have settled with you. [*She hands him a ticket*].

THE TOURIST [*hungrily*] Thank you.

He takes the ticket and goes into the laboratory.

THE GENTLEMAN. He will be a heaven-sent treasure.

THE GIRL. I dont agree. He seems to me to be a conceited fool who thinks himself a genius.

THE GENTLEMAN. Exactly. We shall go by his secretions and reactions: not by his own notions.

A young man in rags, unshaven, and disreputable looking, comes along.

THE GIRL. Who is this awful looking tramp? [*To him*] Hello! Who are you; and what are you doing here?

HE. I'm doing nothing here because nobody will give me anything to do. I'm devilishly hungry. Have you by any chance a crust of bread to spare?

THE MATRON. How did you get into this island? Why were you allowed to land?

HE. I was a stowaway, madam. They wanted to send me

back; but the captain of the return boat would not take me: he said I was too dirty and probably infectious and verminous. The medical officer quarantined me; but I convinced him that I am only a harmless tramp, fit for nothing better; so he let me go. And here I am.

THE MATRON. Do you do nothing to earn your bread?

THE TRAMP. I ask for it. People mostly give it to me. If not, I sing for it. Then they give me a penny or two to stop singing and go away. It's a way of life like any other. It suits me. I'm good for nothing else.

THE GENTLEMAN. How do you know you are good for nothing else?

THE TRAMP. Well, what else am I good for? You can take me into your laboratory and try if you like. There is a canteen there, isnt there?

THE GENTLEMAN. I see you are not unintelligent. You are not uneducated. You could surely work for your living.

THE TRAMP. No. Anything but that. Working is not living. If you are on that tack you wont give me anything: I know your sort. Good morning. [*He starts to go*].

THE GIRL. Stop. You are hungry. I'll get you some bread. [*She goes into the laboratory*].

THE TRAMP. Look at that, now! Ask; and it shall be given to you.

THE GENTLEMAN. Listen to me. I'll give you five guineas if youll submit to a test of your capacity in our laboratory.

THE TRAMP. It would be robbing you. I tell you I have no capacity. I'm an out-and-out Goodfornothing. And five guineas is too much to give a tramp. I must live from hand to mouth. All the joy of life goes when you have five guineas in your pocket.

THE GENTLEMAN. You need not keep it in your pocket. You can buy a decent suit of clothes with it. You need one badly. You are in rags.

THE TRAMP. Of course I'm in rags. Who would give alms to a well-dressed man? It's my business to be in rags.

THE GENTLEMAN. Very well. I'll have you arrested and put through the laboratory and classified. That is the law, compulsory for everybody. If you refuse you may be classed as irresponsible. That means that youll be enlisted in the military police or kept under tutelage in a Labor Brigade. Or you may be classed as dangerous and incorrigible, in which case youll be liquidated.

THE TRAMP. I know all that. What good will it do you? Why are you offering me five guineas when you have only to call the police and put me through the mill for nothing?

THE GENTLEMAN. You have ability enough to cross-examine me. You may have administrative ability, and be cunning enough to shirk its responsibilities. You may be one of the Artful Dodgers who know that begging is easier and happier than bossing.

THE TRAMP. Ha! ha! ha! You suspect me of being a heaven-born genius! Very well: test me til you are black in the face. Youll only be wasting your time; but that wont hurt me, because time is of no value to me: it's my profession to waste it. Youll find I can do nothing. Mind: I'm not a fool: youre quite right there; but I'm a duffer, a hopeless duffer. I can always see what the other fellows ought to do; but I cant do it. Ive tried my hand at everything: no use: Ive failed every time. Ive tastes but no talents. I'd like to be a Shakespear; but I cant write plays. I'd like to be a Michael Angelo or a Raphael; but I can neither draw nor paint. I'd love to be a Mozart or a Beethoven; but I can neither compose a symphony nor play a concerto. I envy Einstein his mathematical genius; but beyond the pence table I cant add two and two together. I know a lot, and can do nothing. When I tell the clever chaps what to do, they wont do it, and tell me I'm ignorant and crazy. And so I am: I know it only too well. Youd better give me a meal or the price of one, and let me jog on the footpath way. My name's not Prospero: it's Autolycus.

THE GENTLEMAN. If you know what other people ought to do, youll be too busy telling them, and making laws for them, to do any of it yourself. In with you into the canteen; and get your bread there.

THE TRAMP. I fly for the bread. You are the boss here: the archpriest, chooser of rulers, lord of human destiny. And your choice is a government of tramps! Ha! ha! ha! ha! ha! ha! ha! [*He goes into the laboratory roaring with laughter*].

THE GENTLEMAN. Two big catches for today. A nincompoop who thinks he's a genius; and a genius who thinks he's a nincompoop.

THE MATRON. I prefer nincompoops. I can always depend on them to do what was done last time. But I never know what a genius will be up to next, except that it will be something upsetting.

FOURTH FABLE

THE same place in the Isle of Wight: but the building is now inscribed DIET COMMISSIONERS. A Commissioner in cap and gown sits at a writing table talking into a dictaphone. He has earphones hanging from his ears.

COMMISSIONER. What I am going to dictate is for the printer; so keep a carbon copy. It is for the new edition of my book on Human Diet. Are you ready? . . . Right. The heading is Chapter four. Living on Air. Now for the text. Ahem!

In the twentieth century the tribes of New Zealand had, under the influence of British colonists, left off eating their prisoners of war. The British themselves, influenced by a prophet whose name has come down to us in various forms as Shelley, Shakespear, and Shavius, had already, after some centuries of restricted cannibalism in which only fishes, frogs, birds, sheep, cows, pigs, rabbits, and whales were eaten, been gradually persuaded to abstain from these also, and to live on plants and fruits, and even on grass, honey, and nuts: a diet which they called vegetarian. Full stop. New paragraph. Ahem!

As this change saved the labor of breeding animals for food, and supported human health and longevity quite as well, if not better, than the eating of dead animals, it was for some time unchallenged as a step forward in civilization. But some unforeseen consequences followed. When cattle were no longer bred and slaughtered for food, milk and butter, cheese and eggs, were no longer to be had. Grass, leaves, and nettles became the staple diet. This was sufficient for rude physical health. At the Olympic Games grass eating athletes broke all the records. This was not surprising, as it had long been known that bulls and elephants, fed on grass and leaves, were the strongest, most fertile, most passionate animals known. But they were also the most ferocious, being so dangerous that nobody dared cross a field in which a bull was loose, and every elephant had to have an armed keeper to restrain it. It had also been noticed that

504

human vegetarians were restless, pugnacious, and savagely abusive in their continual controversies with the remaining meat eaters, who found it easy and pleasant to lead sedentary lives in stuffy rooms whilst the vegetarians could not live without much exercise in the fresh air. When grass eating became general men became more ferocious and dangerous than bulls. Happily they also became less capable of organized action of any kind. They could not or would not make political alliances, nor engage in industrial mass production or wage world wars. Atomic bombs and poison gases and the like were quite beyond their powers of cooperation: their ferocities and animosities, like those of the bull, did not go beyond trespassers within sight and reach. With the ending of wars their numbers increased enormously; but to the few born thinkers who still cropped up among them and ruled them as far as they were capable of being ruled, it was apparent that they were changing into supergorillas through eating grass and leaves. And though they lived longer than the meat eaters, they still suffered from certain deadly diseases and from decay of teeth, failure of eyesight, and decrepitude in old age. Their ablest biologists had to agree that the human race, having tried eating everything on earth that was eatable, had found no food that did not sooner or later poison them. This was challenged by a Russian woman, a noted vegetarian athlete. She pointed out that there was a diet that had not been tried: namely, living on air and water. The supergorillas ridiculed her, alleging that air is not food: it is nothing; and mankind cannot live on nothing in empty space. But a famous mathematician shewed just then that there is no such thing as nothing, and that space is not emptiness and in fact does not exist. There is substance, called matter, everywhere: in fact, the universe consists of nothing else; but whether we can perceive it, or eat and drink it, depends on temperature, rate of radiation, and the sensitiveness of the instruments for detecting and measuring it. As temperature rises, water changes from solid ice to liquid fluid, from liquid fluid to steam, from steam to gas; but it is none the less substantial even at temperatures that are quite immeasurable and hardly conceivable. It followed logically that living on air is as possible as living on flesh or on grass and chopped carrots, though as men cannot live under water, nor fishes out of it, each phase of substance has its appropriate form of life and diet and set of habits. Such creatures as angels are as possible as whales and minnows, elephants and microbes.

The Russian woman claimed that she had lived for months on air and water, but on condition that the air was fresh and that she took the hardest physical exercise daily. It was already known that the vigils and fasts of saints did not weaken them when their spiritual activity was intense enough to produce a state of ecstasy. Full stop: new paragraph.

This briefly is the history of the epoch-making change in social organization produced by the ending of the food problem which had through all recorded history made men the slaves of nature, and defeated all their aspirations to be free to do what they like instead of what they must. The world became a world of athletes, artists, craftsmen, physicists, and mathematicians, instead of farmers, millers, bakers, butchers, bar tenders, brewers, and distillers. Hunger and thirst, which had for centuries meant the need for bread and onions, cheese and beer, beef and mutton, became a search for knowledge of nature and power over it, and a desire for truth and righteousness. The supergorilla became the soldier and servant of Creative Evolution. Full stop. Postscript.

Stop typing and listen to instructions. What I have just dictated is for the tenth edition of my primer for infant schools in the rudimentary biology series. I have dictated only the full stops at the end of the paragraphs. I will fill in the commas and colons and semicolons on the typescript. Leave the type and the format and the illustrations to the printer: he is a better artist in books than I am. He will need paper for two hundred million copies. Goodbye.

He takes off his headphones; puts the cover on the dictaphone; sighs with relief at having done a tedious job; and goes into the building.

FIFTH FABLE

THE scene is unchanged; but the building is now labelled GENETIC INSTITUTE. *On the terrace, seated round a table loaded with old books, are four persons of uncertain age, apparently in the prime of life. Two of them are male, one female, the fourth a hermaphrodite. They wear white sleeveless tunics like heralds' tabards on which are embroidered different flower designs, the two men being distinguished by a thistle and a shamrock respectively, the woman by a rose, and the hermaphrodite by an elm with a vine round its trunk. The sleeves of the men are red, of the woman green, of the hermaphrodite the two colors in a chequered harlequin pattern. The men are close-cropped and cleanshaven: the woman's hair is dressed like that of the Milo Venus. They are in animated discussion, each with an open book on which they occasionally thump to emphasize their points.*

SHAMROCK. I cannot make head or tail of this nineteenth century stuff. They seem to have considered our business unmentionable, and tried to write books about it in which it was not mentioned. [*He shuts the book impatiently.*]

ROSE. That seems hardly possible. Our business is the very first business of any human society: the reproduction of the human race, the most mentionable subject in the world and the most important.

SHAMROCK. Well, Ive been through every scrap of nineteenth century writing that remains; and I tell you that their textbooks on physiology dont mention the reproductive organs nor hint at such a thing as sex. You would not guess from them that it existed.

HERM. To say nothing of hermaphrodites. Being myself a hermaphrodite I have looked myself up in the nineteenth century books; and I simply wasnt there.

THISTLE. Oh, they were the damnedest fools: it is impossible to understand how they kept going for a week, much less for years. They had not brains enough to make an alphabet capable of spelling their language. They counted their goods in twelves but could not count their money in

507

more than tens because they had only ten fingers and could not invent the two missing figures. They could not change their working hours by the sun oftener than twice a year; and it took one of the worst of the killing matches they called wars to make them go even that far. Their calendar is incomprehensible: they could not fix their festivals nor make their months tally with the moon. In music their keyboards had only twelve notes in the octave instead of our sixty-four. One would think they might at least have managed nineteen to play their babyish thirds and sixths bearably in tune. They wasted millions of hours every day because they could not or would not do the simplest things; and when their five per cent of geniuses made wonderful machines for them: big machines that could rise from the ground and fly, and little ones that could think and calculate, they accepted them as gifts from some imaginary paradise they called heaven. When one of their bodily organs went wrong they did not set it right: they just cut it out, and left the patient to recover from the shock or die. When the patient was ill all over and could not be cut to pieces they dosed him with poisons: I hunted out a case of a well-known woman who was given nine different poisons for some trouble they called typhoid. The amazing thing is that she survived it. She must have had the constitution of a bear. It was in the nineteenth century that they gave up believing in idols and priests, and took to believing in medicine men and surgeons. Let us drop digging into this past that is unconceivable, and start from what we really know of the present.

He shuts his book and throws it away.

SHAMROCK [*shutting his book*] Agreed. But why did they consider sex unmentionable?

ROSE. Simply because their methods were so disgusting that they had no decent language for them. You think their methods were like ours, and their passions like ours. You could not make a greater mistake. The seminal fluids which our chemists make in the laboratory, and which it is our business to experiment with, were unknown to them: they had to use glandular excretions from the living body to perpetuate the race. To initiate births they had to practise personal contacts which I would rather not describe. Strangest of all, they seem to have experienced in such contacts the ecstasies which are normal with us in our pursuit of knowledge and power, and culminate in our explorations and discoveries. The religions they believed in were so wildly absurd that one would suppose they could believe anything.

SHAMROCK. Oh, come! They must have had some common sense or they couldnt have lived.

ROSE. They had gleams of it. In spite of their sensual ecstasies, they had decency enough to reserve their highest veneration for persons who abstained from them, exalting them under the special titles of saints, nuns, priests, angels, gods and the like.

HERM. Not always. There were people called Greeks who had dozens of gods whose adventures were scandalously sensual. They poisoned an old man for trying to teach their young men to reason. Serve him right, too; for some of his reasonings were sheer logomachies: in England called puns.

ROSE. True. Another set of them, called Jews or Israelites, tortured a young man to death for trying to persuade them that the divinity they worshipped was in themselves, and promising that if they killed him he would rise from the dead and establish a kingdom of righteousness not among angels in the clouds but on earth among human men and women.

HERM. That was not why they killed him: they believed anyone who promised that much. They killed him because he made a riot in their temple and drove out the money changers, whom he mistook for thieves, being too young and not enough of a financier to know how useful and necessary they were to pilgrims. His name was Hitler, poor chap!

ROSE. All the same, utterly as we are unlike these primitive savages, we are descended from them; and though we manufacture ourselves scientifically, we are not yet agreed as to the sort of mankind we ought to make, nor how many at a time, nor how long they ought to last. We all want the Just Man Made Perfect; but when our chemists ask us for an exact prescription of the necessary protoplasms, hormones, vitamins, enzymes and the rest, we never agree on the last milligram of each ingredient; and it is that milligram that determines whether the resulting product will be a poet or a mathematician.

HERM. I'm against all that. It revolts me. I tell you again and again we shall never make decent human beings out of chemical salts. We must get rid of our physical bodies altogether, except for stuffed specimens in the Natural History Museum. I dont want to be a body: I want to be a mind and nothing but a mind. In the sixteenth century men made it their first article of religion to worship a god who had neither body, parts, nor passions: sensual passions. Even in the dark ages of the nineteenth and twentieth centuries there was a man who aspired to be a vortex in thought, and a woman who declared that the mind made the body and not the body the mind. Demolish all the laboratories. Build temples in which we can pray and pray and pray for deliverance from our bodies until the change occurs naturally as all real changes do.

ROSE. My child, how much farther would that take us? We should still be unable to agree on what sort of mind we needed. Prayer, we know, is a great creative power; but to pray effectively you must know what to pray for. In the sixteenth century there was a famous mathematician who declared that our utmost knowledge was no more than a grain of sand picked up on the margin of the ocean of our ignorance. He was a silly fellow who thought that the world was only forty centuries old and that straight lines were ethically right; but the utmost that we know is still no more than his grain of sand. I would like to be a mind without a body; but that has not happened to me yet; and meanwhile, as another sixteenth sage said, the world must be peopled; and as we can no longer endure the old unmentionable methods we must make material citizens out of material substances in biochemical laboratories. I was manufactured that way myself; and so were you, my boy.

HERM. My body was, and my mind such as it is. But my desire to get rid of my body was not. Where did that come from? Can you tell me?

ROSE. No; but when we know even that, it will be only another grain of sand on the seashore. But it will be worth picking up; and so will all the other grains.

SHAMROCK. In the infinity of time, when the oceans dry up and make no more sand, we shall pick them all up. What then?

ROSE. The pursuit of knowledge and power will never end.

SIXTH AND LAST FABLE
As before, except that the building is now labelled

On the terrace are five students in class, wearing uniforms with six sleeve stripes. Their individual numbers are on their caps. Numbers 1, 2, 3, are youths. 4 and 5 are maidens. Number 1 is older than number 2, number 4 than number 5.

The teacher, a matron, in cap and gown, enters from the building and takes her place.

TEACHER. Let me introduce myself. You have just been promoted to the sixth form. I am your teacher. Explain to me how and why the sixth form differs from the fifth.

YOUTH 1. We shall explain nothing to you. If you are our teacher it is for us to question you: not for you to question us.

MAIDEN 5. Do not be prehistoric. Savages thousands of years ago schooled their children by asking them conundrums and beating them if they could not answer them. You are not going to start that game on us, are you?

YOUTH 3. If you do, Mother Hubbard, youll not have a happy time with us.

TEACHER. You are quite right. It is what I expected you to say. My question was a test. Three of you have shewn that you understand the relation between us as teacher and pupils in the sixth form. The rest of you, if you also agree, will signify the same in the usual manner.

All the students raise their hands in assent.

TEACHER. Good. Now fire away. Ask your questions.

YOUTH 3. What questions shall we ask?

TEACHER. Aha! You see it is not so easy to ask questions. Is there nothing you want to know? If not, the sixth form is not for you: it is out of your mental range; and you can go back to the fifth form and take your leaving certificate.

YOUTH 3. Oh I say! Give me time to think of something.

512

TEACHER. Two minutes; or back to the fifth you go.

YOUTH 2 [*prompting*] Ask her whether when a pine cone disappears into the ground it is the ground that wraps the pine cone up or the cone that buries itself into the clay.

TEACHER. Good, Number Two. I dont know; and neither does anyone else. And you, Number Three, do you really want to know?

YOUTH 3. No. I didnt know that cones bury themselves; and I dont care a dump whether they do or not.

TEACHER. Dont care a dump is vulgar. You should say dont care a dam.

YOUTH 3. Oh, I'm not literary. What does dam mean?

TEACHER. It means a negligible trifle.

YOUTH 2. Wrong, Teacher. My Dark Ages dictionary defines it as a form of profanity in use among clergymen.

TEACHER. In the sixth form, the teacher is always wrong.

YOUTH 1. You are both wrong. It means an animal's mother.

MAIDEN 5. No it doesnt. It means a wall across a river valley to pen it up as a lake.

YOUTH 3. All I meant is what the teacher says.

TEACHER. And so the teacher is always right. For announcing this, Number Three, I'll give you another minute to ask me a question that you do really care about.

YOUTH 3. Why are you so down on me? I am not the only one who hasnt a question ready for you.

TEACHER. The sixth form should be bursting with questions. I'll come to the others presently. I pick on you because your looks do not suggest more than fifth form brains.

YOUTH 1. Dont look at his face. Look at his fingers.

TEACHER. Fingers are not brains.

YOUTH 3. Yes they are. My brains are in my fingers: yours are only in your head. Have you ever invented a machine and constructed it?

TEACHER. No. Have you?

YOUTH 3. Yes.

TEACHER. How?

YOUTH 3. I dont know. I cant find words for it: I'm no talker. But I can do things. And I wont go down to the fifth.

Here I am and here I stick, whatever you say.

TEACHER. So you shall. You know your own mind, though you cannot speak it.

YOUTH 3. I have no mind. I can only do things.

MAIDEN 4. I have a question, Teacher.

TEACHER. Out with it.

MAIDEN 4. How is it that the things that come into Number Three's head never come into mine? Why can he do things that I cant do? Why can I do things that he cant do? I can write an essay: he cant write even a specification of the machines he invents. If you ask him to, he can only twiddle his fingers as if they were wheels and levers? He has to employ a Third Form patent agent to describe it for him.

TEACHER. Ah, now we are coming to the riddle of the universe. You young things always ask it, and will not take "I dont know" for an answer. Can any of you tell me the story of the Sphinx?

MAIDEN 5. I can. The Sphinx was a quadruped with a woman's head and breasts, who put conundrums to everyone who came along, and devoured them if they could not answer them.

TEACHER. Yes: that is the story. But where is the interest of it for you?

MAIDEN 5. Well, a story is a story. I like stories.

MAIDEN 4. She does, Teacher: she is always reading them. And she tells stories about herself. All lies.

YOUTH 2. Why does she tell lies? That is what I want to know.

YOUTH 3. The Sphinx story is rot. Why should the Sphinx eat everybody who couldnt answer its riddles?

YOUTH 1. Why should it kill itself if anyone did answer them? Tell me that.

TEACHER. Never ask why. Ask what, when, where, how, who, which; but never why. Only first form children, who think their parents know everything, ask why. In the sixth form you are supposed to know that why is unanswerable.

YOUTH 3. Nonsense. Why is not unanswerable. Why does water boil? Because its temperature has been raised to

100 Centigrade. What is wrong with that?

TEACHER. That is not why: it is how. Why was it boiled?

YOUTH 2. Because some fellow wanted to boil an egg and eat it. That is why.

TEACHER. Why did he want to eat it?

YOUTH 2. Because he wanted to live and not starve.

TEACHER. That is a fact, not a reason. Why did he want to live?

YOUTH 2. Like everybody else, I suppose.

TEACHER. Why does everybody want to live, however unhappily? Why does anybody want to live?

YOUTH 3. How the devil does anybody know? You dont know. I dont know.

TEACHER. Why dont we know?

YOUTH 2. Because we dont. Thats why.

TEACHER. No. Why is beyond knowledge. All the whys lead to the great interrogation mark that shines for ever across the sky like a rainbow. Why do we exist? Why does the universe exist?

YOUTH 1. If you ask me I should say the universe is a big joke.

MAIDEN 4. I do not see any fun in it. I should say it is a big mistake.

YOUTH 2. A joke must have a joker. A mistake must have a blunderer. If the world exists it must have a creator.

TEACHER. Must it? How do you know? One of the ancient gods, named Napoleon, pointed to the sky full of stars and said "Who made all that?" His soothsayers replied "Whoever it was, who made Him?"

MAIDEN 4. Or Her? Why—

TEACHER. Order, order! Let us have no more whys. They only set you chasing your own tails, like cats. Let us get to work. I call for questions beginning with how.

MAIDEN 5. How do thoughts come into our heads? I dont have a lot of thoughts like Number Four here. She is a highbrow; but I was born quite emptyheaded. Yet I get thoughts that nobody ever suggested to me. Where did they come from?

TEACHER. As to that, there are many theories. Have you

515

none of your own, any of you?

YOUTH 2. My grandfather lectured about the theory of the Disembodied Races. I picked it up from him when I was a kid. Of course the old man is now out-of-date: I dont take him seriously; but the theory sticks in my head because Ive never thought of anything better.

YOUTH 1. Our biology professor in the fifth swore by it. But I cannot quite stomach it.

TEACHER. Can you give me a reason for that?

YOUTH 1. Well, I was brought up to consider that we are the vanguard of civilization, the last step in creative evolution. But according to the theory we are only a survival of the sort of mankind that existed in the twentieth century, no better than black beetles compared to the supermen who evolved into the disembodied. I am not a black beetle.

YOUTH 3. Rot! If we were black beetles, the supermen would have tramped on us and killed us, or poisoned us with phosphorus.

YOUTH 1. They may be keeping us for their amusement, as we keep our pets. I told you the universe is a joke. That is my theory.

MAIDEN 5. But where do our thoughts come from? They must be flying about in the air. My father never said "I think." He always said "It strikes me." When I was a child I thought that something in the air had hit him.

YOUTH 1. What is the use of talking such utter nonsense? How could people get rid of their bodies?

TEACHER. People actually did get rid of their bodies. They got rid of their tails, of their fur, of their teeth. They acquired thumbs and enlarged their brains. They seem to have done what they liked with their bodies.

YOUTH 2. Anyhow, they had to eat and drink. They couldnt have done so without stomachs and bowels.

TEACHER. Yes they could: at least so the histories say. They found they could live on air, and that eating and drinking caused diseases of which their bodies died.

YOUTH 2. You believe that!!!

TEACHER. I believe nothing. But there is the same evidence for it as for anything else that happened millions of years before we were born. It is so written and recorded. As I can neither witness the past nor foresee the future I must take such history as there is as part of my framework of thought. Without such a framework I cannot think any more than a carpenter can cut wood without a saw.

YOUTH 2. Now you are getting beyond me, Teacher. I dont understand.

TEACHER. Do not try to understand. You must be content with such brains as you have until more understanding comes to you. Your question is where our thoughts come from and how they strike us, as Number Five's father put it. The theory is that the Disembodied Races still exist as Thought Vortexes, and are penetrating our thick skulls in their continual pursuit of knowledge and power, since they need our hands and brains as tools in that pursuit.

MAIDEN 4. Some of our thoughts are damnably mischievous. We slaughter one another and destroy the cities we build. What puts that into our heads? Not the pursuit of knowledge and power.

TEACHER. Yes; for the pursuit of knowledge and power involves the slaughter and destruction of everything that opposes it. The disembodied must inspire the soldier and the hunter as well as the pacifist and philanthropist.

YOUTH 1. But why should anybody oppose it if all thoughts come from well meaning vortexes?

TEACHER. Because even the vortexes have to do their work by trial and error. They have to learn by mistakes as well as by successes. We have to destroy the locust and the hook worm and the Colorado beetle because, if we did not, they would destroy us. We have to execute criminals who have no conscience and are incorrigible. They are old experiments of the Life Force. They were well intentioned and perhaps necessary at the time. But they are no longer either useful or necessary, and must now be exterminated. They cannot be exterminated by disembodied thought. The mongoose must be inspired to kill the cobra, the chemist to distil poisons, the physicist to make nuclear bombs, others to be big game hunters, judges, executioners, and killers of

517

all sorts, often the most amiable of mortals outside their specific functions as destroyers of vermin. The ruthless fox-hunter loves dogs: the physicists and chemists adore their children and keep animals as pets.

YOUTH 2. Look here, Teacher. Talk sense. Do these disembodied thoughts die when their number is up, as we do? If not, there can hardly be room for them in the universe after all these millions of centuries.

MAIDEN 5. Yes: that is what I want to know. How old is the world?

TEACHER. We do not know. We lost count in the dark ages that followed the twentieth century. There are traces of many civilizations that followed; and we may yet discover traces of many more. Some of them were atavistic.

MAIDEN 5. At a what?

TEACHER. Atavistic. Not an advance on the civilization before it, but a throw-back to an earlier one. Like those children of ours who cannot get beyond the First Form, and grow up to be idiots or savages. We kill them. But we are ourselves a throw-back to the twentieth century, and may be killed as idiots and savages if we meet a later and higher civilization.

YOUTH 1. I dont believe it. We are the highest form of life and the most advanced civilization yet evolved.

YOUTH 2. Same here. Who can believe this fairy tale about disembodied thoughts? There is not a scrap of evidence for it. Nobody can believe it.

MAIDEN 4. Steady, Number Two: steady. Lots of us can believe it and do believe it. Our schoolfellows who have never got beyond the third or fourth form believe in what they call the immortality of the soul.

YOUTH 1 [*contemptuously*] Yes, because they are afraid to die.

TEACHER. That makes no difference. What is an immortal soul but a disembodied thought? I have received this morning a letter from a man who tells me he was for nineteen years a chain smoker of cigarets. He had no religious faith; but one day he chanced on a religious meeting in the park, and heard the preacher exhorting his flock to listen to
518

the voice of God. He said it would surely come to them and guide them. The smoker tried the experiment of listening just for fun; and soon his head was filled with the words "Quit smoking. Quit smoking." He quitted without the least difficulty, and has never smoked since, though he had tried before and always failed. What was that but the prompting of a disembodied thought? Millions of our third and fourth form people believe it.

YOUTH 2. Well, I am sixth form; and I dont believe it. Your correspondent is just a liar.

MAIDEN 4. What rubbish you talk, Number Two! Do fourth form people let themselves be eaten by lions in the circus, burnt at the stake, or live lives of unselfish charity rather than stop telling lies? It is much more likely that you are a fool.

YOUTH 2. May be; but that does not answer the question.

MAIDEN 5. Hear hear! The smoker may be a liar or Number Two a fool; but where did the thoughts come from? What puts them into our heads? The preachers say they are whispered by God. Anyhow they are whispered; and I want to know exactly how.

TEACHER. Like all young things you want to begin by knowing everything. I can give you only the advice of the preachers: listen until you are told.

A youth, clothed in feathers like a bird, appears suddenly.

TEACHER. Hullo! Who are you? What are you doing here?

THE FEATHERED ONE. I am an embodied thought. I am what you call the word made flesh.

YOUTH 3. Rats! How did you get here? Not by your wings: you havnt got any. You are a Cockyolly Bird.

THE FEATHERED ONE. I do not fly: I levitate. Call me Cockyolly if you like. But it would be more respectful to call me Raphael.

MAIDEN 4. Why should we respect you in that ridiculous costume?

THE TEACHER. Do you seriously wish us to believe that

you are one of the disembodied, again incarnate?

RAPHAEL. Why not? Evolution can go backwards as well as forwards. If the body can become a vortex, the vortex can also become a body.

THE TEACHER. And you are such a body?

RAPHAEL. I am curious to know what it is like to be a body. Curiosity never dies.

MAIDEN 4. How do you like it so far?

RAPHAEL. I do not like nor dislike. I experience.

YOUTH 3. That nonsense will not go down here, Cocky. It sounds smart enough; but it means nothing. Why should we respect you?

RAPHAEL. You had better. I am restraining my magnetic field. If I turned it on it would kill you.

MAIDEN 5. Dont provoke him, Number Three. I feel awful.

MAIDEN 4. You cannot experience bodied life unless you have a girl, and marry, and have children, as we do. Have you brought a girl with you?

RAPHAEL. No. I stop short of your eating and drinking and so forth, and of your reproductive methods. They revolt me.

MAIDEN 4. No passions, then?

RAPHAEL. On the contrary: intellectual passion, mathematical passion, passion for discovery and exploration: the mightiest of all the passions.

THE TEACHER. But none of our passions?

RAPHAEL. Yes. Your passion for teaching.

YOUTH 2. Then you have come to teach us?

RAPHAEL. No. I am here to learn, not to teach. I pass on. [*He vanishes*].

ALL [*screaming*] Hi! Stop! Come back! We have a lot to ask you. Dont go yet. Wait a bit, Raphael.

YOUTH 3. No use. He has invented some trick of vanishing before he is found out. He is only a Confidence Trick man.

THE TEACHER. Nonsense! He did not ask us for anything.

MAIDEN 4. He was just sampling us.

FARFETCHED FABLES

YOUTH 1. He told us nothing. We know nothing.

YOUTH 3. Rot! You want to know too much. We know how to make cyclotrons and hundred inch telescopes. We have harnessed atomic energy. He couldn't make a safety pin or a wheelbarrow to save his life.

THE TEACHER. Enough. We can never want to know too much. Attention! [*All rise*]. You will get at the schoolbook counter copies of an old poem called The Book of Job. You will read it through; and—

YOUTH 2. I read it through when I was thirteen. It was an argument between an old josser named Job and one of the old gods, who pretended he had made the universe. Job said if so he had made it very unfairly. But what use is all that to me? I dont believe the old god made the universe.

TEACHER. You will read the book over again from the point of view that the old god made no such pretence, and crushed Job by shewing that he could put ten times as many unanswerable questions to Job as Job could put to him. It will teach you that I can do the same to you. All will read the book and ask questions or write essays before next Friday.

A jubilant march is heard.

TEACHER. Lunch. March. [*Beating time*] Left-right, left-right, left-right.

They tramp out rhythmically.

THE SIMPLETON OF
THE UNEXPECTED ISLES

A PLAY IN A PROLOGUE AND TWO ACTS
(A VISION OF JUDGMENT)

Written in 1934

First Performed New York 1935

PREFACE ON DAYS OF JUDGMENT

THE increasing bewilderment of my journalist critics as to why I should write such plays as The Simpleton culminated in New York in February 1935, when I was described as a dignified old monkey throwing coco-nuts at the public in pure senile devilment. This is an amusing and graphic description of the effect I produce on the newspapers; but as a scientific criticism it is open to the matter-of-fact objection that a play is not a coco-nut nor I a monkey. Yet there is an analogy. A coco-nut is impossible without a suitable climate; and a play is impossible without a suitable civilization. If author and journalist are both placid Panglossians, convinced that their civilization is the best of all possible civilizations, and their countrymen the greatest race on earth: in short, if they have had a university education, there is no trouble: the press notices are laudatory if the play is entertaining. Even if the two are pessimists who agree with Jeremiah that the heart of man is deceitful above all things and desperately wicked, and with Shakespear that political authority only transforms its wielders into angry apes, there is still no misunderstanding; for that dismal view, or a familiar acquaintance with it, is quite common.

Such perfect understanding covers much more than nine hundred and ninety cases out of every thousand new plays. But it does not cover the cases in which the author and the journalist are not writing against the same background. The simplest are those in which the journalist is ignorant and uncultivated, and the author is assuming a high degree of knowledge and culture in his audience. This occurs oftener than it should; for some newspaper editors think that any reporter who has become stage struck by seeing half a dozen crude melodramas is thereby qualified to deal with Sophocles and Euripides, Shakespear and Goethe, Ibsen and Strindberg, Tolstoy and Tchekov, to say nothing of myself. But the case with which I am concerned here is one in which a reasonably well equipped critic shoots wide because he cannot see the target nor even conceive its existence. The two parties have not the same vision of the world. This sort of vision varies enormously from individual to individual. Between the superstatesman whose vision embraces the whole politically organized world, or the astronomer whose vision of the universe transcends the range of our utmost telescopes, and the peasant who fiercely resists a main drainage scheme for his village because others as well as he will benefit by it, there are many degrees. The Abyssinian Danakil kills a stranger at sight and is continually seeking for an excuse to kill a friend to acquire trophies enough to attract a wife. Livingstone risked his life in Africa every day to save a black man's soul. Livingstone did not say to the sun colored tribesman "There is between me and thee a gulf that nothing can fill": he proposed to fill it by instructing the tribesman on the assumption that the tribesman was as capable mentally as himself, but ignorant. That is my attitude when I write prefaces. My newspaper critics may seem incapable of anything better than the trash they write; but I believe they are capable enough and only lack instruction.

I wonder how many of them have given serious thought to the curious changes that take place in the operation of human credulity and incredulity. I have pointed out on a former occasion that there is just as much evidence for a law of the Conservation of Credulity as of the Conservation of Energy. When we refuse to believe in the miracles of religion for no better reason fundamentally than that we are no longer in the humor for them we refill our minds with the miracles of science, most of which the authors of the Bible would have refused to believe. The humans who have lost their simple childish faith in a flat earth and in Joshua's feat of stopping the sun until he had finished his battle with the Amalekites, find no difficulty in swallowing an expanding boomerang universe. They will refuse to have their children baptized or circumcized, and insist on their being vaccinated, in the teeth of overwhelming evidence that vaccination has killed thousands of children in a quite horrible way whereas no child has ever been a penny the worse for baptism since John the Baptist recommended it. Religion is the mother of scepticism: Science is the mother of credulity. There is nothing that people will not believe nowadays if only it be presented to them as Science, and nothing they will not disbelieve if it be presented to them as religion. I myself began like that; and I am ending by receiving every scientific statement with dour suspicion whilst giving very respectful consideration to the inspirations and revelations of the prophets and poets. For the shift of credulity from religious divination to scientific invention is very often a relapse from comparatively harmless romance to mischievous and even murderous quackery.

Some credulities have their social uses. They have been invented and imposed on us to secure certain lines of behavior as either desirable for the general good or at least convenient to our rulers. I learned this early in life. My nurse induced me to abstain from certain troublesome activities by threatening that if I indulged in them the cock would come down the chimney. This event seemed to me so apocalyptic that I never dared to provoke it nor even to ask myself in what way I should be the worse for it. Without this device my nurse could not have ruled me when her back was turned. It was the first step towards making me rule myself.

Mahomet, one of the greatest of the prophets of God, found himself in the predicament of my nurse in respect of having to rule a body of Arab chieftains whose vision was not co-extensive with his own, and who therefore could not be trusted, when his back was turned, to behave as he himself would have behaved spontaneously. He did not tell them that if they did such and such things the cock would come down the chimney. They did not know what a chimney was. But he threatened them with the most disgusting penances in a future life if they did not live according to his word, and promised them very pleasant times if they did. And as they could not understand his inspiration otherwise than as a spoken communication by a personal messenger he allowed them to believe that the angel Gabriel acted as a celestial postman between him and Allah, the fountain of all inspiration. Except in this way he could not have made them believe in anything but sacred stones and the seven deadly sins.

The Christian churches and the Christian Kings were driven to the same device; and when I evolved beyond the cock and chimney stage I found myself possessed with a firm belief that all my Roman Catholic fellow children would inevitably burn in blazing brimstone to all eternity, and even that I myself, in spite of my Protestant advantages, might come to the same endless end if I were not careful. The whole civilized world seemed to be governed that way in those days. It is so to a considerable extent still. A friend of mine lately asked a leading Irish statesman why he did not resort to a rather soulless stroke of diplomacy. Because, replied the statesman, I happen to believe that there is such a place as hell.

Anywhere else than in Ireland the obsolescence of this explanation would have been startling. For somehow there has been a shift of credulity from hell to perishing suns and the like. I am not thinking of the humanitarian revolt against everlasting brimstone voiced by the late Mrs Bradlaugh Bonner, nor of Tolstoy's insistence on the damnation on earth of the undetected, unpunished, materially prosperous criminal. I am leaving out of the question also the thoughtful, sentimental, honorable, conscientious people who need no hell to intimidate them into considerate social behavior, and who have naturally outgrown the devil with his barbed tail and horns just as I outgrew the cock in the chimney.

But what of the people who are capable of no restraint except that of intimidation? Must they not be either restrained or, as the Russians gently put it, liquidated. No

State can afford the expense of providing policemen enough to watch them all continually; consequently the restraint must, like the fear of hell, operate when nobody is looking. Well, a shift of credulity has destroyed the old belief in hell. How then is the social work previously done by that belief to be taken up and carried on? It is easy to shirk the problem by pointing out that the belief in hell did not prevent even the most superstitious people from committing the most damnable crimes. But though we know of these failures of infernal terrorism we have no record of its successes. We know that naïve attempts to bribe divine justice led to a trade in absolutions, pardons, and indulgences which proved by the hardness of the cash the sinners put down and the cost of the cathedrals they put up that there was a continual overdrawing of salvation accounts by firm believers in the brimstone; but we do not know, and never shall know, how many crimes were refrained from that would have been committed but for the dread of damnation. All we can do is to observe and grapple with the effect of the shift of credulity which has robbed hell of its terrors.

No community, however devout, has ever trusted wholly to damnation and excommunication as deterrents. They have been supplemented by criminal codes of the most hideous barbarity (I have been contemporary with Europeans whose amusements included seeing criminals broken on the wheel). Therefore their effect on conduct must be looked for in that very extensive part of it which has not been touched by the criminal codes, or in which the codes actually encourage anti-social action and penalize its opposite, as when the citizen is forced by taxation or compulsory military service to become an accomplice in some act of vulgar pugnacity and greed disguised as patriotism.

Unless and until we get a new column in the census papers on the point we can only guess how far the shift of credulity has actually taken place in countries like our own in which children, far from being protected against the inculcation of the belief in brimstone, are exposed to it in

every possible way, and are actually, when they have been
confirmed, legally subject to ruinous penalties for question-
ing it. It happens, however, that in one of the largest States
in the world, Russia, the children are protected from
proselytizing (otherwise than by the State itself) not only
by the negative method called Secular Education, but by
positive instruction that there is no personal life after death
for the individual, the teaching being that of Ecclesiastes in
our own canon "Whatsoever thy hand findeth to do, do it
with thy might; for there is no work, nor device, nor
knowledge, nor wisdom, in the grave whither thou goest."
We may take it that no civilized Russian born within the
last twenty years has any apprehension of having to suffer
after death for sins committed before it. At the same time
the list of activities blacklisted by the Russian State as
felonious has been startlingly extended; for the Russian
Government has turned the country's economic morals
downside up by breaking away from our Capitalist Utopia
and adopting instead the views of the Bolshevist prophets
whose invectives and warnings fill the last books of the Old
Testament, and the Communist principles of Jesus, Peter,
and Paul. Not that the Soviet Republic allows the smallest
authority to Jesus or Peter, Jeremiah or Micah the Moras-
thite. They call their economic system, not Bolshevik
Christianity, but Scientific Socialism. But as their conclusions are the same, they have placed every Russian under
a legal obligation to earn his own living, and made it a
capital crime on his part to compel anyone else to do it for
him. Now outside Russia the height of honor and success
is to be a gentleman or lady, which means that your living
is earned for you by other people (mostly untouchables),
and that, far from being under an obligation to work, you
are so disgraced by the mere suggestion of it that you dare
not be seen carrying a parcel along a fashionable thorough-
fare. Nobody has ever seen a lady or gentleman carrying
a jug of milk down Bond Street or the *rue de la Paix*. A
white person doing such a thing in Capetown would be

socially ruined. The physical activities called Sport, which are needed to keep the gentry in health, must be unpaid and unproductive; if payment is accepted for such activities the payee loses caste and is no longer called Mister. Labor is held to be a cross and a disgrace; and the lowest rank known is that of laborer. The object of everyone's ambition is an unearned income; and hundreds of millions of the country's income are lavished annually on ladies and gentlemen whilst laborers are underfed, ill clothed, and sleeping two or three in a bed and ten in a room.

Eighteen years ago this anti-labor creed of ours was the established religion of the whole civilized world. Then suddenly, in one seventh of that world, it was declared a damnable heresy, and had to be rooted out like any other damnable heresy. But as the heretics were carefully taught at the same time that there is no such thing as damnation, how were they to be dealt with? The well-to-do British Liberal, clamoring for freedom of conscience, objects to heretics being restrained in any way: his panacea for that sort of difficulty is Toleration. He thinks that Quakers and Ritualists should tolerate oneanother; and this solution works quite well because it does not now matter a penny to the State or the individual whether a citizen belongs to one persuasion or the other. But it was not always so. George Fox, the heroic founder of the Quakers, could not hear a church bell without dashing into the church and upsetting the service by denouncing the whole business of ritual religion as idolatrous. The bell, he said, "struck on his heart." Consequently it was not possible for the Churches to tolerate George Fox, though both Cromwell and Charles II liked the man and admired him.

Now the heretic in Russia is like Fox. He is not content with a quiet abstract dissent from the State religion of Soviet Russia: he is an active, violent, venomous saboteur. He plans and carries out breakages of machinery, falsifies books and accounts to produce insolvencies, leaves the fields unsown or the harvests to rot unreaped, and slaughters

531

farm stock in millions even at the cost of being half starved
(sometimes wholly starved) by the resultant "famine" in
his fanatical hatred of a system which makes it impossible
for him to become a gentleman. Toleration is impossible:
the heretic-saboteur will not tolerate the State religion;
consequently the State could not tolerate him even if it
wanted to.

This situation, though new to our generation of Liberal
plutocrats, is not new historically. The change from pagan-
ism and Judaism to Christianity, from the worship of consecrated stones to an exalted monotheism under Mahomet,
and from world catholicism to national individualism at the
Reformation, all led to the persecution and virtual out-
lawry of the heretics who would not accept the change. The
original official Roman Catholic Church, which had perhaps the toughest job, was compelled to develop a new
judicial organ, called the Inquisition or Holy Office, to
deal with heresy; and though in all the countries in which
the Reformation triumphed the Inquisition became so unpopular that its name was carefully avoided when similar
organs were developed by the Protestant and later on by
the Secularist governments, yet the Holy Office cropped
up again under all sorts of disguises. Protestant England
would never have tolerated the Star Chamber if it had
called itself an Inquisition and given Laud the official title
borne by Torquemada. In the end all the specific Inquisitions petered out, not in the least through a growth of real
tolerance, but because, as the world settled down into the
new faiths, and the heretics stopped sabotaging and slaughtering, it was found that the ordinary courts could do all
the necessary persecution, such as transporting laborers for
reading the works of Thomas Paine, or imprisoning poor
men for making sceptical jokes about the parthenogenesis
of Jesus.

Thus the Inquisition came to be remembered in England only as an obsolete abomination which classed respectable Protestants with Jews, and burned both. Con-

ceive, then, our horror when the Inquisition suddenly rose
up again in Russia. It began as the Tcheka; then it became
the Gay-pay-oo (Ogpu); now it has settled down as part
of the ordinary police force. The worst of its work is over:
the heretics are either liquidated, converted, or intimidated.
But it was indispensable in its prime. The Bolsheviks, infected as they were with English Liberal and Agnostic
notions, at first tried to do without it; but the result was
that the unfortunate Commissars who had to make the Russian industries and transport services work, found themselves obliged to carry pistols and execute saboteurs and
lazy drunkards with their own hands. Such a Commissar
was Djerjinsky, now, like Lenin, entombed in the Red
Square. He was not a homicidally disposed person; but
when it fell to his lot to make the Russian trains run at all
costs, he had to force himself to shoot a station master who
found it easier to drop telegrams into the waste paper
basket than to attend to them. And it was this gentle
Djerjinsky who, unable to endure the duties of an executioner (even had he had time for them), organized the
Tcheka.

Now the Tcheka, being an Inquisition and not an ordinary police court dealing under written statutes and established precedents with defined offences, and sentencing the
offenders to prescribed penalties, had to determine whether
certain people were public spirited enough to live in a
Communist society, and, if not, to blow their brains out as
public nuisances. If you would not work and pull your
weight in the Russian boat, then the Tcheka had to make
you do it by convincing you that you would be shot if you
persisted in your determination to be a gentleman. For
the national emergencies were then desperate; and the
compulsion to overcome them had to be fiercely in earnest.

I, an old Irishman, am too used to Coercion Acts, sus-
pensions of the Habeas Corpus Act, and the like, to have
any virtuous indignation left to spare for the blunders and
excesses into which the original Tcheka, as a body of well

533

intentioned amateurs, no doubt fell before it had learnt the limits of its business by experience. My object in citing it is to draw attention to the legal novelty and importance of its criterion of human worth. I am careful to say legal novelty because of course the criterion must have been used in the world long before St Paul commanded that "if any would not work, neither should he eat." But our courts have never taken that Communist view: they have always upheld unconditional property, private property, real property, do-what-you-like-with-your-own property, which, when it is insanely extended to the common earth of the country, means the power to make landless people earn the proprietors' livings for them. Such property places the social value of the proprietor beyond question. The propertyless man may be challenged as a rogue and a vagabond to justify himself by doing some honest work; but if he earns a gentleman's living for him he is at once vindicated and patted on the back. Under such conditions we have lost the power of conceiving ourselves as responsible to society for producing a full equivalent of what we consume, and indeed more. On the contrary, every inducement to shirk that primary duty is continually before us. We are taught to think of an Inquisition as a tribunal which has to decide whether we accept the divinity of Christ or are Jews, whether we believe in transubstantiation or merely in the Supper, whether we are prelatists or Presbyterians, whether we accept the authority of the Church or the conclusions of our private judgments as the interpreters of God's will, whether we believe in a triune godhead or a single one, whether we accept the 39 Articles or the Westminster Confession, and so on. Such were the tests of fitness to live accepted by the old Inquisitions. The public never dreams of an economic test except in the form of a Means Test to baffle the attempts of the very poor to become sinecurists like ladies and gentlemen.

My own acquaintance with such a possibility began early in life and shocked me somewhat. My maternal grandfather, a country gentleman who was an accomplished sportsman, was out shooting one day. His dog, growing old, made a mistake: its first. He instantly shot it. I learnt that he always shot his sporting dogs when they were past their work. Later on I heard of African tribes doing the same with their grandparents. When I took seriously to economic studies before electric traction had begun I found that tramway companies had found that the most profitable way of exploiting horses was to work them to death in four years. Planters in certain districts had found the like profitable term for slaves to be eight years. In fully civilized life there was no provision except a savagely penal Poor Law for workers thrown out of our industrial establishments as "too old at forty."

As I happen to be one of those troublesome people who are not convinced that whatever is is right these things set me thinking. My thoughts would now be attributed to Bolshevik propaganda; and pains would be taken by our rulers to stop the propaganda under the impression that this would stop the thoughts; but there was no Bolshevik propaganda in those days; and I can assure the Foreign Office that the landed gentry in the person of my grandfather, the tramway companies, and the capitalist planters, made the question of whether individual dogs and men are worth their salt familiar to me a whole generation before the Tcheka ever existed.

It still seems to me a very pertinent question, as I have to pay away about half my earnings in tribute to the lady-and-gentleman business in order to get permission to live on this earth; and I consider it money very ill spent. For if the people who live on my earnings were changed by some Arabian Nights magician into dogs, and handed over to the sporting successors of my grandfather, they would be shot; and if they were changed into horses or slaves they would be worn out by overwork before their natural time. They are now worn out by underwork.

Nevertheless I do not plead a personal grievance, because though I still amuse myself with professional pursuits and make money by them, I also have acquired the position of a gentleman, and live very comfortably on other people's earnings to an extent which more than compensates me for the depredations of which I am myself the victim. Now my grandfather's dog had no such satisfaction. Neither had the tramway horses nor the slaves, nor have the discarded "too old at forty." In their case there was no proper account keeping. In the nature of things a human creature must incur a considerable debt for its nurture and education (if it gets any) before it becomes productive. And as it can produce under modern conditions much more than it need consume it ought to be possible for it to pay off its debt and provide for its old age in addition to supporting itself during its active period. Of course if you assume that it is no use to itself and is there solely to support ladies and gentlemen, you need not bother about this: you can just leave it to starve when it ceases to be useful to its superiors. But if, discarding this view, you assume that a human creature is created for its own use and should have matters arranged so that it shall live as long as it can, then you will have to go into people's accounts and make them all pay their way. We need no Bolshevik propaganda to lead us to this obvious conclusion; but it makes the special inquisitionary work of the Tcheka intelligible. For the Tcheka was simply carrying out the executive work of a constitution which had abolished the lady and gentleman exactly as the Inquisition carried out the executive work of a catholic constitution which had abolished Jupiter and Diana and Venus and Apollo.

Simple enough; and yet so hard to get into our genteel heads that in making a play about it I have had to detach it altogether from the great Russian change, or any of the actual political changes which threaten to raise it in the National-Socialist and Fascist countries, and to go back to the old vision of a day of reckoning by divine justice for all mankind.

PREFACE ON DAYS OF JUDGMENT

Now the ordinary vision of this event is almost pure bugaboo: we see it as a colossal Old Bailey trial, with the good people helped up into heaven and the bad ones cast headlong into hell; but as to what code of law will govern the judgment and classify the judged as sheep or goats as the case may be, we have not troubled to ask. We are clear about Judas Iscariot going to hell and Florence Nightingale to heaven; but we are not so sure about Brutus and Cromwell. Our general knowledge of mankind, if we dare bring it into play, would tell us that an immense majority of the prisoners at the bar will be neither saints nor scoundrels, but borderland cases of extreme psychological complexity. It is easy to say that to divine justice nothing is impossible; but the more divine the justice the more difficult it is to conceive how it could deal with every case as one for heaven or hell. But we think we need not bother about it; for the whole affair is thought of as a grand finish to the human race and all its problems, leaving the survivors in a condition of changeless unprogressive bliss or torment for the rest of eternity.

To me this vision is childish; but I must take people's minds as I find them and build on them as best I can. It is no use my telling them that their vision of judgment is a silly superstition, and that there never will be anything of the kind. The only conclusion the pious will draw is that I, at all events, will go to hell. As to the indifferent and the sceptical, I may do them the mischief against which Jesus vainly warned our missionaries. I may root out of their minds the very desirable conception that they are all responsible to divine justice for the use they make of their lives, and put nothing in its place except a noxious conceit in their emancipation and an exultant impulse to abuse it. The substitution of irresponsibility for responsibility may present itself as an advance; but it is in fact a retreat which may leave its victim much less eligible as a member of a civilized community than the crudest Fundamentalist. A prudent banker would lend money on personal security

to Bunyan rather than to Casanova. Certainly I should if
I were a banker.

Who shall say, then, that an up-to-date Vision of Judgment is not an interesting subject for a play, especially as
events in Russia and elsewhere are making it urgently
desirable that believers in the Apocalypse should think out
their belief a little? In a living society every day is a day
of judgment; and its recognition as such is not the end of
all things but the beginning of a real civilization. Hence the
fable of The Simpleton of the Unexpected Isles. In it I still
retain the ancient fancy that the race will be brought to
judgment by a supernatural being, coming literally out of
the blue; but his inquiry is not whether you believe in
Tweedledum or Tweedledee but whether you are a social
asset or a social nuisance. And the penalty is liquidation.
He has appeared on the stage before in the person of
Ibsen's button moulder. And as history always follows the
stage, the button moulder came to life as Djerjinsky. My
Angel comes a day after the fair; but time enough for our
people, who know nothing of the button moulder and have
been assured by our gentleman-ladylike newspapers that
Djerjinsky was a Thug.

The button moulder is a fiction; and my Angel is a
fiction. But the pressing need for bringing us to the bar for
an investigation of our personal social values is not a fiction. And Djerjinsky is not a fiction. He found that as there
are no button moulders and no angels and no heavenly
tribunals available, we must set up earthly ones, not to
ascertain whether Mr Everyman in the dock has committed
this or that act or holds this or that belief, but whether he
or she is a creator of social values or a parasitical consumer
and destroyer of them.

Unfortunately the word tribunal immediately calls up
visions not only of judgment but of punishment and
cruelty. Now there need be no more question of either of
these abominations than there was in the case of my grandfather's dog. My grandfather would have been horribly

ashamed of himself if the dog's death had not been instantaneous and unanticipated. And the idea of punishment never entered either his mind or the dog's. (Djerjinsky, by the way, is believed to have devised a similar method of painless liquidation.) It may be expedient that one man should die for the people; but it does not follow in the least that he should be tortured or terrified. Public savagery may demand that the law shall torment a criminal who does something very provoking; for the Sermon on The Mount is still a dead letter in spite of all the compliments we pay it. But to blow a man's brains out because he cannot for the life of him see why he should not employ labor at a profit, or buy things solely to sell them again for more than he gave for them, or speculate in currency values: all of them activities which have for centuries enjoyed the highest respectability, is an innovation which should be carried out with the utmost possible delicacy if public opinion is to be quite reconciled to it. We have also to reckon with the instinctive shrinking from outright killing which makes so many people sign petitions for the reprieve of even the worst murderers, and take no further interest if a reprieve decrees that their lives shall be taken by the slow torture of imprisonment. Then we have a mass of people who think that murderers should be judicially killed, but that the lives of the most mischievous criminals should be held sacred provided they do not commit murder. To overcome these prejudices we need a greatly increased intolerance of socially injurious conduct and an uncompromising abandonment of punishment and its cruelties, together with a sufficient school inculcation of social responsibility to make every citizen conscious that if his life costs more than it is worth to the community the community may painlessly extinguish it.

The result of this, however, will finally be a demand for codification. The citizen will say "I really must know what I may do and what I may not do without having my head shot off." The reply "You must keep a credit balance always at the national bank" is sufficiently definite if the national accountancy is trustworthy and compulsory unemployment made impossible. In fact it is so definite that it finally takes the matter out of the hands of the Inquisition and makes an overdraft an ordinary offence to be dealt with by the police. But police measures are not enough. Any intelligent and experienced administrator of the criminal law will tell you that there are people who come up for punishment again and again for the same offence, and that punishing them is a cruel waste of time. There should be an Inquisition always available to consider whether these human nuisances should not be put out of their pain, or out of their joy as the case may be. The community must drive a much harder bargain for the privilege of citizenship than it now does; but it must also make the bargain not only practicable but in effect much easier than the present very imperfect bargain. This involves a new social creed. A new social creed involves a new heresy. A new heresy involves an Inquisition. The precedents established by Inquisition furnish the material for a new legal code. Codification enables the work of the Inquisition to be done by an ordinary court of law. Thereupon the Inquisition, as such, disappears, precisely as the Tcheka has disappeared. Thus it has always been; and thus it ever shall be.

The moral of the dramatic fable of The Simpleton is now clear enough. With amateur Inquisitions under one name or another or no name at work in all directions, from Fascist *autos-da-fé* to American Vigilance Committees with lynching mobs as torturers and executioners, it is time for us to reconsider our Visions of Judgment, and see whether we cannot change them from old stories in which we no longer believe and new stories which are only too horribly true to serious and responsible public tribunals.

By the way, I had better guard myself against the assumption that because I have introduced into my fable a eugenic experiment in group marriage I am advocating the immediate adoption of that method of peopling the world

PREFACE ON DAYS OF JUDGMENT

for immediate practice by my readers. Group marriage is a form of marriage like any other; and it is just as well to remind our western and very insular Imperialists that marriage in the British Empire is startlingly different in the east from marriage in the British Isles; but I have introduced it only to bring into the story the four lovely phantasms who embody all the artistic, romantic, and military ideals of our cultured suburbs. On the Day of Judgment not merely do they cease to exist like the useless and predatory people: it becomes apparent that they never did exist. And, enchanting as they may be to our perfumers, who give us the concentrated odor of the flower without the roots or the clay or even the leaves, let us hope they never will.

On the Indian Ocean,
April 1935.

THE SIMPLETON OF
THE UNEXPECTED ISLES
PROLOGUE

THE *emigration office at a tropical port in the British Empire. The office is an annex of the harbor and customs sheds on one side and of the railway station on the other. Placards direct passengers TO THE CUSTOMS and TO THE TRAINS through the open doors right and left respectively. The emigration officer, an unsatisfactory young man of unhealthy habits, is sitting writing at his table in the middle of the room. His clerk is at a standing desk against the wall on the customs side. The officer wears tropical clothes, neither too tidy nor too clean. The clerk is in a shabby dark lounge suit.*

THE E. O. [*finishing his writing*] Is that the lot?

CLERK. It's the lot from the French ship; but there is that case standing over from the Liverpool one.

THE E. O. [*exasperated*] Now look here, Wilks. Are you the emigration officer here or am I? Did I tell you that that girl was to be sent back or did I not?

WILKS. Well, I thought—

THE E. O. What business had you to think? I told you she was to go back. I suppose she tipped you to let her come here and make a scene on the chance of getting round me.

WILKS [*hotly*] Youll either take that back or prove it.

THE E. O. I will neither take it back nor prove it until you explain why you are letting this girl bother me again, though she has no papers, no passports, and is in excess of the quota without any excuse for it.

WILKS. Who's letting her bother you again? She told the High Commissioner that you had turned her down; and he told her she had better see you again.

THE E. O. And why the devil didnt you tell me that at first, instead of blithering about her as if she was a common case?

WILKS. The High Commissioner's daughter was on the ship coming back from school. He came down to meet her.

This girl had made friends with her or taken care of her or something.

THE E. O. Thats no good. We cant let her through on that.

WILKS. Well, will you see her?

THE E. O. Is she waiting to see me?

WILKS. She says she's waiting to see what will happen to her.

THE E. O. Same thing, isnt it?

WILKS. I suppose so. But she put it as if there was a difference. I think she's a bit mad. But the Medical Officer says she passes all his tests of sanity, though I could see that he has his doubts.

THE E. O. Oh, shut up. You need a medical test yourself, I think. Fetch her in.

Wilks goes out sulkily through the customs door and returns with a young woman. He leads her to the table and then goes back to his desk.

THE Y. W. Good morning, sir. You dont look as well as you did yesterday. Did you stay up too late?

THE E. O. [*nonplussed for the moment*] I— er— [*Collecting himself*] Look here, young lady. You have to answer questions here, not to ask them.

THE Y. W. You have been drinking.

THE E. O. [*springing up*] What the hell do you mean?

THE Y. W. You have. I smell it.

THE E. O. Very well. Back you go by the next boat, my lady.

THE Y. W. [*unmoved*] At this hour of the morning too! Dont you know you shouldnt?

THE E. O. [*to Wilks*] Take her away, you. [*To the young woman*] Out you go.

THE Y. W. I ought to speak to somebody about it. And look at the state the office is in! Whose business is it to see that it's properly dusted? Let me talk to them for you.

THE E. O. What concern is it of yours?

THE Y. W. I hate to see dust lying about. Look! You

could write your name in it. And it's just awful to see a young man drinking before eleven in the morning.

WILKS [*propitiatory*] Dont say anything about it, Miss: I will see to the dust. Everybody starts the day with a drink here. Dont go talking, Miss, will you?

THE E. O. [*suddenly breaking down in tears*] You can go and tell who you damn well please. For two pins I'd chuck myself into the harbor and have done with it. This climate is hell: you cant stand it unless you drink till you see blue monkeys.

WILKS. Never mind him, Miss: he has nerves. We all have them here sooner or later, off and on. Here! I'll give you a landing ticket; and you just clear off and say nothing. [*He takes a ticket from the table and gives it to her*].

THE E. O. [*weeping*] A man's a slave here worse than a nigger. Spied on, reported on, checked and told off til he's afraid to have a pound note in his pocket or take a glass in his hand for fear of being had up for bribery or drinking. I'm fed up with it. Go and report me and be damned to you: what do I care? [*He sniffs and blows his nose, relieved by his outburst*].

WILKS. Would you have the kindness to clear out, Miss. We're busy. Youre passed all right: nothing to do but shew the ticket. You wont have to go back: we was only joking.

THE Y. W. But I want to go back. If this place is what he says, it is no place for me. And I did so enjoy the voyage out: I ask nothing better than to begin it all over again.

THE E. O. [*with the calm of despair*] Let her have her own way, Wilks. Shew her the way to the ship and shew her the way to the dock gate. She can take which she pleases. But get her out of this or I shall commit suicide.

THE Y. W. Why? Arnt you happy? It's not natural not to be happy. I'd be ashamed not to be happy.

THE E. O. What is there to make a man happy here?

THE Y. W. But you dont need to be made happy. You

545

ought to be happy from the inside. Then you wouldnt need things to make you happy.

THE E. O. My inside! Oh Lord!

THE Y. W. Well, you can make your inside all right if you eat properly and stop drinking and keep the office dusted and your nice white clothes clean and tidy. You two are a disgrace.

THE E. O. [*roaring with rage*] Chuck that woman out.

WILKS. Chuck her yourself. What can *I* do? [*Imploringly to her*] If youd only have the goodness to go, Miss. We're so busy this morning.

THE Y. W. But I am a stranger here: I have nobody else to talk to. And you have nothing to do until the next boat comes in.

THE E. O. The next boat is due the day after tomorrow at five in the afternoon. Do you expect us to sit here talking to you until then?

THE Y. W. Well, it's I who have to do most of the talking, isnt it? Couldnt you shew me round the town? I'll pay for the taxi.

THE E. O. [*feebly rebellious*] Look here: you cant go on like this, you know.

THE Y. W. What were you going to do with yourself this morning if I hadnt come?

THE E. O. I—I— Whats that to you?

THE Y. W. I see you hadnt made up your mind. Let me make it up for you. Put on your hat and come along and shew me round. I seem to spend my life making up other people's minds for them.

THE E. O. [*helplessly*] All right, all right, all right. You neednt make a ballyhoo about it. But I ask myself—

THE Y. W. Dont ask yourself anything, my child. Let life come to you. March.

THE E. O. [*at the railway door, to Wilks, in a last effort to assert himself*] Carry on, you. [*He goes*].

THE Y. W. Wouldnt you like to come too?

WILKS. Yes, Miss; but somebody must stay in the

office; and it had better be me than him. I am indispensable.

THE Y. W. What a word! Dispensables and indispensables: there you have the whole world. I wonder am I a dispensable or an indispensable. [*She goes out through the railway door*].

WILKS [*alone*] Let life come to you. Sounds all right, that. Let life come to you. Aye; but suppose life doesnt come to you! Look at me! What am I? An empire builder: thats what I am by nature. Cecil Rhodes: thats me. Why am I a clerk with only two shirts to my back, with that young waster wiping his dirty boots on me for doing the work he cant do himself, though he gets all the praise and all the pudding? Because life never came to me like it came to Rhodes. Found his backyard full of diamonds, he did; and nothing to do but wash the clay off them and be a millionaire. I had Rhodes's idea all right. Let the whole earth be England, I said to the school teacher; and let Englishmen govern it. Nobody put that into my head: it came of itself. But what did I find in my backyard? Next door's dead cat. Could I make myself head of a Chartered Company with a dead cat? And when I threw it back over the wall my mother said "You have thrown away your luck, my boy" she says "you shouldnt have thrown it back: you should have passed it on, like a chain letter. Now you will never have no more luck in this world." And no more I have. I says to her "I'll be in the papers yet some day" I says "like Cecil Rhodes: you see if I'm not." "Not you, my lad" she says. "Everything what comes to you you throw it back." Well, so I do. Look at this girl here. "Come with me" she says. And I threw the cat back again. "Somebody must be left in the office" I says. "I am indispensable" I says. And all the time I knew that nobody neednt be in the office, and that any Jew boy could do all I do here and do it better. But I promised my mother I'd get into the papers; and I will. I have that much of the Rhodes touch in me. [*He sits at the table and writes on*

547

a luggage label; then reads what he has written] "Here lies a man who might have been Cecil Rhodes if he had had Rhodes's luck. Mother, farewell: your son has kept his word." [*He ties the label to the lapel of his coat*] Wheres that fool's gun? [*He opens a drawer and takes out a brandy flask and an automatic pistol, which he throws on the table*]. I'll damned well shew em whether I'm an empire builder or not. That lassie shant say that I didnt leave the place tidy either, though she can write in the dust of it with her finger. [*He shuts the drawer, and places the chair trimly at the table. Then he goes to his desk and takes out a duster, with which he wipes first the desk and then the table. He replaces the duster in the desk, and takes out a comb and a hand mirror. He tidies his hair; replaces the comb and glass in the desk; closes it and sets the stool in its place before it. He then returns to the table, and empties the flask at a draught*]. Now for it. The back of the head: thats the Russian touch. [*He takes the pistol and presents it over his shoulder to his occiput*]. Let the whole earth be England; and let Englishmen rule it. [*Singing*] Rule Britannia: Britannia rules the wa—

He blows his brains out and falls dead. The Station Master enters.

THE STATION MASTER. Here! Who's been shooting here? [*He sees the body*] Wilks!! Dear! dear! dear! What a climate! The fifth this month. [*He goes to the door*]. Hallo there, Jo. Bring along the stretcher and two or three with you. Mr. Wilks has shot himself.

Jo. [*without, cheerfully*] Right you are, sir.

THE STATION MASTER. What a climate! Poor old Wilks!

SCENE II

A GRASSY *cliff top overhanging the sea. A seat for promenaders. The young woman and the emigration officer stand on the brink.*

THE Y. W. Pity theres no beach. We could bathe.

THE E. O. Not us. Not likely. Theres sharks there. And killer whales, worse than any sharks.

THE Y. W. It looks pretty deep.

THE E. O. I should think it is. The biggest liners can get close up. Like Plymouth. Like Lulworth Cove. Dont stand so close. Theres a sort of fascination in it; and you might get giddy.

They come away from the edge and sit on the seat together: she on his left, he nearest the sea.

THE Y. W. It's lovely here. Better than the town.

THE E. O. Dont deceive yourself. It's a horrible place. The climate is something terrible. Do you know that if you hadnt come in this morning I'd have done myself in.

THE Y. W. Dont talk nonsense. Why should you do yourself in?

THE E. O. Yes I should. I had the gun ready in the drawer of that table. I'd have shot Wilks and then shot myself.

THE Y. W. Why should you shoot poor Wilks? What has he done?

THE E. O. I hate him. He hates me. Everybody here hates everybody else. And the fellow is so confoundedly smug and happy and satisfied: it drives me mad when I can hardly bear my own life. No fear of him shooting himself: not much. So I thought I'd save him the trouble.

THE Y. W. But that would be murder.

THE E. O. Not if I shot myself after. That would make us quits.

THE Y. W. Well, I am surprised to hear a young man like you, in the prime of life as you might say, talking like that. Why dont you get married?

THE E. O. My salary's too small for a white woman.

THE SIMPLETON

Theyre all snobs; and they want a husband only to take them home out of this.

THE Y. W. Why, it's an earthly paradise.

THE E. O. Tell them so; and see what theyll say to you.

THE Y. W. Well, why not marry a colored woman?

THE E. O. You dont know what youre talking about. Ive tried. But now theyre all educated they wont look at a white man. They tell me I'm ignorant and that I smell bad.

THE Y. W. Well, so you do. You smell of drink and indigestion and sweaty clothes. You were quite disgusting when you tried to make up to me in the taxi. Thats why I got out, and made for the sea air.

THE E. O. [*rising hurriedly*] I cant stand any more of this. [*He takes a wallet of papers from his breast pocket and throws them on the seat*]. Hand them in at the office, will you: theyll be wanted there. I am going over.

He makes for the edge of the cliff. But there is a path down the cliff face, invisible from the seat. A native priest, a handsome man in the prime of life, beautifully dressed, rises into view by this path and bars his way.

PRIEST. Pardon, son of empire. This cliff contains the temple of the goddess who is beyond naming, the eternal mother, the seed and the sun, the resurrection and the life. You must not die here. I will send an acolyte to guide you to the cliff of death, which contains the temple of the goddess's brother, the weeder of the garden, the sacred scavenger, the last friend on earth, the prolonger of sleep and the giver of rest. It is not far off: life and death dwell close together: you need prolong your unhappiness only a bare five minutes. The priest there will attend to your remains and see they are disposed of with all becoming rites.

THE E. O. [*to the young woman*] Is he real; or is it the drink?

THE Y. W. He's real. And, my word! isnt he jolly good looking? [*To the priest*] You'll excuse this young man, sir, wont you? He's been drinking pretty hard.

550

THE SIMPLETON

THE PRIEST [*advancing between them*] Blame him not, sweet one. He comes from a strange mad country where the young are taught languages that are dead and histories that are lies, but are never told how to eat and drink and clothe themselves and reproduce their species. They worship strange ancient gods; and they play games with balls marvellously well; but of the great game of life they are ignorant. Here, where they are in the midst of life and loveliness, they die by their own hands to escape what they call the horrors. We do not encourage them to live. The empire is for those who can live in it, not for those who can only die in it. Take your friend to the cliff of death; and bid him farewell tenderly; for he is very unhappy.

THE E. O. Look here: I am an Englishman; and I shall commit suicide where I please. No nigger alive shall dictate to me.

THE PRIEST. It is forbidden.

THE E. O. Who's to stop me? Will you?

The priest shakes his head and makes way for him.

THE Y. W. Oh, you are not going to let him do it, are you?

THE PRIEST. [*holding her back*] We never offer violence to the unhappy. Do not interfere with his destiny.

THE E. O. [*planting himself on the edge and facing the abyss*] I am going to do it: see? Nobody shall say that I lived a dog's life because I was afraid to make an end of it. [*He bends his knees to spring, but cannot*]. I WILL. [*He makes another effort, bending almost to his haunches, but again fails to make the spring-up a spring-over*].

THE PRIEST. Poor fellow! Let me assist you. [*He shoots his foot against the E. O.'s posterior and sends him over the cliff*].

THE E. O. [*in a tone of the strongest remonstrance as he is catapulted into the void*] Oh! [*A prodigious splash*].

THE Y. W. Murderer!

THE SIMPLETON

THE PRIEST. Not quite. There are nets below, and a palisade to keep out the sharks. The shock will do him good.

THE Y. W. Well, I never!

THE PRIEST. Come, young rose blossom, and feast with us in the temple.

THE Y. W. Not so much rose blossom, young man. Are there any priestesses down there?

THE PRIEST. Of course. How can men feast without women?

THE Y. W. Well, let life come to you I always say; and dont cry out until youre hurt. After you, sir.

They descend.

SCENE III

A SHELF *of rock half way down the cliff forms an esplanade between the sea and a series of gigantic images of oriental deities in shallow alcoves cut in the face of the wall of rock. A feast of fruit and bread and soft drinks is spread on the ground. The young woman is sitting at it between the priest on her right nearest the sea and a very handsome young native priestess in robes of dusky yellow silk on her left nearest the images.*

THE Y. W. You know, to me this is a funny sort of lunch. You begin with the dessert. We begin with the entrées. I suppose it's all right; but I have eaten so much fruit and bread and stuff that I dont feel I want any meat.

THE PRIEST. We shall not offer you any. We dont eat it.

THE Y. W. Then how do you keep up your strength?

THE PRIEST. It keeps itself up.

THE Y. W. Oh, how could that be? [*To the priestess*] You wouldnt like a husband that didnt eat plenty of meat, would you? But then youre a priestess; so I suppose it doesnt matter to you, as you cant marry.

THE PRIESTESS. I am married.

THE Y. W. Oh! And you a priestess!

THE PRIESTESS. I could not be a priestess if I were not married. How could I presume to teach others without a completed human experience? How could I deal with children if I were not a mother?

THE Y. W. But that isn't right. My sister was a teacher; but when she married they took her job away from her and wouldnt let her teach any more.

THE PRIESTESS. The rulers of your country must be mad.

THE Y. W. Oh no. Theyre all right: just like other people. [*To the priest*] I say, reverend. What about the poor lad you kicked over the cliff? Is he really safe? I dont feel easy about him.

553

THE PRIEST. His clothes are drying in the sun. They will lend him some clothes and send him up here as soon as he has recovered from his ducking.

An English lady tourist, Baedeker in hand, has wandered in, trying to identify the images with the aid of her book. She now comes behind the seated group and accosts the priest.

THE L. T. Excuse me; but can you tell me which of these figures is the principal god?

THE PRIEST [*rising courteously*] The principal one? I do not understand.

THE L. T. I get lost among all these different gods: it is so difficult to know which is which.

THE PRIEST. They are not different gods. They are all god.

THE L. T. But how can that be? The figures are different.

THE PRIEST. God has many aspects.

THE L. T. But all these names in the guide book?

THE PRIEST. God has many names.

THE L. T. Not with us, you know.

THE PRIEST. Yes: even with you. The Father, the Son, the Spirit, the Immaculate Mother—

THE L. T. Excuse me. We are not Catholics.

THE PRIESTESS [*sharply*] Are your temples then labelled "For men only"?

THE L. T. [*shocked*] Oh, really! So sorry to have troubled you. [*She hurries away*].

THE PRIEST [*resuming his seat*] You should not be rude to the poor lady. She is English, and doesnt understand.

THE PRIESTESS. I find these heathen idolaters very trying. Is it really kind to treat them according to their folly instead of to our wisdom?

THE Y. W. Here! Steady on, you. Who are you calling heathen idolaters? Look at all those images. I should say, if you ask me, that the boot is on the other leg.

THE PRIEST. Those images are not idols: they are personifications of the forces of nature by which we all live. But of course to an idolater they are idols.

THE Y. W. You talk a lot about religion here. Cant you think of something livelier? I always say let life come to you; and dont bother about religion.

THE PRIESTESS. An excellent rule. But the more you let life come to you, the more you will find yourself bothering about religion.

The Emigration Officer rises into view in a spotless white robe. He is clean and rather pale, but looks regenerated.

THE Y. W. Oh boy, you do look the better for your dip. Why, he's an angel, a lamb. What have you done to him?

THE E. O. [*seating himself at the end of the table with his back to the sea*] Well, if you want to know, this blighter kicked me into the sea; and when I'd swallowed a ton or two of your best salt water they fished me out in a net and emptied me out. I brought up my immortal soul. They gave me what I thought was a nice cup of their tea to settle my stomach; but it made me ten times as sick as I was before. Theres nothing of the man you met this morning left except his skin and bones. You may regard me as to all intents and purposes born again.

THE PRIEST. Do you still wish to kill yourself?

THE E. O. When you have been through what I have been through since they fished me out of the water you wont worry about trifles as I used to, old man.

THE Y. W. Thats right. Let life come to you, I always say.

THE E. O. Yes, let life come. The premises are quite empty.

THE LADY TOURIST [*returning and addressing the priest*] Excuse me; but I have been thinking so much about you since you spoke to me. Would you mind accepting and reading this little tract?

THE PRIEST [*rising and coming forward to her, mean-*

555

while reading the title with a polite show of interest]
"Where will you spend eternity?"

THE L. T. [*strangely moved*] I have been haunted by
your face. I could not bear to think of your spending
eternity in torment. I feel sure it is a Christian face.

THE PRIEST. It is very kind of you. I will read the tract
with the greatest attention. Thank you.

*The lady, having no excuse for staying, moves away
reluctantly towards the images.*

THE PRIESTESS [*calling after her imperiously*] Where
have you spent eternity so far, may I ask? That which has
no end can have no beginning?

THE L. T. Excuse me: I have no desire to speak to you.

THE Y. W. [*indicating the priest*] Fallen in love with
him, have you? Well, let yourself rip. Let life come to
you.

THE L. T. Oh! How dare you? Really! Really!! [*She
goes out indignantly*].

THE PRIESTESS. Another conquest, Pra?

THE Y. W. Is his name Pra?

THE PRIESTESS. He has many names; but he answers to
Pra when you call him.

THE Y. W. Oh, what a way to put it! The man isn't
a dog, is he?

THE PRIESTESS. He inspires a doglike devotion in
women. He once did in me; so I know.

THE PRIEST. Dont be vindictive, Prola. I dont do it on
purpose. [*He sits down again, this time next her on her
left*].

THE PRIESTESS. No: you do it by instinct. That, also,
is rather doglike.

THE PRIEST. No matter: I shall soon get the poor lady
beyond the doglike stage.

THE E. O. [*who has been unable to take his eyes off the
priestess*] Is your name Prola?

THE PRIEST. She has many names: some of them terrible ones; but she answers to Prola when you call her.

THE PRIESTESS. Young man: are my eyes like the fish-pools of Heshbon?

THE E. O. Well, I have never seen the fishpools of Heshbon; but your eyes make me feel like that.

THE Y. W. Seems to me theres some sort of magic about this old cave thats dangerous. If you dont mind, I'll bid you all good morning. I always say let life come to you; but here it's coming a bit too thick for me. [*She rises*].

THE PRIESTESS. Wait. We can share him.

THE Y. W. Well I never! [*She flops back into her seat, flabbergasted*].

THE PRIESTESS. Hush. Look.

The Lady Tourist returns and again goes to the priest.

THE L. T. Excuse me; but could I have a word with you alone?

THE PRIEST [*rising*] Certainly. Come with me.

They go into the caves together.

THE E. O. What about a word with me alone, Prola?

THE Y. W. [*with redoubled emphasis*] Well I NEVER!!

THE PRIESTESS [*to the Officer*] You are not yet sufficiently regenerated. But you may hope.

THE Y. W. You take care, boy. I think youve got a touch of the sun. You cant be too careful in the tropics.

An English male tourist enters from among the images. He is on the young side of middle age, with pleasant aristocratic appearance and manners.

THE M. T. Excuse me: I have mislaid my wife. English lady with a guide book. Wears glasses. Bi-focals.

THE Y. W. Her husband! Oh, I say!

THE E. O. [*rising deferentially*] Just left us, Sir Charles.

THE M. T. Hallo! Weve met before, I think, havnt we?

THE E. O. When you landed, Sir Charles. I am the emigration officer.

SIR CHARLES. Ah, of course: yes. You know Lady Farwaters by sight. Which way did she go?

THE E. O. I am sorry: I didnt notice.

SIR CHARLES [*worried*] I wonder what she can be doing.

THE Y. W. So do I.

SIR CHARLES. I beg your pardon?

THE Y. W. Granted.

THE PRIESTESS [*rising and coming to him*] May I shew you round the temple, Sir Charles? We shall probably find her there.

SIR CHARLES [*who has not yet hitherto looked particularly at her*] No thank you, no, no.

THE PRIESTESS. It is interesting. I am not a professional guide: I am a priestess; and I will see that you are not asked for anything. You had better come with me.

SIR CHARLES. No: I— [*he looks at her. His tone changes instantly*]. Well, yes, if you will be so good. Certainly. Thank you.

They go into the alcoves together.

THE Y. W. [*leaving the table*] Oh boy, what do you think of this abode of love? Lady Farwaters, as white as Canterbury veal, has fallen for a brown bishop; and her husband, the whitest English west-end white, has been carried off to her den by an amber colored snake charmer. Lets get out of it while we're safe.

THE E. O. I feel quite safe, thank you. I have been cleaned up. You havnt.

THE Y. W. What do you mean, I havnt?

THE E. O. I mean that you were quite right to object to me half an hour ago. Your offensive personal remarks were fully justified. But now the tables are turned. I havnt gone through the fire; but Ive gone through the water. And the water has gone through me. It is for me now to object and to make personal remarks.

THE Y. W. Make as much as one; and you will get your face smacked.

THE E. O. [*seizing her by the wrist and the back of*

her collar] Go and get cleaned up, you disgusting little devil. [*He rushes her to the edge*].

THE Y. W. [*screaming*] No.

THE E. O. Yes. [*He hurls her over*].

A scream cut short by a splash. The E. O. sits down at the table and attacks the remains of the feast ravenously.

THE PROLOGUE ENDS

ACT I

THE lawn of a stately house on the north coast of a tropical island in the Pacific commands a fine view of the ocean and of a breakwater enclosing a harbor, large enough to accommodate a fleet, but at present shipless. The western face of the house is reached by a terrace and a flight of steps. The steps lead down to a crescent formed by two curved stone seats separated by a patch of sward surrounding a circular well with a low marble parapet. This parapet, like the stone seats, has silk cushions scattered about it.

Behind the crescent the lawn is banked to a higher level and becomes a flower garden, sheltered from the wind by shrubberies. To the west of the flower garden the lawn falls away to the sea, but not to sea level, all that is visible of the port being the top of the lighthouse. There are trees enough in all directions to provide shade everywhere.

However, the raised flower garden is the centre of interest; for in it are four shrines marking the corners of a square. In the two foremost shrines two girl-goddesses sit crosslegged. In the two further ones two youthful gods are sitting in the same fashion. The ages of the four appear to be between 17 and 20. They are magically beautiful in their Indian dresses, softly brilliant, making the tropical flowers of the garden seem almost crude beside them. Their expressions are intent, grave, and inscrutable. They face south with their backs to the sea. The goddess to the east has raven black hair, a swarthy skin, and robes of a thousand shades of deep carnation, in contrast to the younger one on her right, who is a ravishing blonde in a diaphanous white and gold sari. There is a parallel contrast between the two youths, the one on the west being the younger and more delicate, and the one on his left older and more powerfully framed.

The four figures give the garden a hieratic aspect which has its effect on a young English clergyman, who wan-

*ders into the grounds at the north west corner, looking
curiously and apprehensively about him with the air of
a stranger who is trespassing. When he catches sight of the
four figures he starts nervously and whips off his hat;
then approaches them on tiptoe. He has a baby complexion, and a childish expression, credulous and dis-
armingly propitiatory. His age is at most 24.*

*Down the steps at this moment comes Pra, about
twenty years older than when we saw him last, but splen-
didly preserved. His approach is dignified and even cour-
teous, though not warmly so. He evidently wants to know
what the stranger is doing in his garden.*

THE CLERGYMAN [*nervously, hat in hand*] I beg your
pardon. I fear I am trespassing. I am a stranger here; and
I could not find a road up from the beach. I thought I
might cut across through your grounds. [*Indicating the
figures*] But I assure you I had no idea I was intruding
on consecrated ground.

PRA. You are not on consecrated ground, except in so
far as all ground is consecrated.

THE CLERGYMAN. Oh, excuse me. I thought—those
idols—

PRA. Idols!

THE CLERGYMAN. No, of course not idols. I meant
those gods and goddesses—

PRA. They are very beautiful, are they not? [*He
speaks without awe or enthusiasm, with a touch of pity
for the parson and weariness on his own part*].

THE CLERGYMAN. They are most beautiful. Quite marvellous even to me, an English clergyman. I can hardly
wonder at your worshipping them, though of course you
shouldnt.

PRA. Beauty is worshipful, within limits. When you
have worshipped your fill may I shew you the shortest
way out? It is through the house. Where do you wish to
go, by the way?

THE CLERGYMAN. I dont know. I am lost.

561

THE SIMPLETON

PRA. Lost?

THE CLERGYMAN. Yes, quite lost. I dont know where I am. I mean I dont even know what country I am in.

PRA. You are in the Unexpected Isles, a Crown Colony of the British Empire.

THE CLERGYMAN. Do you mean the isles that came up out of the sea when I was a baby.

PRA. Yes. [*Pointing to the breakwater*] That is the harbor of the port of Good Adventure.

THE CLERGYMAN. They put me on shore there.

PRA. Who put you on shore?

THE CLERGYMAN. The pirates.

PRA. Pirates!

THE CLERGYMAN. Yes. I was their chaplain.

PRA. You were their—! [*He turns to the house and calls*] Prola. Prola.

PROLA'S VOICE. Yes. What is it?

PRA. Come out here.

Prola comes down the steps. She, like Pra, is twenty years older; but the years have only made her beauty more impressive.

THE CLERGYMAN [*gaping at her in undisguised awe and admiration*] Oh dear! Is this the lady of the house?

PROLA [*coming past Pra to the Clergyman*] Who is this gentleman?

PRA. He does not seem to know. I think he has escaped from the asylum.

THE CLERGYMAN [*distressed*] Oh, dear beautiful lady, I am not mad. Everybody thinks I am. Nobody believes what I say, though it is the simple truth. I know it is very hard to believe.

PROLA. In the Unexpected Isles nothing is unbelievable. How did you get in here?

THE CLERGYMAN. I lost my way trying to find a short cut up from the beach. I climbed the fence. I am so sorry.

PROLA. Really sorry?

THE CLERGYMAN. I did not mean to intrude. I apologize most sincerely.

PROLA. I did not ask you to apologize: you are quite welcome. I asked were you really sorry. Do you regret finding yourself in this garden?

THE CLERGYMAN. Oh no. It's like the Garden of Eden: I should like to stay here forever. [*Suddenly breaking down to the verge of tears*] I have nowhere to go.

PROLA. Perhaps he is weak with hunger.

THE CLERGYMAN. No: it's not that. I have been under a great strain for a long time; and now that I have escaped—and the beauty of those four—and your lovely awfulness—and—oh [*collapsing on the stone seat*] I am making a fool of myself. I always make a fool of myself. Dont mind me.

PRA. He thinks he has been chaplain in a pirate ship.

THE CLERGYMAN [*rising in desperate protest*] But I have. I have. They kidnapped me at Weston Super Mare where I was doing locum tenens for the Rector of Saint Biddulphs. It was on a Sunday afternoon: I had my clerical clothes on after taking the afternoon service. "You look so innocent and respectable" they said. "Just what we want!" They took me all over the world, where I couldnt speak the language and couldnt explain.

PRA. And they wanted you to minister to them spiritually?

THE CLERGYMAN. No no: that was what was so dreadful. They were crooks, racketeers, smugglers, pirates, anything that paid them. They used me to make people believe that they were respectable. They were often so bored that they made me hold a service and preach; but it was only to make themselves ill laughing at me. Though perhaps I shouldnt say that. Some of them were such dear nice fellows: they assured me it did them no end of good. But they got tired of me and put me ashore here. [*He again resorts to the stone seat, clasping his temples distractedly*] Oh dear! oh dear! nothing ever happens to me that happens to other people. And all because I was not a natural baby. I was a nitrogen baby.

PROLA. A nitrogen baby!

PRA [*to Prola*] Steady. There may be something in this.
[*He goes to the clergyman and sits down beside him*] What
do you mean by a nitrogen baby?

THE CLERGYMAN. You see, my father is a famous biological chemist.

PROLA. I do not see. Your father may be a biological
chemist; but biological chemists' children are like other
people's children.

THE CLERGYMAN. No. No, I assure you. Not my father's children. You dont know my father. Even my Christian name is Phosphor.

PRA. Is what?

THE CLERGYMAN. Phosphor. [*He spells it*] P.H.O.S.
P.H.O.R. The name of the morning star. Phosphorus, you
know. The stuff they make matches with. Such a name to
baptize a boy by! Please dont call me by it.

PRA. Come come! Neither your father nor your god-
fathers and godmothers could change your human nature
by giving you an unusual name in baptism.

THE CLERGYMAN. But it wasnt only the name. My father fed our cows on nitrogen grass.

PRA. Nitrogen gas, you mean.

THE CLERGYMAN. No: nitrogen grass. Some sort of
grass that came up when he sprinkled our fields with
chemicals. The cows ate it; and their butter was very yellow and awfully rich. So was the milk. I was fed on that
sort of milk and butter. And the wheat in my bread was
grown from special nitrates that my father made.

PRA [*to Prola*] I believe he is not mad after all.

THE CLERGYMAN. I assure you I am not. I am weakminded; but I am not mad.

PRA. I have read some very interesting articles about
this by an English chemist named Hammingtap.

THE CLERGYMAN. Thats my father. My name is Hammingtap. The old family name is Hummingtop; but my
564

grandfather changed it when he was at Oxford.

PRA. Prola: our young friend here may really be a new sort of man. Shall we go in and tell the others about him? We might take him into the family for a while, as an experiment.

THE CLERGYMAN [*alarmed*] Oh please, no. Why does everyone want to make an experiment of me?

PROLA. All men and women are experiments. What is your religion?

THE CLERGYMAN. The Christian religion, of course. I am a clergyman.

PROLA. What is the Christian religion?

THE CLERGYMAN. Well, it is—well, I suppose it is the Christian religion. I thought everybody knew. But then of course you are a heathen.

PROLA. What does the Christian religion mean to you?

THE CLERGYMAN. Oh, to me it means everything that is good and lovely and kind and holy. I dont profess to go any further than that.

PROLA. You need not. You had better not. Wait here until we return. We may find some use for you. Come, Pra.

She goes up the steps into the house, followed by Pra. The Clergyman, left with the four figures, looks at them, looks round to make sure that nobody is watching. Then he steals up to the fair goddess.

THE CLERGYMAN. Oh, how lovely you are! How I wish you were alive and I could kiss your living lips instead of the paint on a hard wooden image. I wonder is it idolatry to adore you? St Peter in Rome is only a bronze image; but his feet have been worn away by the kisses of Christian pilgrims. You make me feel as I have never felt before. I must kiss you. [*He does so and finds that she is alive. She smiles as her eyes turn bewitchingly towards him*]. Oh!!! [*He stands gasping, palpitating*].

THE ELDER YOUTH. Beware.

THE YOUNGER. On guard.

THE SIMPLETON

THE FAIR GIRL. Let him worship. His lips are sweet and pure.

THE DARK ONE. "For he on honey dew hath fed"—

THE FAIR ONE. —"and drunk the milk of paradise."

THE DARK ONE. I, Vashti, can see his aura. It is violet.

THE FAIR ONE. I, Maya, can see his halo. It is silvery.

VASHTI. Blessed are the shining ones!

MAYA. Blessed are the simple ones!

THE ELDER YOUTH. Beware. I, Janga, warn thee.

THE YOUNGER YOUTH. On guard. I, Kanchin, shew thee the red light.

JANGA. Their eyebrows are drawn bows.

KANCHIN. Their arrows feel sweet in the heart—

JANGA. —but are deadly.

KANCHIN. The ground within reach of their arms is enchanted.

JANGA. Vashti is lovely even to her brothers.

KANCHIN. Little children would die for Maya.

JANGA. Beware.

KANCHIN. On guard.

JANGA. Trust them not.

KANCHIN. They will break thy spear.

JANGA. They will pierce thy shield.

VASHTI. Fear not, beginner: I will strengthen thee.

MAYA. Strive not, beloved: I will keep thy soul for thee.

THE 2 YOUTHS [*together, fortissimo*] Beware.

The two girl-goddesses suddenly and simultaneously spring from their shrines and march down upon him, Vashti to his left, Maya to his right.

VASHTI. Dare you tread the plains of heaven with us, young pilgrim?

MAYA. We are waves of life in a sea of bliss. Dare you breast them, young swimmer?

THE CLERGYMAN. Oh, I dont know whether you are gods and goddesses or real people. I only know that you fill my heart with inexpressible longings.

MAYA. We are the awakening.

566

VASHTI. We are the way.

MAYA. We are the life.

VASHTI. I am the light. Look at me. [*She throws her arm round him and turns his face to hers*].

MAYA. I am the fire. Feel how it glows [*She also throws her arm round him*].

LADY FARWATERS *comes from the house, and pauses at the top of the steps to take in what is going on.*

THE CLERGYMAN. Oh, one at a time, please.

VASHTI. Perfect love casteth out choice.

MAYA. In love there is neither division nor measure.

LADY FARWATERS [*rushing to him and dragging him away from them*] Stop it, children: you are driving the man mad. Go away, all of you.

The two youths spring from their pedestals and whirl the girls away through the shrubberies.

VASHTI [*invisible, calling*] I will return in dreams.

MAYA [*similarly*] I leave my arrow in your heart.

LADY FARWATERS. You mustnt mind them.

Prola and Pra come down the steps, followed by Sir Charles Farwaters and by Hugo Hyering C.B. and Mrs. Hyering. Hyering is the former emigration officer, now an elderly and very different man, disciplined, responsible and well groomed. His wife is the emigrant girl twenty years older and better drilled socially, but still very much her old self. Lady Farwaters, once a gaunt and affected tourist visiting cave temples and distributing tracts to the heathen, is now a bland and attractive matron.

PRA. Mr Hammingtap: let me introduce you to the Governor of the Unexpected Isles, Sir Charles Farwaters.

SIR CHARLES [*offering his hand*] How do you do, Mr Hammingtap?

THE CLERGYMAN [*jerkily nervous*] Very pleased. [*They shake hands*].

Sir Charles sits down in the middle of the stone seat nearest the steps.

PRA. Lady Farwaters.

THE SIMPLETON

LADY FARWATERS [*smiles and proffers her hand*]!

THE CLERGYMAN. Most kind—er. [*He shakes*].

Lady Farwaters sits down in the middle of the other stone seat.

PRA. This is Mr Hugo Hyering, political secretary to the Isles.

THE CLERGYMAN. How do you do, Sir Hugo?

HYERING [*shaking hands*] Not Sir Hugo. [*Introducing*] Mrs Hyering.

MRS HYERING [*shaking hands*] C.B., in case you are addressing a letter. [*She sits down on Sir Charles's left*].

THE CLERGYMAN. Oh, I am so sorry.

HYERING. Not at all. [*He sits on Lady Farwaters' right*].

PRA [*indicating the parapet of the well*] You had better sit here.

THE CLERGYMAN [*sitting down as directed*] Thank you.

Prola sits down on Sir Charles's left, and Pra on Lady Farwaters' left.

LADY FARWATERS. You have made the acquaintance of our four children, Mr Hammingtap?

THE CLERGYMAN. I couldnt help it. I mean—

PROLA. We know what you mean. You need not explain.

THE CLERGYMAN. But I assure you I—that is—

MRS HYERING. Dont apologize, Mr Hammingtap. We know quite well what our daughters are capable of when they are attracted by a young stranger.

THE CLERGYMAN. I did not understand. They are so sunburnt, and their dresses are so eastern: I thought they were orientals.

SIR CHARLES. They are half orientals. You see, the family is a mixed one. This lady, whom you may address as Prola, and this gentleman, known as Pra, are both entirely oriental, and very dominant personalities at that; so that naturally our children would have a strong oriental

568

strain, would they not?

THE CLERGYMAN [*hastily*] Oh, of course. Quite. Certainly. [*He looks piteously at their gracious unconcerned faces, which tell him nothing*]. I beg your pardon. I am frightfully sorry; but my nerves are in rags; and I cannot follow what you are saying.

HYERING. Oh yes you can. It's all right: you have understood perfectly.

MRS HYERING. Buck up, Mr Hammingtap. Let life come to you.

LADY FARWATERS. Our family arrangements are not those usual in England. We are making a little domestic experiment—

THE CLERGYMAN. Oh, not an experiment, I hope. Chemical experiments are bad enough: I am one myself; but they are scientific. I dont think I could countenance a domestic experiment. And in spite of what you say I am not sure that I am not going mad.

SIR CHARLES. We are distracting you. Let us change the subject. Would you like to be a bishop?

THE CLERGYMAN. Oh dear! Can you make me one?

SIR CHARLES. Well, my recommendation would probably be decisive. A bishop is needed here: a bishop in partibus infidelium. Providence seems to have thrown you on this shore for the purpose, like Jonah. Will you undertake it?

THE CLERGYMAN. I should like to have a bishop's salary, certainly. But unfortunately I am weakminded.

SIR CHARLES. Many bishops are; and they are the best sort. A strongminded bishop is a horror.

THE CLERGYMAN. I am too young.

SIR CHARLES. You will not remain so. Most bishops are too old.

THE CLERGYMAN [*tempted*] It would be rather a lark, wouldnt it?

MRS HYERING. Thats right, Mr Hammingtap: let life come to you.

PRA. What objection have you to be a bishop?

569

THE SIMPLETON

THE CLERGYMAN. Oh, none, I assure you. Of course no clergyman could object to be a bishop. But why do you want to make me one?

SIR CHARLES. I will be quite frank with you, Mr Hammingtap. Twenty years ago my wife and I, with Mr and Mrs Hyering, joined this eastern gentleman and his colleague in a eugenic experiment. Its object was to try out the result of a biological blend of the flesh and spirit of the west with the flesh and spirit of the east. We formed a family of six parents.

THE CLERGYMAN. Six?

SIR CHARLES. Yes, six. The result has been a little disappointing from the point of view of numbers; but we have produced four children, two of each sex, and educated them in the most enlightened manner we were capable of. They have now grown up; consequently the time has arrived when the family group must be extended by young persons of their own age, so that the group may produce a second generation. Now sooner or later this extension of the family group will set people talking.

THE CLERGYMAN. It would strike my people dumb, if I grasp your meaning rightly.

SIR CHARLES. You do. I mean exactly what I say. There will be a struggle with public opinion in the empire. We shall not shirk it: it is part of our plan to open people's minds on the subject of eugenics and the need for mixing not only western and eastern culture but eastern and western blood. Still, we do not want to be stopped, as the Mormons were, or as the Oneida Community would have been if it had not voluntarily broken up. We want to set the intelligent people talking, and to strike the stupid people dumb. And we think we could do both by adding a bishop to the family.

MRS HYERING. And that is where you come in, young man.

PRA. There is another consideration that weighs with us: at least with me. I am convinced that there is something lacking in the constitution of the children. It may be a deficiency of nitrogen. It certainly is a deficiency of something that is essential to a complete social human being.

THE CLERGYMAN. Oh, I cannot believe that. They seemed to me to be quite perfect. I cannot imagine anyone more perfect than Maya.

PRA. Well, what did you think of Maya's conscience, for example?

THE CLERGYMAN [*bewildered*] Her conscience? I suppose—I dont know—I—

PRA. Precisely. You dont know. Well, we do know. Our four wonderful children have all sorts of talents, all sorts of accomplishments, all sorts of charms. And we are heartily tired of all their attractions because, though they have artistic consciences, and would die rather than do anything ugly or vulgar or common, they have not between the whole four of them a scrap of moral conscience. They have been very carefully fed: all the vitamins that the biological chemists have discovered are provided in their diet. All their glands are scientifically nourished. Their physical health is perfect. Unfortunately the biological chemists have not yet discovered either the gland that produces and regulates the moral conscience or the vitamins that nourish it. Have you a conscience, Mr Hammingtap?

THE CLERGYMAN. Oh yes: I wish I hadnt. It tortures me. You know, I should have enjoyed being a pirate's chaplain sometimes if it hadnt been for my terrible conscience. It has made my life one long remorse; for I have never had the strength of mind to act up to it.

PRA. That suggests very strongly that the conscientious man is, chemically speaking, the nitrogenic man. Here, then, we have four young adults, insufficiently nitrogenized, and therefore deficient in conscience. Here also we have a young adult saturated with nitrogen from his cradle, and suffering from a morbid excess of conscience. A union between him and our girls is clearly indicated.

THE CLERGYMAN. You mean that I ought to marry one

of them?

PRA. Not at all. They would regard that as an invidious proceeding.

THE CLERGYMAN. Invidious! I dont understand.

LADY FARWATERS [*goodnaturedly*] Let me try to break it to you, Mr Hammingtap. The two girls attract you very much, dont they?

THE CLERGYMAN. How can one help being attracted, Lady Farwaters? Theyre quite beautiful.

LADY FARWATERS. Both of them?

THE CLERGYMAN. Oh, as a clergyman I could not be attracted by more than one at a time. Still, somehow, I seem to love them all in an inexpressible sort of way. Only, if there were any question of marriage, I should have to choose.

PROLA. And which would you choose?

THE CLERGYMAN. Oh, I should choose Maya.

PROLA. Maya would at once reject you.

THE CLERGYMAN [*much dejected*] I suppose so. I know I am no catch for Maya. Still, she was very kind to me. In fact—but perhaps I oughtnt to tell you this—she kissed me.

SIR CHARLES. Indeed? That shews that she contemplates a union with you.

LADY FARWATERS. You must not think she would reject you on the ground of any personal unworthiness on your part.

THE CLERGYMAN. Then on what ground? Oh, I shouldnt have kissed her.

MRS HYERING. Oho! You said it was she who kissed you.

THE CLERGYMAN. Yes: I know I should have explained that. But she let me kiss her.

MRS HYERING. That must have been a thrill, Mr Hammingtap. Life came to you that time, didnt it?

THE CLERGYMAN. Oh please, I cant speak of it. But why should she reject me if I make her an honorable proposal?

LADY FARWATERS. Because she will consider your honorable proposal dishonorable, Mr Hammingtap, unless it includes all the ladies of the family. You will not be allowed to pick and choose and make distinctions. You marry all or none.

THE CLERGYMAN. Oh dear! My poor little brain is giving way. I cant make sense of what you are saying. I know that your meaning must be perfectly right and respectable, Lady Farwaters; but it sounds like a dreadful sort of wickedness.

LADY FARWATERS. May I try to explain?

THE CLERGYMAN. Please do, Lady Farwaters. But I wish you wouldnt call me Mr Hammingtap. I am accustomed to be called Iddy among friends.

MRS HYERING. What does Iddy stand for?

THE CLERGYMAN. Well, in our home I was known as the idiot.

MRS HYERING. Oh! I am sorry: I didn't know.

THE CLERGYMAN. Not at all. My sister was the Kiddy; so I became the Iddy. Do please call me that. And be kind to me. I am weakminded and lose my head very easily; and I can see that you are all wonderfully clever and strongminded. That is why I could be so happy here. I can take in anything if you will only tell it to me in a gentle hushabyebaby sort of way and call me Iddy. Now go on, Lady Farwaters. Excuse me for interrupting you so long.

LADY FARWATERS. You see, Iddy—

IDDY. Oh, thanks!

LADY FARWATERS [*continuing*] —our four children are not like European children and not like Asiatic children. They have the east in their brains and the west in their blood. And at the same time they have the east in their blood and the west in their brains. Well, from the time when as tiny tots they could speak, they invented fairy stories. I thought it silly and dangerous, and wanted to stop them; but Prola would not let me: she taught them

THE SIMPLETON

a game called the heavenly parliament in which all of them told tales and added them to the general stock until a fairyland was built up, with laws and religious rituals, and finally a great institution which they called the Superfamily. It began by my telling them in my old conventional English way to love oneanother; but they would not have that at all: they said it was vulgar nonsense and made them interfere with oneanother and hate oneanother. Then they hit out for themselves the idea that they were not to love oneanother, but that they were to be oneanother.

IDDY. To be oneanother! I dont understand.

SIR CHARLES. Neither do I. Pra and Prola think they understand it; but Lady Farwaters and I dont; and we dont pretend to. We are too English. But the practical side of it—the side that concerns you—is that Vashti and Maya are now grown up. They must have children. The boys will need a young wife.

IDDY. You mean two wives.

LADY FARWATERS. Oh, a dozen, if so many of the right sort can be found.

IDDY. But—but—but that would be polygamy.

PROLA. You are in the east, Mr Iddy. The east is polygamous. Try to remember that polygamists form an enormous majority of the subjects of the British Empire, and that you are not now in Clapham.

IDDY. How dreadful! I never thought of that.

LADY FARWATERS. And the girls will need a young husband.

IDDY [imploringly] Two young husbands, Lady Farwaters. Oh please, two.

LADY FARWATERS. I think not, at first.

IDDY. Oh! But I am not an oriental. I am a clergyman of the Church of England.

HYERING. That means nothing to Vashti.

PRA. And still less to Maya.

IDDY. But—but—oh dear! don't you understand? I want to marry Maya. And if I marry Maya I cannot marry

574

Vashti. An English clergyman could not marry two women.

LADY FARWATERS. From their point of view they are not two women: they are one. Vashti is Maya; and Maya is Vashti.

IDDY. But even if such a thing were possible how could I be faithful to Vashti without being unfaithful to Maya? I couldn't bear to be unfaithful to Maya.

LADY FARWATERS. Maya would regard the slightest unfaithfulness to Vashti as a betrayal of herself and a breach of your marriage vow.

IDDY. But thats nonsense: utter nonsense. Please dont put such things into my head. I am trying so hard to keep sane; but you are terrifying me. If only I could bring myself never to see Maya again I should rush out of this garden and make for home. But it would be like rushing out of heaven. I am most unhappy; and yet I am dreadfully happy. I think I am under some sort of enchantment.

MRS HYERING. Well, stick to the enchantment while it lasts. Let life come to you.

PRA. May I remind you that not only Vashti and Maya, but all the ladies here, are included in the superfamily compact.

IDDY. Oh, how nice and comfortable that would be! They would be mothers to me.

PROLA [rebuking Pra] Let him alone, Pra. There is such a thing as calf love. Vashti and Maya are quite enough for him to begin with. Maya has already driven him half mad. There is no need for us old people to drive him quite out of his senses. [She rises] This has gone far enough. Wait here alone, Mr Hammingtap, to collect your thoughts. Look at the flowers; breathe the air; open your soul to the infinite space of the sky. Nature always helps.

IDDY [rising] Thank you, Lady Prola. Yes: that will be a great help.

PROLA. Come. [She goes up the steps and into the house].

THE SIMPLETON

They all rise and follow her, each bestowing a word of counsel or comfort on the distracted clergyman.

PRA. Relax. Take a full breath and then relax. Do not strangle yourself with useless anxieties. [*He goes*].

LADY FARWATERS. Cast out fear, Iddy. Warm heart. Clear mind. Think of having a thousand friends, a thousand wives, a thousand mothers. [*She pats him on the shoulder and goes*].

SIR CHARLES. Stand up to it, my boy. The world is changing. Stand up to it. [*He goes*].

MRS HYERING. Dont let that conscience of yours worry you. Let life come to you. [*She goes*].

HYERING. Try to sleep a little. The morning has been too much for you. [*He goes*].

IDDY. Sleep! I will not sleep. They want me to disgrace my cloth; but I wont. I wont relax: I wont disobey my conscience: I wont smell those flowers: I wont look at the sky. Nature is not good for me here. Nature is eastern here: it's poison to an Englishman. I will think of England and tighten myself up and pull myself together. England! The Malverns! the Severn plain! the Welsh border! the three cathedrals! England that is me: I that am England! Damn and blast all these tropical paradises: I am an English clergyman; and my place is in England. Floreat Etona! Back to England and all that England means to an Englishman! In this sign I shall conquer. [*He turns resolutely to go out as he came in, and finds himself face to face with Maya, who has stolen in and listened gravely and intently to his exhortation*].

IDDY [*collapsing in despair on the parapet of the well*] Oh, Maya, let me go, let me go.

MAYA [*sinking beside him with her arm round his neck*] Speak to me from your soul, and not with words that you have picked up in the street.

IDDY. Respect my cloth, Miss Farwaters.

MAYA. Maya. Maya is my name. I am the veil of the temple. Rend me in twain.

576

IDDY. I wont. I will go home and marry some honest English girl named Polly Perkins. [*Shuddering in her embrace*] Oh, Maya, darling: speak to me like a human being.

MAYA. That is how I speak to you; but you do not recognize human speech when you hear it: you crave for slang and small talk, and for readymade phrases that mean nothing. Speak from your soul; and tell me: do you love Vashti? Would you die for Vashti?

IDDY. No.

MAYA [*with a flash of rage, springing up*] Wretch! [*Calmly and conclusively*] You are free. Farewell [*She points his way through the house*].

IDDY [*clutching at her robe*] No, no. Do not leave me. I love you—you. I would die for you. That sounds like a word picked up in the street; but it is true. I would die for you ten times over.

MAYA. It is not true. Words, words, words out of the gutter. Vashti and Maya are one: you cannot love me if you do not love Vashti: you cannot die for me without dying for Vashti.

IDDY. Oh, I assure you I can.

MAYA. Lies, lies. If you can feel one heart throb for me that is not a throb for Vashti: if for even an instant there are two women in your thoughts instead of one, then you do not know what love can be.

IDDY. But it's just the contrary. I—

VASHTI [*who has entered silently, sits beside him and throws an arm round his shoulders*] Do you not love me? Would you not die for me?

IDDY [*mesmerized by her eyes*] Oh DEAR!!! Yes: your eyes make my heart melt: your voice opens heaven to me: I love you. I would die a thousand times for you.

VASHTI. And Maya? You love Maya. You would die a million times for Maya?

IDDY. Yes, yes. I would die for either, for both: for one, for the other—

MAYA. For Vashti Maya?

THE SIMPLETON

IDDY. For Vashti Maya, for Maya Vashti.

VASHTI. Your lives and ours are one life.

MAYA [*sitting down beside him*] And this is the King-dom of love.

The three embrace with interlaced arms and vanish in black darkness.

ACT II

A FINE *forenoon some years later. The garden is unchanged; but inside the distant breakwater the harbor is crowded with cruisers; and on the lawn near the steps is a writing table littered with papers and furnished with a wireless telephone. Sir Charles is sitting at the end of it with his back to the house. Seated near him is Pra. Both are busy writing. Hyering enters.*

SIR CHARLES. Morning, Hyering.

HYERING. Morning. [*He sits at the other end of the table after waving an acknowledgment of Pra's indication of a salaam*]. Anything fresh?

SIR CHARLES [*pointing to the roadstead*] Look! Five more cruisers in last night. The papers say it is the first time the fleets of the British Empire have ever assembled in one place.

HYERING. I hope it will never happen again. If we dont get rid of them quickly there will be the biggest naval battle on record. They are quarrelling already like Kilkenny cats.

SIR CHARLES. What about?

HYERING. Oh, about everything. About moorings, about firing salutes: which has the right to fire first? about flags, about shore parties, about nothing. We shall never be able to keep the peace between them. The Quebec has got alongside the Belfast. The Quebec has announced Mass at eleven on All Saints Day; and the Belfast has announced firing practice at the same hour. Do you see that sloop that came in last night?

SIR CHARLES. What is it?

HYERING. The Pitcairn Island fleet. They are Seventh Day Adventists, and are quite sure the Judgment Day is fixed for five o'clock this afternoon. They propose to do nothing until then but sing hymns. The Irish Free State admiral threatens to sink them if they dont stop. How am I to keep them quiet?

PRA. Dont keep them quiet. Their squabbles will make

579

them forget what they were sent here for.

HYERING. Forget! not they. I have six ultimatums from their admirals, all expiring at noon today. Look. [*He takes a batch of letters from his pocket and throws them on the table*].

SIR CHARLES [*pointing to the letters on the table*] Look at these!

PRA. All about Iddy.

SIR CHARLES. Iddy has got into the headlines at home. The cables are humming with Iddy. Iddy has convulsed the Empire, confound him!

HYERING. Anything fresh from London or Delhi?

SIR CHARLES. The same old songs. The Church of England wont tolerate polygamy on any terms, and insists on our prosecuting Iddy if we cannot whitewash him. Delhi declares that any attempt to persecute polygamy would be an insult to the religions of India.

PRA. The Cultural Minister at Delhi adds a postscript to say that as he has been married two hundred and thirty-four times, and could not have lived on his salary without the dowries, the protest of the Church of England shews a great want of consideration for his position. He has a hundred and seventeen children surviving.

SIR CHARLES. Then there's a chap I never heard of, calling himself the Caliph of British Islam. He demands that Iddy shall put away all his wives except four.

HYERING. What does the Foreign Office say to that?

PRA. The Foreign Office hails it as a happy solution of a difficulty that threatened to be very serious.

HYERING. What do you think about it all yourself, Pra?

PRA. Think! Thought has no place in such discussions. Each of them must learn that its ideas are not everybody's ideas. Here is a cablegram from the League of British Imperial Womanhood, Vancouver and Pretoria. "Burn him alive and his hussies with him." Do you expect me to think about such people?

HYERING. Nobody has made any practical suggestion,

580

I suppose?

PRA. The United States intervene with a friendly suggestion that the parties should be divorced. But the Irish Free State will not hear of divorce, and points out that if the parties become Catholics their marriages can be annulled with the greatest ease.

HYERING. Oh, the west! the west! the west!

PRA. Oh, the east! the east! the east! I tried to reconcile them; and I had only two successes: you and Lady Farwaters.

HYERING. You kicked me into the sea.

SIR CHARLES. You made love to Lady Farwaters.

PRA. I had to use that method with very crude novices; and Lady Farwaters, with her English ladylike bringing-up, was so crude that she really could not understand any purely intellectual appeal. Your own mind, thanks to your public school and university, was in an even worse condition; and Prola had to convert you by the same elementary method. Well, it has worked, up to a point. The insight you obtained into eastern modes of thought has enabled you to govern the eastern crown colonies with extraordinary success. Downing Street hated you; but Delhi supported you; and since India won Dominion status Delhi has been the centre of the British Empire. You, Hyering, have had the same diplomatic success in the east for the same reason. But beyond this we have been unable to advance a step. Our dream of founding a millennial world culture: the dream which united Prola and Pra as you first knew them, and then united us all six, has ended in a single little household with four children, wonderful and beautiful, but sterile. When we had to find a husband for the blossoming girls, only one man was found capable of merging himself in the unity of the family: a man fed on air from his childhood. And how has this paragon turned out? An impotent simpleton. It would be impossible to conceive a human being of less consequence in the world. And yet, look! There is the Imperial Armada, in which every petty province insists on its separate fleet, every trumpery islet its battleship, its cruiser, or at least its sloop or gunboat! Why are they here, armed to the teeth, threatening what they call their sanctions? a word that once meant the approval of the gods, and now means bombs full of poison gas. Solely on account of the simpleton. To reform his morals, half of them want to rain destruction on this little household of ours, and the other half is determined to sink them if they attempt it.

HYERING. They darent use their bombs, you know.

PRA. True; but what is to prevent them from taking to their fists and coming ashore to fight it out on the beach with sticks and bottles and stones, or with their fists? What do the ultimatums say, Hyering?

HYERING [*reading them*] Number one from the English admiral. "If the polygamist-adulterer Hammingtap is not handed over by noon tomorrow" that is today "I shall be obliged to open fire on Government House." Number two, from the commander of the Bombay Squadron. "Unless an unequivocal guarantee of the safety and liberty of Mr Hammingtap be in my hands by noon today" that came this morning "I shall land a shore party equipped with machine guns and tear gas bombs to assist the local police in the protection of his person." Number three: "I have repeatedly informed you that the imperial province of Holy Island demands the immediate and exemplary combustion of the abominable libertine and damnable apostate known as Phosfor Hammingtap. The patience of the Holy Island fleet will be exhausted at noon on the 13th" today "and the capital of the Unexpected Islands must take the consequences." Number four—

SIR CHARLES. Oh, bother number four! They are all the same: not one of them has originality enough to fix half-past-eleven or a quarter-to-one.

HYERING. By the way, Pra, have you taken any steps? I havnt.

PRA. Yes I have. Dont worry. I have sent a message.

SIR CHARLES. What message?

PRA. The Mayor of the Port earnestly begs the commanders of the imperial fleet to suspend action for another day, as his attention is urgently occupied by a serious outbreak of smallpox in the harbor district.

SIR CHARLES. Good. [*The boom of a cannon interrupts him*] There goes the noonday cannon!

HYERING. I hope they got the message in time.

The garden and its occupants vanish. When they reappear, the harbor is empty: not a ship is visible. The writing table, with its chairs and papers, has been removed and replaced by a small tea-table. Tea is ready. The wireless telephone is still there.

Vashti and Maya are in their shrines. Lady Farwaters is sitting on the western stone seat, with Mrs Hyering beside her on her right. Prola is sitting on the eastern seat. All five ladies are taking tea.

Pra comes from the house with Sir Charles and Hyering. They help themselves to tea. Pra abstains.

SIR CHARLES. Not a blessed ship left in the harbor! Your message certainly did the trick, Pra. [*He sits down beside Prola, on her left*].

PRA [*sitting down between the two British ladies*] They may come back.

HYERING [*sitting beside Prola, on her right*] Not a bit of it. By the time the fleet realizes that it has been humbugged the Empire will be tired of Iddy.

VASHTI. The world is tired of Iddy.

MAYA. *I* am tired of Iddy.

VASHTI. Iddy is a pestilence.

MAYA. Iddy is a bore.

VASHTI. Let us throw ourselves into the sea to escape from Iddy.

MAYA. Let us throw Iddy into the sea that he may escape from himself.

VASHTI. You are wise, Prola. Tell us how to get rid of

THE SIMPLETON

Iddy.

MAYA. We cannot endure Iddy for ever, Prola.

PROLA. You two chose him, not I.

MAYA. We were young: we did not know.

VASHTI. Help us, Pra. You have lost faith in us; but your wits are still keen.

MAYA. Pra: we beseech thee. Abolish the incubus.

VASHTI. Give him peace that we may have rest.

MAYA. Give him rest that we may have peace.

VASHTI. Let him be as he was before we knew him.

MAYA. When we were happy.

VASHTI. When he was innocent.

PRA. You raised this strange spirit. I cannot exorcise him.

VASHTI. Rather than endure him I will empty the heavens of their rain and dew.

MAYA. Silence him, O ye stars.

Iddy comes from the house in a condition of lazy self-complacence. He is received in dead silence. Nobody looks at him. He pours himself out a cup of tea. The silence becomes grim. He sits down on the grass at Prola's feet, and sips his tea. The silence continues.

IDDY [*at last*] I am a futile creature.

They all turn as if stung and look at him. Then they resume their attitudes of deadly endurance.

IDDY. It is a terrible thing to be loved. I dont suppose any man has ever been loved as I have been loved, or loved as I have loved. But there's not so much in it as people say. I am writing a sermon about it. It is a sermon on Eternity.

They look at him as before.

IDDY. The line I am going to take is this. We have never been able to imagine eternity properly. St. John of Patmos started the notion of playing harps and singing praises for ever and ever. But the organist tells me that composers have to use the harp very sparingly because, though it makes a very pretty effect at first, you get tired

584

of it so soon. You couldnt go on playing the harp for ever; and if you sang "Worthy is the Lamb" for ever you would drive the Lamb mad. The notion is that you cant have too much of a good thing; but you can: you can bear hardship much longer than you could bear heaven. Love is like music. Music is very nice: the organist says that when the wickedness of mankind tempts him to despair he comforts himself by remembering that the human race produced Mozart; but a woman who plays the piano all day is a curse. A woman who makes love to you all day is much worse; and yet nothing is lovelier than love, up to a point. We all love one another here in a wonderful way: I love Vashti, I love Maya, I love Prola; and they all love me so wonderfully that their three loves are only one love. But it is my belief that some day we'll have to try something else. If we dont we'll come to hate one another.

VASHTI. If it is any consolation to you, Iddy, I can assure you that I already hate you so intensely that if it were in my nature to kill anything I should kill you.

IDDY. There now! I ought to be wounded and horrified; but I'm not: I feel as if youd given me a strawberry ice. Thank you, dear Vashti, thank you. You give me hope that even Maya will get tired of me someday.

MAYA. I have been on the point of beating you to a jelly for ever so long past; but just as my fists were clenched to do it you always managed to come out with some stroke of idiocy that was either so funny or so piteous that I have kissed you instead.

IDDY. You make me happier than I have been for months. But, you know, that does not settle my difficulties. I dont know whether other people are like me or not—

LADY FARWATERS. No, Iddy: you are unique.

IDDY. Anyhow, I have made a discovery as regards myself.

VASHTI. Enough is known already.

MAYA. Seek no further: there is nothing there.

VASHTI. There never has been anything.

IDDY. Shut up, you two. This is something really interesting. I am writing a second sermon.

ALL THE REST [*gasp*]!!!!!!!!

PRA. Was eternity not long enough for one sermon?

IDDY. This one is on love.

VASHTI [*springing up*] I will cast myself down from a precipice.

MAYA [*springing up*] I will gas myself.

IDDY. Oh, not until you have heard my sermon, please.

PROLA. Listen to him, children. Respect the wisdom of the fool.

VASHTI [*resuming her goddess-in-a-shrine attitude*] The oracles of the wise are unheeded Silence for the King of Idiots.

MAYA [*also enshrining herself*] Speak, Solomon.

IDDY. Well, the discovery I have made is that we were commanded to love our enemies because loving is good for us and dreadfully bad for them. I love you all here intensely; and I enjoy loving you. I love Vashti; I love Maya; and I adore Prola with a passion that grows and deepens from year to year.

PROLA. Dolt! I am too old.

IDDY. You were never young and you will never be old. You are the way and the light for me. But you have never loved me and never will love me. You have never loved anything human: why should you? Nothing human is good enough to be loved. But every decent human creature has some capacity for loving. Look at me! What a little worm I am! My sermons are wretched stuff, except these last two, which I think really have something in them. I cannot bear being loved, because I know that I am a worm, and that nobody could love me unless they were completely deluded as to my merits. But I can love, and delight in loving. I love Vashti for hating me, because she is quite right to hate me: her hatred is a proof of her beautiful clear judgment. I love Maya for being out of all patience with me, because I know that I am enough to

586

drive anybody mad, and she is wise enough to know how worthless I am. I love Prola because she is far above loving or hating me; and there is something about her dark beauty that—

PROLA [*kicking him*] Silence, simpleton. Let the unspeakable remain unspoken.

IDDY. I dont mind your kicking me, Prola: you understand; and that is enough for me. And now you see what a jolly fine sermon it will be, and why I shall be so happy here with you from this day on. For I have the joy of loving you all without the burden of being loved in return, or the falsehood of being idolized.

MAYA. Solomon has spoken.

VASHTI. Stupendous.

LADY FARWATERS. Do not mock, darlings. There is something in what he says.

MAYA [*desperately*] But how are we to get rid of him? He is settling down with us for life.

VASHTI. We have brought him on ourselves.

MAYA. We cannot make him hate us.

VASHTI. He will go with us to heaven.

MAYA. In the depths of hell he will find us.

Kanchin and Janga enter processionally, reading newspapers.

KANCHIN. News!

JANGA. News!

They sit enshrined, foursquare with their sisters.

KANCHIN. By wireless.

JANGA. Tomorrow's three o'clock edition.

KANCHIN. The land that brought forth Iddy begins the Apocalypse.

HYERING. What do you mean? Has anything happened in England?

KANCHIN. England has broken loose.

SIR CHARLES. What do you mean? broken loose. Read the news, man. Out with it.

KANCHIN [*reading the headlines*] Dissolution of the

British Empire.

JANGA [*reading*] Withdrawal of England from the Empire.

KANCHIN. England strikes for independence.

JANGA. Downing Street declares for a right little tight little island.

KANCHIN. The British Prime Minister cuts the cable and gives the new slogan.

JANGA. Back to Elizabeth's England; and to hell with the empire!

KANCHIN. Ireland to the rescue!

JANGA. Free State President declares Ireland cannot permit England to break the unity of the Empire. Ireland will lead the attack on treason and disruption.

KANCHIN. The Prime Minister's reply to the President suppressed as unprintable.

JANGA. Canada claims position of premier Dominion left vacant by the secession of England.

KANCHIN. Australia counterclaims as metropolitan dominion.

JANGA. New Zealand proclaims a butter blockade until its claim to precedence is recognized by Australia.

KANCHIN. South Africa renames Capetown Empire City, and gives notice to all Britishers to clear out of Africa within ten days.

JANGA. His Holiness the Pope calls on all Christendom to celebrate the passing away of the last vain dream of earthly empire, and the unity of all living souls in the Catholic Kingdom of God and his Church.

LADY FARWATERS. That sounds like the voice of a grown-up man through the whooping of a pack of schoolboys.

JANGA [*prosaically*] So far, there have been no disturbances and little popular interest.

KANCHIN. The various international Boards are carrying on as usual.

JANGA. Today's football—

PROLA. No, Janga: certainly not.

SIR CHARLES. But what becomes of our jobs as Governor and political secretary, Hyering? Will this affect our salaries?

HYERING. They will stop: that is all. We had better proclaim the Unexpected Isles an independent republic and secure the new jobs for ourselves.

VASHTI. The world is tired of republics and their jobberies. Proclaim a kingdom.

MAYA. Or a queendom.

IDDY. Oh yes: let us make Prola queen. And I shall be her chaplain.

PRA. By all means, as far as I am concerned. Prola has always been the real ruler here.

VASHTI. Prola is she who decides.

MAYA. Prola is she who unites.

VASHTI. Prola is she who knows.

MAYA. No one can withstand Prola.

PROLA. Be quiet, you two. You shall not make an idol of me.

KANCHIN. We shall make you Empress of the Isles.

JANGA. Prola the First.

VASHTI. Homage, Prola.

MAYA. Love, Prola.

KANCHIN. Obedience, Prola.

JANGA. Absolute rule, Prola.

PROLA. All your burdens on me. Lazy idle children.

KANCHIN. Hurrah! All burdens on Prola.

JANGA. The burden of thought.

VASHTI. The burden of knowledge.

MAYA. The burden of righteousness.

VASHTI. The burden of justice.

MAYA. The burden of mercy.

PROLA. Cease, cease: these are not burdens to me: they are the air I breathe. I shall rule you as I have always done because you are too lazy to rule yourselves.

HYERING. You can rule us, Prola. But will the public

ever understand you?

PRA. They will obey her. They would not do that if they understood.

IDDY. I have just been thinking—

MAYA. Solomon has been thinking.

VASHTI. Thoughts without brains.

IDDY. Will the Antiphonal Quartet, if it wants to give another concert, kindly remove itself out of hearing.

KANCHIN. Silence for the Prophet.

JANGA. Mum!

VASHTI. Dumb.

MAYA. Tiddy iddy um. Carry on, darling.

IDDY. Prola can rule this house because she knows what is happening in it. But how is she to be an Empress if she doesnt know what is happening everywhere?

MRS HYERING. She can read the newspapers, cant she? silly?

IDDY. Yes; but fifteen years later, when the statesmen write their memoirs and autobiographies and publish them, we shall find that it never happened at all and what really happened was quite different. We dont know the truth about any of our statesmen until they are dead and cant take libel actions. Nobody knows the sort of people we really are. The papers have been full of us for weeks past; and not a single word they say about us is true. They think I am a sort of Mahdi or Mad Mullah, and that Prola and Vashti and Maya are a troop of immoral dancing girls, and that Sir Charles is a voluptuous sultan and Hyering a co-respondent. They dont live in a world of truth: they live in a world of their own ideas, which have nothing to do with our ideas. Consequently— Therefore— er—er— What was I going to say, Pra? My brain is not strong enough to keep the thread of my remarks. I ought to have written it down.

PRA. What you have arrived at is that we cannot live in a world of political facts, because we shall not know the political facts for years to come. We must therefore live

590

in a world of original ideas, created by ourselves out of our own nature.

IDDY. Yes. We mustnt pretend to be omniscient. Even God would not be omniscient if He read the newspapers. We must have an ideal of a beautiful and good world. We must believe that to establish that beautiful and good world on earth is the best thing we can do, and the only sort of religion and politics that is worth bothering about.

PROLA. What about the people who have no original ideas, Iddy?

PRA. The great majority of mankind?

IDDY. Theyll be only too glad to do what you tell them, Prola, if you can make them feel that it's right.

PROLA. And if they are incapable of feeling it?

JANGA. Kill.

KANCHIN. Kill.

VASHTI. Kill.

MAYA. Kill.

PROLA. They can do that as easily as I. Any fool can. And there are more of them.

JANGA. Set them to kill one another; and rule.

KANCHIN. Divide and govern.

VASHTI. Feed them on splendid words.

MAYA. Dazzle them with our beauty.

MRS HYERING. Well I never!

IDDY [*rising*] Excuse me. I'm going into the house to get the field glass. [*He goes up the steps*].

MRS HYERING. Whatever do you want the field glass for?

IDDY [*pointing to the sky*] There's a strange bird flying about there. I think it's an albatross. [*He goes into the house*].

VASHTI, MAYA, KANCHIN, JANGA [*hissing after him*] Liar. Baby. Dastard. Hypocrite.

SIR CHARLES [*laughing*] An albatross! Now would anybody in the world, over the age of six, except Iddy, invent

THE SIMPLETON

such a ridiculous excuse for going to his room to indulge in his poor little secret vice of cigaret smoking?

MAYA. Faugh! The unkissable.

VASHTI. The air poisoner.

KANCHIN. The albatrocity.

MAYA. VASHTI. JANGA [shocked by the pun] Oh!!

LADY FARWATERS. Cant you four darlings do something useful instead of sitting there deafening us with your slogans?

KANCHIN [springing erect] Yes, action. Action!

JANGA [rising similarly] No more of this endless talk! talk! talk!

VASHTI. Yes, action! daring! Let us rob.

MAYA. Let us shoot.

KANCHIN. Let us die for something.

JANGA. For our flag and for our Empress.

VASHTI. For our country, right or wrong.

MAYA. Let there be sex appeal. Let the women make the men brave.

KANCHIN. We must defend our homes.

JANGA. Our women.

VASHTI. Our native soil.

MAYA. It is sweet to die for one's country.

VASHTI. It is glorious to outface death.

ALL FOUR. Yes. Death! death! Glory! glory!

PROLA. Hold your tongues, you young whelps. Is this what we have brought you up for?

PRA. Stop screaming about nothing, will you. Use your minds.

MAYA. We have no minds.

VASHTI. We have imaginations.

KANCHIN. We have made this house a temple.

JANGA. We have made Prola its goddess.

MAYA. We have made it a palace.

VASHTI. A palace for Queen Prola.

KANCHIN. She shall reign.

JANGA. For ever and ever.

592

THE SIMPLETON

VASHTI AND MAYA [*in unison*] Hail, Prola, our goddess!

KANCHIN AND JANGA [*in unison*] Hail, Prola, our empress!

ALL FOUR [*rushing down to the lawn and throwing themselves on their knees before her*] Hail!

PROLA. Will you provoke me to box your ears, you abominable idolaters. Get up this instant. Go and scrub the floors. Do anything that is dirty and grubby and smelly enough to shew that you live in a real world and not in a fool's paradise. If I catch you grovelling to me, a creature of the same clay as yourselves, but fortunately for you with a little more common sense, I will beat the slavishness out of your bones.

MAYA. Oh, what ecstasy to be beaten by Prola!

VASHTI. To feel her rule in the last extremity of pain!

KANCHIN. To suffer for her!

JANGA. To die for her!

PROLA. Get out, all four. My empire is not of such as you. Begone.

MAYA. How lovely is obedience! [*She makes an obeisance and runs away through the garden*].

VASHTI. Obedience is freedom from the intolerable fatigue of thought. [*She makes her obeisance and sails away, disappearing between the garden and the house*].

KANCHIN. You speak as an empress should speak. [*He salaams and bounds off after Maya*].

JANGA. The voice of authority gives us strength and unity. Command us always thus: it is what we need and love. [*He strides away in Vashti's footsteps*].

PROLA. An excuse for leaving everything to me. Lazy, lazy, lazy! Someday Heaven will get tired of lazy people; and the Pitcairn Islanders will see their Day of Judgment at last.

A distant fusillade of shotguns answers her.

SIR CHARLES. Shooting! What can the matter be?
They all rise and listen anxiously.

THE SIMPLETON

A trumpet call rings out from the sky.

HYERING. Where on earth did that come from? There is not such a thing as a trumpet in the island.

The four come rushing back into the garden, wildly excited.

KANCHIN. Look, look, quick! The albatross.

PRA. [*rising*] The albatross!!

MAYA. Yes: Iddy's albatross. Look!

JANGA. Flying all over the town.

VASHTI [*pointing*] There it goes. See.

A second fusillade of shotguns, much nearer.

MAYA. Oh, theyre all trying to shoot it. Brutes!

KANCHIN. They havnt hit it. Here it comes.

MAYA. It's flying this way.

VASHTI. It's swooping down.

Iddy comes from the house and trots down the steps with a field glass in his hand.

IDDY. Ive been looking at it through the window for the last five minutes. It isnt an albatross. Look at it through this. [*He hands the glass to Pra*].

KANCHIN. Then what is it?

IDDY. I think it's an angel.

JANGA. Oh get out, you silly idiot.

PRA [*looking through the glass*] That is no bird.

An angel flies down into the middle of the garden. General stupefaction. He shakes himself. Quantities of bullets and small shot fall from his wings and clothes.

THE ANGEL. Really, your people ought to know better than to shoot at an angel.

MAYA. Are you an angel?

THE ANGEL. Well, what do you suppose I am?

VASHTI. Of course he is an angel. Look at his wings.

THE ANGEL. Attention, please! Have you not heard the trumpet? This is the Judgment Day.

594

THE SIMPLETON

ALL THE REST. The what???!!!

THE ANGEL. The Judgment Day. The Day of Judgment.

SIR CHARLES. Well I'll be damned!

THE ANGEL. Very possibly.

HYERING. Do you mean that the Pitcairn Islanders were right after all?!

THE ANGEL. Yes. You are all now under judgment, in common with the rest of the English speaking peoples. Dont gape at me as if you had never seen an angel before.

PROLA. But we never have.

THE ANGEL [*relaxing*] True. Ha ha ha! Well, you thoroughly understand, dont you, that your records are now being looked into with a view to deciding whether you are worth your salt or not.

PRA. And suppose it is decided that we are not worth our salt?

THE ANGEL [*reassuring them in a pleasantly offhanded manner*] Then you will simply disappear: that is all. You will no longer exist. Dont let me keep you all standing. Sit down if you like. Never mind me: sitting and standing are all alike to an angel. However—[*he sits down on the parapet of the well*].

They sit as before, the four superchildren enshrining themselves as usual.

The telephone rings. Hyering rises and takes it.

HYERING [*to the angel*] Excuse me. [*To the telephone*] Yes? Hyering speaking. . . . Somebody what? . . . Oh! Somebody fooling on the wireless. Well, theyre not fooling: an angel has just landed here to tell us the same thing. . . . An angel. A for arrowroot, N for nitrogen, G for—thats it: an angel. . . . Well, after all, the Judgment Day had to come some day, hadnt it? Why not this day as well as another? . . . I'll ask the angel about it and ring you later. Goodbye. [*He rings off*]. Look here, angel. The wireless has been on all over Europe. London reports the Judgment Day in full swing;

595

but Paris knows nothing about it; Hilversum knows nothing about it; Berlin, Rome, Madrid, and Geneva know nothing about it; and Moscow says the British bourgeoisie has been driven mad by its superstitions. How do you account for that? If it is the Judgment Day in England it must be the Judgment Day everywhere.

THE ANGEL. Why?

HYERING [*sitting down*] Well, it stands to reason.

THE ANGEL. Does it? Would it be reasonable to try cases in hundreds of different lands and languages and creeds and colors on the same day in the same place? Of course not. The whole business will last longer than what you call a year. We gave the English speaking folk the first turn in compliment to one of your big guns—a dean —name of Inge, I think, I announced it to him last night in a dream, and asked him whether the English would appreciate the compliment. He said he thought they would prefer to put it off as long as possible, but that they needed it badly and he was ready. The other languages will follow. The United States of America will be tried tomorrow, Australasia next day, Scotland next, then Ireland—

LADY FARWATERS. But excuse me: they do not speak different languages.

THE ANGEL. They sound different to us.

SIR CHARLES. I wonder how they are taking it in England.

THE ANGEL. I am afraid most of them are incapable of understanding the ways of heaven. They go motoring or golfing on Sundays instead of going to church; and they never open a Bible. When you mention Adam and Eve, or Cain and Abel, to say nothing of the Day of Judgment, they dont know what you are talking about. The others—the pious ones—think we have come to dig up all the skeletons and put them through one of their shocking criminal trials. They actually expect us to make angels of them for ever and ever.

MRS HYERING. See here, angel. This isnt a proper sort

596

of Judgment Day. It's a fine day. It's like Bank Holiday.

THE ANGEL. And pray why should the Day of Judgment not be a fine day?

MRS HYERING. Well, it's hardly what we were led to expect, you know.

JANGA. "The heavens shall pass away with a great noise."

KANCHIN. "The elements shall melt with fervent heat."

JANGA. "The earth also and the works that are therein shall be burnt up."

VASHTI. The stars are fixed in their courses. They have not fallen to the earth.

MAYA. The heavens are silent. Where are the seven thunders?

VASHTI. The seven vials full of the wrath of God?

JANGA. The four horses?

KANCHIN. The two witnesses?

THE ANGEL. My good people, if you want these things you must provide them for yourselves. If you want a great noise, you have your cannons. If you want a fervent heat to burn up the earth you have your high explosives. If you want vials of wrath to rain down on you, they are ready in your arsenals, full of poison gases. Some years ago you had them all in full play, burning up the earth and spreading death, famine, and pestilence. But the spring came and created life faster than you could destroy it. The birds sang over your trenches; and their promise of summer was fulfilled. The sun that shone undisturbed on your pitiful Day of Wrath shines today over Heaven's Day of Judgment. It will continue to light us and warm us; and there will be no noise nor wrath nor fire nor thunder nor destruction nor plagues nor terrors of any sort. I am afraid you will find it very dull.

LADY FARWATERS [*politely*] Not at all. Pray dont think that.

MRS HYERING. Well, a little good manners never does

597

THE SIMPLETON

any harm; but I tell you straight, Mister Angel, I cant feel as if there was anything particular happening, in spite of you and your wings. Ive only just had my tea; and I cant feel a bit serious without any preparation or even an organ playing.

THE ANGEL. You will feel serious enough presently when things begin to happen.

MRS HYERING. Yes; but what things?

THE ANGEL. What was foretold to you. "His angels shall gather together his elect. Then shall two be in the field: the one shall be taken and the other left. Two women shall be grinding at the mill. The one shall be taken and the other left."

MRS HYERING. But which? Thats what I want to know.

PROLA. There is nothing new in this taking of the one and leaving the other: natural death has always been doing it.

THE ANGEL. Natural death does it senselessly, like a blind child throwing stones. We angels are executing a judgment. The lives which have no use, no meaning, no purpose, will fade out. You will have to justify your existence or perish. Only the elect shall survive.

MRS HYERING. But where does the end of the world come in?

THE ANGEL. The Day of Judgment is not the end of the world, but the end of its childhood and the beginning of its responsible maturity. So now you know; and my business with you is ended. [He rises]. Is there any way of getting out on the roof of this house?

SIR CHARLES [rising] Certainly: it is a flat roof where we often sit. [He leads the way to the house].

KANCHIN. In theory.

JANGA. In fact we never sit there.

THE ANGEL. That does not matter. All I want is a parapet to take off from. Like the albatross, I cannot rise from the ground without great difficulty. An angel is far from being the perfect organism you imagine. There is

598

always something better.

VASHTI. Excelsior.

ALL FOUR [*rising and singing vociferously*] Eck-cel-see-orr! Eck-cel-see-or!

THE ANGEL [*putting his fingers in his ears*] Please, no. In heaven we are tired of singing. It is not done now. [*He follows Sir Charles out*].

KANCHIN. Lets see him take off.

The four rush up the garden and look up at the roof. The others rise and watch.

JANGA [*calling up*] Start into the wind, old man. Spring off hard, from the ball of the foot. Dont fall on us.

KANCHIN. Oopsh! Off he goes.

The beating of the angel's wings is heard.

VASHTI. He makes a noise like a vacuum cleaner.

MAYA [*wafting kisses*] Goodbye, silly old Excelsior. *The noise stops.*

JANGA. His wings have stopped beating. He is soaring up the wind.

KANCHIN. He is getting smaller and smaller. His speed must be terrific.

MAYA. He is too small for an albatross.

VASHTI. He is smaller than a canary.

KANCHIN. He is out of sight.

MAYA. There! One last glint of the sun on his wings. He is gone.

The four troop back and resume their seats. The others sit as before, except that Iddy deserts Prola and sits on the well parapet. Sir Charles returns from the house with a batch of wireless messages in his hand.

SIR CHARLES [*sitting in his former place*] Well, my dears: the Judgment Day is over, it seems.

IDDY. I cant believe it was really the Judgment Day.

PRA. Why?

IDDY. Well, I thought some special notice would have been taken of the clergy. Reserved seats or something like that. But he treated me as if I were only the organ blower.

SIR CHARLES. There are such a lot of priests in the world, Iddy. It would be impossible to reserve seats for them all.

IDDY. Oh, I meant only the clergy of the Church of England, of course.

MRS HYERING. What I cant get over is their sending along just one angel to judge us, as if we didnt matter.

LADY FARWATERS. He actually went away and forgot to judge us.

PRA. I am not so sure of that.

IDDY. Well, are we sheep or goats? tell me that.

MAYA. You are a sheep, Iddy, my sweet: there can be no doubt about that.

IDDY [*bursting into tears*] I love you, Maya; and you always say unkind things to me. [*He rushes away through the garden, sobbing*].

MAYA. Oh, poor Iddy! I'll go and soothe him with a thousand kisses. [*She runs after him*].

HYERING [*to Sir Charles*] What have you got there? Any news from London?

SIR CHARLES. Yes; Exchange Telegraph and Reuters. Copyright reserved.

HYERING. Lets have it.

SIR CHARLES [*reading*] "Judgment Day. Widespread incredulity as to anything having really happened. Reported appearance of angels in several quarters generally disbelieved. Several witnesses are qualifying or withdrawing their statements in deference to the prevailing scepticism."

HYERING. We shall have to be careful too, Charles. Who will believe us if we tell this yarn of an angel flying down into the garden?

SIR CHARLES. I suppose so. I never thought of it in that way. Still, listen to this. [*Reading*] "Policeman who attempted to arrest angel in Leicester Square removed to mental hospital. Church Assembly at Lambeth Palace decides by a large majority that there has been a Visitation. Dissenting minority, led by the Bishop of Edgbaston, denounces the reports as nonsense that would not impose even on the Society for Psychical Research. His Holiness the Pope warns Christendom that supernatural communications reaching the earth otherwise than through the Church are contrary to the Catholic faith, and, if authentic, must be regarded as demoniacal, Cabinet hastily summoned to discuss the situation. Prime Minister, speaking in emergency meeting at the Mansion House, declares that reports of utterances by angels are hopelessly contradictory, and that alleged verbatim reports by shorthand writers contain vulgar expressions. The Government could not in any case allow the British Empire to be placed in the position of being judged by a commission of a few angels instead of by direct divine authority. Such a slight to the flag would never be tolerated by Englishmen; and the Cabinet was unanimous in refusing to believe that such an outrage had occurred. The Prime Minister's speech was received with thunderous applause, the audience rising spontaneously to sing the National Anthem."

PRA. They would.

SIR CHARLES [*looking at another paper*] Hallo! Whats this? [*Reading*] "Later. During the singing of the second verse of the National Anthem at the Mansion House the proceedings were interrupted by the appearance of an angel with a flaming sword who demanded truculently what they meant by ordering God about to do their dirty political work. He was accompanied by unruly cherubim who floated about tweaking the Lord Mayor's nose, pouring ink into the Prime Minister's hat, and singing derisively Con-Found Their Poll-It-Ticks. Part of the audience fell to their knees, repeating the Confession. Others rushed frantically to the doors. Two Salvation lasses stemmed the rush, at great personal danger to themselves, by standing in the doorway and singing Let Angels Prostrate Fall. Order was restored by the Prime Minister, who offered the angel an unreserved apology and an undertaking that the offending verse should not be sung again. A new one is to be provided by the Poet Laureate. The Premier's last words were lost through the misconduct of a cherub who butted him violently in the solar plexus. A wave of the angel's sword and a terrible thunderclap then threw the entire audience prone to the floor. When they rose to their feet the angel and the cherubs had disappeared."

HYERING. Oh, an invention. We cant swallow those cherubs, really.

SIR CHARLES [*taking up a third paper*] This sounds a little more plausible. "A representative of the Fascist Press has called at the War Office to ask whether any steps are being taken to defend the right of public meeting, and to deal with the angelic peril. The Commander-in-Chief, whilst denying that there is any such thing as a right of public meeting by undisciplined and irresponsible persons, declared that the Mansion House incident was quite incomprehensible to him, as he could not conceive how the only really practical part of the National Anthem could give any offence. Any suggestion that it was not the plain duty of the Ruler of the Universe to confound England's enemies could only lead to widespread atheism. The First Lord of the Admiralty, interviewed last night, said that he could not make head or tail of the reports, but that he could assure the public that whatever had really happened, the British Navy would not take it lying down. Later. A Hyde Park orator was thrown into the Serpentine for saying that the British Empire was not the only pebble on the beach. He has been fined thirty shillings for being in unlawful possession of a life buoy, the property of the Royal Humane Society. There can be no doubt that the disparaging remarks and assumed superiority of the angels has started a wave of patriotism throughout the country which is bound to lead to action of some sort."

PRA. Which means, if it means anything, that England's next war will be a war with heaven.

602

PROLA. Nothing new in that. England has been at war with heaven for many a long year.

VASHTI [*inspired*] The most splendid of all her wars!

KANCHIN. The last conquest left to her to achieve!

VASHTI. To overcome the angels!

JANGA. To plant the flag of England on the ramparts of Heaven itself! that is the final glory.

PROLA. Oh go away, children: go away. Now that Maya has gone to kiss somebody, there is nothing left for you to glorify but suicide.

VASHTI [*rising*] I rebel.

JANGA [*rising*] We rebel against Prola, the goddess empress.

KANCHIN [*rising*] Prola has turned back from the forlorn hope.

VASHTI. Prola is a coward. She fears defeat and death.

KANCHIN. Without death there can be no heroism.

JANGA. Without faith unto death there can be no faith.

VASHTI. Prola has failed us in the great Day of Judgment.

KANCHIN. Our souls have been called to their final account.

ALL THREE [*marching away through the garden*] Guilty, Prola: guilty. Adieu, Prola!

PROLA. Oh, adieu until you all want your tea.

PRA. We have taught them everything except common sense.

LADY FARWATERS. We have taught them everything except how to work for their daily bread instead of praying for it.

PROLA. It is dangerous to educate fools.

PRA. It is still more dangerous to leave them uneducated.

MRS HYERING. There just shouldnt be any fools. They wernt born fools: we made fools of them.

PRA. We must stop making fools.

Iddy returns alone. Something strange has happened

603

*to him. He stares at them and tries to speak; but no sound
comes from his lips.*

LADY FARWATERS. What on earth is the matter with
you, Iddy? Have you been drinking?

IDDY [*in a ghastly voice*] Maya.

PROLA. What has happened to Maya?

IDDY. Heaven and earth shall pass away; but I shall
not pass away. That is what she said. And then there was
nothing in my arms. Nothing. Nothing in my arms.
Heaven and earth would pass away; but the love of Maya
would never pass away. And there was nothing. [*He collapses on the well parapet, overcome, not in tears but in
a profound awe*].

PRA. Do you mean that she died in your arms?

IDDY. Died? No. I tell you there was nothing. Dont
you understand? Where she had just been there was nothing. There never had been anything.

PROLA. And the others? Quick, Pra: go and find the
others.

PRA. What others?

PROLA. The other three: our children. I forget their
names.

IDDY. They said "Our names shall live forever." What
were their names?

HYERING. They have gone clean out of my head.

SIR CHARLES. Most extraordinary. I cant for the life
of me remember. How many of them did you say there
were, Prola?

PROLA. Four. Or was it four hundred?

IDDY. There were four. Their names were Love, Pride,
Heroism and Empire. Love's pet name was Maya. I loved
Maya. I loved them all; but it was through love of Maya
that I loved them. I held Maya in my arms. She promised
to endure for ever; and suddenly there was nothing in
my arms. I have searched for the others; but she and they
were one: I found nothing. It is the Judgment.

PROLA. Has she left a great void in your heart, Iddy,

that girl who turned to nothing in your arms?

IDDY. No. This is a beautiful climate; and you are beautiful people; but you are not real to me; and the sun here is not what it is in the valley of the Severn. I am glad I am an English clergyman. A village and a cottage: a garden and a church: these things will not turn to nothing. I shall be content with my little black coat and my little white collar and my little treasure of words spoken by my Lord Jesus. Blessed be the name of the Lord: I shall not forget it as I shall forget Maya's. [*He goes out seaward like a man in a trance*].

LADY FARWATERS [*troubled, half rising*] But, Iddy,—

PROLA. Let him go. The pigeon knows its way home.

Lady Farwaters sinks back into her seat. There is a moment of rather solemn silence. Then the telephone rings.

PRA [*taking up the receiver*] Yes? . . . What? . . . Yes: amazing news: we know all about that. What is the latest? . . . Yes: "plot to destroy our most valuable citizens": I got that; but what was the first word? What plot? . . . Oh, Russian plot. Rubbish! havnt you some sensible reports? . . . Special news broadcast just coming in? . . . Good: put me on to it. [*To the others*] Im through to London Regional. Listen: I'll repeat it as it comes. [*He echoes the news*]. Extraordinary disappearances. Indescribable panic. Stock Exchange closes: only two members left. House of Commons decimated: only fourteen members to be found: none of Cabinet rank. House of Lords still musters fifty members; but not one of them has ever attended a meeting of the Chamber. Mayfair a desert: six hotels left without a single guest. Fresh disappearances. Crowded intercession service at Westminster Abbey brought to a close by disappearance of the congregation at such a rate that the rest fled leaving the dean preaching to the choir. At the Royal Institution Sir Ruthless Bonehead, Egregious Professor of Mechanistic Biology to the Rockefeller Foundation, drew a crowded audience to hear his address on "Whither have they gone?"

THE SIMPLETON

He disappeared as he opened his mouth to speak. Noted Cambridge professor suggests that what is happening is a weeding-out of nonentities. He has been deprived of his Chair; and The Times, in a leading article, points out that the extreme gravity of the situation lies in the fact that not only is it our most important people who are vanishing, but that it is the most unquestionably useful and popular professions that are most heavily attacked, the medical profession having disappeared almost en bloc, whilst the lawyers and clergy are comparatively immune. A situation of terrible suspense has been created everywhere. Happy husbands and fathers disappear from the family dinner with the soup. Several popular leaders of fashion and famous beauties, after ringing their bells for their maids, have been found non-existent when the bells were answered. More than a million persons have disappeared in the act of reading novels. The Morning Post contains an eloquent protest by Lady Gushing president of the Titled Ladies' League of Social Service, on the inequality of sacrifice as between the west end and the east, where casualties have been comparatively few. Lady Gushing has since disappeared. There is general agreement that our losses are irreparable, though their bad effects are as yet unfelt. But before long—

HYERING. Whats the use of going on, Pra? The angels are weeding the garden. The useless people, the mischievous people, the selfish somebodies and the noisy nobodies, are dissolving into space, which is the simplest form of matter. We here are awaiting our own doom.

MRS HYERING. What was it the angel said?

PROLA. The lives which have no use, no meaning, no purpose, will fade out. We shall have to justify our existences or perish. We shall live under a constant sense of that responsibility. If the angels fail us we shall set up tribunals of our own from which worthless people will not come out alive. When men no longer fear the judgment of God, they must learn to judge themselves.

606

SIR CHARLES. I seem to remember somebody saying "Judge not, that ye be not judged."

PROLA. That means "Punish not, that ye be not punished." This is not punishment, but judgment.

HYERING. What is judgment?

PRA. Judgment is valuation. Civilizations live by their valuations. If the valuations are false, the civilization perishes as all the ancient ones we know of did. We are not being punished today: we are being valued. That is the Newest Dispensation.

LADY FARWATERS. I feel an absolute conviction that I shall not disappear and that Charles will not disappear. We have done some queer things here in the east perhaps; but at bottom we are comfortable commonsense probable English people; and we shall not do anything so improbable as disappear.

SIR CHARLES [*to his wife*] Do not tempt the angels, my dear. Remember: you used to distribute tracts before you met Pra.

LADY FARWATERS. Ssh-sh-sh! Dont remind the angels of those tracts.

HYERING [*rising*] Look here. I have an uneasy feeling that we'd better get back to our work. I feel pretty sure that we shant disappear as long as we're doing something useful; but if we only sit here talking, either we shall disappear or the people who are listening to us will. What we have learnt here today is that the day of judgment is not the end of the world but the beginning of real human responsibility. Charles and I have still our duties: the Unexpected Islands have to be governed today just as they had to be yesterday. Sally: if you have given your orders for the housework today, go and cook something or sew something or tidy up the books. Come on, Charles. Lets get to work. [*He goes into the house*].

SIR CHARLES [*to his wife, rising*] You might take a turn in the garden, dear: gardening is the only unquestionably useful job. [*He follows Hyering into the house*].

LADY FARWATERS [*rising*] Prola: shall I bring you some knitting to occupy you?

PROLA. No, thank you. I have some thinking to do.

LADY FARWATERS. Well, dear: I hope that will count as work. I shall feel safer with my gardening basket. [*She goes into the house*].

MRS HYERING. J'you think itll be all right if I go and do some crossword puzzles? It cultivates the mind so, dont you think?

PROLA. Does it? Well, do the puzzles and see what will happen. Let life come to you. Goodbye.

MRS HYERING [*alarmed*] Why do you say goodbye? Do you think I am going to disappear?

PROLA. Possibly. Or possibly *I* may.

MRS HYERING. Oh then for heaven's sake dont do it in my presence. Wait til Ive gone.

She scuttles up the steps into the house, leaving Prola and Pra alone together.

PRA. Tell me the truth, Prola. Are you waiting for me to disappear? Do you feel that you can do better without me? Have you always felt that you could do better without me?

PROLA. That is a murderer's thought. Have you ever let yourself think it? How often have you said to yourself "I could do better alone, or with another woman"?

PRA. Fairly often, my dear, when we were younger. But I did not murder you. Thats the answer. And you?

PROLA. All that stuff belongs to the past: to the childhood of our marriage. We have now grown together until we are each of us a part of the other. I no longer think of you as a separate possibility.

PRA. I know. I am part of the furniture of your house. I am a matter of course. But was I always that? Was I that in the childhood of our marriage?

PROLA. You are still young enough and manlike enough to ask mischievous questions.

PRA. No matter: we shall both disappear presently; and

I have still some curiosity left. Did you ever really care for me? I know I began as a passion and have ended as a habit, like all husbands; but outside that routine there is a life of the intellect that is quite independent of it. What have I been to you in that life? A help or a hindrance?

PROLA. Pra: I always knew from the very beginning that you were an extraordinarily clever fool.

PRA. Good. That is exactly what I am.

PROLA. But I knew also that nobody but a fool would be frivolous enough to join me in doing all the mad things I wanted to do. And no ordinary fool would have been subtle enough to understand me, nor clever enough to keep off the rocks of social ruin. Ive grown fond enough of you for all practical purposes;—

PRA. Thank you.

PROLA.—but Ive never allowed you or any other man to cut me off my own stem and make me a parasite on his. That sort of love and sacrifice is not the consummation of a capable woman's existence: it is the temptation she must resist at all costs.

PRA. That temptation lies in the man's path too. The worst sacrifices I have seen have been those of men's highest careers to women's vulgarities and follies.

PROLA. Well, we two have no reproaches and no regrets on that score.

PRA. No. We are awaiting judgment here quite simply as a union of a madwoman with a fool.

PROLA. Who thought they had created four wonderful children. And who are now brought to judgment and convicted of having created nothing. We have only repeated the story of Helen and Faust and their beautiful child Euphorion. Euphorion also vanished, in his highest flight.

PRA. Yes; but Helen was a dream. You are not a dream. The children did not vanish like Euphorion in their infancy. They grew up to bore me more intensely than I have ever been bored by any other set of human creatures.

609

THE SIMPLETON

Come, confess: did they not bore you?

PROLA. Have I denied it? Of course they bored me. They must have bored one another terribly in spite of all their dressing up and pretending that their fairyland was real. How they must have envied the gardener's boy his high spirits!

PRA. The coming race will not be like them. Meanwhile we are face to face with the fact that we two have made a precious mess of our job of producing the coming race by a mixture of east and west. We are failures. We shall disappear.

PROLA. I do not feel like that. I feel like the leader of a cavalry charge whose horse has been shot through the head and dropped dead under him. Well, a dead hobby horse is not the end of the world. Remember: we are in the Unexpected Isles; and in the Unexpected Isles all plans fail. So much the better: plans are only jigsaw puzzles: one gets tired of them long before one can piece them together. There are still a million lives beyond all the Utopias and the Millenniums and the rest of the jigsaw puzzles: I am a woman and I know it. Let men despair and become cynics and pessimists because in the Unexpected Isles all their little plans fail: women will never let go their hold on life. We are not here to fulfil prophecies and fit ourselves into puzzles, but to wrestle with life as it comes. And it never comes as we expect it to come.

PRA. It comes like a thief in the night.

PROLA. Or like a lover. Never will Prola go back to the Country of the Expected.

PRA. There is no Country of the Expected. The Unexpected Isles are the whole world.

PROLA. Yes, if our fools only had vision enough to see that. I tell you this is a world of miracles, not of jigsaw puzzles. For me every day must have its miracle, and no child be born like any child that ever was born before. And to witness this miracle of the children I will abide the uttermost evil and carry through it the seed of the uttermost good.

PRA. Then I, Pra, must continue to strive for more knowledge and more power, though the new knowledge always contradicts the old, and the new power is the destruction of the fools who misuse it.

PROLA. We shall plan common wealths when our empires have brought us to the brink of destruction; but our plans will still lead us to the Unexpected Isles. We shall make wars because only under the strain of war are we capable of changing the world; but the changes our wars will make will never be the changes we intended them to make. We shall clamor for security like frightened children; but in the Unexpected Isles there is no security; and the future is to those who prefer surprise and wonder to security. I, Prola, shall live and grow because surprise and wonder are the very breath of my being, and routine is death to me. Let every day be a day of wonder for me and I shall not fear the Day of Judgment. [*She is interrupted by a roll of thunder*]. Be silent: you cannot frighten Prola with stage thunder. The fountain of life is within me.

PRA. But you have given the key of it to me, the Man.

PROLA. Yes: I need you and you need me. Life needs us both.

PRA. All hail, then, the life to come!

PROLA. All Hail. Let it come.

They pat hands, eastern fashion.

YOU NEVER CAN TELL

A PLEASANT PLAY IN FOUR ACTS

Written during 1895 and 1896

First Performed London 1899

See Preface to the Second Volume of Plays:
Pleasant and Unpleasant (*Volume III, page 107*)

YOU NEVER CAN TELL

ACT I

IN a dentist's operating room on a fine August morning in
1896. It is the best sitting room of a furnished lodging in a
terrace on the sea front at a watering place on the coast of
Torbay in Devon. The operating chair, with a gas pump and
cylinder beside it, is half way between the center of the room and
one of the corners. If you could look into the room through the
window facing the chair, you would see the fireplace in the middle
of the wall opposite you, with the door beside it to your left, a
dental surgeon's diploma in a frame above the mantelshelf,
an easy chair on the hearth, and a neat stool and bench, with
vice, tools, and a mortar and pestle, in the corner to the right. In
the wall on your left is a broad window looking on the sea.
Beneath it a writing table with a blotter and a diary on it, and
a chair. Also a sofa, farther along. A cabinet of instruments is
handy to the operating chair. The furniture, carpet, and wall-
paper are those of a mid-Victorian drawing room, formally
bright and festive, not for everyday use.

Two persons just now occupy the room. One of them, a very
pretty woman in miniature, her tiny figure dressed with the
daintiest gaiety, is hardly eighteen yet. This darling little creature clearly does not belong to the room, or even to the country; for
her complexion, though very delicate, has been burnt biscuit color
by some warmer sun than England's. She has a glass of water
in her hand, and a rapidly clearing cloud of Spartan endurance
on her small firm set mouth and quaintly squared eyebrows.

The dentist, contemplating her with the self-satisfaction of a
successful operator, is a young man of thirty or thereabouts. He
does not give the impression of being much of a workman: the
professional manner of the newly set-up dentist in search of
patients is underlain by a thoughtless pleasantry which betrays
the young gentleman, still unsettled and in search of amusing adventures. He is not without gravity of demeanor; but the strained
nostrils stamp it as the gravity of the humorist. His eyes are clear,
alert, of sceptically moderate size, and yet a little rash; his forehead is an excellent one, with plenty of room behind it; his nose

and chin are cavalierly handsome. On the whole, an attractive noticeable beginner, of whose prospects a man of business might form a tolerably favorable estimate.

THE YOUNG LADY [*handing him the glass*] Thank you. [*In spite of the biscuit complexion she has not the slightest foreign accent*].

THE DENTIST [*putting it down on the ledge of his cabinet of instruments*] That was my first tooth.

THE YOUNG LADY [*aghast*] Your first! Do you mean to say that you began practising on me?

THE DENTIST. Every dentist has to begin with somebody.

THE YOUNG LADY. Yes: somebody in a hospital, not people who pay.

THE DENTIST [*laughing*] Oh, the hospital doesnt count. I only meant my first tooth in private practice. Why didnt you let me give you gas?

THE YOUNG LADY. Because you said it would be five shillings extra.

THE DENTIST [*shocked*] Oh, dont say that. It makes me feel as if I had hurt you for the sake of five shillings.

THE YOUNG LADY [*with cool insolence*] Well, so you have. [*She gets up*]. Why shouldnt you? it's your business to hurt people. [*It amuses him to be treated in this fashion: he chuckles secretly as he proceeds to clean and replace his instruments. She shakes her dress into order: looks inquisitively about her; and goes to the broad window*]. You have a good view of the sea from your rooms! Are they expensive?

THE DENTIST. Yes.

THE YOUNG LADY. You dont own the whole house, do you?

THE DENTIST. No.

THE YOUNG LADY. I thought not. [*Tilting the chair which stands at the writing-table and looking critically at it as she spins it round on one leg*] Your furniture isnt quite the latest thing, is it?

THE DENTIST. It's my landlord's.

THE YOUNG LADY. Does he own that toothache chair?

[*pointing to the operating chair*].

THE DENTIST. No: I have that on the hire-purchase system.

THE YOUNG LADY [*disparagingly*] I thought so. [*Looking about in search of further conclusions*] I suppose you havnt been here long?

THE DENTIST. Six weeks. Is there anything else you would like to know?

THE YOUNG LADY [*the hint quite lost on her*] Any family?

THE DENTIST. I am not married.

THE YOUNG LADY. Of course not: anybody can see that. I meant sisters and mother and that sort of thing.

THE DENTIST. Not on the premises.

THE YOUNG LADY. Hm! If youve been here six weeks, and mine was your first tooth, the practice cant be very large, can it?

THE DENTIST. Not as yet. [*He shuts the cabinet, having tidied up everything*].

THE YOUNG LADY. Well, good luck! [*She takes out her purse*]. Five shillings, you said it would be?

THE DENTIST. Five shillings.

THE YOUNG LADY [*producing a crown piece*] Do you charge five shillings for everything?

THE DENTIST. Yes.

THE YOUNG LADY. Why?

THE DENTIST. It's my system. I'm whats called a five shilling dentist.

THE YOUNG LADY. How nice! Well, here! [*holding up the crown piece*] a nice new five-shilling piece! your first fee! Make a hole in it with the thing you drill people's teeth with; and wear it on your watch-chain.

THE DENTIST. Thank you.

THE PARLOR MAID [*appearing at the door*] The young lady's brother, sir.

A handsome man in miniature, obviously the young lady's twin, comes in eagerly. He wears a suit of terra cotta cashmere, the elegantly cut frock coat lined in brown silk, and carries in his hand a brown tall hat and tan gloves to match. He has his sister's delicate biscuit complexion, and is built on the same small scale; but he is elastic and strong in muscle, decisive in movement, unexpectedly deeptoned and trenchant in speech, and with perfect manners and a finished personal style which might be envied by a man twice his age. Suavity and self-possession are points of honor with him; and though this, rightly considered, is only a mode of boyish self-consciousness, its effect is none the less staggering to his elders, and would be quite insufferable in a less prepossessing youth. He is promptitude itself, and has a question ready the moment he enters.

THE YOUNG GENTLEMAN. Am I in time?

THE YOUNG LADY. No: it's all over.

THE YOUNG GENTLEMAN. Did you howl?

THE YOUNG LADY. Oh, something awful. Mr Valentine: this is my brother Phil. Phil: this is Mr Valentine, our new dentist. [*Valentine and Phil bow to one another. She proceeds, all in one breath*] He's only been here six weeks and he's a bachelor the house isnt his and the furniture is the landlord's but the professional plant is hired he got my tooth out beautifully at the first go and he and I are great friends.

PHILIP. Been asking a lot of questions?

THE YOUNG LADY [*as if incapable of doing such a thing*] Oh no.

PHILIP. Glad to hear it. [*To Valentine*] So good of you not to mind us, Mr Valentine. The fact is, weve never been in England before; and our mother tells us that the people here simply wont stand us. Come and lunch with us.

Valentine, bewildered by the leaps and bounds with which their acquaintanceship is proceeding, gasps, but has no time to reply, as the conversation of the twins is swift and continuous.

THE YOUNG LADY. Oh, do, Mr Valentine.

PHILIP. At the Marine Hotel: half past one.

THE YOUNG LADY. We shall be able to tell mamma that a respectable Englishman has promised to lunch with us.

PHILIP. Say no more, Mr Valentine: youll come.

VALENTINE. Say no more! I havnt said anything. May I

ask whom I have the pleasure of entertaining? It's really quite impossible for me to lunch at the Marine Hotel with two perfect strangers.

THE YOUNG LADY [*flippantly*] Ooooh! what bosh! One patient in six weeks! What difference does it make to you?

PHILIP [*maturely*] No, Dolly: my knowledge of human nature confirms Mr Valentine's judgment. He is right. Let me introduce Miss Dorothy Clandon, commonly called Dolly. [*Valentine bows to Dolly. She nods to him*]. I'm Philip Clandon. We're from Madeira, but perfectly respectable, so far.

VALENTINE. Clandon! Are you related to—

DOLLY [*unexpectedly crying out in despair*] Yes we are.

VALENTINE [*astonished*] I beg your pardon?

DOLLY. Oh, we are, we are. It's all over, Phil: they know all about us in England. [*To Valentine*] Oh, you cant think how maddening it is to be related to a celebrated person, and never be valued anywhere for our own sakes.

VALENTINE. But excuse me: the gentleman I was thinking of is not celebrated.

DOLLY AND PHILIP [*staring at him*] Gentleman!

VALENTINE. Yes. I was going to ask whether you were by any chance a daughter of Mr Densmore Clandon of Newbury Hall.

DOLLY [*vacantly*] No.

PHILIP. Well, come, Dolly: how do you know youre not?

DOLLY [*cheered*] Oh, I forgot. Of course. Perhaps I am.

VALENTINE. Dont you know?

PHILIP. Not in the least.

DOLLY. It's a wise child—

PHILIP [*cutting her short*] Sh! [*Valentine starts nervously; for the sound made by Phil, though but momentary, is like cutting a sheet of silk in two with a flash of lightning. It is the result of long practice in checking Dolly's indiscretions*]. The fact is, Mr Valentine, we are the children of the celebrated Mrs Lanfrey Clandon, an authoress of great repute—in Madeira. No household is complete without her works. We came to

619

England to get away from them. They are called the Twentieth Century Treatises.

DOLLY. Twentieth Century Cooking.

PHILIP. Twentieth Century Creeds.

DOLLY. Twentieth Century Clothing.

PHILIP. Twentieth Century Conduct.

DOLLY. Twentieth Century Children.

PHILIP. Twentieth Century Parents.

DOLLY. Cloth limp, half a dollar.

PHILIP. Or mounted on linen for hard family use, two dollars. No family should be without them. Read them, Mr Valentine: theyll improve your mind.

DOLLY. But not till weve gone, please.

PHILIP. Quite so: we prefer people with unimproved minds. Our own minds have successfully resisted all our mother's efforts to improve them.

VALENTINE [*dubiously*] Hm!

DOLLY [*echoing him inquiringly*] Hm? Phil: he prefers people whose minds are improved.

PHILIP. In that case we shall have to introduce him to the other member of the family: the Woman of the Twentieth Century: our sister Gloria!

DOLLY [*dithyrambically*] Nature's masterpiece!

PHILIP. Learning's daughter!

DOLLY. Madeira's pride!

PHILIP. Beauty's paragon!

DOLLY [*suddenly descending to prose*] Bosh! No complexion.

VALENTINE [*desperately*] May I have a word?

PHILIP [*politely*] Excuse us. Go ahead.

DOLLY [*very nicely*] So sorry.

VALENTINE [*attempting to take them paternally*] I really must give a hint to you young people—

DOLLY [*breaking out again*] Oh come! I like that. How old are you?

PHILIP. Over thirty.

DOLLY. He's not.

PHILIP [*confidently*] He is.

DOLLY [*emphatically*] Twenty-seven.

PHILIP [*imperturbably*] Thirty-three.

DOLLY. Stuff.

PHILIP [*to Valentine*] I appeal to you, Mr Valentine.

VALENTINE [*remonstrating*] Well, really—[*resigning himself*] Thirty-one.

PHILIP [*to Dolly*] You were wrong.

DOLLY. So were you.

PHILIP [*suddenly conscientious*] We're forgetting our manners, Dolly.

DOLLY [*remorseful*] Yes, so we are.

PHILIP [*apologetic*] We interrupted you, Mr Valentine.

DOLLY. You were going to improve our minds, I think.

VALENTINE. The fact is, your—

PHILIP [*anticipating him*] Our manners?

DOLLY. Our appearance?

VALENTINE [*ad misericordiam*] Oh do let me speak.

DOLLY. The old story. We talk too much.

PHILIP. We do. Shut up, both. [*He seats himself on the arm of the operating chair*].

DOLLY. Mum! [*She sits down in the writing-table chair, and closes her lips with the tips of her fingers*].

VALENTINE. Thank you. [*He brings the stool from the bench in the corner; places it between them; and sits down with a judicial air. They attend to him with extreme gravity. He addresses himself first to Dolly*] Now may I ask, to begin with, have you ever been in an English seaside resort before? [*She shakes her head slowly and solemnly. He turns to Phil, who shakes his head quickly and expressively*]. I thought so. Well, Mr Clandon, our acquaintance has been short; but it has been voluble; and I have gathered enough to convince me that you are neither of you capable of conceiving what life in an English seaside resort is. Believe me, it's not a question of manners and appearance. In those respects we enjoy a freedom unknown in Madeira. [*Dolly shakes her head vehemently*]. Oh yes, I assure you. Lord de Cresci's sister bicycles in knicker-bockers; and the rector's wife advocates dress reform and

621

wears hygienic boots. [*Dolly furtively looks at her own shoe: Valentine catches her in the act, and deftly adds*] No, thats not the sort of boot I mean. [*Dolly's shoe vanishes*]. We dont bother much about dress and manners in England, because, as a nation, we dont dress well and weve no manners. But— and now will you excuse my frankness? [*They nod*]. Thank you. Well, in a seaside resort theres one thing you m u s t have before anybody can afford to be seen going about with you; and thats a father, alive or dead. Am I to infer that you have omitted that indispensable part of your social equipment? [*They confirm him by melancholy nods*]. Then I'm sorry to say that if you are going to stay here for any length of time, it will be impossible for me to accept your kind invitation to lunch. [*He rises with an air of finality, and replaces the stool by the bench*].

PHILIP [*rising with grave politeness*] Come, Dolly. [*He gives her his arm*].

DOLLY. Good morning. [*They go together to the door with perfect dignity*].

VALENTINE [*overwhelmed with remorse*] Oh stop! stop! [*They halt and turn, arm in arm*]. You make me feel a perfect beast.

DOLLY. Thats your conscience: not us.

VALENTINE [*energetically, throwing off all pretence of a professional manner*] My conscience! My conscience has been my ruin. Listen to me. Twice before I have set up as a respectable medical practitioner in various parts of England. On both occasions I acted conscientiously, and told my patients the brute truth instead of what they wanted to be told. Result, ruin. Now Ive set up as a dentist, a five shilling dentist; and Ive done with conscience for ever. This is my last chance. I spent my last sovereign on moving in; and I havnt paid a shilling of rent yet. I'm eating and drinking on credit; my landlord is as rich as a Jew and as hard as nails; and Ive made five shillings in six weeks. If I swerve by a hair's breadth from the straight line of the most rigid respectability, I'm done for. Under such circumstances is it fair to ask me to lunch with you when you dont know your own father?

DOLLY. After all, our grandfather is a canon of Lincoln Cathedral.

VALENTINE [*like a castaway mariner who sees a sail on the horizon*] What! Have you a grandfather?

DOLLY. Only one.

VALENTINE. My dear good young friends, why on earth didnt you tell me that before? A canon of Lincoln! That makes it all right, of course. Just excuse me while I change my coat. [*He reaches the door in a bound and vanishes*].

Dolly and Phil stare after him, and then at one another. Missing their audience, they discard their style at once.

PHILIP [*throwing away Dolly's arm and coming ill-humoredly towards the operating chair*] That wretched bankrupt ivory snatcher makes a compliment of allowing us to stand him a lunch: probably the first square meal he has had for months. [*He gives the chair a kick, as if it were Valentine*].

DOLLY. It's too beastly. I wont stand it any longer, Phil. Here in England everybody asks whether you have a father the very first thing.

PHILIP. I wont stand it either. Mamma m u s t tell us who he was.

DOLLY. Or who he is. He may be alive.

PHILIP. I hope not. No man alive shall father me.

DOLLY. He might have a lot of money, though.

PHILIP. I doubt it. My knowledge of human nature leads me to believe that if he had a lot of money he wouldnt have got rid of his affectionate family so easily. Anyhow, let's look at the bright side of things. Depend on it, he's dead.

He goes to the hearth and stands with his back to the fireplace. The parlormaid appears.

THE PARLORMAID. Two ladies for you, miss. Your mother and sister, miss, I think.

Mrs Clandon and Gloria come in. Mrs Clandon is a veteran of the Old Guard of the Women's Rights movement which had for its Bible John Stuart Mill's treatise on The Subjection of

623

YOU NEVER CAN TELL

Women. She has never made herself ugly or ridiculous by affecting masculine waistcoats, collars, and watchchains, like some of her old comrades who had more aggressiveness than taste; and she is too militant an Agnostic to care to be mistaken for a Quaker. She therefore dresses in as businesslike a way as she can without making a guy of herself, ruling out all attempt at sex attraction and imposing respect on frivolous mankind and fashionable womankind. She belongs to the forefront of her own period (say 1860–80) in a jealously assertive attitude of character and intellect, and in being a woman of cultivated interests rather than passionately developed personal affections. Her voice and ways are entirely kindly and humane; and she lends herself conscientiously to the occasional demonstrations of fondness by which her children mark their esteem for her; but displays of personal sentiment secretly embarrass her: passion in her is humanitarian rather than human: she feels strongly about social questions and principles, not about persons. Only, one observes that this reasonableness and intense personal privacy, which leaves her relations with Gloria and Phil much as they might be between her and the children of any other woman, breaks down in the case of Dolly. Though almost every word she addresses to her is necessarily in the nature of a remonstrance for some breach of decorum, the tenderness in her voice is unmistakeable; and it is not surprising that years of such remonstrance have left Dolly hopelessly spoiled.

Gloria, who is hardly past twenty, is a much more formidable person than her mother. She is the incarnation of haughty high-mindedness, raging with the impatience of a mettlesome dominative character paralyzed by the inexperience of her youth, and unwillingly disciplined by the constant danger of ridicule from her irreverent juniors. Unlike her mother, she is all passion; and the conflict of her passion with her obstinate pride and intense fastidiousness results in a freezing coldness of manner. In an ugly woman all this would be repulsive; but Gloria is attractive. A dangerous girl, one would say, if the moral passions were not also marked, and even nobly marked, in a fine brow. Her tailormade skirt-and-jacket dress, of saffron brown cloth, seems conventional when her back is turned; but it displays in front a blouse of sea-

624

green silk which scatters its conventionality with one stroke, and sets her apart as effectually as the twins from the ordinary run of fashionable seaside humanity.

Mrs Clandon comes a little way into the room looking round to see who is present. Gloria, who studiously avoids encouraging the twins by betraying any interest in them, wanders to the window and looks out to sea with her thoughts far away. The parlor-maid, instead of withdrawing, shuts the door and waits at it.

MRS CLANDON. Well, children? How is the toothache, Dolly?

DOLLY. Cured, thank Heaven. Ive had it out. [*She sits down on the step of the operating chair*].

Mrs Clandon takes the writing-table chair.

PHILIP [*striking in gravely from the hearth*] And the dentist, a first rate professional man of the highest standing, is coming to lunch with us.

MRS CLANDON [*looking round apprehensively at the servant*] Phil!

THE PARLORMAID. Beg pardon, maam. I'm waiting for Mr Valentine. I have a message for him.

DOLLY. Who from?

MRS CLANDON [*shocked*] Dolly!

Dolly catches her lips suppressively with her finger tips.

THE PARLORMAID. Only the landlord, maam.

Valentine, in a blue serge suit, with a straw hat in his hand, comes back in high spirits, out of breath with the haste he has made. Gloria turns from the window and studies him with chilling attention.

PHILIP. Let me introduce you, Mr Valentine. My mother, Mrs Lanfrey Clandon. [*Mrs Clandon bows. Valentine bows, self-possessed and quite equal to the occasion*]. My sister Gloria. [*Gloria bows with cold dignity and sits down on the sofa*].

Valentine falls abjectly in love at first sight. He fingers his hat nervously, and makes her a sneaking bow.

MRS CLANDON. I understand that we are to have the pleasure of seeing you at luncheon today, Mr Valentine.

VALENTINE. Thank you—er—if you dont mind—I mean

if you will be so kind—[*to the parlormaid, testily*] What is it?

THE PARLORMAID. The landlord, sir, wishes to speak to you before you go out.

VALENTINE. Oh, tell him I have four patients here. [*The Clandons look surprised, except Phil, who is imperturbable*]. If he wouldnt mind waiting just two minutes, I—I'll slip down and see him for a moment. [*Throwing himself confidentially on her sense of the position*] Say I'm busy, but that I w a n t to see him.

THE PARLORMAID [*reassuringly*] Yes, sir. [*She goes*].

MRS CLANDON [*on the point of rising*] We are detaining you, I am afraid.

VALENTINE. Not at all, not at all. Your presence here will be the greatest help to me. The fact is, I owe six weeks rent; and Ive had no patients until today. My interview with my landlord will be considerably smoothed by the apparent boom in my business.

DOLLY [*vexed*] Oh, how tiresome of you to let it all out! And weve just been pretending that you were a respectable professional man in a first rate position.

MRS CLANDON [*horrified*] Oh Dolly! D o l l y! My dearest: how can you be so rude? [*To Valentine*] Will you excuse these barbarian children of mine, Mr Valentine?

VALENTINE. Dont mention it: I'm used to them. Would it be too much to ask you to wait five minutes while I get rid of my landlord downstairs?

DOLLY. Dont be long. We're hungry.

MRS CLANDON [*again remonstrating*] Dolly, d e a r!

VALENTINE [*to Dolly*] All right. [*To Mrs Clandon*] Thank you: I shant be long. [*He steals a look at Gloria as he turns to go. She is looking gravely at him. He falls into confusion*]. I—er—er—yes—thank you [*he succeeds at last in blundering himself out of the room; but the exhibition is a pitiful one*].

PHILIP. Did you observe? [*Pointing to Gloria*] Love at first sight. Another scalp for your collection, Gloria. Number fifteen.

MRS CLANDON. Sh—sh pray, Phil. He may have heard

626

you.

PHILIP. Not he. [*Bracing himself for a scene*] And now look here, mamma. [*He takes the stool from the bench; and seats himself majestically in the middle of the room, copying Valentine's recent demonstration. Dolly, feeling that her position on the step of the operating chair is unworthy the dignity of the occasion, rises, looking important and uncompromising. She crosses to the window, and stands with her back to the end of the writing-table, her hands behind her and on the table. Mrs Clandon looks at them, wondering what is coming. Gloria becomes attentive. Phil straightens his back; places his knuckles symmetrically on his knees; and opens his case*]. Dolly and I have been talking over things a good deal lately; and I dont think, judging from my knowledge of human nature—we dont think that you [*speaking very pointedly, with the words detached*] quite. Appreciate. The fact—

DOLLY [*seating herself on the end of the table with a spring*] That weve grown up.

MRS CLANDON. Indeed? In what way have I given you any reason to complain?

PHILIP. Well, there are certain matters upon which we are beginning to feel that you might take us a little more into your confidence.

MRS CLANDON [*rising, with all the placidity of her age suddenly breaking up into a curious hard excitement, dignified but dogged, ladylike but implacable: the manner of the Old Guard*] Phil: take care. What have I always taught you? There are two sorts of family life, Phil; and your experience of human nature only extends, so far, to one of them. [*Rhetorically*] The sort you know is based on mutual respect, on recognition of the right of every member of the household to independence and privacy [*her emphasis on "privacy" is intense*] in their personal concerns. And because you have always enjoyed that, it seems such a matter of course to you that you dont value it. But [*with biting acrimony*] there is another sort of family life: a life in which husbands open their wives' letters, and call on them to account for every farthing of

627

YOU NEVER CAN TELL

their expenditure and every moment of their time; in which women do the same to their children; in which no room is private and no hour sacred; in which duty, obedience, affection, home, morality and religion are detestable tyrannies, and life is a vulgar round of punishments and lies, coercion and rebellion, jealousy, suspicion, recrimination— Oh! I cannot describe it to you: fortunately for you, you know nothing about it. [*She sits down, panting*].

DOLLY [*inaccessible to rhetoric*] See Twentieth Century Parents, chapter on Liberty, passim.

MRS CLANDON [*touching her shoulder affectionately, softened even by a gibe from her*] My dear Dolly: if you only knew how glad I am that it is nothing but a joke to you, though it is such bitter earnest to me. [*More resolutely, turning to Phil*] Phil: I never ask you questions about your private concerns. You are not going to question me, are you?

PHILIP. I think it due to ourselves to say that the question we wanted to ask is as much our business as yours.

DOLLY. Besides, it cant be good to keep a lot of questions bottled up inside you. You did it, mamma; but see how awfully it's broken out again in me.

MRS CLANDON. I see you want to ask your question. Ask it.

DOLLY AND PHILIP [*beginning simultaneously*] Who— [*They stop*].

PHILIP. Now look here, Dolly: am I going to conduct this business or are you?

DOLLY. You.

PHILIP. Then hold your mouth. [*Dolly does so, literally*]. The question is a simple one. When the ivory snatcher—

MRS CLANDON [*remonstrating*] Phil!

PHILIP. Dentist is an ugly word. The man of ivory and gold asked us whether we were the children of Mr Densmore Clandon of Newbury Hall. In pursuance of the precepts in your treatise on Twentieth Century Conduct, and your repeated personal exhortations to us to curtail the number of unnecessary lies we tell, we replied truthfully that we

628

didnt know.

DOLLY. Neither did we.

PHILIP. Sh! The result was that the gum architect made considerable difficulties about accepting our invitation to lunch, although I doubt if he has had anything but tea and bread and butter for a fortnight past. Now my knowledge of human nature leads me to believe that we had a father, and that you probably know who he was.

MRS CLANDON [*her agitation returning*] Stop, Phil. Your father is nothing to you, nor to me. [*Vehemently*] That is enough.

The twins are silenced, but not satisfied. Their faces fall. But Gloria, who has been following the altercation attentively, suddenly intervenes.

GLORIA [*advancing*] Mother: we have a right to know.

MRS CLANDON [*rising and facing her*] Gloria! "We"! Who is "we"?

GLORIA [*steadfastly*] We three. [*Her tone is unmistakeable: she is pitting her strength against her mother's for the first time. The twins instantly go over to the enemy*].

MRS CLANDON [*wounded*] In your mouth "we" used to mean you and I, Gloria.

PHILIP [*rising decisively and putting away the stool*] We're hurting you: let's drop it. We didnt think youd mind. *I* dont want to know.

DOLLY [*coming off the table*] I'm sure *I* dont. Oh, dont look like that, mamma. [*She looks angrily at Gloria and flings her arms round her mother's neck*].

MRS CLANDON. Thank you, my dear. Thanks, Phil. [*She detaches Dolly gently and sits down again*].

GLORIA [*inexorably*] We have a right to know, mother.

MRS CLANDON [*indignantly*] Ah! You insist.

GLORIA. Do you intend that we shall never know?

DOLLY. Oh Gloria, dont. It's barbarous.

GLORIA [*with quiet scorn*] What is the use of being weak? You see what has happened with this gentleman here, mother. The same thing has happened to me.

MRS CLANDON   ⎰   ⎱ What do you mean?
DOLLY   ⎨ [all ⎬ Oh, tell us!
PHILIP   ⎩ together]⎭ What happened to you?

GLORIA. Oh, nothing of any consequence. [*She turns away from them and strolls up to the easy chair at the fireplace, where she sits down, almost with her back to them. As they wait expectantly, she adds, over her shoulder, with studied indifference*] On board the steamer, the first officer did me the honor to propose to me.

DOLLY. No: it was to me.

MRS CLANDON. The first officer! Are you serious, Gloria? What did you say to him? [*Correcting herself*] Excuse me: I have no right to ask that.

GLORIA. The answer is pretty obvious. A woman who does not know who her father was cannot accept such an offer.

MRS CLANDON. Surely you did not want to accept it!

GLORIA [*turning a little and raising her voice*] No; but suppose I h a d wanted to!

PHILIP. Did that difficulty strike you, Dolly?

DOLLY. No. I accepted him.

GLORIA   ⎰   ⎱ Accepted him!
MRS CLANDON   ⎨ [all crying ⎬ Dolly!
PHILIP   ⎩ out together] ⎭ Oh, I say!

DOLLY [*naïvely*] He did look such a fool!

MRS CLANDON. But why did you do such a thing, Dolly?

DOLLY. For fun, I suppose. He had to measure my finger for a ring. Youd have done the same thing yourself.

MRS CLANDON. No, Dolly, I would not. As a matter of fact the first officer d i d propose to me; and I told him to keep that sort of thing for women who were young enough to be amused by it. He appears to have acted on my advice. [*She rises and goes to the hearth*]. Gloria: I am sorry you think me weak; but I cannot tell you what you want. You are all too young.

PHILIP. This is rather a startling departure from Twentieth Century principles.

DOLLY [*quoting*] "Answer all your children's questions, and answer them truthfully, as soon as they are old enough to ask them." See Twentieth Century Motherhood—

PHILIP. Page one.

DOLLY. Chapter one.

PHILIP. Sentence one.

MRS CLANDON. My dears: I do not mean that you are too young to know. I mean that you are too young to be taken into my confidence. You are very bright children, all of you; but you are still very inexperienced and consequently sometimes very unsympathetic. There are experiences of mine that I cannot bear to speak of except to those who have gone through what I have gone through. I hope you will never be qualified for such confidences.

PHILIP. Another grievance, Dolly!

DOLLY. We're not sympathetic.

GLORIA [*leaning forward in her chair and looking earnestly up at her mother*] Mother: I did not mean to be unsympathetic.

MRS CLANDON [*affectionately*] Of course not, dear. I quite understand!

GLORIA [*rising*] But, mother—

MRS CLANDON [*drawing back a little*] Yes?

GLORIA [*obstinately*] It is nonsense to tell us that our father is nothing to us.

MRS CLANDON [*provoked to sudden resolution*] Do you remember your father?

GLORIA [*meditatively, as if the recollection were a tender one*] I am not quite sure. I think so.

MRS CLANDON [*grimly*] You are not sure?

GLORIA. No.

MRS CLANDON [*with quiet force*] Gloria: if I had ever struck you [*Gloria recoils: Phil and Dolly are disagreeably shocked: all three stare at her, revolted, as she continues mercilessly*]—struck you purposely, deliberately, with the intention of hurting you, with a whip bought for the purpose! would you remember that, do you think? [*Gloria utters an exclamation of indignant repulsion*]. That would have been

631

your last recollection of your father, Gloria, if I had not taken you away from him. I have kept him out of your life: keep him now out of mine by never mentioning him to me again.

Gloria, with a shudder, covers her face with her hands until, hearing someone at the door, she recomposes herself. Mrs Clandon sits down on the sofa. Valentine returns.

VALENTINE. I hope Ive not kept you waiting. That landlord of mine is really an extraordinary old character.

DOLLY [*eagerly*] Oh, tell us. How long has he given you to pay?

MRS CLANDON [*distracted by her child's manners*] Dolly, Dolly, Dolly dear! You must not ask questions.

DOLLY [*demurely*] So sorry. Youll tell us, wont you, Mr Valentine?

VALENTINE. He doesnt want his rent at all. He's broken his tooth on a Brazil nut; and he wants me to look at it and to lunch with him afterwards.

DOLLY. Then have him up and pull his tooth out at once; and we'll bring him to lunch too. Tell the maid to fetch him along. [*She runs to the bell and rings it vigorously. Then, with a sudden doubt, she turns to Valentine and adds*] I suppose he's respectable? really respectable?

VALENTINE. Perfectly. Not like me.

DOLLY. Honest Injun?

Mrs Clandon gasps faintly; but her powers of remonstrance are exhausted.

VALENTINE. Honest Injun!

DOLLY. Then off with you and bring him up.

VALENTINE [*looking dubiously at Mrs Clandon*] I dare say he'd be delighted if—er—?

MRS CLANDON [*rising and looking at her watch*] I shall be happy to see your friend at lunch if you can persuade him to come; but I cant wait to see him now: I have an appointment at the hotel at a quarter to one with an old friend whom I have not seen since I left England eighteen years ago. Will you excuse me?

VALENTINE. Certainly, Mrs Clandon.

GLORIA. Shall I come?

MRS CLANDON. No, dear. I want to be alone. [*She goes out, evidently still a good deal troubled*].

Valentine opens the door for her and follows her.

PHILIP [*significantly to Dolly*] Hmhm!

DOLLY [*significantly to Phil*] Ahah!

The parlormaid answers the bell.

DOLLY. Shew the old gentleman up.

THE PARLORMAID [*puzzled*] Madam?

DOLLY. The old gentleman with the toothache.

PHILIP. The landlord.

THE PARLORMAID. Mr Crampton, sir?

PHILIP. Is his name Crampton?

DOLLY [*to Phil*] Sounds rheumaticky, doesnt it?

PHILIP. Chalkstones, probably.

DOLLY. Shew Mr Crampstones up.

THE PARLORMAID [*going out*] Mr Crampton, miss.

DOLLY [*repeating it to herself like a lesson*] Crampton, Crampton, Crampton, Crampton, Crampton. [*She sits down studiously at the writing-table*] I must get that name right, or Heaven knows what I shall call him.

GLORIA. Phil: can you believe such a horrible thing as that about our father? what mother said just now.

PHILIP. Oh, there are lots of people of that kind. Old Chamico used to thrash his wife and daughters with a cart whip.

DOLLY [*contemptuously*] Yes, a Portuguese!

PHILIP. When you come to men who are brutes, there is much in common between the Portuguese and the English variety, Doll. Trust my knowledge of human nature. [*He resumes his position on the hearth-rug with an elderly and responsible air*].

GLORIA [*with angered remorse*] I dont think we shall ever play again at our old game of guessing what our father was to be like. Dolly: are you sorry for y o u r father? the father with lots of money!

633

DOLLY. Oh come! What about your father? the lonely old man with the tender aching heart! He's pretty well burst up, I think.

PHILIP. There can be no doubt that the governor is an exploded superstition. [*Valentine is heard talking to somebody outside the door*]. But hark! he comes.

GLORIA [*nervously*] Who?

DOLLY. Chalkstones.

PHILIP. Sh! Attention! [*They put on their best manners. Phil adds in a lower voice to Gloria*] If he's good enough for the lunch, I'll nod to Dolly; and if she nods to you, invite him straight away.

Valentine comes back with his landlord. Mr Fergus Crampton is a man of about sixty, with an atrociously obstinate ill tempered grasping mouth, and a dogmatic voice. There is no sign of straitened means or commercial diffidence about him: he is well dressed, and would be classed at a guess as a prosperous master-manufacturer in a business inherited from an old family in the aristocracy of trade. His navy blue coat is not of the usual fashionable pattern. It is not exactly a pilot's coat; but it is cut that way, double breasted, and with stout buttons and broad lappels: a coat for a shipyard rather than a counting house. He has taken a fancy to Valentine, who cares nothing for his crossness of grain, and treats him with a disrespectful humanity for which he is secretly grateful.

VALENTINE. May I introduce? This is Mr Crampton: Miss Dorothy Clandon, Mr Philip Clandon, Miss Clandon. [*Crampton stands nervously bowing. They all bow*]. Sit down, Mr Crampton.

DOLLY [*pointing to the operating chair*] That is the most comfortable chair, Mr Ch—crampton.

CRAMPTON. Thank you; but wont this young lady—[*indicating Gloria, who is close to the chair*]?

GLORIA. Thank you, Mr Crampton: we are just going.

VALENTINE [*bustling him across to the chair with good-humored peremptoriness*] Sit down, sit down. Youre tired.

CRAMPTON. Well, perhaps as I am considerably the oldest person present, I—[*he finishes the sentence by sitting down a little rheumatically in the operating chair. Meanwhile Phil, having studied him critically during his passage across the room, nods to Dolly; and Dolly nods to Gloria*].

GLORIA. Mr Crampton: we understand that we are preventing Mr Valentine from lunching with you by taking him away ourselves. My mother would be very glad indeed if you would come too.

CRAMPTON [*gratefully, after looking at her earnestly for a moment*] Thank you. I will come with pleasure.

GLORIA ⎰ [*politely* ⎱ Thank you very much—er—
DOLLY ⎱ *murmuring*] ⎰ So glad—er—
PHILIP   Delighted, I'm sure—er—

The conversation drops. Gloria and Dolly look at one another; then at Valentine and Phil. Valentine and Phil, unequal to the occasion, look away from them at one another, and are instantly so disconcerted by catching one another's eye, that they look back again and catch the eyes of Gloria and Dolly. Thus, catching one another all round, they all look at nothing and are quite at a loss. Crampton looks at them, waiting for them to begin. The silence becomes unbearable.

DOLLY [*suddenly, to keep things going*] How old are you, Mr Crampton?

GLORIA [*hastily*] I am afraid we must be going, Mr Valentine. It is understood, then, that we meet at half past one. [*She makes for the door. Phil goes with her. Valentine retreats to the bell*].

VALENTINE. Half past one. [*He rings the bell*]. Many thanks. [*He follows Gloria and Phil to the door, and goes out with them*].

DOLLY [*who has meanwhile stolen across to Crampton*] Make him give you gas. It's five shillings extra; but it's worth it.

CRAMPTON [*amused*] Very well. [*Looking more earnestly at her*] So you want to know my age, do you? I'm fifty seven.

DOLLY [*with conviction*] You look it.

CRAMPTON [*grimly*] I dare say I do.

DOLLY. What are you looking at me so hard for? Any-

635

thing wrong? [*She feels whether her hat is right*].

CRAMPTON. Youre like somebody.

DOLLY. Who?

CRAMPTON. Well, you have a curious look of my mother.

DOLLY [*incredulously*] Your mother!!! Quite sure you dont mean your daughter?

CRAMPTON [*suddenly blackening with hate*] Yes: I'm q u i t e sure I dont mean my daughter.

DOLLY [*sympathetically*] Tooth bad?

CRAMPTON. No, no: nothing. A twinge of memory, Miss Clandon, not of toothache.

DOLLY. Have it out. "Pluck from the memory a rooted sorrow." With gas, five shillings extra.

CRAMPTON [*vindictively*] No, not a sorrow. An injury that was done me once: thats all. I dont forget injuries; and I dont want to forget them. [*His features settle into an implacable frown*].

DOLLY [*looking critically at him*] I dont think we shall like you when you are brooding over your injuries.

PHILIP [*who has entered the room unobserved, and stolen behind her*] My sister means well, Mr Crampton; but she is indiscreet. Now Dolly: outside! [*He takes her towards the door*].

DOLLY [*in a perfectly audible undertone*] He says he's only fifty seven and he thinks me the image of his mother and he hates his daughter and—[*She is interrupted by the return of Valentine*].

VALENTINE. Miss Clandon has gone on.

PHILIP. Dont forget half past one.

DOLLY. Mind you leave Mr Crampton enough teeth to eat with. [*They go out*].

Valentine comes to his cabinet, and opens it.

CRAMPTON. Thats a spoiled child, Mr Valentine. Thats one of your modern products. When I was her age, I had many a good hiding fresh in my memory to teach me manners.

VALENTINE [*taking up his dental mirror and probe*] What

636

did you think of her sister?

CRAMPTON. You liked her better, eh?

VALENTINE [*rhapsodically*] She struck me as being—[*He checks himself, and adds, prosaically*] However, thats not business. [*He assumes his professional tone*]. Open, please. [*Crampton opens his mouth. Valentine puts the mirror in, and examines his teeth*]. Hm! Youve smashed that one. What a pity to spoil such a splendid set of teeth! Why do you crack nuts with them? [*He withdraws the mirror, and comes forward to converse with his patient*].

CRAMPTON. Ive always cracked nuts with them: what else are they for? [*Dogmatically*] The proper way to keep teeth good is to give them plenty of use on bones and nuts, and wash them every day with soap: plain yellow soap.

VALENTINE. Soap! Why soap?

CRAMPTON. I began using it as a boy because I was made to; and Ive used it ever since. And Ive never had toothache in my life.

VALENTINE. Dont you find it rather nasty?

CRAMPTON. I found that most things that were good for me were nasty. But I was taught to put up with them, and made to put up with them. I'm used to it now: in fact I like the taste when the soap is really good.

VALENTINE [*making a wry face in spite of himself*] You seem to have been very carefully educated, Mr Crampton.

CRAMPTON [*grimly*] I wasnt spoiled, at all events.

VALENTINE [*smiling a little to himself*] Are you quite sure?

CRAMPTON [*crustily*] What d'y' mean?

VALENTINE. Well, your teeth are good, I admit. But Ive seen just as good in very self-indulgent mouths. [*He goes to the cabinet and changes the probe for another one*].

CRAMPTON. It's not the effect on the teeth: it's the effect on the character.

VALENTINE [*placably*] Oh, the character! I see. [*He recommences operations*]. A little wider, please. Hm! Why do you bite so hard? youve broken the tooth worse than you broke the Brazil nut. It will have to come out: it's past

637-

saving. [*He withdraws the probe and again comes to the side of the chair to converse*]. Dont be alarmed: you shant feel anything. I'll give you gas.

CRAMPTON. Rubbish, man: I want none of your gas. Out with it! People were taught to bear necessary pain in my day.

VALENTINE. Oh, if you like being hurt, all right. I'll hurt you as much as you like, without any extra charge for the beneficial effect on your character.

CRAMPTON [*rising and glaring at him*] Young man: you owe me six weeks rent.

VALENTINE. I do.

CRAMPTON. Can you pay me?

VALENTINE. No.

CRAMPTON [*satisfied with his advantage*] I thought not. [*He sits down again*]. How soon d'y' think youll be able to pay me if you have no better manners than to make game of your patients?

VALENTINE. My good sir: my patients havnt all formed their characters on kitchen soap.

CRAMPTON [*suddenly gripping him by the arm as he turns away again to the cabinet*] So much the worse for them! I tell you you dont understand my character. If I could spare all my teeth, I'd make you pull them out one after another to shew you what a properly hardened man can go through with when he's made up his mind to it. [*He nods at Valentine to emphasize this declaration, and releases him*].

VALENTINE [*his careless pleasantry quite unruffled*] And you want to be more hardened, do you?

CRAMPTON. Yes.

VALENTINE [*strolling away to the bell*] Well, youre quite hard enough for me already—as a landlord. [*Crampton receives this with a growl of grim humor. Valentine rings the bell, and remarks in a cheerful casual way, whilst waiting for it to be answered*] Why did you never get married, Mr Crampton? A wife and children would have taken some of the hardness out of you.

CRAMPTON [*with unexpected ferocity*] What the devil is

638

that to you?

The parlormaid appears at the door.

VALENTINE [*politely*] Some warm water, please. [*She retires; and Valentine comes back to the cabinet, not at all put out by Crampton's rudeness, and carries on the conversation whilst he selects a forceps and places it ready to his hand with a gag and a tumbler*]. You were asking me what the devil that was to me. Well, I have an idea of getting married myself.

CRAMPTON [*with grumbling irony*] Naturally, sir, naturally. When a young man has come to his last farthing, and is within twenty four hours of having his furniture distrained upon by his landlord, he marries. Ive noticed that before. Well, marry; and be miserable.

VALENTINE. Oh come! what do you know about it?

CRAMPTON. I'm not a bachelor.

VALENTINE. Then there is a Mrs Crampton?

CRAMPTON [*wincing with a pang of resentment*] Yes: damn her!

VALENTINE [*unperturbed*] Hm! A father, too, perhaps, as well as a husband, Mr Crampton?

CRAMPTON. Three children.

VALENTINE [*politely*] Damn them? eh?

CRAMPTON [*jealously*] No, sir: the children are as much mine as hers.

The parlormaid brings in a jug of hot water.

VALENTINE. Thank you. [*She gives him the jug and goes out. He brings it to the cabinet, continuing in the same idle strain*] I really should like to know your family, Mr Crampton. [*He pours some hot water into the tumbler*].

CRAMPTON. Sorry I cant introduce you, sir. I'm happy to say that I dont know where they are, and dont care, so long as they keep out of my way. [*Valentine, with a hitch of his eyebrows and shoulders, drops the forceps with a clink into the hot water*]. You neednt warm that thing to use on me. I'm not afraid of the cold steel. [*Valentine stoops to arrange the gas pump and cylinder beside the chair*]. Whats that heavy thing?

VALENTINE. Oh, never mind. Something to put my foot

639

on, to get the necessary purchase for a good pull. [*Crampton looks alarmed in spite of himself. Valentine stands upright and places the glass with the forceps ready to his hand, chatting on with provoking indifference*]. And so you advise me not to get married, Mr Crampton? [*He puts his foot on the lever by which the chair is raised and lowered*].

CRAMPTON [*irritably*] I advise you to get my tooth out and have done reminding me of my wife. Come along, man. [*He grips the arms of the chair and braces himself*].

VALENTINE. What do you bet that I dont get that tooth out without your feeling it?

CRAMPTON. Your six weeks rent, young man. Dont you gammon me.

VALENTINE [*jumping at the bet and sending him aloft vigorously*] Done! Are you ready?

Crampton, who has lost his grip of the chair in his alarm at its sudden ascent, folds his arms; sits stiffly upright; and prepares for the worst. Valentine suddenly lets down the back of the chair to an obtuse angle.

CRAMPTON [*clutching at the arms of the chair as he falls back*] P! take care, man! I'm quite helpless in this po—

VALENTINE [*deftly stopping him with the gag, and snatching up the mouthpiece of the gas machine*] Youll be more helpless presently.

He presses the mouthpiece over Crampton's mouth and nose, leaning over his chest so as to hold his head and shoulders well down on the chair. Crampton makes an inarticulate sound in the mouthpiece and tries to lay hands on Valentine, whom he supposes to be in front of him. After a moment his arms wave aimlessly, then subside and drop. He is quite insensible. Valentine throws aside the mouthpiece quickly; picks the forceps adroitly from the glass; and—.

ACT II

ON the terrace at the Marine Hotel. It is a square flagged platform, glaring in the sun, and fenced on the seaward edge by a parapet. The head waiter, busy laying napkins on a luncheon table with his back to the sea, has the hotel on his right, and on his left, in the corner nearest the sea, a flight of steps leading down to the beach. When he looks down the terrace in front of him he sees, a little to his left, a middle aged gentleman sitting on a chair of iron laths at a little iron table with a bowl of lump sugar on it, reading an ultra-Conservative newspaper, with his umbrella up to defend him from the sun, which, in August and at less than an hour after noon, is toasting his protended insteps. At the hotel side of the terrace, there is a garden seat of the ordinary esplanade pattern. Access to the hotel for visitors is by an entrance in the middle of its façade. Nearer the parapet there lurks a way to the kitchen, masked by a little trellis porch. The table at which the waiter is occupied is a long one, set across the terrace with covers and chairs for five, two at each side and one at the end next the hotel. Against the parapet another table is prepared as a buffet to serve from.

The waiter is a remarkable person in his way. A silky old man, white haired and delicate looking, but so cheerful and contented that in his encouraging presence ambition stands rebuked as vulgarity, and imagination as treason to the abounding sufficiency and interest of the actual. He has a certain expression peculiar to men who are pre-eminent in their callings, and who, whilst aware of the vanity of success, are untouched by envy.

The gentleman at the iron table is not dressed for the seaside. He wears his London frock coat and gloves; and his tall silk hat is on the table beside the sugarbowl. The excellent condition and quality of these garments and the gold-rimmed folding spectacles through which he is reading, testify to his respectability. He is about fifty, clean-shaven and close-cropped, with the corners of his mouth turned down purposely, as if he suspected them of wanting to turn up, and was determined not to let them have their way. He keeps his brow resolutely wide open, as if, again, he had resolved in his youth to be truthful, magnanimous, and *incorruptible, but had never succeeded in making that habit of mind automatic and unconscious. Still, he is by no means to be laughed at. There is no sign of stupidity or infirmity of will about him: on the contrary, he would pass anywhere at sight as a man of more than average professional capacity and responsibility. Just at present he is enjoying the weather and the sea too much to be out of patience; but he has exhausted all the news in his paper, and is at present reduced to the advertisements, which are not sufficiently succulent to induce him to persevere with them.*

THE GENTLEMAN [*yawning and giving up the paper as a bad job*] Waiter!

WAITER. Sir? [*coming to him*].

THE GENTLEMAN. Are you quite sure Mrs Clandon is coming back before lunch?

WAITER. Quite sure, sir. She expects you at a quarter to one, sir. [*The gentleman, soothed at once by the waiter's voice, looks at him with a lazy smile. It is a quiet voice, with a gentle melody in it that gives sympathetic interest to his most commonplace remark; and he speaks with the sweetest propriety, neither dropping his aitches nor misplacing them, nor committing any other vulgarism. He looks at his watch as he continues*] Not that yet, sir, is it? 12.43, sir. Only two minutes more to wait, sir. Nice morning, sir!

THE GENTLEMAN. Yes: very fresh after London.

WAITER. Yes, sir: so all our visitors say, sir. Very nice family, Mrs Clandon's, sir.

THE GENTLEMAN. You like them, do you?

WAITER. Yes, sir. They have a free way with them that is very taking, sir, very taking indeed: especially the young lady and gentleman.

THE GENTLEMAN. Miss Dorothea and Mr Philip, I suppose.

WAITER. Yes, sir. The young lady, in giving an order, or the like of that, will say, "Remember, William: we came to this hotel on your account, having heard what a perfect waiter you are." The young gentleman will tell me that I remind him strongly of his father [*the gentleman starts at this*] and that he expects me to act by him as such. [*With a sooth-ing sunny cadence*] Oh, very pleasant, sir, very affable and pleasant indeed!

THE GENTLEMAN. You like his father! [*He laughs at the notion*].

WAITER. Oh sir, we must not take what they say too seri-ously. Of course, sir, if it were true, the young lady would have seen the resemblance too, sir.

THE GENTLEMAN. Did she?

WAITER. No, sir. She thought me like the bust of Shake-spear in Stratford Church, sir. That is why she calls me William, sir. My real name is Walter, sir. [*He turns to go back to the table, and sees Mrs Clandon coming up to the terrace from the beach by the steps*]. Here is Mrs Clandon, sir. [*To Mrs Clandon in an unobtrusively confidential tone*] Gentleman for you, maam.

MRS CLANDON. We shall have two more gentlemen at lunch, William.

WAITER. Right, maam. Thank you, maam. [*He withdraws into the hotel*].

Mrs Clandon comes forward looking for her visitor, but passes over the gentleman without any sign of recognition.

THE GENTLEMAN [*peering at her quaintly from under the umbrella*] Dont you know me?

MRS CLANDON [*incredulously, looking hard at him*] Are you Finch M'Comas?

M'COMAS. Cant you guess? [*He shuts the umbrella; puts it aside; and jocularly plants himself with his hands on his hips to be inspected*].

MRS CLANDON. I believe you are. [*She gives him her hand. The shake that ensues is that of old friends after a long separa-tion*]. Wheres your beard?

M'COMAS [*humorously solemn*] Would you employ a soli-citor with a beard?

MRS CLANDON [*pointing to the silk hat on the table*] Is that your hat?

M'COMAS. Would you employ a solicitor with a sombrero?

MRS CLANDON. I have thought of you all these eighteen years with the beard and the sombrero. [*She sits down on the garden seat. M'Comas takes his chair again*]. Do you go to the meetings of the Dialectical Society still?

M'COMAS [*gravely*] I do not frequent meetings now.

MRS CLANDON. Finch: I see what has happened. You have become respectable.

M'COMAS. Havnt you?

MRS CLANDON. Not a bit.

M'COMAS. You hold to our old opinions still?

MRS CLANDON. As firmly as ever.

M'COMAS. Bless me! And you are still ready to make speeches in public, in spite of your sex [*Mrs Clandon nods*]; to insist on a married woman's right to her own separate property [*she nods again*]; to champion Darwin's view of the origin of species and John Stuart Mill's Essay on Liberty [*nod*]; to read Huxley, Tyndall, and George Eliot [*three nods*]; and to demand University degrees, the opening of the professions, and the parliamentary franchise for women as well as men?

MRS CLANDON [*resolutely*] Yes: I have not gone back one inch; and I have educated Gloria to take up my work when I must leave it. That is what has brought me back to England. I felt I had no right to bury her alive in Madeira: my St Helena, Finch. I suppose she will be howled at as I was; but she is prepared for that.

M'COMAS. Howled at! My dear good lady: there is nothing in any of those views nowadays to prevent her marrying an archbishop. You reproached me just now for having become respectable. You were wrong: I hold to our old opinions as strongly as ever. I dont go to church; and I dont pretend I do. I call myself what I am: a Philosophic Radical standing for liberty and the rights of the individual, as I learnt to do from my master Herbert Spencer. Am I howled at? No: I'm indulged as an old fogey. I'm out of everything, because Ive refused to bow the knee to Socialism.

MRS CLANDON [*shocked*] Socialism!

M'COMAS. Yes: Socialism. Thats what Miss Gloria will be up to her ears in before the end of the month if you let her loose here.

MRS CLANDON [*emphatically*] But I can prove to her that Socialism is a fallacy.

M'COMAS [*touchingly*] It is by proving that, Mrs Clandon, that I have lost all my young disciples. Be careful what you do: let her go her own way. [*With some bitterness*] We're old fashioned: the world thinks it has left us behind. There is only one place in all England where your opinions would still pass as advanced.

MRS CLANDON [*scornfully unconvinced*] The Church, perhaps?

M'COMAS. No: the theatre. And now to business! Why have you made me come down here?

MRS CLANDON. Well, partly because I wanted to see you—

M'COMAS [*with good-humored irony*] Thanks.

MRS CLANDON. —and partly because I want you to explain everything to the children. They know nothing; and now that we have come back to England it is impossible to leave them in ignorance any longer. [*Agitated*] Finch: I cannot bring myself to tell them. I—

She is interrupted by the twins and Gloria. Dolly comes tearing up the steps, racing Phil, who combines terrific speed with an unhurried propriety of bearing which, however, costs him the race, as Dolly reaches her mother first and almost upsets the garden seat by the precipitancy of her embrace.

DOLLY [*breathless*] It's all right, mamma. The dentist is coming; and he's bringing his old man.

MRS CLANDON. Dolly, dear: dont you see Mr M'Comas? [*M'Comas rises, smiling*].

DOLLY [*her face falling with the most disparagingly obvious disappointment*] This! Where are the flowing locks?

PHILIP [*seconding her warmly*] Where the beard? the cloak? the poetic exterior?

DOLLY. Oh, Mr M'Comas, youve gone and spoiled yourself. Why didnt you wait til we'd seen you?

m'comas [*taken aback, but rallying his humor to meet the emergency*] Because eighteen years is too long for a solicitor to go without having his hair cut.

gloria [*at the other side of M'Comas*] How do you do, Mr M'Comas? [*He turns; and she takes his hand and presses it, with a frank straight look into his eyes*]. We are glad to meet you at last.

m'comas. Miss Gloria, I presume? [*Gloria smiles assent; releases his hand after a final pressure; and retires behind the garden seat, leaning over the back beside Mrs Clandon*]. And this young gentleman?

philip. I was christened in a comparatively prosaic mood. My name is—

dolly [*completing his sentence for him declamatorily*] "Norval. On the Grampian hills"—

philip [*declaiming gravely*] "My father feeds his flock, a frugal swain"—

mrs clandon [*remonstrating*] Dear, dear children: dont be silly. Everything is so new to them here, Finch, that they are in the wildest spirits. They think every Englishman they meet is a joke.

dolly. Well, so he is: it's not our fault.

philip. My knowledge of human nature is fairly extensive, Mr M'Comas; but I find it impossible to take the inhabitants of this island seriously.

m'comas. I presume, sir, you are Master Philip [*offering his hand*].

philip [*taking M'Comas's hand and looking solemnly at him*] I was Master Philip: was so for many years; just as you were once Master Finch. [*He gives the hand a single shake and drops it; then turns away, exclaiming meditatively*] How strange it is to look back on our boyhood!

dolly [*to Mrs Clandon*] Has Finch had a drink?

mrs clandon [*remonstrating*] Dearest: Mr M'Comas will lunch with us.

dolly. Have you ordered for seven? Dont forget the old gentleman.

MRS CLANDON. I have not forgotten him, dear. What is his name?

DOLLY. Chalkstones. He'll be here at half past one. [*To M'Comas*] Are we like what you expected?

MRS CLANDON [*earnestly, even a little peremptorily*] Dolly: Mr M'Comas has something more serious than that to tell you. Children: I have asked my old friend to answer the question you asked this morning. He is your father's friend as well as mine; and he will tell you the story of my married life more fairly than I could. Gloria: are you satisfied?

GLORIA [*gravely attentive*] Mr M'Comas is very kind.

M'COMAS [*nervously*] Not at all, my dear young lady: not at all. At the same time, this is rather sudden. I was hardly prepared—er—

DOLLY [*suspiciously*] Oh, we dont want anything prepared.

PHILIP [*exhorting him*] Tell us the truth.

DOLLY [*emphatically*] Bald headed.

M'COMAS [*nettled*] I hope you intend to take what I have to say seriously.

PHILIP [*with profound gravity*] I hope it will deserve it, Mr M'Comas. My knowledge of human nature teaches me not to expect too much.

MRS CLANDON [*remonstrating*] Phil—

PHILIP. Yes, mother: all right. I beg your pardon, Mr M'Comas: dont mind us.

DOLLY [*in conciliation*] We mean well.

PHILIP. Shut up, both.

Dolly holds her lips. M'Comas takes a chair from the luncheon table; places it between the little table and the garden seat, with Dolly on his right and Phil on his left; and settles himself in it with the air of a man about to begin a long communication. The Clandons watch him expectantly.

M'COMAS. Ahem! Your father—

DOLLY. How old is he?

PHILIP. Sh!

MRS CLANDON [*softly*] Dear Dolly: dont let us interrupt Mr M'Comas.

647

M'COMAS [*emphatically*] Thank you, Mrs Clandon. Thank you. [*To Dolly*] Your father is fifty-seven.

DOLLY [*with a bound, startled and excited*] Fifty-seven!! Where does he live?

MRS CLANDON [*remonstrating*] Dolly! Dolly!

M'COMAS [*stopping her*] Let me answer that, Mrs Clandon. The answer will surprise you considerably. He lives in this town.

Mrs Clandon rises, intensely angry, but sits down again, speechless: Gloria watching her perplexedly.

DOLLY [*with conviction*] I knew it. Phil: Chalkstones is our father!

M'COMAS. Chalkstones!

DOLLY. Oh, Crampstones, or whatever it is. He said I was like his mother. I knew he must mean his daughter.

PHILIP [*very seriously*] Mr M'Comas: I desire to consider your feelings in every possible way; but I warn you that if you stretch the long arm of coincidence to the length of telling me that Mr Crampton of this town is my father, I shall decline to entertain the information for a moment.

M'COMAS. And pray why?

PHILIP. Because I have seen the gentleman; and he is entirely unfit to be my father, or Dolly's father, or Gloria's father, or my mother's husband.

M'COMAS. Oh, indeed! Well, sir, let me tell you that whether you like it or not, he is your father, and your sisters' father, and Mrs Clandon's husband. Now! What have you to say to that?

DOLLY [*whimpering*] You neednt be so cross. Crampton isnt your father.

PHILIP. Mr M'Comas: your conduct is heartless. Here you find a family enjoying the unspeakable peace and freedom of being orphans. We have never seen the face of a relative: never known a claim except the claim of freely chosen friendship. And now you wish to thrust into the most intimate relationship with us a man whom we dont know—

DOLLY [*vehemently*] An awful old man! [*Reproachfully*]

648

And you began as if you had quite a nice father for us!

M'COMAS [*angrily*] How do you know that he is not nice? And what right have you to choose your own father? [*Raising his voice*] Let me tell you, Miss Clandon, that you are too young to—

DOLLY [*interrupting him suddenly and eagerly*] Stop: I forgot! Has he any money?

M'COMAS. He has a great deal of money.

DOLLY [*delighted*] Oh, what did I always say, Phil?

PHILIP. Dolly: we have perhaps been condemning the old man too hastily. Proceed, Mr M'Comas.

M'COMAS. I shall not proceed, sir. I am too hurt, too shocked, to proceed.

MRS CLANDON [*struggling with her temper*] Finch: do you realize what is happening? Do you understand that my children have invited that man to lunch, and that he will be here in a few moments?

M'COMAS [*completely upset*] What! Do you mean? am I to understand? is it—

PHILIP [*impressively*] Steady, Finch. Think it out slowly and carefully. He's coming: coming to lunch.

GLORIA. Which of us is to tell him the truth? Have you thought of that?

MRS CLANDON. Finch: you must tell him.

DOLLY. Oh, Finch is no good at telling things. Look at the mess he has made of telling us.

M'COMAS. I have not been allowed to speak. I protest against this.

DOLLY [*taking his arm coaxingly*] Dear Finch: dont be cross.

MRS CLANDON. Gloria: let us go in. He may arrive at any moment.

GLORIA [*proudly*] Do not stir, mother. *I* shall not stir. We must not run away.

MRS CLANDON. My dear: we cannot sit down to lunch just as we are. We shall come back again. We must have no bravado. [*Gloria winces, and goes into the hotel without a word*]. Come, Dolly. [*As she goes to the hotel door, the*

649

waiter comes out with a tray of plates, etc. for two additional covers].

WAITER. Gentlemen come yet, maam?

MRS CLANDON. Two more to come still, thank you. They will be here immediately. [*She goes into the hotel*].

The waiter takes his tray to the service table.

PHILIP. I have an idea. Mr M'Comas: this communication should be made, should it not, by a man of infinite tact?

M'COMAS. It will require tact, certainly.

PHILIP. Good! Dolly: whose tact were you noticing only this morning?

DOLLY [*seizing the idea with rapture*] Oh yes, I declare!

PHILIP. The very man! [*Calling*] William!

WAITER. Coming, sir.

M'COMAS [*horrified*] The waiter! Stop! stop! I will not permit this. I—

WAITER [*presenting himself between Phil and M'Comas*] Yes, sir.

M'Comas's complexion fades into stone grey: all movement and expression desert his eyes. He sits down stupefied.

PHILIP. William: you remember my request to you to regard me as your son?

WAITER [*with respectful indulgence*] Yes, sir. Anything you please, sir.

PHILIP. William: at the very outset of your career as my father, a rival has appeared on the scene.

WAITER. Your real father, sir? Well, that was to be expected, sooner or later, sir, wasnt it? [*Turning with a happy smile to M'Comas*] Is it you, sir?

M'COMAS [*renerved by indignation*]. Certainly not. My children know how to behave themselves.

PHILIP. No, William: this gentleman was very nearly my father: he wooed my mother, but wooed her in vain.

M'COMAS [*outraged*] Well, of all the—

PHILIP. Sh! Consequently, he is only our solicitor. Do you know one Crampton, of this town?

WAITER. Cock-eyed Crampton, sir, of the Crooked Billet,

is it?

PHILIP. I dont know. Finch: does he keep a public house?

M'COMAS [*rising, scandalized*] No, no, no. Your father, sir, is a well known yacht builder, an eminent man here.

WAITER [*impressed*] Oh! Beg pardon, sir, I'm sure. A son of Mr Crampton's! Dear me!

PHILIP. Mr Crampton is coming to lunch with us.

WAITER [*puzzled*] Yes, sir. [*Diplomatically*] Dont usually lunch with his family, perhaps, sir?

PHILIP [*impressively*] William: he does not know that we are his family. He has not seen us for eighteen years. He wont know us. [*To emphasize the communication, Phil seats himself on the iron table with a spring, and looks at the waiter with his lips compressed and his legs swinging*].

DOLLY. We want you to break the news to him, William.

WAITER. But I should think he'd guess when he sees your mother, miss.

Phil's legs become motionless. He contemplates the waiter raptly.

DOLLY [*dazzled*] I never thought of that.

PHILIP. Nor I. [*Coming off the table and turning reproach fully on M'Comas*] Nor you!

DOLLY. And you a solicitor!

PHILIP. Finch: your professional incompetence is appalling. William: your sagacity puts us all to shame.

DOLLY. You really are like Shakespear, William.

WAITER. Not at all, sir. Dont mention it, miss. Most happy, I'm sure, sir. [*He goes back modestly to the luncheon table and lays the two additional covers, one at the end next the steps, and the other so as to make a third on the side furthest from the balustrade*].

PHILIP [*abruptly seizing M'Comas's arm and leading him towards the hotel*] Finch: come and wash your hands.

M'COMAS. I am thoroughly vexed and hurt, Mr Clandon—

PHILIP [*interrupting him*] You will get used to us. Come, Dolly. [*M'Comas shakes him off and marches into the hotel. Phil*

651

follows with unruffled composure].

DOLLY [*turning for a moment on the steps as she follows them*]
Keep your wits about you, William. There will be fireworks.

WAITER. Right, miss. You may depend on me, miss. [*She goes into the hotel*].

Valentine comes lightly up the steps from the beach, followed doggedly by Crampton. Valentine carries a walking stick. Crampton, either because he is old and chilly, or with some idea of extenuating the unfashionableness of his reefer jacket, wears a light overcoat. He stops at the chair left by M'Comas in the middle of the terrace, and steadies himself for a moment by placing his hand on the back of it.

CRAMPTON. Those steps make me giddy. [*He passes his hand over his forehead*]. I have not got over that infernal gas yet.

He goes to the iron chair, so that he can lean his elbows on the little table to prop his head as he sits. He soon recovers, and begins to unbutton his overcoat. Meanwhile Valentine interviews the waiter.

VALENTINE. Waiter!

WAITER [*coming forward between them*] Yes, sir.

VALENTINE. Mrs Lanfrey Clandon.

WAITER [*with a sweet smile of welcome*] Yes, sir. We're expecting you, sir. That is your table, sir. Mrs Clandon will be down presently, sir. The young lady and gentleman were just talking about your friend, sir.

VALENTINE. Indeed!

WAITER [*smoothly melodious*] Yes, sir. Great flow of spirits, sir. A vein of pleasantry, as you might say, sir. [*Quickly, to Crampton, who has risen to get the overcoat off*] Beg pardon, sir; but if youll allow me [*helping him to get the overcoat off, and taking it from him*]. Thank you, sir. [*Crampton sits down again; and the waiter resumes the broken melody*]. The young gentleman's latest is that youre his father, sir.

CRAMPTON. What!

WAITER. Only his joke, sir, his favorite joke. Yesterday, *I* was to be his father. Today, as soon as he knew you were coming, sir, he tried to put it up on me that you were his father: his long lost father! Not seen you for eighteen years, he said.

CRAMPTON [*startled*] Eighteen years!

WAITER. Yes, sir. [*With gentle archness*] But I was up to his tricks, sir. I saw the idea coming into his head as he stood there, thinking what new joke he'd have with me. Yes, sir: thats the sort he is: very pleasant, ve—ry offhand and affable indeed, sir. [*Again changing his tempo to say to Valentine, who is putting his stick down against the corner of the garden seat*] If youll allow me, sir? [*He takes Valentine's stick*]. Thank you, sir. [*Valentine strolls up to the luncheon table and looks at the menu. The waiter turns to Crampton and continues his lay*]. Even the solicitor took up the joke, although he was in a manner of speaking in my confidence about the young gentleman, sir. Yes, sir, I assure you, sir. You would never imagine what respectable professional gentlemen from London will do on an outing, when the sea air takes them, sir.

CRAMPTON. Oh, theres a solicitor with them, is there?

WAITER. The family solicitor, sir: yes, sir. Name of M'Comas, sir. [*He goes towards the hotel entrance with the coat and stick, happily unconscious of the bomblike effect the name has produced on Crampton*].

CRAMPTON [*rising in angry alarm*] M'Comas! [*Calling to Valentine*] Valentine! [*Again, fiercely*] Valentine!! [*Valentine turns*]. This is a plant, a conspiracy. This is my family! my children! my infernal wife.

VALENTINE [*coolly*] Oh indeed! Interesting meeting! [*He resumes his study of the menu*].

CRAMPTON. Meeting! Not for me. Let me out of this. [*Calling across to the waiter*] Give me that coat.

WAITER. Yes, sir. [*He comes back; puts Valentine's stick carefully down against the luncheon table; and delicately shakes the coat out and holds it for Crampton to put on*]. I seem to have done the young gentleman an injustice, sir, havnt I, sir?

CRAMPTON. Rrrh! [*He stops on the point of putting his arms into the sleeves, and turns on Valentine with sudden suspicion*].

653

Valentine: you are in this. You made this plot. You—

VALENTINE [*decisively*] Bosh! [*He throws the menu down and goes round the table to look out unconcernedly over the parapet*].

CRAMPTON [*angrily*] What d'ye—

M'Comas, followed by Phil and Dolly, comes out, but recoils on seeing Crampton.

WAITER [*softly interrupting Crampton*] Steady, sir. Here they come, sir. [*He takes up Valentine's stick and makes for the hotel, throwing the coat across his arm.*]

M'Comas turns the corners of his mouth resolutely down and crosses to Crampton, who draws back and glares, with his hands behind him. M'Comas, with his brow opener than ever, confronts him in the majesty of a spotless conscience.

WAITER [*aside, as he passes Phil on his way out*] Ive broke it to him, sir.

PHILIP. Invaluable William! [*He passes on to the table*].

DOLLY [*aside to the waiter*] How did he take it?

WAITER [*aside to her*] Startled at first, miss; but resigned: very resigned indeed, miss. [*He takes the stick and coat into the hotel*].

M'COMAS [*having stared Crampton out of countenance*] So here you are, Mr Crampton.

CRAMPTON. Yes, here: caught in a trap: a mean trap. Are those my children?

PHILIP [*with deadly politeness*] Is this our father, Mr M'Comas?

M'COMAS [*stoutly*] He is.

DOLLY [*conventionally*] Pleased to meet you again. [*She wanders idly round the table, exchanging a grimace with Valentine on the way*].

PHILIP. Allow me to discharge my first duty as host by ordering your wine. [*He takes the wine list from the table. His polite attention, and Dolly's unconcerned indifference, leave Crampton on the footing of a casual acquaintance picked up that morning at the dentist's. The consciousness of it goes through the father with so keen a pang that he trembles all over; his brow be-*

comes wet; and he stares dumbly at his son, who, just sensible enough of his own callousness to intensely enjoy the humor and adroitness of it, proceeds pleasantly] Finch: some crusted old port for you, as a respectable family solicitor, eh?

M'COMAS [*firmly*] Apollinaris only. Nothing heating. [*He walks away to the side of the terrace, like a man putting temptation behind him*].

PHILIP. Valentine—?

VALENTINE. Would Lager be considered vulgar?

PHILIP. Probably. We'll order some. [*Turning to Crampton with cheerful politeness*] And now, Mr Crampton, what can we do for you?

CRAMPTON. What d'ye mean, boy?

PHILIP. Boy! [*Very solemnly*] Whose fault is it that I am a boy?

Crampton snatches the wine list rudely from him and irresolutely pretends to read it. Philip abandons it to him with perfect politeness.

DOLLY [*looking over Crampton's right shoulder*] The whisky's on the last page but one.

CRAMPTON. Let me alone, child.

DOLLY. Child! No, no: you may call me Dolly if you like; but you musnt call me child. [*She slips her arm through Phil's; and the two stand looking at Crampton as if he were some eccentric stranger*].

CRAMPTON [*mopping his brow in rage and agony, and yet relieved even by their playing with him*] M'Comas: we are— ha!—going to have a pleasant meal.

M'COMAS [*resolutely cheerful*] There is no reason why it should not be pleasant.

PHILIP. Finch's face is a feast in itself.

Mrs Clandon and Gloria come from the hotel. Mrs Clandon advances with courageous self-possession and marked dignity of manner. She stops at the foot of the steps to address Valentine, who is in her path. Gloria also stops, looking at Crampton with a certain repulsion.

MRS CLANDON. Glad to see you again, Mr Valentine. [*He

655

smiles. She passes on and confronts Crampton, intending to address him with complete composure; but his aspect shakes her. She stops suddenly and says anxiously, with a touch of remorse] Fergus: you are greatly changed.

CRAMPTON [*grimly*] I daresay. A man does change in eighteen years.

MRS CLANDON [*troubled*] I—I did not mean that. I hope your health is good.

CRAMPTON. Thank you. No: it's not my health. It's my happiness: thats the change you meant, I think. [*Breaking out suddenly*] Look at her, McComas! Look at her; and [*with a half laugh, half sob*] look at me!

PHILIP. Sh! [*Pointing to the hotel entrance, where the waiter has just appeared*] Order before William!

DOLLY [*touching Crampton's arm warningly*] Ahem!

The waiter goes to the service table and beckons to the kitchen entrance, whence issue a young waiter with soup plates, and a cook, in white apron and cap, with the soup tureen. The young waiter remains and serves: the cook goes out, and reappears from time to time bringing in the courses. He carves, but does not serve. The waiter comes to the end of the luncheon table next the steps.

MRS CLANDON [*as they assemble at the table*] I think you have all met one another already today. Oh no: excuse me. [*Introducing*] Mr Valentine: Mr M'Comas. [*She goes to the end of the table nearest the hotel*]. Fergus: will you take the head of the table, please.

CRAMPTON. Ha! [*Bitterly*] The head of the table!

WAITER [*holding the chair for him with inoffensive encouragement*] This end, sir. [*Crampton submits, and takes his seat*]. Thank you, sir.

MRS CLANDON. Mr Valentine: will you take that side [*indicating the side next the parapet*] with Gloria? [*Valentine and Gloria take their places, Gloria next Crampton and Valentine next Mrs Clandon*]. Finch: I must put you on this side, between Dolly and Phil. You must protect yourself as best you can.

The three take the remaining side of the table, Dolly next

656

her mother, Phil *next his father. Soup is served.*

WAITER [*to Crampton*] Thick or clear, sir?

CRAMPTON [*to Mrs Clandon*] Does nobody ask a blessing in this household?

PHILIP [*interposing smartly*] Let us first settle what we are about to receive. William!

WAITER. Yes, sir. [*He glides swiftly round the table to Phil's left elbow. On his way he whispers to the young waiter*] Thick.

PHILIP. Two small Lagers for the children as usual, William; and one large for this gentleman [*indicating Valentine*]. Large Apollinaris for Mr M'Comas.

WAITER. Yes, sir.

DOLLY. Have a six of Irish in it, Finch?

M'COMAS [*scandalized*] No. No, thank you.

PHILIP. Number 413 for my mother and Miss Gloria as before; and—[*turning inquiringly to Crampton*] Eh?

CRAMPTON [*scowling and about to reply offensively*] I—

WAITER [*striking in mellifluously*] All right, sir. We know what Mr Crampton likes here, sir. [*He goes into the hotel*].

PHILIP [*looking gravely at his father*] You frequent bars. Bad habit!

The cook, followed by a waiter with hot plates, brings in the fish from the kitchen to the service table, and begins slicing it.

CRAMPTON. You have learnt your lesson from your mother, I see.

MRS CLANDON. Phil: will you please remember that your jokes are apt to irritate people who are not accustomed to us, and that your father is our guest today.

CRAMPTON [*bitterly*] Yes: a guest at the head of my own table. [*The soup plates are removed*].

DOLLY [*sympathetically*] It's embarrassing, isnt it? It's just as bad for us, you know.

PHILIP. Sh! Dolly: we are both wanting in tact. [*To Crampton*] We mean well, Mr Crampton; but we are not yet strong in the filial line. [*The waiter returns from the hotel with the drinks*]. William: come and restore good feeling.

WAITER [*cheerfully*] Yes, sir. Certainly, sir. Small Lager

657

for you, sir. [*To Crampton*] Seltzer and Irish, sir. [*To M'Comas*] Apollinaris, sir. [*To Dolly*] Small Lager, miss. [*To Mrs Clandon, pouring out wine*] 413, madam. [*To Valentine*] Large Lager for you, sir. [*To Gloria*] 413, miss.

DOLLY [*drinking*] To the family!

PHILIP [*drinking*] Hearth and Home!

Fish is served.

M'COMAS. We are getting on very nicely after all.

DOLLY [*critically*] After all! After all what, Finch?

CRAMPTON [*sarcastically*] He means that you are getting on very nicely in spite of the presence of your father. Do I take your point rightly, Mr M'Comas?

M'COMAS [*disconcerted*] No, no. I only said "after all" to round off the sentence. I—er—er—er—

WAITER [*tactfully*] Turbot, sir?

M'COMAS [*intensely grateful for the interruption*] Thank you, waiter: thank you.

WAITER [*sotto voce*] Dont mention it, sir. [*He returns to the service table*].

CRAMPTON [*to Phil*] Have you thought of choosing a profession yet?

PHILIP. I am keeping my mind open on that subject. William!

WAITER. Yes, sir.

PHILIP. How long do you think it would take me to learn to be a really smart waiter?

WAITER. Cant be learnt, sir. It's in the character, sir. [*Confidentially to Valentine, who is looking about for something*] Bread for the lady, sir? yes, sir. [*He serves bread to Gloria, and resumes, at his former pitch*] Very few are born to it, sir.

PHILIP. You dont happen to have such a thing as a son, yourself, have you?

WAITER. Yes, sir: oh yes, sir. [*To Gloria, again dropping his voice*] A little more fish, miss? you wont care for the joint in the middle of the day.

GLORIA. No, thank you.

The fish plates are removed, and the next course served.

658

YOU NEVER CAN TELL

DOLLY. Is your son a waiter too, William?

WAITER [*serving Gloria with fowl*] Oh no, miss: he's too impetuous. He's at the Bar.

M'COMAS [*patronizingly*] A potman, eh?

WAITER [*with a touch of melancholy, as if recalling a disappointment softened by time*] No, sir: the other bar. Your profession, sir. A Q.C., sir.

M'COMAS [*embarrassed*] I'm sure I beg your pardon.

WAITER. Not at all, sir. Very natural mistake, I'm sure, sir. I've often wished he w a s a potman, sir. Would have been off my hands ever so much sooner, sir. [*Aside to Valentine, who is again in difficulties*] Salt at your elbow, sir. [*Resuming*] Yes, sir: had to support him until he was thirty-seven, sir. But doing well now, sir: very satisfactory indeed, sir. Nothing less than fifty guineas, sir.

M'COMAS. Democracy, Crampton! Modern democracy!

WAITER [*calmly*] No, sir, not democracy: only education, sir. Scholarships, sir. Cambridge Local, sir. Sidney Sussex College, sir. [*Dolly plucks his sleeve and whispers as he bends down*]. Stone ginger, miss? Right, miss. [*To M'Comas*] Very good thing for him, sir: he never had any turn for real work, sir. [*He goes into the hotel, leaving the company somewhat overwhelmed by his son's eminence*].

VALENTINE. Which of us dare give that man an order again!

DOLLY. I hope he wont mind my sending him for ginger-beer.

CRAMPTON [*doggedly*] While he's a waiter it's his business to wait. If you had treated him as a waiter ought to be treated, he'd have held his tongue.

DOLLY. What a loss that would have been! Perhaps he'll give us an introduction to his son and get us into London society.

The waiter reappears with the ginger-beer.

CRAMPTON [*growling contemptuously*] London society! London society!! Youre not fit for any society, child.

DOLLY [*losing her temper*] Now look here, Mr Crampton.

659

YOU NEVER CAN TELL

If you think—

WAITER [*softly, at her elbow*] Stone ginger, miss.

DOLLY [*taken aback, recovers her good humor after a long breath, and says sweetly*] Thank you, d e a r William. You were just in time. [*She drinks*].

M'COMAS. If I may be allowed to change the subject, Miss Clandon, what is the established religion in Madeira?

GLORIA. I suppose the Portuguese religion. I never inquired.

DOLLY. The servants come in Lent and kneel down before you and confess all the things theyve done; and you have to pretend to forgive them. Do they do that in England, William?

WAITER. Not usually, miss. They may in some parts; but it has not come under my notice, miss. [*Catching Mrs Clandon's eye as the young waiter offers her the salad bowl*] You like it without dressing, maam: yes, maam, I have some for you. [*To his young colleague, motioning him to serve Gloria*] This side, Jo. [*He takes a special portion of salad from the service table and puts it beside Mrs Clandon's plate. In doing so he observes that Dolly is making a wry face*]. Only a bit of watercress, miss, got in by mistake [*he takes her salad away*]. Thank you, miss. [*To the young waiter, admonishing him to serve Dolly afresh*] Jo. [*Resuming*] Mostly members of the Church of England, miss.

DOLLY. Members of the Church of England? Whats the subscription?

CRAMPTON [*rising violently amid general consternation*] You see how my children have been brought up, M'Comas. You see it: you hear it. I call all of you to witness— [*He becomes inarticulate, and is about to strike his fist recklessly on the table when the waiter considerately takes away his plate*].

MRS CLANDON [*firmly*] Sit down, Fergus. There is no occasion at all for this outburst. You must remember that Dolly is just like a foreigner here. Pray sit down.

CRAMPTON [*subsiding unwillingly*] I doubt whether I ought to sit here and countenance all this. I doubt it.

660

WAITER. Cheese, sir? or would you like a cold sweet?

CRAMPTON [*taken aback*] What? Oh! Cheese, cheese.

DOLLY. Bring a box of cigarets, William.

WAITER. All ready, miss. [*He takes a box of cigarets from the service table and places them before Dolly, who selects one and prepares to smoke. He then returns to his table for the matches*].

CRAMPTON [*staring aghast at Dolly*] Does she smoke?

DOLLY [*out of patience*] Really, Mr Crampton, I'm afraid I'm spoiling your lunch. I'll go and have my cigaret on the beach. [*She leaves the table with petulant suddenness and goes to the steps. The waiter strikes a match and adroitly lights her cigaret*]. Thank you, dear William. [*She vanishes down the steps*].

CRAMPTON [*furiously*] Margaret: call that girl back. Call her back, I say.

M'COMAS [*trying to make peace*] Come, Crampton: never mind. She's her father's daughter: thats all.

MRS CLANDON [*with deep resentment*] I hope not, Finch. [*She rises: they all rise a little*]. Mr Valentine: will you excuse me? I am afraid Dolly is hurt and put out by what has passed. I must go to her.

CRAMPTON. To take her part against me, you mean.

MRS CLANDON [*ignoring him*] Gloria: will you take my place whilst I am away, dear. [*She crosses to the steps and goes down to the beach*].

Crampton's expression is one of bitter hatred. The rest watch her in embarrassed silence, feeling the incident to be a very painful one. The waiter discreetly shepherds his assistant along with him into the hotel by the kitchen entrance, leaving the luncheon party to themselves.

CRAMPTON [*throwing himself back in his chair*] Theres a mother for you, M'Comas! Theres a mother for you!

GLORIA [*steadfastly*] Yes: a good mother.

CRAMPTON. And a bad father? Thats what you mean, eh?

VALENTINE [*rising indignantly and addressing Gloria*] Miss Clandon: I—

CRAMPTON [*turning on him*] That girl's name is Crampton, Mr Valentine, not Clandon. Do you wish to join them in insulting me?

VALENTINE [*ignoring him*] I'm overwhelmed, Miss Clandon. It's all my fault: I brought him here: I'm responsible for him. And I'm ashamed of him.

CRAMPTON. What d'y'mean?

GLORIA [*rising coldly*] No harm has been done, Mr Valentine. We have all been a little childish, I am afraid. Our party has been a failure: let us break it up and have done with it. [*She puts her chair aside and turns to the steps, adding, with slighting composure, as she passes Crampton*] Goodbye, father.

She descends the steps with cold disgusted indifference. They all look after her, and so do not notice the return of the waiter from the hotel, laden with Crampton's coat, Valentine's stick, a couple of shawls and parasols, and some camp stools, which he deposits on the bench.

CRAMPTON [*to himself, staring after Gloria with a ghastly expression*] Father! Father!! [*He strikes his fist violently on the table*]. Now—

WAITER [*offering the coat*] This is yours, sir, I think, sir. [*Crampton glares at him; then snatches it rudely and comes down the terrace towards the garden seat, struggling with the coat in his angry efforts to put it on. M'Comas rises and goes to his assistance: then takes his hat and umbrella from the little iron table, and turns towards the steps. Meanwhile the waiter, after thanking Crampton with unruffled sweetness for taking the coat, picks up the other articles and offers the parasols to Phil*]. The ladies' sunshades, sir. Nasty glare off the sea today, sir: very trying to the complexion, sir. I shall carry down the camp stools myself, sir.

PHILIP. You are old, Father William; but you are the most thoughtful of men. No: keep the sunshades and give me the camp stools [*taking them*].

WAITER [*with flattering gratitude*] Thank you, sir.

PHILIP. Finch: share with me [*giving him a couple*]. Come along. [*They go down the steps together*].

YOU NEVER CAN TELL

VALENTINE [*to the waiter*] Leave me something to bring down. One of these [*offering to take a sunshade*].

WAITER [*discreetly*] Thats the younger lady's, sir. [*Valentine lets it go*]. Thank you, sir. If youll allow me, sir, I think you had better take this. [*He puts down his burden on Crampton's chair, and produces from the tail pocket of his dress coat a book with a lady's handkerchief between the leaves to mark the page*]. The elder young lady is reading it at present. [*Valentine takes it eagerly*]. Thank you, sir. The Subjection of Women, sir, you see. [*He takes up the burden again*]. Heavier reading than you and I would care for at the seaside, sir. [*He goes down the steps*].

VALENTINE [*coming rather excitedly to Crampton*] Now look here, Crampton: are you at all ashamed of yourself?

CRAMPTON [*pugnaciously*] Ashamed of myself! What for?

VALENTINE. For behaving like a bear. What will your daughter think of me for having brought you here?

CRAMPTON. I was not thinking of what my daughter was thinking of you.

VALENTINE. No, you were thinking of yourself. Youre a perfect egomaniac.

CRAMPTON [*heartrent*] She told you what I am: a father: a father robbed of his children. What are the hearts of this generation like? Am I to come here after all these years? to see what my children are for the first time! to hear their voices! and carry it all off like a fashionable visitor; drop in to lunch; be Mr Crampton? Mister Crampton! What right have they to talk to me like that? I'm their father: do they deny that? I'm a man, with the feelings of our common humanity: have I no rights, no claims? In all these years who have I had round me? Servants, clerks, business acquaintances. Ive had respect from them: aye, kindness. Would one of them have spoken to me as that girl spoke? Would one of them have laughed at me as that boy was laughing at me all the time? [*Frantically*] My own children! Mister Crampton! My—

VALENTINE. Come, come! theyre only children. She

663

called you father.

CRAMPTON. Yes: "goodbye, father." Goodbye! Oh yes: she got at my feelings: with a stab!

VALENTINE [*taking this in very bad part*] Now look here, Crampton: you just let her alone: she's treated you very well. I had a much worse time of it at lunch than you.

CRAMPTON. You!

VALENTINE [*with growing impetuosity*] Yes: I. I sat next her; and I never said a single thing to her the whole time: couldnt think of a blessed word. And not a word did she say to me.

CRAMPTON. Well?

VALENTINE. Well? Well??? [*Tackling him very seriously, and talking faster and faster*] Crampton: do you know whats been the matter with me today? You dont suppose, do you, that I'm in the habit of playing such tricks on my patients as I played on you?

CRAMPTON. I hope not.

VALENTINE. The explanation is that I'm stark mad, or rather that Ive never been in my real senses before. I'm capable of anything: Ive grown up at last: I'm a Man; and it's your daughter thats made a man of me.

CRAMPTON [*incredulously*] Are you in love with my daughter?

VALENTINE [*his words now coming in a perfect torrent*] Love! Nonsense: it's something far above and beyond that. It's life, it's faith, it's strength, certainty, paradise—

CRAMPTON [*interrupting him with acrid contempt*] Rubbish, man! What have you to keep a wife on? You cant marry her.

VALENTINE. Who wants to marry her? I'll kiss her hands; I'll kneel at her feet; I'll live for her; I'll die for her; and thatll be enough for me. Look at her book! See! [*He kisses the handkerchief*]. If you offered me all your money for this excuse for going down to the beach and speaking to her again, I'd only laugh at you. [*He rushes buoyantly off to the steps, where he bounces right into the arms of the waiter, who is*

664

coming up from the beach. The two save themselves from falling by clutching one another tightly round the waist and whirling one another round].

WAITER [*delicately*] Steady, sir, steady!

VALENTINE [*shocked at his own violence*] I beg your pardon.

WAITER. Not at all, sir, not at all. Very natural, sir, I'm sure, sir, at your age. The lady has sent me for her book, sir. Might I take the liberty of asking you to let her have it at once, sir.

VALENTINE. With pleasure. And if you will allow me to present you with a professional man's earnings for six weeks —[*offering him Dolly's crown piece*]?

WAITER [*as if the sum were beyond his utmost expectations*] Thank you, sir: much obliged. [*Valentine dashes down the steps*]. Very high-spirited young gentleman, sir: very manly and straight set up.

CRAMPTON [*in grumbling disparagement*] And making his fortune in a hurry, no doubt. *I* know what his six weeks' earnings come to. [*He crosses the terrace to the iron table, and sits down*].

WAITER [*philosophically*] Well, sir, you never can tell. Thats a principle in life with me, sir, if youll excuse my having such a thing, sir. [*Delicately sinking the philosopher in the waiter for a moment*] Perhaps you havnt noticed that you hadnt touched that seltzer and Irish, sir, when the party broke up. [*He takes the tumbler from the luncheon table and sets it before Crampton*]. Yes, sir, you never can tell. There was my son, sir! who ever thought that he would rise to wear a silk gown, sir? And yet, today, sir, nothing less than fifty guineas. What a lesson, sir!

CRAMPTON. Well, I hope he is grateful to you, and recognizes what he owes you, as a son should.

WAITER. We get on together very well, very well indeed, sir, considering the difference in our stations. [*Crampton is about to take a drink*]. A small lump of sugar, sir, will take the flatness out of the seltzer without noticeably sweetening the drink, sir. Allow me, sir. [*He drops a lump of sugar into the tumbler*]. But as I say to him, wheres the difference after all? If I must put on a dress coat to shew what I am, sir, he must put on a wig and gown to shew what he is. If my income is mostly tips, and theres a pretence that I dont get them, why, his income is mostly fees, sir; and I understand theres a pretence that h e dont get them! If he likes society, and his profession brings him into contact with all ranks, so does mine too, sir. If it's a little against a barrister to have a waiter for his father, sir, it's a little against a waiter to have a barrister for a son: many people consider it a great liberty, sir, I assure you, sir. Can I get you anything else, sir?

CRAMPTON. No, thank you. [*With bitter humility*] I suppose theres no objection to my sitting here for a while: I cant disturb the party on the beach here.

WAITER [*with emotion*] Very kind of you, sir, to put it as if it was not a compliment and an honor to us, Mr Crampton, very kind indeed. The more you are at home here, sir, the better for us.

CRAMPTON [*in poignant irony*] Home!

WAITER [*reflectively*] Well, yes, sir: thats a way of looking at it too, sir. I have always said that the great advantage of a hotel is that it's a refuge from home life, sir.

CRAMPTON. I missed that advantage today, I think.

WAITER. You did, sir: you did. Dear me! It's the unexpected that always happens, isnt it? [*Shaking his head*] You never can tell, sir: you never can tell.[*He goes into the hotel*].

CRAMPTON [*his eyes shining hardly as he props his drawn miserable face on his hands*] Home! Home!! [*Hearing someone approaching he hastily sits bolt upright. It is Gloria, who has come up the steps alone, with her sunshade and her book in her hands. He looks defiantly at her, with the brutal obstinacy of his mouth and the wistfulness of his eyes contradicting each other pathetically. She comes to the corner of the garden seat and stands with her back to it, leaning against the end of it, and looking down at him as if wondering at his weakness: too curious about him to be cold, but supremely indifferent to their kinship. He greets her with a growl*]. Well?

GLORIA. I want to speak to you for a moment.

CRAMPTON [*looking steadily at her*] Indeed? Thats surprising. You meet your father after eighteen years; and you actually want to speak to him for a moment! Thats touching: isnt it?

GLORIA. All that is what seems to me so nonsensical, so uncalled for. What do you expect us to feel for you? to do for you? What is it you want? Why are you less civil to us than other people are? You are evidently not very fond of us: why should you be? But surely we can meet without quarrelling.

CRAMPTON [*a dreadful grey shade passing over his face*] Do you realize that I am your father?

GLORIA. Perfectly.

CRAMPTON. Do you know what is due to me as your father?

GLORIA. For instance—?

CRAMPTON [*rising as if to combat a monster*] For instance! For instance!! For instance, duty, affection, respect, obedience—

GLORIA [*quitting her careless leaning attitude and confronting him promptly and proudly*] I obey nothing but my sense of what is right. I respect nothing that is not noble. That is my duty. [*She adds, less firmly*] As to affection, it is not within my control. I am not sure that I quite know what affection means. [*She turns away with an evident distaste for that part of the subject, and goes to the luncheon table for a comfortable chair, putting down her book and sunshade*].

CRAMPTON [*following her with his eyes*] Do you really mean what you are saying?

GLORIA [*turning on him quickly and severely*] Excuse me: that is an uncivil question. I am speaking seriously to you; and I expect you to take me seriously. [*She takes one of the luncheon chairs; turns it away from the table; and sits down a little wearily, saying*] Can you not discuss this matter coolly and rationally?

CRAMPTON. Coolly and rationally! No I cant. Do you understand that? I cant.

667

GLORIA [*emphatically*] No. That I cannot understand. I have no sympathy with—

CRAMPTON [*shrinking nervously*] Stop! Dont say anything more yet: you dont know what youre doing. Do you want to drive me mad? [*She frowns, finding such petulance intolerable. He adds hastily*] No: I'm not angry: indeed I'm not. Wait, wait: give me a little time to think. [*He stands for a moment, screwing and clinching his brows and hands in his perplexity; then takes the end chair from the luncheon table and sits down beside her, saying, with a touching effort to be gentle and patient*] Now I think I have it. At least I'll try.

GLORIA [*firmly*] You see! Everything comes right if we only think it resolutely out.

CRAMPTON [*in sudden dread*] No: dont think. I want you to feel: thats the only thing that can help us. Listen! Do you —but first—I forgot. Whats your name? I mean your pet name. They cant very well call you Sophronia.

GLORIA [*with astonished disgust*] Sophronia! My name is Gloria. I am always called by it.

CRAMPTON [*his temper rising again*] Your name is Sophronia, girl: you were called after your aunt Sophronia, my sister: she gave you your first Bible with your name written in it.

GLORIA. Then my mother gave me a new name.

CRAMPTON [*angrily*] She had no right to do it. I will not allow this.

GLORIA. You had no right to give me your sister's name. I dont know her.

CRAMPTON. Youre talking nonsense. There are bounds to what I will put up with. I will not have it. Do you hear that?

GLORIA [*rising warningly*] Are you resolved to quarrel?

CRAMPTON [*terrified, pleading*] No, no: sit down. Sit down, wont you? [*She looks at him, keeping him in suspense. He forces himself to utter the obnoxious name*]. Gloria. [*She marks her satisfaction with a slight tightening of the lips, and sits down*]. There! You see I only want to shew you that I am your father, my—my dear child. [*The endearment is so plaintively inept that she smiles in spite of herself, and resigns herself to indulge him a little*]. Listen now. What I want to ask you is this. Dont you remember me at all? You were only a tiny child when you were taken away from me; but you took plenty of notice of things. Cant you remember someone whom you loved, or [*shyly*] at least liked in a childish way? Come! someone who let you stay in his study and look at his toy boats, as you thought them? [*He looks anxiously into her face for some response, and continues less hopefully and more urgently*] Someone who let you do as you liked there, and never said a word to you except to tell you that you must sit still and not speak? Someone who was something that no one else was to you—who was your father?

GLORIA [*unmoved*] If you describe things to me, no doubt I shall presently imagine that I remember them. But I really remember nothing.

CRAMPTON [*wistfully*] Has your mother never told you anything about me?

GLORIA. She has never mentioned your name to me. [*He groans involuntarily. She looks at him rather contemptuously, and continues*] Except once; and then she did remind me of something I had forgotten.

CRAMPTON [*looking up hopefully*] What was that?

GLORIA [*mercilessly*] The whip you bought to beat me with.

CRAMPTON [*gnashing his teeth*] Oh! To bring that up against me! To turn you from me! When you need never have known. [*Under a grinding, agonized breath*] Curse her!

GLORIA [*springing up*] You wretch! [*With intense emphasis*] You wretch!! You d a r e curse my mother!

CRAMPTON. Stop; or youll be sorry afterwards. I'm your father.

GLORIA. How I hate the name! How I love the name of mother! You had better go.

CRAMPTON. I—I'm choking. You want to kill me. Some —I—[*His voice stifles: he is almost in a fit*].

669

GLORIA [*going up to the balustrade with cool quick resource-fulness, and calling over it to the beach*] Mr Valentine!

VALENTINE [*answering from below*] Yes.

GLORIA. Come here for a moment, please. Mr Crampton wants you. [*She returns to the table and pours out a glass of water*].

CRAMPTON [*recovering his speech*] No: let me alone. I dont want him. I'm all right, I tell you. I need neither his help nor yours. [*He rises and pulls himself together*]. As you say, I had better go. [*He puts on his hat*]. Is that your last word?

GLORIA. I hope so.

He looks stubbornly at her for a moment; nods grimly, as if he agreed to that; and goes into the hotel. She looks at him with equal steadiness until he disappears, when, with a gesture of relief, she turns to Valentine, who comes running up the steps.

VALENTINE [*panting*] Whats the matter? [*Looking round*] Wheres Crampton?

GLORIA. Gone. [*Valentine's face lights up with sudden joy, dread, and mischief as he realizes that he is alone with Gloria. She continues indifferently*] I thought he was ill; but he recovered himself. He wouldnt wait for you. I am sorry. [*She goes for her book and parasol*].

VALENTINE. So much the better. He gets on my nerves after a while. [*Pretending to forget himself*] How could that man have so beautiful a daughter!

GLORIA [*taken aback for a moment; then answering him with polite but intentional contempt*] That seems to be an attempt at what is called a pretty speech. Let me say at once, Mr Valentine, that pretty speeches make very sickly conversation. Pray let us be friends, if we are to be friends, in a sensible and wholesome way. I have no intention of getting married; and unless you are content to accept that state of things, we had much better not cultivate each other's acquaintance.

VALENTINE [*cautiously*] I see. May I ask just this one question? Is your objection an objection to marriage as an institution, or merely an objection to marrying me personally?

GLORIA. I do not know you well enough, Mr Valentine,

to have any opinion on the subject of your personal merits. [*She turns away from him with infinite indifference, and sits down with her book on the garden seat*]. I do not think the conditions of marriage at present are such as any self-respecting woman can accept.

VALENTINE [*instantly changing his tone for one of cordial sincerity, as if he frankly accepted her terms and was delighted and reassured by her principles*] Oh, then thats a point of sympathy between us already. I q u i t e agree with you: the conditions are most unfair. [*He takes off his hat and throws it gaily on the iron table*]. No: what I want is to get rid of all that nonsense. [*He sits down beside her, so naturally that she does not think of objecting, and proceeds, with enthusiasm*] Dont you think it a horrible thing that a man and a woman can hardly know one another without being supposed to have designs of that kind? As if there were no other interests! no other subjects of conversation! As if women were capable of nothing better!

GLORIA [*interested*] Ah, now you are beginning to talk humanly and sensibly, Mr Valentine.

VALENTINE [*with a gleam in his eye at the success of his hunter's guile*] Of course! two intelligent people like us! Isnt it pleasant, in this stupid convention-ridden world, to meet with someone on the same plane? someone with an unprejudiced enlightened mind?

GLORIA [*earnestly*] I hope to meet many such people in England.

VALENTINE [*dubiously*] Hm! There are a good many people here: nearly forty millions. Theyre not all consumptive members of the highly educated classes like the people in Madeira.

GLORIA [*now full of her subject*] Oh, everybody is stupid and prejudiced in Madeira: weak sentimental creatures. I hate weakness; and I hate sentiment.

VALENTINE. Thats what makes you so inspiring.

GLORIA [*with a slight laugh*] Am I inspiring?

VALENTINE. Yes. Strength's infectious.

GLORIA. Weakness is, I know.

YOU NEVER CAN TELL

VALENTINE [*with conviction*] Youre strong. Do you know that you changed the world for me this morning? I was in the dumps, thinking of my unpaid rent, frightened about the future. When you came in, I was dazzled. [*Her brow clouds a little. He goes on quickly*] That was silly, of course; but really and truly something happened to me. Explain it how you will, my blood got—[*he hesitates, trying to think of a sufficiently unimpassioned word*]—oxygenated: my muscles braced; my mind cleared; my courage rose. Thats odd, isnt it? considering that I am not at all a sentimental man.

GLORIA [*uneasily, rising*] Let us go back to the beach.

VALENTINE [*darkly: looking up at her*] What! you feel it too?

GLORIA. Feel what?

VALENTINE. Dread.

GLORIA. Dread!

VALENTINE. As if something were going to happen. It came over me suddenly just before you proposed that we should run away to the others.

GLORIA [*amazed*] Thats strange: very strange! I had the same presentiment.

VALENTINE [*solemnly*] How extraordinary! [*Rising*] Well: shall we run away?

GLORIA. Run away! Oh no: that would be childish. [*She sits down again. He resumes his seat beside her, and watches her with a gravely sympathetic air. She is thoughtful and a little troubled as she adds*] I wonder what is the scientific explanation of those fancies that cross us occasionally!

VALENTINE. Ah, I wonder! It's a curiously helpless sensation: isnt it?

GLORIA [*rebelling against the word*] Helpless?

VALENTINE. Yes, helpless. As if Nature, after letting us belong to ourselves and do what we judged right and reasonable for all these years, were suddenly lifting her great hand to take us—her two little children—by the scruffs of our little necks, and use us, in spite of ourselves, for her own purposes, in her own way.

GLORIA. Isnt that rather fanciful?

VALENTINE [*with a new and startling transition to a tone of utter recklessness*] I dont know. I dont care. [*Bursting out reproachfully*] Oh, Miss Clandon, Miss Clandon: how could you?

GLORIA. What have I done?

VALENTINE. Thrown this enchantment on me. I'm honestly trying to be sensible and scientific and everything that you wish me to be. But—but—oh, dont you see what you have set to work in my imagination?

GLORIA. I hope you are not going to be so foolish—so vulgar—as to say love.

VALENTINE. No, no, no, no, no. Not love: we know better than that. Let's call it chemistry. You cant deny that there is such a thing as chemical action, chemical affinity, chemical combination: the most irresistible of all natural forces. Well, youre attracting me irresistibly. Chemically.

GLORIA [*contemptuously*] Nonsense!

VALENTINE. Of course it's nonsense, you stupid girl. [*Gloria recoils in outraged surprise*]. Yes, stupid girl: thats a scientific fact, anyhow. Youre a prig: a feminine prig: thats what you are. [*Rising*] Now I suppose youve done with me for ever. [*He goes to the iron table and takes up his hat*].

GLORIA [*with elaborate calm, sitting up like a High-school-mistress posing to be photographed*]. That shews how very little you understand my real character. I am not in the least offended. [*He pauses and puts his hat down again*]. I am always willing to be told my own defects, Mr Valentine, by my friends, even when they are as absurdly mistaken about me as you are. I have many faults—very serious faults—of character and temper; but if there is one thing that I am not, it is what you call a prig. [*She closes her lips trimly and looks steadily and challengingly at him as she sits more collectedly than ever*].

VALENTINE [*returning to the end of the garden seat to confront her more emphatically*] Oh yes, you are. My reason tells

673

me so: my knowledge tells me so: my experience tells me so.

GLORIA. Excuse my reminding you that your reason and your knowledge and your experience are not infallible. At least I hope not.

VALENTINE. I must believe them. Unless you wish me to believe my eyes, my heart, my instincts, my imagination, which are all telling me the most monstrous lies about you.

GLORIA [*the collectedness beginning to relax*] Lies!

VALENTINE [*obstinately*] Yes, lies. [*He sits down again beside her*]. Do you expect me to believe that you are the most beautiful woman in the world?

GLORIA. That is ridiculous, and rather personal.

VALENTINE. Of course it's ridiculous. Well, thats what my eyes tell me. [*Gloria makes a movement of contemptuous protest*]. No: I'm not flattering. I tell you I dont believe it. [*She is ashamed to find that this does not quite please her either*]. Do you think that if you were to turn away in disgust from my weakness, I should sit down here and cry like a child?

GLORIA [*beginning to find that she must speak shortly and pointedly to keep her voice steady*] Why should you, pray?

VALENTINE. Of course not: I'm not such an idiot. And yet my heart tells me I should: my fool of a heart. But I'll argue with my heart and bring it to reason. If I loved you a thousand times, I'll force myself to look the truth steadily in the face. After all, it's easy to be sensible: the facts are the facts. Whats this place? it's not heaven: it's the Marine Hotel. Whats the time? it's not eternity: it's about half past one in the afternoon. What am I? a dentist: a five shilling dentist!

GLORIA. And I am a feminine prig.

VALENTINE [*passionately*] No, no: I cant face that: I must have one illusion left: the illusion about you. I love you. [*He turns towards her as if the impulse to touch her were ungovernable: she rises and stands on her guard wrathfully. He springs up impatiently and retreats a step*]. Oh, what a fool I am! an idiot! You dont understand: I might as well talk to the stones on the beach. [*He turns away, discouraged*].

GLORIA [*reassured by his withdrawal, and a little remorse-*

674

ful] I am sorry. I do not mean to be unsympathetic, Mr Valentine; but what can I say?

VALENTINE [*returning to her with all his recklessness of manner replaced by an engaging and chivalrous respect*] You can say nothing, Miss Clandon. I beg your pardon: it was my own fault, or rather my own bad luck. You see, it all depended on your naturally liking me. [*She is about to speak: he stops her deprecatingly*] Oh, I know you musnt tell me whether you like me or not; but—

GLORIA [*her principles up in arms at once*] Must not! Why not? I am a free woman: why should I not tell you?

VALENTINE [*pleading in terror, and retreating*] Dont. I'm afraid to hear.

GLORIA [*no longer scornful*] You need not be afraid. I think you are sentimental, and a little foolish; but I like you.

VALENTINE [*dropping into the nearest chair as if crushed*] Then it's all over. [*He becomes the picture of despair*].

GLORIA [*puzzled, approaching him*] But why?

VALENTINE. Because liking is not enough. Now that I think down into it seriously, I dont know whether I like you or not.

GLORIA [*looking down at him with wondering concern*] I'm sorry.

VALENTINE [*in an agony of restrained passion*] Oh, dont pity me. Your voice is tearing my heart to pieces. Let me alone, Gloria. You go down into the very depths of me, troubling and stirring me. I cant struggle with it. I cant tell you—

GLORIA [*breaking down suddenly*] Oh, stop telling me what you feel: I cant bear it.

VALENTINE [*springing up triumphantly, the agonized voice now solid, ringing, and jubilant*] Ah, it's come at last: my moment of courage. [*He seizes her hands: she looks at him in terror*]. Our moment of courage! [*He draws her to him; kisses her with impetuous strength; and laughs boyishly*]. Now youve done it, Gloria. It's all over: we're in love with one another. [*She can only gasp at him*]. But what a dragon you were! And how hideously afraid I was!

PHILIP'S VOICE [*calling from the beach*] Valentine!

DOLLY'S VOICE. Mr Valentine!

VALENTINE. Goodbye. Forgive me. [*He rapidly kisses her hands, and runs away to the steps, where he meets Mrs Clandon ascending*].

Gloria, quite lost, can only stare after him.

MRS CLANDON. The children want you, Mr Valentine. [*She looks anxiously round*]. Is he gone?

VALENTINE [*puzzled*] He? [*Recollecting*] Oh, Crampton. Gone this long time, Mrs Clandon. [*He runs off buoyantly down the steps*].

GLORIA [*sinking upon the bench*] Mother!

MRS CLANDON [*hurrying to her in alarm*] What is it, dear?

GLORIA [*with heartfelt appealing reproach*] Why didnt you educate me properly?

MRS CLANDON [*amazed*] My child: I did my best.

GLORIA. Oh, you taught me nothing: n o t h i n g.

MRS CLANDON. What is the matter with you?

GLORIA [*with the most intense expression*] Only shame! shame!! shame!!! [*Blushing unendurably, she covers her face with her hands and turns away from her mother*].

ACT III

THE Clandons' sitting room in the hotel. An expensive apartment on the ground floor, with a French window leading to the gardens. In the centre of the room is a substantial table, surrounded by chairs, and draped with a maroon cloth on which opulently bound hotel and railway guides are displayed. A visitor entering through the window and coming down to this central table would have the fireplace on his left, and a writing table against the wall on his right, next the door, which is further down. He would, if his taste lay that way, admire the wall decoration of Lincrusta Walton in plum color and bronze lacquer, with dado and cornice; the ormolu consoles in the corners; the vases on pillar pedestals of veined marble with bases of polished black wood, one on each side of the window; the ornamental cabinet next the vase on the side nearest the fireplace, its centre compartment closed by an inlaid door, and its corners rounded off with curved panes of glass protecting shelves of cheap blue and white pottery; the bamboo tea table, with folding shelves, in the corresponding space on the other side of the window; the photogravures after Burton and Stacy Marks; the saddlebag ottoman in line with the door but on the other side of the room; the two comfortable seats of the same pattern on the hearth-rug; and finally, on turning round and looking up, the massive brass pole above the window, sustaining a pair of maroon rep curtains with decorated borders of staid green. Altogether, a room well arranged to flatter the middle-class occupant's sense of gentility, and reconcile him to a charge of a pound a day for its use.

Mrs Clandon sits at the writing table, correcting proofs. Gloria is standing at the window, looking out in a tormented revery.

The clock on the mantelpiece strikes five with a sickly clink, the bell being unable to bear up against the black marble cenotaph in which it is immured.

MRS CLANDON. Five! I dont think we need wait any longer for the children. They are sure to get tea somewhere.

GLORIA [wearily] Shall I ring?

MRS CLANDON. Do, my dear. [Gloria goes to the hearth

and rings]. I have finished these proofs at last, thank good-ness!

GLORIA [*strolling listlessly across the room and coming behind her mother's chair*] What proofs?

MRS CLANDON. The new edition of Twentieth Century Women.

GLORIA [*with a bitter smile*] Theres a chapter missing.

MRS CLANDON [*beginning to hunt among her proofs*] Is there? Surely not.

GLORIA. I mean an unwritten one. Perhaps I shall write it for you—when I know the end of it. [*She goes back to the window*].

MRS CLANDON. Gloria! More enigmas!

GLORIA. Oh no. The same enigma.

MRS CLANDON [*puzzled and rather troubled; after watching her for a moment*] My dear?

GLORIA [*returning*] Yes.

MRS CLANDON. You know I never ask questions.

GLORIA [*kneeling beside her chair*] I know. I know. [*She suddenly throws her arm about her mother and embraces her almost passionately*].

MRS CLANDON [*gently, smiling but embarrassed*] My dear, you are getting quite sentimental.

GLORIA [*recoiling*] Ah no, no. Oh, dont say that. Oh! [*She rises and turns away with a gesture as if tearing herself*].

MRS CLANDON [*mildly*] My dear: what is the matter? What—

The waiter enters with the tea-tray.

WAITER [*balmily*] Was this what you rang for, maam?

MRS CLANDON. Thank you, yes. [*She turns her chair away from the writing table, and sits down again. Gloria crosses to the hearth and sits crouching there with her face averted*].

WAITER [*placing the tray temporarily on the centre table*] I thought so, maam. Curious how the nerves seem to give out in the afternoon without a cup of tea. [*He fetches the tea table and places it in front of Mrs Clandon, conversing meanwhile*]. The young lady and gentleman have just come back, maam:

678

they have been out in a boat, maam. Very pleasant on a fine afternoon like this: very pleasant and invigorating indeed. [*He takes the tray from the centre table and puts it on the tea table*]. Mr M'Comas will not come to tea, maam: he has gone to call upon Mr Crampton. [*He takes a couple of chairs and sets one at each end of the tea table*].

GLORIA [*looking round with an impulse of terror*] And the other gentleman?

WAITER [*reassuringly, as he unconsciously drops for a moment into the measure of "Ive been roaming," which he sang when a boy*] Oh, he's coming, miss: he's coming. He has been rowing the boat, miss, and has just run down the road to the chemist's for something to put on the blisters. But he will be here directly, miss: directly. [*Gloria, in ungovernable apprehension, rises and hurries towards the door*].

MRS CLANDON [*half rising*] Glo—

Gloria goes out. Mrs Clandon looks perplexedly at the waiter, whose composure is unruffled.

WAITER [*cheerfully*] Anything more, maam?

MRS CLANDON. Nothing, thank you.

WAITER. Thank you, maam. [*As he withdraws, Phil and Dolly, in the highest spirits, come tearing in. He holds the door open for them: then goes out and closes it*].

DOLLY [*ravenously*] Oh, give me some tea. [*Mrs Clandon pours out a cup for her*]. Weve been out in a boat. Valentine will be here presently.

PHILIP. He is unaccustomed to navigation. Wheres Gloria?

MRS CLANDON [*anxiously, as she pours out his tea*] Phil: there is something the matter with Gloria. Has anything happened? [*Phil and Dolly look at one another and stifle a laugh*]. What is it?

PHILIP [*sitting down on her left*] Romeo—

DOLLY [*sitting down on her right*]—and Juliet.

PHILIP [*taking his cup of tea from Mrs Clandon*] Yes, my dear mother: the old, old story. Dolly: dont take all the milk [*he deftly takes the jug from her*]. Yes: in the spring—

DOLLY. —a young man's fancy—

PHILIP. —lightly turns to— thank you [*to Mrs Clandon, who has passed the biscuits*] —thoughts of love. It also occurs in the autumn. The young man in this case is—

DOLLY. Valentine.

PHILIP. And his fancy has turned to Gloria to the extent of—

DOLLY. —kissing her—

PHILIP. —on the terrace—

DOLLY [*correcting him*] —on the lips, before everybody.

MRS CLANDON [*incredulously*] Phil! Dolly! Are you joking? [*They shake their heads*]. Did she allow it?

PHILIP. We waited to see him struck to earth by the lightning of her scorn; but—

DOLLY. —but he wasnt.

PHILIP. She appeared to like it.

DOLLY. As far as we could judge. [*Stopping Phil, who is about to pour out another cup*] No: youve sworn off two cups.

MRS CLANDON [*much troubled*] Children: you must not be here when Mr Valentine comes. I must speak very seriously to him about this.

PHILIP. To ask him his intentions? What a violation of Twentieth Century principles!

DOLLY. Quite right, mamma: bring him to book. Make the most of the nineteenth century while it lasts.

PHILIP. Sh! Here he is.

VALENTINE [*entering*] Very sorry to be late, Mrs Clandon. [*She takes up the tea-pot*]. No, thank you: I never take any. No doubt Miss Dolly and Phil have explained what happened to me.

PHILIP [*momentously, rising*] Yes, Valentine: we have explained.

DOLLY [*significantly, also rising*] We have explained very thoroughly.

PHILIP. It was our duty. [*Very seriously*] Come, Dolly. [*He offers Dolly his arm, which she takes. They look sadly at him, and go out gravely arm in arm, leaving Valentine staring*].

MRS CLANDON [*rising and leaving the tea table*] Will you sit down, Mr Valentine. I want to speak to you a little, if you will allow me. [*Valentine goes slowly to the ottoman, his conscience presaging a bad quarter of an hour. Mrs Clandon takes Phil's chair, and seats herself with gentle dignity. Valentine sits down*]. I must begin by throwing myself somewhat on your consideration. I am going to speak of a subject of which I know very little: perhaps nothing. I mean love.

VALENTINE. Love!

MRS CLANDON. Yes, love. Oh, you need not look so alarmed as that, Mr Valentine: I am not in love with you.

VALENTINE [*overwhelmed*] Oh, really, Mrs—[*Recovering himself*] I should be only too proud if you were.

MRS CLANDON. Thank you, Mr Valentine. But I am too old to begin.

VALENTINE. Begin! Have you never—?

MRS CLANDON. Never. My case is a very common one, Mr Valentine. I married before I was old enough to know what I was doing. As you have seen for yourself, the result was a bitter disappointment for both my husband and myself. So you see, though I am a married woman, I have never been in love; I have never had a love affair; and, to be quite frank with you Mr Valentine, what I have seen of the love affairs of other people has not led me to regret that deficiency in my experience. [*Valentine, looking very glum, glances sceptically at her, and says nothing. Her color rises a little; and she adds, with restrained anger*] You do not believe me?

VALENTINE [*confused at having his thought read*] Oh, why not? Why not?

MRS CLANDON. Let me tell you, Mr Valentine, that a life devoted to the Cause of Humanity has enthusiasms and passions to offer which far transcend the selfish personal infatuations and sentimentalities of romance. Those are not your enthusiasms and passions, I take it? [*Valentine, quite aware that she despises him for it, answers in the negative with a melancholy shake of his head*]. I thought not. Well, I am equally at a disadvantage in discussing those so-called affairs

681

of the heart in which you appear to be an expert.

VALENTINE [*restlessly*] What are you driving at, Mrs Clandon?

MRS CLANDON. I think you know.

VALENTINE. Gloria?

MRS CLANDON. Yes. Gloria.

VALENTINE [*surrendering*] Well, yes: I'm in love with Gloria. [*Interposing as she is about to speak*] I know what youre going to say: Ive no money.

MRS CLANDON. I care very little about money, Mr Valentine.

VALENTINE. Then youre very different to all the other mothers who have interviewed me.

MRS CLANDON. Ah, now we are coming to it, Mr Valentine. You are an old hand at this. [*He opens his mouth to protest: she cuts him short with some indignation*]. Oh, do you think, little as I understand these matters, that I have not common sense enough to know that a man who could make as much way in one interview with such a woman as my daughter, can hardly be a novice?

VALENTINE. I assure you—

MRS CLANDON [*stopping him*] I am not blaming you, Mr Valentine. It is Gloria's business to take care of herself; and you have a right to amuse yourself as you please. But—

VALENTINE [*protesting*] Amuse myself! Oh, Mrs Clandon!

MRS CLANDON [*relentlessly*] On your honor, Mr Valentine, are you in earnest?

VALENTINE [*desperately*] On my honor I am in earnest. [*She looks searchingly at him. His sense of humor gets the better of him; and he adds quaintly*] Only, I always have been in earnest; and yet—! Well, here I am, you see.

MRS CLANDON. This is just what I suspected. [*Severely*] Mr Valentine: you are one of those men who play with women's affections.

VALENTINE. Well, why not, if the Cause of Humanity is the only thing worth being serious about? However, I understand. [*Rising and taking his hat with formal politeness*]

682

You wish me to discontinue my visits.

MRS CLANDON. No: I am sensible enough to be well aware that Gloria's best chance of escape from you now is to become better acquainted with you.

VALENTINE [*unaffectedly alarmed*] Oh, dont say that, Mrs Clandon. You dont think that, do you?

MRS CLANDON. I have great faith, Mr Valentine, in the sound training Gloria's mind has had since she was a child.

VALENTINE [*amazingly relieved*] O-oh! Oh, thats all right. [*He sits down again and throws his hat flippantly aside with the air of a man who has no longer anything to fear*].

MRS CLANDON [*indignant at his assurance*] What do you mean?

VALENTINE [*turning confidentially to her*] Come! shall I teach you something, Mrs Clandon?

MRS CLANDON [*stiffly*] I am always willing to learn.

VALENTINE. Have you ever studied the subject of gunnery? artillery? cannons and war-ships and so on?

MRS CLANDON. Has gunnery anything to do with Gloria?

VALENTINE. A great deal. By way of illustration. During this whole century, my dear Mrs Clandon, the progress of artillery has been a duel between the maker of cannons and the maker of armor plates to keep the cannon balls out. You build a ship proof against the best gun known: somebody makes a better gun and sinks your ship. You build a heavier ship, proof against that gun: somebody makes a heavier gun and sinks you again. And so on. Well, the duel of sex is just like that.

MRS CLANDON. The duel of sex!

VALENTINE. Yes: youve heard of the duel of sex, havnt you? Oh, I forgot: youve been in Madeira: the expression has come up since your time. Need I explain it?

MRS CLANDON [*contemptuously*] No.

VALENTINE. Of course not. Now what happens in the duel of sex? The old fashioned daughter received an old fashioned education to protect her against the wiles of man. Well, you know the result: the old fashioned man got round her. The old fashioned mother resolved to protect her daughter more effectually—to find some armor too strong for the old fashioned man. So she gave her daughter a scientific education: your plan. That was a corker for the old fashioned man: he thought it unfair, and tried to howl it down as unwomanly and all the rest of it. But that didnt do him any good. So he had to give up his old fashioned plan of attack: you know: going down on his knees and swearing to love, honor, and obey and so on.

MRS CLANDON. Excuse me: that was what the woman swore.

VALENTINE. Was it? Ah, perhaps youre right. Yes: of course it was. Well, what did the man do? Just what the artillery man does: went one better than the woman: educated himself scientifically and beat her at that game just as he had beaten her at the old game. I learnt how to circumvent the Women's Rights woman before I was twenty-three: it's all been found out long ago. You see, my methods are thoroughly modern.

MRS CLANDON [*with quiet disgust*] No doubt.

VALENTINE. But for that very reason theres one sort of girl against whom they are of no use.

MRS CLANDON. Pray which sort?

VALENTINE. The thoroughly old fashioned girl. If you had brought up Gloria in the old way, it would have taken me eighteen months to get to the point I got to this afternoon in eighteen minutes. Yes, Mrs Clandon: the Higher Education of Women delivered Gloria into my hands; and it was you who taught her to believe in the Higher Education of Women.

MRS CLANDON [*rising*] Mr Valentine: you are very clever.

VALENTINE [*rising also*] Oh, Mrs Clandon!

MRS CLANDON. And you have taught me—nothing. Goodbye.

VALENTINE [*horrified*] Goodbye! Oh, maynt I see her before I go?

MRS CLANDON. I am afraid she will not return until you
684

have gone, Mr Valentine. She left the room expressly to avoid you.

VALENTINE [*thoughtfully*] Thats a good sign. Goodbye. [*He bows and makes for the door, apparently well satisfied*].

MRS CLANDON [*alarmed*] Why do you think it a good sign?

VALENTINE [*turning near the door*] Because I am mortally afraid of her; and it looks as if she were mortally afraid of me.

He turns to go and finds himself face to face with Gloria, who has just entered. She looks steadfastly at him. He stares helplessly at her; then round at Mrs Clandon; then at Gloria again, completely at a loss.

GLORIA [*white, and controlling herself with difficulty*] Mother: is what Dolly told me true?

MRS CLANDON. What did she tell you, dear?

GLORIA. That you have been speaking about me to this gentleman?

VALENTINE [*murmuring*] This gentleman! Oh!

MRS CLANDON [*sharply*] Mr Valentine: can you hold your tongue for a moment?

He looks piteously at them; then, with a despairing shrug, goes back to the ottoman and throws his hat on it.

GLORIA [*confronting her mother, with deep reproach*] Mother: what right had you to do it?

MRS CLANDON. I dont think I have said anything I have no right to say, Gloria.

VALENTINE [*confirming her officiously*] Nothing. Nothing whatever. [*The two women look at him crushingly*]. I beg your pardon. [*He sits down ignominiously on the ottoman*].

GLORIA. I cannot believe that anyone has any right even to think about things that concern me only. [*She turns away from them to conceal a painful struggle with her emotion*].

MRS CLANDON. My dear: if I have wounded your pride—

GLORIA [*turning on them for a moment*] My pride! My pride! Oh, it's gone: I have learnt now that I have no strength to be proud of. [*Turning away again*] But if a woman cannot protect herself, no one can protect her. No one has any right to try: not even her mother. I know I

585

have lost your confidence, just as I have lost this man's respect;—[*She stops to regain command of her voice*].

VALENTINE. This man! Oh!

MRS CLANDON. Pray be silent, sir.

GLORIA [*continuing*] —but I have at least the right to be left alone in my disgrace. I am one of those weak creatures born to be mastered by the first man whose eye is caught by them; and I must fulfil my destiny, I suppose. At least spare me the humiliation of trying to save me. [*She sits down, with her handkerchief to her eyes, at the further end of the table*].

VALENTINE [*jumping up*] Look here—

MRS CLANDON [*severely*] Mr Va—

VALENTINE [*recklessly*] No: I will speak: Ive been silent for nearly thirty seconds. [*He goes resolutely to Gloria*]. Miss Clandon—

GLORIA [*bitterly*] Oh, not Miss Clandon: you have found it quite safe to call me Gloria.

VALENTINE. No I wont: youll throw it in my teeth afterwards and accuse me of disrespect. I say it's a heartbreaking falsehood that I dont respect you. It's true that I didnt respect your old pride: why should I? it was nothing but cowardice. I didnt respect your intellect: Ive a better one myself: it's a masculine speciality. But when the depths stirred! when my moment came! when you made me brave! ah, then! then!! then!!!

GLORIA. Then you respected me, I suppose.

VALENTINE. No I didnt: I adored you. [*She rises quickly and turns her back on him*]. And you can never take that moment away from me. So now I dont care what happens. [*He comes back to the ottoman, addressing a cheerful explanation to nobody in particular*] I'm perfectly aware that I'm talking nonsense. I cant help it. [*To Mrs Clandon*] I love Gloria; and theres an end of it.

MRS CLANDON [*emphatically*] Mr Valentine: you are a most dangerous man. Gloria: come here. [*Gloria, wondering a little at the command, obeys, and stands, with drooping head, on her mother's right hand, Valentine being on the opposite side.*

Mrs Clandon then begins, with intense scorn] Ask this man whom you have inspired and made brave, how many women have inspired him before [*Gloria looks up suddenly with a flash of jealous anger and amazement*]; how many times he has laid the trap in which he has caught you; how often he has baited it with the same speeches; how much practice it has taken to make him perfect in his chosen part in life as the Duellist of Sex.

VALENTINE. This isnt fair. Youre abusing my confidence, Mrs Clandon.

MRS CLANDON. Ask him, Gloria.

GLORIA [*in a flush of rage, going over to him with her fists clenched*] Is that true?

VALENTINE. Dont be angry—

GLORIA [*interrupting him implacably*] Is it true? Did you ever say that before? Did you ever feel that before? for another woman?

VALENTINE [*bluntly*] Yes.

Gloria raises her clenched hands.

MRS CLANDON [*horrified, catching her uplifted arm*] Gloria!! My dear! Youre forgetting yourself.

Gloria, with a deep expiration, slowly relaxes her threatening attitude.

VALENTINE. Remember: a man's power of love and admiration is like any other of his powers: he has to throw it away many times before he learns what is really worthy of it.

MRS CLANDON. Another of the old speeches, Gloria. Take care.

VALENTINE [*remonstrating*] Oh!

GLORIA [*to Mrs Clandon, with contemptuous self-possession*] Do you think I need to be warned now? [*To Valentine*] You have tried to make me love you.

VALENTINE. I have.

GLORIA. Well, you have succeeded in making me hate you: passionately.

VALENTINE [*philosophically*] It's surprising how little difference there is between the two. [*Gloria turns indignantly away from him. He continues, to Mrs Clandon*] I know men whose wives love them; and they go on exactly like that.

MRS CLANDON. Excuse me, Mr Valentine; but had you not better go?

GLORIA. You need not send him away on my account, mother. He is nothing to me now; and he will amuse Dolly and Phil. [*She sits down with slighting indifference, at the end of the table nearest the window*].

VALENTINE [*gaily*] Of course: thats the sensible way of looking at it. Come, Mrs Clandon! you cant quarrel with a mere butterfly like me!

MRS CLANDON. I very greatly mistrust you, Mr Valentine. But I do not like to think that your unfortunate levity of disposition is mere shamelessness and worthlessness;—

GLORIA [*to herself, but aloud*] It is shameless; and it is worthless.

MRS CLANDON [*continuing*] so perhaps we had better send for Phil and Dolly, and allow you to end your visit in the ordinary way.

VALENTINE [*as if she had paid him the highest compliment*] You overwhelm me, Mrs Clandon. Thank you.

The waiter returns.

WAITER. Mr M'Comas, maam.

MRS CLANDON. Oh, certainly. Bring him in.

WAITER. He wishes to see you in the reception-room, maam.

MRS CLANDON. Why not here?

WAITER. Well, if you will excuse my mentioning it, maam, I think Mr M'Comas feels that he would get fairer play if he could speak to you away from the younger members of your family, maam.

MRS CLANDON. Tell him they are not here.

WAITER. They are within sight of the door, maam; and very watchful, for some reason or other.

MRS CLANDON [*going*] Oh, very well: I'll go to him.

WAITER [*holding the door open for her*] Thank you, maam. [*She goes out. He comes back into the room, and meets the eye of*

688

YOU NEVER CAN TELL

Valentine, who wants him to go]. All right, sir. Only the tea-things, sir. [*Taking the tray*] Excuse me, sir. Thank you, sir. [*He goes out*].

VALENTINE [*to Gloria*] Look here. Youll forgive me, sooner or later. Forgive me now.

GLORIA [*rising to level the declaration more intensely at him*] Never! While grass grows or water runs, never! never!! never!!!

VALENTINE [*unabashed*] Well, I dont care. I cant be unhappy about anything. I shall never be unhappy again, never, never, never, while grass grows or water runs. The thought of you will always make me wild with joy. [*Some quick taunt is on her lips: he interposes swiftly*] No: I never said that before: thats new.

GLORIA. It will not be new when you say it to the next woman.

VALENTINE. Oh dont, Gloria, dont. [*He kneels at her feet*].

GLORIA. Get up! Get up! How dare you?

Phil and Dolly, racing, as usual, for first place, burst into the room. They check themselves on seeing what is passing. Valentine springs up.

PHILIP [*discreetly*] I beg your pardon. Come, Dolly. [*He offers her his arm and turns to go*].

GLORIA [*annoyed*] Mother will be back in a moment, Phil. [*Severely*] Please wait here for her. [*She turns away to the window, where she stands looking out with her back to them*].

PHILIP [*significantly*] Oh, indeed. Hmhm!

DOLLY. Ahah!

PHILIP. You seem in excellent spirits, Valentine.

VALENTINE. I am. [*He comes between them*]. Now look here. You both know whats going on: dont you?

Gloria turns quickly, as if anticipating some fresh outrage.

DOLLY. Perfectly.

VALENTINE. Well, it's all over. Ive been refused. Scorned. I'm here on sufferance only. You understand? it's all over. Your sister is in no sense entertaining my addresses, or condescending to interest herself in me in any way. [*Gloria,*

689

satisfied, turns back contemptuously to the window]. Is that clear?

DOLLY. Serve you right. You were in too great a hurry.

PHILIP [*patting him on the shoulder*] Never mind: youd never have been able to call your soul your own if she'd married you. You can now begin a new chapter in your life.

DOLLY. Chapter seventeen or thereabouts, I should imagine.

VALENTINE [*much put out by this pleasantry*] No: dont say things like that. Thats just the sort of thoughtless remark that makes a lot of mischief.

DOLLY. Oh, indeed? Hmhm!

PHILIP. Ahah! [*He goes to the hearth and plants himself there in his best head-of-the-family attitude*].

M'Comas, looking very serious, comes in quickly with Mrs Clandon, whose first anxiety is about Gloria. She looks round to see where she is, and is going to join her at the window when Gloria comes down to meet her with a marked air of trust and affection. Finally Mrs Clandon takes her former seat, and Gloria posts herself behind it. M'Comas, on his way to the ottoman, is hailed by Dolly.

DOLLY. What cheer, Finch?

M'COMAS [*sternly*] Very serious news from your father, Miss Clandon. Very serious news indeed. [*He passes impressively to the ottoman, and sits down*].

Dolly, duly impressed, follows and sits beside him on his right.

VALENTINE. Perhaps I had better go.

M'COMAS. By no means, Mr Valentine. You are deeply concerned in this. [*Valentine takes a chair from the table and sits astride of it, leaning over the back, near the ottoman*]. Mrs Clandon: your husband demands the custody of his two younger children, who are not of age.

MRS CLANDON [*in quick alarm*] To take Dolly from me?

DOLLY [*touched*] But how nice of him! He likes us, mamma.

M'COMAS. I am sorry to have to disabuse you of any such illusion, Miss Dorothea.

DOLLY [*cooing ecstatically*] Dorothee-ee-ee-a! [*Nestling*

690

against his shoulder, quite overcome]. Oh, Finch!

M'COMAS [*nervously, shrinking away*] No, no, no, no!

MRS CLANDON. The deed of separation gives me the custody of the children.

M'COMAS. It also contains a covenant that you are not to approach or molest him in any way.

MRS CLANDON. Well: have I done so?

M'COMAS. Whether the behavior of your younger children amounts to legal molestation is a question on which it may be necessary to take counsel's opinion. At all events, Mr Crampton not only claims to have been molested; but he believes that he was brought here by a plot in which Mr Valentine acted as your agent.

VALENTINE. Whats that? Eh?

M'COMAS. He alleges that you drugged him, Mr Valentine.

VALENTINE. So I did.

M'COMAS. But what did you do that for?

DOLLY. Five shillings extra.

M'COMAS [*to Dolly, short-temperedly*] I must really ask you, Miss Clandon, not to interrupt this very serious conversation with irrelevant interjections. [*Vehemently*] I insist on having earnest matters earnestly and reverently discussed. [*This outburst produces an apologetic silence, and puts M'Comas himself out of countenance. He coughs, and starts afresh, addressing himself to Gloria*]. Miss Clandon: it is my duty to tell you that your father has also persuaded himself that Mr Valentine wishes to marry you—

VALENTINE [*interposing adroitly*] I do.

M'COMAS [*huffily*] In that case, sir, you must not be surprised to find yourself regarded by the young lady's father as a fortune hunter.

VALENTINE. So I am. Do you expect my wife to live on what I earn? tenpence a week!

M'COMAS [*revolted*] I have nothing more to say, sir. I shall return and tell Mr Crampton that this family is no place for a father. [*He makes for the door*].

691

MRS CLANDON [*with quiet authority*] Finch! [*He halts*]. If Mr Valentine cannot be serious, you can. Sit down. [*M'Comas, after a brief struggle between his dignity and his friendship, succumbs, seating himself this time midway between Dolly and Mrs Clandon*]. You know that all this is a made up case—that Fergus does not believe in it any more than you do. Now give me your real advice: your sincere, friendly advice. You know I have always trusted your judgment. I promise you the children will be quiet.

M'COMAS [*resigning himself*] Well, well! What I want to say is this. In the old arrangement with your husband, Mrs Clandon, you had him at a terrible disadvantage.

MRS CLANDON. How so, pray?

M'COMAS. Well, you were an advanced woman, accustomed to defy public opinion, and with no regard for what the world might say of you.

MRS CLANDON [*proud of it*] Yes: that is true.

Gloria, behind the chair, stoops and kisses her mother's hair, a demonstration which disconcerts her extremely.

M'COMAS. On the other hand, Mrs Clandon, your husband had a great horror of anything getting into the papers. There was his business to be considered, as well as the prejudices of an old fashioned family.

MRS CLANDON. Not to mention his own prejudices.

M'COMAS. Now no doubt he behaved badly, Mrs Clandon.

MRS CLANDON [*scornfully*] No doubt.

M'COMAS. But was it altogether his fault?

MRS CLANDON. Was it mine?

M'COMAS [*hastily*] No. Of course not.

GLORIA [*observing him attentively*] You do not mean that, Mr M'Comas.

M'COMAS. My dear young lady, you pick me up very sharply. But let me just put this to you. When a man makes an unsuitable marriage (nobody's fault, you know, but purely accidental incompatibility of tastes); when he is deprived by that misfortune of the domestic sympathy which,

692

I take it, is what a man marries for; when, in short, his wife
is rather worse than no wife at all (through no fault of her
own, of course), is it to be wondered at if he makes matters
worse at first by blaming her, and even, in his desperation,
by occasionally drinking himself into a violent condition or
seeking sympathy elsewhere?

MRS CLANDON. I did not blame him: I simply rescued
myself and the children from him.

M'COMAS. Yes; but you made hard terms, Mrs Clandon.
You had him at your mercy: you brought him to his knees
when you threatened to make the matter public by applying
to the Courts for a judicial separation. Suppose he had
had that power over you, and used it to take your children
away from you and bring them up in ignorance of your very
name, how would you feel? what would you do? Well, wont
you make some allowance for his feelings? in common
humanity.

MRS CLANDON. I never discovered his feelings. I discovered his temper, and his—[*she shivers*] the rest of his common humanity.

M'COMAS [*wistfully*]Women can be very hard, Mrs Clandon.

VALENTINE. Thats true.

GLORIA [*angrily*] Be silent. [*He subsides*].

M'COMAS [*rallying all his forces*] Let me make one last appeal. Mrs Clandon: believe me, there are men who have a
good deal of feeling, and kind feeling too, which they are not
able to express. What you miss in Crampton is that mere
veneer of civilization, the art of shewing worthless atten-
tions and paying insincere compliments in a kindly charming way. If you lived in London, where the whole system is
one of false good-fellowship, and you may know a man for
twenty years without finding out that he hates you like poison,
you would soon have your eyes opened. There we do unkind
things in a kind way: we say bitter things in a sweet voice:
we always give our friends chloroform when we tear them to
pieces. But think of the other side of it! Think of the people

who do kind things in an unkind way! people whose touch
hurts, whose voices jar, whose tempers play them false, who
wound and worry the people they love in the very act of trying to conciliate them, and who yet need affection as much
as the rest of us. Crampton has an abominable temper, I
admit. He has no manners, no tact, no grace. He'll never
be able to gain anyone's affection unless they will take his
desire for it on trust. Is he to have none? not even pity?
from his own flesh and blood?

DOLLY [*quite melted*] Oh how beautiful, Finch! How nice
of you!

PHILIP [*with conviction*] Finch: this is eloquence: positive eloquence.

DOLLY. Oh mamma, let us give him another chance. Let
us have him to dinner.

MRS CLANDON [*unmoved*] No, Dolly: I hardly got any
lunch. My dear Finch: there is not the least use in talking to
me about Fergus. You have never been married to him: I
have.

M'COMAS [*to Gloria*] Miss Clandon: I have hitherto refrained from appealing to you, because, if what Mr Crampton told me be true, you have been more merciless even than
your mother.

GLORIA [*defiantly*] You appeal from her strength to my
weakness!

M'COMAS. Not your weakness, Miss Clandon. I appeal
from her intellect to your heart.

GLORIA. I have learnt to mistrust my heart. [*With an
angry glance at Valentine*] I would tear my heart out and
throw it away if I could. My answer to you is my mother's
answer.

M'COMAS [*defeated*] Well, I am sorry. Very sorry. I have
done my best. [*He rises and prepares to go, deeply dissatisfied*].

MRS CLANDON. But what did you expect, Finch? What do
you want us to do?

M'COMAS. The first step for both you and Crampton is to
694

obtain counsel's opinion as to whether he is bound by the deed of separation or not. Now why not obtain this opinion at once, and have a friendly meeting [*her face hardens*] or shall we say a neutral meeting? to settle the difficulty? Here? In this hotel? To-night? What do you say?

MRS CLANDON. But where is the counsel's opinion to come from?

M'COMAS. It has dropped down on us out of the clouds. On my way back here from Crampton's I met a most eminent Q.C.: a man whom I briefed in the case that made his name for him. He has come down here from Saturday to Monday for the sea air, and to visit a relative of his who lives here. He has been good enough to say that if I can arrange a meeting of the parties he will come and help us with his opinion. Now do let us seize this chance of a quiet friendly family adjustment. Let me bring my friend here and try to persuade Crampton to come too. Come: consent.

MRS CLANDON [*rather ominously, after a moment's consideration*] Finch: I dont want counsel's opinion, because I intend to be guided by my own opinion. I dont want to meet Fergus again, because I dont like him, and dont believe the meeting will do any good. However [*rising*], you have persuaded the children that he is not quite hopeless. Do as you please.

M'COMAS [*taking her hand and shaking it*] Thank you, Mrs Clandon. Will nine o'clock suit you?

MRS CLANDON. Perfectly. Phil: will you ring, please. [*Phil rings the bell*]. But if I am to be accused of conspiring with Mr Valentine, I think he had better be present.

VALENTINE [*rising*] I quite agree with you. I think it's most important.

M'COMAS. There can be no objection to that, I think. I have the greatest hopes of a happy settlement. Goodbye for the present. [*He goes out, meeting the waiter, who holds the door open for him*].

MRS CLANDON. We expect some visitors at nine, William. Can we have dinner at seven instead of half past?

WAITER [*at the door*] Seven, maam? Certainly, maam. It will be a convenience to us this busy evening, maam. There will be the band and the arranging of the fairy lights and one thing or another, maam.

DOLLY. Fairy lights!

PHILIP. A band! William: what mean you?

WAITER. The fancy ball, miss.

DOLLY AND PHILIP [*simultaneously rushing at him*] Fancy ball!!!

WAITER. Oh yes, sir. Given by the regatta committee for the benefit of the Life-boat, sir. [*To Mrs Clandon*] We often have them, maam: Chinese lanterns in the garden, maam: very bright and pleasant, very gay and innocent indeed. [*To Phil*] Tickets downstairs at the office, sir, five shillings: ladies half price if accompanied by a gentleman.

PHILIP [*seizing his arm to drag him off*] To the office, William!

DOLLY [*breathlessly, seizing his other arm*] Quick, before theyre all sold. [*They rush him out of the room between them*].

MRS CLANDON [*following them*] But they mustnt go off dancing this evening. They must be here to meet—[*She disappears*].

Gloria stares coolly at Valentine, and then deliberately looks at her watch.

VALENTINE. I understand. Ive stayed too long. I'm going.

GLORIA [*with disdainful punctiliousness*] I owe you some apology, Mr Valentine. I am conscious of having spoken to you somewhat sharply. Perhaps rudely.

VALENTINE. Not at all.

GLORIA. My only excuse is that it is very difficult to give consideration and respect when there is no dignity of character on the other side to command it.

VALENTINE. How is a man to look dignified when he's infatuated?

GLORIA [*angrily*] Dont say those things to me. I forbid you. They are insults.

VALENTINE. No: theyre only follies. I cant help them.

GLORIA. If you were really in love, it would not make you foolish: it would give you dignity! earnestness! even beauty.

VALENTINE. Do you really think it would make me beautiful? [*She turns her back on him with the coldest contempt*]. Ah, you see youre not in earnest. Love cant give any man new gifts. It can only heighten the gifts he was born with.

GLORIA [*sweeping round at him again*] What gifts were you born with, pray?

VALENTINE. Lightness of heart.

GLORIA. And lightness of head, and lightness of faith, and lightness of everything that makes a man.

VALENTINE. Yes, the whole world is like a feather dancing in the light now; and Gloria is the sun [*She rears her head haughtily*]. Beg pardon: I'm off. Back at nine. Goodbye. [*He runs off gaily, leaving her standing in the middle of the room staring after him*].

GLORIA [*at the top of her voice; suddenly furious with him for leaving her*] Idiot!

ACT IV

THE same room. Nine o'clock. Nobody present. The lamps are lighted; but the curtains are not drawn. The window stands wide open; and strings of Chinese lanterns are glowing among the trees outside, with the starry sky beyond. The band is playing dance-music in the garden, drowning the sound of the sea.

The waiter enters, shewing in Crampton and M'Comas. Crampton looks cowed and anxious. He sits down wearily and timidly on the ottoman.

WAITER. The ladies have gone for a turn through the grounds to see the fancy dresses, sir. If you will be so good as to take seats, gentlemen, I shall tell them. [*He is about to go into the garden through the window when M'Comas stops him*].

M'COMAS. Stop a bit. If another gentlman comes, shew him in without any delay: we are expecting him.

WAITER. Right, sir. What name, sir?

M'COMAS. Boon. Mr Boon. He is a stranger to Mrs Clandon; so he may give you a card. If so, the name is spelt B.O.H.U.N. You will not forget.

WAITER [*smiling*] You may depend on me for that, sir. My own name is Boon, sir, though I am best known down here as Balmy Walters, sir. By rights I should spell it with the aitch you, sir; but I think it best not to take that liberty, sir. There is Norman blood in it, sir; and Norman blood is not a recommendation to a waiter.

M'COMAS. Well, well: "True hearts are more than coronets, and simple faith than Norman blood."

WAITER. That depends a good deal on one's station in life, sir. If you were a waiter, sir, youd find that simple faith would leave you just as short as Norman blood. I find it best to spell myself B. double-O.N., and to keep my wits pretty sharp about me. But I'm taking up your time, sir. Youll excuse me, sir: your own fault for being so affable, sir. I'll tell the ladies youre here, sir. [*He goes out into the garden through the window*].

698

M'COMAS. Crampton: I can depend on you, cant I?

CRAMPTON. Yes, yes. I'll be quiet. I'll be patient. I'll do my best.

M'COMAS. Remember: Ive not given you away. Ive told them it was all their fault.

CRAMPTON. You told me that it was all my fault.

M'COMAS. I told you the truth.

CRAMPTON [*plaintively*] If they will only be fair to me!

M'COMAS. My dear Crampton, they wont be fair to you: it's not to be expected from them at their age. If youre going to make impossible conditions of this kind, we may as well go back home at once.

CRAMPTON. But surely I have a right—

M'COMAS [*intolerantly*] You wont get your rights. Now, once for all, Crampton, did your promise of good behavior only mean that you wont complain if theres nothing to complain of? Because, if so— [*He moves as if to go*].

CRAMPTON [*miserably*] No, no: let me alone, cant you? Ive been bullied enough: Ive been tormented enough. I tell you I'll do my best. But if that girl begins to talk to me like that and to look at me like— [*He breaks off and buries his head in his hands*].

M'COMAS [*relenting*] There, there: itll be all right, if you will only bear and forbear. Come: pull yourself together: theres someone coming. [*Crampton, too dejected to care much, hardly changes his attitude. Gloria enters from the garden. M'Comas goes to meet her at the window: so that he can speak to her without being heard by Crampton*]. There he is, Miss Clandon. Be kind to him. I'll leave you with him for a moment. [*He goes into the garden*].

Gloria comes in and strolls coolly down the middle of the room.

CRAMPTON [*looking round in alarm*] Wheres M'Comas?

GLORIA [*listlessly, but not unsympathetically*] Gone out. To leave us together. Delicacy on his part, I suppose. [*She stops beside him and looks quaintly down at him*]. Well, father?

CRAMPTON [*submissively*] Well, daughter?

They look at one another with a melancholy sense of humor,
though humor is not their strong point.

GLORIA. Shake hands. [*They shake hands*].

CRAMPTON [*holding her hand*] My dear: I'm afraid I
spoke very improperly of your mother this afternoon.

GLORIA. Oh, dont apologize. I was very high and mighty
myself; but Ive come down since: oh, yes: Ive been brought
down. [*She sits down on the floor beside his chair*].

CRAMPTON. What has happened to you, my child?

GLORIA. Oh, never mind. I was playing the part of my
mother's daughter then; but I'm not: I'm my father's
daughter. [*Looking at him forlornly*] Thats a come down, isnt
it?

CRAMPTON [*angry*] What! [*Her expression does not alter.
He surrenders*]. Well, yes, my dear: I suppose it is, I sup-
pose it is. I'm afraid I'm sometimes a little irritable; but
I know whats right and reasonable all the time, even when
I dont act on it. Can you believe that?

GLORIA. Believe it! Why, thats myself: myself all over.
I know whats right and dignified and strong and noble, just
as well as she does; but oh, the things I do! the things I do!
the things I let other people do!!

CRAMPTON [*a little grudgingly in spite of himself*] As well as
she does? You mean your mother?

GLORIA [*quickly*] Yes, mother. [*She turns to him on her
knees and seizes his hands*]. Now listen. No treason to h e r: no
word, no thought against her. She is our superior: yours
and mine: high heavens above us. Is that agreed?

CRAMPTON. Yes, yes. Just as you please, my dear.

GLORIA [*not satisfied, letting go his hands and drawing back
from him*] You dont like her?

CRAMPTON. My child: you havnt been married to her. I
have. [*She raises herself slowly to her feet, looking at him with
growing coldness*]. She did me a great wrong in marrying me
without really caring for me. But after that, the wrong was
all on my side, I dare say. [*He offers her his hand again*].

GLORIA [*taking it firmly and warningly*] Take care. Thats

700

my dangerous subject. My feelings—my miserable cowardly womanly feelings—may be on your side; but my conscience is on hers.

CRAMPTON. I'm very well content with that division, my dear. Thank you.

Valentine arrives. Gloria immediately becomes deliberately haughty.

VALENTINE. Excuse me; but it's impossible to find a servant to announce one: even the never failing William seems to be at the ball. I should have gone myself; only I havnt five shillings to buy a ticket. How are you getting on, Crampton? Better, eh?

CRAMPTON. I am myself again, Mr Valentine, no thanks to you.

VALENTINE. Look at this ungrateful parent of yours, Miss Clandon! I saved him from an excruciating pang; and he reviles me!

GLORIA [*coldly*] I am sorry my mother is not here to receive you, Mr Valentine. It is not quite nine o'clock; and the gentleman of whom Mr M'Comas spoke, the lawyer, has not yet come.

VALENTINE. Oh yes he has. Ive met him and talked to him. [*With gay malice*] Youll like him, Miss Clandon: he's the very incarnation of intellect. You can hear his mind working.

GLORIA [*ignoring the jibe*] Where is he?

VALENTINE. Bought a false nose and gone to the fancy ball.

CRAMPTON [*crustily, looking at his watch*] It seems that everybody has gone to this fancy ball instead of keeping to our appointment here.

VALENTINE. Oh, he'll come all right enough: that was half an hour ago. I didnt like to borrow five shillings from him and go in with him; so I joined the mob and looked through the railings until Miss Clandon disappeared into the hotel through the window.

GLORIA. So it has come to this, that you follow me about

in public to stare at me.

VALENTINE. Yes: somebody ought to chain me up.

Gloria turns her back on him and goes to the fireplace. He takes the snub very philosophically, and goes to the opposite side of the room. The waiter appears at the window, ushering in Mrs Clandon and M'Comas.

MRS CLANDON. I am so sorry to have kept you all waiting.

A grotesquely majestic stranger, in a domino and false nose with goggles, appears at the window.

WAITER [*to the stranger*] Beg pardon, sir; but this is a private apartment, sir. If you will allow me, sir, I will shew you the American bar and supper rooms, sir. This way, sir.

He goes into the garden, leading the way under the impression that the stranger is following him. The majestic one, however, comes straight into the room to the end of the table, where, with impressive deliberation, he takes off the false nose and then the domino, rolling up the nose in the domino and throwing the bundle on the table like a champion throwing down his glove. He is now seen to be a tall stout man between forty and fifty, clean shaven, with a midnight oil pallor emphasized by stiff black hair, cropped short and oiled, and eyebrows like early Victorian horsehair upholstery. Physically and spiritually a coarsened man: in cunning and logic a ruthlessly sharpened one. His bearing as he enters is sufficiently imposing and disquieting; but when he speaks, his powerful menacing voice, impressively articulated speech, strong inexorable manner, and a terrifying power of intensely critical listening, raise the impression produced by him to absolute tremendousness.

THE STRANGER. My name is Bohun. [*General awe*]. Have I the honor of addressing Mrs Clandon? [*Mrs Clandon bows. Bohun bows*]. Miss Clandon? [*Gloria bows. Bohun bows*]. Mr Clandon?

CRAMPTON [*insisting on his rightful name as angrily as he dares*] My name is Crampton, sir.

BOHUN. Oh, indeed. [*Passing him over without further notice and turning to Valentine*] Are you Mr Clandon?

VALENTINE [*making it a point of honor not to be impressed by him*] Do I look like it? My name is Valentine. I did the drugging.

BOHUN. Ah, quite so. Then Mr Clandon has not yet arrived?

WAITER [*entering anxiously through the window*] Beg pardon, maam; but can you tell me what became of that— [*He recognizes Bohun, and loses all his self-possession. Bohun waits rigidly for him to pull himself together*]. Beg pardon, sir, I'm sure, sir. [*Brokenly*] Was—was it you, sir?

BOHUN [*remorselessly*] It was I.

WAITER [*Unable to restrain his tears*] You in a false nose, Walter! [*He clings to a chair to support himself*]. I beg your pardon, maam. A little giddiness—

BOHUN [*commandingly*] You will excuse him, Mrs Clandon, when I inform you that he is my father.

WAITER [*heartbroken*] Oh no, no, Walter. A waiter for your father on top of a false nose! What will they think of you?

MRS CLANDON. I am delighted to hear it, Mr Bohun. Your father has been an excellent friend to us since we came here.

Bohun bows gravely.

WAITER [*shaking his head*] Oh no, maam. It's very kind of you: very ladylike and affable indeed, maam; but I should feel at a great disadvantage off my own proper footing. Never mind my being the gentleman's father, maam: it is only the accident of birth after all, maam. Youll excuse me, I'm sure, having interrupted your business. [*He begins to make his way along the table, supporting himself from chair to chair, with his eye on the door*].

BOHUN. One moment. [*The waiter stops, with a sinking heart*]. My father was a witness of what passed today, was he not, Mrs Clandon?

MRS CLANDON. Yes, most of it, I think.

BOHUN. In that case we shall want him.

WAITER [*pleading*] I hope it may not be necessary, sir. Busy evening for me, sir, with that ball: very busy evening

703

indeed, sir.

BOHUN [*inexorably*] We shall want you.

MRS CLANDON [*politely*] Sit down, wont you?

WAITER [*earnestly*] Oh, if you please, maam, I really must draw the line at sitting down. I couldnt let myself be seen doing such a thing, maam: thank you, I am sure, all the same. [*He looks round from face to face wretchedly, with an expression that would melt a heart of stone*].

GLORIA. Dont let us waste time. William only wants to go on taking care of us. I should like a cup of coffee.

WAITER [*brightening perceptibly*] Coffee, miss? [*He gives a little gasp of hope*]. Certainly, miss. Thank you, miss: very timely, miss, very thoughtful and considerate indeed. [*To Mrs Clandon, timidly but expectantly*] Anything for you, maam?

MRS CLANDON. Er—oh yes: it's so hot, I think we might have a jug of claret cup.

WAITER [*beaming*] Claret cup, maam! Certainly, maam.

GLORIA. Oh well, I'll have claret cup instead of coffee. Put some cucumber in it.

WAITER [*delighted*] Cucumber, miss! yes miss. [*To Bohun*] Anything special for you, sir? You dont like cucumber, sir.

BOHUN. If Mrs Clandon will allow me: syphon: Scotch.

WAITER. Right, sir. [*To Crampton*] Irish for you, sir, I think, sir? [*Crampton assents with a grunt. The waiter looks inquiringly at Valentine*].

VALENTINE. I like cucumber.

WAITER. Right, sir. [*Summing up*] Claret cup, syphon, one Scotch and one Irish?

MRS CLANDON. I think thats right.

WAITER [*himself again*] Right, maam. Directly, maam. Thank you. [*He ambles off through the window, having sounded the whole gamut of human happiness, from despair to ecstasy, in fifty seconds*].

M'COMAS. We can begin now, I suppose.

BOHUN. We had better wait until Mrs Clandon's husband arrives.

704

CRAMPTON. What d'y'mean? I'm her husband.

BOHUN [*instantly pouncing on the inconsistency between this and his previous statement*] You said just now that your name was Crampton.

CRAMPTON. So it is.

MRS CLANDON	[*all four*	I—
GLORIA	*speaking*	My—
M'COMAS	*simul-*	Mrs—
VALENTINE	*taneously*]	You—

BOHUN [*drowning them in two thunderous words*] One moment. [*Dead silence*]. Pray allow me. Sit down, everybody. [*They obey humbly. Gloria takes the saddle-bag chair on the hearth. Valentine slips round to her side of the room and sits on the ottoman facing the window, so that he can look at her. Crampton sits on the ottoman with his back to Valentine's. Mrs Clandon, who has all along kept at the opposite side of the room in order to avoid Crampton as much as possible, sits near the door, with M'Comas beside her on her left. Bohun places himself magisterially in the centre of the group, near the corner of the table on Mrs Clandon's side. When they are settled, he fixes Crampton with his eye, and begins*] In this family, it appears, the husband's name is Crampton: the wife's, Clandon. Thus we have on the very threshold of the case an element of confusion.

VALENTINE [*getting up and speaking across to him with one knee on the ottoman*] But it's perfectly simple—

BOHUN [*annihilating him with a vocal thunderbolt*] It is. Mrs Clandon has adopted another name. That is the obvious explanation which you feared I could not find out for myself. You mistrust my intelligence, Mr Valentine— [*stopping him as he is about to protest*] no: I dont want you to answer that: I want you to think over it when you feel your next impulse to interrupt me.

VALENTINE [*dazed*] This is simply breaking a butterfly on a wheel. What does it matter? [*He sits down again*].

BOHUN. I will tell you what it matters, sir. It matters that if this family difference is to be smoothed over as we all

705

hope it may be, Mrs Clandon, as a matter of social convenience and decency, will have to resume her husband's name
[*Mrs Clandon assumes an expression of the most determined
obstinacy*] or else Mr Crampton will have to call himself Mr
Clandon. [*Crampton looks indomitably resolved to do nothing of
the sort*]. No doubt you think that an easy matter, Mr Valentine. [*He looks pointedly at Mrs Clandon, then at Crampton*]. I
differ from you. [*He throws himself back in his chair, frowning
heavily*].

M'COMAS [*timidly*] I think, Bohun, we had perhaps better
dispose of the important questions first.

BOHUN. M'Comas: there will be no difficulty about the
important questions. There never is. It is the trifles that will
wreck you at the harbor mouth. [*M'Comas looks as if he considered this a paradox*]. You dont agree with me, eh?

M'COMAS [*flatteringly*] If I did—

BOHUN [*interrupting him*] If you did, you would be me,
instead of being what you are.

M'COMAS [*fawning on him*] Of course, Bohun, your speciality—

BOHUN [*again interrupting him*] My speciality is being
right when other people are wrong. If you agreed with me I
should be no use here. [*He nods at him to drive the point home;
then turns suddenly and forcibly on Crampton*]. Now you, Mr
Crampton: what point in this business have you most at
heart?

CRAMPTON [*beginning slowly*] I wish to put all considera-
tions of self aside in this matter—

BOHUN [*cutting him short*] So do we all, Mr Crampton.
[*To Mrs Clandon*] You wish to put self aside, Mrs Clandon?

MRS CLANDON. Yes: I am not consulting my own feelings
in being here.

BOHUN. So do you, Miss Clandon?

GLORIA. Yes.

BOHUN. I thought so. We all do.

VALENTINE. Except me. My aims are selfish.

BOHUN. Thats because you think an affectation of sin-

706

YOU NEVER CAN TELL

cerity will produce a better effect on Miss Clandon than an affectation of disinterestedness. [*Valentine, utterly dismantled and destroyed by this just remark, takes refuge in a feeble speechless smile. Bohun, satisfied at having now effectually crushed all rebellion, again throws himself back in his chair, with an air of being prepared to listen tolerantly to their grievances*]. Now, Mr Crampton, go on. It's understood that self is put aside. Human nature always begins by saying that.

CRAMPTON. But I mean it, sir.

BOHUN. Quite so. Now for your point.

CRAMPTON. Every reasonable person will admit that it's an unselfish one. It's about the children.

BOHUN. Well? What about the children?

CRAMPTON [*with emotion*] They have—

BOHUN [*pouncing forward again*] Stop. Youre going to tell me about your feelings, Mr Crampton. Dont. I sympathize with them; but theyre not my business. Tell us exactly what you want: thats what we have to get at.

CRAMPTON [*uneasily*] It's a very difficult question to answer, Mr Bohun.

BOHUN. Come: I'll help you out. What do you object to in the present circumstances of the children?

CRAMPTON. I object to the way they have been brought up.

Mrs Clandon's brow contracts ominously.

BOHUN. How do you propose to alter that now?

CRAMPTON. I think they ought to dress more quietly.

VALENTINE. Nonsense.

BOHUN [*instantly flinging himself back in his chair, outraged by the interruption*] When you are done, Mr Valentine: when you are quite done.

VALENTINE. Whats wrong with Miss Clandon's dress?

CRAMPTON [*hotly to Valentine*] My opinion is as good as yours.

GLORIA [*warningly*] Father!

CRAMPTON [*subsiding piteously*] I didnt mean you, my dear. [*Pleading earnestly to Bohun*] But the two younger ones!

707

you have not seen them, Mr Bohun; and indeed I think you would agree with me that there is something very noticeable, something almost gay and frivolous in their style of dressing.

MRS CLANDON [*impatiently*] Do you suppose I choose their clothes for them? Really, this is childish.

CRAMPTON [*furious, rising*] Childish!

Mrs Clandon rises indignantly.

M'COMAS [*all rising and speaking together*] Crampton, you promised—

VALENTINE Ridiculous. They dress charmingly.

GLORIA Pray let us behave reasonably.

Tumult. Suddenly they hear a warning chime of glasses in the room behind them. They turn guiltily and find that the waiter has just come back from the bar in the garden, and is jingling his tray as he comes softly to the table with it. Dead silence.

WAITER [*to Crampton, setting a tumbler apart on the table*] Irish for you, sir. [*Crampton sits down a little shamefacedly. The waiter sets another tumbler and a syphon apart, saying to Bohun*] Scotch and syphon for you, sir. [*Bohun waves his hand impatiently. The waiter places a large glass jug and three tumblers in the middle*]. And claret cup. [*All subside into their seats. Peace reigns*].

MRS CLANDON. I am afraid we interrupted you, Mr Bohun.

BOHUN [*calmly*] You did. [*To the waiter, who is going out*] Just wait a bit.

WAITER. Yes, sir. Certainly, sir. [*He takes his stand behind Bohun's chair*].

MRS CLANDON [*to the waiter*] You dont mind our detaining you, I hope. Mr Bohun wishes it.

WAITER [*now quite at his ease*] Oh no, maam, not at all, maam. It is a pleasure to me to watch the working of his trained and powerful mind: very stimulating, very entertaining and instructive indeed, maam.

BOHUN [*resuming command of the proceedings*] Now, Mr Crampton: we are waiting for you. Do you give up your objection to the dressing or do you stick to it?

CRAMPTON [*pleading*] Mr Bohun: consider my position for a moment. I havnt got myself alone to consider: theres my sister Sophronia and my brother-in-law and all their circle. They have a great horror of anything that is at all—at all—well——

BOHUN. Out with it. Fast? Loud? Gay?

CRAMPTON. Not in any unprincipled sense, of course; but—but— [*blurting it out desperately*] those two children would shock them. Theyre not fit to mix with their own people. Thats what I complain of.

MRS CLANDON [*with suppressed anger*] Mr Valentine: do you think there is anything fast or loud about Phil and Dolly?

VALENTINE. Certainly not. It's utter bosh. Nothing can be in better taste.

CRAMPTON. Oh yes: of course you say so.

MRS CLANDON. William: you see a great deal of good English society. Are my children overdressed?

WAITER [*reassuringly*] Oh dear no, maam. [*Persuasively*] Oh no, sir, not at all. A little pretty and tasty no doubt, but very choice and classy, very genteel and high toned indeed. Might be the son and daughter of a Dean, sir, I assure you, sir. You have only to look at them, sir, to——

At this moment a harlequin and columbine, waltzing to the band in the garden, whirl one another into the room. The harlequin's dress is made of lozenges, an inch square, of turquoise blue silk and gold alternately. His bat is gilt and his mask turned up. The columbine's petticoats are the epitome of a harvest field, golden orange and poppy crimson, with a tiny velvet jacket for the poppy stamens. They pass, an exquisite and dazzling apparition, between M'Comas and Bohun, and then back in a circle to the end of the table, where, as the final chord of the waltz is struck, they make a tableau in the middle of the company, the harlequin down on his left knee, and the columbine standing on his right knee, with her arms curved over her head. Unlike their dancing, which is charmingly graceful, their attitudinizing is

709

hardly a success, and threatens to end in a catastrophe.

THE COLUMBINE [*screaming*] Lift me down, somebody: I'm going to fall. Papa: lift me down.

CRAMPTON [*anxiously running to her and taking her hands*] My child!

DOLLY[*jumping down, with his help*] Thanks: so nice of you. [*Phil sits on the edge of the table and pours out some claret cup. Crampton returns to the ottoman in great perplexity*]. Oh, what fun! Oh dear! [*She seats herself with a vault on the front edge of the table, panting*]. Oh, claret cup! [*She drinks*].

BOHUN [*in powerful tones*] This is the younger lady, is it?

DOLLY [*slipping down off the table in alarm at his formidable voice and manner*] Yes, sir. Please, who are you?

MRS CLANDON. This is Mr Bohun, Dolly, who has very kindly come to help us this evening.

DOLLY. Oh, then he comes as a boon and a blessing—

PHILIP. Sh!

CRAMPTON. Mr Bohun—M'Comas: I appeal to you. Is this right? Would you blame my sister's family for objecting to it?

DOLLY [*flushing ominously*] Have you begun again?

CRAMPTON [*propitiating her*] No, no. It's perhaps natural at your age.

DOLLY [*obstinately*] Never mind my age. Is it pretty?

CRAMPTON. Yes, dear, yes. [*He sits down in token of submission*].

DOLLY [*insistently*] Do you like it?

CRAMPTON. My child: how can you expect me to like it or to approve of it?

DOLLY [*determined not to let him off*] How can you think it pretty and not like it?

M'COMAS [*rising, scandalized*] Really I must say—

Bohun, who has listened to Dolly with the highest approval, is down on him instantly.

BOHUN. No: dont interrupt, M'Comas. The young lady's method is right. [*To Dolly, with tremendous emphasis*] Press your questions, Miss Clandon: press your questions.

DOLLY [*turning to Bohun*] Oh dear, you a r e a regular overwhelmer! Do you always go on like this?

BOHUN [*rising*] Yes. Dont you try to put me out of countenance, young lady: youre too young to do it. [*He takes M'Comas's chair from beside Mrs Clandon's, and sets it beside his own*]. Sit down. [*Dolly, fascinated, obeys; and Bohun sits down again. M'Comas, robbed of his seat, takes a chair on the other side, between the table and the ottoman*]. Now, Mr Crampton, the facts are before you: both of them. You think youd like to have your two youngest children to live with you. Well, you wouldnt— [*Crampton tries to protest; but Bohun will not have it on any terms*] no you wouldnt: you think you would; but I know better than you. Youd want this young lady here to give up dressing like a stage columbine in the evening and like a fashionable columbine in the morning. Well, she wont: never. She thinks she will; but—

DOLLY [*interrupting him*] No I dont. [*Resolutely*] I'll n e v e r give up dressing prettily. Never. As Gloria said to that man in Madeira, never, never, never! while grass grows or water runs.

VALENTINE [*rising in the wildest agitation*] What! What! [*Beginning to speak very fast*] When did she say that? Who did she say that to?

BOHUN [*throwing himself back with massive pitying remonstrance*] Mr Valentine—

VALENTINE [*pepperily*] Dont you interrupt me, sir: this is something really serious. I i n s i s t on knowing who Miss Clandon said that to.

DOLLY. Perhaps Phil remembers. Which was it, Phil? number three or number five?

VALENTINE. Number five!!!

PHILIP. Courage, Valentine! It wasnt number five: it was only a tame naval lieutenant who was always on hand: the most patient and harmless of mortals.

GLORIA [*coldly*] What are we discussing now, pray?

VALENTINE [*very red*] Excuse me: I am sorry I interrupted. I shall intrude no further, Mrs Clandon. [*He bows *to Mrs Clandon and marches away into the garden, boiling with suppressed rage].*

DOLLY. Hmhm!

PHILIP. Ahah!

GLORIA. Please go on, Mr Bohun.

DOLLY [*striking in as Bohun, frowning formidably, collects himself for a fresh grapple with the case*] Youre going to bully us, Mr Bohun.

BOHUN. I—

DOLLY [*interrupting him*] Oh yes you are: you think youre not; but you are. I know by your eyebrows.

BOHUN [*capitulating*] Mrs Clandon: these are clever children: clear headed well brought up children. I make that admission deliberately. Can you, in return, point out to me any way of inducing them to hold their tongues?

MRS CLANDON. Dolly, dearest—!

PHILIP. Our old failing, Dolly. Silence!

Dolly holds her mouth.

MRS CLANDON. Now, Mr Bohun, before they begin again—

WAITER [*softly*] Be quick, sir: be quick.

DOLLY [*beaming at him*] Dear William!

PHILIP. Sh!

BOHUN [*unexpectedly beginning by hurling a question straight at Dolly*] Have you any intention of getting married?

DOLLY. I! Well, Finch calls me by my Christian name.

M'COMAS [*starting violently*] I will not have this. Mr Bohun: I use the young lady's Christian name naturally as an old friend of her mother's.

DOLLY. Yes, you call me Dolly as an old friend of my mother's. But what about Dorothee-ee-a?

M'Comas rises indignantly.

CRAMPTON [*anxiously, rising to restrain him*] Keep your temper, M'Comas. Dont let us quarrel. Be patient.

M'COMAS. I will not be patient. You are shewing the most wretched weakness of character, Crampton. I say this is monstrous.

712

YOU NEVER CAN TELL

DOLLY. Mr Bohun: please bully Finch for us.

BOHUN. I will. M'Comas: youre making yourself ridiculous. Sit down.

M'COMAS. I—

BOHUN [*waving him down imperiously*] No: sit down, sit down.

M'Comas sits down sulkily; and Crampton, much relieved, follows his example.

DOLLY [*to Bohun, meekly*] Thank you.

BOHUN. Now listen to me, all of you. I give no opinion, M'Comas, as to how far you may or may not have committed yourself in the direction indicated by this young lady. [*M'Comas is about to protest*]. No: dont interrupt me: if she doesnt marry you she will marry somebody else. That is the solution of the difficulty as to her not bearing her father's name. The other lady intends to get married.

GLORIA [*flushing*] Mr Bohun!

BOHUN. Oh yes you do: you dont know it; but you do.

GLORIA [*rising*] Stop. I warn you, Mr Bohun, not to answer for my intentions.

BOHUN [*rising*] It's no use, Miss Clandon: you cant put me down. I tell you your name will soon be neither Clandon nor Crampton; and I could tell you what it will be if I chose. [*He goes to the table and takes up his domino. They all rise; and Phil goes to the window. Bohun, with a gesture, summons the waiter to help him to robe*]. Mr Crampton: your notion of going to law is all nonsense: your children will be of age before you can get the point decided. [*Allowing the waiter to put the domino on his shoulders*] You can do nothing but make a friendly arrangement. If you want your family more than they want you, youll get the worst of the arrangement: if they want you more than you want them youll get the better of it. [*He shakes the domino into becoming folds and takes up the false nose. Dolly gazes admiringly at him*]. The strength of their position lies in their being very agreeable people personally. The strength of your position lies in your income. [*He claps on the false nose, and is again grotesquely transfigured*].

713

DOLLY [*running to him*] Oh, now you look quite like a human being. Maynt I have just one dance with you? Can you dance?

Phil, resuming his part of harlequin, waves his bat as if casting a spell on them.

BOHUN [*thunderously*] Yes: you think I cant; but I can. Allow me. [*He seizes her and dances off with her through the window in a most powerful manner, but with studied propriety and grace*].

PHILIP. "On with the dance: let joy be unconfined." William.

WAITER. Yes, sir.

PHILIP. Can you procure a couple of dominos and false noses for my father and Mr M'Comas?

M'COMAS. Most certainly not. I protest—

CRAMPTON. Yes, yes. What harm will it do, just for once, M'Comas? Dont let us be spoil-sports.

M'COMAS. Crampton: you are not the man I took you for. [*Pointedly*] Bullies are always cowards. [*He goes disgustedly towards the window*].

CRAMPTON [*following him*] Well, never mind. We must indulge them a little. Can you get us something to wear, waiter?

WAITER. Certainly, sir. [*He precedes them to the window, and stands aside there to let them pass out before him*]. This way, sir. Dominos and noses, sir?

M'COMAS [*angrily, on his way out*] I shall wear my own nose.

WAITER [*suavely*] Oh dear yes, sir: the false one will fit over it quite easily, sir: plenty of room, sir, plenty of room. [*He goes out after M'Comas*].

CRAMPTON [*turning at the window to Phil with an attempt at genial fatherliness*] Come along, my boy. Come along. [*He goes*].

PHILIP [*cheerily, following him*] Coming, dad, coming. [*On the window threshold he stops; looks after Crampton; then turns fantastically with his bat bent into a halo round his head, and says with lowered voice to Mrs Clandon and Gloria*] Did you feel the pathos of that? [*He vanishes*].

MRS CLANDON [*left alone with Gloria*] Why did Mr Valentine go away so suddenly, I wonder?

GLORIA [*petulantly*] I dont know. Yes, I do know. Let us go and see the dancing.

They go towards the window, and are met by Valentine, who comes in from the garden walking quickly, with his face set and sulky.

VALENTINE [*stiffly*] Excuse me. I thought the party had quite broken up.

GLORIA [*nagging*] Then why did you come back?

VALENTINE. I came back because I am penniless. I cant get out that way without a five-shilling ticket.

MRS CLANDON. Has anything annoyed you, Mr Valentine?

GLORIA. Never mind him, mother. This is a fresh insult to me: that is all.

MRS CLANDON [*hardly able to realize that Gloria is deliberately provoking an altercation*] Gloria!

VALENTINE. Mrs Clandon: have I said anything insulting? Have I done anything insulting?

GLORIA. You have implied that my past has been like yours. That is the worst of insults.

VALENTINE. I imply nothing of the sort. I declare that my past has been blameless in comparison with yours.

MRS CLANDON [*most indignantly*] Mr Valentine!

VALENTINE. Well, what am I to think when I learn that Miss Clandon has made exactly the same speeches to other men that she has made to me? Five former lovers, with a tame naval lieutenant thrown in! Oh, it's too bad.

MRS CLANDON. But you surely do not believe that these affairs—mere jokes of the children's—were serious, Mr Valentine?

VALENTINE. Not to you. Not to her, perhaps. But I know what the men felt. [*With ludicrously genuine earnestness*] Have you ever thought of the wrecked lives, the unhappy marri-

715

ages contracted in the recklessness of despair, the suicides, the—the—the—

GLORIA [*interrupting him contemptuously*] Mother: this man is a sentimental idiot. [*She sweeps away to the fireplace*].

MRS CLANDON [*shocked*] Oh, my dearest Gloria, Mr Valentine will think that rude.

VALENTINE. I am not a sentimental idiot. I am cured of sentiment for ever. [*He turns away in dudgeon*].

MRS CLANDON. Mr Valentine: you must excuse us all. Women have to unlearn the false good manners of their slavery before they acquire the genuine good manners of their freedom. Dont think Gloria vulgar [*Gloria turns, astonished*]: she is not really so.

GLORIA. Mother! You apologize for me to him!

MRS CLANDON. My dear: you have some of the faults of youth as well as its qualities; and Mr Valentine seems rather too old fashioned in his ideas about his own sex to like being called an idiot. And now had we not better go and see what Dolly is doing? [*She goes towards the window*].

GLORIA. Do you go, mother. I wish to speak to Mr Valentine alone.

MRS CLANDON [*startled into a remonstrance*] My dear! [*Recollecting herself*] I beg your pardon, Gloria. Certainly, if you wish. [*She goes out*].

VALENTINE. Oh, if your mother were only a widow! She's worth six of you.

GLORIA. That is the first thing I have heard you say that does you honor.

VALENTINE. Stuff! Come: say what you want to say and let me go.

GLORIA. I have only this to say. You dragged me down to your level for a moment this afternoon. Do you think, if that had ever happened before, that I should not have been on my guard? that I should not have known what was coming, and known my own miserable weakness?

VALENTINE [*scolding at her passionately*] Dont talk of it in that way. What do I care for anything in you but your weakness, as you call it? You thought yourself very safe, didnt you, behind your advanced ideas? I amused myself by upsetting t h e m pretty easily.

GLORIA [*insolently, feeling that now she can do as she likes with him*] Indeed!

VALENTINE. But why did I do it? Because I was being tempted to awaken your heart: to stir the depths in you. Why was I tempted? Because Nature was in deadly earnest with me when I was in jest with her. When the great moment came, who was awakened? who was stirred? in whom did the depths break up? In myself—m y s e l f. *I* was transported: y o u were only offended—shocked. You are just an ordinary young lady, too ordinary to allow tame lieutenants to go as far as I went. Thats all. I shall not trouble you with conventional apologies. Goodbye. [*He makes resolutely for the door*].

GLORIA. Stop. [*He hesitates*]. Oh, will you understand, if I tell you the truth, that I am not making advances to you?

VALENTINE. Pooh! I know what youre going to say. You think youre not ordinary: that I was right: that you really have those depths in your nature. It flatters you to believe it. [*She recoils*]. Well, I grant that you are not ordinary in some ways: you are a clever girl [*Gloria stifles an exclamation of rage, and takes a threatening step towards him*]; but youve not been awakened yet. You didnt care: you dont care. It was my tragedy, not yours. Goodbye. [*He turns to the door. She watches him, appalled to see him slipping from her grasp. As he turns the handle, he pauses; then turns again to her, offering his hand*]. Let us part kindly.

GLORIA [*enormously relieved, and immediately turning her back on him deliberately*] Goodbye. I trust you will soon recover from the wound.

VALENTINE [*brightening up as it flashes on him that he is master of the situation after all*] I shall recover: such wounds heal more than they harm. After all, I still have my own Gloria.

GLORIA [*facing him quickly*] What do you mean?

VALENTINE. The Gloria of my imagination.

GLORIA [*proudly*] Keep your own Gloria: the Gloria of your imagination. [*Her emotion begins to break through her pride*]. The real Gloria: the Gloria who was shocked, offended, horrified—oh yes, quite truly—who was driven almost mad with shame by the feeling that all her power over herself had broken down at her first real encounter with—with—[*The color rushes over her face again. She covers it with her left hand, and puts her right on his left arm to support herself*].

VALENTINE. Take care. I'm losing my senses again. [*Summoning all her courage, she takes away her hand from her face and puts it on his right shoulder, turning him towards her and looking him straight in the eyes. He begins to protest agitatedly*]. Gloria: be sensible: it's no use: I havnt a penny in the world.

GLORIA. Cant you earn one? Other people do.

VALENTINE [*half delighted, half frightened*] I never could: youd be unhappy. My dearest love: I should be the merest fortune-hunting adventurer if—[*Her grip of his arms tightens; and she kisses him*]. Oh Lord! [*Breathless*] Oh, I—[*he gasps*] I dont know anything about women: twelve years experience is not enough. [*In a gust of jealousy she throws him away from her; and he reels back into a chair like a leaf before the wind*].

Dolly dances in, waltzing with the waiter, followed by Mrs Clandon and Finch, also waltzing, and Phil pirouetting by himself.

DOLLY [*sinking on the chair at the writing-table*] Oh, I'm out of breath. How beautifully you waltz, William!

MRS CLANDON [*sinking on the saddle-bag seat on the hearth*] Oh, how could you make me do such a silly thing, Finch! I havnt danced since the soirée at South Place twenty years ago.

GLORIA [*peremptorily to Valentine*] Get up. [*Valentine gets up abjectly*]. Now let us have no false delicacy. Tell my mother that we have agreed to marry one another.

A silence of stupefaction ensues. Valentine, dumb with panic, looks at them with an obvious impulse to run away.

YOU NEVER CAN TELL

DOLLY [*breaking the silence*] Number Six!

PHILIP. Sh!

DOLLY [*tumultuously*] Oh, my feelings! I want to kiss somebody; and we bar it in the family. Wheres Finch?

M'COMAS. No, positively.

Crampton appears at the window.

DOLLY [*running to Crampton*] Oh, youre just in time. [*She kisses him*]. Now [*leading him forward*] bless them.

GLORIA. No. I will have no such thing, even in jest. When I need a blessing, I shall ask my mother's.

CRAMPTON [*to Gloria, with deep disappointment*] Am I to understand that you have engaged yourself to this young gentleman?

GLORIA [*resolutely*] Yes. Do you intend to be our friend or—

DOLLY. —or our father?

CRAMPTON. I should like to be both, my child. But surely—! Mr Valentine: I appeal to your sense of honor.

VALENTINE. Youre quite right. It's perfect madness. If we go out to dance together I shall have to borrow five shillings from her for a ticket. Gloria: dont be rash: youre throwing yourself away. I'd much better clear straight out of this, and never see any of you again. I shant commit suicide: I shant even be unhappy. Itll be a relief to me: I— I'm frightened, I'm positively frightened; and that's the plain truth.

GLORIA [*determinedly*] You shall not go.

VALENTINE [*quailing*] No, dearest: of course not. But— oh, will somebody only talk sense for a moment and bring us all to reason! *I* cant. Where's Bohun? Bohun's the man. Phil: go and summon Bohun.

PHILIP. From the vasty deep. I go. [*He makes his bat quiver in the air and darts away through the window*].

WAITER [*harmoniously to Valentine*] If you will excuse my putting in a word, sir, do not let a matter of five shillings stand between you and your happiness, sir. We shall be only too pleased to put the ticket down to you; and you can settle

719

at your convenience. Very glad to meet you in any way, very happy and pleased indeed, sir.

PHILIP [*reappearing*] He comes. [*He waves his bat over the window*].

Bohun comes in, taking off his false nose and throwing it on the table in passing as he comes between Gloria and Valentine.

VALENTINE. The point is, Mr Bohun—

M'COMAS [*interrupting from the hearthrug*] Excuse me, sir: the point must be put to him by a solicitor. The question is one of an engagement between these two young people. The lady has some property, and [*looking at Crampton*] will probably have a good deal more.

CRAMPTON. Possibly. I hope so.

VALENTINE. And the gentleman hasnt a rap.

BOHUN [*nailing Valentine to the point instantly*] Then insist on a settlement. That shocks your delicacy: most sensible precautions do. But you ask my advice; and I give it to you. Have a settlement.

GLORIA [*proudly*] He shall have a settlement.

VALENTINE. My good sir, I dont want advice for myself. Give h e r some advice.

BOHUN. She wont take it. When youre married, she wont take yours either—[*turning suddenly on Gloria*] oh no you wont: you think you will; but you wont. He'll set to work and earn his living— [*turning suddenly on Valentine*] oh yes you will: you think you wont; but you will. She'll make you.

CRAMPTON [*only half persuaded*] Then, Mr Bohun, you dont think this match an unwise one?

BOHUN. Yes I do: all matches are unwise. It's unwise to be born; it's unwise to be married; it's unwise to live; and it's wise to die.

WAITER [*insinuating himself between Crampton and Valentine*] Then, if I may respectfully put a word in, sir, so much the worse for wisdom!

PHILIP. Allow me to remark that if Gloria has made up her mind—

DOLLY. The matter's settled; and Valentine's done for.

And we're missing all the dances.

VALENTINE [*to Gloria, gallantly making the best of it*] May I have a dance—

BOHUN [*interposing in his grandest diapason*] Excuse me: I claim that privilege as counsel's fee. May I have the honor? thank you. [*He dances away with Gloria, and disappears among the lanterns, leaving Valentine gasping*].

VALENTINE [*recovering his breath*] Dolly: may I— [*offering himself as her partner*]?

DOLLY. Nonsense! [*eluding him and running round the table to the fireplace*]. Finch: my Finch! [*She pounces on M'Comas and makes him dance*].

M'COMAS [*protesting*] Pray restrain—really— [*He is borne off dancing through the window*].

VALENTINE [*making a last effort*] Mrs Clandon: may I—

PHILIP [*forestalling him*] Come, mother. [*He seizes his mother and whirls her away*].

MRS CLANDON [*remonstrating*] Phil, Phil— [*She shares M'Comas's fate*].

CRAMPTON [*following them with senile glee*] Ho! ho! He! he! he! [*He goes into the garden chuckling*].

VALENTINE [*collapsing on the ottoman and staring at the waiter*] I might as well be a married man already.

WAITER [*contemplating the defeated Duellist of Sex with ineffable benignity*] Cheer up, sir, cheer up. Every man is frightened of marriage when it comes to the point; but it often turns out very comfortable, very enjoyable and happy indeed, sir—from time to time. *I* never was master in my own house, sir: my wife was like your young lady: she was of a commanding and masterful disposition, which my son has inherited. But if I had my life to live twice over, I'd do it again: I'd do it again, I assure you. You never can tell, sir: you never can tell.

THE PHILANDERER

A TOPICAL COMEDY IN FOUR ACTS OF THE EARLY
EIGHTEEN-NINETIES

Written in 1893

First Performed London 1905

See Preface to the First Volume of Plays:
Pleasant and Unpleasant (*Volume III, page vii*)

PREFATORY NOTE

THERE is a disease to which plays as well as men become liable with advancing years. In men it is called doting, in plays dating. The more topical the play the more it dates. The Philanderer suffers from this complaint. In the eighteen-nineties, when it was written, not only dramatic literature but life itself was staggering from the impact of Ibsen's plays, which reached us in 1889. The state of mind represented by the Ibsen Club in this play was familiar then to our Intelligentsia. That far more numerous body which may be called the Unintelligentsia was as unconscious of Ibsen as of any other political influence: quarter of a century elapsed before an impatient heaven rained German bombs down on them to wake them from their apathy. That accustomed them to much more startling departures from Victorian routine than those that shock the elderly colonel and the sentimental theatre critic in The Philanderer; but they do not associate their advance in liberal morals with the great Norwegian. Even the Intelligentsia have forgotten that the lesson that might have saved the lives of ten million persons hideously slaughtered was offered to them by Ibsen.

I make no attempt to bring the play up to date. I should as soon think of bringing Ben Johnson's Bartholomew Fair up to date by changing the fair into a Woolworth store. The human nature in it is still in the latest fashion: indeed I am far from sure that its ideas, instead of being 36 years behind the times, are not for a considerable section of the community 36 years ahead of them. My picture of the past may be for many people a picture of the future. At all events I shall leave the play as it is; for all the attempts within my experience to modernize ancient plays have only produced worse anachronisms than those they aimed at remedying.

1930.

724

THE PHILANDERER

ACT I

A LADY and gentleman are making love to one another
in the drawing room of a flat in Ashley Gardens in the
Victoria district of London. It is past ten at night. The
walls are hung with theatrical engravings and photographs:
Kemble as Hamlet, Mrs Siddons as Queen Katherine pleading
in court, Macready as Werner (after Maclise), Sir Henry Irving
as Richard III (after Long), Ellen Terry, Mrs Kendal, Ada
Rehan, Sarah Bernhardt, Henry Arthur Jones, Sir Arthur
Pinero, Sydney Grundy, and so on, but not Eleonora Duse nor
any one connected with Ibsen. The room is not rectangular, one
corner being cut off diagonally by the doorway, and the opposite
one rounded by a turret window filled up with a stand of
flowers surrounding a statuet of Shakespear. The fireplace is
on the doorway side, with an armchair near it. A small round
table, further from the door on the same side, with a chair beside
it, has a yellow backed French novel lying open on it. The piano,
a grand, is on the Shakespear side, open, with the keyboard at
right angles to the wall. The piece of music on the desk is When
Other Lips. Incandescent lights, well shaded, are on the piano
and mantelpiece. Near the piano is a sofa, on which the lady
and gentleman are seated affectionately side by side, in one
another's arms.

The lady, Grace Tranfield, is about 32, slight of build, delicate of feature, and sensitive in expression. She is just now given
up to the emotion of the moment; but her well closed mouth, proudly
set brows, firm chin, and elegant carriage shew plenty of determination and self-respect. She is in evening dress.

The gentleman, Leonard Charteris, a few years older, is un-
conventionally but smartly dressed in a velvet jacket and cashmere trousers. His collar, dyed Wotan blue, is part of his shirt,
and turns over a garnet colored scarf of Indian silk, secured by a
turquoise ring. He wears blue socks and leather sandals. The
arrangement of his tawny hair, and of his moustaches and short
beard, is apparently left to Nature; but he has taken care that
Nature shall do him the fullest justice. His amative enthusiasm,

at which he is himself laughing, and his clever, imaginative, humorous ways, contrast strongly with the sincere tenderness and dignified quietness of the woman.

CHARTERIS [*impulsively clasping Grace*] My dearest love.

GRACE [*responding affectionately*] My darling. Are you happy?

CHARTERIS. In Heaven.

GRACE. My own.

CHARTERIS. My heart's love. [*He sighs happily, and takes her hands in his, looking quaintly at her*]. That must positively be my last kiss, Grace; or I shall become downright silly. Let us talk. [*He releases her and sits a little apart*]. Grace: is this your first love affair?

GRACE. Have you forgotten that I am a widow? Do you think I married Tranfield for money?

CHARTERIS. How do I know? Besides, you might have married him not because you loved him, but because you didnt love anybody else. When one is young, one marries out of mere curiosity, just to see what it's like.

GRACE. Well, since you ask me, I never was in love with Tranfield, though I only found that out when I fell in love with you. But I used to like him for being in love with me. It brought out all the good in him so much that I have wanted to be in love with someone ever since. I hope, now that I am in love with you, you will like me for it just as I liked Tranfield.

CHARTERIS. My dear: it is because I like you that I want to marry you. I could love anybody—any pretty woman, that is.

GRACE. Do you really mean that, Leonard?

CHARTERIS. Of course. Why not?

GRACE [*reflecting*] Never mind. Now tell me, is this your first love affair?

CHARTERIS [*amazed at the simplicity of the question*] No, bless my soul, no; nor my second, nor my third.

GRACE. But I mean your first serious one?

CHARTERIS [*with a certain hesitation*] Yes. [*There is a pause.*

She is not convinced. He adds, with a very perceptible load on his conscience] It is the first in which *I* have been serious.

GRACE [*searchingly*] I see. The other parties were always serious.

CHARTERIS. Not always. Heaven forbid!

GRACE. How often?

CHARTERIS. Well, once.

GRACE. Julia Craven?

CHARTERIS [*recoiling*] Who told you that? [*She shakes her head mysteriously. He turns away from her moodily and adds*] You had much better not have asked.

GRACE [*gently*] I'm sorry, dear. [*She puts out her hand and pulls softly at him to bring him near her again*].

CHARTERIS [*yielding mechanically to the pull, and allowing her hand to rest on his arm, but sitting squarely without the least attempt to return the caress*] Do I feel harder to the touch than I did five minutes ago?

GRACE. What nonsense!

CHARTERIS. I feel as if my body had turned into the toughest hickory. That is what comes of reminding me of Julia Craven. [*Brooding, with his chin on his right hand and his elbow on his knee*] I have sat alone with her just as I am sitting with you—

GRACE [*shrinking from him*] Just!

CHARTERIS [*sitting upright and facing her steadily*] Just exactly. She has put her hands in mine, and laid her cheek against mine, and listened to me saying all sorts of silly things. [*Grace, chilled to the soul, rises from the sofa and sits down on the piano stool, with her back to the keyboard*]. Ah, you dont want to hear any more of the story. So much the better.

GRACE [*deeply hurt, but controlling herself*] When did you break it off?

CHARTERIS [*guiltily*] Break it off?

GRACE [*firmly*] Yes: break it off.

CHARTERIS. Well: let me see. When did I fall in love with you?

GRACE. Did you break it off then?

727

THE PHILANDERER

CHARTERIS [*making it plainer and plainer that it has not been broken off*] It was clear then, of course, that it must be broken off.

GRACE. And did you break it off?

CHARTERIS. Oh, yes: *I* broke it off.

GRACE. But did s h e break it off?

CHARTERIS [*rising*] As a favor to me, dearest, change the subject. Come away from the piano: I want you to sit here with me. [*He takes a step towards her*].

GRACE. No. I also have grown hard to the touch: much harder than hickory for the present. Did she break it off?

CHARTERIS. My dear, be reasonable. It was fully explained to her that it was to be broken off.

GRACE. Did she accept the explanation?

CHARTERIS. She did what a woman like Julia always does. When I explained personally, she said it was not my better self that was speaking, and that she knew I still really loved her. When I wrote it to her with brutal explicitness, she read the letter carefully and then sent it back to me with a note to say that she had not had the courage to open it, and that I ought to be ashamed of having written it. [*He comes beside Grace, and puts his left hand caressingly round her neck*]. You see, dearie, she wont look the situation in the face.

GRACE [*shaking off his hand and turning a little away on the stool*] I am afraid, from the light way you speak of it, you did not sound the right chord.

CHARTERIS. My dear: when you are doing what a woman calls breaking her heart, you may sound the very prettiest chords you can find on the piano; but to her ears it is just like this. [*He sits down on the bass end of the keyboard. Grace puts her fingers in her ears. He rises and moves away from the piano, saying*] No, my dear: Ive been kind; Ive been frank; Ive been everything that a goodnatured man can be; but she only takes it as the making up of a lovers' quarrel. [*Grace winces*]. Frankness and kindness: one is as bad as the other. Especially frankness. Ive tried both. [*He crosses to the fireplace, and stands facing the fire, looking at the ornaments on*

728

the mantelpiece, and warming his hands].

GRACE [*her voice a little strained*] What are you going to try now?

CHARTERIS [*on the hearthrug, turning to face her*] Action, my dear. Marriage. In that she must believe. She wont be convinced by anything short of it; because, you see, Ive had some tremendous philanderings before, and have gone back to her after them.

GRACE. And so that is why you want to marry me?

CHARTERIS. I cannot deny it, my love. Yes: it is your mission to rescue me from Julia.

GRACE [*rising*] Then, if you please, I decline to be made use of for any such purpose. I will not steal you from another woman. [*She walks up and down the room with ominous disquiet*].

CHARTERIS. Steal me! [*He comes towards her*]. Grace: I have a question to put to you as an advanced woman. Mind! as an advanced woman. Does Julia belong to me? Am I her owner—her master?

GRACE. Certainly not. No woman is the property of a man. A woman belongs to herself and to nobody else.

CHARTERIS. Quite right. Ibsen for ever! Thats exactly my opinion. Now tell me, do I belong to Julia; or have I a right to belong to myself?

GRACE [*puzzled*] Of course you have; but—

CHARTERIS [*interrupting her triumphantly*] Then how can you steal me from Julia if I dont belong to her? [*He catches her by the shoulders and holds her out at arms length in front of him*]. Eh, little philosopher? No, my dear: if Ibsen sauce is good for the goose, it's good for the gander as well. Besides [*coaxing her*] it was nothing but a philander with Julia. Nothing else in the world, I assure you.

GRACE [*breaking away from him*] So much the worse! I hate your philanderings: they make me ashamed of you and of myself. [*She goes to the sofa and sits in the corner furthest from the piano, leaning gloomily on her elbow with her face averted*].

729

CHARTERIS. Grace: you utterly misunderstand the origin of my philanderings. [*He sits down beside her*]. Listen to me. Am I a particularly handsome man?

GRACE [*astonished at his conceit*] No.

CHARTERIS [*triumphantly*] You admit it. Am I a well dressed man?

GRACE. Not particularly.

CHARTERIS. Of course not. Have I a romantic mysterious charm about me? do I look as if a secret sorrow preyed on me? am I gallant to women?

GRACE. Not in the least.

CHARTERIS. Certainly not. No one can accuse me of it. Then whose fault is it that half the women I speak to fall in love with me? Not mine: I hate it: it bores me to distraction. At first it flattered me—delighted me—that was how Julia got me, because she was the first woman who had the pluck to make me a declaration. But I soon had enough of it; and at no time have I taken the initiative and persecuted women with my advances as women have persecuted me. Never. Except, of course, in your case.

GRACE. Oh, you need not make any exception. I had a good deal of trouble to induce you to come and see us. You were very coy.

CHARTERIS [*fondly, taking her hand*] With you, dearest, the coyness was sheer coquetry. I loved you from the first, and fled only that you might pursue. But come! let us talk about something really interesting. [*He takes her in his arms*]. Do you love me better than anyone else in the world?

GRACE. I dont think you like to be loved too much.

CHARTERIS. That depends on who the person is. You [*pressing her to his heart*] cannot love me too much: you cannot love me half enough. I reproach you every day for your coldness, your—[*A violent double knock without. They start and listen, still in one another's arms, hardly daring to breathe*]. Who the deuce is calling at this hour?

GRACE. I cant imagine. [*They listen guiltily. The door of the flat is opened without. They hastily get away from one another*].

A WOMAN'S VOICE OUTSIDE. Is Mr Charteris here?

CHARTERIS [*springing up*] Julia! The devil! [*He stands at the end of the sofa with his eyes fixed on the door and his heart beating very unpleasantly*].

GRACE [*rising also*] What can she want?

THE VOICE. Never mind: I will announce myself. [*A beautiful, dark, tragic looking woman, in mantle and toque, appears at the door, raging*]. Oh, this is charming. I have interrupted a pretty tête-à-tête. Oh, you villain! [*She comes straight at Grace. Charteris runs across behind the sofa, and stops her. She struggles furiously with him. Grace preserves her self-possession, but retreats quietly to the piano. Julia, finding Charteris too strong for her, gives up her attempt to get at Grace, but strikes him in the face as she frees herself*].

CHARTERIS [*shocked*] Oh, Julia, Julia! This is too bad.

JULIA. Is it, indeed, too bad? What are you doing up here with that woman? You scoundrel! But now listen to me, Leonard: you have driven me to desperation; and I dont care what I do, or who hears me: I'll not bear it. She shall not have my place with you—

CHARTERIS. Sh-sh!

JULIA. No, no: I dont care: I will expose her true character before everybody. You belong to me: you have no right to be here; and she knows it.

CHARTERIS. I think you had better let me take you home, Julia.

JULIA. I will not. I am not going home: I am going to stay here—h e r e—until I have made you give her up.

CHARTERIS. My dear: you must be reasonable. You really cannot stay in Mrs Tranfield's house if she objects. She can ring the bell and have us both put out.

JULIA. Let her do it then. Let her ring the bell if she dares. Let us see how this pure virtuous creature will face the scandal of what I will declare about her. Let us see how y o u will face it. I have nothing to lose. Everybody knows how you have treated me: you have boasted of your conquests, you poor pitiful vain creature: I am the common talk of your acquaintances and hers. Oh, I have calculated my advantage [*she tears off her mantle*]: I am a most unhappy and injured woman; but I am not the fool you take me to be. I am going to stay: see? [*She flings the mantle on the round table; puts her toque on it; and sits down*]. Now, Mrs Tranfield: theres the bell [*pointing to the button beside the fireplace*]: why dont you ring? [*Grace, looking attentively at Charteris, does not move*]. Ha! ha! I thought so.

CHARTERIS [*quietly, without relaxing his watch on Julia*] Mrs Tranfield: I think you had better go into another room. [*Grace makes a movement towards the door, but stops and looks inquiringly at Charteris as Julia springs up to intercept her. He advances a step to guard the way to the door*].

JULIA. She shall not. She shall stay here. She shall know what you are, and how you have been in love with me: how it is not two days since you kissed me and told me that the future would be as happy as the past. [*Screaming at him*] You did: deny it if you dare.

CHARTERIS [*to Grace in a low voice*] Go.

GRACE [*with nonchalant disgust, going*] Get her away as soon as you can, Leonard.

Julia, with a stifled cry of rage, rushes at Grace, who is crossing behind the sofa towards the door. Charteris seizes Julia, and prevents her from getting past the sofa. Grace goes out. Charteris, holding Julia fast, looks round to the door to see whether Grace is safely out of the room.

JULIA [*suddenly ceasing to struggle, and speaking with the most pathetic dignity*] Oh, there is no need to be violent. [*He passes her across to the sofa, and leans against the end of it, panting and mopping his forehead*]. That is worthy of you! to use brute force! to humiliate me before her! [*She bursts into tears*].

CHARTERIS [*to himself, with melancholy conviction*] This is going to be a cheerful evening. Now patience! patience! patience! [*He sits down on a chair near the round table*].

JULIA [*in anguish*] Leonard: have you no feeling for me?

THE PHILANDERER

CHARTERIS. Only an intense desire to get you safely out of this.

JULIA [*fiercely*] I am not going to stir.

CHARTERIS [*wearily*] Well, well. [*He heaves a long sigh*].

They sit silent for a while: Julia striving, not to regain her self-control, but to maintain her rage at boiling point.

JULIA [*rising suddenly*] I am going to speak to that woman.

CHARTERIS [*jumping up*] No, no. Hang it, Julia, dont lets have another wrestling match. Remember: I'm getting on for forty: youre too young for me. Sit down; or else let me take you home. Suppose her father comes in!

JULIA. I dont care. It rests with you. I am ready to go if she will give you up: until then I stay. Those are my terms: you owe me that. [*She sits down determinedly*].

Charteris looks at her for a moment; then, making up his mind, goes resolutely to the sofa; sits down near the end of it, she being at the opposite end; and speaks with biting emphasis.

CHARTERIS. I owe you just exactly nothing.

JULIA [*reproachfully*] Nothing! You can look me in the face and say that? Oh, Leonard!

CHARTERIS. Let me remind you, Julia, that when first we became acquainted, the position you took up was that of a woman of advanced views.

JULIA. That should have made you respect me the more.

CHARTERIS [*placably*] So it did, my dear. But that is not the point. As a woman of advanced views, you were determined to be free. You regarded marriage as a degrading bargain, by which a woman sells herself to a man for the social status of a wife and the right to be supported and pensioned in old age out of his income. Thats the advanced view: our view. Besides, if you had married me, I might have turned out a drunkard, a criminal, an imbecile, a horror to you; and you couldnt have released yourself. Too big a risk, you see. Thats the rational view: our view. Accordingly, you reserved the right to leave me at any time if you found our companionship incompatible with—what was the expression you used?—with your full development as a

733

human being. I think that was how you put the Ibsenist view: our view. So I had to be content with a charming philander, which taught me a great deal, and brought me some hours of exquisite happiness.

JULIA. Leonard: you confess then, that you owe me something?

CHARTERIS [*haughtily*] No: what I received, I paid. Did you learn nothing from me? was there no delight for you in our friendship?

JULIA [*vehemently and movingly; for she is now sincere*] No. You made me pay dearly for every moment of happiness. You revenged yourself on me for the humiliation of being the slave of your passion for me. I was never sure of you for a moment. I trembled whenever a letter came from you, lest it should contain some stab for me. I dreaded your visits almost as much as I longed for them. I was your plaything, not your companion. [*She rises, exclaiming*] Oh, there was such suffering in my happiness that I hardly knew joy from pain. [*She sinks on the piano stool, and adds, as she buries her face in her hands and turns away from him*] Better for me if I had never met you!

CHARTERIS [*rising indignantly*] You ungenerous wretch! Is this your gratitude for the way I have just been flattering you? What have I not endured from you? endured with angelic patience? Did I not find out, before our friendship was a fortnight old, that all your advanced views were merely a fashion picked up and followed like any other fashion, without understanding or meaning a word of them? Did you not, in spite of your care for your own liberty, set up claims on me compared to which the claims of the most jealous wife would have been trifles? Have I a single woman friend whom you have not abused as old, ugly, vicious—

JULIA [*quickly looking up*] So they are.

CHARTERIS. Well, then, I'll come to grievances that even you can understand. I accuse you of habitual and intolerable jealousy and ill temper; of insulting me on imaginary provocation; of positively beating me; of stealing letters of mine—

JULIA. Yes, nice letters!

CHARTERIS. —of breaking your solemn promises not to do it again; of spending hours—aye, days! piecing together the contents of my waste paper basket in your search for more letters; and then representing yourself as an ill used saint and martyr wantonly betrayed and deserted by a selfish monster of a man.

JULIA [*rising*] I was justified in reading your letters. Our perfect confidence in one another gave me the right to do it.

CHARTERIS. Thank you. Then I hasten to break off a confidence which gives such rights. [*He sits down sulkily on the sofa*].

JULIA [*bending over him threateningly*] You have no right to break it off.

CHARTERIS. I have. You refused to marry me because—

JULIA. I did not. You never asked me. If we were married, you would never dare treat me as you are doing now.

CHARTERIS [*laboriously going back to his argument*] It was understood between us as people of advanced views that we were not to marry; because, as the law stands, I might have become a drunkard, a—

JULIA. —a criminal, an imbecile or a horror. You said that before. [*She sits down beside him with a fling*].

CHARTERIS [*politely*] I beg your pardon, my dear. I know I have a habit of repeating myself. The point is that you reserved your freedom to give me up when you pleased.

JULIA. Well, what of that? I do not please to give you up; and I will not. You have not become a drunkard or a criminal.

CHARTERIS. You dont see the point yet, Julia. You seem to forget that in reserving your freedom to leave me in case I should turn out badly, you also reserved my freedom to leave you in case you should turn out badly.

JULIA. Very ingenious. And pray, have *I* become a drunkard, or a criminal, or an imbecile?

CHARTERIS. You have become what is infinitely worse

735

than all three together: a jealous termagant.

JULIA [*shaking her head bitterly*] Yes: abuse me: call me names.

CHARTERIS. I now assert the right I reserved: the right of breaking with you when I please. Advanced views, Julia, involve advanced duties: you cannot be an advanced woman when you want to bring a man to your feet, and a conventional woman when you want to hold him there against his will. Advanced people form charming friendships: conventional people marry. Marriage suits a good many people; and its first duty is fidelity. Friendship suits some people; and its first duty is unhesitating uncomplaining acceptance of a notice of change of feeling from either side. You chose friendship instead of marriage. Now do your duty, and accept your notice.

JULIA. Never. We are engaged in the eye of—the eye of—

CHARTERIS. Yes, Julia? Cant you get it out? In the eye of something that advanced women dont believe in, eh?

JULIA [*throwing herself at his feet*] Oh, Leonard, dont be cruel. I'm too miserable to argue—to think. I only know I love you. You reproach me with not wanting to marry you. I would have married you at any time after I came to love you, if you had asked me. I will marry you now if you will.

CHARTERIS. I wont, my dear. Thats flat. We're intellectually incompatible.

JULIA. But why? We could be so happy. You love me: I know you love me. I feel it. You say "My dear" to me: you have said it several times this evening. I know I have been wicked, odious, bad: I say nothing in defence of myself. But dont be hard on me. I was distracted by the thought of losing you. I cant face life without you, Leonard. I was happy when I met you: I had never loved any one; and if you had only let me alone, I could have gone on contentedly by myself. But I cant now. I must have you with me. Dont cast me off without a thought of all I have at stake. I could be a friend to you if you would only let me; if you would only

736

tell me your plans; give me a share in your work; treat me as something more than the amusement of an idle hour. Oh, Leonard, Leonard, youve never given me a chance: indeed you havnt. I'll take pains; I'll read; I'll try to think; I'll conquer my jealousy; I'll—[*she breaks down, rocking her head desperately on his knees and writhing*]. Oh, I'm mad: I'm mad: youll kill me if you desert me.

CHARTERIS [*petting her*] My dear love, dont cry: dont go on in this way. You know I cant help it.

JULIA [*sobbing as he rises and tenderly lifts her with him*] Oh, you can, you can. One word from you will make us happy for ever.

CHARTERIS [*diplomatically*] Come, my dear: we really must go. We cant stay until Cuthbertson comes. [*He releases her gently, and takes her mantle from the table*]. Here is your mantle: put it on and be good. You have given me a terrible evening: you must have some consideration for me.

JULIA [*dangerous again*] Then I am to be cast off?

CHARTERIS [*coaxingly*] You are to put on your bonnet, dearest. [*He puts the mantle on her shoulders*].

JULIA [*with a bitter half laugh, half sob*] Well, I suppose I must do what I am told. [*She goes to the table, and looks for her toque. She sees the yellow backed French novel*]. Ah, look at that [*holding it out to him*]! Look at what the creature reads! filthy, vile French stuff that no decent woman would touch. And you—you have been reading it with her.

CHARTERIS. You recommended that book to me yourself.

JULIA. Faugh! [*She dashes it on the floor*].

CHARTERIS [*running anxiously to the book*] Dont damage property, Julia. [*He picks it up and dusts it*]. Making scenes is an affair of sentiment: damaging property is serious. [*He replaces it on the table*]. And now do pray come along.

JULIA [*implacably*] You can go: there is nothing to prevent you. I will not stir. [*She sits down stubbornly on the sofa*].

CHARTERIS [*losing patience*] Oh come! I am not going to begin all this over again. There are limits even to my for-

THE PHILANDERER

bearance. Come on.

JULIA. I will not, I tell you.

CHARTERIS. Then goodnight. [*He makes resolutely for the door. With a rush, she gets there before him and bars his way*]. I thought you wanted me to go.

JULIA [*at the door*] You shall not leave me here alone.

CHARTERIS. Then come with me.

JULIA. Not until you have sworn to me to give up that woman.

CHARTERIS. My dear: I will swear anything if youll only come away and put an end to this.

JULIA [*perplexed, doubting him*] You will swear?

CHARTERIS. Solemnly. Propose the oath. I have been on the point of swearing for the last half hour.

JULIA [*despairingly*] You are only making fun of me. I want no oaths. I want your promise: your sacred word of honor.

CHARTERIS. Certainly: anything you demand, on condition that you come away immediately. On my sacred word of honor as a gentleman—as an Englishman—as anything you like—I will never see her again, never speak to her, never think of her. Now come.

JULIA. But are you in earnest? Will you keep your word?

CHARTERIS [*smiling subtly*] Now you are getting unreasonable. Do come along without any more nonsense. At any rate, I am going. I am not strong enough to carry you home; but I am strong enough to make my way through that door in spite of you. You will then have a new grievance against me for my brutal violence. [*He takes a step towards the door*].

JULIA [*solemnly*] If you do, I swear I will throw myself from that window, Leonard, as you pass out.

CHARTERIS [*unimpressed*] That window is at the back of the building. I shall pass out at the front; so you will not hurt me. Goodnight. [*He approaches the door*].

JULIA. Leonard: have you no pity?

CHARTERIS. Not the least. When you condescend to these

antics you force me to despise you. How can a woman who behaves like a spoiled child and talks like a sentimental novel have the audacity to dream of being a companion for a man of any sort of sense or character? [*She gives an inarticulate cry, and throws herself sobbing on his breast*]. Come! dont cry, my dear Julia: you dont look half so beautiful as when youre happy; and it makes me all damp. Come along.

JULIA [*affectionately*] I'll come, dear, if you wish it. Give me one kiss.

CHARTERIS [*exasperated*] This is too much. No: I'm dashed if I will. Here: let me go, Julia. [*She clings to him*]. Will you come without another word if I give you a kiss?

JULIA. I will do anything you wish, darling.

CHARTERIS. Well, here. [*He takes her in his arms and gives her an unceremonious kiss*]. Now remember your promise. Come along.

JULIA. That was not a nice kiss, dearest. I want one of our old real kisses.

CHARTERIS [*furious*] Oh, go to the deuce. [*He disengages himself impulsively; and she, as if he had flung her down, falls pathetically with a stifled moan. With an angry look at her, he strides out and slams the door. She raises herself on one hand, listening to his retreating footsteps. They stop. Her face lights up with eager, triumphant cunning. The steps return hastily. She throws herself down again as before. Charteris reappears, in the utmost dismay, exclaiming*] Julia: we're done. Cuthbertson's coming upstairs with your father [*she sits up quickly*]. Do you hear? the two fathers!

JULIA [*sitting on the floor*] Impossible. They dont know one another.

CHARTERIS [*desperately*] I tell you theyre coming up together like twins. What on earth are we to do?

JULIA [*scrambling up with the help of his hand*] Quick: the lift: we can go down in that. [*She rushes to the table for her toque*].

CHARTERIS. No: the man's gone home; and the lift's locked.

739

THE PHILANDERER

JULIA [*putting on her toque at express speed*] Let's go up to the next floor.

CHARTERIS. Theres no next floor. We're at the top of the house. No, no: you must invent some thumping lie. I cant think of one: you can, Julia. Exercise all your genius. I'll back you up.

JULIA. But—

CHARTERIS. Sh-sh! Here they are. Sit down and look at home. [*Julia tears off her toque and mantle; throws them on the table; and darts to the piano, at which she seats herself*].

JULIA. Come and sing.

She plays the symphony to When Other Lips. Charteris stands at the piano, as if about to sing. Two elderly gentlemen enter. Julia stops playing.

The elder of the two newcomers, Colonel Daniel Craven, affects the bluff simple veteran, and carries it off pleasantly and well, having a fine upright figure, and being, in fact, a good-naturedly impulsive credulous person who, after an entirely thoughtless career as an officer and a gentleman, is now being startled into some sort of self-education by the surprising proceedings of his children.

His companion, Mr Joseph Cuthbertson, Grace's father, has none of the Colonel's boyishness. He is a man of fervent idealistic sentiment, so frequently outraged by the facts of life that he has acquired an habitually indignant manner, which unexpectedly becomes enthusiastic or affectionate when he speaks.

The two men differ greatly in expression. The Colonel's face is lined with weather, with age, with eating and drinking, and with the cumulative effect of many petty vexations, but not with thought: he is still fresh, still full of expectations of pleasure and novelty. Cuthbertson has the lines of sedentary London brain work, with its chronic fatigue and longing for rest and recreative emotion, and its disillusioned indifference to adventure and enjoyment, except as a means of recuperation. His vigilant, irascible eye, piled-up hair, and the honorable seriousness with which he takes himself, give him an air of considerable consequence.

They are both in evening dress. Cuthbertson has not taken off

THE PHILANDERER

his fur-collared overcoat.

CUTHBERTSON [*with a hospitable show of delight at finding visitors*] Dont stop, Miss Craven. Go on, Charteris.

He comes behind the sofa, and hangs his overcoat on it, after taking an opera glass and a theatre program from the pockets, and putting them down on the piano. Craven meanwhile goes to the fireplace, and plants himself on the hearthrug.

CHARTERIS. No, thank you. Miss Craven has just been taking me through an old song; and Ive had enough of it. [*He takes the song off the piano desk and lays it aside; then closes the lid over the keyboard*].

JULIA [*passing between the sofa and piano to shake hands with Cuthbertson*] Why, youve brought Daddy! What a surprise! [*Looking across to Craven*] So glad youve come, Dad. [*She takes a chair near the window, and sits there*].

CUTHBERTSON. Craven: let me introduce you to Mr Leonard Charteris, the famous Ibsenist philosopher.

CRAVEN. Oh, we know one another already. Charteris is quite at home in our house, Jo.

CUTHBERTSON. I beg both your pardons. He's quite at home here too. [*Charteris sits down on the piano stool*]. By the bye, wheres Grace?

JULIA AND CHARTERIS. Er— [*They stop and look at one another*].

JULIA [*politely*] I beg your pardon, Mr Charteris: I interrupted you.

CHARTERIS. Not at all, Miss Craven. [*An awkward pause*].

CUTHBERTSON [*to help them out*] You were going to tell us about Grace, Charteris.

CHARTERIS. I was only going to say that I didnt know that you and Craven were acquainted.

CRAVEN. Why, *I* didnt know it until tonight. It's a most extraordinary thing. We met by chance at the theatre; and he turns out to be my oldest friend.

CUTHBERTSON [*energetically*] Yes, Craven; and do you see how this proves what I was saying to you about the

741

break-up of family life? Here are all our young people bosom friends, inseparables; and yet they never said a word of it to us. We two, who knew each other before they were born, might never have met again if you hadnt popped into the stall next mine tonight by pure chance. Come: sit down [*bustling over to him affectionately, and pushing him into the armchair above the fire*]: theres your place, by my fireside, whenever you choose to fill it. [*He posts himself at the end of the sofa, leaning against it and admiring Craven*]. Just imagine you being Dan Craven!

CRAVEN. Just imagine you being Jo Cuthbertson, though! Thats a far more extraordinary coincidence; because I'd got it into my head that your name was Tranfield.

CUTHBERTSON. Oh, thats my daughter's name. She's a widow, you know. How uncommonly well you look, Dan! The years havnt hurt you much.

CRAVEN [*suddenly becoming unnaturally gloomy*] I look well. I even feel well. But my days are numbered.

CUTHBERTSON [*alarmed*] Oh. dont say that, my dear fellow. I hope not.

JULIA [*with anguish in her voice*] Daddy! [*Cuthbertson looks inquiringly round at her*].

CRAVEN. There, there, my dear: I was wrong to talk of it. It's a sad subject. But it's better that Cuthbertson should know. We used to be very close friends, and are so still, I hope. [*Cuthbertson goes to Craven and presses his hand silently; then returns to the sofa and sits down, pulling out his handkerchief, and displaying some emotion*].

CHARTERIS [*a little impatiently*] The fact is, Cuthbertson, Craven's a devout believer in the department of witchcraft called medical science. He's celebrated in all the medical schools as an example of the newest sort of liver complaint. The doctors say he cant last another year; and he has fully made up his mind not to survive next Easter, just to oblige them.

CRAVEN [*with military affectation*] It's very kind of you to try to keep up my spirits by making light of it, Charteris.

742

But I shall be ready when my time comes. I'm a soldier. [*A sob from Julia*]. Dont cry, Julia.

CUTHBERTSON [*huskily*] I hope you may long be spared, Dan.

CRAVEN. To oblige me, Jo, change the subject. [*He gets up, and again posts himself on the hearthrug with his back to the fire*].

CHARTERIS. Persuade him to join our club, Cuthbertson. He mopes.

JULIA. It's no use. Sylvia and I are always at him to join; but he wont.

CRAVEN. My child: I have my own club.

CHARTERIS [*contemptuously*] Yes: the Junior Army and Navy! Do you call that a club? Why, they darent let a woman cross the doorstep!

CRAVEN [*a little ruffled*] Clubs are a matter of taste, Charteris. You like a cock-and-hen club: I dont. It's bad enough to have Julia and her sister—a girl under twenty!—spending half their time at such a place. Besides, now really, such a name for a club! The Ibsen club! I should be laughed out of London. The Ibsen club! Come, Cuthbertson! back me up. I'm sure you agree with me.

CHARTERIS. Cuthbertson's a member.

CRAVEN [*amazed*] No! Why, he's been talking to me all the evening about the way in which everything is going to the dogs through advanced ideas in the younger generation.

CHARTERIS. Of course. He's been studying it in the club. He's always there.

CUTHBERTSON [*warmly*] Not always. Dont exaggerate, Charteris. You know very well that though I joined the club on Grace's account, thinking that her father's presence there would be a protection and a—a sort of sanction, as it were, I never approved of it.

CRAVEN [*tactlessly harping on Cuthbertson's inconsistency*] Well, you know, this is unexpected: now it's really very unexpected. I should never have thought it from hearing you

743

talk, Jo. Why, you said the whole modern movement was abhorrent to you because your life had been passed in witnessing scenes of suffering nobly endured and sacrifice willingly rendered by womanly women and manly men and deuce knows what else. Is it at the Ibsen club that you see all this manliness and womanliness?

CHARTERIS. Certainly not: the rules of the club forbid anything of the sort. Every candidate for membership must be nominated by a man and a woman, who both guarantee that the candidate, if female, is not womanly, and if male, not manly.

CRAVEN [*chuckling cunningly, as he stoops to press his heated trousers against his legs, which are chilly*] Wont do, Charteris. Cant take me in with so thin a story as that.

CUTHBERTSON [*vehemently*] It's true. It's monstrous; but it's true.

CRAVEN [*with rising indignation, as he begins to draw the inevitable inferences*] Do you mean to say that somebody had the audacity to guarantee that my Julia is not a womanly woman?

CHARTERIS [*darkly*] It sounds incredible; but a man was found ready to take that inconceivable lie on his conscience.

JULIA [*firing up*] If he has nothing worse than that on his conscience, he may sleep pretty well. In what way am I more womanly than any of the rest of them, I should like to know? They are always saying things like that behind my back: I hear of them from Sylvia. Only the other day a member of the committee said I ought never to have been elected—that you [*to Charteris*] had smuggled me in. I should like to see her say it to my face: thats all.

CRAVEN. But, my precious, I most sincerely hope she was right. She paid you the highest compliment. Why, the place must be a den of infamy.

CUTHBERTSON [*emphatically*] So it is, Craven: so it is.

CHARTERIS. Exactly. Thats what keeps it so select: nobody but people whose reputations are above suspicion dare belong to it. If we once got a good name, we should become a mere whitewashing shop for all the shady characters in London. Better join us, Craven. Let me put you up.

CRAVEN. What! Join a club where theres some scoundrel who guaranteed my daughter to be an unwomanly woman! If I werent an invalid, I'd kick him.

CHARTERIS. Oh dont say that. It was I.

CRAVEN [*reproachfully*] You! Now upon my soul, Charteris, this is very vexing. Now how could you bring yourself to do such a thing?

CHARTERIS. She made me. Why, I had to guarantee Cuthbertson as unmanly; and he's the leading representative of manly sentiment in London.

CRAVEN. That didnt do Jo any harm; but it took away my Julia's character.

JULIA [*outraged*] Daddy!

CHARTERIS. Not at the Ibsen club: quite the contrary. After all, what can we do? You know what breaks up most clubs for men and women. Theres a quarrel—a scandal—cherchez la femme—always a woman at the bottom of it. Well, we knew this when we founded the club; but we noticed that the woman at the bottom of it was always a womanly woman. The unwomanly women who work for their living, and know how to take care of themselves, never give any trouble. So we simply said we wouldnt have any womanly women; and when one gets smuggled in she has to take care not to behave in a womanly way. We get on all right. [*He rises*]. Come to lunch with me there tomorrow and see the place.

CUTHBERTSON [*rising*] No: he's engaged to me. But you can join us.

CHARTERIS. What hour?

CUTHBERTSON. Any time after twelve. [*To Craven*] It's at 90 Cork Street, at the other end of the Burlington Arcade.

CRAVEN [*making a note on his cuff*] 90, you say. After twelve. [*Suddenly relapsing into gloom*] By the bye, dont order anything special for me. I'm not allowed wine: only Apol-

745

linaris. No meat either: only a scrap of fish occasionally. I'm to have a short life, but not a merry one. [*Sighing*] Well, well! [*Bracing himself up*] Now, Julia: it's time for us to be off. [*Julia rises*].

CUTHBERTSON. But where on earth is Grace? I must go and look for her. [*He turns to the door*].

JULIA [*stopping him*] Oh pray dont disturb her, Mr Cuthbertson. She's so tired.

CUTHBERTSON. But just for a moment, to say goodnight. [*Julia and Charteris look at one another in dismay. Cuthbertson looks quickly at them, perceiving that something is wrong*].

CHARTERIS. We must make a clean breast of it, I see.

CUTHBERTSON. Of what?

CHARTERIS. The truth is, Cuthbertson, Mrs Tranfield, who is, as you know, the most thoughtful of women, took it into her head that I—well, that I particularly wanted to speak to Miss Craven alone. So she said she was tired, and went to bed.

CRAVEN [*scandalized*] Tut! tut!

CUTHBERTSON. Oho! is that it? Then it's all right: she never goes to bed as early as this. I'll fetch her in a moment. [*He goes out confidently, leaving Charteris aghast*].

JULIA. Now youve done it. [*She rushes to the round table, and snatches up her mantle and toque*]. I'm off. [*She makes for the door*].

CRAVEN [*horrified*] What are you doing, Julia? You cant go until youve said goodnight to Mrs Tranfield. It'd be horribly rude.

JULIA. You can stay if you like, Daddy: I cant. I'll wait for you in the hall. [*She hurries out*].

CRAVEN [*following her*] But what on earth am I to say? [*She disappears, shutting the door behind her in his face. He turns to Charteris, grumbling*]. Now really you know, Charteris, this is devilish awkward: upon my life it is. That was a most indelicate thing of you to say plump out before us all: that about you and Julia.

CHARTERIS. I'll explain it all tomorrow. Just at present

we'd really better follow Julia's example and bolt. [*He starts for the door*].

CRAVEN [*intercepting him*] Stop! dont leave me like this: I shall look like a fool. Now I shall really take it in bad part if you run away, Charteris.

CHARTERIS. All right. I'll stay. [*He lifts himself on to the shoulder of the grand piano and sits there swinging his legs and contemplating Craven resignedly*].

CRAVEN [*pacing up and down*] I'm excessively vexed about Julia's conduct: I am indeed. She cant bear to be crossed in the slightest thing, poor child. I'll have to apologize for her, you know: her going away is a downright slap in the face for these people here. Cuthbertson may be offended already for all I know.

CHARTERIS. Oh, never mind about him. Mrs Tranfield bosses this establishment.

CRAVEN [*cunningly*] Ah, thats it, is it? He's just the sort of fellow that would have no control over his daughter. [*He goes back to his former place on the hearthrug with his back to the fire*]. By the bye, what the dickens did he mean by all that about passing his life amid—what was it?—"scenes of suffering nobly endured and sacrifice willingly rendered by womanly women and manly men" and a lot more of the same sort? I suppose he's something in a hospital.

CHARTERIS. Hospital! Nonsense! he's a dramatic critic. Didnt you hear me say he was the leading representative of manly sentiment in London?

CRAVEN. You dont say so! Now really, who'd have thought it! How jolly it must be to be able to go to the theatre for nothing! I must ask him to get me a few tickets occasionally. But isnt it ridiculous for a man to talk like that? I'm hanged if he dont take what he sees on the stage quite seriously.

CHARTERIS. Of course: thats why he's a good critic. Besides, if you take people seriously off the stage, why shouldnt you take them seriously on it, where theyre under some sort of decent restraint? [*He jumps down from the piano, and goes*

747

to the window].

Cuthbertson comes back.

CUTHBERTSON [*to Craven, rather sheepishly*] The fact is, Grace has gone to bed. I must apologize to you and Miss— [*He turns to Julia's seat, and stops on seeing it vacant*].

CRAVEN [*embarrassed*] It is I who have to apologize for Julia, Jo. She—

CHARTERIS [*interrupting*] She said she was quite sure that if we didnt go, youd persuade Mrs Tranfield to get up to say goodnight for the sake of politeness; so she went straight off.

CUTHBERTSON. Very kind of her indeed. I'm really ashamed—

CRAVEN. Dont mention it, Jo: dont mention it. She's waiting for me below. [*Going*] Goodnight. Goodnight, Charteris.

CHARTERIS. Goodnight.

CUTHBERTSON [*seeing Craven out*] Goodnight. Say goodnight and thanks to Miss Craven for me. Tomorrow any time after twelve, remember. [*They go out.*]

Charteris, with a long sigh, crosses to the fireplace, thoroughly tired out.

CRAVEN [*outside*] All right.

CUTHBERTSON [*outside*] Take care of the stairs: theyre rather steep. Goodnight. [*The outside door shuts*].

Cuthbertson returns. Instead of entering, he stands impressively in the doorway with one hand in the breast of his waistcoat, eyeing Charteris sternly.

CHARTERIS. Whats the matter?

CUTHBERTSON [*sternly*] Charteris: what has been going on here? I insist on knowing. Grace has not gone to bed: I have seen and spoken with her. What is it all about?

CHARTERIS. Ask your theatrical experience, Cuthbertson. A man, of course.

CUTHBERTSON [*coming forward and confronting him*] Dont play the fool with me, Charteris: I'm too old a hand to be amused by it. I ask you, seriously, what is the matter?

748

CHARTERIS. I tell you, seriously, I'm the matter. Julia wants to marry me: I want to marry Grace. I came here tonight to sweetheart Grace. Enter Julia. Alarums and excursions. Exit Grace. Enter you and Craven. Subterfuges and excuses. Exeunt Craven and Julia. And here we are. Thats the whole story. Sleep over it. Goodnight. [*He leaves*].

CUTHBERTSON [*staring after him*] Well I'll be—

ACT II

NEXT day at noon, in the library of the Ibsen club. A long room, with glass doors half-way down on both sides, leading respectively to the dining room corridor and the main staircase. At the end, in the middle, is the fireplace, surmounted by a handsome mantelpiece, with a bust of Ibsen, and decorative inscriptions of the titles of his plays. There are circular recesses at each side of the fireplace, with divan seats running round them, the space above the divans lined with books. A long settee faces the fire. Along the back of the settee, and touching it, is a green table, littered with journals. Ibsen, looking down the room, has the dining room door on his left, and further on, nearly in the middle of the library, a revolving bookcase, with an easy chair close to it. On his right, between the door and the recess, is a light library step-ladder. Further on, past the door an easy chair, and a smaller one between it and the middle of the room. Placards inscribed SILENCE are conspicuously exhibited here and there.

Cuthbertson is seated in the easy chair at the revolving bookstand, reading The Daily Graphic. Dr Paramore is on the divan in the recess on Ibsen's right, reading The British Medical Journal. He is young as age is counted in the professions: barely forty. His hair is wearing bald on his forehead; and his dark arched eyebrows, coming rather close together, give him a conscientiously sinister appearance. He wears the frock coat of the fashionable physician, and cultivates the professional bedside manner with scrupulous conventionality. Not at all a happy or frank man, but not consciously unhappy nor intentionally insincere, and highly self-satisfied intellectually.

Sylvia Craven is sitting in the middle of the settee before the fire, reading a volume of Ibsen, only the back of her head being visible from the middle of the room. She is a pretty girl of eighteen, small and trim, wearing a mountaineering suit of Norfolk jacket and breeches with neat town stockings and shoes. A detachable cloth skirt lies ready to her hand across the end of the settee.

A page boy's voice, monotonously calling for Dr Paramore, is heard approaching outside on the right.

THE PAGE [outside] Dr Paramore, Dr Paramore, Dr Para-

THE PHILANDERER

more [*he enters, carrying a salver with a card on it*] Dr Par—

PARAMORE [*sharply, sitting up*] Here, boy. [*The boy presents the salver. Paramore takes the card and looks at it*]. All right: I'll come down to him. [*The boy goes. Paramore rises, and comes from the recess, throwing his paper on the table*]. Good morning, Mr Cuthbertson [*stopping to pull out his cuffs, and shake his coat straight*]. Mrs Tranfield quite well, I hope?

SYLVIA [*turning her head indignantly*] Sh—sh—sh!

Paramore turns, surprised. Cuthbertson rises energetically and looks across the bookstand to see who is the author of this impertinence.

PARAMORE [*to Sylvia, stiffly*] I beg your pardon, Miss Craven: I did not mean to disturb you.

SYLVIA [*flustered and self-assertive*] You may talk as much as you like if you will have the common consideration to ask first whether the other people object. What I protest against is your assumption that my presence doesnt matter because I'm only a female member. Thats all. Now go on, pray: you dont disturb me in the least. [*She turns to the fire, and again buries herself in Ibsen*].

CUTHBERTSON [*with emphatic dignity*] No gentleman would have dreamt of objecting to our exchanging a few words, madam. [*She takes no notice. He resumes angrily*] As a matter of fact I was about to say to Dr Paramore that if he would care to bring his visitor up here, *I* should not object. The impudence! [*He dashes his paper down on the chair*].

PARAMORE. Oh, many thanks; but it's only an instrument maker.

CUTHBERTSON. Any new medical discoveries, doctor?

PARAMORE. Well, since you ask me, yes: perhaps a most important one. I have discovered something that has hitherto been overlooked: a minute duct in the liver of the guinea pig. Miss Craven will forgive my mentioning it when I say that it may throw an important light on her father's case. The first thing, of course, is to find out what the duct is there for.

751

THE PHILANDERER

CUTHBERTSON [*reverently, feeling that he is in the presence of Science*] Indeed? How will you do that?

PARAMORE. Oh, easily enough, by simply cutting the duct, and seeing what will happen to the guinea pig. [*Sylvia rises, horrified*]. I shall require a knife specially made to get at it. The man who is waiting for me downstairs has brought me a few handles to try before fitting it and sending it to the laboratory. I am afraid it would not do to bring such weapons up here.

SYLVIA. If you attempt such a thing, Dr Paramore, I will complain to the committee. A majority of the members are anti-vivisectionists. You ought to be ashamed of yourself. [*She snatches up the detachable skirt, and begins buttoning it on as she flounces out at the staircase door*].

PARAMORE [*with patient contempt*] Thats the sort of thing we scientific men have to put up with nowadays, Mr Cuthbertson. Ignorance, superstition, sentimentality: they are all one. A guinea pig's convenience is set above the health and lives of the entire human race.

CUTHBERTSON [*vehemently*] It's not ignorance nor superstition, Paramore: it's sheer downright Ibsenism: thats what it is. Ive been wanting to sit comfortably at that fire the whole morning; but Ive never had a chance with that girl there. I couldnt go and plump myself down on a seat beside her: goodness knows what she'd think I wanted! Thats one of the delights of having women in the club: when they come in here they all want to sit at the fire and adore that bust. I sometimes feel that I should like to take the poker, and fetch it a wipe across the nose. Ugh!

PARAMORE. I must say I prefer the elder Miss Craven to her sister.

CUTHBERTSON [*his eye lighting up*] Ah, Julia! I believe you. A splendid fine creature: every inch a woman. No Ibsenism about her!

PARAMORE. I quite agree with you there, Mr Cuthbertson. Er—by the way, do you think is Miss Craven attached to Charteris at all?

752

CUTHBERTSON. What! that fellow! Not he. He hangs about after her; but he's not man enough for her. A woman of that sort likes a strong, manly, deep throated, broad chested man.

PARAMORE [*anxiously*] Hm! a sort of sporting character, you think?

CUTHBERTSON. Oh, no, no. A scientific man, perhaps, like yourself. But you know what I mean: a MAN. [*He strikes himself a sounding blow on the chest*].

PARAMORE. Of course; but Charteris is a man.

CUTHBERTSON. Pah! you dont see what I mean.

The page boy returns with his salver.

THE PAGE [*calling monotonously as before*] Mr Cuthbertson, Mr Cuthbertson, Mr Cuth—

CUTHBERTSON. Here, boy. [*He takes a card from the salver*]. Bring the gentleman up here. [*The boy goes out*]. It's Craven. He's coming to lunch with me and Charteris. You might join us if youve nothing better to do, when youve finished with the instrument man. If Julia turns up I'll ask her too.

PARAMORE [*flushing with pleasure*] I shall be very pleased. Thank you. [*He is going out at the staircase door when Craven enters*]. Good morning, Colonel Craven.

CRAVEN [*at the door*] Good morning: glad to see you. I'm looking for Cuthbertson.

PARAMORE [*smiling*] There he is. [*He goes out*].

CUTHBERTSON [*greeting Craven effusively*] Delighted to see you. Now will you come to the smoking room; or will you sit down here, and have a chat while we're waiting for Charteris? If you like company, the smoking room's always full of women. Here in the library we shall have it pretty well all to ourselves until about three o'clock.

CRAVEN. I dont like to see women smoking. I'll make myself comfortable here. [*He sits in the easy chair on the staircase side*].

CUTHBERTSON [*taking the smaller chair on his left*] Neither do I. Theres not a room in this club where I can enjoy a pipe quietly without a woman coming in and beginning to roll a cigaret. It's a disgusting habit in a woman: it's not natural to her sex.

CRAVEN [*sighing*] Ah, Jo, times have changed since we both courted Molly Ebden all those years ago. I took my defeat well, old chap, didnt I?

CUTHBERTSON [*with earnest approval*] You did, Dan. The thought of it has often helped me to behave well myself: it has, on my honor.

CRAVEN. Yes: you always believed in hearth and home, Jo: in a true English wife, and a happy wholesome fireside. How did Molly turn out?

CUTHBERTSON [*trying to be fair to Molly*] Well, not bad. She might have been worse. You see, I couldnt stand her relations: all the men were roaring cads; and she couldnt get on with my mother. And then she hated being in town; and of course I couldnt live in the country on account of my work. But we hit it off as well as most people until we separated.

CRAVEN [*taken aback*] Separated! [*He is irresistibly amused*]. Oh! that was the end of the hearth and home, Jo, was it?

CUTHBERTSON [*warmly*] It was not my fault, Dan. [*Sentimentally*] Some day the world will know how I loved that woman. But she was incapable of valuing a true man's affection. Do you know, she often said she wished she'd married you instead.

CRAVEN [*sobered by the suggestion*] Dear me! dear me! Well, perhaps it was better as it was. You heard about my marriage, I suppose.

CUTHBERTSON. Oh yes: we all heard of it.

CRAVEN. Well, Jo, I may as well make a clean breast of it: everybody knew it. *I* married for money.

CUTHBERTSON [*encouragingly*] And why not, Dan? Why not? We cant get on without it, you know.

CRAVEN [*with sincere feeling*] I got to be very fond of her, Jo. I had a home until she died. Now everything's changed.

754

Julia's always here. Sylvia's of a different nature; but she's always here too.

CUTHBERTSON [*sympathetically*] I know. It's the same with Grace. She's always here.

CRAVEN. And now they want me to be always here. Theyre at me every day to join the club. To stop my grumbling, I suppose. Thats what I want to consult you about. Do you think I ought to join?

CUTHBERTSON. Well, if you have no conscientious objection—

CRAVEN [*testily interrupting him*] I object to the existence of the place on principle; but whats the use of that? Here it is in spite of my objection; and I may as well have the benefit of any good that may be in it.

CUTHBERTSON [*soothing him*] Of course: thats the only reasonable view of the matter. Well, the fact is, it's not so inconvenient as you might think. When youre at home, you have the house more to yourself; and when you want to have your family about you, you can dine with them at the club.

CRAVEN [*not much attracted by this*] True.

CUTHBERTSON. Besides, if you dont want to dine with them, you neednt.

CRAVEN [*convinced*] True, very true. But dont they carry on here, rather?

CUTHBERTSON. Oh no: they dont exactly carry on. Of course the usual tone of the club is low, because the women smoke, and earn their own living, and all that; but still theres nothing actually to complain of. And it's convenient, certainly.

Charteris comes in, looking round for them.

CRAVEN [*rising*] Do you know, Ive a great mind to join, just to see what it's like.

CHARTERIS [*coming between them*] Do so by all means. I hope I havnt disturbed your chat by coming too soon.

CRAVEN. Not at all. [*He shakes his hand cordially*].

CHARTERIS. Thats right. I'm earlier than I intended. The fact is, I have something rather pressing to say to Cuthbertson.

CRAVEN. Private?

CHARTERIS. Not particularly. [*To Cuthbertson*] Only what we were speaking of last night.

CUTHBERTSON. Well, Charteris, I think that is private, or ought to be.

CRAVEN [*retiring discreetly towards the table*] I'll just take a look at The Times—

CHARTERIS [*stopping him*] Oh, it's no secret: everybody in the club guesses it. [*To Cuthbertson*] Has Grace never mentioned to you that she wants to marry me?

CUTHBERTSON [*indignantly*] She has mentioned that you want to marry her.

CHARTERIS. Ah; but then it's not what I want, but what Grace wants, that will weigh with you.

CRAVEN [*a little shocked*] Excuse me, Charteris: this is private. I'll leave you to yourselves [*again moving towards the table*].

CHARTERIS. Wait a bit, Craven: youre concerned in this. Julia wants to marry me too.

CRAVEN [*in a tone of the strongest remonstrance*] Now really! Now upon my life and soul!

CHARTERIS. It's a fact, I assure you. Didnt it strike you as rather odd, our being up there last night, and Mrs Tranfield not with us?

CRAVEN. Well, yes it did. But you explained it. And now really, Charteris, I must say your explanation was in shocking bad taste before Julia.

CHARTERIS. Never mind. It was a good, fat, healthy, bouncing lie.

CRAVEN AND CUTHBERTSON. Lie!

CHARTERIS. Didnt you suspect that?

CRAVEN. Certainly not. Did you, Jo?

CUTHBERTSON. Not at the moment.

CRAVEN. Whats more, I dont believe you. I'm sorry to have to say such a thing; but you forget that Julia was present, and didnt contradict you.

CHARTERIS. She didnt want to.

CRAVEN. Do you mean to say that my daughter deceived me?

CHARTERIS. Delicacy towards me compelled her to, Craven.

CRAVEN [*taking a very serious tone*] Now look here, Charteris: have you any proper sense of the fact that youre standing between two fathers?

CUTHBERTSON. Quite right, Dan, quite right. I repeat the question on my own account.

CHARTERIS. Well, I'm a little dazed still by standing for so long between two daughters; but I think I grasp the situation. [*Cuthbertson flings away with an exclamation of disgust*].

CRAVEN. Then I'm sorry for your manners, Charteris: thats all. [*He turns away sulkily; then suddenly flares up and comes back at Charteris*]. How dare you tell me my daughter wants to marry you? Who are you, pray, that she should have any such ambition?

CHARTERIS. Just so: you're quite right: she couldnt have made a worse choice. But she wont listen to reason. I assure you, my dear Craven, Ive said everything that fifty fathers could have said; but it's no use: she wont give me up. And if she wont listen to me, what likelihood is there of her listening to you?

CRAVEN [*in angry bewilderment*] Cuthbertson: did you ever hear anything like this?

CUTHBERTSON. Never! Never!

CHARTERIS. Oh, bother! Come! dont behave like a couple of conventional old fathers: this is a serious affair. Look at these letters [*producing a letter and a letter-card*]! This [*shewing the card*] is from Grace—by the way, Cuthbertson, I wish youd ask her not to write on letter-cards: the blue color makes it so easy for Julia to pick the bits out of my waste paper basket and piece them together. Now listen. "My dear Leonard: Nothing could make it worth my while to be exposed to such scenes as last night's. You had much better go back to Julia, and forget me. Yours sincerely,

Grace Tranfield."

CUTHBERTSON. I approve of every word of that letter.

CHARTERIS [*turning to Craven and preparing to read the letter*] Now for Julia. [*The Colonel turns away to hide his face from Charteris, anticipating a shock, and puts his hand on a chair to steady himself*]. "My dearest boy: Nothing will make me believe that this odious woman can take my place in your heart. I send some of the letters you wrote me when we first met; and I ask you to read them. They will recall what you felt when you wrote them. You cannot have changed so much as to be indifferent to me: whoever may have struck your fancy for the moment, your heart is still mine"—and so on: you know the sort of thing—"Ever and always your loving Julia." [*The Colonel sinks on the chair, and covers his face with his hand*]. You dont suppose she's serious, do you? thats the sort of thing she writes me three times a day. [*To Cuthbertson*] Grace is in earnest though, confound it. [*He holds out Grace's letter*]. A blue card as usual! This time I shall not trust the waste paper basket. [*He goes to the fire, and throws the letters into it*].

CUTHBERTSON [*facing him with folded arms as he comes back to them*] May I ask, Mr Charteris, is this the New Humor?

CHARTERIS [*still too preoccupied with his own affairs to have any sense of the effect he is producing on the others*] Oh, stuff! Do you suppose it's a joke to be situated as I am? Youve got your head so stuffed with the New Humor and the New Woman and the New This, That, and The Other, all mixed up with your own old Adam, that youve lost your senses.

CUTHBERTSON [*strenuously*] Do you see that old man, grown grey in the honored service of his country, whose last days you have blighted?

CHARTERIS [*surprised, looking at Craven and realizing his distress with genuine concern*] I'm very sorry. Come, Craven: dont take it to heart. [*Craven shakes his head*]. I assure you it means nothing: it happens to me constantly.

CUTHBERTSON. There is only one excuse for you. You

758

THE PHILANDERER

are not fully responsible for your actions. Like all advanced people, you have got neurasthenia.

CHARTERIS [*appalled*] Great Heavens! whats that?

CUTHBERTSON. I decline to explain. You know as well as I do. I'm going downstairs now to order lunch. I shall order it for three; but the third place is for Paramore, whom I have invited, not for you. [*He goes out through the dining room door*].

CHARTERIS [*putting his hand on Craven's shoulder*] Come, Craven: advise me. Youve been in this sort of fix yourself probably.

CRAVEN. Charteris: no woman writes such a letter to a man unless he has made advances to her.

CHARTERIS [*mournfully*] How little you know the world, Colonel! The New Woman is not like that.

CRAVEN. I can only give you very oldfashioned advice, my boy; and that is that it's well to be off with the Old Woman before youre on with the New. I'm sorry you told me. You might have waited for my death: it's not far off now. [*His head droops again*].

Julia and Paramore come in from the staircase. Julia stops as she catches sight of Charteris, her face clouding, and her breast heaving. Paramore, seeing the Colonel apparently ill, hurries down to him with his bedside manner in full play.

CHARTERIS [*seeing Julia*] Oh, Lord! [*He retreats under the lee of the revolving bookstand*].

PARAMORE [*sympathetically to the Colonel, taking his wrist, and beginning to count his pulse*] Allow me.

CRAVEN [*looking up*] Eh? [*He withdraws his hand and rises rather crossly*]. No, Paramore: it's not my liver now: it's private business.

A chase begins between Julia and Charteris, all the more exciting to them because the huntress and her prey alike must conceal the real object of their movements from the others. Charteris first makes for the staircase door. Julia immediately retreats to it, barring his path. He doubles back round the bookstand, setting it whirling as he makes for the other door, Julia crossing in pursuit

759

of him. He is about to escape when he is cut off by the return of Cuthbertson. Turning back, he sees Julia close upon him. There being nothing else for it, he bolts into the recess on Ibsen's left.

CUTHBERTSON. Good morning, Miss Craven. [*They shake hands*]. Wont you join us at lunch? Paramore's coming too.

JULIA. Thanks: I shall be very pleased. [*She strolls with affected purposelessness towards the recess. Charteris, almost trapped in it, crosses to the opposite recess by way of the fender, knocking down the fireirons with a crash as he does so*].

CRAVEN [*who has crossed to the whirling bookcase and stopped it*] What the dickens are you doing there, Charteris?

CHARTERIS. Nothing. It's such a confounded room to get about in.

JULIA [*maliciously*] Yes: isnt it? [*She is about to move to guard the staircase door when Cuthbertson offers her his arm*].

CUTHBERTSON. May I take you down?

JULIA. No, really: you know it's against the rules of the club to coddle women in any way. Whoever is nearest the door goes first.

CUTHBERTSON. Oh, well, if you insist. Come, gentlemen: let us go to lunch in the Ibsen fashion: the unsexed fashion. [*He turns and goes out, followed by Paramore, who raises his politest consulting-room laugh. Craven goes last*].

CRAVEN [*at the door, gravely*] Come, Julia.

JULIA [*with patronizing affection*] Yes, Daddy dear, presently. Dont wait for me: I'll come in a moment. [*The Colonel hesitates*]. It's all right, Daddy.

CRAVEN [*very gravely*] Dont be long, my dear. [*He goes out*].

CHARTERIS. I'm off. [*He makes a dash for the staircase door*].

JULIA [*darting at him and seizing his wrist*] Arnt you coming?

CHARTERIS. No. Unhand me, Julia. [*He tries to get away: she holds him*]. If you dont let me go, I'll scream for help.

JULIA [*reproachfully*] Leonard! [*He breaks away from her*]. Oh, how can you be so rough with me, dear! Did you get

760

my letter?

CHARTERIS. Burnt it—

Julia turns away, struck to the heart, and buries her face in her hands.

CHARTERIS [*continuing*]—along with hers.

JULIA [*quickly turning again*] Hers! Has she written to you?

CHARTERIS. Yes: to break off with me on your account!

JULIA [*her eyes gleaming*] Ah!

CHARTERIS. You are pleased. Wretch! Now you have lost the last scrap of my regard. [*He turns to go, but is stopped by the return of Sylvia. Julia turns away and stands pretending to read a paper which she picks up from the table*].

SYLVIA [*offhandedly*] Hallo, Charteris! how are you getting on? [*She takes his arm familiarly, and walks down the room with him*]. Have you seen Grace Tranfield this morning? [*Julia drops the paper, and comes a step nearer to listen*]. You generally know where she's to be found.

CHARTERIS. I shall never know any more, Sylvia. She's quarrelled with me.

SYLVIA. Sylvia! How often am I to tell you that I am not Sylvia at the club?

CHARTERIS. I forgot. I beg your pardon, Craven, old chap [*slapping her on the shoulder*].

SYLVIA. Thats better. A little overdone, but better.

JULIA. Dont be a fool, Silly.

SYLVIA. Remember, Julia, if you please, that here we are members of the club, not sisters. I dont take liberties with you here on family grounds: dont you take any with me. [*She goes to the settee, and resumes her former place*].

CHARTERIS. Quite right, Craven. Down with the tyranny of the elder sister!

JULIA. You ought to know better than to encourage a child to make herself ridiculous, Leonard, even at my expense.

CHARTERIS [*seating himself on the edge of the table*] Your lunch will be cold, Julia.

761

Julia is about to retort furiously when she is checked by the reappearance of Cuthbertson at the dining room door.

CUTHBERTSON. What has become of you, Miss Craven? Your father is getting quite uneasy. We're all waiting for you.

JULIA. So I have just been reminded, thank you. [*She goes out angrily past him, Sylvia looking round to see*].

CUTHBERTSON [*looking first after her, then at Charteris*] More neurasthenia! [*He follows her*].

SYLVIA [*jumping up on her knees on the settee, and speaking over the back of it*] Whats up, Charteris? Julia been making love to you?

CHARTERIS [*speaking to her over his shoulder*] No. Jealous of Grace.

SYLVIA. Serve you right. You are an awful devil for philandering.

CHARTERIS [*calmly*] Do you consider it good club form to talk that way to a man who might nearly be your father?

SYLVIA [*knowingly*] Oh, I know you, my lad.

CHARTERIS. Then you know that I never pay any special attention to any woman.

SYLVIA [*thoughtfully*] Do you know, Leonard, I really believe you. I dont think you care a bit more for one woman than for another.

CHARTERIS. You mean I dont care a bit less for one woman than another.

SYLVIA. That makes it worse. But what I mean is that you never bother about their being only women: you talk to them just as you do to me or any other fellow. Thats the secret of your success. You cant think how sick they get of being treated with the respect due to their sex.

CHARTERIS. Ah, if Julia only had your wisdom, Craven! [*He gets off the table with a sigh, and perches himself reflectively on the step ladder*].

SYLVIA. She cant take things easy: can she, old man? But dont you be afraid of breaking her heart: she gets over her little tragedies. We found that out at home when our great sorrow came.

CHARTERIS. What was that?

SYLVIA. I mean when we learned that poor papa had Paramore's disease.

CHARTERIS. Paramore's disease! Why, whats the matter with Paramore?

SYLVIA. Oh, not a disease that he suffers from, but one that he discovered.

CHARTERIS. The liver business?

SYLVIA. Yes: thats what made Paramore's reputation, you know. Papa used to get bad occasionally; but we always thought that it was partly his Indian service, and partly his eating and drinking too much. He used to wolf down a lot in those days, did Dad. The doctor never knew what was wrong with him until Paramore discovered a dreadful little microbe in his liver. There are forty millions of them to every square inch of liver. Paramore discovered them first; and now he declares that everybody should be inoculated against them as well as vaccinated. But it was too late to inoculate poor papa. All they could do was to prolong his life for two years more by putting him on a strict diet. Poor old boy! they cut off his liquor; and he's not allowed to eat meat.

CHARTERIS. Your father appears to me to be uncommonly well.

SYLVIA. Yes: you would think he was a great deal better. But the microbe is at work, slowly but surely. In another year it will be all over. Poor old Dad! it's unfeeling to talk about him in this attitude: I must sit down properly. [She comes down from the settee, and takes the chair near the bookstand]. I should like papa to live for ever just to take the conceit out of Paramore. I believe he's in love with Julia.

CHARTERIS [starting up excitedly] In love with Julia! A ray of hope on the horizon! Do you really mean it?

SYLVIA. I should think I do. Why do you suppose he's hanging about the club today in a beautiful new coat and tie instead of attending to his patients? That lunch with Julia

763

will finish him. He'll ask Daddy's consent before they come back: I'll bet you three to one he will, in anything you please.

CHARTERIS. Gloves?

SYLVIA. No: cigarets.

CHARTERIS. Done! But what does she think about it? Does she give him any encouragement?

SYLVIA. Oh, the usual thing. Enough to keep any other woman from getting him.

CHARTERIS. Just so. I understand. Now listen to me: I am going to speak as a philosopher. Julia is jealous of everybody: everybody. If she saw you flirting with Paramore she'd begin to value him directly. You might play up a little, Craven, for my sake: eh?

SYLVIA [rising] Youre too awful, Leonard. For shame! However, anything to oblige a fellow Ibsenite. I'll bear your affair in mind. But I think it would be more effective if you got Grace to do it.

CHARTERIS. Think so? Hm! perhaps youre right.

THE PAGE [outside as before] Dr Paramore, Dr Paramore, Dr Paramore—

SYLVIA. They ought to get that boy's voice properly cultivated: it's a disgrace to the club. [She goes into the recess on Ibsen's left].

The page enters, carrying The British Medical Journal.

CHARTERIS [calling to the page] Dr Paramore is in the dining room.

THE PAGE. Thank you, sir. [He is about to go into the dining room when Sylvia swoops on him].

SYLVIA. Here: where are you taking that paper? It belongs to this room.

THE PAGE. It's Dr Paramore's particular orders, miss. The British Medical Journal has always to be brought to him dreckly it comes.

SYLVIA. What cheek! Charteris: oughtnt we to stop this on principle?

CHARTERIS. Certainly not. Principle's the poorest reason I know for making yourself nasty.

SYLVIA. Bosh! Ibsen!

CHARTERIS [*to the page*] Off with you, my boy: Dr Paramore's waiting breathless with expectation.

THE PAGE [*seriously*] Indeed, sir? [*He hurries off*].

CHARTERIS. That boy will make his way in this country. He has no sense of humor.

Grace comes in. Her dress, very convenient and businesslike, is made to please herself and serve her own purposes without the slightest regard to fashion, though by no means without a careful concern for her personal elegance. She enters briskly, like an habitually busy woman.

SYLVIA [*running to her*] Here you are at last, Tranfield, old girl. Ive been waiting for you this last hour. I'm starving.

GRACE. All right, dear. [*To Charteris*] Did you get my letter?

CHARTERIS. Yes. I w i s h you wouldnt write on those confounded blue letter-cards.

SYLVIA [*to Grace*] Shall I go down first, and secure a table?

CHARTERIS [*taking the reply out of Grace's mouth*] Do, old boy.

SYLVIA. Dont be too long. [*She goes into the dining room*].

GRACE. Well?

CHARTERIS. I'm afraid to face you after last night. Can you imagine a more horrible scene? Dont you hate the very sight of me after it?

GRACE. Oh no.

CHARTERIS. Then you ought to. Ugh! it was hideous: an insult: an outrage. A nice end to all my plans for making you happy: for making you an exception to all the women who swear I have made them miserable!

GRACE [*sitting down placidly*] I am not at all miserable. I'm sorry; but I shant break my heart.

CHARTERIS. No: yours is a thoroughbred heart: you dont scream and cry every time it's pinched. Thats why you are the only possible woman for me.

GRACE [*shaking her head*] Not now. Never any more.

CHARTERIS. Never! What do you mean?

THE PHILANDERER

GRACE. What I say, Leonard.

CHARTERIS. Jilted again! The fickleness of the women I love is only equalled by the infernal constancy of the women who love me. Well, well! I see how it is, Grace: you cant forget that horrible scene last night. Imagine her saying I had kissed her within the last two days!

GRACE [*rising eagerly*] Was that not true?

CHARTERIS. True! No: a thumping lie.

GRACE. Oh, I'm so glad. That was the only thing that really hurt me.

CHARTERIS. Just why she said it. How adorable of you to care! My darling. [*He seizes her hands, and presses them to his breast*].

GRACE. Remember! it's all broken off.

CHARTERIS. Ah yes: you have my heart in your hands. Break it. Throw my happiness out of the window.

GRACE. Oh, Leonard, does your happiness really depend on me?

CHARTERIS [*tenderly*] Absolutely. [*She beams with delight. A sudden revulsion comes to him at the sight: he recoils, dropping her hands and crying*] Ah no: why should I lie to you? [*He folds his arms and adds firmly*] My happiness depends on nobody but myself. I can do without you.

GRACE [*nerving herself*] So you shall. Thank you for the truth. Now *I* will tell you the truth.

CHARTERIS [*unfolding his arms in terror*] No, please. Dont. As a philosopher, it's my business to tell other people the truth; but it's not their business to tell it to me. I dont like it: it hurts.

GRACE [*quietly*] It's only that I love you.

CHARTERIS. Ah! thats not a philosophic truth. You may tell me that as often as you like. [*He takes her in his arms*].

GRACE. Yes, Leonard; but I'm an advanced woman. [*He checks himself, and looks at her in some consternation*]. I'm what my father calls the New Woman. [*He lets her go, and stares at her*]. I quite agree with all your ideas.

CHARTERIS [*scandalized*] Thats a nice thing for a respect-

766

able woman to say! You ought to be ashamed of yourself.

GRACE. I am quite in earnest about them too, though you are not. That is why I will never marry a man I love too much. It would give him a terrible advantage over me: I should be utterly in his power. Thats what the New Woman is like. Isnt she right, Mr Philosopher?

CHARTERIS. The struggle between the Philosopher and the Man is fearful, Grace. But the Philosopher says you are right.

GRACE. I know I am right. And so we must part.

CHARTERIS. Not at all. You must marry some one else; and then I'll come and philander with you.

Sylvia comes back.

SYLVIA [*holding the door open*] Oh, I say: c o m e along. I'm starving.

CHARTERIS. So am I. I'll lunch with you if I may.

SYLVIA. I thought you would. Ive ordered soup for three. [*Grace passes out. Sylvia continues, to Charteris*] You can watch Paramore from our table: he's pretending to read the British Medical Journal; but he must be making up his mind for the plunge: he looks green with nervousness. [*She goes out*].

CHARTERIS. Good luck to him! [*He follows her*].

The library remains unoccupied for ten minutes.

Then Julia, angry and miserable, comes in from the dining room, followed by Craven. She crosses the room tormentedly, and throws herself into a chair.

CRAVEN [*impatiently*] What is the matter? Has every one gone mad today. What do you mean by suddenly getting up from the table and tearing away like that? What does Paramore mean by reading his paper, and not answering when he's spoken to? [*Julia writhes impatiently*]. Come, come [*tenderly*]: wont my pet tell her own Daddy what— [*irritably*] what the devil is wrong with everybody. Do pull yourself together, Julia, before Cuthbertson comes. He's only paying the bill: he'll be here in a moment.

JULIA. I couldnt bear it any longer. Oh, to see them sit-

767

ting there at lunch together, laughing, chatting, making game of me! I should have screamed out in another moment. I should have taken a knife and killed her. I should have—

Cuthbertson appears, stuffing the luncheon bill into his waist-coat pocket as he comes to them. He begins speaking the moment he enters.

CUTHBERTSON. I'm afraid youve had a very poor lunch, Dan. It's disheartening to see you picking at a few beans, and drinking soda water. I wonder how you live!

JULIA. Thats all he ever takes, Mr Cuthbertson, I assure you. He hates to be bothered about it.

CRAVEN. Wheres Paramore?

CUTHBERTSON. Reading his paper. I asked him wasnt he coming; but he didnt hear me. It's amazing how anything scientific absorbs him. Clever man! Monstrously clever man!

CRAVEN [*pettishly*] Oh yes, thats all very well, Jo; but it's not good manners at table: he should shut up the shop sometimes. Heaven knows I am only too anxious to forget his science, since it has pronounced my doom. [*He sits down with a melancholy air*].

CUTHBERTSON [*compassionately*] You musnt think about that, Craven: perhaps he was mistaken. [*He sighs deeply and sits down*]. But he certainly is a very clever fellow. He thinks twice before he commits himself.

They sit in silence, full of gloom. Suddenly Paramore enters, pale and in the utmost disorder, with The British Medical Journal in his clenched hand. They rise in alarm. He tries to speak, but chokes, clutches at his throat, and staggers. Cuthbertson quickly takes his chair and places it behind Paramore, who sinks into it as they crowd about him, Craven at his right shoulder, Cuthbertson on his left, and Julia behind.

CRAVEN. Whats the matter, Paramore?

JULIA. Are you ill?

CUTHBERTSON. No bad news, I hope?

PARAMORE [*despairingly*] The worst of news! Terrible news! Fatal news! My disease—

CRAVEN [*quickly*] Do you mean my disease?

PARAMORE [*fiercely*] I mean my disease: Paramore's disease: the disease I discovered: the work of my life! Look here [*he points to the journal with a ghastly expression of horror*]! If this is true, it was all a mistake: there is no such disease.

Cuthbertson and Julia look at one another, hardly daring to believe the good news.

CRAVEN [*in strong remonstrance*] And you call this bad news! now really, Paramore—

PARAMORE [*cutting him short hoarsely*] It's natural for you to think only of yourself. I dont blame you: all invalids are selfish. Only a scientific man can feel what I feel now. [*Writhing under a sense of intolerable injustice*] It's the fault of the wickedly sentimental laws of this country. I was not able to make experiments enough: only three dogs and a monkey. Think of that, with all Europe full of my professional rivals! men burning to prove me wrong! There is freedom in France: enlightened republican France! One Frenchman experiments on two hundred monkeys to disprove my theory. Another sacrifices £36—three hundred dogs at three francs apiece—to upset the monkey experiments. A third proves them both wrong by a single experiment in which he gets the temperature of a camel's liver sixty degrees below zero. And now comes this cursed Italian who has ruined me. He has a government grant to buy animals with, besides having the run of the largest hospital in Italy. [*With desperate resolution*] But I wont be beaten by any Italian. I'll go to Italy myself. I'll rediscover my disease: I know it exists; I feel it; and I'll prove it if I have to experiment on every mortal animal thats got a liver at all. [*He folds his arms and breathes hard at them*].

CRAVEN [*his sense of injury growing on him*] Am I to understand, Paramore, that you took it on yourself to pass sentence of death on me: yes, of Death! on the strength of three dogs and an infernal monkey?

PARAMORE [*utterly contemptuous of Craven's narrow personal view of the matter*] Yes. That was all I could get a license for.

CRAVEN. Now upon my soul, Paramore, I'm vexed at this. I dont wish to be unfriendly; but I'm extremely vexed, really. Why, confound it, do you realize what youve done! Youve cut off my meat and drink for a year! made me an object of public scorn! a miserable vegetarian and teetotaller.

PARAMORE [*rising*] Well, you can make up for lost time now. [*Bitterly, shewing Craven the Journal*] There! you can read for yourself. The camel was fed on beef dissolved in alcohol; and he gained half a ton on it. Eat and drink as much as you please. [*Still unable to stand without support, he makes his way past Cuthbertson to the revolving bookcase, and stands there with his back to them, leaning on it with his head on his hands*].

CRAVEN [*grumbling*] Oh yes: it's very easy for you to talk, Paramore. But what am I to say to the Humanitarian societies and the Vegetarian societies that have made me Vice President?

CUTHBERTSON [*chuckling*] Aha! You made a virtue of it, did you, Dan?

CRAVEN [*warmly*] I made a virtue of necessity, Jo. No one can blame me.

JULIA [*soothing him*] Well, never mind, Daddy. Come back to the dining room, and have a good beefsteak.

CRAVEN [*shuddering*] Ugh! [*Plaintively*] No: Ive lost my old manly taste for it. My very nature's been corrupted by living on pap. [*To Paramore*] Thats what comes of all this vivisection. You go experimenting on horses; and of course the result is that you try to get me into condition by feeding me on beans.

PARAMORE [*curtly, without changing his position*] Well, if theyve done you good, so much the better for you.

CRAVEN [*querulously*] Thats all very well; but it's very vexing. You dont half see how serious it is to make a man believe that he has only another year to live: you really dont, Paramore: I cant help saying it. Ive made my will, which was altogether unnecessary; and Ive been reconciled to a lot of people I'd quarrelled with: people I cant stand under ordinary circumstances. Then Ive let the girls get round me at home to an extent I should never have done if I'd had my life before me. Ive done a lot of serious thinking and reading and extra church going. And now it turns out simple waste of time. On my soul, it's too disgusting: I'd far rather die like a man when I said I would.

PARAMORE [*as before*] Perhaps you may. Your heart's shaky, if thats any satisfaction to you.

CRAVEN [*offended*] You must excuse me, Paramore, if I say that I no longer feel any confidence in your opinion as a medical man. [*Paramore's eye flashes: he straightens himself and listens*]. I paid you a pretty stiff fee for that consultation when you condemned me; and I cant say I think you gave me value for it.

PARAMORE [*turning and facing Craven with dignity*] Thats unanswerable, Colonel Craven. I shall return the fee.

CRAVEN. Oh, it's not the money; but I think you ought to realize your position. [*Paramore turns stiffly away. Craven follows him impulsively, exclaiming remorsefully*] Well, perhaps it was a nasty thing of me to allude to it. [*He offers Paramore his hand*].

PARAMORE [*conscientiously taking it*] Not at all. You are quite in the right, Colonel Craven: my diagnosis was wrong; and I must take the consequences.

CRAVEN [*holding his hand*] No, dont say that. It was natural enough: my liver is enough to set any man's diagnosis wrong. [*A long handshake, very trying to Paramore's nerves. Paramore then retires to the recess on Ibsen's left, and throws himself on the divan with a half suppressed sob, bending over The British Medical Journal with his head on his hands and his elbows on his knees*].

CUTHBERTSON [*who has been rejoicing with Julia at the other side of the room*] Well, let's say no more about it. I congratulate you, Craven, and hope you may long be spared. [*Craven offers his hand*]. No, Dan: your daughter first. [*He takes Julia's hand gently and hands her across to Craven, into whose arms she flies with a gush of feeling].*

JULIA. Dear old Daddy!

CRAVEN. Ah, is Julia glad that the old Dad is let off for a few years more?

JULIA [*almost crying*] Oh, so glad! so glad!

Cuthbertson sobs audibly. The Colonel is affected. Sylvia, entering from the dining room, stops abruptly at the door on seeing the three. Paramore, in the recess, escapes her notice.

SYLVIA. Hallo!

CRAVEN. Tell her the news, Julia: it would sound ridiculous from me. [*He goes to the weeping Cuthbertson, and pats him consolingly on the shoulder*].

JULIA. Silly: only think! Dad's not ill at all. It was only a mistake of Dr Paramore's. Oh, dear! [*She catches Craven's left hand and stoops to kiss it, his right hand being still on Cuthbertson's shoulder*].

SYLVIA [*contemptuously*] I knew it. Of course it was nothing but eating too much. I always said Paramore was an ass. [*Sensation. The group of Cuthbertson, Craven and Julia breaks up as they turn in dismay*].

PARAMORE [*without malice*] Never mind, Miss Craven. That is what is being said all over Europe now. Never mind.

SYLVIA [*a little abashed*] I'm so sorry, Dr Paramore. You must excuse a daughter's feelings.

CRAVEN [*huffed*] It evidently doesnt make much difference to you, Sylvia.

SYLVIA. I'm not going to be sentimental over it, Dad, you may bet. [*Coming to Craven*] Besides, I knew it was nonsense all along. [*Petting him*] Poor dear old Dad! why should your days be numbered any more than any one else's? [*He pats her cheek, mollified. Julia impatiently turns away from them*]. Come to the smoking room; and lets see what you can do after teetotalling for a year.

CRAVEN [*playfully*] Vulgar little girl! [*He pinches her ear*]. Shall we come, Jo! Youll be the better for a pick-me-up after all this emotion.

CUTHBERTSON. I'm not ashamed of it, Dan. It has done

me good. [*He goes up to the table and shakes his fist at the bust over the mantelpiece*]. It would do y o u good too, if you had eyes and ears to take it in.

CRAVEN [*astonished*] Who?

SYLVIA. Why, good old Henrik, of course.

CRAVEN [*puzzled*] Henrik?

CUTHBERTSON [*impatiently*] Ibsen, man: Ibsen. [*He goes out by the staircase door, followed by Sylvia, who kisses her hand to the bust as she passes. Craven stares blankly after her, and then at the bust. Giving the problem up as insoluble, he shakes his head and follows them. Near the door, he checks himself, and comes back*].

CRAVEN [*softly*] By the way, Paramore?

PARAMORE [*rousing himself with an effort*] Yes?

CRAVEN. You werent in earnest that time about my heart, were you?

PARAMORE. Oh nothing, nothing. Theres a slight murmur: mitral valves a little worn perhaps; but theyll last your time if youre careful. Dont smoke too much.

CRAVEN. What! More privations! Now really, Paramore, really—

PARAMORE [*rising distractedly*] Excuse me: I cant pursue the subject. I—I—

JULIA. Dont worry him now, Daddy.

CRAVEN. Well, well: I wont. [*He comes to Paramore, who is pacing restlessly up and down the middle of the room*]. Come, Paramore! I'm not selfish, believe me: I can feel for your disappointment. But you must face it like a man. And after all, now really, doesnt this shew that theres a lot of rot about modern science? Between ourselves, you know, it's horribly cruel: you must admit that it's a deuced nasty thing to go ripping up and crucifying camels and monkeys. It must blunt all the finer feelings sooner or later.

PARAMORE [*turning on him*] How many camels and horses and men were ripped up in that Soudan campaign where you won your Victoria Cross, Colonel Craven?

CRAVEN [*firing up*] That was fair fighting: a very different

773

thing, Paramore.

PARAMORE. Yes: Martinis and machine guns against naked spearmen.

CRAVEN [*hotly*] Naked spearmen can kill, Paramore. I risked my life: dont forget that.

PARAMORE [*with equal spirit*] And I have risked mine, as all doctors do, oftener than any soldier.

CRAVEN [*handsomely*] Thats true. I didnt think of that. I beg your pardon, Paramore: I'll never say another word against your profession. But I hope youll let me stick to the good oldfashioned shaking-up treatment for my liver: a clinking run across country with the hounds.

PARAMORE [*with bitter irony*] Isnt that rather cruel? a pack of dogs ripping up a fox?

JULIA [*coming coaxingly between them*] Oh please dont begin arguing again. Do go to the smoking room, Daddy: Mr Cuthbertson will wonder what has become of you.

CRAVEN. Very well, very well: I'll go. But youre really not reasonable today, Paramore, to talk that way of fair sport—

JULIA. Sh—sh [*coaxing him towards the door*].

CRAVEN. Well, well, I'm off. [*He goes goodhumoredly, pushed out by Julia*].

JULIA [*turning at the door with her utmost witchery of manner*] Dont look so disappointed, Dr Paramore. Cheer up. Youve been most kind to us; and youve done papa a lot of good.

PARAMORE [*delighted, rushing over to her*] How beautiful it is of you to say that to me, Miss Craven!

JULIA. I hate to see any one unhappy. I cant bear unhappiness. [*She runs out, casting a Parthian glance at him as she flies*].

Paramore stands enraptured, gazing after her through the glass door. Whilst he is thus absorbed, Charteris comes in from the dining room and touches him on the arm.

PARAMORE [*starting*] Eh? Whats the matter?

CHARTERIS [*significantly*] Charming woman, isnt she,

Paramore? [*Looking admiringly at him*] How have you managed to fascinate her?

PARAMORE. I! Do you really mean— [*He looks at him; then recovers himself, and adds coldly*] Excuse me: this is a subject I do not care to jest about. [*He walks away from Charteris, and sits down in the nearest easy chair, reading his journal to intimate that he does not wish to pursue the conversation*].

CHARTERIS [*ignoring the hint, and coolly sitting down beside him*] Why dont you get married, Paramore? You know it's a scandalous thing for a man in your profession to be single.

PARAMORE [*shortly, still pretending to read*] Thats my own business: not yours.

CHARTERIS. Not at all: it's pre-eminently a social question. Youre going to get married, arnt you?

PARAMORE. Not that I am aware of.

CHARTERIS [*alarmed*] No! Dont say that. Why?

PARAMORE [*rising angrily and rapping one of the* SILENCE *placards*] Allow me to call your attention to that. [*He crosses the room to the easy chair near the revolving bookstand, and flings himself into it with determined hostility*].

CHARTERIS [*following him, too deeply concerned to mind the rebuff*] Paramore: you alarm me more than I can say. Youve muffed this business somehow. I fully expected to find you a joyful accepted suitor.

PARAMORE [*angrily*] Yes, you have been watching me because you admire Miss Craven yourself. Well, you may go in and win now. You will be pleased to hear that I am a ruined man.

CHARTERIS. You! Ruined! How? The turf?

PARAMORE [*contemptuously*] The turf!! Certainly not.

CHARTERIS. Paramore: if the loan of all I possess will help you over this difficulty, you have only to ask.

PARAMORE [*rising in surprise*] Charteris! I—[*Suspiciously*] Are you joking?

CHARTERIS. Why on earth do you always suspect me of joking? I never was more serious in my life.

775

PARAMORE [*shamed by Charteris's generosity*] Then I beg your pardon. I thought the news would please you.

CHARTERIS [*deprecating this injustice to his good feeling*] My dear fellow!

PARAMORE. I see I was wrong. I am really very sorry. [*They shake hands*]. And now you may as well learn the truth. I had rather you heard it from me than from the gossip of the club. My liver discovery has been—er—er—[*he cannot bring himself to say it*].

CHARTERIS [*helping him out*] Confirmed? [*Sadly*] I see: the poor Colonel's doomed.

PARAMORE. No: on the contrary, it has been—er—called in question. The Colonel now believes himself to be in perfectly good health; and my friendly relations with the Cravens are entirely spoilt.

CHARTERIS. Who told him about it?

PARAMORE. I did, of course, the moment I read the news in this. [*He shews the journal, and puts it down on the bookstand*].

CHARTERIS. Why, man, youve been a messenger of glad tidings! Didnt you congratulate him?

PARAMORE [*scandalized*] Congratulate him! Congratulate a man on the worst blow pathological science has received for the last three hundred years!

CHARTERIS. No, no, no. Congratulate him on having his life saved. Congratulate Julia on having her father spared. Swear that your discovery and your reputation are as nothing to you compared with the pleasure of restoring happiness to the household in which the best hopes of your life are centred. Confound it, man, youll never get married if you cant turn things to account with a woman in these little ways.

PARAMORE [*gravely*] Excuse me; but my self-respect is dearer to me even than Miss Craven. I cannot trifle with scientific questions for the sake of a personal advantage. [*He turns away coldly, and goes towards the table*].

CHARTERIS. Well, this beats me! The Nonconformist

conscience is bad enough; but the scientific conscience is the very devil. [*He follows Paramore, and puts his arm familiarly round his shoulder, bringing him back again whilst he speaks*]. Now look here, Paramore: I have no conscience in that sense at all: I loathe it as I loathe all the snares of idealism; but I have some common humanity and common sense. [*He replaces him in the easy chair, and sits down opposite him*]. Come! what is a really scientific theory? A true theory, isnt it?

PARAMORE. No doubt.

CHARTERIS. For instance, you have a theory about Craven's liver, eh?

PARAMORE. I still believe that to be a true theory, though it has been upset for the moment.

CHARTERIS. And you have a theory that it would be pleasant to be married to Julia?

PARAMORE. I suppose so. In a sense.

CHARTERIS. That theory also will be upset, probably, before youre a year older.

PARAMORE. Always cynical, Charteris.

CHARTERIS. Never mind that. Now it's a perfectly damnable thing for you to hope that your liver theory is true, because it amounts to hoping that Craven will die an agonizing death.

PARAMORE. And always paradoxical, Charteris.

CHARTERIS. Well, at least youll admit that it's amiable and human to hope that your theory about Julia is right, because it amounts to hoping that she may live happily ever after.

PARAMORE. I do hope that with all my soul—[*correcting himself*] I mean with all my function of hoping.

CHARTERIS. Then, since both theories are equally scientific, why not devote yourself, as a humane man, to proving the amiable theory rather than the damnable one?

PARAMORE. But how?

CHARTERIS. I'll tell you. You think I'm fond of Julia myself. So I am; but then I'm fond of everybody; so I dont count. Besides, if you try the scientific experiment of asking

777

her whether she loves me, she'll tell you that she hates and despises me. So I'm out of the running. Nevertheless, like you, I hope that she may be happy with all my—what did you call your soul?

PARAMORE [*impatiently*] Oh, go on, go on: finish what you were going to say.

CHARTERIS [*suddenly affecting complete indifference, and rising carelessly*] I dont know that I was going to say anything more. If I were you I should invite the Cravens to tea in honor of the Colonel's escape from a horrible doom. By the way, if youve done with that British Medical Journal, I should like to see how theyve smashed your theory up.

PARAMORE [*wincing as he also rises*] Oh, certainly, if you wish it. I have no objection. [*He takes the journal from the bookstand*]. I admit that the Italian experiments apparently upset my theory. But please remember that it is doubtful—extremely doubtful—whether anything can be proved by experiments on animals. [*He hands Charteris the journal*].

CHARTERIS [*taking it*] It doesnt matter: I dont intend to make any. [*He retires to the recess on Ibsen's right, picking up the step-ladder as he passes and placing it so that he is able to use it for a leg rest as he settles himself to read on the divan with his back to the corner of the mantelpiece*].

Paramore goes to the dining room door, and is about to leave the library when he meets Grace entering.

GRACE. How do you do, Dr Paramore? So glad to see you. [*They shake hands*].

PARAMORE. Thanks. Quite well, I hope?

GRACE. Quite, thank you. Youre looking overworked. We must take more care of you, Doctor.

PARAMORE. You are too kind.

GRACE. It is you who are too kind—to your patients. You sacrifice yourself. Have a little rest. Come and talk to me. Tell me all about the latest scientific discoveries, and what I ought to read to keep myself up to date. But perhaps youre busy.

PARAMORE. No, not at all. Only too delighted. [*They go*

788

into the recess on Ibsen's left, and sit there chatting in whispers, very confidentially].

CHARTERIS. How they all love a doctor! They can say what they like to him. [*Julia returns, but does not look his way. He takes his feet from the ladder and sits up*]. Whew! [*Julia wanders along his side of the room, apparently looking for some one. Charteris steals after her*].

CHARTERIS [*in a low voice*] Looking for me, Julia?

JULIA [*starting violently*] Oh! How you startled me!

CHARTERIS. Sh! I want to shew you something. Look! [*He points to the pair in the recess*].

JULIA [*jealously*] That woman!

CHARTERIS. My young woman, carrying off your young man.

JULIA. What do you mean? Do you dare insinuate—

CHARTERIS. Sh—sh—sh! Dont disturb them.

Paramore rises; takes down a book; and sits on a footstool at Grace's feet.

JULIA. Why are they whispering like that?

CHARTERIS. Because they dont want any one to hear what they are saying to one another.

Paramore shews Grace a picture in the book. They both laugh heartily over it.

JULIA. What is he shewing her?

CHARTERIS. Probably a diagram of the liver. [*Julia, with an exclamation of disgust, makes for the recess. Charteris catches her sleeve*]. Stop: be careful, Julia. [*She frees herself by giving him a push which upsets him into the easy chair; then crosses to the recess, and stands looking down at Grace and Paramore from the corner next the fireplace*].

JULIA [*with suppressed fury*] You seem to have found a very interesting book, Dr Paramore. [*They look up, astonished*]. May I ask what it is? [*She stoops swiftly; snatches the book from Paramore; and comes down to the table quickly to look at it whilst they rise in amazement*]. Good Words! [*She flings it on the table, and sweeps back past Charteris, exclaiming contemptuously*] You fool! [*Paramore and Grace, meanwhile,*

THE PHILANDERER

come from the recess: Paramore bewildered: Grace very determined].

CHARTERIS [*aside to Julia as he gets out of the easy chair*] Idiot! She'll have you turned out of the club for this.

JULIA [*terrified*] She cant: can she?

PARAMORE. What is the matter, Miss Craven?

CHARTERIS [*hastily*] Nothing. My fault: a stupid practical joke. I beg your pardon and Mrs Tranfield's.

GRACE [*firmly*] It is not your fault in the least, Mr Charteris. Dr Paramore: will you oblige me by finding Sylvia Craven for me, if you can?

PARAMORE [*hesitating*] But—

GRACE. I want you to go n o w, if you please.

PARAMORE [*succumbing*] Certainly. [*He bows and goes out by the staircase door*].

GRACE. You are going with him, Charteris.

JULIA. You will not leave me here to be insulted by this woman, Mr Charteris. [*She takes his arm as if to go with him*].

GRACE. When two ladies quarrel in this club, it is against the rules to settle it when there are gentlemen present: especially the gentleman they are quarrelling about. I presume you do not wish to break that rule, Miss Craven. [*Julia sullenly drops Charteris's arm. Grace turns to Charteris, and adds*] Now! Trot off.

CHARTERIS. Certainly. Certainly. [*He follows Paramore ignominiously*].

GRACE [*to Julia, with quiet peremptoriness*] Now: what have you to say to me?

JULIA [*suddenly throwing herself tragically on her knees at Grace's feet*] Dont take him from me. Oh dont—dont be so cruel. Give him back to me. You dont know what youre doing—what our past has been—how I love him. You dont know—

GRACE. Get up; and dont be a fool. Suppose any one comes in and sees you in that ridiculous attitude!

JULIA. I hardly know what I'm doing. I dont care what I'm doing: I'm too miserable. Oh, wont you listen to me?

780

GRACE. Do you suppose I am a man, to be imposed on by this sort of rubbish?

JULIA [*getting up and looking darkly at her*] You intend to take him from me, then?

GRACE. Do you expect me to help you to keep him after the way you have behaved?

JULIA [*trying her theatrical method in a milder form: reasonable and impulsively goodnatured instead of tragic*] I know I was wrong to act as I did last night. I beg your pardon. I am sorry. I was mad.

GRACE. Not a bit mad. You calculated to an inch how far you could go. When he is present to stand between us and play out the scene with you, I count for nothing. When we are alone, you fall back on your natural way of getting anything you want: crying for it like a baby until it is given to you.

JULIA [*with unconcealed hatred*] You learnt this from him.

GRACE. I learnt it from yourself, last night and now. How I hate to be a woman when I see, by you, what wretched childish creatures we are! Those two men would cut you dead and have you turned out of the club if you were a man, and had behaved in such a way before them. But because you are only a woman, they are forbearing! sympathetic! gallant! Oh, if you had a scrap of self-respect, their indulgence would make you creep all over. I understand now why Charteris has no respect for women.

JULIA. How dare you say that?

GRACE. Dare! I love him. And I have refused his offer to marry me.

JULIA [*incredulous, but hopeful*] You have refused!

GRACE. Yes; because I will not give myself to any man who has learnt how to treat women from you and your like. I can do without his love, but not without his respect; and it is your fault that I cannot have both. Take his love then; and much good may it do you! Run to him, and beg him to take you back.

JULIA. Oh, what a liar you are! He loved me before he

ever saw you—before he ever dreamt of you, you pitiful thing. Do you think *I* need go down on my knees to men to make them come to me? That may be your experience, you creature with no figure: it is not mine. There are dozens of men who would give their souls for a look from me. I have only to lift my finger.

GRACE. Lift it then; and see whether he will come.

JULIA. How I should like to kill you! I dont know why I dont.

GRACE. Yes: you like to get out of your difficulties at other people's expense. It is something to boast of, isnt it, that dozens of men would make love to you if you invited them?

JULIA [*sullenly*] I suppose it's better to be like you, with a cold heart and a serpent's tongue. Thank Heaven, I have a heart: that is why you can hurt me as I cannot hurt you. And you are a coward. You are giving him up to me without a struggle.

GRACE. Yes: it is for you to struggle. I wish you success. [*She turns away contemptuously, and is going to the dining room door when Sylvia enters on the opposite side, followed by Cuthbertson and Craven, who come to Julia, whilst Sylvia crosses to Grace*].

SYLVIA. Here I am, sent by the faithful Paramore. He hinted that I'd better bring the elder members of the family too: here they are. Whats the row?

GRACE [*quietly*] Nothing, dear. Theres no row.

JULIA [*hysterically, tottering and stretching out her arms to Craven*] Daddy!

CRAVEN [*taking her in his arms*] My precious! Whats the matter?

JULIA [*through her tears*] She's going to have me expelled from the club; and we shall all be disgraced. Can she do it, Daddy?

CRAVEN. Well, really, the rules of this club are so extraordinary that I dont know. [*To Grace*] May I ask, madam, whether you have any complaint to make of my daughter's conduct?

GRACE. Yes, sir. I am going to complain to the committee.

SYLVIA. I knew youd overdo it some day, Julia.

CRAVEN. Do you know this lady, Jo?

CUTHBERTSON. This is my daughter, Mrs Tranfield, Dan. Grace: this is my old friend Colonel Craven.

Grace and Craven bow to one another constrainedly.

CRAVEN. May I ask the ground of complaint, Mrs Tranfield?

GRACE. Simply that Miss Craven is essentially a womanly woman, and, as such, not eligible for membership.

JULIA. It's false. I'm not a womanly woman. I was guaranteed when I joined just as you were.

GRACE. By Mr. Charteris, I think, at your own request. I shall call him as a witness to your thoroughly womanly conduct just now in his presence and Dr Paramore's.

CRAVEN. Cuthbertson: are they joking? or am I dreaming?

CUTHBERTSON [*grimly*] It's real, Dan: youre awake.

SYLVIA [*taking Craven's left arm, and hugging it affectionately*] Dear old Rip Van Winkle!

CRAVEN. Well, Mrs Tranfield, all I can say is that I hope you will succeed in establishing your complaint, and that Julia may soon see the last of this most outrageous institution.

Charteris returns.

CHARTERIS [*at the door*] May I come in?

SYLVIA. Yes: youre wanted here as a witness. [*Charteris comes in, and places himself with evident misgiving between Julia and Grace*]. It's a bad case of womanliness.

GRACE [*half aside to him, significantly*] You understand? [*Julia, watching them jealously, leaves her father and gets close to Charteris. Grace adds aloud*] I shall expect your support before the committee.

JULIA. If you have a scrap of manhood in you you will take my part.

CHARTERIS. But then I shall be expelled for being a

783

manly man. Besides, I'm on the committee myself: I cant act as judge and witness too. You must apply to Paramore: he saw it all.

GRACE. Where is Dr Paramore?

CHARTERIS. Just gone home.

JULIA [*with sudden resolution*] What is Dr Paramore's number in Savile Row?

CHARTERIS. Seventy-nine.

Julia goes out quickly by the staircase door, to their astonishment. Charteris follows her to the door, which swings back in his face, leaving him staring after her through the glass.

SYLVIA [*running to Grace*] Grace: go after her. Dont let her get beforehand with Paramore. She'll tell him the most heartbreaking stories about how she's been treated, and get round him completely.

CRAVEN [*thundering*] Sylvia! Is that the way to speak of your sister, miss? [*Grace squeezes Sylvia's hand to console her; takes a magazine from the table; and sits down calmly. Sylvia posts herself behind Grace's chair, leaning over the back to watch the ensuing colloquy between the three men*]. I assure you, Mrs Tranfield, Dr. Paramore has just invited us all to take afternoon tea with him; and if my daughter has gone to his house, she is simply taking advantage of his invitation to extricate herself from a very embarrassing scene here. We're all going there. Come, Sylvia. [*He turns to go, followed by Cuthbertson*].

CHARTERIS [*in consternation*] Stop! [*He gets between Craven and Cuthbertson*]. What hurry is there? Cant you give the man time?

CRAVEN. Time! What for?

CHARTERIS [*talking foolishly in his agitation*] Well, to get a little rest, you know: a busy professional man like that! He's not had a moment to himself all day.

CRAVEN. But Julia's with him.

CHARTERIS. Well, no matter: she's only one person. And she ought to have an opportunity of laying her case before him. As a member of the committee, I think thats only just. Be reasonable, Craven: give him half an hour.

CUTHBERTSON [*sternly*] What do you mean by this, Charteris?

CHARTERIS. Nothing, I assure you. Only common consideration for poor Paramore.

CUTHBERTSON. Youve some motive. Craven: I strongly advise that we go at once. [*He grasps the door handle*].

CHARTERIS [*coaxingly*] No, no. [*He puts his hand persuasively on Craven's arm, adding*] It's not good for your liver, Craven, to rush about immediately after lunch.

CUTHBERTSON. His liver's cured. Come on, Craven. [*He opens the door*].

CHARTERIS [*catching Cuthbertson by the sleeve*] Cuthbertson: youre mad. Paramore's going to propose to Julia. We must give him time: he's not the man to come to the point in three seconds as you or I would. [*Turning to Craven*] Dont you see? that will get me out of the difficulty we were speaking of this morning: you and I and Cuthbertson. You remember?

CRAVEN. Now is this a thing to say plump out before everybody, Charteris? Confound it, have you no decency?

CUTHBERTSON [*severely*] None whatever.

CHARTERIS [*turning to Cuthbertson*] No: dont be unkind, Cuthbertson. Back me up. My future, her future, Mrs Tranfield's future, Craven's future, everybody's future depends on Julia being Paramore's affianced bride when we arrive. He's certain to propose if youll only give him time. You know youre a kindly and sensible man as well as a deucedly clever one, Cuthbertson, in spite of all the nonsense you pick up in the theatre. Say a word for me.

CRAVEN. I'm quite willing to leave the decision to Cuthbertson; and I have no doubt whatever as to what that decision will be.

Cuthbertson carefully shuts the door, and comes back into the room with an air of weighty reflection.

CUTHBERTSON. I am now going to speak as a man of the world: that is, without moral responsibility.

CRAVEN. Quite so, Jo. Of course.

THE PHILANDERER

CUTHBERTSON. Therefore, though I have no sympathy whatever with Charteris's views, I think we can do no harm by waiting—say ten minutes or so. [*He sits down*].

CHARTERIS [*delighted*] Ah, there's nobody like you after all, Cuthbertson, when theres a difficult situation to be judged. [*He sits down on the settee back*].

CRAVEN [*deeply disappointed*] Oh well, Jo, if that is your decision, I must keep my word and abide by it. Better sit down and make ourselves comfortable, I suppose. [*He sits also, under protest*].

A pause, very trying for the three men.

GRACE [*looking up from her magazine*] Dont fidget, Leonard.

CHARTERIS [*slipping off the settee back*] I cant help it: I'm too restless. The fact is, Julia has made me so nervous that I cant answer for myself until I know her decision. Mrs Tranfield will tell you what a time Ive had lately. Julia's really a most determined woman, you know.

CRAVEN [*starting up*] Well, upon my life! Upon my honor and conscience!! Now really!!! I shall go this instant. Come on, Sylvia. Cuthbertson: I hope youll mark your sense of this sort of thing by coming on to Paramore's with us at once. [*He marches to the door*].

CHARTERIS [*desperately*] Craven: youre trifling with your daughter's happiness. I ask only five minutes more.

CRAVEN. Not five seconds, sir. Fie for shame, Charteris! [*He goes out*].

CUTHBERTSON [*to Charteris, as he passes him on his way to the door*] Bungler! [*He follows Craven*].

SYLVIA. Serve you right, you duffer! [*She follows Cuthbertson*].

CHARTERIS. Oh, these headstrong old men! [*To Grace*] Nothing to be done now but go with them, and delay the Colonel as much as possible. So I'm afraid I must leave you.

GRACE [*rising*] Not at all. Paramore invited me, too.

CHARTERIS [*aghast*] You dont mean to say youre coming!

GRACE. Most certainly. Do you suppose I will let that

786

woman think I am afraid to meet her? [*Charteris sinks on a chair with a prolonged groan*]. Come: dont be silly: youll not overtake the Colonel if you delay any longer.

CHARTERIS. Why was I ever born, child of misfortune that I am! [*He rises despairingly*]. Well, if you must come, you must. [*He offers his arm, which she takes*]. By the way, what happened after I left you?

GRACE. I gave her a lecture on her behavior which she will remember to the last day of her life.

CHARTERIS [*approvingly*] That was right, darling. [*He slips his arm round her waist*] Just one kiss. To soothe me.

GRACE [*complacently offering her cheek*] Foolish boy! [*He kisses her*]. Now come along. [*They go out together*].

ACT III

PARAMORE'S *reception room in Savile Row. Viewing the room from the front windows, the door is seen in the opposite wall near the left hand corner. Another door, a light noiseless one covered with green baize, leading to the consulting room, is in the right hand wall towards the back. The fireplace is on the left. At the nearer corner of it a couch is placed at right angles to the wall, settlewise. At the other corner, an easy chair. On the right the wall is occupied by a bookcase, further forward than the green baize door. Beyond the door is a cabinet of anatomical preparations, with a framed photograph of Rembrandt's School of Anatomy hanging on the wall above it. In front, a little to the right, a teatable.*

Paramore is seated in a round-backed chair, on castors, pouring out tea. Julia sits opposite him, with her back to the fire. He is in high spirits: she very downcast.

PARAMORE [*handing her the cup he has just filled*] There! Making tea is one of the few things I consider myself able to do thoroughly well. Cake?

JULIA. No, thank you. I dont like sweet things. [*She sets down the cup untasted*].

PARAMORE. Anything wrong with the tea?

JULIA. No. It's very nice.

PARAMORE. I'm afraid I'm a bad entertainer. The fact is, I am too professional. I shine only in consultation. I almost wish you had something serious the matter with you; so that you might call out my knowledge and sympathy. As it is, I can only admire you, and feel how pleasant it is to have you here.

JULIA [*bitterly*] And pet me, and say pretty things to me. I wonder you dont offer me a saucer of milk at once.

PARAMORE [*astonished*] Why?

JULIA. Because you seem to regard me very much as if I were a Persian cat.

PARAMORE [*in strong remonstrance*] Miss Cra—

JULIA [*cutting him short*] Oh, you neednt protest. I'm used to it: it's the sort of attachment I seem always to inspire.

788

THE PHILANDERER

[*Ironically*] You cant think how flattering it is.

PARAMORE. My dear Miss Craven, what a cynical thing to say! You! who are loved at first sight by the people in the street as you pass. Why, in the club I can tell by the faces of the men whether you have been lately in the room or not.

JULIA [*shrinking fiercely*] Oh, I hate that look in their faces. Do you know that I have never had one human being care for me since I was born?

PARAMORE. Thats not true, Miss Craven. Even if it were true of your father, and of Charteris, who loves you madly in spite of your dislike for him, it is not true of me.

JULIA [*startled*] Who told you that about Charteris?

PARAMORE. Why, he himself.

JULIA [*with deep, poignant conviction*] He cares for only one person in the world; and that is himself. There is not in his whole nature one unselfish spot. He would not spend one hour of his real life with— [*a sob chokes her: she rises passionately, crying*] You are all alike, every one of you. Even my father only makes a pet of me. [*She goes away to the fireplace, and stands with her back to him to hide her face*].

PARAMORE [*following her humbly*] I dont deserve this from you: indeed I do not.

JULIA [*rating him*] Then why do you gossip about me behind my back with Charteris?

PARAMORE. We said nothing disparaging of you. Nobody shall ever do that in my presence. We spoke of the subject nearest our hearts.

JULIA. His heart! Oh God, his heart! [*She sits down on the couch, and covers her face*].

PARAMORE [*sadly*] I am afraid you love him, for all that, Miss Craven.

JULIA [*raising her head instantly*] If he says that, he lies. If ever you hear it said that I cared for him, contradict it: it is false.

PARAMORE [*quickly advancing to her*] Miss Craven: is the way clear for me then?

JULIA [*losing interest in the conversation, and looking crossly*

789

THE PHILANDERER

away from him]. What do you mean?

PARAMORE [*impetuously*] You must see what I mean. Contradict the rumor of your attachment to Charteris, not by words—it has gone too far for that—but by becoming my wife. [*Earnestly*] Believe me: it is not merely your beauty that attracts me [*Julia, interested, looks up at him quickly*]: I know other beautiful women. It is your heart, your sincerity, your sterling reality, [*Julia rises and gazes at him, breathless with a new hope*] your great gifts of character that are only half developed because you have never been understood by those about you.

JULIA [*looking intently at him, and yet beginning to be derisively sceptical in spite of herself*] Have you really seen all that in me?

PARAMORE. I have felt it. I have been alone in the world; and I need you, Julia. That is how I have divined that you, also, are alone in the world.

JULIA [*with theatrical pathos*] You are right there. I am indeed alone in the world.

PARAMORE [*timidly approaching her*] With you I should not be alone. And you? with me?

JULIA. You! [*She gets quickly out of his reach, taking refuge at the teatable*]. No, no. I cant bring myself— [*She breaks off, perplexed, and looks uneasily about her*]. Oh, I dont know what to do. You will expect too much from me. [*She sits down*].

PARAMORE. I have more faith in you than you have in yourself. Your nature is richer than you think.

JULIA [*doubtfully*] Do you really believe that I am not the shallow, jealous, devilish tempered creature they all pretend I am?

PARAMORE. I am ready to place my happiness in your hands. Does that prove what I think of you?

JULIA. Yes: I believe you really care for me. [*He approaches her eagerly: she has a violent revulsion, and rises with her hands up as if to beat him off, crying*] No, no, no, no. I cannot. It's impossible. [*She goes towards the door*].

790

PARAMORE [*looking wistfully after her*] Is it Charteris?

JULIA [*stopping and turning*] Ah, you think that! [*She comes back*]. Listen to me. If I say yes, will you promise not to touch me? Will you give me time to accustom myself to our new relations?

PARAMORE. I promise most faithfully. I would not press you for the world.

JULIA. Then—then— Yes: I promise.

PARAMORE. Oh, how unspeakably hap—

JULIA [*stopping his raptures*] No: not another word. Let us forget it. [*She resumes her seat at the table*]. I havnt touched my tea. [*He hastens to his former seat. As he passes, she puts her left hand on his arm and says*] Be good to me, Percy: I need it sorely.

PARAMORE [*transported*] You have called me Percy! Hurrah!

Charteris and Craven come in. Paramore hastens to meet them, beaming.

PARAMORE. Delighted to see you here with me, Colonel Craven. And you too, Charteris. Sit down. [*The Colonel sits down on the end of the couch*]. Where are the others?

CHARTERIS. Sylvia has dragged Cuthbertson off into the Burlington Arcade to buy some caramels. He likes to encourage her in eating caramels: he thinks it's a womanly taste. Besides, he likes them himself. Theyll be here presently. [*He strolls across to the cabinet, and pretends to study the Rembrandt photograph, so as to be as far out of Julia's reach as possible*].

CRAVEN. Yes; and Charteris has been trying to persuade me that theres a short cut between Cork Street and Savile Row somewhere in Conduit Street. Now did you ever hear such nonsense? Then he said my coat was getting shabby, and wanted me to go into Poole's and order a new one. Paramore: is my coat shabby?

PARAMORE. Not that I can see.

CRAVEN. I should think not. Then he wanted to draw me into an argument about the Egyptian war. We should have

791

been here quarter of an hour ago only for his nonsense.

CHARTERIS [*still contemplating Rembrandt*] I did my best to keep him from disturbing you, Paramore.

PARAMORE [*gratefully*] You kept him exactly the right time, to a second. [*Formally*] Colonel Craven: I have something very particular to say to you.

CRAVEN [*springing up in alarm*] In private, Paramore: now really it must be in private.

PARAMORE [*surprised*] Of course. I was about to suggest my consulting room: theres nobody there. Miss Craven: will you excuse me: Charteris will entertain you until I return. [*He leads the way to the green baize door*].

CHARTERIS [*aghast*] Oh, I say, hadnt you better wait until the others come?

PARAMORE [*exultant*] No need for further delay now, my best friend. [*He wrings Charteris's hand*]. Will you come, Colonel?

CRAVEN. At your service, Paramore: at your service.

Craven and Paramore go into the consulting room. Julia turns her head, and stares insolently at Charteris. His nerves play him false: he is completely out of countenance in a moment. She rises suddenly. He starts, and comes hastily forward between the table and the bookcase. She crosses to that side behind the table; and he immediately crosses to the opposite side in front of it, dodging her.

CHARTERIS [*nervously*] Dont, Julia. Now dont abuse your advantage. Youve got me here at your mercy. Be good for once; and dont make a scene.

JULIA [*contemptuously*] Do you suppose I am going to touch you?

CHARTERIS. No. Of course not.

She comes forward on her side of the table. He retreats on his side of it. She looks at him with utter scorn; sweeps across to the couch; and sits down imperially. With a great sigh of relief he drops into Paramore's chair.

JULIA. Come here. I have something to say to you.

CHARTERIS. Yes? [*He rolls the chair a few inches towards*

THE PHILANDERER

her].

JULIA. Come here, I say. I am not going to shout across the room at you. Are you afraid of me?

CHARTERIS. Horribly. [*He moves the chair slowly, with great misgiving, to the end of the couch*].

JULIA [*with studied insolence*] Has that woman told you that she has given you up to me without an attempt to defend her conquest?

CHARTERIS [*whispering persuasively*] Shew that you are capable of the same sacrifice. Give me up too.

JULIA. Sacrifice! And so you think I'm dying to marry you, do you?

CHARTERIS. I am afraid your intentions have been honorable, Julia.

JULIA. You cad!

CHARTERIS [*with a sigh*] I confess I am something either more or less than a gentleman, Julia. You once gave me the benefit of the doubt.

JULIA. Indeed! I never told you so. If you cannot behave like a gentleman, you had better go back to the society of the woman who has given you up: if such a coldblooded, cowardly creature can be called a woman. [*She rises majestically: he makes his chair fly back to the table*]. I know you now, Leonard Charteris, through and through, in all your falseness, your petty spite, your cruelty and your vanity. The place you coveted has been won by a man more worthy of it.

CHARTERIS [*springing up, and coming close to her, gasping with eagerness*] What do you mean? Out with it. Have you accep—

JULIA. I am engaged to Dr Paramore.

CHARTERIS [*enraptured*] My own Julia! [*He attempts to embrace her*].

JULIA [*recoiling: he catching her hands and holding them*] How dare you! Are you mad? Do you wish me to call Dr Paramore?

CHARTERIS. Call everybody, my darling—everybody in London. Now I shall no longer have to be brutal; to defend myself; to go in fear of you. How I have looked forward to this day! You know now that I dont want you to marry me or to love me: Paramore can have all that. I only want to look on and rejoice disinterestedly in the happiness of [*kissing her hand*] my dear Julia [*kissing the other*] my beautiful Julia. [*She tears her hands away and raises them as if to strike him, as she did the night before at Cuthbertson's: he faces them with joyous recklessness*]. No use to threaten me now: I am not afraid of those hands: the loveliest hands in the world.

JULIA. How have you the face to turn round like this after insulting and torturing me?

CHARTERIS. Never mind, dearest: you never did understand me; and you never will. Our vivisecting friend has made a successful experiment at last.

JULIA [*earnestly*] It is you who are the vivisector: a far crueller, more wanton vivisector than he.

CHARTERIS. Yes; but then I learn so much more from my experiments than he does! And the victims learn as much as I do. Thats where my moral superiority comes in.

JULIA [*sitting down again on the couch with rueful humor*] Well, you shall not experiment on me any more. Go to your Grace if you want a victim. She'll be a tough one.

CHARTERIS [*reproachfully, sitting down beside her*] And you drove me to propose to her to escape from you! Suppose she had accepted me, where should I be now?

JULIA. Where *I* am, I suppose, now that I have accepted Paramore.

CHARTERIS. But I should have made Grace unhappy. [*Julia sneers*]. However, now I come to think of it, youll make Paramore unhappy. And yet if you refused him he would be in despair. Poor devil!

JULIA [*her temper flashing up for a moment again*] He is a better man than you.

CHARTERIS [*humbly*] I grant you that, my dear.

JULIA [*impetuously*] Dont call me your dear. And what do you mean by saying that I shall make him unhappy? Am I not good enough for him?

794

THE PHILANDERER

CHARTERIS [*dubiously*] Well, that depends on what you mean by good enough.

JULIA [*earnestly*] You might have made me good if you had chosen to. You had a great power over me. I was like a child in your hands; and you knew it.

CHARTERIS. Yes, my dear. That means that whenever you got jealous and flew into a tearing rage, I could always depend on its ending happily if I only waited long enough, and petted you very hard all the time. When you had had your fling, and called the object of your jealousy every name you could lay your tongue to, and abused me to your heart's content for a couple of hours, then the reaction would come; and you would at last subside into a soothing rapture of affection which gave you a sensation of being angelically good and forgiving. Oh, I know that sort of goodness! You may have thought on these occasions that I was bringing out your latent amiability; but I thought you were bringing out mine, and using up rather more than your fair share of it.

JULIA. According to you, then, I have no good in me. I am an utterly vile worthless woman. Is that it?

CHARTERIS. Yes, if you are to be judged as you judge others. From the conventional point of view, theres nothing to be said for you, Julia: nothing. Thats why I have to find some other point of view to save my self-respect when I remember how I have loved you. Oh, what I have learnt from you! from you! who could learn nothing from me! I made a fool of you; and you brought me wisdom: I broke your heart; and you brought me joy: I made you curse your womanhood; and you revealed my manhood to me. Blessings for ever and ever on my Julia's name! [*With genuine emotion, he takes her hand to kiss it again*].

JULIA [*snatching her hand away in disgust*] Oh, stop talking that nasty sneering stuff.

CHARTERIS [*laughingly appealing to the heavens*] She calls it nasty sneering stuff! Well, well: I'll never talk like that to you again, dearest. It only means that you are a beautiful woman, and that we all love you.

795

JULIA. Dont say that: I hate it. It sounds as if I were a mere animal.

CHARTERIS. Hm! A fine animal is a very wonderful thing. Dont let us disparage animals, Julia.

JULIA. That is what you really think me.

CHARTERIS. Come, Julia! you dont expect me to admire you for your moral qualities, do you?

Julia turns and looks hard at him. He starts up apprehensively, and backs away from her. She rises and follows him up slowly and intently.

JULIA [*deliberately*] I have seen you very much infatuated with this depraved creature who has no moral qualities.

CHARTERIS [*retreating*] Keep off, Julia. Remember your new obligations to Paramore.

JULIA [*overtaking him in the middle of the room*] Never mind Paramore: that is my business. [*She grasps the lappels of his coat in her hands, and looks fixedly at him*]. Oh, if the people you talk so cleverly to could only know you as I know you! Sometimes I wonder at myself for ever caring for you.

CHARTERIS [*beaming at her*] Only sometimes?

JULIA. You fraud! You humbug! You miserable little plaster saint! [*He looks delighted*]. Oh! [*In a paroxysm half of rage, half of tenderness, she shakes him, growling over him like a tigress over her cub*].

Paramore and Craven return from the consulting room, and are thunderstruck at the spectacle.

CRAVEN [*shouting, utterly scandalized*] Julia!!

Julia releases Charteris, but stands her ground disdainfully as they come forward, Craven on her left, Paramore on her right.

PARAMORE. Whats the matter?

CHARTERIS. Nothing, nothing. Youll soon get used to this, Paramore.

CRAVEN. Now really, Julia, this is a very extraordinary way to behave. It's not fair to Paramore.

JULIA [*coldly*] If Dr Paramore objects, he can break off our engagement. [*To Paramore*] Pray dont hesitate.

PARAMORE [*looking doubtfully and anxiously at her*] Do you

wish me to break it off?

CHARTERIS [*alarmed*] Nonsense! dont act so hastily. It was my fault. I annoyed Miss Craven—insulted her. Hang it all, dont go and spoil everything like this.

CRAVEN. This is most infernally perplexing. I cant believe that you insulted Julia, Charteris. Ive no doubt you annoyed her: youd annoy anybody: upon my soul you would; but insult! now what do you mean by that?

PARAMORE [*very earnestly*] Miss Craven: in all delicacy and sincerity I ask you to be frank with me. What are the relations between you and Charteris?

JULIA [*enigmatically*] Ask him. [*She goes to the fireplace, turning her back on them*].

CHARTERIS. Certainly: I'll confess. I'm in love with Miss Craven. Ive persecuted her with my addresses ever since I knew her. It's been no use: she utterly despises me. A moment ago the spectacle of a rival's happiness stung me to make a nasty sneering speech; and she—well, she just shook me a little, as you saw.

PARAMORE [*chivalrously*] I shall never forget that you helped me to win her, Charteris. [*Julia turns quickly, a spasm of fury in her face*].

CHARTERIS. Sh! For Heaven's sake dont mention it.

CRAVEN. This is a very different story to the one you told Cuthbertson and myself this morning. Youll excuse my saying that it sounds much more like the truth. Come! you were humbugging us, werent you?

CHARTERIS [*enigmatically*] Ask Julia.

Paramore and Craven turn to Julia. Charteris remains doggedly looking straight before him.

JULIA. It's quite true. He has been in love with me; he has persecuted me; and I utterly despise him.

CRAVEN. Dont rub it in, Julia: it's not kind. No man is quite himself when he's crossed in love. [*To Charteris*] Now listen to me, Charteris. When I was a young fellow, Cuthbertson and I fell in love with the same woman. She preferred Cuthbertson. I was taken aback: I wont deny it. But

I knew my duty; and I did it. I gave her up, and wished Cuthbertson joy. He told me this morning, when we met after many years, that he has respected and liked me ever since for it. And I believe him, and feel the better for it. [*Impressively*] Now, Charteris: Paramore and you stand today where Cuthbertson and I stood on a certain July evening thirty-five years ago. How are you going to take it?

JULIA [*indignantly*] How is he going to take it, indeed! Really, papa, this is too much. If Mrs Cuthbertson wouldnt have you, it may have been very noble of you to make a virtue of giving her up, just as you made a virtue of being a teetotaller when Percy cut off your wine. But h e shant be virtuous over m e. I have refused him; and if he doesnt like it he can—he can—

CHARTERIS. I can lump it. Precisely. Craven: you can depend on me. I'll lump it. [*He moves off nonchalantly, and leans against the bookcase with his hands in his pockets*].

CRAVEN [*hurt*] Julia: you dont treat me respectfully. I dont wish to complain; but that was not a becoming speech.

JULIA [*bursting into tears, and throwing herself into the easy chair*] Is there any one in the world who has any feeling for me? who does not think me utterly vile?

Craven and Paramore hurry to her in the greatest consternation.

CRAVEN [*remorsefully*] My pet: I didnt for a moment mean—

JULIA. Must I stand to be bargained for by two men—passed from one to the other like a slave in the market, and not say a word in my own defence?

CRAVEN. But, my love—

JULIA. Oh, go away, all of you. Leave me. I—oh—[*she gives way to a passion of tears*].

PARAMORE [*reproachfully to Craven*] Youve wounded her cruelly, Colonel Craven. Cruelly.

CRAVEN. But I didnt mean to: I said nothing. Charteris: was I harsh?

CHARTERIS. You forget the revolt of the daughters, Craven. And you certainly wouldnt have gone on like that to any grown-up woman who was n o t your daughter.

CRAVEN. Do you mean to say that I am expected to treat my daughter the same as I would any other girl?

PARAMORE. I should say certainly, Colonel Craven.

CRAVEN. Well, dash me if I will. There!

PARAMORE. If you take that tone, I have nothing more to say. [*He crosses the room with offended dignity, and posts himself with his back to the bookcase beside Charteris*].

JULIA [*with a sob*] Daddy.

CRAVEN [*turning solicitously to her*] Yes, my love.

JULIA [*looking up at him tearfully, and kissing his hand*] Dont mind them. You didnt mean it, Daddy, did you?

CRAVEN. No, no, my precious. Come: dont cry.

PARAMORE [*to Charteris, looking at Julia with delight*] How beautiful she is!

CHARTERIS [*throwing up his hands*] Oh, Lord help you, Paramore! [*He leaves the bookcase, and sits at the end of the couch farthest from the fire*].

Sylvia arrives.

SYLVIA [*contemplating Julia*] Crying again! Well, you a r e a womanly one!

CRAVEN. Dont worry your sister, Sylvia. You know she cant bear it.

SYLVIA. I speak for her good, Dad. All the world cant be expected to know that she's the family baby.

JULIA. You will get your ears boxed presently, Silly.

CRAVEN. Now! now! now! my dear children, really now! Come, Julia: put up your handkerchief before Mrs Tranfield sees you. She's coming along with Jo.

JULIA [*rising*] That woman again!

SYLVIA. Another row! Go it, Julia!

CRAVEN. Hold your tongue, Sylvia. [*He turns commandingly to Julia*]. Now look here, Julia.

CHARTERIS. Hallo! A revolt of the fathers!

CRAVEN. Silence, Charteris. [*To Julia, unanswerably*] The test of a man's or woman's breeding is how they behave

799

in a quarrel. Anybody can behave well when things are going smoothly. Now you said today, at that iniquitous club, that you were not a womanly woman. Very well: I dont mind. But if you are not going to behave like a lady when Mrs Tranfield comes into this room, youve got to behave like a gentleman; or fond as I am of you, I'll cut you dead exactly as I would if you were my son.

PARAMORE [*remonstrating*] Colonel Craven—

CRAVEN [*cutting him short*] Dont be a fool, Paramore.

JULIA [*tearfully excusing herself*] I'm sure, Daddy—

CRAVEN. Stop snivelling. I'm not speaking as your Daddy now: I'm speaking as your commanding officer.

SYLVIA. Good old Victoria Cross! [*Craven turns sharply on her; and she darts away behind Charteris, and presently seats herself on the couch, so that she and Charteris are shoulder to shoulder, facing opposite ways*].

Cuthbertson arrives with Grace, who remains near the door whilst her father joins the others.

CRAVEN. Ah, Jo, here you are. Now, Paramore: tell em the news.

PARAMORE. Mrs Tranfield: Cuthbertson: allow me to introduce you to my future wife.

CUTHBERTSON [*coming forward to shake hands with Paramore*] My heartiest congratulations! Miss Craven: you will accept Grace's congratulations as well as mine, I hope.

CRAVEN. She will, Jo. [*Peremptorily*] Now, Julia.

Julia slowly rises.

CUTHBERTSON. Now, Grace. [*He conducts her to Julia's right; then posts himself on the hearthrug, with his back to the fire, watching them, whilst the Colonel keeps guard on the other side*].

GRACE [*speaking in a low voice to Julia alone*] So you have shewn him that you can do without him! Now I take back everything I said. Will you shake hands with me? [*Julia gives her hand painfully, with her face averted*]. They think this a happy ending, Julia, these men: our lords and masters!

The two stand silent hand in hand.

THE PHILANDERER

SYLVIA [*leaning back across the couch, aside to Charteris*] Has she really chucked you? [*He nods assent. She looks at him dubiously, and adds*] I expect you chucked her.

CUTHBERTSON. And now, Paramore, mind you dont stand any chaff from Charteris about this. He's in the same predicament himself. He's engaged to Grace.

JULIA [*dropping Grace's hand, and speaking with breathless anguish, but not violently*] Again!

CHARTERIS [*rising hastily*] Dont be alarmed. It's all off.

SYLVIA [*rising indignantly*] What! Youve chucked Grace too! What a shame! [*She goes to the other side of the room, fuming*].

CHARTERIS [*following her, and putting his hand soothingly on her shoulder*] She wont have me, old chap. That is [*turning to the others*], unless Mrs Tranfield has changed her mind again.

GRACE. No: we shall remain very good friends, I hope; but nothing would induce me to marry you. [*She takes the easy chair at the fireplace, and sits down with perfect composure*].

JULIA. Ah! [*She sits down on the couch with a great sigh of relief*].

SYLVIA [*consoling Charteris*] Poor old Leonard!

CHARTERIS. Yes: this is the doom of the philanderer. I shall have to go on philandering now all my life. No domesticity, no fireside, no little ones, nothing at all in Cuthbertson's line! Nobody will marry me—unless you, Sylvia: eh?

SYLVIA. Not if I know it, Charteris.

CHARTERIS [*to them all*] You see!

CRAVEN [*coming between Charteris and Sylvia*] Now you really shouldnt make a jest of these things: upon my life and soul you shouldnt, Charteris.

CUTHBERTSON [*on the hearthrug*] The only use he can find for sacred things is to make a jest of them. Thats the New Order. Thank Heaven, we belong to the Old Order, Dan!

CHARTERIS. Cuthbertson: dont be symbolic.

CUTHBERTSON [*outraged*] Symbolic! That is an accusation of Ibsenism. What do you mean?

CHARTERIS. Symbolic of the Old Order. Dont persuade yourself that you represent the Old Order. There never was any Old Order.

CRAVEN. There I flatly contradict you, and stand up for Jo. I'd no more have behaved as you do when I was a young man than I'd have cheated at cards. *I* belong to the Old Order.

CHARTERIS. Youre getting old, Craven; and you want to make a merit of it, as usual.

CRAVEN. Come now, Charteris: youre not offended, I hope. [*With a conciliatory outburst*] Well, perhaps I shouldnt have said that about cheating at cards. I withdraw it [*offering his hand*].

CHARTERIS [*taking Craven's hand*] No offence, my dear Craven: none in the world. I didnt mean to shew any temper. But [*aside, after looking round to see whether the others are listening*] only just consider! the spectacle of a rival's happiness! the—

CRAVEN [*aloud, decisively*] Charteris: now youve got to behave like a man. Your duty's plain before you. [*To Cuthbertson*] Am I right, Jo?

CUTHBERTSON [*firmly*] You are, Dan.

CRAVEN [*to Charteris*] Go straight up and congratulate Julia. And do it like a gentleman, smiling.

CHARTERIS. Colonel: I will. Not a quiver shall betray the conflict within.

CRAVEN. Julia: Charteris has not congratulated you yet. He's coming to do it.

Julia rises, and fixes a dangerous look on Charteris.

SYLVIA [*whispering quickly behind Charteris as he is about to advance*] Take care. She's going to hit you. I know her.

Charteris stops and looks cautiously at Julia, measuring the situation. They regard one another steadfastly for a moment. Grace softly rises and gets close to Julia.

CHARTERIS [*whispering over his shoulder to Sylvia*] I'll chance it. [*He walks confidently up to Julia*]. Julia? [*He proffers his hand*].

THE PHILANDERER

JULIA [*exhausted, allowing herself to take it*] You are right. I am a worthless woman.

CHARTERIS [*triumphant, and gaily remonstrating*] Oh, why?

JULIA. Because I am not brave enough to kill you.

GRACE [*taking her in her arms as she sinks, almost fainting, away from him*] Oh no. Never make a hero of a philanderer.

Charteris, amused and untouched, shakes his head laughingly. The rest look at Julia with concern, and even a little awe, feeling for the first time the presence of a keen sorrow.

CHRONOLOGY OF THE PLAYS

The birth date of a play in this chronology is considered
to be the probable date when the author finished writing it.
Copyright performance, amateur or professional performance, and publication dates may all be different.

1892	WIDOWERS' HOUSES
1893	THE PHILANDERER
1894	MRS WARREN'S PROFESSION
1894	ARMS AND THE MAN
1895	CANDIDA
1895	THE MAN OF DESTINY
1896	YOU NEVER CAN TELL
1897	THE DEVIL'S DISCIPLE
1898	CAESAR AND CLEOPATRA
1899	CAPTAIN BRASSBOUND'S CONVERSION
1901	THE ADMIRABLE BASHVILLE
1903	MAN AND SUPERMAN
1904	JOHN BULL'S OTHER ISLAND
1904	HOW HE LIED TO HER HUSBAND
1905	MAJOR BARBARA
1905	PASSION, POISON, AND PETRIFACTION
1906	THE DOCTOR'S DILEMMA
1907	THE INTERLUDE AT THE PLAYHOUSE (*playlet*)
1908	GETTING MARRIED
1909	THE SHEWING-UP OF BLANCO POSNET
1909	PRESS CUTTINGS
1909	THE FASCINATING FOUNDLING
1909	THE GLIMPSE OF REALITY
1910	MISALLIANCE
1910	THE DARK LADY OF THE SONNETS
1911	FANNY'S FIRST PLAY

CHRONOLOGY OF THE PLAYS

INDEX

The italicized Roman numeral following each entry refers to the Volume of Complete Plays With Prefaces in which the material appears.

INDEX

808

INDEX

INDEX

DATE DUE

GAYLORD   PRINTED IN U.S.A.

Vasiliu